Reviews of *Get Free Cash for College*

"Upbeat, well-organized and engaging, this comprehensive tool is an exceptional investment for the college-bound."
–Publishers Weekly

"A present for anxious parents."
–Mary Kaye Ritz, The Honolulu Advertiser

"Helpful, well-organized guide, with copies of actual letters and essays and practical tips. A good resource for all students."
–KLIATT

"Upbeat tone and clear, practical advice."
–Book News

"Unlike other authors, the Tanabes use their experiences and those of other students to guide high school and college students and their parents through the scholarship and financial aid process."
–Palo Alto Daily News

Praise for authors Gen and Kelly Tanabe

"What's even better than all the top-notch tips is that the book is written in a cool, conversational way."
–College Bound Magazine

"A 'must' for any prospective college student."
–Midwest Book Review

"Invaluable information ranging from the elimination of admission myths to successfully tapping into scholarship funds."
–Leonard Banks, The Journal Press

"The Tanabes literally wrote the book on the topic."
–Bull & Bear Financial Report

"Offers advice on writing a good entrance essay, taking exams and applying for scholarships and other information on the college experience–start to finish."
–Town & Country Magazine

"The Tanabes, experts on the application process, can discuss such topics as how to get into the college of your choice, ways to finance your college education, applying online and what universities are looking for in a student."
–Asbury Park Press

"The first book to feature the strategies and stories of real students."
–New Jersey Spectator Leader

GET FREE CASH FOR COLLEGE

- 2008 -

- **A comprehensive Scholarship Directory and Scholarship Strategy Guide**
- **Step-by-step instructions on how to find, apply for and win scholarships**
- **Learn from the successes and failures of real students**
- **The only resource you will need on scholarships**

Gen and Kelly Tanabe

Winners of over $100,000 in scholarships and authors of
1001 Ways to Pay for College and *How to Write a Winning Scholarship Essay*

Get Free Cash for College 2008
By Gen and Kelly Tanabe

Published by SuperCollege, LLC
3286 Oak Court
Belmont, CA 94002
650-618-2221
www.supercollege.com

ISBN-13: 978-1-9326-6216-0
ISBN-10 1-932662-16-2

Manufactured in the United States of America
10 9 8 7 6 5 4 3 2 1

Cataloging-in-Publication Data
Gen S. Tanabe, Kelly Y. Tanabe
    Get Free Cash for College 2008 / by Gen S. Tanabe and Kelly Y. Tanabe.

        p.   cm.
    Includes appendices and index.
    ISBN-13: 978-1-9326-6216-0
    ISBN-10 1-932662-16-2
    1. College Guides   I. Title
    2. Reference   3. Personal Finance

Contents at a Glance

Table of Contents

Chapter 10. Strategies for Specific Scholarships / 123

Chapter 11. Guaranteed Scholarships / 137

Chapter 12. Unleash the Power of the Internet / 143

Chapter 13. Financial Aid Workshop / 149

Chapter 14. Free Cash for Graduate School / 169

Chapter 15. How to Keep the Money You Win / 181

Part II. Scholarship Directory

Scholarship Directory / 185

Awards for high school, college, graduate and adult students

Special Features

Stories from Real Life

These stories about the successes and failures of real students are entertaining and enlightening. They serve as valuable lessons about how the scholarship process really works!

Special Highlights

As a step-by-step strategy guide, we have created easy-to-follow practical methods for key areas of the scholarship process.

To our families for shaping who we are.

To Harvard for four of the best years of our lives.

To the many students and friends who made this book possible by sharing their scholarship experiences, secrets, successes and failures.

To all the students and parents who understand that paying for college is a challenging but worthwhile endeavor.

How to Get Free Cash for College

In this chapter, you'll learn:

- How this book guides you through the entire scholarship process

- How this book is different from traditional scholarship books

- The seven myths of scholarships

- Why all financial aid is not created equal

- How scholarships are judged and what you can do to maximize your chances of winning

How to Get Free Cash for College

About the Authors

Gen and Kelly Tanabe won more than $100,000 in scholarships and graduated from Harvard debt-free.

When I received my acceptance letter from Harvard, I proudly showed it to my parents. After calming down from the excitement, they asked that question you don't really want to ask, "How are we going to pay for this education?" This is when my father—always the pragmatist—made me an offer that was difficult to refuse.

"Son," he began, "why don't you go to our state university and I'll buy you a brand new car?" Given the price of a private college, it would have been much cheaper for my family to pay state tuition and buy a new car. In fact, for what Harvard charged, we could have purchased a whole fleet of cars.

So there I was: Harvard in one hand but a brand new ride in the other. It was a difficult decision.

When my coauthor, Kelly, received her acceptance letter from Harvard, she and her family were similarly torn. She had also been accepted to the University of Southern California and offered a full-tuition scholarship. Harvard, on the other hand, didn't offer any assistance.

So why, you might wonder as our parents certainly did, would we both choose to attend one of the most expensive colleges in the country and turn down (both literally and figuratively) free rides? We made the decision because we were fanatical in our belief that we could find scholarships to pay our mind-boggling tuition bills. There was only one, tiny problem with this decision: We had no idea where to start.

We began our journey the only way we knew. We bought a scholarship book. (Sound familiar?) After flipping through hundreds of pages of scholarships, we were disappointed to find that few awards fit us. Even more discouraging was that when we found a scholarship, we didn't have a clue on how to actually win the award. Through a long process of trial and error we slowly developed a workable system for finding and winning scholarships.

In the end we won more than $100,000 in scholarships, ranging from local awards from the Lions Club, high school PTA and local newspaper to national awards from Tylenol, Shell Oil Company and Knight Ridder newspapers. These scholarships allowed us not only to fulfill our dream of attending Harvard but (to our parents' delight) to graduate debt-free.

This book is based on the hard lessons we learned during our struggle to fund our own educations. In addition, we have done years of research collecting the strategies used by hundreds of students who have successfully won scholarships. (We've included samples of their scholarship applications, resumes and essays in this book.) We've interviewed scholarship judges to learn how they pick scholarship winners and what you can do to improve your chances in a competition. We then distilled these experiences, strategies and advice into a system that we believe will help you find and win scholarships. In short, this is the knowledge that we wish had been available when we were applying for scholarships.

Scholarships Are Not Just for Superstars

Whether you are just starting out or are an experienced veteran of the battle for scholarships, this book has a great deal to offer. Each chapter is filled with valuable advice, strategies, shortcuts and real life examples. Through the lessons in this book you can emulate our successes while avoiding our most tragic blunders in your own scholarship quest.

Don't think you need to be the class valedictorian or star athlete to win a scholarship. If you have the desire, you have everything you need to win free cash for college. We will help you make this happen. The goal of this book is to teach you the skills and provide you with the resources to be able to pay for the college of your dreams and graduate, as we did, debt-free.

Why Most Scholarship Books and Websites Can Be Soooooooooooooo Frustrating

Chances are that you found this book nestled among dozens of others on scholarships. If you look at the other books, you will notice something interesting: They all look like telephone directories. Flip through one, and you will find that it doesn't contain much more than award listings. This is the traditional format of the scholarship book, and it has been around for decades. The Internet has not done much to improve on things. You can go to various websites that list scholarships but again you are just viewing raw scholarships—and often many may not even fit you that well.

Unfortunately, it is this directory format that has caused so much dissatisfaction among students. While any single book or website may contain thousands of listings, few of those awards actually apply to you. To make matters worse, even when you do find an award, these books and websites leave you on your own to figure out how to create an application that will win the scholarship. What's the point of spending all this time and effort to find a scholarship when you don't know how to win it?

As we wrote this book, we vowed not to perpetuate the mistakes of other scholarship book authors. Go ahead and flip through a few chapters. What do you see? Holy cow! You see actual paragraphs and real examples of applications, scholarship resumes and essays. In fact, the whole first half of this book is a detailed scholarship strategy guide. You will learn all the ins and outs of scholarships, grants and financial aid. You will also learn what works when applying for scholarships and how to get the best financial aid offer. We have loaded this book with examples so you can see what a scholarship essay looks like and read a preview of questions you may be asked in a scholarship interview. We equip you with the knowledge and tools to actually win the scholarships that you spend valuable time finding.

But that's not all. Traditional scholarship directories can be very helpful and save a lot of time *if* they contain awards that you actually qualify for. In the second half of this book you will find the largest directory of awards on the current market that you can actually win.

By definition, all scholarships have eligibility requirements. However, we have selected awards with the least restrictive eligibility criteria. This means you will find

---

How This Book Is Different from Every Other Scholarship Book

The scholarships that appear in this directory are open to almost all students. You won't find awards open only to the third son of an actuary from Bumstead, North Dakota.

Just as important, this book doesn't abandon you once you find an award. The entire first half is a comprehensive strategy guide that shows you how to create a winning scholarship application. After all, why bother applying if you don't know how to maximize your chances of winning?

more awards that fit you in our publication than in a traditional scholarship book. We didn't bulk up our directory with useless scholarships such as the one for descendents of one-armed Confederate soldiers who were taken prisoner at the battle of Gettysburg. We've selected awards that we feel the majority of our readers could apply for and have a reasonable chance of winning. And in case you are interested in the more obscure awards–especially if you happen to have a great grand uncle from Virginia who lost an arm at Gettysburg–we'll show you how to find them.

Get Free Cash for College is our attempt to fix the outdated format of traditional scholarship books and websites that have been found lacking by so many students. In doing so, we believe that this book will provide you with the maximum advantage possible when it comes to finding and winning free cash for college.

The Big Picture

Don't you hate it when you are given instructions on how to do something without knowing what the final result is supposed to be? We do too, which is why at the start of each chapter you will find what we call *The Big Picture*. This is an overview of our approach or strategy. Seeing the big picture first will help you understand how all the smaller pieces fit together.

So in the spirit of giving you the big picture, we would like to share our general view of scholarships. Through our own experience and that of helping thousands of students and interviewing dozens of scholarship judges, we have come to firmly believe that the biggest misconception about scholarships is that you have to be an academic, athletic or extracurricular superstar to win one.

This is just plain untrue.

There are scholarships that reward every background, talent and achievement that you can imagine. Plus, most don't even consider grades, or if they do, it is the least important factor. It is true that winning a scholarship is not easy. There will be competition because scholarships are essentially free cash with no strings attached. But like most everything in life, you can greatly improve your chances of winning by learning as much as you can about these competitions and applying what you learn to your applications. Matched with the right scholarships and armed with this knowledge, you can set yourself up to win.

The bottom line is that scholarship winners are not superstars but are those who have prepared and invested the time to create an application that highlights their strengths while minimizing their weaknesses.

It's really sad to see students who don't apply for scholarships because they mistakenly assume that they don't have a chance to win. The truth is that regardless of what kind of student you are, winning comes down to whether or not you have a solid strategy. We believe you can learn this strategy. In fact, we're sure of it!

Not a Superstar, Not a Problem

You don't have to be a straight-A student or star athlete to win a scholarship. The strategies in this book and the students you will meet clearly prove that any student can win a scholarship. What is required is the desire and willingness to put in the time and effort to find awards that fit your background and write applications that show scholarship judges why you deserve to win. Don't worry, you'll learn how in the following chapters.

The Mind-Boggling Cost of a Good Education

We don't need to tell you that college is expensive. But have you actually seen the numbers? Are you ready for some major sticker shock? The price tag is staggering–an average of $12,796* per year for tuition and room and board at four-year public schools and $30,367* at private schools. These costs have grown approximately 30 percent over the past 10 years and have consistently risen faster than inflation. Ouch!

That is the bad news. The good news is that more than $134 billion was awarded in scholarships and financial aid last year. That's a lot of cash! You only need to get a small slice of this pie to be able to afford college. At this amount, even getting a small piece of crust is appealing!

So if you're ready to get your piece of the scholarship pie, let's begin by debunking some of the most common myths about scholarships that often prevent even the most motivated students from applying.

Seven Scholarship Myths Busted

Did you know that Walt Disney is cryogenically frozen and awaiting the day medical science can revive him? Or, you do know to be careful when walking the city at night since there are gangs of organ thieves who will knock you unconscious and steal your kidneys, right? We have all heard urban legends like these, and on the subject of scholarships there are no shortages of such stories.

You may have heard myths like these: You need to have near zero dinero in order to qualify for a scholarship, or you have to be the record holder for three-point shots, to win a full-ride award. To help you sort the truth from the tall tale, here are some common scholarship myths and the truth behind them:

Myth #1: You need to be financially destitute to be eligible to apply for scholarships.

The Truth: While it is true that financial need is a consideration for some scholarships, the definition of "need" varies considerably. Given the cost of a college education, many families who consider themselves to be "middle class" actually qualify for need-based scholarships. Plus, there are many scholarships where financial need is not even a factor. These "merit-based" scholarships are based on achievements, skills, career goals, family background and a host of other considerations that have nothing to do with a family's financial situation. You really could be the son or daughter of Donald Trump and still win a scholarship.

*The College Board

Myth #2: You can only win scholarships as a high school senior.

The Truth: It is never too early or too late to apply for scholarships. There are awards for students as young as seventh grade. (If you win these awards, the money may be paid to you directly or put into a trust account until you head off to college.) Also, many students stop applying for scholarships after they graduate from high school. Big mistake. There are many awards for college students. Once you are in college you should continue to apply for scholarships, especially those geared toward specific majors and careers.

More Truth: Most scholarships are aimed at students who are getting their first degree, regardless of age. If you're 92 and working toward your bachelor's degree, you are just as eligible for scholarships as the 17-year-old high school student. In fact, today more than 20 percent of all students on campus are over the age of 35, so it's easy to understand why the rules for many scholarships have been modified to no longer limit an applicant based on age.

Myth #3: Only star athletes get scholarships, especially full-tuition scholarships.

The Truth: While full-tuition scholarships for star running backs often make the news, the majority of scholarships awarded by colleges are not for athletics. As you will see in the Scholarship Directory in this book, there are literally thousands of scholarships for those of us who don't know the difference between a touchdown and a touchback.

If you are an athlete, you might also be surprised to know that many colleges give scholarships to student athletes even if they are not the next Michael Jordan. Depending on the level of the school's athletic team, you may find that while at one college your soccer skill wouldn't earn you a place on the team as a bench warmer, at another school you would not only be a starter but also could earn a half-tuition scholarship.

Myth #4: You need straight A's to win money for college.

The Truth: While straight A's certainly don't hurt your chances of winning, most students assume that grades are the primary means for picking scholarship winners. This is just not true. Most scholarships are based on criteria other than grades and reward specific skills or talents such as linguistic, athletic or artistic ability. Even for scholarships in which grades are considered, they are often not the most important factor. What's more important is that you best match the qualities the scholarship committee seeks. Most students who win scholarships do not have the highest GPA. Don't let the lack of a perfect transcript prevent you from applying for scholarships.

Myth #5: You should get involved in as many extracurricular activities as possible to win a scholarship.

The Truth: Scholarship competitions are not pie eating contests where you win through volume. They are more like baking contests in which you create an exquisite dessert with an appearance and flavor that matches the tastes of the judges. Scholarships are won by quality, not quantity.

Scholarship judges are looking for students who have made quality contributions. For example, for a public service scholarship, the judges would be more impressed if you organized a school-wide volunteer day than if you were a member of 20 volunteer organizations but did little to distinguish yourself in them. Scholarship judges are looking for meaningful involvement, not a laundry list of clubs that you've joined.

Myth #6: You should apply to every scholarship you find.

The Truth: When you turn 35, you technically are eligible to run for President of the United States. This hardly means you should start packing your bags for the White House. Just because you are technically eligible for a scholarship does not mean you should apply for it. Why? You have a limited amount of time to spend on scholarship applications. It is necessary to allocate your time to those in which you have the best chance of winning. You may find that you are eligible for 500 scholarships. Unless you're willing to make applying to scholarships your full-time avocation, it's unlikely that you can apply to more than several dozen awards. Thus, you need to be selective about which scholarships fit you best. One caveat: This does not mean that you should only apply to two or three scholarships. You should still apply to as many scholarships as you can—just make sure you have them prioritized.

Myth #7: There's nothing you can do to increase your chances of winning a scholarship.

The Truth: We would not be here today if it weren't for the fact that there are many techniques you can use to improve your chances of winning scholarships. In the following chapters you will learn how to select scholarships that best fit you and your background, create a powerful application, write winning essays and successfully present yourself in interviews. We will teach you what successful students have done that worked for them. While there is no magic formula that guarantees you'll win a scholarship, our strategies have worked for others and can work for you too.

What about Federal Financial Aid?

You may think that the terms *scholarship* and *financial aid* are interchangeable. They are not. Financial aid refers to money from the government (both federal and state) and the college. It comes in several forms. Each type of aid has its own requirements, advantages and disadvantages. When we talk about financial aid, we mean one of the following:

Grants: Money with no strings attached—meaning you don't have to pay it back. This is really the equivalent of hitting the financial aid jackpot. Grants are almost always based on financial need.

> *Advantages:* Grants do not need to be repaid.
> *Disadvantages:* They are limited to those with financial need.

Student Loans: Money you borrow and are required to pay back with interest. In most cases the terms are more generous than other types of consumer loans. Some student loans are also based on financial need.

Scholarships: The Ultimate in Financial Aid

Scholarships are the only form of aid that comes with virtually no strings attached and that you can receive regardless of your family's finances.

Advantages: Loans are usually the easiest form of financial aid to obtain. Often you do not need to repay them until after you graduate or leave school.

Disadvantages: Unlike the other forms of financial aid, loans need to be repaid.

Work-Study: Money you earn the old-fashioned way—by working. This federal program subsidizes on-campus employment while you are enrolled in school. The program is based on financial need.

Advantages: Work-study allows you to gain valuable work experience (like how to shelve books, scrub dishes or serve a mean cup of coffee) while in school and opens up employment opportunities that are not available to other students.

Disadvantages: You will need to balance schoolwork with a part-time job. The program is limited to those with financial need.

In this book we will explain how financial aid works and what you need to get your share. We will also cover some important techniques on how to make sure you are receiving the most financial aid that you deserve from the college. To successfully pay for college, keep all your options open by applying for both financial aid and scholarships.

The Big Disadvantage of Federal Financial Aid

With so much financial aid available, why would anyone want to apply for a scholarship? The downside to financial aid is that most of the programs are based on need. This means that a family's income and assets are examined. Unfortunately, many middle class families find that they don't qualify for grants. Or, even if they do qualify, the amount they receive falls far short of what they need. This is where scholarships can be a lifesaver. Most scholarships don't consider a family's finances and therefore can bridge the gap between what a family has saved (including what they get from financial aid) and what the college actually costs them.

Scholarships: The Real Financial Aid Jackpots

While financial aid is important, we consider scholarships to be the true jackpots. With few, if any, strings attached to the money, scholarships represent free cash that does not have to be paid back. Best of all, students can win scholarships regardless of their parents' income!

In general, scholarships range in size from $100 to more than $100,000. Scholarships come from diverse organizations including schools, colleges, churches, state and local governments, companies and civic, political, service and athletic organizations. Often, these groups provide awards to promote their cause. For businesses, the cause may be to contribute to the communities in which they operate or to build relationships with future potential employees. For colleges, the motive may be to recruit certain types of students, to create a diverse student population by attracting those

"How We Choose Our Scholarship Winners"
Mary Hawkins, Scholarship Judge

The first thing you should understand about national scholarships like ours is the magnitude. We don't just get a box of applications for our scholarship. We get truckloads of applications. I am on the small team of people who sift through this mountain of paperwork.

Our first step is to make a quick first pass. We spend about 10 to 20 seconds taking a brief look at the applications. Even though we don't spend much time on each application, we quickly eliminate applications that don't meet the basic requirements. We purge applications that are not complete, missing information or materials, illegible or sloppily completed. We're pretty rigid in our decisions because we've found that if students don't even follow our award's simple directions, they probably aren't that attentive to their studies either.

After this first pass, we separate the applications into two piles. One is the pile of students we send thank you notes for entering. The other is the pile with potential. We spend on average between one and three minutes per application, hitting the highlights of the application form and reading the first few paragraphs of the essay. If we are impressed, we place the application in a separate pile.

Our last step is to separate the truly outstanding applications from the merely great ones. This is always the most difficult part. There are always so many more students with superb qualifications than we have scholarships to give. It's not easy to point out exactly what makes an application rise above the rest, but here are some qualities I've found common to our winners:

Academics. There are some scholarships in which academics is not the most important factor. For us, academic excellence is a prerequisite. Students don't have to have perfect grade point averages, but they do have to be committed to their schoolwork and take challenging courses. This should be reflected in the application.

Leadership. We look for students who have made a difference by being leaders in their activities. You don't have to be student body president to be a leader. You can show leadership by serving your community, speaking out for what you believe in or being an example for other students. We want students who will make a difference both in college and beyond.

Originality. Students with an original approach to their essays rise to the top. Creativity shows intelligence and a readiness to think differently.

Results. In the students' activities, we seek students who have demonstrated that they can deliver results. We don't care what area these results are in (i.e., music, service, science, sports) but we do want to see that there are actions that support the applicants' words.

Personality. One of the most important things we want are students who we feel like we know after reading their applications. It's important that students convey a piece of who they really are and that we feel like we've gotten to know them a little better through their applications.

Some scholarship judges have the luxury of being able to interview their finalists. Personally, I think it would help to meet the person behind the application. However, I think we do a great job relying on the applications, essays and recommendations. It's amazing how well you can get to know someone just through their written words.

with different backgrounds or to encourage students to enter nontraditional fields. Local and civic organizations often promote the missions of their organizations. For example, an equestrian club might sponsor a scholarship to reward students who love horseback riding.

The possibilities are truly limitless. And here's a secret: For practically every cause, occupation, hobby and passion that exists there is at least one scholarship. Often there are more. With some detective work, you can find many awards that match

Scholarships Are Everywhere

There are scholarships for practically every cause, talent and interest. While some are based on your financial background (need-based) others are based on almost any criteria that you can imagine (merit-based).

your particular skills, talents, achievements, goals and background. As you are searching, you will discover that most scholarships can be divided into two major categories: Need-based and Merit-based.

Need-based scholarships are those in which financial need is a criterion. The importance of financial need and the definition of financial need in the selection process vary by scholarship. For some scholarships, financial need may be the most important factor or may be required for eligibility. For others, it may be one of many factors that are used to pick a winner. Also, the definition of a student with financial need varies widely. One scholarship may consider a family that makes less than $50,000 a year "needy" while another may set the limit at $100,000.

Most scholarships are **merit-based**, which means financial need is not a requirement to apply. These scholarships are based on qualities such as skills, talents or accomplishments. "Merit" does not automatically equal academic merit, either. In the context of scholarships, "merit" can really mean anything from being a part of a specific ethnic group to being able to ride a skateboard. The only thing a merit-based scholarship really signifies is that your family's financial status is not a consideration.

It's no secret that we believe scholarships are the best way to pay for college. This does not mean that you should ignore other forms of financial aid. However, there are some real advantages that scholarships offer over other forms of financial aid.

First, you don't have to hold down a job to win a scholarship. For work-study, you need to work part-time. For loans, you need to toil after graduating to pay them off. Scholarships are free cash that does not need to be paid back. We love it (and so will you)!

Scholarships are open to students from all financial backgrounds. Most financial aid programs are based on your parents' and your financial background, something that you have little control over. While some scholarships are based on financial need, the vast majority are not.

Scholarships may be renewable. You need to apply for financial aid each year that you are in college. What you receive for your first year may not be the same for your second, third or fourth years. However, if a scholarship is "renewable" as long as you meet the requirements (often maintaining a 3.0 GPA) you will get the money each and every year that you are in school. A $1,000 "renewable" scholarship may actually be worth $4,000 over the course of your college career.

Most important, unlike other types of financial aid, scholarships allow you the greatest opportunity to control your chances of winning. You create the application and write the essay, and you control how you present yourself to the scholarship judges during the interview. The bottom line is that you determine through your own efforts the chances of receiving free cash for college.

Scholarship Competitions Are Not Lotteries

Unlike a lottery jackpot, scholarships are not based on luck. To win scholarships, you need to show the scholarship judges how you fit the award. Often this is through the scholarship application, essay and interview. In fact, almost all scholarship competitions come down to one key factor—how well you can show that you fit the mission of the scholarship. In this respect you have tremendous influence over the outcome. Through what you choose to highlight (and ignore) in the scholarship application, you are able to show your fit with the scholarship's mission. We hope that you feel empowered by the fact that you have so much control over the scholarship process!

In the following chapters you will learn how to use this opportunity to tailor your application to fit a scholarship's mission and thereby maximize your chances of winning it. Now turn the page and let's get started!

Chapter 1 Summary: How to Get Free Cash for College

Not a superstar? Not a problem. Remember that you don't have to be an academic, athletic or extracurricular superstar to win scholarships. Different scholarships reward different strengths. However, you do need a solid strategy for applying for scholarships. Discover the ins and outs of creating a winning strategy in the next chapters, including selecting scholarships that fit, creating outstanding applications and keeping the money you win.

Benefit from the experiences of others. The best way to learn anything is to study and draw from the knowledge of those who have already been through a similar experience. We will share the successes (and a few disasters) of students who have been through the scholarship process. You can choose to emulate their feats and avoid their failures.

Not all money is the same. Financial aid comes in a number of different forms, each with its own advantages and disadvantages. Loans are repaid while grants and scholarships are not. Work-study allows you to hold a part-time job while attending college.

Debunk scholarship urban legends. Separate the truth from the tall tale about scholarships. Among the truths in this chapter are the following:

You don't have to be financially destitute, participate in every extracurricular activity or apply for every scholarship for which you remotely qualify.

Scholarships for everyone. There are scholarships for almost every skill, experience, career aspiration and field of study you can imagine. Find those that fit you best in our massive Scholarship Directory.

Take advantage of your influence. Scholarships are based on factors such as your fit with the mission, essays, interviews, recommendations and financial need. Understand that you can positively affect nearly all these requirements.

Know what the judges want. In the first round, superficial factors are important such as neatness and completeness. Next, judges divide applications between good and excellent based on factors such as academics, leadership, originality, strength, results, maturity and personality.

Judging criteria. One of the most important things to remember when applying for scholarships is that you must show how you fulfill the mission of the award. In the following chapters, you will learn more about defining the mission and using it to your advantage throughout your applications, essays and interviews.

Find the Best Scholarships You Can Win

In this chapter, you'll learn:

- The best places to find scholarships

- Truly outrageous scholarships

- How to determine which scholarships you have the best chance of winning

- How to read the minds of the judges

- The magic number of scholarships

Where to Find the Best Scholarships

There's a saying: "If you give a man a fish, you feed him for a day. If you teach a man to fish, you feed him for life." In the second half of this book you will find a massive Scholarship Directory with hundreds of scholarships for which you can apply to win. That's our way of giving you a barrel full of fish! We do, however, want to make sure that we also teach you how to catch your own scholarships. So before you skip to the directory, master the techniques in this chapter to guarantee yourself a lifetime supply of scholarships.

Learning how to find scholarships is a skill. Unfortunately, we learned this through painful trial and error. For example, when we first started to search for scholarships, we applied for nearly every one that we found as long as we remotely met the eligibility requirements. Big mistake. We wasted a lot of time filling out applications that we should have passed on. Even worse, we spent a lot of time tracking down scholarships that we later discovered were listed in resources that were free for the asking. But we did learn from each mistake and eventually developed an efficient strategy for finding scholarships.

In this chapter we will teach you everything we learned about unearthing scholarships, including how to avoid common time-wasting mistakes. Let's begin with an overview of our scholarship-finding technique.

The Big Picture

Our approach to finding scholarships consists of two important steps. First, you must create a list of as many scholarships as possible that fit you. The Scholarship Directory in the second half of this book is a great place to start. However, don't stop here. Use the techniques in this chapter to seek out other scholarships–especially local awards given in your community. The goal is to compile as large a list as possible from as many sources as possible.

Second, once you have a big list of scholarships, prioritize the awards. Here is where you will do some detective work. Decide which scholarships from the list are most worth your time in filling out applications. To help process your choices and maximize your time, you need to learn as much as you can about each scholarship and the goal of the awarding organization. You also need to determine if your own background, skills and experience match what the scholarship wants to reward. Don't worry, this is much easier than it sounds and we'll show you how to do it quickly.

By following this two-step technique you will end up with a prioritized list of scholarships that are closely matched to your background and achievements. So, even before you fill out a single scholarship application form, you have greatly improved your chances of winning. Plus, you saved time by not wasting energy on awards that you won't win.

The Best Places to Find Scholarships

When we began to look for scholarships, we made what is perhaps the biggest mistake of every novice scholarship hunter—we started by looking as far away as possible. We were mesmerized by the big prizes of the large (and often well-publicized) national awards. We even thought, "If I won just one of these national scholarship competitions, I'd be set and could end my search." This turned out to be a big mistake and an even bigger time-waster. It seemed that everyone and his brother, sister and second cousin were also applying to these competitions. The Coca-Cola scholarship competition, for example, receives more than 100,000 applications each year.

It turned out that the last place we looked for scholarships was our most lucrative source. Best of all, this place turned out to be in our own backyard!

Fantastic Backyard Scholarships

What are backyard scholarships and where do you find them? Think about all the groups, clubs, businesses, churches and organizations in your community. Each of these is a potential source for scholarships. (If you are already in college, you have two communities: your hometown and the city in which you go to school.) Since these awards are usually only available to students in your community, the competition is a lot less fierce.

You may be thinking, "Yeah, but what good is a $500 Lions Club scholarship when my college costs 20 grand a year?" It's true that local scholarships don't award the huge prizes that some of the national competitions do. You already know that we won over $100,000 in scholarships. What we haven't told you is that the majority of this money came from local scholarships! We literally won $500 here and $1,500 there. By the time we graduated from Harvard and added up all the awards, it turned out to be a huge amount. Plus, some of the local scholarships that we won were "renewable," which meant that we received that money each year we were in college. So a $500 renewable scholarship was really worth $2,000 over four years.

If you still can't get over the fact that some of the local awards seem small compared to the cost of tuition, try this exercise: Take the amount of the award and divide it by the time you invested in the application. For the $500 Lions Club award, let's say that you spent one hour each night for three days to complete the application and write the essay. $500 divided by three hours works out to a little over $166 per hour. (Now imagine that the award was for $1,000 instead. That would make it $333 per hour!) Surprised? If you can find a job that pays you more than $166 an hour, then take it and forget applying to scholarships. If not, then get back to applying for scholarships—even the little ones!

As you begin the search for scholarships, make your community the first place you look. Begin with the following places to find your own backyard scholarships:

High school counselor or college financial aid office. If you are a high school student, start with your counselor. Ask if he or she has a list of

Be a Detective

Take off your "thinking cap" as your elementary school teacher used to call it and put on your "detective hat." When researching scholarships, be willing to look high and low to find out whatever you can about the mission of the award and goal of the organization that is giving away the money.

Find the Binder

Your counselor probably has a binder full of local scholarships. Many high school counselors we spoke with lament the fact that not very many students take advantage of the legwork they have done compiling local scholarships. Make your counselor's day and ask to see their list of scholarships.

scholarship opportunities. Most counselors have a binder filled with local scholarships. It's helpful if before your meeting, you prepare information about your family's financial background as well as special interests or talents you have that would make you eligible for scholarships. Don't forget that your own high school will have a variety of scholarships from such places as the parent-teacher organization, alumni group and athletic booster clubs.

If you are a college student, make an appointment with your school's financial aid advisor. Before the appointment, think about what interests and talents you have and what field you may want to enter after graduation. If you have one, take a copy of your Free Application for Federal Student Aid (FAFSA) as background. Mention any special circumstances about your family's financial situation. Ask your advisor for recommendations of scholarships offered by the college or by community organizations. Also, if you have already declared a major, check with the department's administrative assistant or chair for any awards that you might be eligible to win.

It's important whenever you speak to a counselor (either in high school or college) that you inquire about any scholarships that require nomination. Often these scholarships are easier to win since the applicant pool is smaller. You have nothing to lose by asking, and if anything, it shows how serious you are about financing your education.

High school websites. You may not visit your school's website daily, but when you are looking for scholarships, it pays to search the site for lists of scholarships. Most high schools post scholarship opportunities for students on their websites. (You may have to dig down a few levels to find this list.) If your school does not do this, surf over to the websites of other high schools in the area. You'll find that many are a wealth of scholarship resources.

Nearby colleges. While your college has great scholarship resources, wouldn't it be great if you had double or triple these resources? You can. Simply seek the resources of other local colleges. Ask permission first, but you'll find that most neighboring schools are more than willing to help you. If you are in high school, nothing prevents you from visiting all the local colleges and asking for scholarship information. Because you are a prospective student, these colleges will be happy to provide whatever assistance they can.

Student clubs and organizations. Here's a reason to enjoy your extracurricular activities even more. One benefit of participating may be a scholarship sponsored by the organization. Inquire with the officers or advisors of the organization about scholarship funds. Bands, newspapers, academic clubs, athletic organizations and service organizations often have scholarships that are awarded to outstanding members. If the organization has a national parent organization (e.g. National Honor Society) visit the national organization website. There are often awards that are given by the parent organization for members of local chapters.

Community organizations. If you've ever wondered why community organizations have so many breakfast fundraisers, one reason is that some provide money for scholarships. You usually don't have to be a member of these organizations to apply. In fact, many community groups sponsor scholarships that are open to all students who live in the area. As we have mentioned, college students really have two communities: your hometown and where you go to college. Don't neglect either of these places.

How do you find these organizations? Many local government websites list them. Visit the websites for your town, city and state. Also visit or call your community association or center. Local or state affiliates should be able to provide the names and contact information for groups that disburse college funds to deserving students. If contact information is lacking for some of the groups, follow up by using the phone book to look up the organizations. Some phone books even have a calendar of annual events that are sponsored by various civic groups. Finally, don't forget to pay a visit to the public library and ask the reference librarian for help. Here is a brief list of some of the more well-known civic groups to track down:

- Altrusa
- American Legion and American Legion Auxiliary
- American Red Cross
- Association of Junior Leagues International
- Boys and Girls Clubs
- Boy Scouts and Girl Scouts
- Circle K
- Civitan
- Elks Club
- Lions Club
- 4-H Clubs
- Fraternal Order of Eagles
- Friends of the Library
- Kiwanis International
- Knights of Columbus
- National Exchange Club
- National Grange
- Optimist International
- Performing arts center
- Rotary Club
- Rotaract and Interact
- Ruritan
- Sertoma International
- Soroptimist International of the Americas
- U.S. Jaycees
- USA Freedom Corps
- Veterans of Foreign Wars
- YMCA and YWCA
- Zonta International

Local businesses. Businesses like to return some of their profits to employees and students in the community. Many offer scholarships as a way to reward students who both study and work. Ask your manager if your employer has a scholarship fund and how you can apply. Some compa-

---

Ask to Be Nominated

Sometimes the biggest hurdle to winning a scholarship from your school or college is that you need to be nominated. Don't be afraid to ask teachers or professors if they will nominate you.

nies–particularly large companies that have offices, distributorships or factories in your community–offer scholarships that all students in the community are eligible to win. Check with the chamber of commerce for a list of the largest employers in the area. You can call the public relations or community outreach department in these companies to inquire about any scholarship opportunities. Visit the large department and chain stores in the area and ask the store manager or customer service manager about scholarships.

Parents' employer. Your parents may hate their bosses, but they'll love the fact that many companies award scholarships to the children of their employees as a benefit. They should speak with someone in the human resources department or their direct managers about scholarships and other educational programs offered by their company.

Parents' or grandparents' military service. If your parents or grandparents served in the U.S. Armed Forces, you may qualify for a scholarship from a military association. Each branch of the service and even specific divisions within each branch have associations. Speak with your parents and grandparents about their military service and see if they belong to or know of these military associations.

Your employer. Flipping burgers may have an up side. Even if you work only part-time, you may qualify for an educational scholarship given by your employer. For example, McDonald's offers the National Employee Scholarship to reward the accomplishments of its student-employees. There is even a McScholar of the Year prize that includes a $5,000 scholarship. If you have a full- or part-time job, ask your employer about scholarships.

Parents' union. Some unions sponsor scholarships for the children of their members. Ask your parents to speak with the union officers about scholarships and other educational programs sponsored by their union.

Interest clubs. Performing arts centers, city orchestras, equestrian associations and amateur sports leagues are just a few of the many special interest clubs that may offer scholarships. While some limit their awards to members, many simply look for students who are interested in what they support. A city performing arts center, for example, may offer an award for a talented performing artist in the community.

Professional sports teams. They may not have won a World Series since the 1950s, but many local professional athletic teams offer community awards (and not necessarily for athletes) as a way to contribute to the cities in which they are based.

Church or religious organizations. Religious organizations may provide scholarships for members. If you or your parents are members of a religious organization, check with the leaders to see if a scholarship is offered.

Local government. Some cities and counties provide scholarships specifically designated for local students. Often, local city council members and state representatives sponsor a scholarship fund. Even if you didn't vote for them, call their offices and ask if they offer a scholarship.

Local newspaper. Local newspapers often print announcements about students who win scholarships. Keep a record of the scholarships featured or go to the library or look online at back issues of the newspaper. Check last year's spring issues (between March and June) for announcements of scholarship recipients. Contact the sponsoring organizations to see if you're eligible to enter the next competition.

Searching Beyond Your Own Backyard

Once you have exhausted the opportunities in the community, it is time to broaden your search. Although the applicant pool is often larger with national awards, you shouldn't rule them out.

Because many national award programs have marketing budgets, finding these awards may actually be a little easier than the local awards. Most national awards will be advertised and the following places will help you track them down:

Internet. The Internet is more than a place to instant message and trade music. (Legally, of course!) One of the benefits of online scholarship directories is that they can be updated at any time. Thus, if you search an online scholarship directory, you can usually find up-to-date information on new scholarships. We recommend that you use as many online scholarship databases as possible as long as they are free. There are enough quality free databases that you should not have to pay for any online search. Here are a few we recommend:

- SuperCollege (www.supercollege.com)
- CollegeAnswer (www.collegeanswer.com)
- BrokeScholar (www.brokescholar.com)
- Careers and Colleges (www.careersandcolleges.com)
- The College Board (www.collegeboard.com)
- Free Scholarship Information (www.freschinfo.com)
- Scholarships.com (www.scholarships.com)

"Smaller Is Sometimes Better"
John Chin, Scholarship Winner

I had two friends who were determined to beat each other at winning scholarships. One decided to apply for only the top national scholarships and spent his time crafting a handful of great applications. My other friend, who knew that he would not be able to compete on a national level, concentrated only on local scholarships and applied to as many as he could.

At first it looked like my friend who applied to the big nationwide scholarships would win. He made the semifinals in several competitions and won a couple of $1,000 prizes.

However, his glory was short-lived. My other friend was constantly winning small $100 to $250 prizes. When everything was finally totaled, his collection of small but plentiful loot was $500 more!

When I became a senior guess which strategy I used to win scholarships!

The Hidden Scholarship Application

Almost all colleges use your application for admission to judge you for scholarships. When applying you are not just trying to get in but to get in with a scholarship.

- AdventuresinEducation (www.adventuresineducation.org)
- CollegeNet (www.collegenet.com)
- Mario Einaudi Center for International Studies (www.einaudi.cornell.edu/funding/search.asp)

Just remember that while many online databases claim to have billions of dollars in scholarships listed, they represent only a tiny fraction of what is available. We have personally used nearly every free scholarship database on the Internet and know from experience that none of them (including our own at www.supercollege.com) lists every scholarship that you might win. Think of these databases as starting points, that they are not the only places to find awards.

Professional associations. There is an association for every profession you can imagine. Whether you want to be a doctor, teacher or helicopter pilot, there are professional organizations that exist not only to advance the profession, but also to encourage students to enter that field by awarding grants and scholarships.

To find these associations, contact people who are already in the profession. If you think you want to become a computer programmer, ask computer programmers about the associations to which they belong. Also look at the trade magazines that exist for the profession since they have advertisements for various professional organizations.

Another way to find associations is through books like *The Encyclopedia of Associations.* This multi-volume set found at most college libraries lists nearly every professional association in the United States. Once you find these associations, contact them or visit their websites to see if they offer scholarships.

Professional associations often provide scholarships for upper-level college students, graduate school or advanced training. But even high school students who know what they want to do after college can find money from associations.

Big business. If you've never received a personal "thank you" from large companies like Coca-Cola, Calgon, Tylenol or Microsoft, here it is. A lot of these have charitable foundations that award scholarships. Companies give these awards to give something back to the community (and the positive PR sure doesn't hurt either). When you visit company websites, look for links to their foundations, which often manage the scholarship programs.

Many companies offer similar types of scholarships. What if you're a student film maker? Think about all the companies that make money or sell products to you from cameras to film to tripods. Are you into industrial music? What special software or instruments do you use? How about the makers of audio equipment? Consider the companies that will benefit from more people using their products and services.

Some companies also offer awards to attract future employees. For example, Microsoft, the software company, sponsors a scholarship program for student programmers. Be sure to investigate companies that employ

people in your field of study—especially if it is highly competitive—to see if they offer scholarships.

Colleges. You may think that checks only travel from your pocket to your college to pay for tuition. But colleges actually give a lot of money to students. Some of this money comes from the college itself while other money is from generous donations of alumni. Every college administers a number of scholarships, some based on financial need and some based on merit. What many students don't know is that often a student's application for admission is also used by the college to determine if he or she may win a scholarship. This is one reason it is worth the submission of any optional essay suggested on a college application. Even if the essay does not impact your admission, it could be used to award you some scholarship dollars.

Truly Outrageous Scholarships

Believe it or not there are scholarships for students who are left-handed or even skilled at using duct tape. You've probably heard rumors of outrageous scholarships with criteria so specific or outlandish that few students qualify. It may be seductive to think that there might be an award with such specific criteria that only you qualify. But don't spend too much time looking for these types of scholarships. You will win more money if you search for more normal awards that reward your specific range of interests, achievements and background.

Nevertheless, as you search for scholarships, you will discover some strange awards. We certainly did. We want to share a few of these choice awards with you. Keep in mind that the majority of scholarships do not have criteria as outrageous as these. But reading about them is certainly entertaining.

The Unathletic Scholarship

We have all heard of athletic scholarships. But how about one for those of us who don't participate in any sports? Bucknell University in Lewisburg, Pennsylvania, has an award for those who are unathletic. It was created by a frugal bachelor who left $1 million to create a scholarship for students who don't drink or smoke and, most important, do not participate in any "strenuous" athletics whatsoever. To qualify, you also need to be from certain counties in Pennsylvania.

The Lefty Award

Lefties put up with a lot of inconveniences—from hard-to-use scissors to smeared ink when writing in notebooks. Now, there is a scholarship that rewards the roughly 10 percent of students who are left-handed. The Mary Francis Beckley scholarship provides up to $1,500 for students at Juniata College in Huntingdon, Pennsylvania. The scholarship is in honor of Mary Francis, a left-hander who met her future husband (also a lefty) while both were attending college.

The Stuck at Prom Scholarship

The makers of "Duck" brand duct tape sponsor this award. The prize is a $6,000 scholarship for the couple that goes to their high school prom in the most original attire made from—you guessed it—duct tape. This award will give new meaning to the next time you seal a box with the sticky stuff.

Million Dollar Name

Did you know that there is one last name in America that can win you a full-tuition scholarship to Loyola University in Chicago? If you are Catholic and have the following last name you can get a four-year scholarship. Ready? The winning name is Zolp. And to prevent any of you from changing your last name, we should warn you that the school does require that this be the name on your birth certificate.

While these awards are good for a laugh, remember that they are not common, and you should not spend your time trying to find an obscure award that only you can win. Focus instead on creating a list of awards that match your entire range of interests and achievements.

I Have My Big List of Scholarships. Now What?

Until now, we have focused on places to find scholarships. If you invest time exploring these areas, you should have a fairly long list of potential scholarships. It may be tempting to start cranking out applications. However, this would waste valuable time. Just because you find an award for which you qualify does not mean that you should immediately apply. You want to focus your energies (and limited time) only on those awards that you have the best chance of winning.

How to Choose Scholarships You Can Win

It would save a lot of time if you knew beforehand which scholarships you'd win and which you wouldn't. With this information, you'd only spend time applying for the scholarships you knew would result in cash in your pocket.

There is no way to be 100 percent certain that you'll win any scholarship. But if you know enough about the scholarship and the organization giving away the money, you can determine if your background, interests and achievements make you a strong contender. By doing the detective work to uncover the purpose of the scholarships on your list, you will be able to focus time on those that fit you best and therefore offer the best chance of winning.

#1. Heed the Words from the Sponsors

When you're watching television, it's perfectly acceptable to get up and grab a soda or munchies during the commercial breaks. Advertisers cer-

---

Don't Write Off the Big Competitions

Don't be discouraged from applying to a scholarship that attracts a lot of students. After all, somebody has to win these awards, and there is no reason that it can't be you.

Thinking Like a Judge

Train yourself to think from the perspective of the scholarship judges. What are they trying to accomplish by awarding the scholarship? What kind of student are they seeking? What is the organization's goal and mission?

tainly don't like it, but there are no negative repercussions for ignoring the sponsors' messages. This is not the case for scholarships.

Scholarships, of course, don't have commercial breaks, but they do have sponsors–the organizations that are providing the money. Nobody, and we mean nobody, gives away money without a reason. Every sponsor has a mission for giving away their hard-earned cash. This mission may be a goal they are trying to achieve or ideology they are trying to promote.

For example, a teachers' organization might award a scholarship because its members want to encourage students to enter the teaching profession. The scholarship fulfills this mission since it helps support students who want to major in education. An environmental group might sponsor a scholarship with the mission of promoting environmental awareness. It might reward students who have done environmental work in school. A local bank might give money to a student who has done a great deal of public service as a way to give back to the community in which it does business.

It is critical that you find the mission of the scholarship since it will tell you exactly what kind of student the selection committee is seeking. Take our example of the teachers' scholarship. By knowing that the organization wants to encourage students to become teachers, you can surmise (if they don't explicitly say so) that they want to give their money to students who are committed to becoming teachers and can show this through qualifications such as being an education major, student teacher or volunteer tutor. You can also guess that when picking a winner, the selection committee will look for students who enjoy interacting with young people and who value education.

The mission of a scholarship is your best clue to what the selection committee wants in a winner. As you go through each award on your list, uncover its mission. In other words, your mission is to find their mission.

#2. Do the Detective Work

To uncover the mission of a scholarship you need to do some detective work. Begin by carefully reading the description of the scholarship. Sometimes the answer is clearly stated in the award description. Also look at the eligibility requirements to see what kind of questions the scholarship sponsors are asking. Is there a GPA requirement? If there is and it's relatively high, grades are probably important. If the GPA requirement is low, then grades are probably not important. Does the application ask for a list of extracurricular activities? If so, they are probably a significant part of the selection criteria. Do you need to submit an essay on a specific topic or a project to demonstrate proficiency in a field of study? All these requirements are clues about what the scholarship judges think will (and won't) be important.

For example, a public service scholarship may be based only on your philanthropic acts. If that is the case, the entire application will most likely be focused on descriptions of your selfless deeds. On the other hand, a scholarship given by a major corporation may be based on a combination of grades, leadership and personal integrity. The eligibility requirements will provide clues about what criteria the organization will use to judge you and therefore what they consider important.

After you have scanned the application requirements, ask yourself: What is the purpose of the awarding organization? Whether it's helping students who dream of becoming circus performers or rewarding students for their religious fervor, every organization has a reason for its existence. If you're lucky, the goal is clearly stated in the description of the organization, but sometimes you need to look deeper. For example, even if the scholarship description does not directly state it, you can be sure that an award given by an organization that is composed of local physicians will probably prefer that the winner have a connection with medicine or an intention to enter the medical field.

Just as your friends are a reflection of you, most clubs and organizations want to reach students who are similar to their membership. If you don't know much about the organization, contact them to learn background information regarding the history, purpose or contributions of the group. Check out the organization's website to get a sense of their mission and membership. Read their brochures or publications. The more you know about why the organization is giving the award, the better you'll understand how you may or may not fit.

Once you have a sense of whom the scholarship committee is looking for, you can determine if you can make a strong case that you are that person. The only way to do this is to be honest about yourself.

#3. Be Realistic About How Great You Are

Here's where you need to separate reality in your mom's eyes from the rest of the world's reality. From Mom's perspective, you are the next Bill Gates, Albert Einstein or Amelia Earhart. Mom may be right. But as you are applying for scholarships, take a realistic, un-momlike look at yourself. You know what your strengths are and aren't better than anyone else.

Be careful not to be too hard on yourself. After working with thousands of students, we have learned that students more often underestimate their abilities than overestimate. Try to be realistic, but also don't sell yourself short. Remember that scholarship judges are not looking for the perfect match. There are a lot of factors that will influence their decision, and many of these things like personality or motivation are difficult to measure. However, you do want to find a match between the mission of the scholarship and some of your own interests, goals and achievements.

If you are your school's star journalist, naturally you should apply for journalism scholarships. But if all you have done is write a single letter to the editor, spend your time applying to scholarships that better match what you have accomplished. You can still apply for a journalism scholarship, especially if you only

---

> **Balance Quality and Quantity When Choosing Awards**
>
> *When deciding how many scholarships to apply for, create a balance between the quality and quantity of your applications. Don't apply for 75 awards sending in the same application to each. At the same time, don't apply to one or two scholarships and spend four weeks perfecting each application.*

recently realized that you want to become a journalist, but you will be at a disadvantage compared to the other applicants and therefore should place this award below other awards on your to-do list.

As you go through your list of scholarships, move to the bottom those in which you have the weakest matches to the goal of the scholarships. Make those awards that fit you best your highest priority. These are the ones that you want to focus on first.

#4. Size Up the Competition

Sometimes knowing how tough your competition is will also help you choose which scholarships to select as your focus (and hence your first applications). Your competition can be as broad as every student in America or as limited as the members of your school's Delta Phi Epsilon. As you can guess, the larger your competition, the more outstanding you need to be to win the scholarship. Look at your accomplishments and think about how they compare to others at your school, in your city and in your state.

If you are a pianist and the highest honor you've won is your school's talent show, you probably have a reasonable chance of winning a musical scholarship provided by your school. If your highest honor is winning a state competition, you will want to apply for state and even national-level music scholarships. By understanding how you match up to others who will apply for awards, you can spend your time on scholarships that you have a strong shot to win.

#5. Remember the Clock Never Stops

Scholarship deadlines are not like tax deadlines, where there is a single day when all forms are due. The deadlines for scholarships vary. Be aware of these crucial dates. Unless you plan carefully, you may miss out on a scholarship simply because you don't have the time to create a decent application. Sandwiched among studying, sleeping and everything else in your busy life, there is limited time to spend on applying for scholarships. If you find a great scholarship that is due next week but requires a yet-to-be-written original composition that would take a month, you should probably pass on the competition. If you know that, given the amount of time available, you won't be able to do an acceptable job, it's better to pass and move on to awards in which you have the time to put together a winning application. Remember, too, that you may be able to apply for the award next year.

The Magic Number of Scholarships

The truth is that there is no magic number of scholarships for which you should apply. But you should avoid the extremes. Don't select only a couple of scholarships with the intention of spending countless hours crafting the perfect application. While it is true that to win you need to turn in quality applications, there is also a certain amount of subjective decision making. So even with the perfect application, you may not win. This means that you need to apply to more than a few scholarships. On the other hand, don't apply for 75 awards, sending in the same application to each. You'll just waste your time. You need to strike a balance between quantity and quality.

After you prioritize your scholarships with the ones you feel fit you best at the top of the list, push yourself to apply to as many as you can, working from top to bottom. You probably won't get to the end. This is okay since you have the least chance of winning the awards at the bottom anyway. By prioritizing and working methodically down your list, you will have hedged your bets by making sure that your first applications are for the scholarships that you have the best chance of winning while also not limiting yourself to only a handful of awards.

Don't Look for Scholarships Alone

Many students treat searching for scholarships like a spy game, where they keep the scholarships that they find top secret. They probably feel that the fewer people who know about the scholarship, the better chance they have of winning.

This is totally counterproductive.

While researching this book, we interviewed hundreds of students and only a small handful actually collaborated with others on their scholarship search. Yet, the students who did work with others found it much easier to find awards and to stay motivated. Ultimately, they won more money than the students who decided to go it alone.

Think about it. You are applying to a scholarship along with thousands of other students from across your state. Does it really matter if your friend applies? Absolutely not. What do you have to gain by working in a group and sharing the awards that you find? Plenty. The students who worked with others discovered that by sharing the awards they found and pooling their resources, they were able to find more scholarships in less time than they would have if they had worked alone. The end result was that these students had more scholarships to apply to and more time to focus on their applications. Hence, they won more money.

Look around you and find others who are also hunting for scholarships. Agree to share awards and even come up with assignments for spreading around the task of searching different sources for scholarships.

You will also find that an additional benefit of being part of a group is that it will keep you motivated. It's easier to stay focused when you have others depending on you. There is no reason why the scholarship process should be one that you embark on alone.

Chapter 2 Summary: Find Scholarships You Can Win

Use the two-prong approach to select scholarships. First, find as many as you can. Then screen and prioritize them based on whether or not you can present yourself as the ideal candidate.

Find scholarships all around you. To find scholarships, investigate the surroundings such as your school, community organizations, the Internet, your parents' and your employers, local and state governments and local newspapers and publications. Don't neglect your own backyard.

Don't count on outrageous awards. Look at all your talents and interests.

Choose scholarships you can win. Some tips: Try to understand what the judges want to achieve by awarding the scholarship and what they are looking for in the winner. Survey your qualifications, and be realistic about how well you fit the awards. Size up the competition both past and present.

Apply to as many as time allows. There are two factors that limit the number of scholarships you apply for: the amount of time you have to apply and your fit with the scholarship criteria. Apply for as many scholarships as you can that are appropriate and for which you have the time to develop quality applications.

Don't go it alone. Form your own network of scholarship searchers to spread out the work and find more awards.

Avoid Scholarship Scams

In this chapter, you'll learn:

- The false promises of scholarship scam artists and how to avoid them

- How to recognize the telltale signs of a scholarship scam

- How one student got taken by an offer that was too good to be true

Scholarships That Steal

Now that you know where to find scholarships, you need to be aware of some dangers that may be lurking nearby. While the great majority of scholarship providers and services have philanthropic intentions, not all do. There are some scholarship services and even scholarships themselves that you need to avoid. According to the Federal Trade Commission, in one year there were more than 175,000 cases reported of scholarship scams, costing consumers $22 million. And this is a low estimate since most scholarship scams go unreported!

While we were fortunate to have not been victims of a scholarship scam, we have to admit that the offers we received were tempting. We both received letters in high school and college from companies that promised to help us find and win "unclaimed" scholarships. The pitch was tempting: There is money out there that no one is claiming. All we needed to do was purchase their service to get a list of these awards. Had we done so, we would have been $400 poorer and certainly none the richer.

In this chapter, we will describe some of the common scams that you may encounter. You must avoid these offers, no matter how glamorous they seem.

The Big Picture

The key to avoiding a scholarship scam is to understand the motivation of the people behind these scams. Those who operate financial aid rip-offs know that paying for college is something that makes you extremely nervous. They also know that most people don't have extensive experience when it comes to scholarships and may therefore believe that there are such things as "hidden" or "unclaimed" scholarships. These charlatans take advantage of your fears and discomfort by offering an easy answer with a price tag that seems small compared to the promised benefits.

Be aware that you are vulnerable to these kinds of inducements. Think about it this way. If you have a weakness for buying clothes, you need to be extra vigilant when you are at the shopping mall. Similarly, because you need money for college, you are more susceptible to tempting scholarship offers. Acknowledging that these fears make you a target of scam artists is the first step to spotting their traps.

How to Spot a Scholarship Scam

Imagine one day you open your mailbox and find a letter from a very official-sounding organization offering a personalized analysis of your financial aid opportunities and expert recommendations of scholarships you should apply for—all for the low cost of a few hundred dollars. You may think that is not much, considering that the cost of your education could run into six digits. That's exactly what these companies want

Avoid All Guarantees

You can usually detect a scholarship scam if the promise is too good to be true, if you are "guaranteed" to win or if payment is required.

you to think. The truth is that the information they provide is free public information (like descriptions of various loan programs) and none of it is truly personalized—unless you call typing your name on top of a photocopy personalized.

In most cases there is nothing illegal about these offers, which is why they continue to exist, but they are certainly a waste of money. Our advice is to save your money and invest a little time in researching financial aid opportunities yourself.

The following are some examples of "tempting" offers that you should avoid. Remember while the words may change, the message is still the same: Pay us and you won't have to worry about how to pay for tuition.

"Pay us $$$ and we will create a personalized financial aid plan for your child. We have a library of hundreds of resources that we will use to create an individualized financial aid plan for you." What they don't tell you is that the resources they use can easily be found for free on the Internet or in your library. In fact, the scholarships listed in this book are probably their "resources." Save yourself hundreds of dollars and find the scholarships yourself. Plus, you'll do a more thorough job and actually be able to find scholarships that you can win.

"Pay us $$$ and we will research and identify the 20 scholarships that fit you best. Why spend weeks researching scholarships when our specialized researchers can do it for you? We have scholarship sources that no one else does. Plus, you are guaranteed to win at least one." You would receive a list of 20 scholarships you could have found on your own for free. Plus, any scholarship that is a "guaranteed" win is a scam as we'll explain later.

"I Lost $500 from a Scholarship Scam"
Steven Hecht, Scam Victim

My parents and I attended a free seminar sponsored by a college financial aid service company. During the seminar, the speaker explained how competitive it was to win scholarships and how many dollars aren't awarded each year because students just don't know about the scholarships. He said that his company would use its comprehensive national database to produce a personalized scholarship program for me. Even better, if I didn't win $2,500 in scholarships from their program, they would refund the fee of $495. My parents and I thought that because we could get our money back, there was no risk in trying the program. Along with most of the other families at the seminar, we signed up for the program.

A week later, we received a packet in the mail. It contained some articles about scholarships and financial aid and a one-page document with scholarships listed. I applied for each of the scholarships. Within the next few months, I won none of them.

My parents remembered the guarantee and we wrote a letter requesting our refund of the $495. Were we surprised when our request was refused. The company said we needed to read the small print of the contract we signed. The guarantee was that I would either win $2,500 in scholarships or that the company's program would provide opportunities that could be worth $2,500. In our excitement on the night of the seminar, we never bothered to read the small print. We were out almost $500. We definitely could have used the money toward my tuition instead of toward a bogus scholarship scam.

"Each year millions of dollars in scholarships are not awarded. Pay us $$$ and we will locate unclaimed scholarship dollars that your son or daughter can win." The reality is that there are very few "unclaimed" scholarships. Those that are have such specific eligibility requirements that almost no one can qualify. Plus, you can find thousands of scholarships on your own in books and on the Internet without paying a search fee. You'll also do a much better job.

"You're a finalist in our scholarship. Pay us $$$ for your registration fee. You're guaranteed to win!" The truth is that you are not guaranteed to win, or if you did win, the prize would be less than the registration fee. Real scholarships never require any fee from applicants.

"You've won our scholarship, guaranteed! All we need is your credit card number to verify your eligibility." Instead of winning a "guaranteed" scholarship, you would get some surprise charges on your next credit card bill.

"You qualify for our exclusive, incredibly low-interest loan program. All you need to do is pay us $$$ to lock in the rate." The truth is that you would pay the fee but not get the loan. Or you might get the loan, but the interest rate could be much higher than if you shopped around.

"Come to our very informative financial aid seminar, where you'll learn our secret strategies for scholarships found nowhere else in the world." Seminars like these may actually be sales pitches for any combination of the above. Not all seminars are scams or rip-offs, so you'll have to use your own judgment. However, one giveaway is if the seminar sounds like a sales pitch or contains promises that sound too good to be true. If you feel like the seminar is just a live version of a late-night infomercial, you are probably looking at a seminar where you will be asked to part with your money for what may be totally worthless information.

In general, the major telltale sign that you are about to be taken by a dubious offer is if you are asked to pay any significant amount of money. Particularly if you are applying for a scholarship, never part with your money. Scholarships are meant to pay *you* money, not the other way around.

Red Flags That Indicate a Scam

Here are some common red flags to watch for:

- **Registration, entry or administrative fee:** Legitimate scholarship and financial aid programs do not require an upfront fee. Do not pay for anything more than the cost of postage. Remember, real scholarships are about giving you money, not taking funds *from* you.

- **Soliciting your credit card number or bank account:** Never give out this kind of financial information to anyone who contacts you from a scholarship organization. No scholarship needs this information to award you money for college.

Red Flag

The biggest tip-off to a scholarship scam is that you must part with your money. Any time that you are asked to open your wallet, be wary.

- **Refusal to reveal name, address or phone number:** You know that something is wrong when the person on the telephone won't reveal his or her name or contact information.

- **Guarantee:** There is no such thing as a guaranteed scholarship in exchange for a fee. Legitimate scholarships are based on merit or need, not your willingness to pay a registration fee.

If you discover that you have been the victim of one of these scams, don't be embarrassed. This happens to thousands of parents and students every year. Report your experience to the Better Business Bureau and Federal Trade Commission (www.ftc.gov) to help prevent it from happening to others. Also, be sure to write us about it in care of SuperCollege, 3286 Oak Court, Belmont, CA 94002. We maintain lists of dishonest and worthless programs and would like to know if you encounter any new ones.

The adage of consumer protection applies to scholarships. If an offer sounds too good to be true, it probably is.

Chapter 3 Summary: Avoid Scholarship Scams

Know when a guarantee is not a guarantee. What is tempting about scholarship scams is that they promise guaranteed money or a money-back guarantee. Read the small print—there is no such thing as a guaranteed scholarship.

Recognize your weakness. If you are stressed about paying for college, realize that you are es-pecially susceptible to unrealistic promises to help solve your problem.

Keep your wallet closed. Scholarship services and applications should always be free. If a service sounds too good to be true, it probably is.

Create a Stunning Scholarship Application

CHAPTER 4

In this chapter, you'll learn:

- To create a plan of attack

- How to present your achievements to captivate the attention of the judges

- Which accomplishments to highlight and which to hide

- Top 10 scholarship application do's and don'ts

Scholarship Applications: Your Entry Ticket

At first glance, scholarship applications look easy–most are only a single page in length. Piece of cake, right? Don't let their diminutive size fool you. The application is a vital part of winning any scholarship. Scholarship judges must sift through hundreds or even thousands of applications, and the application form is what they use to determine which applicants continue to the next stage. It's crucial that you ace your application to make this first cut.

In this chapter, we'll look at strategies you can use to transform an ordinary scholarship application form into a screaming testament of why you deserve to win free cash for college. Along the way, you'll meet students just like you who have used well-crafted applications to win incredible amounts of money. We'll also introduce you to a few who made fatal application blunders that you'll want to avoid.

The Big Picture

Our strategy for the application form is simple. Although you can't control the questions that are asked or even the activities and achievements you already have, you can control how you describe each accomplishment, whether to include or omit information and the order in which you present each item. In short, you control how you portray yourself on paper.

This is why the application form is deceptively simple. Most students rush through the application since they believe it's an unimportant part of the scholarship process. They don't spend the time to consider which activities, honors and awards to list and how each contributes to conveying who they are to the judges. Big mistake! Even though there is limited space on applications, you want to be deliberate in what you write to maximize your application's impact on the scholarship judges. Our approach requires more work, but it will dramatically improve your chances of winning a scholarship.

Create Your Plan of Attack

With thousands of scholarships available and only one you, it makes sense to develop an overall strategy before you begin tackling scholarship applications. So, let's start with some highlevel planning.

Prioritize the scholarships to which you think you are a match. In Chapter 2, you learned how to select scholarships that best match your background and experience. Be sure you have your list of scholarship opportunities prioritized so that you know in which order to apply. If time runs out and you can't get to all the awards on your list, at least you have applied to those you have the best chance of winning.

Don't Underestimate the Application Form

Don't take the application form lightly. It may be short, but it is critical that you ace it if you want to advance to the next round. Most scholarship judges use the application form to separate those who will advance from those who will receive the "Sorry, try again later" letters.

Build a timeline. After you have a prioritized list of scholarships, look at their deadlines and create a schedule for applying. Set deadlines for when you will have the application forms completed, essays written and recommendations, if required, submitted. Post this schedule where you can see it every day. We also recommend that you share it with your parents. Moms and dads are great at nagging (we mean reminding) you to meet deadlines so you might as well use their nagging (we mean motivating) skills to your advantage.

Look for recycling opportunities. The first scholarship for which you apply will take the most time and it will no doubt be the most difficult. But with each application you complete, it will get easier. This is because for each successive application, you can draw on the materials you developed for the previous one. To complete your first application, you need to think about your activities and recall achievements that you have forgotten. If there is an essay component, you will need to find a topic and craft an articulate essay. When you work on your second application, you can benefit from the work you've already done for the first. As you're building your timeline, look for scholarships in which you can recycle information from one application to another. Recycling will save you time. In addition, you can improve on your work each time that you use it. For example, the second time you answer a question about your plans after graduation, you can craft your response more effectively than the first. As you recycle information, don't just reuse it, improve it!

Once you have your prioritized list of scholarships and a schedule that takes advantage of "parental motivation" you are ready to start. Keep recycling opportunities in the back of your mind and you'll save even more time, which will help you apply to more scholarships.

General Rules for Completing the Application

Before you fire up your computer (or typewriter if you're old school), here are a few basic application rules to keep in mind:

Make application form triplets. The first thing to do when you receive scholarship applications is to make three photocopies of them. Why do you need three copies? Your goal is to craft the perfect application. As unlikely as it seems, you probably won't achieve perfection the first time around. A spare copy is your insurance should you make a mistake. It's not uncommon to discover that only four out of your five most important life accomplishments fit within the two-inch space on the form. Regardless of how many copies you make, never use your last clean copy of the application form. Trust us—and every student who has ruined their original at 2 a.m. on the day their application was due. It's well worth your time to have plenty of extra copies.

Be a neat freak. You may have dirty laundry strewn across your room and a pile of papers large enough to be classified as its own life form, but you don't want the scholarship judges to know that. When it comes to applications, neatness does count.

We would not ordinarily be neatness zealots—we admit to having our own mountains of life-imbibed papers—but submitting an application with globs of correction fluid, scratched out words or illegible hieroglyphics will severely diminish your message. Think how much less impressive the Mona Lisa would be if da Vinci had painted it on a dirty old bed sheet. You may have the most incredible thoughts to convey in your applications, but if your form is filled with errors, none of it will matter. In a sea of hundreds and even thousands of other applications, you don't want yours to be penalized by sloppy presentation.

Know when to leave a space blank. An official mom rule from childhood is this: "If you don't have anything nice to say, don't say it." While this is a good lesson on self-restraint, it does not always hold true for scholarship applications. In general, it is not a good idea to leave any area blank. You don't need to fill the entire space, but you should make an effort to list something in every section. However, before you try to explain how the handmade certificate that your mom presented you for being *Offspring of the Year* qualifies as an "award," realize that there are limits. If you've never held a job, don't list anything under work experience. If, however, you painted your grandmother's house one summer and got paid for it, consider listing it if you don't have any other options.

Use your judgment and common sense when trying to decide whether or not to leave an area blank. Ask yourself if what you are including will strengthen or weaken your application. Think like a judge. Is the information relevant? Or does it seem like a stretch? If you cannot convince yourself that what you are listing is justified, it will certainly not go over well with the judges. Remember your mom's advice; leave it blank and move on to the sections where you have something great to say.

Nip and tuck every sentence. Succinct and terse, scholarship application forms bear the well-earned reputation for having less space than you need. Often offering only a page or less, scholarship applications leave little room for much more than just the facts. As you are completing your applications, remember to abbreviate where appropriate and keep your sentences short. Often judges are scanning the application form. If they want an essay, they will ask for one.

Instructions do not have to be taken literally. If the instructions say to list your awards, don't feel like you can't add explanation if you need to. If you have three great awards, it is better to use your space to list those three with short explanations rather than cram in all 15 awards that you've won in your life. (No argument can be made for the timeliness of your *Perfect Attendance Award* from kindergarten.) You are trying to present the most relevant information that shows the scholarship judges why you deserve their money. Use the space to explain how each award, job or activity relates to the scholarship.

Also, feel free to interpret some instructions. Work experience does not have to be limited to traditional jobs. Maybe you started your own free-lance design business or cut lawns on the weekends. The same goes for leadership positions. Who said that leadership has to be an elected position

---

Fill in as Many Blanks as Possible

Blank spaces can bring out the agoraphobia in you—the open space can be frightening. While you want to fill in each space, you don't want to stretch something to the point of looking ridiculous. So if you absolutely don't have anything worthwhile to list, don't stress and just leave the space blank.

within an organization? Just be sure to explain the entry if the relationship is not totally clear. Here's an example:

> Volunteer Wilderness Guide. Led clients through seven-day trek in Catskills. Responsible for all aspects of the trip including group safety.

Always remember that the application is you. A scholarship application is more than a piece of paper. In the eyes of the scholarship judges, it is you. It may not be fair, but in many cases the application is the only thing that the judges will have as a measurement standard. The last thing you want to be is a dry list of academic and extracurricular achievements. You are a living, breathing person. Throughout the application, take every opportunity—no matter how small—to show the judges who you really are. Use descriptions and vocabulary that reveal your passion and commitment. Always remember that the application is a reflection of you.

The Five Steps to Crafting a Winning Application

We have reduced the process for completing your application to five distinct steps. As you read each step think of how you can apply it to the specific applications that you are working on.

Step 1: Use a Little "Spin" to "Wow" Your Audience

Politicians are notorious for telling their constituents what they want to hear. Good politicians never lie, but they do put a flattering "spin" on their words depending on whom they're addressing. While you must never lie on your application forms, you do want to present yourself in the best possible way and appeal to your audience. In other words, employ a little spin.

We know that some politicians have a difficult time distinguishing between lying and spinning. You shouldn't. Let's say you are applying for a scholarship that rewards students who are interested in promoting literacy. You have been a volunteer at your local library where each week one of your responsibilities is to read stories to a dozen children. Here are three ways you could describe this activity on your application:

Non-spin description:

Library volunteer.

Lie:

Library reading program founder. Started a national program that reaches thousands of children every day to promote literacy.

Spin:

Library volunteer. Promoted literacy among children through weekly after-school reading program at public library.

Spin but Don't Lie

You can't change the facts about your accomplishments, but you can change how you describe them. Employ a different spin for each scholarship. Remember, you can spin, but NEVER lie.

At one extreme, you can see that a lie exaggerates well beyond the truth. At the other extreme, the non-spin description is not very impressive because it does not explain how the activity relates to the purpose of the scholarship. The spin version does not stretch the truth, but it does make clear how this activity fits within the context of the goal of the scholarship. It focuses on what is important to the judges while at the same time it ignores other aspects of your job that are not relevant—such as shelving books.

To take this example one step further, let's say that now you are applying for a scholarship that rewards student leaders. One of your other responsibilities as a library volunteer is to maintain the schedule for volunteers and help with the recruitment of new volunteers. Your description for this scholarship might read:

> Library volunteer. Coordinated volunteer schedule and recruited new members for after-school reading program.

"How My Support of Legalizing Marijuana Cost Me"
Mike Porter, Scholarship Applicant

I went to high school in what I thought was a liberal-minded city. Our school principal seemed to be a hippy, straight out of the 1960s, with long hair and even wearing tie-dyed shirts on Fridays. The mayor of our city was constantly in the newspaper for his liberal stands on everything from funding for the homeless to gay rights.

In my senior year I applied for a scholarship for students in my high school. When asked about my leadership in extracurricular activities, I thought nothing of putting down that I was president of our school's Advocate Club. Our club promoted political activism, and we had made local headlines for rallies we held for increasing funding for education, keeping large chain corporations out of our downtown and legalizing the medicinal use of marijuana. There was a photo of me in the local newspaper holding a marijuana plant at a sit-in.

My friends told me they thought I had a really good chance of winning because I had the highest grades in our class and I was one of a handful of students admitted to Berkeley. I hate to brag, but my teachers really liked me because I took the time to get to know them, and they wrote great recommendation letters. I wrote an essay about my experiences with the Advocate Club and my fight to legalize marijuana.

When the winners were announced at our senior banquet, I was disappointed that I did not win any of the three prizes. I was pretty cocky and thought I should have been a shoo-in. I was so distraught that the next day at school I spoke with my counselor, who was one of the judges, and asked her why she thought I didn't win.

At first she was hesitant to give me any information about what happened behind closed doors. After reassuring her that I wasn't going to tell anyone and that I only wanted to know so I could improve my applications in the future, she let me in on the judges' thoughts. She said that everyone knew that I was qualified, but there were three judges who voted against me because while they admired my devotion to causes, they disagreed with my lobbying for the legalization of medicinal uses for marijuana. I couldn't believe what I was hearing—that my political views prevented me from winning.

After I found out who the judges were, it was easy to understand why they voted against me. They were members of our local government who were very conservative compared to the rest of the city's political leaders. The ironic thing was that I could have found out who the judges were before turning in my application. If I had, I might have given less attention to my most controversial belief.

Moral of the Story: *Understanding the awarding organization and who is likely to read your application can give you insight into what to focus on and what to avoid. If Mike had asked some basic questions about the judges, he probably would have won.*

Know Your Audience

You would never give a speech without knowing who your audience is, right? So don't start your applications until you know who will read them.

Notice how you have "spun" your activity so that it highlights a different aspect of what you did and better shows the judges how you fit their criteria. In the application you should use the opportunity to spin your accomplishments to match the goal of the award.

To be able to spin effectively you need to know your audience. When you prioritized your scholarships earlier, you should have discovered the purposes of the scholarships. Remember that in most cases the scholarship judges want to give their money to students who are the best reflections of themselves. For example, the Future Teachers of America judges will want to fund students who seem the most committed to pursuing a teaching career. The American Congress of Surveying and Mapping judges, on the other hand, want to give their money to students who have the strongest interest in cartography.

To determine your audience, ask the following questions. Use your answers to guide your decisions on how much detail to provide, what to include or omit and how to prioritize your achievements. You'll find that just thinking about these questions and putting yourself into the mindset of the judges will enable you to craft a better application.

 What is the mission of the organization giving away the scholarship? Why do they want to give free money to students?

Organizations don't give away scholarships and expect nothing in return. Behind their philanthropic motives lies an ulterior motive–to promote their organization's vision. To find this vision, visit the organization's website, call its offices to ask for more information or request materials to read. If it's a local group, meet some of its members or attend a meeting. Once you know what the organization is all about, you can better decide which of your achievements would make the biggest impression on the scholarship application.

Let's imagine that you are applying for an award given by an organization of professional journalists. In visiting their website you learn that print and broadcast journalists join this group because they are passionate about the profession of journalism and want to encourage public awareness about the importance of a free press. Immediately, you know that you need to highlight those experiences that demonstrate your zeal for journalism and, if possible, your belief in the value of a free press. Among your activities and accomplishments are the following:

Columnist for your high school newspaper
Vice President of the Writers' Club
English essay contest winner
Summer internship at a radio station

As you look at this list, you remember that in the Writers' Club you participated in a workshop that helped a local elementary school start its own newspaper. Since this achievement almost perfectly matches the mission of our hypothetical journalism organization, use your limited space in the application to list it first and to add an explanation.

You might write something like this:

> Writers' Club, Vice President, organized "Writing Counts" workshop at Whitman Elementary School, which resulted in the launch of the school's first student-run newspaper.

Think of the impact this would have on the scholarship judges. "Look here, Fred" one journalist on the judging committee would say. "This student does what we do! Definitely someone we should interview!"

Before you can even begin to evaluate which activities to list and how to describe them, you need to know as much as you can about the organization sponsoring the scholarship. By understanding the purpose of the organization, you can select achievements and spin them in ways that will be sure to attract the attention of the judges.

Q **Who is going to read your scholarship application? What kind of people make up the organization that is giving away the money?**

Let's imagine for a moment that you need to give a speech to two groups of people. Without knowing who your audience is, you would have a difficult time composing a speech that would appeal to them, right?

It would make a big difference in your presentation were one a group of mathematicians and the other a group of fashion designers. To grab the attention of each of these audiences, you'd need to adjust your speech accordingly. References to mathematical theorems would hardly go over well with the designers, just as the mathematicians probably could not care less about how black the new black really is.

It's not always possible to know who your audience is, but you should try to find out who is likely to be on the judging committee. In some instances you may actually know the people by name—such as an administrator at your school, a local congressman or business leader. Often you will have a sense of what kind of people will most likely be judging. Most groups have identifiable traits among their membership. The Veterans of Foreign Wars and American Civil Liberties Union, for example, have members with identifiable beliefs.

In the same way that understanding the mission of an organization helps you to decide how to present certain information, so too does knowing the composition of the judging panel. For example, if you know that members of the community who are committed to public service are on the judging committee, then stress your contributions in that area.

Be sure to avoid things that might be offensive to the organization's members. Just imagine what would happen if you thoughtlessly mentioned that you were the author of an economics project entitled "How Labor Unions Make the U.S. Unable to Compete and Lowers Our Standard of Living" to judges who are members of the International Brotherhood of Teamsters.

It should also be clear to you why you can't use the same list of activities and accomplishments for every scholarship. Take the time to craft a unique list that matches what each of the scholarships is intended to reward.

Find Out Why They Are Giving Away Their Money

Nobody gives away money without a reason. Behind every organization's philanthropic actions lies a motive. Your job is to uncover what this motive is and spin your application accordingly.

Stand Out

To stand out from the competition you need to predict who will enter and imagine what will be on their applications.

Step 2: Stand Out from the Competition

Think of the scholarship competition as a reverse police lineup where you want to stand out and be picked by the people behind the one-way mirror. You want the judge to say without hesitation, "That's the one!" The only way this will happen is if your application is noticed and doesn't get lost in the crowd. One of the best ways to accomplish this is to know what you're up against—in other words, think about who else will be in the lineup with you.

Try to anticipate your competition—even if it's just an educated guess. Depending on to whom the scholarship is offered, you may have a limited or broad pool of competitors. If the award is confined to your school, you may know everyone who will enter on a first-name basis. If it's national, all you may know for a medical scholarship, for instance, is that the applicants are students interested in becoming doctors.

More important than the scope of the competition is the type of students who will apply. One of the biggest challenges in any competition is to break away from the pack. If 500 pre-med students are applying for a $10,000 scholarship from a medical association, you need to make sure that your application stands out from those of the 499 other applicants. If you are lucky, you may have done something that few have done. (Inventing a new vaccine in your spare time would certainly set you apart!) Unfortunately, most of us will have to distinguish ourselves in more subtle ways, such as through the explanation of activities and accomplishments.

Say you are applying for a scholarship given by a national medical association that seeks to promote the medical sciences. It just so happens that you are considering a pre-med major and you have interned at a local hospital. If you hadn't read this book, you might have listed under activities:

Summer Internship at Beth Israel Children's Hospital

But you did read this book! So you know that this is a great activity to elaborate on since it demonstrates your commitment to medicine and shows that you truly are interested in entering the medical field. You also know that you need to stand out from the competition and as great as this activity is, you know that a lot of other applicants will also have volunteered at hospitals. So instead of simply listing the internship, you add detail to make the experience more unique. You could write:

Summer Internship at Beth Israel Children's Hospital, assisted with clinical trial of new allergy medication.

This description is much more unique and memorable. By providing details, you can illustrate to the judges how your volunteer work is different from that of other students. Remember that you can add short descriptions in most applications even if the instructions do not explicitly ask for them.

Let's look at another example. If you know that many applicants for a local public service scholarship have participated in your school's annual canned food drive, you need to highlight contributions that go beyond this program. You'd probably want to highlight the other public service activities you did besides the canned food drive because you know that the food drive alone will not set you apart from the others.

If you can anticipate who your competition will be and what they might write in their applications, you will be able to find a way to go one step further to distinguish yourself from the crowd. Even the simple act of adding a one-sentence description to an activity can make the difference between standing out and getting lost.

Step 3: List Important Accomplishments First

In movies, the most dare-devilish car chase, the most harrowing showdown and the most poignant romantic revelations are usually saved until the end. While this works for Hollywood, it does not for scholarship applications. Since scholarship judges review so many applications and the space on the form is limited, you need to highlight your most impressive points first.

If you have listed four extracurricular activities, assume that some judges won't read beyond the first two. This doesn't mean that all judges will be this rushed, but there are always some who are. It's extremely important that you prioritize the information that you present and rank your accomplishments according to the following—which should not come as too much of a surprise.

> **Fit.** The most important factor in prioritizing your achievements is how they fit with the goal of the scholarship. This is, after all, why these kind people want to hand you some free dough. Emphasize accomplishments that match the purpose of the scholarship. If you are applying for an award that rewards athleticism, stress how well you've done in a particular sport before listing your volunteer activities.

> **Scope.** Prioritize your accomplishments by their scope, or how much of an impact they have made. How many people have been affected by your work? To what extent has your accomplishment affected your community? Did your contribution produce measurable results? In simple terms, put the big stuff before the small stuff.

> **Uniqueness.** Since your application will be compared to those of perhaps thousands of others, include accomplishments that are uncommon. Give priority to those that are unique or difficult to win. Being on your school's honor roll is certainly an achievement, but it is an honor that many others have received. Try to select honors that fewer students have received. Remember the reverse police lineup idea—you want to stand out in order to be selected.

> **Timeliness.** This is the least-important criterion, but if you get stuck and aren't sure how to arrange some of your accomplishments, put the more recent achievements first. Having won an election in the past year is more relevant than having won one three years ago. Some students ask us if they should list junior high or even elementary school achievements. Generally, stick to accomplishments from high school if you're a high school student and to college if you're a college student. An exception is if your accomplishment is extremely impressive and relevant—such as publishing your own book in the eighth grade. Of course, if you run out of recent achievements and there is still space on the form, go ahead and reach back to the past—but try to limit yourself to one or two items.

How to Brag Without Being Conceited

Bragging without sounding conceited is an art. The key is to cite facts and figures to support your statements.

You want your application to be as unforgettable as the best Hollywood movies. The only difference between your work and Spielberg's—besides the millions of dollars—is that you need to place the grand finale first.

Step 4: Write to Impress

The inspiring words of Martin Luther King Jr.'s "I have a dream" speech were punctuated with his dramatic, emotion-filled voice, hopeful expression and confident presence. His delivery would not have been as forceful had he spoken in a drab, monotone with hands stuffed into his pockets and eyes lowered to avoid contact with the audience. Nor would his dramatic presentation have been as effective had his message been unimportant. The lesson? Both content and delivery count.

While you don't have the opportunity for person-to-person delivery with your scholarship applications, you can and should present information in a compelling way. Here are some time-tested writing strategies for creating a positive impression through your applications:

Showcase Your Smarts. There's a reason why your parents wanted you to study and do well in school. In addition to the correlation between studying and success in college, almost all scholarships (even those that are athletic in nature) require some level of academic achievement. College is, after all, about learning (at least that's what you want your parents to believe).

As you are completing your applications, keep in mind that while you may be applying for a public service scholarship, you should also include at least a few academic achievements. For example, it does not hurt to list on an athletic scholarship form that you also came in second place at the science fair. This should not be the first thing you list, but it should be included somewhere to show the committee that you have brains in addition to brawn.

When you describe your intellectual activities, explain how they match the scholarship's goal most closely. For example, if you are applying for a science scholarship, focus on the awards you've won at science fairs and the advanced courses you've taken in the sciences rather than writing awards or advanced literature courses. Use your academic achievements to illustrate why you see your future in the sciences. Scholarship judges ideally want to see that your academic talents are in line with the scholarship's purpose.

Extracurricular Activities and Hobbies Show Your Passion. If your only activity were studying, your life would be severely lacking in excitement. Scholarship organizers recognize this and thus the criteria for many scholarships include extracurricular activities or hobbies. Scholarship committees want evidence that you do more than read textbooks, take exams and watch television. They want to know that you have other interests. This makes you a more well-rounded person.

As always, when completing your applications, select extracurricular activities and hobbies that fit with the scholarship's mission. If you are applying for a music scholarship, describe how you've been involved in your school's orchestra or how you've taken violin lessons. By showing that you not only have taken classes in music theory but have also been involved with music outside of your studies, the scholarship committee will get a more complete picture of your love for music. Remember to use your activities and hobbies to illustrate your passion for a subject.

Leadership Is Always Better Than Membership. If you've ever tried to motivate a group of peers to do anything without taking the easy way out–bribery–you know that it takes courage, intelligence and creativity to be a leader. Because of this, many scholarships give extra points to reward leadership. Scholarship judges want to know that the dollars will be awarded to someone who will not only make a difference in the future but who will also be a leader and motivate others to do the same. Think of it this way: If you were a successful businessperson trying to encourage entrepreneurship, wouldn't you want to give your money to a young person who is not only an entrepreneur but who also motivates others to become entrepreneurs? Scholarship providers believe the return on their investment will be higher when they put their money behind leaders rather than followers.

Describing leadership in your activities or hobbies will also help set you apart from the other applicants. Many students are involved with environmental groups, but what if you are the only one to actually help increase recycling on your campus? Wouldn't that make your application a standout?

To show scholarship judges that you are a leader, list any activities in which you held an office. Describe leadership positions you've had and what your responsibilities were. Use active verbs when describing your work:

> Organized band fundraiser to purchase new instruments
> Led a weeklong nature tour in Yosemite Valley
> Founded first website to list volunteer activities
> Directed independent musical performance

Remember that you don't need to be an elected officer to be a leader. Many students have organized special projects, led teams or helped run events. Even if you didn't have an official title, you can include these experiences. Here's an example:

> Environmental Action Committee Member. Spearheaded committee on reducing waste and increasing recycling on campus.

When describing your leadership, include both formal and informal ways you have led groups. This shows the scholarship committee that you are a worthy investment.

Honors and Awards Validate Your Strengths. There's a reason why all trophies are gold and gaudy. They shout to the world in a deafening roar, "Yes, this glittery gold miniature figure means I am the best!" For applications that ask for your honors and awards, impart some of that victorious roar and attitude. In no way are we recommending that you ship your golden statuettes off with your applications. We are saying that you should highlight honors and awards in a way that gets the scholarship committee to pay attention to your application.

What makes an award impressive is scope. Not a minty mouthwash, scope in this case is the impact and influence of the award. You worked for the award and earned

---

Always Describe an Award

Don't expect the judges to know the ins and outs of the honors or awards you've won. Provide descriptions that illustrate how prestigious the honor is and how it fits with the purpose of the scholarship.

every golden inch of it. Show the committee that they don't just hand these statuettes out to anybody. One way to do this is to point out how many awards are given:

English Achievement Award. Presented to two outstanding juniors
each year.

By itself, the English Achievement Award does not tell the scholarship committee very much. Maybe half the people in your class were given the award. By revealing the scope of the award (particularly if it was given to only a few) it becomes much more impressive.

In competitions that reach beyond your school, it is important to qualify your awards. For example, while everyone at your school may know that the Left Brain Achievement Award is given to creative art students, the rest of the world does not.

Don't write:

Left Brain Achievement Award.

Do write:

Left Brain Achievement Award. Recognized as an outstanding
creative talent in art as conferred upon by vote of art department
faculty.

You've worked hard to earn the honors and awards that you have received, and you should not hesitate to use them in your applications to help you win scholarships.

Step 5: Make Sure the Application Fits

You'd never buy a pair of pants without trying them on. Treat your applications the same way. You have limited space in which to cram a lot of information. You will need to do quite a bit of editing and may even have to omit some accomplishments.

Of course by now you know which ones to include and which can be safely omitted. To make sure that everything fits, start completing one of the photocopies that you made of the application. Here's where you'll appreciate having those backup practice forms.

As you fill out the application, you may find that you are trying to squeeze in too many details or that you have more room and can expand on your most impressive achievements. Don't forget to adjust font sizes and line spacing if necessary–just don't sacrifice readability (i.e., don't go below 10-point fonts).

Only by trying on your application will you know if what you have in mind will fit. Now that you know the five steps to insure that your application is a winner, here is our Top Ten list of application form do's and don'ts which will serve as a final reminder of how to create that stunning application!

(Don't do this!)

Top Ten Application Do's and Don'ts

With money on the table, it's much better to learn from others' successes and mistakes before you risk your own fortunes. From interviews with students and scholarship judges and firsthand experience reviewing scholarship applications, we've developed our Top Ten list of scholarship application do's and don'ts. Let's shed the negative energy first and start with the don'ts.

Don'ts

1. DON'T prioritize quantity over quality. It's not the quantity of your accomplishments that's important. It's the quality of your contributions.

2. DON'T stretch the truth. Tall tales are prohibited.

3. DON'T squeeze to the point of illegibility. Scholarship applications afford minimal space. It's impossible to fit in everything that you want to say. Don't try by sacrificing legibility.

4. DON'T write when you have nothing to say. If you don't have something meaningful to present, leave it blank.

5. DON'T create white-out globs. If it's that sloppy, start over.

6. DON'T procrastinate. Don't think you can finish your applications the night before they're due.

7. DON'T settle for less than perfect. You can have imperfections. Just don't let the selection committee know.

8. DON'T miss deadlines. No matter the reason, if you miss the deadline, you won't win the scholarship.

9. DON'T turn in incomplete applications. Make sure your application is finished before sending it.

10. DON'T underestimate what you can convey. Scholarship applications may appear to be short and simple. Don't undervalue them. In a small space, you can create a powerful story of why you should win.

And now the good stuff.

Do's

1. DO understand the scholarship's mission. Know why they're giving out the dough.

> ### Make Sure Everything Fits
>
> *What you want to write and what you have room to write may be two different things. Use a practice application before the real one to see what fits.*

2. DO remember who your audience is. You need to address animal rights activists and retired dentists differently.

3. DO show how you fit with the scholarship's mission. You're not going to win unless you have what the selection committee wants.

4. DO be proud of your accomplishments. Don't be afraid to brag.

5. DO focus on leadership and contributions. Make your contributions known.

6. DO make your application stand out.

7. DO practice to make sure everything fits. Use your spare copies of the application for trial and error.

8. DO get editors. They'll help you create the best, error-free applications you can.

9. DO include a resume. Whether they ask for it or not, make sure you include a tailored scholarship resume. See the next chapter for how to create a great resume.

10. DO make copies of your finished applications for reference. Save them for next year when you do this all over again.

"My Midnight Scholarship Application"
Charlene Davis, Scholarship Applicant

I've always considered myself a fast person. I speak, walk and move quickly. That's why I didn't think it was out of the question to complete my scholarship application the night before it was due. It was a one-page document with about a dozen questions on it. How difficult could it be?

At about 9 p.m., I whipped out the application. It was a scholarship given by my department, which was sociology. The questions seemed easy enough. They asked about the classes I had taken, my involvement in activities on campus and what I planned to do after graduation.

Boy, did I underestimate the amount of time it would take to answer those dozen questions. I didn't anticipate spending two hours searching for my transcript because I couldn't remember the exact classes and grades that I received in the two previous years. By 11 p.m., I found a copy of my transcript in the very back of a file box I kept in the corner of my closet. I also didn't

think I would make so many errors completing the application. It took forever to white-out each mistake, wait for the white-out to dry and then realign the application to retype my corrected answer.

By 6 a.m., I finished completing the application. Full of poorly worded sentences, it certainly wasn't one of my best pieces of work. I hand-delivered the completed application to the assistant in my department at 9 a.m. She took one look at me and asked, "Pulled an all-nighter, eh?" I nodded lethargically. After crashing, I awoke in the afternoon to look at a copy of what I submitted. There were mistakes everywhere including incomplete sentences and incoherent thoughts.

As expected, I didn't win the scholarship. I knew I would have had a decent chance if I had spent some quality time on the application. My advice: Don't wait until the night before. You may think you can do it, but I am proof that you can't.

Finishing Touches

**Remind Yourself
That the
Application Is You**

*Above everything
else remember that
the application form
is you. Through
this sheet of paper
you are showing
the scholarship
judges why they
should choose you.
If you keep this and
the mission of the
award in mind, you
will create a solid
application.*

Once you've completed your applications, check and double-check for accuracy. Look at every line and every question to make sure you've filled out all the information that is requested on the form. Make sure you have someone else take a look at your application. They will catch mistakes that you invariably will miss. Remember that presentation affects how scholarship judges view applications. You want to convey that you are serious about winning the scholarship by submitting an application that is complete and error-free.

Finally, before handing your applications off to the post office, make application twins. Photocopy all your application materials. If for some reason your scholarship form is lost in the mail, you have a copy you can resend. Plus, you will have a great starting place for when you apply for scholarships next year.

Chapter 4 Summary: Create a Stunning Scholarship Application

Create an application plan of attack. Prioritize the scholarships to which you'd like to apply, build a timeline and schedule for applying and determine recycling opportunities.

Do application pre-work. Before you start, make three copies of the scholarship forms for practice, remember to be neat and realize that the application is a reflection of you.

Give them what they want to hear. Don't lie, but present the truth in a way that matches the mission of the award. Keep in mind why the organization is providing the award and who your audience is as you are completing your applications.

Spin. Use words deliberately to highlight how each accomplishment fits the mission of the award.

Go for the gusto quickly. This means don't bury your main point. Concentrate on how your accomplishments match the scholarship's goal and the scope, uniqueness and timeliness of your achievements.

Write to impress. Focus on academics, leadership, extracurricular achievements, honors and awards.

Make sure the application fits. Get the most important information in your application forms.

Put on those finishing touches. Every question should be answered, and all information requested should be provided.

The Scholarship Resume

In this chapter, you'll learn:

- What goes into a scholarship resume
- How to write a resume that stands out
- What an actual scholarship resume looks like

Scholarship Resumes: One-Page Autobiographies

If your life were a book, then your scholarship resume would be the Cliffs Notes. A scholarship resume is your opportunity to tout your greatest achievements and life's accomplishments. The only catch is that you are limited to one page. Some scholarships require resumes to get a quick overview of your achievements. Others don't, but including a resume will always enhance your application.

A scholarship resume is not the same as one that you would use to get a job. It's unlikely that your work experience (if you have any) will be the focus. However, the principles and format are the same. A good resume that scores you a job shows employers that you have the right combination of work experience and skills to be their next hire. Similarly, your scholarship resume should show the committee why you are the most qualified student to win their award.

The Big Picture

Think of the scholarship resume as a "cheat sheet" that you give to the judges. By looking at your resume the judges get a quick overview of your achievements and interests. The resume is not an exhaustive list of everything you have done. It only highlights and summarizes the most impressive and relevant achievements.

To make sure that it really focuses on the crème de la crème, your resume should fit on a single sheet of paper. This is sometimes harder than it sounds.

Here is the information you need for a scholarship resume:

Contact information. Your vital statistics, including name, address, phone number and email.

Objective. Purpose of the resume.

Education. Schools you've attended beginning with high school, expected or actual graduation dates.

Academic achievements. Relevant coursework, awards and honors received.

Extracurricular experience. Relevant extracurricular activities, locations and dates of participation, job titles, responsibilities and accomplishments.

Work experience. Where and when you've worked, job titles, responsibilities and accomplishments on the job.

Skills and interests. Additional relevant technical, lingual or other skills or talents that do not fit in the categories above.

Your Resume

A scholarship resume is a one-page overview of your most important achievements. It shows the judges why you are the most qualified student to win their scholarship, and it does so in just one page.

There are many good ways to format a resume. Most important, your resume should be easy to skim and be organized in a logical manner.

Here is an example of a well-written scholarship resume. Remember that there are other equally good formats in which to present this information.

Some points to note about this resume:

Notice how this resume is concise and very easy to read. By limiting herself to a single page, Melissa makes sure that even if you just scan her resume you will pick up her key strengths.

See how each description includes examples of leadership as well as awards or special recognition.

Melissa conveys the impact of her work by pointing out concrete results.

Notice how her description of summer jobs highlights some of her key accomplishments.

The final section adds a nice balance by describing some of her other hobbies and interests.

Melissa Lee
1000 University Drive
San Francisco, CA 94134
(415) 555-5555

Objective
To obtain funding for college through the SuperCollege.com Scholarship.

Education
University of San Francisco   San Francisco, CA
B.A. candidate in sociology. Expected graduation in 2011. Honor roll.

Lowell High School   San Francisco, CA
Graduated in 2007 with highest honors. Principal's Honor Roll, 4 years.

Activities and Awards
SF Educational Project   San Francisco, CA
Program Assistant. Recruit and train 120 students for various community service projects in semester-long program. Manage and evaluate student journals, lesson plans and program participation. 2005-present.

Lowell High School Newspaper   San Francisco, CA
Editor-In-Chief. Recruited and managed staff of 50. Oversaw all editorial and business functions. Newspaper was a finalist for the prestigious Examiner Award for excellence in student journalism. 2003-2007.

Evangelical Church   San Francisco, CA
Teacher. Prepared and taught weekly lessons for third grade Sunday School class. Received dedication to service award from congregation. 2003-2007.

Asian Dance Troupe   San Francisco, CA
Member. Perform at community functions and special events. 2005-present.

Employment
Palo Alto Daily News   Palo Alto, CA
Editorial Assistant. Researched and wrote eight feature articles on such topics as education reform, teen suicide and summer fashion. Led series of teen reader response panels. Summer 2007.

Russian Hill Public Library   San Francisco, CA
Library Page. Received "Page of the Month" Award for outstanding performance. Summers 2005-2006.

Interests
Fluent in Mandarin and HTML. Interests include journal writing, creative writing, photography, swimming and aerobics.

Your resume should be descriptive enough for the judges to understand each item but not so wordy that they can't find what they need. It should be neatly organized and easy to follow. Having reviewed hundreds of resumes, here are some simple strategies we've developed:

Don't worry if your resume presents the same information that's in the application form. Some judges will read only the application or your resume, so it's important your key points are in both. However, in the resume, try to expand on areas that you were not able to cover fully in the application.

Include only the important information. Remember to incorporate only the most relevant items and use what you know about the scholarship organization to guide how you prioritize what you share in your resume. For each piece of information, ask yourself: Will including this aid the selection committee in seeing that I am a match for the award? Is this information necessary to convince them that I should receive the award? Only include things that support your fit with the scholarship's mission.

Focus on responsibilities and achievements. In describing your experiences in work and activities, focus on the responsibilities you held and highlight measurable or unique successes. Successes could include starting a project, reaching goals or implementing one of your ideas. For example, if you were the treasurer of the Literary Club, you would want to include that you were responsible for managing a $10,000 annual budget.

Demonstrate in your resume how you showed leadership. Leadership could include leading a project or team, instructing others or mentoring your peers. What's more important than your title or where you worked is the quality of your involvement. Explaining your successes and your role as a leader will provide concrete evidence of your contribution.

Be proud. Your resume is your time to shine. Don't be afraid to draw attention to all that you've accomplished. If you played a key role in a project, say so. If you exceeded your goals, advertise it. No one else is going to do your bragging for you.

Use active verbs. When you are describing your achievements, use active verbs such as: *founded, organized, achieved, created, developed, directed* and, our personal favorite, *initiated.*

Don't tell tall stories. On the flip side of being proud is being untruthful. It's important that you describe yourself in the most glowing way possible, but stay connected with the truth. If you developed a new filing system at your job, don't claim that you single-handedly led a corporate revolution. With your complete scholarship application, selection committees can see through a resume that is exaggerated and doesn't match the rest of the application, essay and recommendations.

Get editors. After the hundredth time reading your resume, you'll probably not notice an error that someone reading it for the first time will catch. Get others to read and edit your resume. Editors can let you know if something doesn't make sense, offer you alternative wording and help

---

Give Your Resume to Your Recommenders

Besides including your scholarship resume in your application you may also give it to your recommenders so that they have a cheat sheet to your accomplishments and can include them in their recommendations.

correct your boo-boos. Some good choices for editors may be teachers or professors, work supervisors or parents. Work supervisors may be especially helpful since part of their job is to review resumes of job applicants. Your school may also offer resume help in the counseling department or career services office.

Avoid an eye test. In trying to squeeze all the information onto a single page, don't make your font size so small that the words are illegible. Try to leave space between paragraphs. The judges may have tired, weary eyes from reading all those applications. Don't strain them even more.

Strive for perfection. It's a given that your resume should be error-free. There's no excuse for mistakes on a one-page document that is meant to exemplify your life's work.

Chapter 5 Summary: The Scholarship Resume

Your one-page autobiography. A resume presents the main highlights of your education and achievements in an easy-to-read format and provides scholarship judges with a brief overview of you.

Remember that your resume is a summary and highlight of your accomplishments. The biggest mistake in writing a resume is to try to be comprehensive and list everything you have done in great detail.

Force yourself to use one page. Without resorting to micro-sized fonts and spacing, force yourself to fit everything onto one page. That will ensure that you only include the most important and relevant information.

Focus on achievements. If possible, quantify your accomplishments.

Use active verbs. Don't be afraid to brag by using active verbs.

Get editors. The best way to make sure your resume is clear and concise is to get feedback from others.

Get the Right Recommendations

In this chapter, you'll learn:

- How to get recommendations that make an impact

- Who makes the best recommender

- Essential information you must provide to guarantee great recommendations

- How to ensure your recommenders meet the deadlines

Getting the Praise of Others

If you need a reason to kiss up to your teachers or professors, here's one—recommendations. Scholarships sometime require that you submit recommendations from teachers, professors, school administrators, employers or others who can vouch for your accomplishments. Scholarship judges use recommendations to get another perspective of your character and accomplishments. Viewed together with your application and essay, the recommendation helps the judges get a more complete picture of who you are. Plus, it's always impressive when someone else extols your virtues.

Many students believe that they have no control over the recommendation. This isn't true. You actually have a lot of control over the letter that your recommenders write. In this chapter we will explore several ways—all perfectly ethical—to ensure that you get great recommendations.

The Big Picture

A recommendation is an important opportunity for someone else to tell scholarship judges why you deserve to win. You may assume that because others do the actual writing, recommendations are completely out of your control. Banish that thought. The secret is to not only pick the right people but to also provide them with all of the information they need to turn out a great letter of recommendation. Many applicants overlook this fact. But not you, right? Armed with superb recommendations, your scholarship application is sure to rise to the top.

Finding People to Say Nice Things about You

Your first task is to find recommenders. Unfortunately, mom, dad and anyone else related to you are excluded. So, how do you get those recommendations without familial ties to sing your praises?

First, think about all the people in your life who can speak meaningfully about you and your accomplishments. Your list may include teachers, professors, advisors, school administrators, employers, religious leaders, coaches or leaders of organizations and activities in which you are involved. While some scholarships require recommendations from specific people (like a teacher or professor), most are pretty liberal and allow you to select anyone who knows you.

Find Someone Who Knows You

As a rule, select recommenders who can speak meaningfully about both your academic abilities and your character.

Second, once you have a list of potential recommenders, analyze which of these people could present information about you that best matches the goals of the scholarships. If you apply for an academic scholarship, you'll want at least one teacher or professor to write a recommendation. If you apply for an athletic scholarship, a coach would be a good choice. Select people who are able to write about the things that are most important to the scholarship judges. A good exercise is to imagine what

Don't Only Pick Teachers Who Gave You A's in Class

Be careful about asking teachers or professors who gave you an A in their class but don't really know you. Some professors will use form letters for students whom they have not had a meaningful conversation with but did well in their classes.

your potential recommender would write and whether or not this would enhance your case for winning the scholarship.

After considering these two questions, you should be left with only a few people from which to choose. If you can't decide between two equally qualified people, choose the one who knows you the best as a person. For example, if you got A's in three classes and are trying to decide which professor to ask for a recommendation, pick the one who can write more than a testament to your academic ability. This is important because a recommendation that contains comments on your character is extremely memorable. Maybe one of the professors knows you well enough to include a few sentences on your drive to succeed or your family background. Ideally, your recommender is able to describe not only your performance in the classroom but also the values and character traits that make you special.

Give Your Recommender the Chance to Say "No"

Once you've selected whom you'd like to write your recommendations, ask them to do so—early. A general rule is to allow at least three weeks before the recommendation is due. Explain that you are applying for scholarships and are required to submit recommendations from people who know you and who can comment on some of your achievements.

It's important to ask the person a question like this: "Do you feel comfortable writing a recommendation letter for me?" This allows the person the opportunity to decline your request if he or she doesn't feel comfortable or doesn't have the time. If you get a negative or hesitant response, don't assume that it's because he or she has a low opinion of you. It could simply be that the person doesn't know you well enough or is too busy to write a thoughtful recommendation. It's much better to have the recommender decline to write a letter than to get one that is rushed or not entirely positive. In most cases, however, potential recommenders are flattered and happy to oblige.

Don't Play the Name Game

From being recognized by strangers to getting preferential reservations at the hottest restaurants, there are a lot of perks to being famous. You might think that this special treatment carries over to recommendations, and that scholarship judges will be star-struck by a letter from someone with a fancy title. However, don't assume that just because you ask someone well known to write your recommendations that you are a shoo-in for the scholarship. In fact, you might be surprised to learn that doing so could actually hurt your chances of winning.

So the question is this: "Should I try to find someone famous to write a letter of recommendation for me?" The answer comes down to the principles outlined above. How well does the person know you, and can he or she write about you in a way that presents you as a viable candidate for the scholarship? If the answer is "yes," then by all means ask the person to help you. However, if you don't know the person very well or if what he or she will write could lack a connection to the qualities that the scholarship committee is looking for, it's better to forgo the value of high name recognition and ask someone who can address what's most important in a letter of recommendation.

For example, if you work as a summer intern for your state senator, you may think that a letter from such a political luminary would give your application the star power to set it apart from others with recommendations from mere mortals. However, if you spent more time photocopying or stuffing envelopes than you did developing keen political strategies and saw the senator as many times as you have fingers on your left hand, chances are that he or she would have very few meaningful things to say about your performance. "A skilled photocopier" and "brewed a mean cup of coffee" are not compliments you want sent to the scholarship judges.

If you ask someone well known to write your recommendations, make sure that he or she really knows you and can speak about your accomplishments personally and meaningfully. The quality of what is said in the recommendations is much more important than whose signature is on the bottom of the page.

Do the Grunt Work for Your Recommenders

Once you've selected your recommenders, give them everything they need to get the job done. Since they are doing you a favor, make the process as easy as possible for them. This is also where you can most influence what they write and actually direct what accomplishments they highlight. But before we delve into the specifics, here is an overview of what you need to provide each recommender:

Cover letter. This describes the scholarships you are applying for. In the letter, you should list deadlines and give the recommenders direct guidance on what to write. More on this in a bit.

Resume. A resume provides a quick overview of your most important achievements in an easy to follow one-page format. It is also what your recommenders will use as they cite your important achievements. (See Chapter 5 for details on creating a scholarship resume.)

Recommendation form. Some scholarships provide an actual form that your recommenders need to complete. Fill in the parts that you can, such as your name and address.

Pre-addressed, stamped envelopes. Read the application materials to find out if you need to submit your recommendations separately or with the rest of your application. For letters that are to be mailed separately, provide your recommenders with envelopes that are stamped and have the scholarship's mailing address on them. If you are supposed to submit the letters with your application, provide your recommenders with envelopes on which you have written your name. Many recommenders prefer to write letters that are confidential and that you don't get to read.

Once you have everything, place it in a folder or envelope and label it with your recommender's name.

Give Your Recommenders a Script

Because you know yourself better than anyone else, you would probably receive the best recommendations if you sat down and wrote them yourself. Unfortunately, this practice is frowned upon by scholarship judges. Short of writing your own recommendations, you can influence how they turn out by providing your recommenders with detailed descriptions of your accomplishments that can help them decide which aspects of you to highlight in their letters. This is best done through the cover letter that you send to the prospective recommender.

This letter provides your recommenders with all the information that they need to write your letters, including details about the scholarships and suggestions for what you'd like the recommendations to address. Since the cover letter also includes other essentials like deadlines, mailing instructions and a thank you, you will not sound as if you are giving orders but rather that you are providing helpful assistance. In fact, your recommenders will appreciate your reminding them what's important and what they should include.

Here are the elements to include in your cover letter:

Details on the scholarships. List the scholarships for which you will use their letters. Give a brief one-paragraph description of the mission of each of the awards and what qualities the scholarship committee seeks. This information will help your recommenders understand which of your qualities are important to convey and who will read the letters.

How you fit the scholarship. This is the most important part of your cover letter because it's your chance to remind your recommenders of your accomplishments and to offer suggestions for what to write. Make sure that you highlight how you match the goals of the scholarships. For example, if you are applying for a scholarship for future teachers, include information about your student teaching experience and the coursework you've taken in education. Leave out the fact that you were on the tennis team.

Deadlines. Inform your recommenders of how long they have to compose the letters. If time permits, ask them to mail the letters a week before the actual deadlines.

What to do with the letters when they're done. Give your recommenders instructions about what to do with the completed letters.

Thank you. Recommendations may take several hours to complete, and your recommenders are very busy people. Don't forget to say thank you in advance for writing you a great letter of recommendation.

To illustrate the power of a good cover letter, read the example on the following page as if you were a recommender. Remember that this is only one example and your cover letter will naturally be different. However, regardless of your individual writing style, your cover letter should include the same points as the following example.

The Cover Letter Is Key

A well-written cover letter is a powerful tool. It allows you to suggest what to write and provides guidance for your recommenders. Craft your cover letters carefully and include everything that you would like your recommenders to mention in their letters.

Some notes about this cover letter:

Dear Dr. Louis,

Thank you again for writing my scholarship recommendations. These awards are very important for my family and me to be able to pay for my education. Here are the scholarships I am applying for:

SuperCollege.com Scholarship   Deadline: July 31

This is a national scholarship based on academic and non-academic achievement, including extracurricular activities and honors. I believe I'm a match for this scholarship because of my commitment to academics (I currently have a 3.85 grade point average) and because of the volunteer work I do with the Youth Literacy Project and the PLUS program.

Beth describes each scholarship she is applying for, its goal and deadline and why she feels she is a fit with the award.

Quill & Scroll Scholarship   Deadline: April 20

This scholarship is for students who want to pursue a career in journalism. Journalism is the field I want to enter after graduation. As you know, I am an editor for our school newspaper, contributing a column each week on issues that affect our student body.

Community Scholarship   Deadline: May 5

This scholarship is for students who have given back to their communities through public service. I have always been committed to public service. Outside of class, I not only formed the Youth Literacy Project but have also volunteered with the PLUS program.

The heart of the cover letter is here, where Beth gives a quick summary of information she suggests her professor include in the letter.

To help you with your recommendation, I've enclosed a resume. Also, here are some highlights of specific accomplishments that I was hoping you might comment on in your letter:

* The essay I wrote for your class that won the Young Hemingway competition

* How I formed the Youth Literacy Project with you as the project's advisor

* My three years of volunteer work with the PLUS program

* The weekly column I've written for the newspaper on school issues

Beth provides instructions about what to do with the letters when completed.

After you've finished, please return the recommendations to me in the envelopes I've enclosed. If you have any questions, please feel free to contact me at 555-5555. Again, thank you very much for taking the time to help me.

This is a well-written cover letter that is brief and easy to understand.

Sincerely,
Beth

Tie a String Around Your Recommenders' Fingers

All recommenders have one thing in common: Too much to do and not enough time. It's important that you check with your recommender a couple of weeks before the letters are due. You need to monitor the progress of your recommendations. You may find that they're complete and already in the mail. A more common discovery is that they won't have been touched. Be polite yet diligent when you ask about the progress. It's crucial that you work with your recommenders to get the letters in on time.

The "You Can't Spell Success Without U" Mug

You now have everything you need to ask for and receive stellar recommendations. It's important to remember that even if it is a part of their job description, your recommenders are spending their time to help you. Remember this as you ask others to write recommendation letters and be sure to let them know that you appreciate their efforts.

"Follow Up or Fall Down"
Marla Sabin, Scholarship Applicant

Last year I applied for a scholarship for women who are planning to go into business. In addition to the application, I needed to get three recommendation letters from previous employers and professors. An obvious choice was my manager from the previous summer. I had interned in the product development department of a national software company. For the other two recommendations, I asked a professor and advisor at school.

I did everything right, providing all three with my resume, pre-addressed envelopes and information on the scholarship and its deadline. I let them know that they were supposed to send the letters directly to the organization. In the meantime, I worked on my part of the application, writing an essay about my summer internship and getting my transcript and other materials together. Amazingly, I completed the application a few days before the deadline and sent it off early. I was feeling pretty good about myself for being so put together. I had to admit that even I felt it was a pretty strong application.

A couple of months later, I received a letter from the women's organization. It said that while I had a very high-quality application, regretfully because my application was incomplete, the organization was unable to award me a scholarship and instead offered the non-paying distinction of honorable mention. I racked my brain trying to think of what was missing. Over and over I replayed my trip to the post office and knew that I hadn't left anything out.

The next day I contacted the organization to find out what was missing. I was able to speak with someone who was on the selection committee. She looked up my file and said that I only had two recommendations on file, one from my professor and the other from my advisor. My previous manager had not submitted my third recommendation! She said that had all my materials been submitted, I probably would have won an award.

I learned my lesson. I had assumed that the three people I asked would be responsible enough to remember to submit the recommendation letters, but I was wrong. Two out of three is not good enough. Had I just reminded them, I probably would have won the scholarship.

Sometimes, a thank you gift is appropriate. Every time my (Kelly) mother wants to say thank you to a friend or acquaintance, she writes a note and gives a small token gift. My favorite is the "You Can't Spell Success Without U" mug because of its campy play on words.

Whether or not you select an equally campy token of appreciation, it's important that you thank your recommenders. After all, they are dedicating their free time to help you win funds for college.

Chapter 6 Summary: Get the Right Recommendations

You have more influence than you think. You can affect what your recommenders write by whom you select, what materials you provide and how you follow up.

Familiar faces. Select people who can write meaningfully about your abilities and experience and who can convey how you fit the mission of the award. Try to choose teachers, professors or others who know you beyond how well you perform on tests.

Do the grunt work. Provide everything the recommenders need to get the job done including cover letter, resume, recommendation paperwork and pre-addressed, stamped envelopes.

A script. You can't write your own recommendation letters, but you can offer reminders to assist your recommenders as they are writing the letters. Include descriptions of the awards, information about accomplishments that they may want to mention and what they should do once they have completed the letters.

Be a watchdog. It's your job to make sure that the letters are submitted on time. Check in with your recommenders and make sure they meet the deadlines.

Say thank you. After all, your recommenders are trying to help you win money!

Secrets to Writing Winning Essays

CHAPTER 7

In this chapter, you'll learn:

- The real question being asked by every scholarship essay question

- Six steps to writing a winning scholarship essay

- How to choose the right topic

- Tips to overcome writer's block

- Strategies for introductions and conclusions

- The seven most important essay writing don'ts

- How to recycle your essays

The Scholarship Essay: Your Ticket to the Finals

Here's a situation repeated a million times each year. A student receives a scholarship application and quickly glances over the form. It looks pretty straightforward, so it's tossed into the "to do" pile. The day before it's due, the student finally gets around to filling it out. Breezing through the application form, the student is about to celebrate finishing when he or she encounters the final requirement. It reads as follows:

> *In 1894 Donald VonLudwig came to America with 10 cents in his pocket and within a decade built an empire. Write an 800-word essay on how you would incorporate the lessons of VonLudwig's success into your life.*

Uh, oh. Life just got harder. Meet the dreaded scholarship essay. And the hypothetical student described above—the one we are poking fun at—was one of us! After a few experiences like this one, (which were usually accompanied by all night writing sessions), we learned to work on the essay first and never underestimate how much time it requires.

For most scholarship competitions it is the essay (not the application or recommendations) that will make or break your chances of winning. Why? Because the essay offers you the best chance to show the scholarship judges why you deserve to win. While your application form will get you to the semifinals, it is the essay that will carry you into the winner's circle.

Since the essay is so important, you must not assume that you can crank out a quality essay the night before it's due. A quality essay will take both time and effort. In this chapter we will take you step by step through the process of crafting a winning essay—don't worry it's easier than you may have imagined. Plus, you will read examples of essays that won thousands of dollars in scholarships. From these, you can see firsthand how the strategies presented in this chapter are actually put to use in real life.

The Big Picture

Regardless of the specific wording, the underlying question for almost all essay questions is the same: "Why do you deserve to win?" (Your answer should not be, "Because I need the money!")

Think about these questions: The Future Teachers of America scholarship asks you to write about the "future of education." The Veterans of Foreign Wars asks you to define "patriotism." The National Sculpture Society asks you to "describe your extracurricular passions." Believe it or not, all these seemingly different questions are asking for the same answer: Why do you deserve to win our money?

Your answers to each must address this underlying question. When writing the Future Teachers of America essay, you can discuss the general state of education and quote a few facts and figures, but you'd better be sure to include how you personally fit into the future of education. If you are planning to be a teacher, you might elaborate on how you will contribute

Put Your Modesty On Hold

Some students find it hard to brag in their essays. Part of the reason is that they have been taught to be modest. It's time to put modesty aside and be proud of your accomplishments.

to shaping students' lives. Similarly use the topic of patriotism to impress the VFW judges with not only what you perceive patriotism to be but also how you have actually acted upon those beliefs. And if you answer the National Sculpture Society question with an essay on how much you love to play the guitar, then you really don't deserve to win!

Our approach is to use the essay to prove to the scholarship committee that you are the worthiest applicant for the award. Often the question will lead you in the right direction. (Would it surprise you to learn that the Amelia Earhart award asks about your interest in aerospace?) But even if the question is not obvious or is general in nature, you should still answer the same question ("Why do you deserve to win?") in every essay.

Six Steps to Writing a Winning Scholarship Essay

By now you should be tired of hearing us repeat our mantra of knowing the mission of the scholarship. You have used this to guide your selection of those scholarships you are most likely to win and how to complete the application form for them. So it shouldn't surprise you that you must also use it to guide your essay. Remember, when you are writing about why you deserve to win, the answer and all the examples that you use should show how you fulfill that mission of the scholarship. With this in mind, let's begin our six steps to writing a winning scholarship essay.

Step 1: Find the Right Topic and Approach

You will encounter two types of essay questions. The first asks you to write about a specific topic. For example, "Why is it important to protect our natural environment?" The second type of question gives you a very broad topic such as, "Tell us about yourself." In the first case you don't need to think about a topic, but you do need to develop an approach to answering the question. In the latter you need to come up with both a topic and an approach. Let's look at how this is done, starting with the more difficult task of finding a topic.

Finding a Topic

Let's imagine that you are applying for a scholarship that presents an essay question so broad that you can essentially choose your own topic. To get the ideas flowing, you should use that idea-generating technique you learned in fifth grade–brainstorming. Take out a notebook or start a new file on your computer and just start listing possible topics and themes. Ask yourself questions like these:

- What was a significant event in my life?
- What teacher, relative or friend has influenced who I am?
- What have I learned from my experiences?
- What are my goals for the future?

- Where will I be 10 years from now?
- What motivates me to achieve my goals?

When brainstorming, don't be critical of the topics you unearth—just let the creativity flow. Ask parents and friends for suggestions.

Once you have a list of topics, you can start to eliminate those that don't help you answer the question of why you deserve to win. For example, if you apply to a scholarship that rewards public service, you would not want to write about the time you got lost in the woods for three days and had to survive on a single candy bar and wild roots. While that might make an interesting and exciting essay, it does not show the scholarship judges why you are the epitome of public service. This topic, however, may come in handy when you need to write an essay for a scholarship based on character or leadership or why you love Snickers bars.

After you whittle down your list to a few topics that will help show why you deserve to win this particular scholarship, then choose the topic that is the most interesting to you or that you care about the most. It seems self-evident, but surprisingly many students do not select topics that excite them. Why is it important to pick a topic that you are passionate about? Because if you truly like your topic, you will write a better essay. In fact, your enthusiasm and excitement will naturally permeate your writing, which will make it interesting and memorable. It's so much easier to stay motivated writing about something you enjoy rather than something you find boring.

Developing a Unique Approach

Whether you have to think of a topic yourself or one is given to you, the next task is to figure out how you are going to approach it. For any given topic there are probably a hundred ways you could address the subject matter in an essay. Most topics are also way too large to completely cover in an 800- to 1,000-word essay, so you are going to have to narrow it down and only share a small part of the larger story. All this involves coming up with an approach to what you will present in your essay—an approach that must convince the judges that you deserve to win their money.

Let's take a look at writing about the traumatic experience of being lost in the woods for three days. You choose this topic since the scholarship wants to reward students with strong character and leadership and this is an experience that you believe shows both. But how do you write about it? If you just retell the story of the ordeal, it will not help the judges see why such an experience reveals the quality of your character or leadership. You need to dig deeper and think about how this experience revealed your strengths. To do this, ask yourself questions like these:

- What does this topic reveal about me?
- How has my life been changed by this experience?
- Why did I do what I did?
- What is the lesson that I learned from this experience?
- What aspect of this topic is most important to making my point?

In thinking about your experience alone in the woods, you may realize that on the second day you came close to breaking down and losing all hope of being rescued. This was the critical point where you had to make a decision to give up or push forward. You decide to focus your essay only on this small sliver of time, what went

---

Pick a Topic You Care About

Finding a good topic can take time. However, the key to writing a good essay is to be passionate about your subject. If you invest the time to pick a good topic, you will find that it is much easier to write the essay.

"How I Beat Writer's Block"
Kevin Meyers, Scholarship Winner

When I first started writing my scholarship essay it was like a scene from TV, where I looked at a single sentence on a piece of paper, didn't like what I saw, crumpled the paper and tossed it into the trash can. I repeated this process many times until the crumpled paper started overflowing and I wanted to stop.

Finally, I told myself that I should just start writing and not stop until I had a complete page. It really worked. It wasn't a masterpiece—I didn't come up with the final version of my essay in a single sitting. But I did get two whole pages written at one time and, more important, I got over my writer's block.

From then on it was much easier because I had something to work with instead of crumpled pieces of paper.

---

through your mind and how you decided that you were not going to give up. The details of how you got lost and of your eventual rescue would be unimportant and may be mentioned in only a sentence or two. Focusing your essay on just the second day—and more particularly on how you were able to conquer your fears and not lose hope—would clearly demonstrate to the judges that even under extreme pressure, your true character was revealed. Since you also need to address the leadership aspect, you decide to focus on how you took charge of your fears on the second day. To do this, your essay will describe specific actions you took to lead yourself successfully through this ordeal.

Finding the right approach is just as important as finding the right topic. This is especially true if you answer a question that provides a specific topic. With every scholarship applicant writing about the same topic, you need to be sure that your approach persuasively shows the judges why you deserve to win more than anyone else.

Step 2: Insure That Your Topic and Approach are Original by Sharing a Slice of Your Life

Now that you have a topic and an idea of your approach, you need to decide how you are going to convey your message on paper. Keep in mind that scholarship judges are going to read hundreds if not thousands of essays. Often the essays will be on similar topics, particularly if the topic was given in the scholarship application. Therefore, you need to make sure that your writing is original.

The best way to do this is to share a "slice of your life" in the essay. Imagine that you are writing about your summer trip to Europe. Travel is a very common topic. If you decide to write about how your trip made your realize people from around the world are really quite similar, then you run the real risk of sounding just like every other travel essay. The same would be true for writing about sports. If you tell the story of how your team rallied and came from behind to win the game, you can be sure that it will sound like many other essays about sports. To make sure your essay is original, you need to share a "slice of life." Find one incident that happened dur-

It's All About You

The essay is about you—your opinions, experiences and thoughts. For every scholarship essay that you write, remember to tie it in some way, directly or indirectly, to yourself.

ing your travels or pick one particular moment in the game and use that to make your point. By focusing on a single day, hour or moment, you greatly reduce your chances of having an essay that sounds like everyone else's. Plus, essays that share a slice of life are usually a lot more interesting and memorable.

Let's look at an example. What if you choose to write about how your mom has been your role model? Moms are one of the most popular role models for essays (and they should be, considering the pain of childbirth). How do you make your mom distinct from all the other applicants writing about their moms? Go ahead and take a moment to think about your mom. Be very specific. Can you find one character trait or incident that really influenced you? Let's say your mom has an obsession with collecting porcelain figurines and this passion led to you becoming interested in collecting baseball cards. Because of this, you are now considering a career in sports management. Now we have something! Imagine that first day when you realized how much your mom loved collecting figurines. Maybe you even bought her one as a present and now she cherishes it above all others. Perhaps it was that moment that jump-started your love for baseball cards, which has now developed into a full blown obsession with sports to the point where you intend to make it a career. You've just succeeded in turning a very popular topic–Mom–into an entirely original essay by finding that slice of life. No two people share the exact same slice of life, so by finding one to share, you are almost always guaranteed to have an original essay.

Want another example? Let's set the stage. Imagine that you are applying to a scholarship for students who major in psychology. The question posed on the application is this: "Tell us about an influential person who inspired you to pursue psychology." As you brainstorm, you list the authors of books you've read and some professors whose classes you have enjoyed. But how many students will be writing about these same people? You would even wager money that every other essay will be about Freud!

As you brainstorm, you recall the worst fight you have ever had with your best friend Susan. As you think about this fight that nearly destroyed a 10-year friendship, you realize that it was one of the first times you applied classroom knowledge to a real-life experience. In analyzing the fight, you realize that those psychology principles you studied have practical applications beyond the textbook. So for your essay you decide to write about the fight and how it made you even more committed than ever to become a psychology major.

You don't have to look far to find originality. We all have experiences that are unique to us. Even common experiences can be made original, depending on how you approach them. So don't exclude a topic just because it is common. By spending some time thinking about how you will write about it, you may be surprised at how original it could be.

Step 3: It's Time to Start Writing

The most challenging part of writing a scholarship essay is getting started. Our advice: Just start writing. The first words you put down on paper may not be brilliant literature, but don't worry. You can always return to edit your work. It's easier to edit words you've already written than words that don't exist.

Do you think you have a bad case of writer's block? If so, the cure may surprise you. The best cure for writer's block is to just start writing!

We all have different writing styles, but certain points should be kept in mind as you are writing something that is focused on winning over a scholarship committee. Think about these things as you craft that winning essay:

Write for the Scholarship Judges

Let's pretend you're a stand-up comedian who has two performances booked: one at the trendiest club in town where all cool college students congregate and the other at a retirement home. As a skilled comedian, you would prepare different material aimed at the different audiences. The college crowd would be able to relate to jokes about relationships and dating, while your jokes about dentures and arthritis would probably—and this is a hunch—go over better with the senior citizens.

The same goes for writing your essays. Since many are given by specialized organizations or for specific purposes, you need to write an essay that is appropriate for the audience. Think about who is going to read your essay. Is your audience natural science professors, circus performers or used car salesmen? Write your essay so it appeals to that audience. This should guide not only your selection of topics but also your word choice, language and tone.

Be Yourself

While you want to present yourself in a way that attracts the attention of the scholarship judges, you don't want to portray yourself as someone you are not. It's okay to present selected highlights from your life that fit with the award, but it's not ethical to exaggerate or outright lie. If you apply for a scholarship to promote the protection of animals, don't write about your deep compassion for helping animals when you've never ventured closer than 10 feet to one because of your allergies. Feel comfortable about everything you write, and don't go overboard trying to mold yourself into being the student you think the scholarship judges want to read about. If you've done your job of picking scholarships that match you best, you already know that you are a good fit. Your task in the essay is to demonstrate this to the judges.

Personalize Your Essay

Think of the scholarship judges as an audience who has come to see your Broadway show. You are the star. To keep them satisfied, give them what they want. In other words, the scholarship judges want to know about your life and experiences. When you write your essay, write about what has happened to you *personally* or about how you *personally* have been affected by something. If you are writing about drug abuse for an essay about a problem that faces college students today, do more than recite the latest national drug use statistics and the benefits of drug rehabilitation programs. Otherwise, your essay may be informative, but it won't be interesting. Instead, write about how a friend nearly overdosed on drugs, how others tried to pressure you into trying drugs or about your volunteer work at a rehabilitation clinic. Instantly, your essay will be more interesting and memorable. Plus, the judges really do want to learn more about you, and the only way for them to do this is if you share something about yourself in your essay.

Positive Is Better Than Negative

Being positive does not mean you have to break out the pompoms, but you should strive to give your essay—whatever the subject—a positive tone and outlook.

Make Sure You Have a Point

Try this exercise: See if you can encapsulate the point of your essay into a single sentence. If you can't, you don't have a main point. So, you'd better get one!

You may think this is obvious, but many students' essays don't have a main point. Use that most basic lesson from *Composition 101*: Have a thesis statement that states the main point of your essay. Let's say you are writing about growing up in the country. You might structure your essay around the idea that growing up in the country gave you a strong work ethic. This is the essay's main point. You can describe all the flat land and brush you like, but unless these descriptions help to support your point, you don't have a quality essay.

Support Your Statement

Once you put your main point out there, you can't abandon it. Like a baby learning to walk, you have to support your thesis statement because it can't stand on its own. This means you have to provide reasons why your statement is true. You can do this by giving detailed and vivid examples from your personal experiences and accomplishments.

Use Examples and Illustrations

When a reader can visualize what you are writing about, it helps to make an impression. Anecdotes and stories accomplish this very effectively. Examples and illustrations also make your ideas clearer. If you want to be a doctor, explain how you became interested in becoming one. You might describe the impact of getting a stethoscope from your father when you were a child. Or maybe you can write about your first day volunteering at the hospital. Examples help readers picture what you are saying and even relate to your experiences. The scholarship judge may have never volunteered at a hospital, but by reading your example that judge can easily understand how such an experience could be so influential.

The one danger of examples is that you need to be sure to keep them concise. It is often too easy to write a long and detailed example when only a few sentences are sufficient. Remember, in an example you are not retelling an entire story but just pulling out a few highlights to illustrate the point you are trying to make.

Show Activity

If you were forced to sit in an empty room with nothing but a bare wall to stare at, you would probably get bored pretty quickly. The same goes for an essay. Don't force the scholarship judges to read an essay that does nothing. Your essay needs activity and movement to bring it to life. This may consist of dialogue, action, stories and thoughts. The last thing you want to do is bore your readers. With action, you won't have to worry about that!

Highlight Your Growth

You may not have grown an inch since seventh grade, but scholarship judges will look for your growth in other ways. They want to see evidence of emotional and intellectual growth, what your strengths are and how you have developed them.

Strengths may include—but certainly aren't limited to—mastery of an academic course, musical talent, helping others, athletic ability, leading a group and more. Overcoming adversity or facing a challenge may also demonstrate your growth.

Be Positive

You don't need to break out the pompoms and do a cheer, but you need to convey a positive attitude in your essay. Scholarship committees want to see optimism, excitement and confidence. They prefer not to read essays that are overly pessimistic, antagonistic or critical. This doesn't mean that you have to put a happy spin on every word written or that you can't write about a serious topic or problem. For example, if you were a judge reading the following essays about the very serious topic of teen pregnancy, to which author's education fund would you rather make a contribution?

> Thesis 1: We could reduce the number of pregnant teens by one-half if we shifted our efforts away from scare tactics to providing responsible sex education combined with frank discussions on the responsibilities of caring for a child.

> Thesis 2: Teen pregnancy is incurable. Teenagers will always act irresponsibly and it would be futile for us to believe that we can control this behavior.

Scholarship committees favor authors who not only recognize problems but also present potential solutions. Leave being pessimistic to adults. You are young, with your entire future ahead of you. Your optimism is what makes you so exciting and why organizations want to give you money to pursue your passion for changing the world. Don't shy away from this opportunity.

Be Concise

The scholarship essay may not have the strict limits of a college admission essay, but that does not give you a license to be verbose. Keep your essay tight, focused and within the recommended length of the scholarship guidelines. If no parameters are given, one or two pages should suffice. You certainly want the readers to get through the entirety of your masterpiece. Remember that most scholarship selection committees are composed of volunteers who are under no obligation to read your entire essay. Make your main points quickly and keep your essay as brief and to the point as possible.

Leave Good First and Last Impressions

Studies have found that in a speech people only really listen to the first minute and last minute. The same is true for essays. Give the judges introductions and conclusions that are unforgettable.

Step 4: Perfect Your Introduction and Conclusion

Studies have found that the most important parts of a speech are the first and last minutes. In between, listeners fade in and out of paying attention. It is the introduction and conclusion that leave a lasting impact. This holds true for scholarship essays as well. You need to have a memorable introduction and conclusion. If you don't, the readers may not make it past your introductory paragraph or they may discount your quality essay after reading a lackluster ending. Spend extra time making sure these two parts deliver the message you want. Here are some tips to create knockout introductions and conclusions:

Get Good Editors

The best way to improve your essay is to find good editors. Good editors provide a different perspective, help you see your work in a fresh light and enhance the message of your writing. Parents, teachers, professors and friends make convenient editors.

Introductions

Create action or movement. Think of the introduction as the high-speed car chase at the beginning of a movie that catches the audience's attention.

Pose a question. Questions draw attention because the readers think about how they would answer them and are curious to see how you will answer them in your essay.

Describe. If you can create a vivid image for readers, they will be more likely to want to read on.

Conclusions

Be thoughtful. Your conclusion should make the second most powerful statement in your essay because this is what your readers will remember. (The most powerful statement should be in your introduction.)

Leave a parting thought. The scholarship committee members have already read your essay (we hope), so you don't need to rehash what you have already said. It's okay to summarize in one sentence, but do more than just summarizing by adding a parting thought. This could be one last observation or idea that ties into the main point of your essay.

Don't be too quick to end. Too many students tack on a meaningless conclusion or even worse, don't have one at all. Have a decent conclusion that goes with the rest of your essay and that doesn't consist of two words, "The End."

Step 5: Find Essay Editors

Despite what you may think, you're not infallible. Stop gasping—it's true. This means it's important to get someone else to edit your work. Roommates, friends, family members, teachers, professors or advisors make great editors. When you get another person to read your essay, he or she will find errors that eluded you, as well as parts that are unclear to someone reading your essay for the first time. Ask your editors to make sure your ideas are clear, that you answer the question appropriately and that your essay is interesting. Take their suggestions seriously. The more input you get from others and the more times you rewrite your work, the better.

You want your essay to be like silk—smooth and elegant. When you read your work, make sure the connections between ideas are logical and the flow of your essay is understandable. (This is where editors can be extremely helpful.) Also check that you have not included any unnecessary details that might obscure the main point of your essay. Be careful to include any information that is vital to your thesis. Your goal is to produce an essay with clear points and supporting examples that logically flow together.

You also want to make sure that your spelling and grammar are perfect. Again, the best way to do this is to have someone else read your work. If you don't have time to ask someone, then do it yourself–but do it carefully. Read your essay at least once with the sole purpose of looking for spelling and grammatical mistakes. (Your computer's spell check is not 100 percent reliable and won't catch when you accidentally describe how you bake bread with one cup of "flower" instead of "flour.") Try reading your work out loud to listen for grammatical mistakes.

Step 6: Recycle Your Essays

This has no relation to aluminum cans or newspapers. In this case recycling means reusing essays you have written for college applications, classes or even other scholarships. Because colleges and scholarship committees usually ask very broad questions, this is generally doable and saves you a tremendous amount of time.

Later in this chapter you will read an example essay. You may be surprised to learn that the author recycled her essay with minimal changes to answer such differing questions as these: "Tell us about one of your dreams," "What is something you believe in strongly?" and "What past experience continues to influence you today?"

However, be careful not to recycle an essay when it just doesn't fit. It's better to spend the extra time to write an appropriate essay than to submit one that doesn't match the scholarship or answer the question.

Seven Sins of the Scholarship Essay

Instead of writing an essay, one student placed the sheet of paper on the floor and tap danced on it. She then wrote that she hoped the scuff marks on the paper were evidence of her enthusiasm. In the judges' eyes, this was a silly stunt and, of course, her application was sent to the rejection pile. While you may not make such an egregious error, there are common mistakes that you need to avoid. Most of these lessons were learned the hard way–through actual experience.

1. DON'T Write a Sob Story

Everyone who applies for a scholarship needs money. Many have overcome obstacles and personal hardships. However, few scholarships are designed to reward students based on the "quantity" of hardships. Scholarship judges are not looking to give their money to those who have suffered the most. On the contrary they want to give money to students who came up with a plan to succeed *despite* an obstacle. Therefore, if you are writing about the hardships you have faced, be sure that you spend as much time, if not more, describing how you have overcome or plan to rise above those challenges.

Use Common Sense When Picking a Topic

While no topic is totally taboo, use common sense and avoid topics that are too radical or risque. The scholarship judges might admire your openness or conviction, but if your essay makes them feel uncomfortable they will probably not select you as the winner.

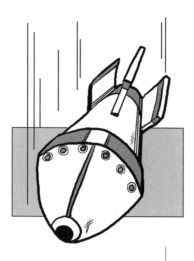

2. DON'T Use the Shotgun Approach

A common mistake is to write one essay and submit it without any changes to dozens of scholarships—hoping that maybe one will be a winner. While we do recommend that you recycle your essays, you should not just photocopy your essays and blast them out to every scholarship committee. This simply does not work. Unless the scholarships have identical questions, missions and goals, your essay cannot be reused verbatim. Spend the time to craft an essay for each scholarship, and you will win more than if you write just one and blindly send it off to many awards.

3. DON'T Be Afraid to Get Words on Paper

One common cause of writer's block is the fear of beginning. When you sit down to write, don't be afraid to write a draft, or even ideas for a draft, that are not perfect. You will have time to revise your work. What you want to do is get words on paper. They can be wonderfully intelligent words or they can be vague concepts. The point is that you should just write. Too many students wait until the last minute and get stuck at the starting line.

4. DON'T Try to Be Someone Else

Since you want to be the one the scholarship judges are seeking to reward with money, you need to highlight achievements and strengths that match the criteria of the scholarship. But you don't want to lie about yourself or try to be someone you are not. Besides being dishonest, the scholarship judges will probably pick up on your affectation and hold it against you.

5. DON'T Try to Impress with Feats of Literary Gymnastics

By this, we mean you won't get any bonus points for overusing clichés, quotes or words you don't understand. Too many students think that quotes and clichés will impress scholarship judges. Unless they are used sparingly and appropriately, they will win you no favors. (Remember that quotes and clichés are not your words and are therefore not original.) The same goes for overusing the thesaurus. Do experiment with words that are less familiar to you, but do not make the thesaurus your co-author. It's better to use simple words correctly than to make blunders with complicated ones.

6. DON'T Stray Too Far from the Topic

A mistake that many students make is that they don't actually answer the question. This is especially true with recycled essays. Make sure that your essays, whether written from scratch or recycled from others, address the question asked.

7. DON'T Write Your Stats

A common mistake is to repeat your statistics from your application form. Often these essays begin with "My name is" and go on to list classes, GPAs and extracurricular activities. All this information is found in your application. On top of that, it's boring. If you are going to write about a class or activity, make it interesting by focusing on a *specific* class or activity.

Putting What You Learned into Practice

Now that you have learned how to write a winning scholarship essay, it's time to put what you learned into practice. Before you head off to write, however, we recommend that you read the essays that appear in the next chapter. These essays were used by students to win tens of thousands of dollars in scholarships. While each essay is unique to the writer, you will be able to see many of the strategies outlined in this chapter being put to use. Once you have read the example essays, you are ready to write your own scholarship essay that will help you get some free cash for college.

Chapter 7 Summary: Secrets to Writing Winning Essays

The real question. There are many questions you may be presented as a topic for a scholarship essay. Whatever it is, remember that you need in some way to convey in your answer why you should win the award.

Choose a topic you care about. You'll write the best essay when it is about something meaningful to you.

Be an original. Don't write about what you think every other student will write about. Or, if you do, take an original approach to the topic. Scholarship essays offer the opportunity for you to set yourself apart from the other applicants.

Write for your audience. Keep in mind who is likely to read your essay and what viewpoint or information you can share to convince each judge that you are a fit with the award.

Your essay is you. Show who you are through your essay by describing an experience, opinion, accomplishment or goal. Paint a more complete portrait of yourself that expands beyond the facts and figures of your application.

It's alive! Use examples, illustrations, dialogue and description to inject life into your essay. Create a narration and develop sights, sounds and emotions that the judges can relate to and envision. Draw them into your work.

Show your strengths and growth. Demonstrate to the selection committee that you have developed the intellectual maturity to take on college and the real world. Describe experiences or traits that show personal growth.

The big two. The two most important paragraphs are the introduction and conclusion. Open with something that will catch the attention of the judges, and close with what you want them to take away from your essay.

Get editors. The best way to enhance your work is to have others read it, and then help you improve it. They can suggest content, structural and technical improvements.

Recycle. Whenever possible, save time and sanity by reusing an essay that you've written before. Remember to modify it to fit the new topic.

Learn by example. Get inspired by the essays that others have written to win scholarships.

Real Winning Scholarship Essays

CHAPTER 8

In this chapter, you'll learn:

- What makes an essay a winner

- Why you don't need to be a great writer to write a money-winning essay

- How to write your own winning essay

Winning Scholarship Essays

It's one thing to study the theory behind the pheromones of love, but it is entirely a different thing to experience the euphoria, quickened heartbeat and walking on clouds of love. In a similar way, you have seen the theory behind writing a powerful scholarship essay. It is now time to see this theory in action.

The following essays were written by students who won scholarships. In each essay you will see how winning principles are put to use. The results are essays that inspire, provoke and most important, win money.

As with any example essay, please remember that this is not necessarily the way your essay should be written. Use these example essays as an illustration of how a good essay might look. Your essay will naturally be different and unique to your own style and personality.

Winning Essay #1: My Two Dads

This essay was written by Gregory James Yee, a graduate of Whitney High School in Cerritos, California. Although Gregory is a student at Stanford University, he wrote this essay as part of his application to the University of Southern California. Besides garnering an acceptance to USC, this essay also earned him a $7,500 per year Trustee Scholarship. Remember that many colleges use your college application to automatically consider you for scholarships they offer.

The topic of the essay is Gregory's musical talent, which was discovered early. At the age of 2, he could hum *The Star-Spangled Banner* in perfect rhythm and pitch, and at age 4 he began piano lessons. Throughout his 15 years of lessons, he won numerous awards including the Raissa Tselentis Award given to one student nationwide for outstanding performance in the Advanced Bach category of the National Guild Audition. He is also a composer.

"Essays in No Time Mean No Money"
Stan Rollins, Scholarship Applicant

I have first-hand experience with the importance of starting early and editing your scholarship essay. I found five scholarships that asked virtually the same question so I procrastinated on writing my essay until a few days before. Then to make matters worse, I quickly wrote the essay while watching *The Simpsons* and sent it to the five scholarship committees. I sent the same exact essay to each one of the scholarships.

I also applied for one other scholarship where I could use an essay that I wrote in my AP English class. I had spent a lot of time and effort on this essay since it was for class. I had asked my teacher for feedback and carefully edited the essay. So it was a good essay and I was lucky that I could also use it for the scholarship application.

Well you can guess what happened. I lost the five scholarships and only won the one where I had used my AP English essay. But what really killed me was that the five I lost were all for awards over $1,000 while the one I won was for a measly 50 bucks!

My Two Dads

I have two fathers. My first and biological father is the one who taught me how to drive a car, throw a baseball and find the area under a curve using integral calculus, among the innumerable other common duties of a good dad. He has been there for me through the ups of my successful piano career and the downs of my first breakup, and has always offered his insightful hand of guidance. My second father is who I connect with on a different level; he is the only person I know who thinks like I do. My second dad is my music composition teacher, Tony Fox, and he shares the one passion that has been a part of my life since the age of two: music.

Tony is a hardworking professor who can spend hours illustrating the meaning of a particular chord in a famous classical composition or ease an extraordinarily stressful situation with his colorful wit. He may appear intimidating to a new student at USC as the Assistant Band Director, but once someone mentions music, there is no one more adept, more creative or more dedicated to making music for the world to hear than Tony.

Tony has touched my life in a way few people have experienced. At my lessons with him, I bring compositions I am in the progress of perfecting, and with a few words of his guidance, I can almost see the changes needed before he mentions them. Almost instantly after I ask a question – such as which chord progression works best at a certain point in the music or why a certain counter melody sounds so beautiful – we agree on what is best for the music. It is almost as if we know what the other is thinking and merely state aloud our thoughts just in case one or the other is caught off guard. It is truly rare to find two people who agree with each other on what it is exactly that makes compositions aesthetically pleasing.

Last year when I was working on a composition, I ran into a discouraging roadblock that could have delayed my progress significantly. No one in my family and none of my friends could help. However, as soon as I shared the piece with Tony, he made some suggestions and together we made the necessary amendments to the music. The result was a finished project, a beautiful mosaic of our collective design, and it was debuted last year by my high school wind ensemble. When I first heard my music performed, I thought back to the hours I had spent tinkering at my piano and Tony's thoughtful guidance. This is how Tony and I relate. It's a common frequency upon which the most advanced radio cannot even begin to comprehend.

Tony has filled in areas of my life where few people, including my real father, could understand. He is the teacher of lessons big and small, from looking into the eyes of those whose hands I shake to recognizing that time is the most valuable gift one can give or receive. Whereas many of my peers have only *one* father, I have been fortunate enough to have two of them.

Why This Essay Won

An accomplished musician like Gregory could have written an essay that was simply a retelling of all the musical awards he won. Instead, Gregory gives insight into what music means to him and takes us into his mind to see the creative and learning process at work. Writing about what he goes through to create a composition allows even those of us who are tone deaf to experience vicariously what it is like to create music.

Notice how Gregory uses powerful imagery to show us how he interacts with his music teacher and overcomes difficulties while composing. Gregory also subtly includes some of his most important musical accomplishments. Although he listed many of his awards in his application, this essay takes us beyond those achievements and really lets us see the wonderful person behind those awards.

Winning Essay #2: Bet You Can't

The next essay was written in response to the question, "What book has had a significant influence on your life?" The scholarship was sponsored by—you guessed it—a local library. The writer, who wishes to remain anonymous here, knew that to stand out she had to write about something original. Forget Twain, Hawthorne or Emerson—she knew every other essay would be about icons like them. She also knew that while she had to write about a unique book she also needed to show how it had affected her life, and she wanted to show the scholarship committee a part of her personality that would demonstrate her future potential. Although the library scholarship committee was not interested in supporting future librarians, it did want to give money to young people who will improve the community in the future. Since she knew that the readers would be librarians volunteering their time after work, she was determined to keep the essay within the 500-word limit. No overworked librarian would be able to get through a 10-page tome. Here is her essay. You can see for yourself how memorable it is.

Bet You Can't

The book offered a simple challenge: "Bet you can't evenly fold a paper more than eight times." So I tried. But, even after constructing a large piece of paper out of four newspaper sheets taped together, I still could make no more than eight even folds. Although this might seem like proof that indeed a paper cannot be folded more than eight times, I still believe that it can be done. In fact I believe that every impossible task listed in the book titled appropriately *Bet You Can't* is possible.

I bought *Bet You Can't,* a short paperback printed on cheap newsprint paper, when I was in elementary school. Yet, it still sits on my bookshelf between *Shakespeare's Greatest Works* and *The History of the American Revolution.* I could never get myself to pack it away with my other childhood books because I could never accept the fact that there were things that could not be done. After all, if we could discover how to split an atom with a laser and perfect a way to bake cheese inside pizza crust, surely we could find a way to fold a paper more than eight times.

I am a firm believer that there are no limits to what men and women can achieve. I truly feel that the only barriers are those that we impose upon ourselves. And this is precisely why I find *Bet You Can't* so frustrating and why I refuse to accept what it claims is impossible.

Some might say that I am ignoring reality, that I am naive to believe that human beings are capable of everything. I imagine that these same people take great pleasure in reading a book like *Bet You Can't* because it emphasizes the limits, reveals man's weakness and validates their pessimistic view of the world. They must love taunting someone like me with such a book. Be that as it may, I refuse to accept their outlook and refuse to let a book like *Bet You Can't* exist uncontested.

Where would we be today if we had listened to those who make words like "impossible," "undoable" and "utterly futile" their mantra? How much poorer would we be if people like Newton, Roosevelt or King had heeded the advice of their contemporaries and abandoned what they were told could not be done?

I know that it may be mathematically true that you cannot fold a paper evenly more than eight times, but that does not keep me from trying. And I know that one day I will achieve that elusive ninth fold.

Why This Essay Won

This essay has three key strengths: First, the writer makes her essay stand out from the rest by selecting a book that most likely no other student selected. (Other students probably chose books they read in school.) When you are writing your essay, remember to write about a unique topic or approach the topic in a creative way.

Second, the writer passionately presents her conviction that there is nothing that people can't accomplish. This optimism and belief in the strength of humanity are traits that scholarship committees like. It is always a good idea to write your essay in a way that highlights your positive characteristics. Plus, taking a stand and being resolute in your ideas will make your essay stand above the many others that stick to vague generalizations and lack conviction.

Third, even though the topic of this essay is a book, the writer keeps her work focused on herself. She spotlights how her life has been affected by the book and does not waste any space with a book report or summary. Remember: You can't answer why you deserve to win if you don't write about yourself.

Winning Essay #3: Public Service

Brian Babcock-Lumish won both the Marshall and Truman Scholarships, highly prestigious awards that draw applicants from across the country. He wrote the following essay for the Truman Scholarship, which awards $30,000 to each of the 80 winners. The Truman places a heavy emphasis on leadership and public service, which is clear from the several essays that each applicant needs to write. In this essay Brian was asked, "Describe your most satisfying public service activity." A graduate of the U.S. Military Academy at West Point, he focuses on the idea that service is embodied in the Army and now is inextricable from his own life. From Bowie, Maryland, he is studying Russian and East European Studies at Oxford as a part of the Marshall Scholarship.

Public Service

Brian's contributions reflect his own opinions, not those of the U.S. military.

My most satisfying public service has been my time as an enlisted soldier in the US Army. Even as a young private, I knew that I was a part of something greater than myself. The nature of the US-Russian relationship has changed in the last decade, yet I was still playing a vital role as a Russian linguist. The military depends on area experts versed in the language, culture and politics of a region. It was my duty to be that expert.

I must admit that my service in the military was not originally motivated by the greater good. I joined as a way to pay for college and pick up a useful skill. West Point and a military career were the last things on my mind. During my year and a half as an enlisted soldier, I grew to appreciate our country's need for those who are willing to make the sacrifices that the military requires. My view began to change from one of self-interest to one of selfless service.

Selfless service is now an explicit part of the Army's core values. As my role in public service has changed from enlisted soldier to future officer, my commitment to public service has only grown. At one time, my life was entrusted to the officers over me. In a short time, I will be that officer. The service that the military renders to society - namely, national security - is one that I am proud to be a part of.

As an officer, I will have a more direct way to impact the bigger picture, whether it be as a tactical commander or strategic adviser. Regardless, the military's ability to fulfill its mission depends on young soldiers — soldiers like the one I once was and the ones I will soon be commanding.

Having been a soldier who understood the Army life and its difficulties, I will be in a better position to lead my own soldiers. My service as a private in the Army in which I will soon be a lieutenant has taught me valuable lessons about my beliefs and myself. That initial period of service gives me greater confidence in my ability to continue my service as an Army officer.

Why This Essay Won

The power of this essay comes from the fact that Brian convinces us that public service is the foundation of both his present career and life. Brian allows us to trace his beginning as a lowly private who had very little appreciation for the concept of service and joined the Army to simply gain skills and pay for college who then grows to understand the value of service to both his country and fellow soldiers. Brian shows us how his commitment to service on various levels has become ingrained in his life and affects almost everything that he does. It is clear that he has a passion for his service in the military.

The essay also shows how Brian's commitment to service will continue to play a significant role in his future as a leader. Although the essay asks about a past experience, Brian successfully lays out a vision of how his own concept of service will be transmitted to the soldiers he will lead. When you finish this essay you not only understand Brain's most significant public service activity but you are also sure that this experience will continue to have an impact on him throughout his future.

Winning Essay #4: Cultural Heritage

When asked to write about her ethnic and cultural heritage, Elisa Tatiana Juárez could have detailed countless influences from her Hispanic background. She chose instead to recount a single event: a trip to Mexico. As you read her essay, you will notice how focusing on this trip allows Elisa to illustrate how her cultural heritage has influenced her and how she weaves in some of her accomplishments. With this essay, she won a scholarship from the Presbyterian Church, USA.

A graduate of Coral Reef Senior High School in Miami, Elisa is a student at Brown University. In addition to this award, she won the National Hispanic Heritage Youth Award for Science and Technology and the Science Silver Knight Award.

Cultural Heritage

The hour hand of the clock is rapidly approaching two in the morning. I look at my clothes thrown about my room. I can't take my shorts so I pull them out of the suitcase. Papi says it's not safe. I tuck a conservative looking blouse in between a box of Equal and a large bag of Jolly Ranchers. We have been buying gifts and treats for my family in Mexico for almost a month, and we still aren't packed. I look at myself in the mirror. Long blonde hair, light skin and clear eyes. Where did I come from?

You look at me and there is no way that I can convince you that my native language is Spanish and that I learned English by watching "Sesame Street" with my Papito. If I tell you that I am Mexican, you would look at me and ask if I was joking. If you ate at my house the chances of eating meat and potatoes are slim to none. Instead, you would find quesadillas con frijoles y salsa ranchera served on our blue and white Mexican dishes.

In just under five hours I will be on a plane to Mexico to see my family. When I get off the airplane the smell of Mexico will make me feel at home. The overcrowding of the streets, the crazy Mexican drivers and the cries of the street vendors all remind me of how lucky I am. Arriving at my abuelita's house I know she will be there to give me un abrazo y un beso. She will then take me by the hand and lead me to the table where we will all sit around and talk about the flight while eating the ever-popular bolillos and pan dulce from the bakery down the street. When I visit I feel like I am the only guera in the whole city. But this never makes me feel singled out or uncomfortable.

I smile at the adventures that await me. Every time I go to Mexico I learn so many new and different things about my past. I do not only focus on events such as the Mexican War of Independence, but I also learn about the people who carry Mexico in their veins. My family is from Mexico, DF (Mexico City), and my maternal great grandfather was one of the first Presbyterian pastors in the country. He helped start a seminary in the north. During the revolution, when he had to leave the country, he started a Presbyterian church in a small town in Arizona that is still there.

During my last visit to Mexico I became even more aware of the extreme poverty conditions in my country. Around that time I had won several awards internationally for my scientific research. Where's the connection? For a long while now I have been considering becoming a doctor as my career. In Mexico I noticed the enormous demand for doctors, but the poverty level among the citizens was incredible. This sparked my interest in possibly becoming a medical missionary. I realized that my potential for becoming a doctor could be used for helping other people less fortunate than I am. I do not think that I would have been able to realize my full potential to help others had I not been from a different culture.

Being Mexican has made me realize the importance of growing up in a multi-cultural home. I am very lucky to be able to share my experiences with other people to assist them in understanding other cultures. I feel like I can be a voice to those who cannot speak. At a recent Montreat Conference I learned that barely 5 percent of the Presbyterian Church (USA) is considered multi-ethnic. In a country where the Anglo population in many cities, like Miami, is a minority, this seems to me to be a critical issue. Because of my background I feel very strongly about this and have been motivated to make a difference. I am on the Montreat Youth Planning Committee and encouraged the team to select a black pastor from South Africa as the pastor for two weeks. I plan on using this experience as a vehicle to share with other students the importance of knowing other cultures. I want to share with them the meaning of my trip to Mexico.

Why This Essay Won

Typically when students write about their ethnic or cultural heritage, they write about predictable topics such as the value of education, a history lesson or the importance of working hard. There is little creativity in these types of essays. Elisa, on the other hand, creates a vivid and memorable story. Reading her essay gives us a mental picture of who she is and the influence of her visit to Mexico. She gives us a slice of her life instead of a long (and unoriginal) description of her entire upbringing.

Notice also how Elisa incorporates some of her achievements within the essay. When describing her reaction to the poverty of Mexico she explains her desire to enter the medical field and alludes to her past achievements in the sciences. She does not have to go into detail about these achievements since they are explained in her application, which the judges would have already read.

The same is true for her description of the importance of growing up in a multi-cultural home. Not only does Elisa cite a national statistic that surprises us, but she also describes how she is working to change that fact through her involvement with the Montreat Youth Planning Committee, a national conference of the Presbyterian Church. Clearly these are issues that are important to the judges (who are affiliated with the Presbyterian Church) and underscore Elisa's leadership within the youth group.

Winning Essay #5: Leadership

Donald H. Matsuda Jr. is the kind of person who doesn't just act. He inspires others to act as well. In his application for the Truman Scholarship, he writes about how he directed community leaders and health professionals to start a series of health insurance drives. This is one of the essays that he wrote to become one of 80 Truman Scholars in the country.

From Sacramento and a graduate of Stanford University, Donald also founded the San Mateo Children's Health Insurance Program, directed the United Students for Veterans' Health and founded the Nepal Pediatric Clinical Internship.

Leadership

A few years ago, I saw a shocking headline on the front page of the New York Times that read: "Forty-Four Million Americans Without Health Insurance." Upon reading the article, I was stunned to discover that one-third of these uninsured Americans were children. Such figures made it clear to me that work needed to be done to remedy this problem, and I was ready to take action.

At this time, I was working at the Health for All Clinic as a public health and community outreach intern, and I decided to approach the director about this problem. He clearly agreed that immediate action needed to be taken to control the growing numbers of America's uninsured. However, he admitted that the clinic did not have the time, energy or the funds to invest into such an ambitious endeavor. I was not discouraged by his response. Instead, I saw this challenge as an opportunity to gain firsthand experience as a change agent in the field of public policy.

After completing extensive research, I discovered a unique program called Healthy Families. The ultimate goal of this government program is to provide low-cost insurance coverage to children who do not qualify for traditional insurance plans. I decided to develop my own project from scratch, proposing to launch a sustainable series of Healthy Families insurance drives at the Health for All Clinic. I applied for funding through the Haas Center for Public Service Fellowship program, and the clinic director signed on as my community partner for the project.

During the next six months, I worked very closely with the clinic staff to organize and plan this series of insurance drives. I recruited various ethnic community leaders and healthcare professionals to help generate support of the program, and assembled several advertising campaigns in the surrounding communities. The clinic director and I also developed a workshop on immigrant health to attract more diverse populations to our insurance drives. After holding three Healthy Families drives, the clinic managed to sign up over 150 children for this program. The director was elated by this turnout and established an entire Healthy Families division to build upon the success of this project. Upon completion of this project, I started directing other insurance drives with the hope of improving the health and well-being of America's children.

Where to Find More Winning Scholarship Essays

We believe that reading real essays is the best way for you to really see what works, and these essays are certainly a start. Unfortunately, we could not include more than a handful of examples in this book. If you want more scholarship essay examples, take a look at our book, *How to Write a Winning Scholarship Essay.* In it you will find 30 additional winning essays from a variety of students and written in many styles. Also, take a look at our website, SuperCollege (www. supercollege.com), where we post additional example essays. We think you'll be inspired.

"An excellent guide for all students."
School Library Journal

How to Write a
Winning
Scholarship
Essay Gen and Kelly Tanabe

30 Essays That Won Over $3 Million in Scholarships

INCLUDES SCHOLARSHIP INTERVIEW STRATEGIES

Why This Essay Won

Donald's essay only scratches the surface of his accomplishments, which is exactly how it should be. Instead of listing every leadership role he has had, Donald explains how he created a health care program in his community.

He begins with his motivation for starting the program and then recounts the initial skepticism that he faced when he first proposed the idea. His essay describes the various difficulties and ultimate success of his project.

Notice that Donald does not describe a typical leadership role, one in which he was elected as a leader. This is an excellent example of how you can take a project in which you played a significant role and show how it demonstrates your leadership abilities. Remember, leadership is not just an elected position.

Be Inspired

We hope the essays in this chapter have inspired you to write your own winning scholarship essay. It's interesting to note that these essays are not masterpieces in terms of pure writing skill. But what all the essays do very well is convey to the scholarship judges why the student deserves to win. The writers have clearly done their homework on the mission of the scholarships and have used that information as a guide on which part of their lives and activities to highlight. You don't need to be a great writer to write a winning scholarship essay, but you do need to spend the time and effort to write an essay that is original, shares a slice of your life, and, most important, gives the scholarship judges a reason to give you their money.

Ace the Interviews

In this chapter, you'll learn:

- The importance of interviews
- What homework you must do before every interview
- The best way to prepare for the interview
- How to remain calm during a stressful interview
- What to wear and how to speak
- Secrets of creating interactive interviews
- The most common interview questions
- Strategies for phone or group interviews

The Face-to-Face Encounter

A judge for the Rotary International Ambassadorial Scholarship shared with us the following true story. For the last phase of the scholarship competition for his region, the finalists met with the selection committee for an interview. The interview was very important and was the final step in determining who would win the $25,000 scholarship.

One finalist was an Ivy League student who flew across the country for the interview. Within the first five minutes, it was painfully clear to all the judges that the applicant didn't have the foggiest idea what the Rotary Club stood for. It's as if the applicant thought that his resume and Ivy League pedigree would make him a winner.

As you can guess, this applicant had a very disappointing flight back to his college. Lesson number one for the scholarship interview: At the very least know what the organization stands for.

Many students dread the interview. If your heart beats faster or your palms moisten when you think about the prospect of sitting face to face with the judges, you are not alone. While the other parts of the scholarship application take time and effort, they can be done in the privacy of your home. Interviews, on the other hand, require interaction with–gasp–a real live human.

The good news is that the interview is usually the final step in the scholarship application process and if you make it that far, you're a serious contender. In this chapter, we show you what most scholarship committees are looking for and how you should prepare to deliver a winning interview. We also show you how to make the most of your nervousness and how to turn it into an asset rather than a liability.

The Big Picture

There are two secrets for doing well in scholarship interviews. The first is: Remind yourself over and over again that scholarship interviewers are real people. Repeat it until you believe it. As such, your goal is to have as normal a conversation as possible, despite the fact that thousands of dollars may hang in the balance. It's essential that you treat interviewers as real people, interact with them and ask them questions.

The second secret is just as important: The best way to have successful interviews is to train for them. The more you practice interviewing, the more comfortable you'll be during the real thing. In this chapter, we'll tell you what kinds of questions to expect and how to perfect your interviewing skills.

Why Human Interaction Is Needed

The first step to delivering a knockout interview is to understand why some scholarships require interviews in the first place. With the popularity of technology like e-mail and instant messaging, there seems to be less need for human interaction. (Believe it or not, there was a time when telephones were answered by a person instead of a maze of touchtone options.)

For some scholarship committees, a few pieces of paper with scores and autobiographical writing are not enough to get a full picture of who the applicants really are. They are giving away a lot of cash and the judges are responsible for making sure they are giving it to the most deserving students possible.

Scholarship judges use interviews as a way to learn how you compare in person versus on paper. Having been on both sides of the interview table, we can attest to the fact that the person you expect based on the written application is not always the person you meet at the interview.

It's important to know that the purpose of interviews is not to interrogate you, but rather for the scholarship committee to get to know you better and probe deeper into the reason why you deserve their money.

Interviewers Are Real People Too

If you've ever met a celebrity, you've probably realized that while their face may grace the covers of magazines and they have houses big enough to merit their own ZIP code, they eat, drink and sleep and have likes and dislikes just like any other person. The same thing holds true for interviewers.

Interviewers can be high-profile professors or high-powered businesspeople, but they are all passionate about some topics and bored with others. They enjoy speaking about themselves and getting to know more about you. Acknowledging this will help keep your nerves under control. Throughout the interview, remind yourself that your interviewer is human, and strive to make the interview a conversation, not an interrogation.

Interview Homework

You'd never walk into a test and expect to do well without studying the material. The same is true for interviews. Don't attempt them without doing your homework. There is basic information you need to know before starting your interviews so that you appear informed and knowledgeable. It's not difficult information to obtain, and it goes a long way in demonstrating that you care enough about winning to have put in some effort. Here are some things you should know before any interview:

Try to Relax

You don't have to picture your interviewers in their underwear to relax. Just keep reminding yourself that they are real people. They may be well known in their field or leaders in the community, but they are still just people.

Purpose of the scholarship. What is the organization hoping to accomplish by awarding the scholarship? Whether it's promoting students to enter a certain career area, encouraging a hobby or interest or rewarding students for leadership, every scholarship has a mission.

Criteria for selecting the winner. From the scholarship materials, you can get information about what the judges are hoping to find in a winner. From the kinds of information they request in the application to the topic of the essay question, each piece is a clue about what is important to the judges. Scholarships can be based on academic achievement, nonacademic achievement or leadership to name a few criteria. Understand what kind of student the organization is seeking and stress that side of yourself during the interview.

Background of the awarding organization. Do a little digging on the organization itself. Check out its website or publications. Attend a meeting or speak with someone who's a member. From this detective work, you will get a better idea of who the organization's members are and what they are trying to achieve. It can also be a great topic of conversation during the interview.

Background of your interviewer. If possible, find out as much as you can about who will be interviewing you. In many cases, you may know little more than their name and occupation, but if you can, find out more. You already have one piece of important information about your interviewers: You know that they are passionate about the organization and its mission. They wouldn't be volunteering their time to interview if they weren't.

Use Your Detective Work to Create an Advantage

Once you've done your detective work on the above topics, it's time to *use* the information you've uncovered. For example, if you are in front of a group of doctors and they ask you about your activities, you would be better off discussing your work at the local hospital than your success on the baseball diamond. As much as possible, focus the conversation on areas where your activities, goals, interests and achievements match the goal of the awarding organization. By discussing what matters most to the scholarship judges, you will insure that this will be a memorable conversation–one that will set you apart from the other applicants that are interviewed.

By knowing something about your interviewers beforehand, you can think of topics and questions that will be interesting for them. Most interviewers allow some time for you to ask questions. Here again your detective work will come in handy since you can ask them more about the organization or their background. By asking intelligent questions (i.e., not the ones that can be answered by simply reading the group's mission statement) you will demonstrate that you've done your homework. You'll also give interviewers something interesting to talk about–either themselves or their organization.

The more information you can get before the interview, the better you will perform. Having this background material will also allow you to answer unexpected ques-

Make Your Interview a Two-Way Conversation

Strive for interactive interviews. Do not do all the talking. Pose questions, ask for advice and have fun.

tions better and come up with thoughtful questions for the judges if you are put on the spot.

You Are Not the Center of the Universe

Despite what Mom or Dad says, the Earth revolves around the sun, not you. It helps to remember this in your interviews. Your life may be the most interesting ever lived, but this is still no excuse for speaking only about you for the duration of the interview.

The secret to successful interviews is simply this: They should be interactive. The surest way to bore your interviewers is to spend the entire time speaking only about yourself. You may have had the unfortunate experience of being on the receiving end of a conversation like this if you have a friend who speaks nonstop about herself and who never seems to be interested in your life or what you have to say. Don't you just hate this kind of conversation? So will your scholarship interviewers.

To prevent a self-centered monologue, constantly look for ways to interact with your interviewers. In addition to answering questions, ask some yourself. Ask about their experiences in school or with the organization. Inquire about their thoughts on some of the questions they pose to you. Take time to learn about your interviewers' experiences and perspectives.

Also, speak about topics that interest your interviewers. You can tell which topics intrigue them by their reactions and body language. From the detective work you've done, you also have an idea of what they are passionate about.

Try to make your interviews a two-way conversation instead of a one-way monologue. Engage your interviewers and keep them interested. If you do this, they will remember your interview as a great conversation and you as a wonderful, intelligent person deserving of their award.

> ### Dress for Success
>
> *No one has ever been penalized for being overdressed. If you have questions about what's appropriate, err on the side of being conservative.*

Look and Sound the Part

Studies have shown that in speeches what's more important than what you say is how you sound and how you look when you say it. It's important that you make a good visual presentation. Here are some tips to make sure that you look and sound your best, an important complement to what you actually say to the judges:

Dress appropriately. A backward-turned baseball cap and baggy jeans slung down to your thighs may be standard fare for the mall (at least they were last season), but they are not appropriate for interviews. You probably don't have to wear a suit, unless you find out through your research that the organization is very conservative, but you should dress appropriately. No-no's include the following: hats, bare midriffs, short skirts or shorts, open-toe shoes and iron-free wrinkles. Think about covering obtrusive tattoos or removing ex-

"The Only Thing in Life that Matters Is Calculus"
Kelly Tanabe, Author and Scholarship Judge

Following is the experience that I had interviewing an applicant for a scholarship based on academic achievement and contributions to extracurricular activities. Mark, the college sophomore I interviewed, is mathematically gifted but lacked in his presentation an attempt to keep the conversation interactive. Learn from his mistakes.— Kelly Tanabe

The student is sitting at the table with his hands covering his face. His mop of stringy, brown hair dangles around his face. I greet him with a cheery, "Hi. How are you?" Absent of enthusiasm, he mumbles under his breath with his hands still partially covering his face, "Fine." He resists making eye contact of any kind and tilts his head even further down. My intuition tells me that this is going to be one very long hour.

With that promising start, I notice what Mark is wearing. I can't help it. I'm human. He is wearing jeans with an orange sweater over a faded green T-shirt. His sweater even has a few holes in it. I have nothing against his holey sweater. I, too, have been known to wear clothes with extra ventilation in the privacy of my home. The thing that bothers me is: Why did he choose to wear mismatching, worn clothes to such an important interview? I'm giving up five hours on a Saturday to interview finalists for this scholarship, and Mark can't even find a decent shirt to wear?

Our conversation is hardly better than his color coordination. When I ask him a question, he replies with short and mumbled single-sentence answers. What gets him mildly excited is calculus. Pretty much everything he says relates back to the subject of calculus. His father is a calculus professor. He tutors other students in calculus. He even named his twin Golden Retrievers Sine and Cosine. His knowledge and the graduate-level coursework he has taken impress me.

After he finishes listing all the calculus classes he has taken and calculus awards he has won, I try to direct the conversation in a different route. I want to find out what more there is to him. I ask him about what he likes to do outside of schoolwork. He continues to tell me how to prove a calculus theory and how he dreams of calculus formulas in his sleep. His calculus barrage is unrelenting.

To again try to get him to change the subject I mention that I was a sociology major, which, by the way, is about the furthest removed from calculus as possible. It has been several years since I've done a calculus problem. I understand that he is very talented in mathematics, but why don't we talk about something else he enjoys? After all, this is not a scholarship for mathematical achievement. It's a scholarship for overall academic and extracurricular achievement.

He doesn't get the hint and continues to carry on about calculus. As I tune out his math lesson, I can't get over the fact that he never makes eye contact, speaks under his breath whenever he talks and never puts together more than two sentences at a time. Getting him to speak about anything other than calculus is virtually impossible. When I ask him what his greatest strength and greatest weakness are, he tells me his strength is (surprise, surprise) his mathematical ability and his weakness is his social skills. At least he is honest!

In the end I give up trying to direct the conversation beyond calculus. My overall impression of him is that he may be a mathematical wizard, but he lacks the ability to hold a normal conversation. At the end of an hour, he has not smiled, made eye contact or asked a single question. As we end the interview I thank Mark for coming in. He does not reply and shuffles out of the room. His head hangs low, and again his stringy, brown hair drapes his hidden face.

In spite of his mathematical talents, I find the other applicants to be much more interesting even if they cannot prove a complex theorem as quickly as Mark. The other interviewers agree, and we award the scholarship to a student who is not only academically strong but can also communicate effectively.

> ### *Don't Be Afraid to Be Animated*
>
> *When you speak, be animated, using gestures and making eye contact. These visual cues tell your interviewer that you are confident, charismatic and interested in the conversation.*

tra ear/nose/tongue/eyebrow rings. Don't dress so formally that you feel uncomfortable, but dress nicely. It may not seem fair, but your dress will affect the impression you make and influence the decision of the judges. Save making a statement of your individuality for a time when money is not in question.

Sit up straight. During interviews, do not slouch. Sitting up straight conveys confidence, leadership and intelligence. It communicates that you are interested in the conversation. Plus, it makes you look taller.

Speak in a positive tone of voice. One thing that keeps interviewers engaged is your tone. Make sure to speak in a positive one. This will not only maintain your interviewers' interest but will also suggest that you have an optimistic outlook. Of course, don't try so hard that you sound fake.

Don't be monotonous. If you've ever had a teacher or professor who speaks at the same rate and tone without variation, you know that this is the surest reason for a nap. Don't give your interviewers heavy eyelids. Tape record yourself and pay attention to your tone of voice. There should be natural variation in your timbre.

Speak at a natural pace. If you're like most people, the more nervous you are, the faster you speak. Be aware of this so that you don't speed talk through your interview.

Make natural gestures. Let your hands and face convey action and emotions. Use them as tools to illustrate anecdotes and punctuate important points.

Make eye contact. Eye contact engages interviewers and conveys self-assurance and honesty. If it is a group interview, make eye contact with all your interviewers—don't just focus on one. Maintaining good eye contact can be difficult, but just imagine little dollar signs in your interviewers' eyes and you shouldn't have any trouble. Ka-ching!

Smile. There's nothing more depressing than having a conversation with someone who never smiles. Don't smile nonstop, but show some teeth at least once in a while.

If you use these tips, you will have a flawless look and sound to match what you're saying. All these attributes together create a powerful portrait of who you are. Unfortunately, not all these things come naturally, and you'll need to practice before they become unconscious actions.

The Practice Interview

One of the best ways to prepare for an interview is to do a dress rehearsal. This allows you to run through answering questions you might be asked and to practice honing your demeanor and style. You will feel more comfortable when it comes time for the actual interview. If anything will help you deliver a winning interview, it's practice. It may be difficult, but force yourself to set aside some time to run through a practice session at least once. Here's how:

> **Find a mock interviewer.** Bribe or coerce a friend or family member to be your mock interviewer. Parents or teachers often make the best interviewers because they are closest in age and perspective to most actual scholarship interviewers.
>
> **Prep your mock interviewer.** Share with your interviewer highlights from this chapter such as the purpose of scholarship interviews, what skills you want to practice and typical interview questions, which are described in the next section. If you're having trouble with eye contact, for example, ask them to take special notice of where you are looking when you speak and to make suggestions for correcting this.
>
> **Set up a video camera.** If you have access to a tape recorder or camcorder, set it up to tape yourself so that you can review your mock interview afterward. Position the camera behind your interviewer so you can observe how you appear from their perspective.
>
> **Do the dress rehearsal.** Grab two chairs and go for it. Answer questions and interact with your mock interviewer as if you were at the real thing.
>
> **Get feedback.** After you are finished, get constructive criticism from your mock interviewer. Find out what you did well and what you need to work on. What were the best parts of the interview? Which of your answers were strong, and which were weak? When did you capture or lose your mock interviewer's attention? Was your conversation one-way or two-way?
>
> **Review the tape.** Evaluate your performance. If you can, watch or listen to the tape with your mock interviewer so you can get additional feedback. Listen carefully to how you answer questions so you can improve on them. Pay attention to your tone of voice. Watch your body language to see what you are unconsciously communicating.
>
> **Do it again.** If you have the time and your mock interviewer has the energy or you can find another mock interviewer, do a second interview. If you can't find anyone, do it solo. Practice your answers, and focus on making some of the weaker ones more interesting.

The bottom line is the more you practice, the better you'll do.

Answers to the Most Common Interview Questions

The best way to ace an exam would be to know the questions beforehand. The same is true for interview questions. From interviewing dozens of judges and applicants as well as having judged dozens of scholarship competitions ourselves, we've developed a list of commonly asked questions along with suggestions for answering them. This list is by no means comprehensive. There is no way to predict every question you will be asked. And in your actual interviews, the questions may not be worded in

---

Practice, Practice, Practice

Practice does make perfect when it comes to interviews. Even if you have to sit in front of a mirror and interview yourself, doing even one mock interview will really boost your performance on the real thing.

exactly the same way. However, the answer that interviewers are seeking is often the same.

Before your interviews, take the time to review this list. Add more questions particular to the specific scholarship to which you are applying. Practice answering these questions to yourself and in your mock interviews with friends and family.

You will find that the answers you prepare to these questions will be invaluable during your real interviews. Even though the questions you are asked may be different, the thought that you put in now will help you formulate better answers. To the interviewer, you will sound incredibly articulate and thoughtful. Let's take a look at those questions.

Why did you choose your major?

- For major-based scholarships and even for general scholarships, interviewers want to know what motivated you to select the major, and they want a sense of how dedicated you are to that area of study. Make sure you have reasons for your decision. Keep in mind that an anecdote will provide color to your answer.

- If you are still in high school, you will probably be asked about your intended major. Make sure you also have reasons why you are considering this major.

Why do you want to enter this career field?

- For scholarships that promote a specific career field, interviewers want to know your inspiration for entering the field and how committed you are to it. You will need to articulate the reasons and experiences that prompted your interest in this career and also anything you have done to prepare yourself for associated studies in this area.

- Be prepared to discuss your plans for after graduation, i.e. how will you use your education in the field you have chosen. You may be asked what kind of job you plan to have and why you would like it.

- Know something about the news in the field associated with the scholarship. For example, if you are applying for an information technology award, read up on the trends in the IT industry. There may be some major changes occurring that you will be asked to comment on.

What are your plans after graduation?

- You are not expected to know precisely what you'll do after graduation, but you need to be able to respond to this common question. Speak about what you are thinking about doing once you have that diploma in hand. The more specific you can be the better.

"Don't Hate Me Because I'm Beautiful and Faultless"
Kelly Tanabe, Author and Scholarship Judge

One student I interviewed was a better fit for a beauty pageant than a scholarship competition. —Kelly Tanabe

From my first impression, she seems promising. I say "Hello," and she responds with a smile, eye contact and a friendly "Hello" in return. I notice she is fashionably dressed in a blue color-coordinated pantsuit. She is strikingly beautiful, with long blond hair and deep blue eyes. Her makeup is perfectly in place.

Maria tells me that her dream is to travel the world. Why? She finds other cultures "interesting." A generic answer. At this point, I envision her on stage in a Miss America pageant. I ask her to explain. Miss California comes out of the soundproof room dressed in her blue-sequined evening gown. It's her turn to answer the question that will show the judges her ability to demonstrate grace and composure while being beautiful and holding up under the pressure.

She says, "I think it's so neat to be able to learn about other cultures. We are so different. I just want to learn about cultures around the world." The judges wince. Nine points for composure, zero for substance.

Miss California, er Maria, tells me she is an aspiring model. "It was so incredible. I was sitting at a cafe when a woman came up to me and gave me her business card. She told me she wanted me to model." That explains the perfect makeup. I can almost hear the singing, "Here she comes, Miss America."

At this point I admit to myself that I am a little envious of this freshman who has spent her life turning the heads of the opposite sex. To make up for my bias, however, I purposely give her the benefit of the doubt. I think that there must be more to her than her good looks and Miss America answers. Throughout the remainder of the interview, however, I find no evidence of this. I ask her what leadership experience she has. She says she is the leader among her friends. Because of her they all now aspire to become models. Ugh. Just what the world needs—another slew of teenage girls starving themselves with noble aspirations of appearing on magazine covers.

I resort to an easy question. What are her grade point average and test scores? She says she can't remember. I wonder if she is telling the truth or if they are so bad she doesn't want me to know.

I ask a standard job interview question. What are your greatest strength and weakness? She replies, "My greatest strength is my ability to get along with my friends. I am good at getting along with pretty much anyone." Her greatest strength is that she is popular?!? "My weakness. Hmm. Well. Um. I can't think of a weakness." What kind of answer is this? Everyone has a weakness! I try to coach her, "Isn't there something that is more challenging for you or that you want to work on?" She answers, " Well, I can't really think of anything I want to work on. If something is more challenging I just work harder." Ladies and gentlemen, not only is Maria perfect looking, but in her mind she is also perfect.

I am tempted to ask something tougher, what recruiters from those high-paying consulting and investment banking firms ask to understand candidates' thought process and to see how they hold up under pressure. If you have a stack of quarters as high as the Empire State Building, how many quarters will you have? How would you figure out how many psychiatrists there are in the Chicago area? I envision the serious look on her perfectly matted face and the furrow of her delicately plucked eyebrows in thought. Then, her head slowly bloats into an oversized, perfectly blond beach ball, and KABOOM! an explosion from brain overexertion.

I return to reality and end the interview asking if she has any questions. Usually students ask at least one. For many, this is one of their best opportunities to learn about the organization that is awarding the scholarship. Maria has none. Not only is she beautiful, folks, but she has all the answers. The host places the sparkling crown on her head. The newly crowned Miss America starts crying the requisite tears and waves to the cheering audience.

I bid farewell to Maria. I wonder if the outcome would have been different had she had a male interviewer. One flash of her pearly toothed smile may have won.

- Provide reasons for your plans. Explain the process in which you developed your plans and what your motivation is.

- It's okay to discuss a couple of possible paths you may take, but don't bring up six very different options. Even if you are deciding among investment banking, the Peace Corps, banana farming and seminary, don't say so. The interviewer will think that you don't have a clear direction of what you want to do. This may very well be true, but it's not something you want to share. Select the one or two possible paths that you are most likely to take.

Why do you think you should win this scholarship?

- Focus your answer on characteristics and achievements that match the mission of the scholarship. For example, if the scholarship is for biology majors, discuss your accomplishments in the field of biology. Your answer may include personal qualities as well as specific accomplishments.

- Be confident but not arrogant. For this type of question, be careful about balancing pride and modesty in your answer. You want to be confident enough to have reasons why you should win the scholarship, but you don't want to sound overly boastful. To avoid sounding pompous, don't say that you are better than all the other applicants or put down your competition. Instead, focus on your strengths independent of the other people who are applying.

- Have three reasons. Three is the magic number that is not too many or too few. To answer this question just right, offer three explanations for why you fulfill the mission of the scholarship.

Tell me about times when you've been a leader.

- Interviewers ask this type of question (although sometimes worded a little differently) to gauge your leadership ability and your accomplishments as a leader. They want to award scholarships to students who will be leaders in the future. When you answer, try to discuss leadership that you've shown that matches what the scholarship is meant to achieve.

- Don't just rattle off the leadership positions you've held. Instead, give qualitative descriptions of what you accomplished as a leader. Did your group meet its goals? Did you start something new? How did you shape the morale of the group you led? For this kind of question, anecdotes and short stories are a good way to illustrate how you've been effective.

- Remember that leadership doesn't have to be a formally elected position. You can describe how you've informally led a special project or group. You could even define how you are a leader among your siblings.

- Be prepared to discuss what *kind* of leader you are. Your interviewer may ask about your approach to leadership or your philosophy on being a good leader. Have examples to explain how you like to lead. For example, do you lead by example? Do you focus on motivating others and getting their buy-in?

What are your strengths? Weaknesses?

● As you are applying for jobs, you will answer this question more times than you will shake hands. It is a common job interview question that you may also get asked in scholarship interviews. Be prepared with three strengths and three weaknesses. Be honest about your weaknesses.

● Your strengths should match the mission of the scholarship and should highlight skills and accomplishments that match the characteristics the judges are seeking.

● You should be able to put a positive spin on your weaknesses. (And you'd better say you have some!) For example, your perfectionism could make you frustrated when things don't go the way you plan but could also make you a very motivated person. Your love of sports could detract from your studies but could provide a needed break and be representative of your belief in balance in your life. Just make sure that the spin you put on your weakness is appropriate and that your weakness is really a weakness.

Where do you see yourself in 10 years?

● We know that nobody knows exactly what he or she is going to be doing in 10 years. The interviewers don't need specific details. They just want a general idea of what your long-term goals are and what you aspire to become. If you have several possibilities, at least one should be in line with the goals of the scholarship.

● Try to be as specific as possible without sounding unrealistic. For example, you can say that you would like to be working at a high-tech company in marketing, but leave out that you plan to have a daughter Rita, son Tom and dog Skip. Too much detail will make your dreams sound too naive.

Tell me about yourself. Or, is there anything you want to add?

● The most difficult questions are often the most open-ended. You have the freedom to say anything. For these kinds of questions, go back to the mission of the scholarship and shape your answer to reflect the characteristics that the judges are seeking in the winner. Practice answering this question several times because it is the one that stumps applicants the most.

● Have three things to say about yourself that match the goal of the scholarship. For example, you could discuss three personal traits you have, such as motivation, leadership skills and interpersonal skills. Or, you could discuss three skills applicable to academics, such as analytical skills, problem-solving skills and your love of a good challenge.

● The alternative, "Is there anything you want to add?" is typically asked at the end of the interview. In this case, make your response brief but

*Ask Your Own
Questions*

*An interview
should not be an
interrogation, with
the interviewer firing
all the questions and
you answering. Ask
some questions to
make the interview
interactive. It will be
more interesting for
both of you.*

meaningful. Highlight the most important thing you want your interviewer to remember.

Other Questions

In addition to these, here are some more common questions:

- What do you think you personally can contribute to this field?
- How do you plan to use what you have studied after graduation?
- Do you plan to continue your studies in graduate school?
- What do you want to specifically focus on within this field of study?
- Do you plan to do a thesis or senior project?
- Who are your role models in the field?
- What do you see as the future of this field?
- How do you see yourself growing in your career?
- What can you add to this field?
- What do you think are the most challenging aspects of this field?
- What is your ideal job after graduating from college?
- Tell me about a time that you've overcome adversity.
- What are your opinions about (fill in political or field-related issue)?
- Tell me about your family.
- What do you hope to gain from college?
- Who is a role model for you?
- What is your favorite book? Why?
- What is the most challenging thing you have done?

Remember that with all these questions your goal is to demonstrate that you are the best fit for the scholarship. Be sure to practice these with your mock interviewer. The more comfortable and confident you feel answering these questions, the better you'll do in your interviews.

Questions for the Questioner

There is a huge difference between an interview and an interrogation. In an interview, you also ask questions. Make certain that your interview does not become an interrogation. Ask questions yourself throughout the conversation. Remember that you want to keep the conversation two-way.

Toward the end of your interview, you will probably have the opportunity to ask additional questions. Take this opportunity. If you don't ask any questions, it will appear that you are uninterested in the conversation or haven't put much thought into your interview. Take time before the interview to develop a list of questions you may want to ask. Of course you don't have to ask all your questions, but you need to be prepared to ask a few.

To get you started, we've developed some suggestions. Adapt these questions to the specific scholarship you are applying for and personalize them.

- How did you get involved with this organization?
- How did you enter this field? What was your motivation?

- Who do you see as your mentors in this field?
- What do you think are the most exciting things about your career?
- What advice do you have for someone starting out?
- What do you see as the greatest challenges for this field?
- What do you think will be the greatest advancements in 10 years?
- What effect do you think technology will have on this field?
- I read that there is a (insert trend) in this field. What do you think?

The best questions are those that come from your detective work. Let's say that in researching an organization you discover that they recently launched a new program to research a cure for diabetes. Inquiring about this new program would be a perfect question to ask. It not only shows that you have done your homework, but it is also a subject about which the organization is deeply concerned.

Use Time to Your Advantage

The best time to ask Mom or Dad for something is when they're in a good mood. It's all about timing. Timing is also important in interviews. If you have more than one scholarship interview, time them strategically. Schedule less important and less demanding interviews first. This will allow you the opportunity to practice before your more difficult interviews. You will improve your skills as you do more interviews. It makes sense to hone your skills on the less important ones first.

If you are one of a series of applicants who will be interviewed, choose the order that fits you best. If you like to get things over with, try to be interviewed in the beginning. If you need more time to prepare yourself mentally, select a time near the end. We recommend that you don't choose to go first because the judges will use your interview as a benchmark for the rest. They may not recognize you as the best applicant even though it turns out to be true.

The Long-Distance Interview

If you've ever been in a long-distance relationship, you know there's a reason why most don't last. You simply can't communicate over the telephone in the same way you can in person. Scholarship interviews are the same. You may find that an interview will not be face-to-face but over the telephone instead. If this happens, here are some strategies to help bridge the distance:

Find a quiet place to do the interview where you won't be interrupted. You need to be able to give your full attention to the conversation you are having.

Know who's on the other end of the line. You may interview with a panel of people. Write down each of their names and positions when they first introduce themselves to you. They will be impressed when you are able to respond to them individually and thank each of them by name.

Role of the Interview

Interviews play an important role in the scholarship selection process. Judges use interviews to see who you are beyond what you write in your application and essay and to select a winner among highly qualified finalists.

Use notes from your practice interviews. One of the advantages of doing an interview over the telephone is that you can refer to notes without your interviewers knowing. Take advantage of this.

Look and sound like you would in person. Pretend that your interviewers are in the room with you, and use the same gestures and facial expressions that you would if you were meeting in person. It may sound strange, but your interviewers will actually be able to hear through your voice when you are smiling, when you are paying attention and when you are enthusiastic about what you're saying. Don't do your interview lying down in your bed or slouched back in a recliner.

Don't use a speaker phone, cordless phone or cell phone. Speaker phones often echo and pick up distracting surrounding noise. Cordless and cell phones can generate static, and the battery can die at the worst possible moment.

Turn off call waiting. Nothing is more annoying than hearing the call waiting beep while you are trying to focus and deliver an important thought. (And, this may sound obvious, never click over to take a second call.)

Use the techniques of regular interviews. You'd be surprised how much is translated over the telephone. Don't neglect good speaking and delivery points just because the interviewers can't see you!

The Group Interview

So it's you on one side of the table and a panel of six on the other side. It's certainly not the most natural way to have a conversation. How do you stay calm when you are interviewed by a council of judges?

Think of the group as individuals. Instead of thinking it's you versus the team, think of each of the interviewers as an individual. Try to connect with each person separately.

Try to get everyone's name if you can. Have a piece of paper handy that you can use to jot down everyone's name and role so that you can refer to them in the conversation. You want to be able to target your answers to each of the constituents. If you are interviewing with a panel of employees from a company and you know that Ms. Sweeny works in accounting while Mr. Duff works in human resources, you can speak about your analytical skills to appeal to Ms. Sweeny and your people skills to appeal to Mr. Duff.

Make eye contact. Look into the eyes of each of the panelists. Don't stare, but show them that you are confident. Be careful not to focus on only one panelist.

Respect the hierarchy. You may find that there is a leader in the group like the scholarship chair or the CEO of the company. Pay a little more attention to stroke the ego of the person in charge. They are used to it, they expect it and a little kissing up never hurt anyone.

Include everyone. In any group situation, there are usually one or two more vocal members who take the lead. Don't focus all your attention only on the loud ones. Spread your attention among the panelists as evenly as possible.

The Disaster Interview

Even if you do your interview homework and diligently practice mock interviewing, you may still find that you and your interviewer just don't connect or that you just don't seem to have the right answers. For students who spend some time preparing, this is a very rare occurrence. Interviewers are not trying to trick you or make you feel bad. They are simply trying to find out more about you and your fit with the award. Still, if you think that you've bombed, here are some things to keep in mind:

Avoid should have, would have, could have. Don't replay the interview in your head again and again, thinking of all the things you should have said. It's too easy to look back and have the best answers. Instead, use what you've learned to avoid making the same mistakes in your next interview.

There are no right answers. Remember that in reality there really are no right answers. Your answers may not have been perfect, but that doesn't mean that they were wrong. There are countless ways to answer the same question.

The toughest judge is you. Realize that you are your own greatest critic. While you may think that you completely bombed an interview, your interviewer will most likely not have as harsh an opinion.

The Post-Interview

After you complete your interviews, follow up with a thank you note. Remember that interviewers are typically volunteers and have made the time to meet with you. If you feel that there is very important information that you forgot to share in your interview, mention it briefly in your thank you note. If not, a simple note will suffice. You will leave a polite, lasting impression on your interviewer.

For More Help

Because the interview is often the last stage in scholarship competitions, it is one of the most important factors. In this chapter, we have shared strategies that should help you to ace interviews. If you would like more help, refer to our book *How to Write a Winning Scholarship Essay*. You'll find advice from scholarship judges about interviews and more than 20 example scholarship questions and answers.

Chapter 9 Summary: Ace the Interviews

Scholarship interviewers are real people. Remember to think of your interview as a conversation with an adult who is interested in your life. This will serve to calm your nerves and to help you relax and be yourself.

Do your interview homework. Before the big day, know the purpose of the scholarship, the criteria for selection, the background of the awarding organization and the background of your interviewer.

Appearances count. Look and act the part by dressing appropriately, sitting up straight and speaking with interest in your voice.

Do a mock interview. The best way to prepare for scholarship interviews is to practice for them. Get a friend or family member to practice interviewing you. The more practice you get, the more you'll know what to expect and the more comfortable you'll be in the real situation.

Get familiar with the questions that you are most likely to be asked. Practice answering these questions. (See the section in this chapter on the answers to the most common interview questions.)

Don't just react. Interact! Create a two-way conversation with your interviewer so that you are not just answering questions but asking them too.

Because of distance, some interviews may not be face-to-face. For telephone interviews, use the same strategies you use for in-person interviews. The person on the other end of the line can't see you but can hear interest in your voice.

Some interviews may be group sessions with you and have more than one interviewer. Remember to direct attention to everyone in the group and try to connect by addressing each person individually and making eye contact.

If you feel like you've blown an interview, remember that you are your toughest judge. Understand that the other pieces of your application count and you probably did better than you think.

Strategies for Specific Scholarships

· ·

In this chapter, you'll learn strategies to apply for scholarships based on:

- Major or academic field

- Career goal

- Leadership

- Athletics

- Community service

- Ethnic background

- Religious background

- Hobbies

- Parents' employer

- Financial need

· ·

College Cash from Your Hobbies and Pastimes

Scholarships provide the perfect opportunity for reaping financial gain as a result of your delight in dogs or your gusto for golf. From automobile aficionados to zephyr zealots, there exists an organization for the love of almost anything you can imagine. And where there are enthusiast organizations, there are often scholarships to promote that interest.

Add to this list organizations that want to promote academic fields, industries, sports, public service, religions, political agendas and education, and you get a large number of scholarships with very specific goals and objectives. This means that the majority of scholarships available to you will reward students with specific backgrounds, skills or achievements. To take the same approach when applying to these scholarships, which have disparate aims, would be a fatal mistake. Each has its own requirements, judging criteria and competition. Each demands an individualized, well-developed plan of attack.

In this chapter, we provide strategies for specific types of scholarships. Depending on the scholarship, there are different twists you can give your application to insure that it fits the goals of the award and has the best chance of winning.

The Big Picture

In our Scholarship Directory, you will find scholarships for nearly every talent, hobby and interest imaginable. There are scholarships for linguistic majors, soccer players and future museum curators. It is tempting to use the same application and essay to apply to all these scholarships. However, if you look carefully, you will notice that while there may be many commonalities among scholarships, each is focused on a specific quality that you need to have in your application. If you hope to win, don't take any shortcuts. Spend the time to tune your applications for each scholarship and you will be rewarded with lots of free cash for college.

Awards Based on Your Current or Future Major

Whether you're majoring in Taisho-period Japanese history or computer science, there are scholarships open to you. Scholarships based on an academic major or concentration of study are some of the most commonly available. Colleges, foundations and associations provide the scholarships to encourage study in these academic areas. The difficult question is this: How do you make your application stand out from those of other students who by definition have similar goals and training as you? Here are some strategies to help you set your application apart from others in your academic field:

Emphasize your passion for the field. Show the scholarship judges that you are not only a good student of Asian history, for example, but that it is a passion and

source of intellectual curiosity that you will pursue for the rest of your life. This does not mean that you need to become a professor of history after you graduate. However, finding some way to tie the skills of the discipline with your future career is essential. In all elements–the application, essay, recommendations and interview–demonstrate your commitment to your major and how it will influence the rest of your life.

To prevent essays from being a list of coursework, one possible approach is to focus on your inspiration for selecting the major. Again, reveal a passion for the subject that goes beyond the fact (true as it may be) that you picked the major because your roommates did too! Ask yourself questions like these: What motivated you to select this field of study? Do you have an interesting anecdote to illustrate how you made your decision? This is something that differs from student to student and that will help personalize your application. Think about how you plan to use the skills from this major in your future. Do you plan to make this major a career? What contributions to the field have you made or are you planning to make? Remember, the goal is to show your commitment to this area of study or career field.

For the essay, do not just reiterate your qualifications as listed in your application or resume. Use the space to add color to your application and to illustrate in a creative way your commitment to the academic field. Think about describing your first interaction with something or someone related to this area of study, a mentor who has influenced your decision or your vision of the future of the field. Anecdotes go a long way since most essays focus solely on the purely academic pursuits of their authors.

Although your focus throughout the application should be on academics, you can also discuss how you have developed skills or interests outside the classroom that relate to the field. For example, if you are studying the sciences, maybe you also volunteer with an organization that helps encourage females to pursue careers in science. Weaving in nonacademic experiences that support your academic goals is very powerful and shows your dedication to the field beyond the classroom.

In interviews, don't just list off the facts that are in your application. Try to add a personal dimension to your academic interests. Explain how you selected your major and what your plans are for utilizing your knowledge. Describe in detail your passion for the field and why it is important to you. Ask your interviewer about his or her commitment and thoughts on its future. Asking a roomful of professors about the state of their field and where it's headed is sure to generate a stimulating conversation. You already know that this is an area of great interest for your interviewers. Use the topic to relate to them.

Recommendations should be from teachers or professors who can vouch for your dedication. Select those who have worked with you in your studies or in developing skills needed in the field. If you apply for a history-related scholarship, you could ask your history teacher or professor for a recommendation. You could also ask a librarian with whom you've worked closely on research, since this is a highly desirable skill for the study of history.

Show Your Commitment

For scholarships based on major, the judges want to see evidence of your commitment to your field and your potential for contributing to it while you are in college and afterward.

Overall, remember that there will be many other students who have taken similar coursework and received similar grades. Be sure that your application presents your qualifications, your devotion to the field and your plans for contributing to its advancement. This is how you can differentiate yourself from the other applicants.

Scholarships for Your Future Career

In most everything, there are the "usual" and the "unusual." It is no different with scholarships. There are the usual scholarships for future accountants, doctors and business-people. Then, there are the unusual scholarships for those who want to seek answers about the existence of aliens or work underwater. But one thing is for sure: In nearly every career field you can imagine—both the expected and unexpected—there are scholarships available.

Companies and professional organizations award career-based scholarships to encourage talented young people to enter their fields. They want to create a relationship with the most promising future leaders in their industries. Your challenge is this: How do you convince the judges that you are the applicant with the most promise? Since these scholarships attract others interested in the industry, you can bet that many will have similar backgrounds as yours. Also, many will say that they intend to enter this career after graduation. These two facts alone will not guarantee a win. You need to distinguish yourself from the pack. Read on to learn how.

As you are completing your applications, keep in mind that you want to show how much promise you have for succeeding in the career field. Describe related work experience, coursework and honors or awards. Relate experiences in which you've developed the skills needed in the career. Even if you aren't absolutely certain that you will enter the field, it's okay to apply for scholarships. Nobody expects you to sign away your life at this point.

Concentrate on what contributions you plan to make within the industry. If you plan to be a graphic designer, what kind of design do you plan to do? What kind of innovative projects would you like to tackle? The more thoughtful your responses are the better. Sharing this will make your future contributions to the field more real.

To differentiate your application from the others, discuss how your interest in the career started. Did you have a mentor who piqued your curiosity? Did your studies influence your interest? Your background will be different from that of other students.

Essays offer you the opportunity to share your personal or emotional dedication to the career. Utilize the space to illustrate your commitment with an anecdote or example. Share your personal motivations, i.e. what attracts you to the field. If you are applying for an accounting scholarship, don't restate the information in your application about the coursework you've taken and internships you've held. Write about how you first became interested in the field or about the most valuable experience you had while interning. Or, you may want to write about your analytical ability. Be sure to connect how your analytical skill will contribute to your future as an accountant.

> ### *Give Examples*
>
> *It's not enough for you to say that you are a leader or committed to XYZ cause. You need to be able to back up your statements with actual actions and results.*

Convey to interviewers information they can't find in your application. Share why you plan to enter the field, highlights from your experience and your plans for the future. Recognize that your plans may change, but outline where you see yourself in the career in the next five or 10 years. Describe your goals and how you hope to make inventive contributions.

Get recommendations from employers if you've had experience in the field. If you haven't, your employers may still be able to describe skills that you've developed that are necessary for the career. Ask teachers or professors who have taught related subjects.

Remember that your overall objective is to demonstrate your devotion to the career and your ability to excel and make useful contributions to it.

Awards That Recognize Leadership

When you were a child, being a leader meant you decided which schoolyard game to play during recess. Now, it may mean leading an organization, heralding a cause or influencing the establishment. In the future, it will mean managing and motivating a team of people or making a difference in your community. Scholarship judges recognize the value of supporting students who are promising leaders—in fact this is a quality that almost all scholarships reward. They want to back those who will move and shake their world.

When you apply for scholarships based on leadership (or any award that values leadership), it's not enough to say that you are a leader. You need to prove it to the scholarship judges by sharing your experiences with them. Here are some strategies for applying for leadership-based scholarships:

To demonstrate your leadership ability, *show* **the scholarship judges how you've been a leader.** Describe leadership positions you've held and your responsibilities in each, but don't stop here. In addition, use examples to illustrate how you've successfully led a group, how you've directed or motivated your peers. Give the scholarship judges shining examples of your leadership in action.

Provide concrete examples of the effects of your leadership. Did your team meet its goals? Did you lead a new or innovative project? Did you increase membership or participation? Were there changes as a result of your efforts? Results provide solid evidence of the effectiveness of your leadership.

Recognize that being a leader doesn't just mean being the president of a class or organization. Leaders are people who are passionate about their cause and who influence other people. Leadership can take many forms, from writing an editorial column to leading a Girl Scout troop. Include both formal and informal leadership roles you've played. This may consist of official positions you've held as well as special projects you've led in which you didn't have an official title. The important thing about leadership is that you have influenced other people and rallied them to take action.

In applications, highlight your main responsibilities and achievements as a leader. This will provide a quick overview of your accomplishments. As always select those that best fit the mission of the scholarship.

In essays, do not just repeat the information that is on your applications. Provide insight into who you are as a leader. Share an anecdote about one of your experiences as a leader. Describe your philosophy on being a leader. Tell the judges when you first realized the power of leadership and what it meant to you to discover qualities of leadership within yourself. Talk about a leader you admire. Let the scholarship judges know what characteristics a position of leadership brings out in you. It's important that you personalize your leadership experience.

In interviews, use the same strategies that you have put into action in your essays and applications forms and don't recount information that your interviewers can easily find and read in those documents. Instead, use the interview time with the judges to provide personal information about your leadership experience or share your personal approach to leadership. Share examples of times you've been a leader. Try to exude confidence in your interview. Since you'll be in the company of other leaders, ask them about their philosophy of leadership, what they did as students and what they find challenging about being a leader in their fields.

Ask recommenders to describe examples of your leadership ability. Remind them of projects and events in which you were a leader so they can complete the portrait of you as a strong leader in their letters to the committee.

Athletic Scholarships

You're the best dribbler, server, runner, pitcher or sprinter at your school. How do you use that talent to pay for college? With an athletic scholarship.

Athletic scholarships are the Holy Grail. At their best, they can cover tuition and fees, room and board and books. That's not bad for doing something you enjoy.

There are two types of athletic scholarships. The first is given by colleges to the best college-bound high school athletes. The second is from organizations that reward high school or college students who participate in athletics but that may or may not base the scholarships on athletic talent.

College Athletic Awards

College athletic scholarships are funded by membership revenue from the National Collegiate Athletic Association (NCAA), which encompasses more than 950 colleges. The colleges are divided into three divisions, with athletic scholarships awarded for Division I and Division II schools. At Division III schools, student athletes receive scholarships based on financial need but not on athletic talent.

However, don't think that every talented athlete is instantly showered with a full-ride scholarship. It takes more than talent to win and to keep one of these awards. Here are some strategies for winning an NCAA scholarship:

Remember that academics rule–even in qualifying for athletic scholarships. You can be the number one player in the country, but if you don't have the grades or tests scores, you won't play competitively in college. The minimum academic requirements for eligibility are that you must do or have the following:

- Graduate from high school.
- Complete a curriculum of at least 14 academic courses including these subjects:
  English: Four years.
  Mathematics: Two years of courses at the level of Algebra I or above.
  Natural or physical science (including at least one laboratory course, if offered by your high school): Two years.
  Additional courses: English, mathematics or natural or physical science: One year.
  Social science: Two years.
  Additional academic courses: In any of the above subject areas or foreign language, philosophy or non-doctrinal religion courses: Three years.
- Have a core-course grade-point average and a combined score on the SAT verbal and math sections or a sum score on the ACT based on the NCAA qualifier index scale. In other words they set minimum scores that you must achieve.

You don't have to be a football or basketball star to win athletic scholarships. In fact, you may have better opportunities to win scholarships for less-publicized sports like crew, rugby, volleyball or field hockey. Competition is often less intense for these sports.

Find schools that match both your athletic and academic goals. Don't choose a college solely because of its athletic program. The great majority of student athletes don't go professional after graduating. They go to graduate school or find jobs. Select a college that fulfills your academic needs so that you will be prepared for the next step.

College coaches may not find you, so you must find them. Unless you are a true superstar, the reality is that coaches don't have the resources to do national searches for student athletes. If you want to be noticed, you are going to need to start the conversation. Do this by writing a letter to coaches at prospective colleges. Build a portfolio as evidence of your athletic ability. Your portfolio should include the following:

- Athletic statistics such as win-loss record, times, averages, etc.
- Records set
- Honors or awards won
- Newspaper clips
- Videotapes of games
- Letters of recommendation from coaches

Keep in touch with the coaches. Follow up to make sure they received your letter and portfolio. Ask if they need additional information. Get your high school coach to call the college coach on your behalf. Try to keep yourself at the top of their list of whom they want on next year's team.

Grades Count Too

For athletic scholarships, your scores on the field are important but so are your scores in the classroom. To qualify, you must meet minimum academic requirements.

If you are fortunate enough to receive an athletic scholarship, realize that you are not guaranteed a free ride for the rest of your academic career. There are no guaranteed four-year athletic scholarships in Division I, II or III. Athletic scholarships are awarded for a maximum of one academic year and may be renewed each year for a maximum of five years within a six-year period.

Don't count on that $7 million contract yet. For a very, very small minority, college segues into professional athletics. According to the NCAA, the odds of a high school football player making it to a professional team are about 6,000 to 1, and the odds for a high school basketball player are 10,000 to 1. Do your best, but keep focused on academics too.

Get more information. The more information you have, the better equipped you'll be for facing the stiff competition for athletic scholarships. Speak with your coach and guidance counselors. Also, get more detailed information on eligibility and a directory of schools that have scholarships for each sport from the NCAA. Contact information for the NCAA can be found in Appendix B.

Athletic Organization Awards

There are also scholarships for high school and college athletic competitors and enthusiasts given by aficionado organizations and athletic associations like your school's booster club.

For these scholarships, the level of athletic talent can vary. For some, athletic ability is the key measurement, while others equally weigh additional qualities like leadership, academic achievement or public service. Adapt your application to fit the criteria on which you will be judged. Here are some strategies to help you:

In your application, concentrate on how you meet the mission of the scholarship. For example, if you are applying for a scholarship that is based on both athletic and academic achievement, outline your accomplishments on the field and in the classroom.

Submit a sports portfolio. Your portfolio brings the judges to the sidelines of your game and enables them to see evidence of your athletic ability. See the previous section for what to include in your portfolio.

Go beyond your stats. Describe your motivation for participating in the sport to provide background for your interest. Outline your goals for the future, and let the scholarship judges know where you are headed. While going off to play in the NFL or NBA may be your goal, consider mentioning alternatives to demonstrate that you understand how difficult going professional is and how much you value a solid education.

Try to make your essays different from what the scholarship committee will expect. Many athletes write about the time they scored the winning touchdown or hit the winning home run. Take a different approach. Depict the first time you recognized your passion for the sport. Describe an unexpected mentor or role model who influenced and shaped you as an athlete. Explain why the sport is important *besides* scoring points and becoming a professional athlete. Use the essay to share something about yourself, not to just glorify your accomplishments. The scholarship judges will know by your portfolio that you are a talented player. You need to show them that you can be self-analytical about your athletic achievements.

In interviews, go beyond the information that is in your applications and essays. Again, don't just recount the winning game or match. Provide insight into your personal motivation and goals. Have anecdotes and examples besides those from game time to illustrate your commitment to the sport. Be ready to discuss your major and classes you'd like to take.

Encourage your coaches to write about your athletic statistics but also about you as a person in their letters of recommendation. You may want to ask a teacher or professor who knows you in a different capacity to write a recommendation as well. Request that he or she comment on your integrity and dedication to academics. This will provide a more complete picture of who you are underneath the jersey.

Scholarships for Public Service

Scholarships offer the opportunity for philanthropy to pay off in cold hard cash. Of course, this should not be your motivation for volunteering, but it is a nice perk of donating your time and service for a worthy cause. Many organizations provide scholarships to encourage public service among youth. Your challenge becomes how you distinguish your application from those of all the other do-gooders.

As with other types of scholarships, what's most important for service-based scholarships is fulfilling the mission. Before you start your application to any one service organization, you must understand what the group is trying to achieve. What is the organization's purpose? Why is it awarding the scholarship? Once you understand this, mold your application to show how you fit the scholarship. Highlight service experience that matches the scholarship's mission.

When completing the application, include details that define the quality of the contributions that you have made. List the number of hours you've contributed in service and what you did. Include any responsibilities or leadership positions that you held. Most important, note the effects of your contributions. Give concrete evidence of how your service has produced results. For example, if you volunteered for an adult literacy program, describe how your students improved their scores on a reading test after working with you. If you volunteered for a voter registration drive, recount how many voters you registered. By providing specific results of your work, scholarship judges will see that you not only volunteer but you also make a difference that is measurable and material.

Personalize your inspiration. Discuss your motivation for serving and why the causes are important to you. Bring your inspiration to a personal level so that the scholarship committee can understand you better as a person. Be illustrative in your essay, providing lively examples or anecdotes. Don't be afraid to be creative.

Take a similar approach with interviews. Go beyond what you have included in your application and essay. Use this time to show interviewers why your volunteer work is important to you personally. Practice sharing experiences and information to illustrate your points. Also take the time to learn about your interviewers' links to public service. Ask members of the scholarship committee how they got involved and what motivates them to continue in areas of service.

Avoid merely stating the facts about your public service in every part of your application. Instead, make your service personal by conveying how it has affected the lives of those you have helped and how it has affected you.

Awards Based on Ethnic Background

No matter what your ethnic background, there is probably a scholarship for you. Scholarships based on ethnic background are awarded to celebrate the history or culture of an ethnic group, increase the number of minorities in college and encourage minorities to enter certain professions. Regardless of the purpose of the award, here are some points to keep in mind when applying:

Meet the goal of the scholarship. It's not enough for you to just be a member of the ethnic group. In other words, if you are applying for an award for Asian Americans, you will not win simply because you are an Asian American. You will win if you fit the mission of the award. If the purpose of the award is to help Asian Americans become leaders in the community, you must not only have the appropriate ethnic background but also demonstrate your leadership skills and show your plans to be involved in the Asian American community in the future.

Personalize your application. Instead of making general statements about the culture of your ethnic group or describing its history in your application, write about how your heritage has affected you personally. The scholarship judges are probably already familiar with the culture and history of the group, so describing these will not tell them anything about you. It's important that your application demonstrates the importance of your background to you, how it has shaped who you are, how you identify with it and how you will use it in the future.

Explain how you will share your knowledge with others. Remember that scholarship judges want to get the most mileage from the awards they are giving. This means they want to reward students who will make an impact on the future. You can show that you will do so by explaining how you have already influenced others.

Religious Scholarships

When you think of money for education, religion is probably the last thing that pops into mind. However, many religious organizations award scholarships to encourage students to get involved in activities of faith and to promote the growth of that religion. We have a few words of advice for applying for religious-based scholarships.

Most important, only apply for a religious scholarship if you are a true believer in the principles and teachings of that religion. We don't suspect that you would do this, but some students have been known to apply for such scholarships even though the only time they attend church is when their parents drag them out of bed on Christmas and Easter mornings. If you are not truly dedicated to the religion, mission or church, don't pretend to be.

That said, let's discuss what you should do when applying for a scholarship that is supported by a religious organization.

Emphasize your participation in religious activities in your application. This may include participating in missionary campaigns, church camps, teaching, volunteering or studying religious traditions. These descriptions will help show the selection committee your dedication to the religion. Also emphasize how religious teaching and faith have helped you in the past and what they mean to your future.

Go beyond your faith. Often, religious scholarships are not just about religion. Many recognize students who have done public service, displayed leadership or excelled academically. Include descriptions about your many nonreligious activities in your application and essays as well.

Awards for Hobbies

You probably didn't know that you can earn money from being an amateur radio operator, a bowler or a Latin speaker, but you can. For almost every hobby there is a scholarship. Organizations composed of enthusiasts want to encourage the growth and popularity of the objects of their affection and thus have established scholarships for students who partake in them.

Insure that you fit the mission of the scholarship. If the scholarship is for true enthusiasts of the hobby, make sure you really are an enthusiast. Don't apply for a philatelic scholarship if the only stamps you've ever touched are those you use to send letters.

In applications, highlight any honors or awards you have won in the hobby. If you haven't won any, provide other evidence of your knowledge or skill level. If you are applying for a sewing scholarship and have never won an award in sewing, describe instead how you started a business in which you sold your sewn products. Convey to the scholarship committee your skill level in the hobby whether it's through awards you've won or other personal accomplishments that you've made.

Use essays as an opportunity to discuss the personal significance of your hobby. Explain your motivation for becoming involved or discuss role models in the hobby. Make your essay personal with anecdotes, dialogues or active experiences. Don't be afraid to be creative. Convey how the hobby has affected you individually.

Utilize essays or interviews to demonstrate that you are committed to continuing your hobby. Discuss your goals so that the selection committee will understand that by awarding the scholarship to you, they will meet their goal of promoting the hobby in the future.

In interviews, provide insight into how the hobby has affected you. Then ask interviewers how they got their start in the hobby and about their experiences as well. You know that this is a topic of conversation they will enjoy.

Get recommendations from those who can vouch for your skill level in the hobby. If you are applying for a sewing scholarship, get a recommendation from your sewing teacher or from a frequent recipient of some of your projects.

Scholarships from Your Parents' Employers

One perk that employers often provide is a scholarship fund for the sons and daughters of their employees. The great thing about employer scholarships is that the children of employees often have good chances of winning. Because it is a requirement to be the child of an employee, there are a limited number of people who can apply. This does not mean that employer scholarships are easy to win, but it does mean that–unlike scholarships in which every student in the country can apply–the competition for these awards will be significantly less. Here are some strategies to help improve your chances even more:

Ask your parents to find out who the judges will be. If the parent(s) who is employed by the provider of the scholarship feels it's appropriate, he or she can informally speak with the judges to get more information on what qualities they are looking for in students who are viable candidates for the award. They might also ask what characteristics were common among students who have won in the past. Warn your parent(s) not to try and lobby for you since this can easily backfire. If your parent(s) is able to gather more information about what the judges are looking for beyond the written guidelines, you will have a better idea of how to shape your application and essay.

Focus on how you fulfill the mission of the scholarship in the application and essay. Often the mission will be general, rewarding students for academic achievement and leadership. Review the information in this chapter on applying for scholarships based on academics and leadership.

"My Hobbies Paid for College"
Russell Duffy, Scholarship Winner

When I was a freshman in college, my parents asked me to apply for scholarships to help pay my tuition bills. I made a list of all my hobbies and interests. I cross-referenced them with scholarships and found three awards that matched my hobbies: writing, singing and public speaking.

In the spring I applied for all three. For the writing scholarship, I described how I wrote for our school's literary magazine and included clips from pieces I had gotten published. When I applied for the singing scholarship, I included audio and videotapes of performances I'd made in high school and college. For the public speaking scholarship, I had to give a speech as a part of the competition.

It turns out that I won two scholarships for public speaking and singing. I never thought that what I love to do in my free time could help me pay for college, but I won $3,000!

Don't Assume You Don't Qualify for Need-Based Awards

Don't count yourself out of need-based scholarships without first understanding how the judges define financial need. For some, there are specific guidelines, while for others a level of need is preferred but not required.

Be careful in the interview how you describe your parents. Be aware that while it's inappropriate and shouldn't happen, what you say could get back to your mom or dad's manager, supervisor or employer. Do not be critical or relate information that could be used against your parents. For example, do not say that your parents dislike their managers or express their beliefs about what changes should be made to the company. Chances are that the judges will not reveal what they learn, but it's better to be cautious.

Know something about the company. You may know where your parents work but have no idea what their companies actually do. Sit down with your parents and ask them to describe their jobs and tell you about the company in general. Visit the website to get more information on what the company does and achievements or products that it is most proud of.

Need-Based Scholarships

Because the purpose of financial aid is to assist those who need help to attend college, it makes sense that financial need is a requirement for many scholarships. To make a case for your need, it's not enough to submit the Free Application for Federal Student Aid (FAFSA) or tax forms. Here is some guidance for applying for need-based scholarships:

First, try to find out how the organization defines "need" and how much of a role it plays in the selection of scholarship recipients. Scholarship benefactors and organizations define need differently. You may find that while you are needy according to the guidelines of one scholarship, you may not be according to another. If you are on the borderline of meeting the financial criteria for a specific scholarship but you find out that financial need does not play a large role in selection, you may still have a good chance of winning. However, if you discover that it is the largest factor, you may choose to spend your time applying to a different scholarship that better fits your background and circumstances.

Tell the truth about how much you will really require to attend college. Most need-based scholarships require documentation of your earnings, taxes paid and projected college expenses so the judges will be able to verify your financial situation.

Build a case that demonstrates your financial need. Concisely highlight the main reasons for your need. By showing that your income and assets are X and you anticipate that your college education will cost Y, you can quickly show the difference between the two. Briefly explain special circumstances that affect your need such as the costs of a sibling's education, medical costs or the support of an elderly or ailing relative. This helps the scholarship committee understand your circumstances.

Money should not be the entire premise of your application. Include information about your financial background, but spend the rest of the application making a case for why you're qualified to win the award. Your financial situation is just one consideration. Once you've established that you need financial help, prove that you meet the mission of the scholarship. Let the financial forms demonstrate your need. Your application, essay, interview and recommendations should focus on how you fit the scholarship, not on why you need money.

Recurring Themes

In this chapter, we have outlined strategies that you should use when applying for specific scholarships. Because each is judged by a different group of people and has different qualifications, take an individualized approach to applying to them. However, in your study of these very different types of scholarships, you'll find some recurring themes to take away. In summary, remember to do the following:

- Build a case for why you fit the mission of the scholarship.
- Tell the truth.
- Use essays and interviews to go beyond facts found in your application.
- Share something personal about yourself.

By following these guidelines, you will create the strongest application possible and therefore the best chance of coming home with the dough.

Chapter 10 Summary: Strategies for Specific Scholarships

There are scholarships for nearly every talent, hobby or interest imaginable. Your job is to find those that best match your skills and experience. Then, create an application that builds a case for why you should win the award.

Scholarships based on major. Directly or indirectly demonstrate your passion for the field and share your plans to use what you learned in college after graduating.

Scholarships based on career goals. Show how much promise you have for contributing to the field in the future and describe your motivation for entering the field as well as your goals for the future.

Scholarships based on leadership. Demonstrate how you've been a leader through examples and illustrations, including the results of your work. Remember that you don't have to hold an official position to be a leader.

College-bound high school athletes. Keep in mind that your scores on the field are important but so are the scores you get in the classroom. Academic achievement is a must for athletic scholarships. With a few exceptions for nationally recognized athletes, the coaches will not find you. You will need to build a portfolio to showcase your talents and start the communication with them.

Be realistic about athletic scholarships. Know that there are many more student athletes than there are scholarships available and that your chances of making it into the professional leagues are about 6,000 to 1 for football and 10,000 to 1 for basketball.

Scholarships based on service. Highlight the results of your service work and any responsibilities or leadership positions that you have held. Explain your motivation for participating in service work.

Scholarships based on ethnic background. Highlight your contributions to your ethnic community and the role you plan to play in the future.

Scholarships based on religious belief. Focus on your contributions to your faith and the community. Share activities and the responsibilities that you have shouldered.

Scholarships based on a hobby or interest. Showcase awards or honors you've won for the hobby and evidence of your skill in it.

Need-based awards. The definition of financial "need" varies by award, which means that you may qualify for awards even if you think you don't. Build a case that illustrates why you need aid by showing the costs of your education and your family's ability to contribute.

Guaranteed Scholarships

In this chapter, you'll learn:

- Why guaranteed scholarships do exist

- How to tell if a guaranteed scholarship is actually a scam

- Getting in-state tuition even if you live out of state

Do Guaranteed Scholarships Really Exist?

Normally, when you hear the words "guaranteed" and "scholarship" used in the same sentence, you should run in the other direction. In previous chapters we warned you about any scholarship that claimed to be "guaranteed." While this is often a sign of a scam, there is one exception. There are scholarships with fixed criteria that are often quantitative. Anyone who meets certain eligibility standards wins one of these scholarships automatically.

This does not mean that anyone <u>can</u> win. You still need to meet the criteria such as getting a specific SAT I score. However, because the criteria for winning are quantitative, it takes the uncertainty out of whether or not you will win.

In this chapter we will introduce you to a variety of guaranteed scholarships so that you know how to recognize them. Keep in mind that many of these awards are limited to students who attend particular colleges or are residents of specific states. However, they are numerous enough that you will probably be able to benefit from some of them.

The Big Picture

The majority of these "guaranteed" awards are sponsored by colleges and state governments. It is important that you carefully research your college, or colleges that you are applying to, as well as your state government to see if they offer any of these awards. Since they are often based on such objective criteria as grades, SAT scores and even state of residency, you don't want to miss any opportunities. Why wouldn't you cash in on a guaranteed scholarship?

National Merit Scholarships

The PSAT (Preliminary Scholastic Assessment Test) can be one of the most lucrative tests you'll take. The National Merit program, administered by the National Merit Scholarship Corporation, a nonprofit organization, receives the scores for all high school juniors who take the PSAT. Using these scores the National Merit organization selects the highest-scoring students to be named National Merit Semifinalists. About 16,000 students out of the more than 1.4 million students who take the PSAT become Semifinalists.

Being selected a semifinalist is an honor in itself because it means that out of all of the juniors who took the PSAT exam, you are among the top scoring echelon. Unfortunately you don't automatically win a scholarship with this honor. However, those who are National Merit Semifinalists are invited to compete for a National

Merit Scholarship. From the 16,000 Semifinalists, about 8,000 win a National Merit Scholarship that might be one of the following:

- $2,500 from the National Merit Scholarships organization
- Corporate-sponsored Merit Scholarship awards
- College-sponsored Merit Scholarship awards

The key to being honored as a National Merit Semifinalist—and thus being able to compete for some money—is to take the PSAT exam during your junior year.

GPA and Exam-Based Scholarships

Some colleges want more brains on campus and offer automatic scholarships to academically talented students. These guaranteed awards are based on SAT I or ACT scores or GPA. For example, Saint Joseph's College in Rensselaer, Indiana, offers an Honors Scholarship worth up to $13,000 to all accepted students who have certain combinations of GPAs and test scores. There's a calculator on the website to see if you qualify. Here's one winning GPA-test score combination:

- SAT I score of 1240 or higher or ACT score of 28 or higher
- GPA of 3.3 or higher

Take a look at your school or the schools in which you are interested, and see if they offer similar guaranteed scholarships. You will find that many colleges offer incentives to attract bright students.

Transfer Student Awards

If you find that your college is not the right fit for you, transferring may be the answer. Unfortunately, your financial aid package does not automatically transfer from one college to another. You will need to reapply. Some colleges make the transition easier.

To encourage students who want to transfer into their college, some schools offer guaranteed awards to incoming transfer students with a minimum GPA in their previous college. For example, Spalding University in Louisville, Kentucky, offers a scholarship for transfer students according to the following scale:

- $3,700 for students with 3.5-4.0
- $3,200 for students with 3.2-3.49
- $2,800 for students with 3.0-3.19

If you are thinking about transferring, speak with someone in the financial aid office at the colleges you are considering. Ask them what kind of financial aid package you may expect as a transfer student and inquire about automatic scholarships for which you may be eligible.

The Real Guaranteed Scholarships

Guaranteed scholarships are usually a scam. But there are a few exceptions to this as you can see from this list of awards that are all but guaranteed if you meet certain requirements.

State Entitlement Awards

Whether or not you like where you live, there's a benefit to living there. States have financial aid programs for their residents. Some of these programs effectively reward students who perform at a specific academic level in high school. Georgia, for example, has the HOPE program that automatically awards money to high school students who have a B average or higher. Ironically, one of the biggest problems with the program is that many students aren't aware that they are eligible for a HOPE Scholarship and don't claim their money.

Many states offer similar entitlement awards. Some are based on academic merit while others have criteria related to financial need. Awards may be designated for high school seniors, adult students or students in certain fields like nursing, medicine or education. Be aware that some require you to use the money only at a college within your state.

We have a listing of all the state agencies that manage scholarships in the Scholarship Directory section of this book. Contact your agency to make sure you are not leaving any money on the table.

In-State Tuition for Out-Of-State Students

Getting in-state tuition at a public university can save you thousands of dollars. Take a look at the additional money needed for the University of California at Berkeley if you are from out of state. Those students who are not residents of California will have to pay a $18,684 non-resident fee.

If you are an out-of-state student, you will need to pay out-of-state tuition until you can establish in-state residency. This is easier in some states than others. Texas, for example, does not like students to move to their state just to use their fine educational system and then leave. One of the residency requirements is that you live in Texas for 12 months without attending a secondary institution. This makes gaining residency for purposes of reduced tuition at a Texas college far less attractive and almost impossible.

The University of California system, on the other hand, makes it possible but not easy. To become a resident you need to show three things:

> **Physical presence.** You must have proof that you remained in the state for more than one year. This means no going home for summer. You actually have to physically be in the state and be able to prove it.

> **Intent.** You must establish ties to the state of California that show you intend to make California your home. This requires giving up any previous residence and getting proof of your move such as a California driver's license.

> **Financial independence.** If both parents are nonresidents, you must show that you are financially independent from your parents. One way is that

you have not been claimed as an income tax deduction by your parents for at least two years.

There is one exception to the problem of establishing residency. Some schools have formed relationships with neighboring states to offer their residents automatic in-state rates from the beginning. The University of Arkansas, for example, offers a Non-Resident Tuition Award for entering freshmen from neighboring states that include Texas, Mississippi, Louisiana, Kansas, Missouri, Oklahoma and Tennessee. You must meet minimum academic criteria of a 3.5 GPA or higher and have an ACT score of at least 25 or an SAT I score of at least 1130. If you meet these academic qualities and are from a neighboring state, you will be granted in-state tuition, which can save you up to $6,000 a year in fees.

All It Takes to Win Is to Apply

These guaranteed scholarships are wonderful. There is no strategy involved in winning. If you meet the established qualifications, you win. The only challenge is to make sure you are aware that the awards exist. Now that you have an idea of what is out there, it shouldn't be hard to find some in your area. So get out there and stake your claim!

Chapter 11 Summary: Guaranteed Scholarships

There really are guaranteed scholarships. While we have warned you about scholarship scams that guarantee that you will win, there are legitimate awards that are based on quantitative criteria.

National Merit Scholarships. You may win scholarships from corporations and colleges based on your performance on the PSAT in your junior year.

Academic scholarships. Some colleges automatically award scholarships based on your grades and test scores. These are available for entering freshmen and transfer students.

State entitlement awards. You may win scholarships from your state based on your academic performance.

In-state tuition for out-of-state students. You can save money by qualifying for residency.

Unleash the Power of the Internet

. . . .

In this chapter, you'll learn:

- How to find more scholarships online

- Strategies for applying for scholarships via the Internet

- The importance of researching awarding organizations and past winners

- How to avoid costly scholarship scams on the Internet

. . . .

Opening the Scholarship Vault with the Internet

In the pre-Internet days, the only way to find out about scholarships was through books. The only way to research the background of awarding organizations was to write or call. In fact, the only way to apply was with typewriter and paper. The Internet has helped open the possibilities for scholarships by providing more access to awards, an easy method to find out about awarding organizations and the means for applying with your computer. In this chapter, we show you how to take advantage of these high-tech options.

**The Big
Picture**

Our view of the Internet is that it is a great tool for finding scholarships. But it is not the only tool. The biggest mistake you can make is assuming that once you do a few Internet searches, you are done. While the Internet has made the typewriter and whiteout obsolete, it sometimes makes applying so easy that students get sloppy. Remember, you should treat online applications with just as much care and attention as you would a paper application. Once you hit that submit button it's too late to make any corrections.

Using the Internet to Find Scholarships

You will find one of the most comprehensive directories of scholarships in the second half of this book. However, no directory has every scholarship available. In fact, new scholarships are formed every day. One of the benefits of using the Internet in your search is that website databases can be updated very quickly. Here are some tips for using the Internet to search for scholarships:

Look for databases of scholarships that you can search for free. We have one on our site at **www.supercollege.com**. Our database works like this: You answer questions about your education, academic goals, career goals, activities, parents' activities and employment, religion, talents, ethnicity and additional background information. Our database uses your answers to search thousands of awards and provide matches for scholarships that fit your individual background.

Searches should always be free. Never pay for a scholarship search.

Before beginning your search, prepare a list of your parents' employers and activities as well as your own activities, talents and interests. This will save time when you are actually using a website to search for scholarships. Having your pertinent information in a concise format will help insure that you don't forget or miss anything.

Don't Get Careless

One unintended consequence of applying to scholarships online is the huge increase in careless mistakes. For some students, filling out an online application is too easy. Without checking spelling and grammar they simply hit the "submit" button. A better idea is to compose your answers to the application separately and then copy and paste them into the online form.

Spend time to complete the questions about your background. There may be a lot of questions, but the more specific and accurate you can be about your background, the better your results will be.

Remember that no database is perfect. Every scholarship database has its shortcomings. The biggest is that none is anywhere near complete. There are millions of scholarships available and online databases only index a few thousand—and often these are the larger national type of awards. Searching the Internet is no substitute for doing your own research. Plus, depending on the quality of the software and your answers to the background questions, you may discover that not all the matches may actually be good fits.

The bottom line is to use the Internet like any good tool. But do realize that it is not perfect and needs to be supplemented with your own detective work.

Zap! Applying for Scholarships Online

In the old days, you had to lug out the typewriter and whiteout correction fluid every time you wanted to complete an application. It's much easier now. Fire up your computer and connect to the Internet. No correction fluid needed! There are many benefits to applying online. It's easy to correct typos and you don't have to make a trip to the Post Office. However, for even the most tech-savvy students, applying for scholarships online can be challenging. To help, here are some tips for applying electronically:

Preview the application. Before you start completing the application, take a sneak peek at it so that you know what questions are asked and what information you'll need to provide.

Consider your options. If you don't feel comfortable completing the application online, use the old-fashioned method. Most scholarships still offer you the option of printing out the application and completing it offline. It's better to spend time perfecting your essay than to lose hours figuring out how to use the Internet to apply.

Prepare your materials and answers in advance. Because you have previewed the questions, you can compose and organize the information in advance. Spend time on your answers. Just because you can apply instantly with the click of a button doesn't mean that you should craft your answers as speedily.

Read the directions regarding timing out to see if you need to complete the entire application in a single sitting or if you can save it, return at another time and complete it. In most cases, you will need to submit all your information at one time.

Compose your essay in a word processing program first, and then upload it. Don't try to write your essay at the same time you are submitting the application. When submitting your essays online, follow the same strategies that are recommended for submitting them offline. Brainstorm topics, write with passion and get editors to review your work. Don't take shortcuts. Review Chapter 7 for essay-writing strategies.

Be careful to avoid typos and mistakes. It's easy to make careless mistakes when you submit your applications online. Take time to review your work.

Print out what you submit so you have a hard copy. You can refer to the hard copy when applying to other scholarships, and you will have a spare in case your electronic copy gets lost.

Read the submission instructions to find any information that you might need to submit offline. For some scholarships, you complete your application online and then print it out and send it. For others, you submit your application online but send additional information like letters of recommendation or transcripts by regular mail. Follow the directions carefully.

Get confirmation. When you submit your application online, most organizations will send you confirmation that they have received your application. If they do not, get confirmation by sending an email.

Our Favorite Free Scholarship Websites

SuperCollege
www.supercollege.com

College Answer
www.collegeanswer.com

BrokeScholar
www.brokescholar.com

Free Scholarship Information
www.freschinfo.com

Mario Einaudi Center for International Studies
www.einaudi.cornell.edu/funding/search.asp

The College Board
www.collegeboard.com

The Princeton Review
www.review.com

FinancialAid.com
www.financialaid.com

How to Be an Internet Private Eye

Use the Internet to Research the Scholarship Organization

One of the best uses of the Internet is to research the organizations that are giving away the money. Visit their website and see what they are all about before you decide to apply for their scholarship.

There's a reason that the Internet was once nicknamed the "Information Super-highway." You can find out the dirt on pretty much anyone, including scholarship organizations. In addition to finding scholarships and applying to them online, use the Internet to research the sponsor organizations and awards. Here are some tips:

Read the sponsor organization's website to learn more about the mission of the organization and the award that they offer. This will help you understand what the organization is trying to accomplish by giving the scholarship.

Request additional information, newsletters or other literature if it's available. Or, read the literature online. Many organizations have their literature and newsletters accessible on their websites.

Get information on past winners. Some organizations list past winners on their websites and include brief biographical information. Again, this will help you understand what kind of student the organization is seeking for its scholarship recipient.

The more you can learn about the organization and the award, the better you can craft your application to fit the scholarship.

Be Cautious of Scams

Both offline and online, there always will be that unscrupulous small minority of people who try to take advantage of students' and parents' fears of the high costs of college. Here are some red flags to watch for when you research scholarship possibilities:

Registration, entry or administrative fee: Legitimate scholarship and financial aid programs do not require an upfront fee. Never pay to search a scholarship database on the Internet.

Soliciting your credit card number: Never give out this kind of financial information to anyone who contacts you.

No name, address or phone number: Legitimate online businesses post their contact information on their websites. If no such information exists, the organization–and its scholarship–could be bogus.

Guarantee: Remember, there is no such thing as a scholarship you are guaranteed to win. Legitimate scholarships are based on merit or need, not your willingness to pay a registration fee.

Read Chapter 3, *Avoid Scholarship Scams,* for more information on scholarship scams in general. While there is a small group of people who try to take advantage of students, a number of great services can provide scholarship and financial aid guidance–for free. We encourage you to visit SuperCollege.com to learn more.

Chapter 12 Summary: Unleash the Power of the Internet

The Internet is a great tool for finding scholarships, applying for scholarships and learning more about the sponsoring organizations. Online scholarship information can be updated very quickly and best of all, it's free! Use it in combination with traditional resources like this book and your high school counselor or financial aid officer.

Find scholarships online through websites with free, searchable scholarship databases and through search engines.

Some scholarships allow you to apply online. Take advantage of this opportunity to save time and headaches. Be as diligent about the quality of your work when you apply online as when you apply on paper.

Do online detective work. Learn more about scholarship sponsors and past winners and use your Internet research skills to improve your application.

Avoid online scholarship scams. Be wary of any scholarship services that require a fee, solicit your credit card number, have no contact information or make "guarantees" that sound too good to be true.

You are welcome to visit our website, SuperCollege.com (www.supercollege.com). Search our free database of thousands of scholarships, learn more scholarship and financial aid tips and strategies and apply for the SuperCollege. com scholarship.

Financial Aid Workshop

In this chapter, you'll learn:

- How to get a share of the $134 billion in financial aid awarded each year

- What you need to qualify for aid and how to apply

- Eligibility requirements of each financial aid program

- Proven strategies for getting more aid from your college

Getting the Most Financial Aid You Deserve

How much financial aid do you think is given out each year? $1 billion? $10 billion? How about $50 billion? The answer is more than $134 billion! That is a lot of money. Some families assume that it's very difficult to claim this money. It's not. All you have to do to find out how much financial aid you deserve is simply this: "Ask for it."

The sad reality is that most families do not ask for financial aid. We've heard almost every excuse why families do not apply. The three most common are these:

"I don't understand how financial aid works so it must be too complicated."

"My family's income or assets must be too high so I won't even bother applying."

"Deadline? What deadline? Did I miss the deadline to apply?!"

Banish these excuses—except for the last one which is important—and we'll make sure that you don't miss the deadline. What surprises many families, even those who consider themselves middle or upper-middle class, is that they do qualify for financial aid. Contrary to what you may believe, financial aid is based on more than just income and assets. Other important factors include family size, parents' age and the cost of your college. In fact, the more expensive your college, the more likely you are to get financial aid. You have nothing to lose and everything to gain by applying for financial aid.

The Big Picture

The term *financial aid* can seem confusing at first since it refers to a cornucopia of money—including grants, loans and even subsidized employment. This money comes from a variety of sources including the federal government, state governments and colleges. These entities have dozens of individual programs (you might have heard of Pell Grants or Stafford Loans) that are under the umbrella term financial aid.

We imagine that right now you are scratching your head and rubbing your temples wondering how you can possibly master the confusing world of financial aid. The good news is that you don't have to. The colleges administer this vast amount of money and decide both the amount and type (i.e., grants or loans) each student receives. Some of these decisions are based on federal guidelines while others are determined by the colleges themselves. But you really don't need to concern yourself with these details. After you apply for financial aid, you will receive an award letter from each college that spells out how much you will get. These award letters will contain everything for which you qualify, including grants, scholarships, student loans and work-study programs. But you won't get this award letter if you don't fill out the applications correctly and submit everything on time.

It is also important to always keep in mind that the financial aid process consists of two phases. The first phase involves mathematical computation. A standard formula calculates how much money your family can contribute to one year of education and therefore how much you qualify for in

financial aid. (This number is known as the Expected Family Contribution or the EFC.) But once this number is determined, the second phase of the process involves a real, live human known as a financial aid officer. Financial aid officers have a lot of power and can significantly affect the size and makeup of your financial aid package. They use their professional judgment for special circumstances that are not adequately addressed by the financial aid formulas and provide a critical check to make sure that aid goes to the right students. These financial aid officers are actually some of your strongest allies in receiving financial aid. So while the first phase of financial aid (filling out the forms and calculating your Expected Family Contribution) can seem very inflexible, the second phase of financial aid is all human and in certain instances is very flexible.

The Financial Aid Cornucopia

The first step to getting your hands on financial aid is to understand what it is. Basically, you may receive any combination of the following types of money. As you read the short description of each, you will see that some forms of aid are better than others.

Grants/Scholarships: Money with no strings attached—meaning you don't have to pay it back. This is really the equivalent of hitting the financial aid jackpot. Grants are sometimes called scholarships, and often these terms are used interchangeably. The major grant program from the federal government is the Pell Grant. However, each state and college may also have its own grant programs.

Loans: Money you borrow and are required to pay back with interest. In most cases the terms are more generous than other types of loans such as home equity loans. For example, the Stafford student loan program does not require that you start to repay your loan until after you graduate. Also, if you qualify for the "subsidized" Stafford loan program, the federal government will pay the interest that you owe while you are in college. It's basically an interest-free loan until after you graduate. There are also loans for parents such as the PLUS. Don't discount loans just because they are borrowed money. A low-interest student loan may be just what you need to make up for any shortfall in your ability to pay for tuition.

Work-Study: Money you earn the old-fashioned way—by working. But work-study is not your typical part-time job. The government subsidizes your pay so that you earn more and can qualify for choice part-time jobs on campus that students who don't have work-study cannot get. Work-study jobs are often in places like the library or student center and offer good wages along with flexible hours that can accommodate your schedule as a student.

Most financial aid packages are a combination of the above. But as you can see, some forms of financial aid (such as grants) are much more desirable than others (such as loans). When it comes to deciding what your specific package will look like, each college's financial aid officer will make the decision based on rules and guidelines as well as how much money they have to give.

Five Steps to Getting Financial Aid

We are going to break down the financial aid process into five easy steps. We will also give you a little inside information on how each step of the process works so you can see what factors will affect your outcome. In many ways applying for financial aid is like doing your federal taxes. There are forms to fill out and rules (even loopholes) that can help or hurt your bottom line. Now, we know that no one enjoys filling out a 1040 tax return, but at least in this case there is a good possibility that you will be getting a nice chunk of change back from the government to help you pay for college, so it's certainly worth your time to tackle it.

Step 1: Fill Out the FAFSA

As with anything from the government, you need to fill out a form. In this case, to be considered for federal financial aid, you will need to complete the Free Application for Federal Student Aid or FAFSA. Most states and many public universities also require this form to be eligible for their aid programs. If you are applying to a private college, you may also have to submit the CSS/PROFILE form, which is similar to the FAFSA. The main difference between the CSS/PROFILE and FAFSA is not in the data it collects, but the formula that is used to determine how much financial aid you deserve. Unfortunately, you don't have a choice in which form the colleges use since they will require either one or both. Also, some colleges have additional forms that you need to fill out.

Since all families should complete the FAFSA (similar to the CSS/PROFILE), let's take a look at it in detail. The FAFSA is a multi-page form that asks for detailed financial information including items from your previous federal income tax return. It's not a difficult form to complete. What is difficult is that you need to collect a lot of information about your income and assets. In fact, the information that you include in your FAFSA should match the numbers on your federal tax return. But here's the kicker: While you have until April 15 to do your taxes, you must turn in the FAFSA to the Department of Education as soon as possible after January 1 of the year you will be starting or continuing school. If you are a high school student applying to college, this means that after January 1 of your senior year you must submit the FAFSA form. If you are already in college, you must submit the FAFSA each year to continue to receive financial aid.

It's also important that you don't miss the colleges' deadlines—and each school sets its own. Most want you to submit the FAFSA sometime in February or March.

Don't let the fact that you haven't completed your taxes prevent you from missing the deadline. It's better to bite the bullet and do your taxes early this year, or if this is impossible, you should use estimates and update the information later. Whether you use actual numbers or estimates, it is vital that you submit the FAFSA as soon as possible. Financial aid is awarded on a first-come, first-served basis. If you wait until April, it is possible that funds may already be depleted even if you do deserve the help.

The CSS/PROFILE

Many private colleges require the CSS/PROFILE. Think of the CSS/PROFILE as the FAFSA for non-federal financial aid. You will be asked many of the same questions, so get your tax forms out and even your completed FAFSA. Follow the same advice that we have for the FAFSA, and make sure you adhere to the deadlines. The colleges provide the deadlines for the CSS/PROFILE, typically October or November if you have applied to colleges early or February for regular decision. If you are already in college, submit the form as soon as possible, or at the latest, four weeks before the priority filing deadline.

There is a big push by the Department of Education, which administers the FAFSA, to get you to fill out the application online. This is not a bad idea since the online form is designed to help prevent errors and give you faster results. You can begin the process by going to the Department of Education's website at www.fafsa.ed.gov. Be sure to download the pre-application worksheets. These will help you collect the information you will need to complete the FAFSA. If you prefer to fill out the FAFSA on paper, get a copy from your school counselor, public library or college financial aid office. You can also request an application by writing to the Federal Student Aid Information Center at P.O. Box 84, Washington, DC 20044.

As with all government forms, at first glance the FAFSA may seem intimidating. However, if you spend some time working on it, you'll find that the information is relatively straightforward. To help, here are some tips for completing the form:

File the FAFSA as soon as possible after January 1. This is an important form. Don't procrastinate. Notice how many times we repeat this!

Complete your income taxes early. Unless you're an accountant, there are more enjoyable things you'd probably rather do, but information from your income tax forms will be very helpful for completing the FAFSA. Plus, while others are stressed and panic-stricken around April 15, you'll already be done with your taxes. If you can't finish your taxes, don't be afraid to use estimates.

Follow directions. The Department of Education reports that delays are caused most often because students or parents don't follow directions when completing the FAFSA. Spend the time to read the directions and follow them completely. If you have questions, don't guess but contact the Federal Student Aid Information Center at 1-800-4-FED-AID.

Be thorough. Answer questions completely. Take the time to find the answers to all the information requested.

Realize that the FAFSA takes time. Set aside half a day to gather the information and complete the form. Don't think that you can complete it during the commercials of "The Simpsons."

Save time with the Renewal FAFSA. If you've applied for federal financial aid before, you can usually use the Renewal FAFSA. This form saves you time because many of the blanks are pre-filled with data from the prior year. Ask your school counselor or an employee of the financial aid office for more information.

If you transfer schools, check with your new school to see what forms you should complete. Your financial aid package does not automatically transfer with you.

Don't think you're on your own. Use the help provided by your school and by the government. The Department of Education has an entire staff of people to assist you with completing the necessary forms and answering your questions about financial aid. Visit their website at www.fafsa. ed.gov and don't hesitate to contact them by phone or email with your questions.

Step 2: Review Your Student Aid Report

After you submit the FAFSA, you will need to wait patiently as the Department of Education computers crunch the numbers to determine your Expected Family Contribution. If you submitted the CSS/PROFILE, the computers at the College Board are also furiously working using a slightly different formula. At this stage, the process is completely computational. The same calculations are applied to every student. If you and your friend submitted FAFSAs with identical numbers, the results would be the same for both of you.

The magic number that the computers spit out is your Expected Family Contribution or EFC. This number represents what your family (you and your parents) are expected to contribute toward one year of your education. Whether or not your EFC is accurate is another topic that we will discuss later. But for now let's look at how your EFC is determined:

Parent income **X** up to 47% +
Parent assets **X** up to 5.65% +
Student income **X** 50% +
Student assets **X** 35% =
Expected Family Contribution

Now don't have a heart attack. Not all your income or assets are subject to the 47 percent and 5.65 percent assessment rate. There are both income and asset protections that effectively shelter some of your money. Plus, depending on your income,

"I Assumed I Wouldn't Get Aid, but I Was Wrong"
Jeffrey Newell, College Student

Before my freshman year I spent an entire weekend dutifully completing all the financial aid forms. After spending all that time on the forms, I thought that I would get a sweet financial aid package. My family certainly wasn't at the poverty level, but it wasn't unheard of for students in similar financial situations as mine to get some significant grants.

I was pretty disappointed that after spending all that time gathering financial information and getting my parents to do their taxes early just to apply, I only received a medium-size loan. Because my parents were doing okay financially—they own a travel agency—we decided not to take the loan and to squeeze by on what we had.

After my experience in my first year, I decided not to apply for financial aid for my sophomore or junior years. I assumed that I would only be offered a loan anyway, so why waste my time? During those couple of years, the

business for my parents went up and down as usual depending on how much people wanted to travel.

Before my senior year, one of my roommates asked how I was doing with my financial aid applications. I said that I don't usually apply. He was shocked and told me I should apply. After some badgering, I obliged and applied just to get him to stop bugging me.

I didn't see a whole lot of difference in my family's financial situation between my first year and my last, but I received an offer for a loan and a grant. A grant? That's money I don't have to repay. After getting the grant, I realized I should have taken the time to apply before. Even though my family's financial situation didn't change dramatically over the years, it changed enough to make the difference between a loan and grant. What I learned: Apply even if you don't think you should.

the assessment rate may not be the full 47 percent or 5.65 percent. In fact, the lower your income and assets, the lower your assessment rate.

The best way to get an estimate of what your Expected Family Contribution will be is to use a free online EFC calculator. These calculators let you enter some numbers and quickly get an estimate of your Expected Family Contribution. The College Board's website has a similar calculator at http://apps.collegeboard.com/fincalc/efc_welcome.jsp. College Answer's website also offers an easy-to-use calculator at http://www.collegeanswer.com/paying/est_efc/efc_index.jsp. You can also adjust the numbers to see how changes in your income and assets affect your EFC.

A few weeks after you submit the FAFSA, you will receive the Student Aid Report (SAR) from the Department of Education. The SAR includes a summary of the information that you submitted in the FAFSA and shows your Estimated Family Contribution (EFC). Carefully review your SAR. If there are any mistakes, you need to correct them immediately.

Step 3: Make the College Aware of Special Circumstances, if Necessary

You are not the only one who receives the information in the SAR. Each college that you apply to or the college that you attend will also receive this information along with your Expected Family Contribution. There, the financial aid officer takes this information and uses it to determine your financial need. Determining financial need is fairly easy. All the financial aid officer does is subtract the Cost Of Attendance (COA) from your Expected Family Contribution (EFC).

> **Cost Of Attendance –**
> **Expected Family Contribution =**
> **Financial Need**

The Cost Of Attendance (COA) is the cost of attending your college or university for one year. These costs include the following: tuition and other fees, room and board, transportation between your home and the college, books and other supplies and estimated personal expenses.

Let's take a look at an example:

> *You have completed the FAFSA. You have also received your SAR that reports an EFC of $8,000. This means that you and your parents are expected to contribute $8,000 to pay for next year's college expenses. If the college costs $7,000 per year, then you would not receive any financial aid since it's assumed that you can afford it. Remember that your EFC is $8,000 so your family is expected to contribute $8,000, which is more than the cost of attending the college. However, if another college costs $20,000 then you would expect to receive an aid package of $12,000. In other words, at the first college you are not considered to have financial need but at the second college you have a financial need of $12,000.*

It's at this point in the process when the computers stop and the humans take over, that any special circumstances may be considered. Financial aid officers at the colleges have the ability to raise or lower the EFC for a variety of reasons. Therefore, it is crucial that you are open about your family's true financial situation to the financial aid officer. Remember too that all financial aid is based on previous year's taxes. A lot may have happened this year that is not reflected by last year's tax return. If you want to share additional information, send a letter to the college financial aid office to explain any unusual circumstances that may affect your family's finances. Most colleges include a space on their financial aid forms for you to describe any relevant information such as this. When you are thinking about writing this letter, consider these three points:

Don't hide the financial dirty laundry. Many parents feel compelled to hide embarrassing circumstances when filling out financial forms. After all, you are revealing financial strengths and weaknesses to a total stranger. However, if there are special circumstances such as large medical bills, current or impending unemployment, recent or ongoing divorce, siblings attending private elementary or high schools or any additional expenses that may not be reflected in the FAFSA or CSS/PROFILE, tell the financial aid officer. Don't be embarrassed. It could cost you big time.

Give the college a reason to give more money. Financial aid officers are numbers people. However, they have wide latitude for interpreting numbers and can apply a variety of standards. They can make exceptions, which can help or hurt your case. To get the most support from these professionals, make a case with numbers. Don't just say that you don't have enough money–show it. Document with numbers why your tax forms don't accurately reflect your true income or expenses.

Don't ever try to trick the college. The human being in the financial aid process is also what keeps it safe from trickery. You could, for example, take all the money in your savings account and plunk it down to buy an around-the-world vacation. On paper you'd have no savings. Yet, when the financial aid officer looks at your income, he or she will think it is very odd that someone who earns a decent living and owns a nice house is so cash poor. Not only would the financial aid officer not give you more financial aid, but you would also have depleted your savings.

Step 4: Compare Award Letters

Every college tries to create a financial aid package that meets your needs using a combination of grants, loans and work-study. However, not every school is able to do this. Some colleges with limited resources may only be able to offer a financial aid package that covers a portion of your entire financial need.

If you are a high school senior, you will receive financial aid award letters several weeks after receiving college acceptance letters. Each details how much and what type of financial aid you are being offered. It's not necessary to accept or reject the whole package. You are free to pick and choose. For example, definitely accept any grants or scholarships, but carefully consider loans or work-study.

You should also compare award letters. While one college may cost twice as much as another, you may find that it is also willing to give twice the financial aid. In that case, the actual costs of the two colleges may be the same.

Step 5: If You Need It, Ask for a Re-evaluation

If you feel that the amount of financial aid you are offered by a college is simply not enough, ask for a re-evaluation. To be effective, provide the financial aid office with concrete reasons why their initial assessment was wrong. Start with a letter or call to the financial aid office. Be sure to have all your documents ready, and remember that the squeaky wheel often gets the grease. If you don't say anything about the package, the college will assume that you are happy with it.

If you do ask for a reassessment, don't make the mistake of approaching it like you would buying a car where you haggle with a salesperson over the cost of floor mats and how much below the sticker price you will pay. Financial aid officers are really on your side and they do want to give you every penny that you deserve. However, to make it feasible for them to do so, you need to make a strong (and documented) case for why their initial evaluation was flawed.

Good reasons to ask for a reassessment include the following:

- Unusual medical expenses
- Tuition for a sibling including private secondary or elementary school
- Unemployment of a spouse or parent
- Ongoing divorce or separation
- Care for an aging relative

There is one other situation that may warrant a reassessment. If one college offers you significantly more than your first choice college, it may be possible to use that to get a better package. For example, if you are accepted to College A and College B, but College B offers a more generous financial aid package, you could try to work with College A to raise or match College B's package. First, write a letter to College A, stating that you would like very much to attend the college but that you may not be able to because of the financial aid package offered. Outline in quick bullet points the financial aid package offered by College B. Provide brief reasons why you need a package like that to be offered by College A. Reiterate that you would prefer to attend College A and would like to know if there is anything the financial aid office can do to increase the package. Follow up with a phone call. This does not always work and some colleges have a strict policy of not matching award offers of other colleges. However, some colleges have the means to be more flexible and just might raise their initial offer.

It's always important to be proactive when it comes to financial aid. If at any point during your time in college your financial circumstances change significantly, contact your school's financial aid office. We recommend first writing a letter that outlines your special circumstances in quick, easy-to-understand bullet points. The financial aid officer will then have all the information he or she needs to reassess your financial situation. Follow up with a telephone call to check on any additional information and on the status of your inquiry.

A Re-evaluation Success Story

If you find it hard to believe that a single letter can result in a larger financial aid package, here is the proof. The following is a letter one student wrote to the Harvard financial aid office while she was a student there. Before writing the letter, she had received only a small loan from Harvard despite the fact that her father had been laid off for over a year. The student composed this letter to explain her family's extenuating circumstances, describing their actual income and expenses. Her letter paid off—she got a $6,500 grant for each semester that she had left in school!

Reassessment Letter to Harvard

Dear Sir or Madam:

I am writing to request that my financial aid package for the fall semester be reconsidered. My family and I were disappointed with the amount we were offered because in addition to my father having been unemployed for over a year, my older sister will be a sophomore in college, and my mother, a part-time teacher, has received no income since June because of summer break.

We understand that nearly every family must undergo an amount of hardship to send its members to college. However, because my parents wish to continue financing my sister's and my education, they are worried about how they will pay for their own expenses. They have been using my mother's income to basically cover their mortgage payments and their savings to pay for everything else. In February, my parents had $33,000 in savings. In the last six months, their savings has decreased by about $15,000. They now have $18,000 to contribute to my sister's and my college expenses as well as to spend on their and my younger brother's food and basic necessities. They don't know how long their savings will last without a change in the amount of aid I will receive.

At the end of this month, my sister will begin her sophomore year at USC. The cost will be $26,998, and she has received $18,758 in financial aid. This makes my parents' contribution amount to $8,240, of which they will borrow $2,625. One of the things you might be able to address is why my sister's financial aid package was dramatically higher than mine.

Since July of last year my father has been unemployed. His severance pay ended in October, and his unemployment benefits have been depleted since February. Although he has applied for over a dozen positions, his prospects for finding a job in his specialty are slim.

My parents and I have discussed the possibility of having me take a year off so that I may work to help pay for tuition, but we'd much rather that I finish school now and work after I have received my degree.

Please contact my parents or me with any further questions you may have. Thank you very much for your time and consideration. I hope that this information is helpful in your review of my application.

Sincerely Yours,

There's no guarantee that a letter like this will work, but if your family's situation changes, get in touch with your financial aid office immediately.

Exchanging One Kind of Money for Another

In an ideal world, you would receive a financial aid package from the school, and any external scholarships you won would be a bonus on top of the package. Unfortunately, most colleges deduct the amount of scholarships that you win from the financial aid package. We believe that this is a huge disservice to students, diminishing the appeal of scholarships.

Fortunately, this trend is not universal and is showing signs of changing. By taking a proactive stance, you can help accelerate this change. If you find yourself in this situation, contact the financial aid office first. Explain that you applied for the scholarships because you needed money in addition to your financial aid package. If they haven't already, ask if they will reduce your student contribution or loans instead of reducing the amount of your grants.

Another course of action is to contact the organization that awarded the scholarship. If they are aware of this problem, some organizations won't award scholarships to students whose colleges reduce their aid package. If you can get the organization to write a letter of support or to provide a copy of its policy, you have a good chance of getting your college to reassess the reduction of your financial aid.

If this does happen and the college will not help you, at the very least let the college know that you are disappointed with their policy and hope that it will change. Also, it is better for you to receive financial aid in the form of scholarships, which you do not need to repay, than nearly any other form of financial aid. Plus, since financial aid budgets and demand vary each year, you may not receive the same amount in financial aid next year. If you have a renewable scholarship, at least you can count on it for all four years.

Declaring Independence

Some students mistakenly believe that if they declare independence from their parents, they will get more financial aid. Unfortunately, declaring independence for the purposes of financial aid is based on strict guidelines. In most cases, you are considered dependent on your parents, and their income and assets are considered in financial aid. You're considered to be independent if one of the following is true:

- You were born before January 1, 1984 (for the 2007-2008 school year).
- You're married.
- You're enrolled in a graduate or professional degree program.
- You have legal dependents other than a spouse.
- You're an orphan or ward of the court.
- You're a veteran of the U.S. Armed Forces.

If you are independent, only you and your spouse's (if you have one) income and assets will be considered. Some parents don't support their children or provide funds toward their college expenses, even though according to the above guidelines they are still considered dependent. If this is your situation, it is vitally important that you include a detailed letter explaining this to the financial aid office.

Strategies That Can Help You Get More Financial Aid

Just like with tax planning, good financial aid planning can help you qualify for more financial aid. Just remember that financial aid is always based on the previous year's taxes, which means that any actions you take must be done a year in advance. The following are generalized strategies that may not be appropriate for your individual situation. These are not hard and fast rules since what might be good for one family may be unworkable for another. Before taking any action, speak with an accountant. Note that these suggestions are directed to both you and your parents.

Limit your child's assets. Looking at the calculation that determines the Expected Family Contribution, you can see that if you put money into a child's name, it will be assessed by 35 percent. But if you keep the money in your name it will only be assessed by up to 5.65 percent. For every $100 in the student's name, you will be expected to spend $35 to pay for college. However, for every $100 in your name, you will be expected to spend only $5.65. That's a big difference. Any money that is in your child's bank account is considered your child's asset. If a relative would like to give a gift of cash or stock to your child, ask if he or she is willing to either give it to you or wait until your child graduates from college. Or your generous relative could make the gift directly to your child's 529 Savings Plan.

Putting money in your child's name is generally a bad idea when it comes to financial aid. Of course, there may be some good tax reasons for doing this, especially if you know that you won't qualify for financial aid. Balance the desire to save on taxes with the effect that putting money into a child's name will have on financial aid. It's important to speak with an accountant about the benefits of this strategy so that your specific situation is considered.

Spend UGMA funds two years before your child graduates. Let's say that you have put some money into a custodial account for your child. Why not spend this money while your child is still in high school instead of leaving it to be counted against your financial need? Now if you go crazy and spend it on luxuries, then this won't help. However, let's say that when your child turns 16 and gets his or her driver's license, you plan to buy a used car. Instead of using your own money, let your child use his or her custodial account. As long as you don't spend more than you normally would and buy a BMW instead of a Corolla, then you'll put your child in a better position to receive more financial aid. If you plan to do this, make sure to withdraw whatever amount of money that you plan to spend before January 1 of your student's junior year. Always keep in mind that financial aid is based on the previous year's tax returns, which for the typical student who enters college in the fall will cover January 1 of the junior year through December 31 of the senior year.

> ### Investment in You
>
> *Don't discount a loan right away. Remember that your education is an investment in your future. It's perfectly normal to borrow some money, and why not do so at the lowest interest rate possible?*

Consider deferring bonuses and raises. Imagine this scenario. It's November 2007 and your child is graduating from high school and starting college in the fall of 2008. Your boss tells you that you will get a bonus or significant raise. If you take the bonus now, then that money will be used when determining your child's financial aid package for the 2008-2009 school year. Remember that financial aid is always based on the previous tax year. If you delay taking the bonus for two months until January 2008, then that money will not be used in your child's student financial aid calculations. It will be counted when he or she applies for financial aid for the second year of college. But since you will have spent some (maybe even a significant amount) to pay for the first year, you will have fewer assets that will be counted during the second year of college. This also buys time to save since you know that the bonus or increase in salary will reduce your financial aid in the following year.

Before you utilize this strategy, be sure that you are going to get financial aid in the first place. Run your numbers through one of the free EFC calculators listed earlier. Also consider other factors. Will your boss still be in the mood to give you a bonus next year? Sometimes it's better to just take the money. This tactic would be much more lucrative if your child were entering his or her senior year in college in 2007. Deferring your raise or bonus in this situation would mean that it would not be counted at all since your son or daughter would be graduating from college *before* you received the raise.

Consider alternative forms of bonuses. If you have the flexibility, it may make sense to take your bonus or even a pay raise in some other form than cash. For example, instead of taking a raise, you might swap one day a week of working from home which would lower childcare costs. Or you might convert your bonus from a cash payment to training or classes that you were planning to pay yourself. A bonus or raise that does not show up as income will not be subjected to financial aid consideration. However, carefully weigh the costs of forgoing a cash bonus or raise. If you can use the money to pay down credit card debt (with its high interest rate), for example, you are probably much better off doing that.

Time stock sales. When you sell a stock can have an impact on financial aid. Let's say you have a stock that has appreciated by $10,000. If you sell the stock after January 1 of your child's junior year in high school, the earnings are considered income for the first year of college and will be assessed at up to 47 percent. From the $10,000 gain, as much as $4,700 can be counted by the financial aid formula as going to pay for college. But let's say that instead you sell the stock before January 1 of your child's junior year. The proceeds will not be counted as income but instead show up as an asset. As a parental asset, this money can only be assessed at a rate up to 5.65 percent, which means only $565 is considered as available to pay for college.

Build your 401K or IRA accounts. Under both the federal and institutional methodologies, your retirement accounts are not considered assets that can be used to pay for college. Plus, under current tax laws you can withdraw money from these accounts and use them to pay for college without paying a penalty. So don't neglect your retirement as you save for your child's college needs.

Use 529 Savings Plans and Coverdell Educational Savings Accounts to build a college nest egg tax free. Both 529 Savings Plans and Coverdell ESAs allow you to invest money without paying taxes on the gain as long as it is used for educational expenses. As a bonus, both of these accounts are considered assets of the parent(s), which means that they have minimal impact on financial aid. Don't neglect these two savings vehicles for building tax-free college savings.

A Quick Word about Saving for College

While this chapter focuses on financial aid, we cannot stress enough how important it is for you to have a strong savings plan. Your personal savings is your best ally when it comes to paying for college. Scholarships will always be competitions with no guarantees that you'll win. Financial aid changes each year, depending on the budgets of the government and college. There is no guarantee—even if you deserve it—that you will receive all the financial aid that you need to pay for school. Plus, since your savings are your money, you have total freedom to use it at whichever college you want. Nothing is as flexible as your own money.

If you want to learn more about saving for college, we recommend *1001 Ways to Pay for College,* which has a whole chapter on how to create a smart savings plan.

The Federal Financial Aid Programs in Detail

The reward for tackling tax forms and financial aid applications is a package that may consist of federal and state aid. To help you understand what you are offered, here are some descriptions of the possibilities.

We begin with the grants. These are like scholarships in that they represent free cash that does not have to be repaid. Just remember that these are only for a year, and you must reapply each year to continue to receive them.

Federal Pell Grants

<u>Details</u>: For undergraduate study, with the exception of post-baccalaureate teacher certification programs. You can be enrolled less than half-time. Provides every eligible student with funds.

<u>Based on</u>: Financial need as determined by your Estimated Family Contribution and Cost Of Attendance, full-time or part-time status and length of enrollment.

<u>Amount</u>: Varies based on funding. The maximum amount for the 2007-08 school year was $4,310.

> ### No Credit, No Problem
>
> *One advantage of federal student loans is that they are guaranteed by the federal government. This means even if you have no credit history you can still qualify for a student loan.*

How you get the money: Grant that can be credited to your school account, pay you directly or do a combination of both.

Federal Supplemental Educational Opportunity Grants (FSEOGs)

Details: Grants for undergraduates with the most financial need, i.e., the lowest Expected Family Contributions. FSEOGs do not need to be repaid. The government provides limited funds for individual schools to administer through this program. This means there is no guarantee that every eligible student will receive an FSEOG.

Based on: Financial need, when you apply and the availability of funds at your school. Priority is given to those who receive Federal Pell Grants.

Amount: $100-$4,000 per year.

How you get the money: The school will credit your account, pay you directly or both.

Academic Competitiveness Grant

Details: Grants for full-time first- and second-year undergraduate students who are eligible for Pell Grants and who have completed an academically rigorous high school program. One way of meeting the academic requirement is by having passing grades in four years of English, three years of math (including Algebra I, Geometry or Data Analysis and Statistics), three years of science (including one year each of at least two of the following: biology, chemistry or physics), three years of social studies and one year of a foreign language. Another way of meeting the academic requirement is by taking two Advanced Placement (AP) or International Baccalaureate (IB) courses and scoring three or higher on the AP exams or four or higher on the IB exams. There are more details at http://studentaid.ed.gov.

Based on: Financial need and high school coursework.

Amount: Up to $750 for the first year of study and up to $1,300 for the second year of study.

How you get the money: Grant that can be credited to your school account, pay you directly or do a combination of both.

National Science and Mathematics Access to Retain Talent Grant (National SMART Grant)

Details: Grants for full-time third- or fourth-year undergraduate students who are majoring in physical, life or computer sciences, math, technology or engineering or in a foreign language determined critical to national security.

<u>Based on</u>: Financial need. Applicants must be Pell Grant recipients and must have a minimum 3.0 GPA.

<u>Amount</u>: Up to $4,000.

<u>How you get the money</u>: Grant that can be credited to your school account, pay you directly or do a combination of both.

After the grants, which are really the best types of free cash for college, comes the work-study program.

Federal Work-Study

<u>Details</u>: Provides jobs for undergraduate and graduate students with financial need, allowing them to earn money while attending school. The focus is on providing work experience in your area of study. Generally, you will work for your school on campus or for a nonprofit organization or public agency if you work off campus. You will have a limit on the hours you can work in this program. The government provides limited funds for individual schools to administer this program.

<u>Based on</u>: Financial need, when you apply and the availability of funds at your school.

<u>Amount</u>: Federal minimum wage or higher.

<u>How you get the money</u>: Paid by the hour if you're an undergraduate. Paid by the hour or a salary if you're a graduate school student.

Student Loans

The last type of aid is a loan. Did we just hear you groan? Before you think that loans are for the birds, you should know that most students who go to college borrow money to pay for tuition. In addition, the terms for most student loans are extremely favorable and better than almost any other type of consumer loan.

There are two types of loans: Subsidized loans are based on financial need. They are subsidized because the government subsidizes the interest payments so that you are not charged interest until repayment, usually after you graduate. Unsubsidized loans are not based on financial need. You are charged interest from the time the loan is disbursed until it is paid off. However, the interest rates are still usually lower than other types of loans. In one school year, you may have both subsidized and unsubsidized loans.

Stafford Loans

<u>Details</u>: There are two types of Stafford Loans: Direct Stafford Loans and FFEL Stafford Loans. For Direct Stafford Loans, the U.S. government is the lender. For FFEL Stafford Loans, the lenders are participating banks, credit unions or other financial institutions.

Amount: For dependent undergraduate students, you can borrow a maximum of $3,500 if you're a first-year student in a full academic year program. You may borrow $4,500 if you have completed your first year of study and are enrolled in a full academic year program or $5,500 a year if you've completed two years of study and are enrolled in a full academic year program. For independent undergraduate students or dependent students whose parents are not able to get a PLUS loan, you can borrow a maximum of $7,500 if you're a first-year student in a full academic year program ($3,500 of this amount can be subsidized). You may borrow $8,500 if you've completed your first year of study and are enrolled in a full academic year program ($4,500 of this amount can be subsidized) or $10,500 a year if you've completed two years of study and are enrolled in a full academic year program ($5,500 of this amount can be subsidized).

Interest and fees: The interest rate is fixed at 6.8 percent for loans disbursed on or after July 1, 2006. There is also a fee of up to 4 percent of the loan.

How you get the money: The money will be disbursed to your school either by the Department of Education for Direct Stafford Loans or by the lender for FFEL Stafford Loans. The money must first be used for tuition, fees and room and board. After these expenses are paid, you will receive the remaining amount by check or cash.

How you repay the money: You will begin to repay your loan after you graduate, leave school or drop below half-time enrollment. For Direct Stafford Loans, you can pay using one of four methods: the Standard Repayment Plan of a fixed amount per month for up to 10 years; the Extended Repayment Plan, which extends the repayment period to generally between 12 and 30 years; the Graduated Repayment Plan, in which your payments start lower and increase generally every two years; or the Income Contingent Plan, in which your income affects the amount of your monthly payments.

For FFEL Stafford Loans, you can pay using one of four methods: Standard Repayment Plan; Graduated Repayment Plan; Income-Sensitive Repayment Plan, in which your income affects the amount of your monthly payments; or Extended Repayment Plan, which extends the payment period up to 25 years.

In certain situations, you can receive a deferment to temporarily postpone payments on your loan. For subsidized loans, you do not pay interest during the deferment period. For unsubsidized loans, you do. Under certain circumstances you can receive forbearance, a limited and temporary postponement or reduction of your payments, if you are unable to meet your repayment schedule and are not eligible for a deferment. These circumstances may include poor health, serving in a medical or dental internship or residency or if the payments exceed 20 percent of your monthly gross income. For both subsidized and unsubsidized loans, you pay interest during the forbearance period. Deferments and forbearance must be approved by the Direct Loan Servicing Center if you have a Direct Stafford Loan or with the lender if you have an FFEL Stafford Loan.

PLUS Loans for Graduate and Professional Degrees

Details: Loans for graduate and professional degree students that are not based on financial need.

Amount: The maximum is the Cost of Attendance minus other financial aid in the FFEL and Direct Loan program.

Other details: The interest and fees and how you get the money is the same as the PLUS Loans below.

PLUS Loans

Details: Loans for parents with good credit histories to pay for their dependent undergraduate students' educations. Available through both the Direct PLUS Loan and FFEL PLUS Loan Program. For FFEL PLUS Loans, you will choose a lender by contacting your school or the Federal Student Aid Information Center. This program is available for parents of undergraduate students who are enrolled at least half time.

Based on: These loans are not based on financial need.

Amount: The maximum is the Cost Of Attendance minus any other financial aid you receive. For example, if your Cost Of Attendance is $10,000 and you receive $6,000 in financial aid, the maximum amount your parents can borrow is $4,000.

Interest and fees: The interest rate is fixed at 7.9 percent for Direct PLUS Loans and 8.5 percent for FFEL PLUS Loans disbursed on or after July 1, 2006. There is also a fee of up to 4 percent of the loan.

How you get the money: The money will be disbursed to your school either by the Department of Education for Direct PLUS Loans or by the lender for FFEL PLUS Loans. The money must first be used for tuition, fees and room and board. After these expenses are paid, your parents will receive the remaining amount by check or cash.

How you repay the money: Repayment begins within 60 days after the first loan disbursement, and interest starts to accumulate from the first disbursement.

For Direct PLUS Loans, you can pay using one of three methods: the Standard Repayment Plan of a fixed amount per month; the Extended Repayment Plan, which extends the repayment period; or the Graduated Repayment Plan, in which your payments start lower and increase every two years. For FFEL PLUS Loans, your parents will follow a repayment schedule provided by the lender.

In specific situations, you can receive a deferment to temporarily postpone payments on your loan or forbearance, a limited and temporary postponement or reduction of your payments if you are unable to meet your repayment schedule and are not eligible for a deferment.

Consolidation Loans

Details: Allows students and parents to consolidate a number of federal financial aid loans into a single loan to simplify repayment. This allows the borrowers to make one payment per month and in some cases obtain a lower interest rate. All the federal loans described in this chapter can be consolidated. Contact the Loan Origination Center's Consolidation Department at 800-557-7392 or the consolidation department of a participating lender.

Direct Consolidation Loans are provided by the U.S. Department of Education. They can be one of three types: Direct Subsidized Consolidation Loans, Direct Unsubsidized Consolidation Loans or Direct PLUS Consolidation Loans.

FFEL Consolidation Loans are provided by participating banks, credit unions, savings and loans and other lenders as either a Subsidized FFEL Consolidation Loan or an Unsubsidized FFEL Consolidation Loan.

Eligibility: You can get a Consolidated Loan once you've started repayment or during deferment or forbearance. If you are in school, you can apply for a Direct Consolidation Loan if you are attending at least half time and have at least one Direct Loan or FFEL Loan in an in-school period. You may be eligible for a Consolidated Loan if you are in default on a Direct Loan.

Interest and fees: The interest rate is fixed throughout the repayment period and is the weighted average of the loans being consolidated.

Federal Perkins Loans

Details: Low-interest loans for undergraduate and graduate students with extreme financial need. Your school provides the loan from funds provided by the government and its own funds. You must repay the loan.

Based on: Financial need, when you apply and availability of funds.

Amount: You can borrow up to $4,000 per year as an undergraduate or $6,000 per year as a graduate student.

Interest and fees: 5 percent interest. There are no additional fees.

How you get the money: Your school will either pay you directly or credit your school account.

How you repay the money: Nine months after you graduate, leave school or drop below half-time enrollment, you will begin repayment.

Under certain circumstances, you can receive a deferment to temporarily postpone payments on your loan. You do not pay interest during the deferment period. Under certain circumstances you can receive forbearance, a limited and temporary postponement or reduction of your payments if you are unable to meet your repayment schedule and are not eligible for a deferment. These circumstances may include poor health, serving in a medical or dental internship or residency or if the payments exceed 20 percent of your monthly gross income. Interest is accrued during the forbearance period. Deferments and forbearance must be approved by your school.

Getting More Help

In this chapter, we have given you a basic understanding of how the financial aid process works and what you need to do to apply. For information on state programs, contact your state's higher education agency, which is listed in the directory. Also, consider our book, *1001 Ways to Pay for College,* since it includes additional material on financial aid, tax advantages and long-term college savings programs. You can also get help with applying for federal financial aid by contacting the Federal Student Aid Information Center at the following address:

Federal Student Aid Information Center
P.O. Box 84
Washington, DC 20044-0084
800-4-FED-AID

Chapter 13 Summary: Financial Aid Workshop

Each year more than $134 billion in financial aid is awarded. Your mission is to make sure some of that money comes to you. Unlike scholarships in which you need to compete for the funds, in most cases, if you qualify for federal financial aid, you will receive it. Your responsibility is to learn about the different options open to you and to apply.

There are three types of financial aid: Grants, which do not need to be repaid; loans, which allow you to borrow money and must be repaid; and work-study, which allows you to work at a part-time job while attending school.

Qualifying for federal financial aid. You need to have financial need, which is determined by the cost of attending your college (Cost Of Attendance) and the amount that the government determines your family can contribute toward your education (Estimated Family Contribution). There are additional requirements including: graduating from high school, working toward an eligible degree program and being a U.S. citizen, U.S. national or U.S. permanent resident.

To apply, you must complete the Free Application for Federal Student Aid (FAFSA) and/or the CSS/PROFILE. Do this online or with old-fashioned paper.

After the FAFSA. You will receive a Student Aid Report (SAR) from the government which determines your Estimated Family Contribution (EFC), or the amount that your family is expected to contribute. Your school's financial aid office will develop a financial aid package using this information that may be a combination of scholarships, loans, grants or work-study.

The scholarship dollars you win may affect your financial aid package. They reduce your Cost Of Attendance. Realize that this may not be bad if your package is composed of more scholarship dollars, which do not need to be repaid, and less loan dollars, which, of course, need to be repaid.

There may be flexibility. Once you've received the financial aid package from your college, especially if there are extenuating circumstances such as medical or dental expenses, tuition for a sibling or a change in your parents' employment situation, things can still change. In some cases, there is also flexibility when you are deciding between two colleges with differences in their financial aid packages.

Free Cash for Graduate School

In this chapter, you'll learn:

- How to adjust your strategy to win graduate financial aid

- Why not all graduate aid is made equal

- Step-by-step strategies for completing fellowship and grant proposals

- Tips for acing the interviews

- How to keep the money you've won

The Long and Expensive Path of Graduate School

Typically spanning two to eight years, graduate school can be a long and arduous path. With the stresses of dissertations, oral exams, board exams, research and the quest to publish, the less you need to worry about paying for your education the better. While grad student life is hardly equated with luxury, there are a lot of financial aid resources available from graduate schools, the government and private organizations. The challenge is to find these resources, and because they are limited, make your work in your particular field stand out so that you get some of this aid.

Your approach to graduate financial aid will be different than it was to undergraduate financial aid. While undergraduate scholarships are often based on involvement in activities, leadership or special skills, the majority of graduate scholarships and fellowships are based primarily on academics and research. Crafting your applications for graduate school aid requires its own set of unique strategies.

Another difference is that the community of applicants and judges is often smaller in graduate studies. Graduate students who apply will have more similar backgrounds than undergraduate students. This means that you will need to be particularly strategic about how to set your application apart from those of other students. Because you know that the selection committee will probably be professors or other specialists in your field of study, you need to craft your application materials to impress this very demanding crowd.

The strategies in this chapter are specifically designed for graduate school scholarships and fellowships. Hopefully we can help ease the stress of at least one aspect of graduate school life. As for the dissertation, we're sorry—you're on your own.

The Big Picture

As you go from undergraduate to graduate school, the intensity of academics increases. The same holds true for financial aid. For graduate school, financial aid is not based on leadership or extracurricular activities. Research and academics count most.

Our approach to graduate financial aid is to focus on demonstrating your long-term commitment to academics and research. Judges are no longer casual members of clubs or volunteers. They are the small circle of leaders in your future career field—professors, deans and academic institutional heads. To win you must show them the intensity of your passion for your field and your ability to contribute to its advancement. You must demonstrate your ability to think critically and innovatively.

Understanding Graduate Financial Aid

The first step to getting graduate school financial aid is to learn about all the options that are available to you. There are several forms of financial aid, each with its own requirements and benefits. Here is a brief overview:

Scholarships: Often given by private organizations, scholarships are typically awarded in general fields of study. They are usually open to both undergraduate and graduate students. Scholarships are based on merit, with some based on financial need as well. They do not need to be repaid.

Grants: Unfortunately, only undergraduate students are eligible for Pell Grants or Federal Supplemental Educational Opportunity Grants (FSEOG) from the government under most circumstances. However, there are special federal grants for students entering the health and medical fields from the National Health Services Corps and the Armed Forces.

In addition, there are various types of research grants for graduate students. Provided by the federal and state governments, graduate schools or private organizations, this form of aid does not need to be repaid. For graduate students, grants often fund a specific project, research study or dissertation. These grants can pay for the costs of materials and sometimes even travel to research centers. They can also provide you with the right to use facilities and libraries to which you might not normally have access.

Fellowships: Provided by graduate school departments, private organizations and states, fellowships support graduate and post-graduate studies, research or work placement. They typically fund research or study in a particular area at a specific university. Only open to graduate students, fellowships are based on academic merit, with a minority based on financial need as well. They do not need to be repaid and can fund tuition and/or research expenses, with many providing stipends for living expenses. However, don't expect to start living a life of luxury–the stipends are still not enough to raise you above the poverty line. Some require recipients to work as Teaching or Research Assistants.

Federal aid: Funded by the government, federal financial aid includes loans and grants. These are based entirely on financial need. For more information, see Chapter 13, *Financial Aid Workshop*.

Employment: Many graduate schools supplement students' education with employment opportunities to research or teach. For some schools, such employment is a requirement to graduate or a part of the financial aid package.

Loan repayment programs: Some cities and states offer loan repayment programs. Under these programs graduate students can have their loans repaid by the city or state if they agree to work in specific occupations. Upon graduation from medical school, a state may agree to repay your student loan if you work in an area of the state that needs more doctors. Some cities are encouraging students to become teachers by agreeing to repay their graduate student loans if they work in certain school districts.

More Than Money

In addition to providing financial relief, scholarships, grants, fellowships and teaching assistantships can assist you in your career and add prestige to your curriculum vitae. As you apply for these programs, you may need to complete an application or make an in-person case to the committee that grants research appointments. In do-

New Approach

Your approach to graduate financial aid should be different than it was to undergraduate financial aid. The majority of graduate scholarships and fellowships are based primarily on academics and research.

ing this, you gain experience presenting your research proposal, and you hone your skills of persuasion, both necessary skills in academia. These financial aid programs also help you build the foundation of your academic reputation and introduce your work to others in your field. You have the prospect of networking with professors and other academics who will be your supporters in the future. Keep these additional opportunities in mind as you apply for graduate financial aid programs.

It's All about Academics

An emphasis on academics is a chief factor that differentiates graduate school grants, scholarships and fellowships from undergraduate awards. Undergraduate awards may be based on criteria like leadership, activities, hobbies, talents or athletic ability. Graduate awards, however, are almost entirely based on academics, achievement in a particular field of study and your potential contribution to the future of that field.

Remember this focus on academics when applying for graduate awards. Throughout applications, proposals, essays and interviews, emphasize your contribution to and passion for the academic field spotlighted by the award. Other factors such as leadership and interpersonal skills are important in how they equip you to succeed in the field, but the main emphasis should be on your ability to contribute to the collective knowledge in a specific area.

When applying to graduate programs, check websites and catalogues to find out who the professors are in the department you wish to join. Familiarize yourself with their books and articles and explain how your plans fit with their academic interests. If you are not able to visit a campus, call individual professors to discuss their program and your plans. They will appreciate your attempts to introduce yourself, your knowledge of their work and your efforts to find out more about the department's program.

Concentrate on the mission of financial aid awards. The mission may be simple: to advance a field by supporting those who study it. Or the mission may be more complex, furthering a specific agenda or encouraging study of specific areas. The government, for example, funds the study of certain languages that are considered to be strategically important. Even if you are studying economics in 17th century Russia, you could qualify for a FLAS award since part of your coursework would include the study of the Russian language.

Learn more about an award's mission by reading the literature published by the organization, viewing its website or speaking with the award administrator. A great way to see the group's mission in action is to find out information about previous winners. Ask the organization for a list of these students. If you are already in graduate school, there are probably some winners in your department who are a few years ahead of you. Contact them to find out details about their background, their approach to applying and any helpful hints they can provide about the award's selection.

By understanding the mission of the award and the awarding organization, you will know how well you fit with what it is trying to

> **Applications Are Building Blocks**
>
> *Use applications as building blocks to construct a case for why you should win the award. Present information that demonstrates your academic commitment and achievements.*

achieve. You will also be able to shape the application, proposal, essay and interview to reflect the mission of the award, making you a stronger candidate in the eyes of the selection committee.

Applications: Your Stats Sheet

Applications are like baseball cards. Flip over a baseball card and you'll find the most important statistics about the player such as his batting averages and home runs. Similarly, applications are the place for the most important statistics about your achievements. Selection committees use them as a quick way to learn the key facts about you. Because you are vying to be noticed and working with both the limited space provided and the limited attention span of selection committees, follow these strategies to make the most of your applications:

Make application triplets. Before starting, make at least three photocopies of each application. Use one for practice to make sure the most important information you need to convey fits in the space given. Keep the others in case you make an egregious error and need to start over, something that will most likely happen at 3 a.m. the day the application is due.

Build a case for how you fit the mission of the award. Always keep the mission of the award at the forefront of your thinking so that you can provide evidence and examples of how you fulfill it. If the award's objective is to support students who show promise in your academic field, highlight your classes, awards and accomplishments in that area.

Know your audience. Try to find out as much information as you can about the selection committee. You will complete an application differently if the selection committee is composed of professors in your department than if it is made up of employers at a biomedical company trying to build relationships for future recruitment. For a selection committee of professors, focus on research, teaching and publishing. On the other hand, for employers at a biomedical company, highlight how your research has commercial applications as well as related work experience. By knowing your audience, you can shape your application accordingly.

Focus on your key achievements. With the limited space applications provide, concentrate on only the most important information. Prioritize information that shows direct contributions or achievements in your field, including classes, awards, lectures given, teaching experience, published works, abstracts, current unpublished projects and related work experience. Give secondary priority to information that demonstrates skills that are not direct achievements but that are still important to the field.

Neatness counts. Remember that a sloppy application conveys that you don't take the award seriously. Committee members may also think that if you are careless in completing your application, you may be equally careless in your studies. Neither of these are impressions that you want to make. If the error is noticeable enough, use the extra copy you made of your application and start over. It will take extra time, but it's worth it.

Make copies after completion. Make a photocopy of your application for your records. The next time you are completing an application, you can use the copy as a cheat sheet which will save you valuable hours in reassembling your information since you've already prioritized and written descriptions of your accomplishments.

Check to make sure you have everything gathered together. Before mailing your applications, insure that you have included everything. You can be disqualified for missing a single piece.

For more information on applications, refer to Chapter 4, *Create a Stunning Scholarship Application.*

Recommendations: Getting Professorial Praise

Throughout your applications you have the opportunity to praise yourself and your accomplishments in glowing words of admiration. Recommendations offer professors and others the opportunity to do the same and to confirm that you are as great as you say you are. To get the most powerful recommendations possible, follow these strategies for selecting and preparing your recommenders:

Be strategic about whom you ask. The most important principle for selecting recommenders is how well they know you. You may have received the highest grade in class, but if your professor couldn't pick you out from a crowd, he or she is not the best person to ask. Select those with whom you've worked closely and who can speak meaningfully about your abilities. An equally important measure is the ability of the recommender to vouch for your talent and achievements in the academic field. Choose professors and others who can describe first-hand how competent you are in your studies. If you are new to graduate work, don't hesitate to ask your former undergraduate professors to write a recommendation. This is perfectly acceptable.

Do the grunt work for your recommenders. To make writing recommendations easier, provide all the background information and forms they need for the task:

> **Cover letter:** A brief letter describing the awards you are applying for, their deadlines and helpful reminders of information they may want to include in the recommendations.

> **Curriculum vitae:** A concise overview of your academic honors, coursework and achievements.

> **Recommendation paperwork:** Any forms that your recommenders need to complete with blanks for your personal information pre-filled by you.

Give this information to your recommenders assembled neatly in a folder so that they have everything they need to get started.

Finally, write a thank you note for their help. Even though writing recommendations is a part of the job for professors, recognize that they have taken time from their busy schedules to help you.

For more recommendation strategies, see Chapter 6, *Get the Right Recommendations.*

Essays: Getting Personal

If the application is your formal introduction to the selection committee, then the essay is like the part of the conversation in which you get more personal. You can use the essay to describe in more detail your academic interests, goals and contributions. Because essays allow you to share more of yourself beyond the application form, they offer your best opportunity to set your application apart from those of other applicants. The following strategies will help you create an essay with impact:

Focus on the progress you have made in your field. The best essay is one that gets the selection committee excited about your work and makes them want to fund your education so that you can complete it. Tempt them with what you have done, reveal some early results even if they are only preliminary or describe the plans for your future research. Give the selection committee a tantalizing view into what you are learning. Take advantage of knowing who is on the committee and what their interests are.

Give them something they can't get anywhere else. Don't just restate what is written in your application or curriculum vitae. If you do this, you will simply waste space. Essays should provide information and insight about you that is not included in the applications.

Get personal. Reveal something about yourself. What motivated you to choose this area of study? What do you feel is the most exciting thing about your field? Who has been a mentor for you? What do you hope to accomplish after you get your degree? Answering a question like one of these will give the selection committee insight into your thoughts and help to distinguish you beyond your achievements.

Know and understand your audience. Adjust your message and level of formality based on who will read your work. Your essay should be more formal and academic in nature if the intended audience is composed of professors than if it is made up of community leaders. As you write, think about who will read your essay.

Get editors. Don't rely on yourself for the entire direction of your essays. Professors, colleagues and family members make great editors. They can offer suggestions for improvement, expand on ideas you have and make sure you don't have any mistakes. They may even remember something great that you did but forgot to mention in your essay. The more help you can get from others, the better your essays will be.

Be creative. When it comes to describing your coursework and achievements in the application, there isn't much room for creativity. Not so for essays. Be as ingenious as you can, as long as it is appropriate. Use anecdotes, dialogue and action to make your essay come alive. If appropriate, discuss your unique approach or how you got started in the field. Use illustrations to show that you have the skills needed or to reflect your dedication to your studies. After reading many essays that are alike, the selection committee will appreciate one that takes chances with a little creativity. If you are worried about being too imaginative, ask a professor for feedback.

Address intellectual issues. Graduate school is a world unto itself. The setting is different from undergraduate school in that specialists devote themselves to technical and intellectual issues in a chosen field. Demonstrate your knowledge of these issues and your ability to discuss the latest developments. You don't need to be long-winded about this–be brief, concise and to the point, just like research–but remember that

---

Focus on the Essay
_____

Selection committees use essays to learn more about you on a personal and professional level beyond the straight facts of your application. Use the essay to explain your motivations and goals and how you view your field of study. Essays are your best opportunity to set your application apart from the others.

it is important to let your readers know that you understand the field in which you, too, will become a specialist.

Be yourself. Most important, make sure that your essay echoes who you really are. Only write what is comfortable for you. In trying to make your essay different from the others, don't do so by adopting an alter ego. Be yourself and use your accomplishments in the field to make you stand out.

Refer to Chapter 7, *Secrets to Writing Winning Essays*, for more help with essays.

Research Grant Proposals: Application Heavies

If scholarship essays are the featherweights of graduate financial aid, grant proposals are the heavyweights. Unlike normal scholarship essays, research grant proposals require outlining specific academic objectives and implementation plans. Provided by the government, graduate schools and private organizations, most graduate grants award aid for a specific project, study or dissertation. Because the awarding organizations have limited funds, their objective is to get the most academic mileage out of the least amount of money. When applying for grants, follow the strategies for essays above, but keep these additional points in mind:

How will your research benefit the field? Awarding grants is not a selfless task. The committee wants the bragging rights for backing research that advances the field. To fulfill this need, explain the potential significance of your research on the field. Show why your research is meaningful. Include specific applications of your research if they are not immediately apparent.

What is your plan of action? It's important to convey that you have goals for your research, but it's equally important to explain how you're going to get there. An essential component of a grant proposal is an outline of your plan of action. Include measurable objectives, a timeline and budget. Make it clear that you have an organized plan for accomplishing your objectives. Everyone knows that research takes more time than you think and costs more than you budget. Show the committee an aggressive but realistic plan and they will be impressed. It is also important to indicate the limits of your project—what you will not address as well as what you propose to accomplish.

How does the grant fit with the future you? The selection committee realizes that few people do research for philanthropic reasons. They want to know what's in it for you, your reasons for being interested in the research and how it fits with your future career plans. Explain how you hope to use what you learn in the future and what your future plans are.

What specifics can you offer? Be as specific as possible to show the seriousness of your efforts. Don't just offer your hypothesis. Describe the line of reasoning that you have taken to reach it. Offer an excerpt of the sources you plan to use. Explain who your advisors will be and their roles. You must show the committee how committed you are to the project. Giving them a taste of what you have found so far is a great way to demonstrate your seriousness.

Be Detailed in Your Proposal

Research grant proposals require more details than regular essays. Impress the selection committee by showing them that you've thought through all the steps and potential obstacles to successfully complete the project.

Interviews: Interaction with a Purpose

For some awards, the interaction gets even more personal than can be conveyed via essays or proposals. Some require interviews with one or more members of the selection committee who will use an interview as a way to get to know you beyond your application. This face-to-face time will also serve as an opportunity for the committee to delve deeper into your academic interests. The most important rule is never go to an interview without having done your homework. Here are your assignments:

Know the purpose. Understand the purpose of the award and the awarding organization. Research both by speaking with members of the organization, reading the group's literature and speaking with past recipients of the award.

Practice. Practice doing mock interviews before the real thing. Ask a friend or family member to ask you questions and practice answering them. To get even more out of mock interviews, tape them for review afterward.

Have an interactive conversation. Don't just speak about yourself and your accomplishments. Your interviewers have probably worked in the field for a number of years. Use this time to find out more about how they got to where they are and to discuss their thoughts on the future of the field. Try to engage them in your project. Ask their opinions on what they think the results might be. Be sure to prepare questions in advance so that you have an arsenal of thoughtful and provocative questions.

Be ready for anything. Most interviews are straightforward, with interviewers asking questions you can generally anticipate. However–especially for graduate awards–interviewers have been known to throw in a curveball or two. Some professors treat interviews as a time to bolster their egos and ask esoteric questions about their fields. If you are surprised with one of these questions, take a second to think and do your best. You can always say that you don't know the answer now but would be happy to get back to the professor. After the interview, find the answer and email it that day. Chances are, if you were stumped, so were the other applicants and it could impress the scholarship judges that you took the time to research the question and find an answer. There really is no fool-proof way to prepare for this kind of question, except to ask your mock interviewer to toss in a few outlandish questions to get you thinking on your feet.

Remind yourself to overlook the prestige of your interviewers. Professors can be intimidating. Remember that they are real people. Treat them with deserved respect but don't be intimidated by them. If you don't have experience speaking with professors or if you find yourself extremely nervous around them, set up some office hours with professors on your campus to talk about the field and to ask about the award. Get used to talking one-on-one with professors before you walk into your first interview.

Know what members of the committee have published. If you know who your interviewers will be, read their work and be conversant about it. The opinions presented in their published work will be useful in predicting how they may react to your work and opinions.

You can find more interview strategies in Chapter 9, *Ace the Interviews*.

Get Paid to Step into a Classroom or Lab

After you've exhausted the resources for winning money for your education, you can always resort to the traditional method: Working for it. Many schools offer opportunities to earn money through on-campus employment. In fact, for some schools and fellowships, it's a requirement.

Typical employment opportunities are teaching or researching. Grad students offer schools an additional pool of young and enthusiastic instructors for undergraduate courses. Grad students also assist professors with conducting research. In the sciences, lab work is a staple of the graduate school education.

To find out about opportunities for employment at your school, go to your department or your school's career services office. Be prepared with a curriculum vitae that outlines your desired type of work and qualifications. If that doesn't work, approach individual professors and ask about opportunities directly. You may even be able to create a position for yourself.

Keep Your Aid Flowing

Despite your wishes, once you win a research grant, fellowship or scholarship, you can't take the money and run. You don't need to pay the money back, but you still have some responsibilities for maintaining your award. Here are some tips for carrying out the responsibilities of your award:

Get to know your grant, fellowship or scholarship administrators. Along with assisting with the administrative paperwork, administrators associated with your award will be able to answer your questions about the details of your award as well as offer advice on how to maximize the benefits of it.

Be aware of your award's term and requirements. Take time to understand the particulars of your award. How long does the award last? What happens if you take a leave of absence, study part time or quit your studies? Is the award renewable? If it is, what do you need to do to renew it?

Learn about restrictions for spending the dough. Some awards are limited to tuition only. Others can be used for books, travel or even living expenses. Some provide the money directly to your school while others provide a check made out to you. Make sure that you understand what you can spend the award money on and what sort of records you need to keep.

Know what happens once you're finished with your studies. Understand who owns the equipment that you purchase and if the awarding organization has any kind of ownership of your work. Keep records of your expenditures including receipts.

Learn the tax implications of your award. Speak with the award administrator or the IRS (www.irs.gov or 800-829-1040).

Keep the awarding organization up to date on your progress. Provide the organization with a summary report or copy of the finished product after you have

---

Renew Your Award

Get to know your award, its requirements and restrictions so that you can keep what you've earned and use it to its fullest potential. Don't ignore the small print when you receive an award to avoid unpleasant surprises.

finished your work. If your work is published, be sure to credit the various groups that have given you awards. This is not only good manners, but it will also help ensure that the award is around in the future.

Getting More Help

Now that you are armed with strategies for winning scholarships and fellowships, don't stop here. Investigate these additional resources to lighten the burden of being a poor grad student. Here are some sources:

Your department. Inquire about awards and employment opportunities. Read newsletters distributed by your department and check the department bulletin board.

Your peers. There's probably a small circle of people who also study your field. Ask fellow students about awards they know of or that they have won themselves.

Award administrators. Speak with award administrators to see if they know of other awards that may be applicable to you.

Professors. Communicate your goals for the future so that if your professors come across an appropriate program or award, they will think of you. Share ideas for research and employment. Your professors may be able to help you develop proposals to fund your ideas.

Financial aid office. Make sure you have the most up-to-date information on programs offered by your school's financial aid office. Meet at least twice a year with a financial aid advisor to review your situation.

Career services office. Use this office to investigate potential employment opportunities.

Internet. Search websites that offer information and scholarship databases for graduate students. Our site, SuperCollege.com (www.supercollege.com), has a free searchable database of thousands of scholarships.

Associations. Professional and academic associations are a great source of awards for advanced studies. For some of them, you don't even need to be a member to apply.

Your surroundings. On-campus organizations, employers and community groups often award scholarships and fellowships. Wherever you are, keep an eye out for opportunities.

Maximize Your Resources

The best way to get money for graduate school is to find out as much information as you can. Look around you—there are resources in your department, on the Internet and on campus. Use them!

Chapter 14 Summary: Free Cash For Graduate School

Priorities change. While undergraduate awards are often based on a combination of academics, leadership and activities, graduate awards are almost always based solely on academics and research. You will need to adjust your strategy to highlight your commitment to your field.

Different types of money. Graduate financial aid comes in several formats: Federal loans need to be repaid, while scholarships, grants and fellowships do not. Some graduate programs require teaching or research as a part of their financial aid packages.

Prestige and money. Graduate financial aid not only provides financial reward but enhances your curriculum vitae as well.

Applications: Your time to shine. Applications offer you the opportunity to build a case for how you fit the mission of the award. Know who your audience will most likely be and present the information that will show them that you are the best fit for the award.

Help your recommenders help you. When asking others to write your recommendation letters, provide everything they need, including a cover letter, curriculum vitae and accompanying paperwork. Make their job as easy as possible.

Show your academic might in essays. Address academic issues and demonstrate how through your research or projects you fit the requirements for the award.

Research grant proposals are the application heavies. You must provide detailed information about the project you propose, your plan of action and the potential benefits you can make to your field of study.

Practice for interviews. Learn as much as you can about the awarding organization and the interviewers themselves. Then practice with mock interviewers.

Responsibly maintain what you've won. Each award has its own requirements and restrictions. Get to know them so you hold onto your winnings and use the award to its fullest extent.

Don't be afraid to ask for help. If you look around your campus, there are many resources for you to use from professors to the financial aid office to fellow students. Take advantage of them all when finding money for grad school.

How to Keep the Money You Win

In this chapter, you'll learn:

- How to ensure you keep the financial aid and scholarship dollars you win

- Our advice for approaching and winning scholarships

- A special request from Gen and Kelly

CHAPTER 15

You're There!

When you learn to skydive, your first lesson does not start with jumping out of an airplane. First you go through training in which you learn techniques and safety measures—on the ground. Only after practicing on the ground can you take to the sky.

In your scholarship education, you have just completed the ground training and are ready to take the plunge. As you move from the strategies for applying for scholarships to actually applying for them, we have a few words of advice on how to keep the dollars you earn and how to stay motivated.

Keeping the Dollars That Are Yours

Let's jump ahead to after you win a cache of scholarship dollars. It would be nice once the scholarship checks were written if you could run off for that well-deserved trip to the Bahamas. Alas, there are restrictions on how you can spend the cash and how you must maintain your scholarship. (Besides, everyone knows that Hawaii is the place to go.) Here are some tips to keep in mind:

Get to know your scholarship and financial aid administrators. These people will be able to answer questions about your award and make sure you are spending it the way you should.

Give the scholarship committee members proof if they want it. Some awards require that you provide proof of enrollment or transcripts. Send it to them.

Be aware of your award's requirements and what happens if something changes. How long does the award last? What happens if you take a leave of absence, study part time, study abroad, transfer schools or quit your studies? College is full of possibilities! Do you have to maintain a minimum grade point average or take courses in a certain field?

Know if there are special requirements for athletic scholarships. If you've won an athletic scholarship, you are most likely required to play the sport. (You didn't get that full ride scholarship for nothing!) Understand the implications of what would happen if you were not able to play because of circumstances such as an injury or not meeting academic requirements.

Find out if the award is a cash cow (renewable). If an award is renewable, you are eligible to get it every year you are in school. If so, find out what you need to do and when you need to do it to renew. Some awards just require a copy of your transcript, while others require you to submit an entirely new application.

Understand restrictions for spending the dough. Some awards are limited to tuition. Others can be used for books, travel or even living expenses. Some provide the money directly to your school; others provide a check made out to you. Understand what you can spend it on and what sort of records you need to keep.

Lessons into Action

You've just learned step-by-step strategies for every piece of the scholarship process from finding scholarships to writing winning applications to using the Internet to expand your search. Now it's time to search our comprehensive Scholarship Directory and put these lessons into action.

Learn the tax implications of your award. Speak with the award administrator or your pals at the IRS (www.irs.gov or 800-829-1040).

Be aware of requirements after you graduate. Some awards such as ROTC scholarships require employment after graduation. Because these arrangements can drastically affect your future, learn about the requirements now.

Keep the awarding organization up to date on your progress. Write the organization a thank you note, and keep them updated on your progress at the end of the year. This is not only good manners, but it will also help ensure that the award is around in the future.

Parting Words

I (Gen) remember when I won the Sterling Scholarship, one of the highest honors for students in Hawaii. The awards ceremony was televised live throughout the state. For weeks before submitting my application, I prepared for the competition, compiling a 50-page application book, practicing for the eight hours of interviews and enlisting the help of no less than three teachers from my high school. Even though the scholarship was only $1,000, my parents still keep the trophy on display and share with unwitting visitors the videotape of my triumph. I realize now that I was able to put in such extensive effort because of my outlook on the award. I knew whether I won or lost, I would gain the experience of building a portfolio, becoming a skilled interviewee, working closely with my teachers and meeting some incredible students.

While scholarships are primarily a source of funding for your education, approach them in the same way you do your favorite sport or hobby. I also played for my school's tennis team—and lost just about every match. Yet, I continued because I enjoyed the sport and found the skills a challenge. If you approach your scholarships in this manner, you'll probably win more of them and have fun in the process. Treat them like a chore, and you'll hate every minute, neglecting to put in the effort required to win.

The bottom line is that if you are going to take the time to apply, you should take the time to win. The secrets, tips and strategies in this book will put you within striking distance. Follow them and you'll win more and more often.

This book is unique in that it really is two books in one. Now that you know how to win, it's time to begin finding scholarships to put these strategies to use. The second half of this book is a complete listing of scholarships and awards and is indexed by various criteria so you can quickly find those that match your interests and qualifications. And, because we know you just can't get enough of us, we also encourage you to visit our website, SuperCollege.com, for the most up-to-date information on scholarships and financial aid.

We both wish you the best of luck.

Neither Easy Nor Quick

Applying for scholarships is not easy. It requires time, patience and perseverance. The competition is tough. As you are applying, remind yourself that the reward is even greater. And when you receive your college diploma, you will feel deep satisfaction from knowing that you played a significant role in paying for this education.

A Special Request

As you jump headlong into the wonderful world of scholarships, we have a special request. We would love to hear about your experiences with scholarships and how this book has helped you. Please send us a note after you've finished raking in your free cash for college.

Gen and Kelly Tanabe
c/o SuperCollege
3286 Oak Court
Belmont, CA 94002

Onward!

Let's fly! Flip the page and start finding scholarships. It's time to put all the strategies and tips you've just learned to work for you!

Scholarship Directory

DIRECTORY

A comprehensive directory to thousands of scholarships, grants and contests including:

- Awards for high school, college, graduate and adult students

- Easy-to-use index to help you find the scholarships that are right for you

The Scholarship Directory

It's time to put into action the secrets, tips, and strategies that you learned in the first half of the book. We've done the hard work of scouring the country to find the best scholarships that you can win. We've made a special effort to select awards with broad eligibility requirements, which means you'll find plenty of scholarships that fit your background, goals and interests.

Before you jump into the directory, spend a few moments to learn how the scholarships are organized so that you don't miss out on any awards.

How to Find the Scholarships that Match You

To help find the awards that match you best, we've conveniently organized our directory of scholarships into 45 major categories. Since some scholarships span several categories we have also listed related scholarships in each of the categories.

Listed below is the complete list of categories, descriptions of the types of awards you'll find in each category and some suggestions on related sections. Remember to also use the various indexes in the back of the book to help you zero in on more scholarships.

Academics/General
Browse this section first since the scholarships listed are open to nearly everyone. While some of the scholarships do have grade requirements, you'll be surprised to learn that often the minimum for applying is very low. There are also plenty of awards that are not based on grades and even a few scholarships that are awarded by random drawing.

Accounting/Finance
Here you will find a lot of specific awards for future accountants and students majoring in finance. Be sure to also look at the related *Business/Management* and *Mathematics* sections.

Aerospace/Aviation
Move over Chuck Yeager. If your dream is to fly, fix, manage, build or serve drinks on any kind of aircraft or rocket, this is the section for you. If you like the technical aspects of aerospace you should also browse the awards listed in *Engineering* and *Mathematics.*

Agriculture/Horticulture/Animals
Awards in this area include agricultural science, animal husbandry, horticulture, floriculture and animals in general. Two related sections you should also explore are *Forestry/Wildlife* and *Biological Sciences/Life Sciences.*

Architecture/Landscape
Includes money for future landscape designers, lighting people and architects. If you are the artistic type (which many architecture and landscape people seem to be) don't forget to also look at the related *Graphic Arts* and *Performing Arts/Music/ Drama/Visual Arts* sections.

Athletics/Outdoors

Yes, there are scholarships for athletes. Whether you are a national champion or dilettante, there are awards for both good (and mediocre) athletes. This section also contains awards for those who love the outdoors. Most students also find related awards in the *Leadership* section.

Biological Sciences/Life Sciences

This category is for students who plan on studying or entering careers in biology, ichthyology, ornithology, entomology and many other "-ologies." Some of the more common majors in this category include:

> Biology, Biochemistry, Biophysics, Botany, Anatomy, Ecology, Neuroscience, Biometrics, Zoology, Entomology, Pathology and Pharmacology.

You should also look for awards in the *Chemistry, Medicine/Nursing/Health Profession, Forestry/Wildlife* and *Agriculture/Horticulture/Animals* sections.

Business/Management

All future CEOs and business types should explore this category. Be sure to also look at some of the business specific categories like *Accounting/Finance, Marketing* and *Hospitality/Travel/Tourism.* And if you're the type that's headed to the corporate boardroom, be sure to look at the *Leadership* category.

Chemistry

There are a wide variety of chemistry awards in this category. Also make sure you look at the *Sciences/Physical Sciences, Medicine/Nursing/Health Professions* and *Engineering* (includes Chemical Engineering) categories.

Communications

Whether you are a ham radio operator, speech giver or mass communications major, this category has scholarships for communications majors and just plain good communicators. Also see the *Journalism/Broadcasting* and *English/Writing* sections.

Computer and Information Science

If you take comfort in the warm glow of a computer screen and your keyboard is practically a fifth appendage, this is the section for you. Be sure to also look at the *Engineering, Mathematics* and *Sciences/Physical Sciences* sections for more computer-related awards.

Construction Trades

This category includes awards for those headed for management positions and those who will work in the industry. If you are looking for money for a two-year or technical school be sure to look at the *Vocational/Technical* section.

Culinary Arts

If cooking or baking is your passion and you need money to feed the habit, take a look at the awards in this category. Also, look at the *Food Services, Hospitality/Travel/ Tourism* and *Business/Management* sections for some related scholarships.

Dentistry

If you dream of drilling holes in people's teeth but are short on cash to learn how to do it correctly, look no further. This section includes awards for both dentists and dental hygienists. Find more awards in *Medicine/Nursing/Health Professions.*

Put Your Knowledge to Work

Use what you've learned in the first half of this book to prioritize the awards and select those that fit you and your background best. Spend the most time on those awards that you are most likely to win.

Use the Indexes

Use the indexes at the end of the directory to search for scholarships that match your specific talents, interests and background.

Disability/Illness

This section has awards for students with physical, hearing, vision, mental and learning disabilities. It also includes awards for students who have been afflicted with certain illnesses.

Education/Teaching

You've been a student for much of your life. If the tables are turning and you now want to teach, here are awards for teaching and education at the elementary, secondary and collegiate level. Also look at the awards listed in *English/Writing, Public Administration/Social Work, Public Service/Community Service* and *State of Residence* since many states give grants to encourage students to become teachers.

Engineering

This is a huge category of awards for engineers of all types. Included are scholarships for such specialties as:

> Mechanical, Electrical, Chemical, Agricultural, Nuclear, Imaging, Geophysics, Plastics and Optics.

Be sure to also look at the awards in the *Aerospace/Aviation, Computer and Information Science* and *Sciences/Physical Sciences* sections.

English/Writing

You don't have to be an English major to win some of these awards. This category is jam packed with awards for writing, public speaking and literature. If this is your section, you may also find awards in *Education/Teaching, Communications, Journalism/Broadcasting* and *Library Science*.

Ethnic and Area Studies

If you're itching to whip out that passport and get out of here, you can find money to help fund your study of different cultures and countries. Also check out the *Foreign Language* and *Social Science/History* sections.

Food Services

We all have to eat, and you could win money to study this essential industry. Remember that the food service industry incorporates more than flipping burgers. There are also careers in business, product development and marketing. Be sure to look at the *Culinary Arts* and *Hospitality/Travel/Tourism* sections as well.

Foreign Language

Sona si latine loqueris. (Translation: Honk if you speak Latin.) If you laughed before reading the translation you could win some cash for your language skills. Also check out the *Ethnic and Area Studies* section.

Forestry/Wildlife

Ah, the great outdoors. Why not get some money to help learn the skills to enter a career that will keep you outside? Be sure to also explore the *Agriculture/Horticulture/Animals* and *Biological Sciences/Life Sciences* sections.

Graphic Arts

Whether you are interested in commercial or fine art there are scholarships to help you become a better artist. Also look at the *Performing Arts/Music/Drama/Visual Arts* category.

Hospitality/Travel/Tourism

From managing a five-star hotel to planning a cruise for a thousand people there are awards that can help you enter this field. Be sure to also look at the *Business/Management* section.

Journalism/Broadcasting

Print, radio, television and the Internet are all well represented in this section for budding journalists. Be sure to also browse the *Communications* and *English/Writing* categories.

Law

If you're studying to become a lawyer you can certainly use your skills to try to argue your way to some financial aid with these scholarships.

Leadership

Are people always following you? Then look at these awards that reward leadership. Remember that you don't have to be the president of your student body to demonstrate leadership. You can show it through informal positions and directing special projects.

Library Science

There is more to working in a library than shelving books. Awards are available for anyone who wants to study this science. Also see the *English/Writing* section.

Marketing

Use your skills to market yourself to some of these fantastic scholarships. Also see the *Business/Management* category.

Mathematics

Simple addition tells you that if you are good in math you should be able to add to your scholarship cache by winning some of these awards. Be sure to look at related sections such as *Engineering, Accounting/Finance, Computer and Information Science, Aerospace/Aviation* and *Sciences/Physical Sciences*.

Medicine/Nursing/Health Professions

Future doctors, nurses and other health care professions should head to this category stat! If you are interested in dentistry, don't forget to look at that specific category.

Military/Police/Fire

Most of these awards require that you have a parent or grandparent who has served in the military or been a police officer or fire fighter. There are also awards if you want to enter one of these professions.

Organizations/Clubs/Employers

Many large companies and service organizations give awards to their members. If you or your parents are members of any of the groups in this category, you may qualify for a scholarship.

Performing Arts/Music/Drama/Visual Arts

This category includes dancing, singing, acting, music, drawing, painting, sculpture, photography and more. Be sure to look at the *Graphic Arts* and *English/Writing* categories for related awards.

Prioritize Your Awards

The best way to read the directory is with a notepad at your side so you can jot down the scholarship numbers of all the awards that you are interested in. You can then easily go back and sort through your list and prioritize what you have found.

Psychology
Analyze these awards to see if you qualify for some free cash. In addition, peruse the *Social Science/History* section for more awards.

Public Administration/Social Work
These awards cover both government work and social work. Also see *Public Service/Community Service*.

Public Service/Community Service
These awards offer you an opportunity to get paid for your volunteer work. Public and community service includes volunteer work, being an active member of a service club or simply being involved in your own community.

Race/Ethnicity/Gender/Family Status
There are a lot of awards for members of minority and nonminority ethnic groups, women and students with unique family situations.

Real Estate
Sold! Find scholarships for future realtors, and look at the *Business/Management* category too.

Religion and Churches
Churches and religious organizations support their members with a variety of scholarships and awards.

Sciences/Physical Sciences
Typically known as the "hard sciences," this category includes:

> Astronomy, Astrophysics, Chemistry, Geology, Paleontology, Metallurgy, Oceanography, Earth and Planetary Sciences, Physics, Nuclear Physics, Optics, Acoustics and more.

Also be sure to browse the *Biological/Life Sciences, Engineering, Chemistry, Mathematics* and *Computer and Information Science* sections.

Social Science/History
Take a close look at this category if you think you'll major in or enter a career in one of the social sciences, which includes:

> Anthropology, Archaeology, Criminology, Economics, Geography, Cartography, History, International Relations and Affairs, Political Science, Sociology, Urban Studies and more.

You may also find related scholarships in *Education/Teaching, English/Writing, Foreign Language* and *Ethnic and Area Studies*.

State of Residence
Here's your opportunity to get something back from your (or your parents') state tax dollars. Every state offers scholarships and grants for their residents. Some states even offer awards to out-of-state students who study in their states. Be sure to look at both your home state as well as any of the states you are planning to go to college in to find the most awards.

Unions
If your parents or grandparents are members of a trade or professional union, you may be eligible for these awards.

Vocational/Technical
Whether it's autobody work or heating and cooling, you can find money for technical or vocational training. You can also find scholarships in the *Construction Trades*, *Engineering* and *Computer and Information Science* sections.

"Take Off the Blinders" to Find the Most Scholarships

Now that you know the categories, the best way to find scholarships is to jump right in and head to the sections that fit you best.

Do you remember when your elementary school teacher would say, "Take off the mental blinders"? Ours did to encourage us to think broadly. In the same way we want to encourage you to "take off the scholarship blinders" and not think about yourself too narrowly. Consider your accomplishments, activities, goals and background as broadly as possible. Look through some of the categories even if you don't immediately see a fit. You might discover that you actually fit one of the leadership scholarships even if you haven't held a formal leadership position. Or you may find an award in the life sciences category in a field that you love but never realized was a life science.

Don't be afraid to be forward-thinking. Write down any scholarships that fit even if you have to wait a year to apply. The awards we have selected are from the larger organizations and businesses, so you can be certain that they are going to be around for a long time.

When you are ready to apply for a scholarship be sure to confirm both the deadline and contact information with the scholarship organization. Some awards change the specific day an application is due each year. Fortunately, most scholarship organizations have websites. You should also be able to download many of the scholarship applications. For the few that don't have websites you will have to send a request by mail. A few scholarships require nominations by your high school or college. Don't be shy about asking your counselor or professor to nominate you for an award.

We are really excited that you can now put everything that you learned to good use to actually help you find and win some free cash for college.

Happy scholarship hunting!

Academics/General

Also See Scholarships Listed Under:
Leadership
Public Service/Community Service

A&E Television Network

P.O. Box 7996
Melville, NY 11775-7267
Website: http://www.aetv.com/class/

1 • A&E Essay Contests

Purpose: To encourage students to research and write about important figures.

Eligibility: Applicants must be in grades 5 to 12 and write an essay on important people in society. There are two levels of competition: grades 5 to 8 and grades 9 to 12. The teachers and schools of the winners also receive prizes. The topic for the essay varies and may be found on the website. A recent topic was, "Lives that Make a Difference."

How to Apply: Applicants send essays and applications by mail.

Deadline: Varies.
Amount: $2,500-$5,000.
Number of Awards: 4.

AAA

1000 AAA Drive
Heathrow, FL 32746
Phone: 407-444-8000
Email: aaatravelchallenge@national.aaa.com
Website: http://www.aaa.com/TravelChallenge/

2 • AAA Traffic Safety Poster Program

Purpose: To encourage students to make posters promoting traffic safety.

Eligibility: Applicants must be in kindergarten through eighth grade. There are three grade-level divisions: K-grade 2, grades 3-5 and grades 6-8. Students must use one of twenty slogans. Entries are judged on originality, presentation, visual impact and relationship to traffic safety. The winning posters will be reproduced in catalogs. There are grand, 1st, 2nd, 3rd and judge's level winners. Local AAA club representatives can provide additional information.

How to Apply: Applications are available at local AAA clubs.
Deadline: January 16.
Amount: $5,000-$25,000.
Number of Awards: 5.

3 • Travel High School Challenge

Purpose: In an effort to increase travel knowledge and geographic literacy, the award recognizes and rewards students in grades 9 to 12 for their travel destination knowledge.

Eligibility: Applicants must be in grades 9 to 12 at a public or private junior high school or high school or be in a certified home school program. Applicants must take an Internet test before going to the next round.

How to Apply: Applications are available online.
Deadline: January.
Amount: $25,000.
Number of Awards: 3.

Academic Finance Corporation

One W. Boylston Street, Chadwick Court
Worcester, MA 01605
Phone: 877-232-4322
Fax: 508-854-9972
Email: info@afclending.com
Website: http://www.50kgiveaway.org

4 • 50k Giveaway Scholarship

Purpose: To assist first-year college or trade-school students with expenses.

Eligibility: This is a random drawing. Entries must be from those entering their first year of an accredited two-year or four-year college or trade school.

How to Apply: Applications are available online.
Deadline: Varies.
Amount: $5,000.
Number of Awards: 10.

Alpha Kappa Alpha

5656 S. Stony Island Avenue
Chicago, IL 60637
Phone: 800-653-6528
Fax: 773-947-0277
Email: akaeaf@akaeaf.net
Website: http://www.akaeaf.org

5 • Educational Advancement Foundation Merit Scholarship

Purpose: To support academically-talented students.

Eligibility: Applicants must be full-time undergraduate sophomores or graduate students at an accredited school. They must have a GPA of at least 3.0 and demonstrate involvement and community service.

How to Apply: Applications are available online.
Deadline: April 15 for undergraduate, September 15 for graduate.
Amount: $1,000.
Number of Awards: Varies.

American Fire Sprinkler Association

9696 Skillman Street
Suite 300
Dallas, TX 75243
Phone: 214-349-5965
Fax: 214-343-8898
Email: afsainfo@firesprinkler.org
Website: http://www.afsascholarship.org

6 • American Fire Sprinkler Association Scholarship Program

Purpose: To provide financial aid to high school seniors and introduce them to the fire sprinkler industry.

Eligibility: Applicants must be high school seniors who plan to attend a U.S. college, university or certified trade school. Students must read the "Fire Sprinkler Essay" available online and then take an online quiz. Applicants receive one entry in the scholarship drawing for each question answered correctly.

How to Apply: Applications are available online.
Deadline: April 12.
Amount: $5,000.
Number of Awards: 4.

American Legion

Attn.: Americanism and Children and Youth Division
P.O. Box 1055
Indianapolis, IN 46206
Phone: 317-630-1249
Fax: 317-630-1369
Email: acy@legion.org
Website: http://www.legion.org

7 • National Oratorical Contest

Purpose: To reward students for their knowledge of government and oral presentation skills.

Eligibility: Applicants must be high school students under the age of 20 who are U.S. citizens or legal residents. Students first give an oration within their state and winners compete at the national level. The oration must be related to the Constitution of the United States focusing on the duties and obligations citizens have to the government. It must be in English and be between eight and ten minutes. There is also an assigned topic which is posted on the website, and it should be between three and five minutes.

How to Apply: Contact your local American Legion post or state headquarters.

Deadline: December 1.

Amount: $18,000.

Number of Awards: Varies.

Apple Computer Inc.

1 Infinite Loop
Cupertino, CA 95014
Website: http://www.apple.com

8 • Apple Scholars Program

Purpose: To provide cash scholarships and technological equipment to students who have demonstrated a prolific use of technology in their schoolwork.

Eligibility: Applicants are evaluated on academic achievement, application of technology, future plans to implement technology and ability to articulate the importance of digital media in academia. The competition is open to all U.S. high school seniors who will be enrolled in a two- or four-year accredited college/university. Apple employees, their families and/or affiliates are not eligible.

How to Apply: Applications are available online and may be submitted online or by mail.

Deadline: May 30.

Amount: $2,000.

Number of Awards: 10.

ArtCarved Class Rings

7211 Circle S. Road
Austin, TX 78745
Website: http://www.artcarved.com

9 • ArtCarved Get Cash for College Scholarship

Purpose: To award high school students in the U.S. with excellent academic achievement and community service.

Eligibility: Applicants must have taken the SAT, ACT or PSAT examinations and must have an ArtCarved store account number from a participating store.

How to Apply: Applications are available online.

Deadline: March 15, May 31, August 31 and December 31.

Amount: $500.

Number of Awards: 4.

Calgon

New York, NY 10016
Website: http://www.takemeaway.com

10 • Calgon, Take Me Away to College Scholarship Competition

Purpose: To provide an opportunity to win money for college based on original expression in writing.

Eligibility: Applicants must be females age 18 and older who are U.S. residents, be enrolled in an undergraduate program at four-year college and have a minimum 3.0 GPA. Applicants must complete one full year of study at the undergraduate level after winning the scholarship to receive the full award.

How to Apply: Applications are available online.

Deadline: February 14.

Amount: $1,000-$7,000.

Number of Awards: 8.

CBC Spouses Program

1720 Massachusetts Avenue NW
Washington, DC 20036
Phone: 800-784-2577
Fax: 202-775-0773
Email: info@cbcfinc.org
Website: http://www.cbcfinc.org

11 • CBC Spouses Program

Purpose: To provide tuition assistance to students in congressional districts of members of the Congressional Black Caucus.

Eligibility: Applicants must be high school seniors, college students or graduate students, have a minimum 2.5 GPA, reside or attend school in a congressional district represented by a Congressional Black Caucus Member and submit a financial statement to determine financial need. Applicants for the performing arts scholarship in particular must be 21 years of age. This is an equal opportunity scholarship program, which considers applicants solely on qualifications and ability without regard to race, religion, sex, age, national origin, disability or veteran status.

How to Apply: Applications are available online and should be submitted to the local selection committee as listed online, not the CBCF office.

Deadline: May 1.

Amount: Varies.

Number of Awards: Varies.

Central Intelligence Agency

Office of Public Affairs
Washington, DC 20505
Phone: 703-482-0623
Fax: 703-482-1739
Website: http://www.cia.gov

12 • CIA Undergraduate Scholarship Program

Purpose: To encourage students to pursue careers with the CIA.

Eligibility: Applicants must be high school students or college sophomores. High school students must have an SAT score of 1000 or higher or an ACT score of 21 or higher, while all applicants must have a GPA of at least 3.0. Applicants must demonstrate financial need, defined as a household income of less than $70,000 for a family of four or $80,000 for a family of five or more. They must meet all criteria for regular CIA employees, including security checks and medical examinations. Applicants must commit to a

work experience each summer during college and agree to CIA employment for at least 1.5 times the length of their CIA-sponsored scholarship.
How to Apply: There is no application form; applicants may submit a resume online.
Deadline: November 1.
Amount: Annual salary including benefits and up to $18,000 for tuition.
Number of Awards: Varies.

Citizens' Scholarship Foundation of America

One Scholarship Way
P.O. Box 297
St. Peter, MN 56082
Phone: 800-537-4180
Website: http://www.csfa.org

13 • Dollars for Scholars Scholarship

Purpose: To encourage students to aim for and achieve loftier educational goals.
Eligibility: Applicants must be members of a local Dollars for Scholars chapter. There are more than 1,200 Dollars for Scholars chapter that award more than $29 million in awards each year.
Deadline: Varies.
Amount: Varies.
Number of Awards: Varies.

Coca-Cola Scholars Foundation

P.O. Box 442
Atlanta, GA 30301
Phone: 800-306-2653
Email: questions@coca-colascholars.org
Website: http://www.coca-colascholars.org

14 • Coca-Cola Two-Year College Scholarship

Purpose: To recognize students enrolled in two-year programs for their academic achievement and community service.
Eligibility: Applicants/nominees should be first- or second-year post-secondary students who intend to complete their education at a two-year degree school. Applicants must be U.S. citizens or permanent residents, but may NOT be children of Coca-Cola employees. Students must have maintained a 2.5 GPA and performed 100+ hours of community service within the 12 months previous to application. Applicants must be planning to enroll in at least two courses at a two-year institution.
How to Apply: Applications are available online.
Deadline: May 31.
Amount: Varies.
Number of Awards: Varies.

College Answer

Sallie Mae
12061 Bluemont Way
Reston, VA 20190
Website: http://www.collegeanswer.com

15 • $1,000 Scholarship Drawing Sponsored by Sallie Mae's CollegeAnswer.com

Purpose: To help students pay for college.
Eligibility: Applicants may be high school, undergraduate or graduate students and must register on the CollegeAnswer website.

Each month one registered user is selected in a random drawing to receive the scholarship.
How to Apply: Register at the website to enter.
Deadline: Varies.
Amount: $1,000.
Number of Awards: 1 per month.

College Prowler Inc.

5001 Baum Boulevard
Suite 750
Pittsburgh, PA 15213
Phone: 800-290-2682
Fax: 412-697-1396
Email: scholarship@collegeprowler.com
Website: http://www.collegeprowler.com

16 • College Prowler Essay Scholarship

Purpose: To award students for their advice on entering college.
Eligibility: Applicants must be high school sophomores, juniors or seniors or college freshmen or recent transfer students. Students must write essays based on the topics stated on the website. There are monthly and annual winners.
How to Apply: Applications are available online.
Deadline: Ongoing.
Amount: $1,000.
Number of Awards: Varies.

CollegeNET Scholarship Review Committee

805 SW Broadway
Suite 1600
Portland, OR 97205
Phone: 503-973-5200
Fax: 503-973-5252
Email: scholarship@collegenet.com
Website: http://www.collegenet.com

17 • CollegeNET Scholarship

Purpose: To assist college applicants.
Eligibility: Applicants must sign up at the website and visit and participate in forums. Recipients are determined by votes on the website.
How to Apply: Applications are available online.
Deadline: February 24.
Amount: $1,000-$4,000.
Number of Awards: 4.

Common Knowledge Scholarship Foundation

P.O. Box 290361
Davie, FL 33329-0361
Website: http://www.cksf.org

18 • CKSF Movie Scholarships

Purpose: To reward students and parents for movie knowledge.
Eligibility: Applicants must be high school or college students or their parents and complete the free online registration. The contest is based on a series of short multiple choice quizzes about a movie. Participants receive 500 points for each correct answer and lose one point for each second taken to finish a question. The top 25 percent of the highest scoring students in the first quiz will be automatically entered into a second quiz round. The highest scoring student at the end of the second quiz wins the scholarship.

How to Apply: Applicants must complete the free online registration.
Deadline: June 1.
Amount: $250.
Number of Awards: 1.

Datatel

4375 Fair Lakes Court
Fairfax, VA 22033
Phone: 800-328-2835
Email: scholars@datatel.com
Website: http://www.datatel.com

19 • Returning Student Scholarship

Purpose: Datatel has created scholarship programs as part of its commitment to higher education and to give back to its clients.
Eligibility: Applicants must be currently attending an eligible Datatel school after an absence of at least five years. Both full-time and part-time (at least six credit hours) students may apply. Applicants must provide a personal statement that includes the impact of being a returning student, the challenges of combining school with such things as work and family and the importance of receiving the scholarship to help achieve a dream.
How to Apply: Applications are available online.
Deadline: January 31.
Amount: $1,500.
Number of Awards: 50.

Davidson Institute for Talent Development

9665 Gateway Drive
Suite B
Reno, NV 89521
Phone: 775-852-3483
Email: davidsonfellows@ditd.org
Website: http://www.davidson-institute.org

20 • Davidson Fellows Award

Purpose: To award young people for their works in mathematics, science, technology, music, literature, philosophy or "outside the box."
Eligibility: Applicants must be under the age of 18 and be able to attend the awards reception in Washington, D.C. In addition to the monetary award, the institute will pay for travel and lodging expenses. Three nominator forms, three copies of a 15-minute DVD or VHS videotape and additional materials are required.
How to Apply: Applications are available online.
Deadline: March 30.
Amount: $50,000.
Number of Awards: Varies.

Davis-Putter Scholarship Fund

P.O. Box 7307
New York, NY 10116
Email: information@davisputter.org
Website: http://www.davisputter.org

21 • Davis-Putter Scholarship Fund

Purpose: To assist students who are both academically capable and who aid the progressive movement for peace and justice both on campus and in their communities.

Eligibility: Applicants must be undergraduate or graduate students who participate in the progressive movement, acting in the interests of issues such as expansion of civil rights and international solidarity, among others. Applicants must also have demonstrated financial need as well as a solid academic record.
How to Apply: Applications are available online.
Deadline: April 1.
Amount: Up to $6,000.
Number of Awards: Varies.

Edfinancial Services

eCampusTours c/o Edsouth
P.O. Box 31549
Knoxville, TN 37930
Website: http://www.ecampustours.com

22 • $1000 Scholarship Drawing

Purpose: Ten entrants will each receive a $1,000 scholarship to help pay for college. Winners will be selected through a random drawing by Edfinancial Services.
Eligibility: Eligible students include U.S. citizens, U.S. nationals and permanent residents or students enrolled in a U.S. institution of higher education. Winners must be enrolled in an eligible institution of higher education, as stipulated in the eligibility requirements, within one year of winning the award. Scholarship awards will be paid directly to the college.
How to Apply: Entries are available online, and registration is required. Entries may be submitted by mail.
Deadline: August 1.
Amount: $1,000.
Number of Awards: 10.

Educational Communications Scholarship Foundation

721 N. Mckinley Road
Lake Forest, IL 60045
Email: school@ecsf.org
Website: http://www.ecsf.org

23 • Educational Communications Scholarship

Purpose: To provide hard-working students with financial assistance for post-secondary education.
Eligibility: Applicants are evaluated on the basis of academic achievement, financial need, work experience and leadership skills. Applicants must be high school students who have taken either the SAT or the ACT.
How to Apply: Applications are available online.
Deadline: May 31.
Amount: $1,000.
Number of Awards: 200+.

EF Educational Tours

EF Center Boston
One Education Street
Cambridge, MA 02141
Phone: 617-619-1300
Fax: 800-318-3732
Email: marisa.talbot@ef.com
Website: http://www.eftours.com

24 • Global Citizen Awards

Purpose: To support students with strong global perspectives.

Eligibility: Applicants must be high school seniors in the United States or Canada nominated by their schools and must write an essay on a topic related to global citizenship. The award includes a scholarship and paid educational trip to Europe.

How to Apply: Applications are available online.

Deadline: February 15.

Amount: Varies.

Number of Awards: 12 (10 American, 2 Canadian).

Elder & Leemaur Publishers

115 Garfield Street #4953
Sumas, WA 98295
Website: http://www.elpublishers.com

25 • Student Authors

Purpose: To support students to explore career opportunities in professional writing.

Eligibility: Applicants must be high school seniors or current undergraduate students in North America and must submit an essay of up to 500 words on one of the provided topics. Students must attend or plan to attend a college/university in either Canada or the United States. Some essays will be featured in the publication.

How to Apply: Essays should be submitted online.

Deadline: July 1.

Amount: Varies.

Number of Awards: Varies.

26 • University Writing Scholarship

Purpose: To promote students to explore career opportunities in professional writing.

Eligibility: Applicants must be high school seniors or current undergraduate students in North America and must submit an essay up to 500 words on one of the provided topics. Students must attend or plan to attend a college/university in either Canada or the United States. Some essays will be featured in the publication.

How to Apply: Essays should be submitted online.

Deadline: Varies.

Amount: Varies.

Number of Awards: Varies.

27 • Young Authors Head Start Program

Purpose: To encourage students to explore career opportunities in professional writing.

Eligibility: Applicants must be high school seniors or current undergraduate students in North America and must write an essay of up to 500 words on one of the provided topics. Students must attend or plan to attend a college/university in either Canada or the United States. Some essays will be featured in the publication.

How to Apply: Essays should be submitted online.

Deadline: Varies.

Amount: Varies.

Number of Awards: Varies.

Elks National Foundation (IL)

2750 N. Lakeview Avenue
Chicago, IL 60614
Phone: 773-755-4732
Fax: 773-755-4733
Email: scholarship@elks.org
Website: http://www.elks.org

28 • Most Valuable Student Scholarships

Purpose: Monetary awards for college education are given to high school seniors who have demonstrated scholarship, leadership, and a financial need.

Eligibility: Applicants must be graduating high school seniors who are U.S. citizens and who plan to pursue a four-year degree on a full-time basis at a U.S. college or university. Selection is based on financial need, leadership and scholarship. Male and female students compete separately.

How to Apply: Contact the scholarship chairman of your local Lodge or the Elks association of your state.

Deadline: January.

Amount: $1,000-$15,000.

Number of Awards: 500.

German Marshall Fund of the United States

1744 R Street NW
Washington, DC 20009
Phone: 202-745-3950
Fax: 202-265-1662
Email: info@gmfus.org
Website: http://www.gmfus.org

29 • Marshall Memorial Fellowship

Purpose: To provide fellowships for future community leaders to travel in Europe and to explore its societies, institutions and people.

Eligibility: Applicants must be between 28 and 40 years of age and demonstrate achievement within their profession, civic involvement and leadership. Candidates should have little or no previous experience traveling through Europe. Fellows visit five or six cities and meet with policy makers, business professionals and other community leaders.

How to Apply: Applications are available online.

Deadline: June 23.

Amount: Varies.

Number of Awards: 100.

Glamour

The Conde Nast Publications Inc.
4 Times Square
New York, NY 10036
Phone: 800-244-4526
Email: ttcw@glamour.com
Website: http://www.glamour.com

30 • Top Ten College Women Competition

Purpose: To recognize outstanding leaders among women who are college juniors.

Eligibility: Applicants must be female junior-year students in an undergraduate program. Judging is based on academics, community service and leadership skills.

How to Apply: Applications are available by email to ttcw@glamour.com.

Deadline: January.

Amount: $1,500.

Number of Awards: 10.

GoCollege.com

Website: http://www.gocollege.com

31 • Scholarship Lucky Draw

Purpose: To provide scholarship opportunities to students who register on the website.
Eligibility: This is a monthly drawing for a $250 college scholarship award.
How to Apply: Enter by registering online and completing a questionnaire.
Deadline: Ongoing.
Amount: $250.
Number of Awards: 1.

Henkel Consumer Adhesives

32150 Just Imagine Drive
Avon, OH 44011-1355
Website: http://www.ducktapeclub.com

32 • Stuck at Prom Scholarship

Purpose: To reward students for their creativity with duct tape.
Eligibility: Applicants must attend a high school prom as a couple in the spring wearing the most original attire that they make from duct tape. Photographs of past winners are available on the website.
How to Apply: Applications are available online.
Deadline: June 9.
Amount: $6,000.
Number of Awards: 3.

Honor Society of Phi Kappa Phi

P.O. Box 16000
Louisiana State University
Baton Rouge, LA 70893-6000
Phone: 800-804-9880 x13
Email: awards@phikappaphi.org
Website: http://www.phikappaphi.org

33 • Study Abroad Grants

Purpose: To provide scholarships for undergraduate students who will study abroad.
Eligibility: Applicants do not have to be members of Phi Kappa Phi but must attend an institution with a Phi Kappa Phi chapter, have between 56 and 90 credit hours and have at least two semesters remaining at their home institution upon return. Students must have been accepted into a study abroad program that demonstrates their academic preparation, career choice and the welfare of others.
How to Apply: Applications are available online.
Deadline: February 15.
Amount: $1,000.
Number of Awards: 38.

Horatio Alger Association

Attn.: Scholarship Department
99 Canal Center Plaza
Alexandria, VA 22314
Phone: 703-684-9444
Fax: 703-684-9445
Website: http://www.horatioalger.com

34 • Horatio Alger Association Scholarship Program

Purpose: To assist students who are committed to pursuing a bachelor's degree and have demonstrated integrity, financial need, academic achievement and community involvement.
Eligibility: Applicants must enter college the fall following their high school graduation, be in need of financial aid ($50,000 or less adjusted gross income per family is preferred) and be involved in extracurricular and community activities.
How to Apply: Applications are available online.
Deadline: October 15.
Amount: Varies.
Number of Awards: Varies.

Institute for Humane Studies at George Mason University

3301 N. Fairfax Drive
Suite 440
Arlington, VA 22201
Phone: 800-697-8799
Fax: 703-993-4890
Email: ihs@gmu.edu
Website: http://www.theihs.org

35 • Hayek Fund for Scholars

Purpose: To make awards of up to $1,000 to graduate students and untenured faculty members for career-enhancing activities.
Eligibility: Applicants must be graduate students or untenured faculty members and must submit a cover letter explaining how participation will advance their careers and how their understanding of the classical liberal/libertarian tradition will be broadened. Applicants must also submit an abstract of the paper they are going to present (if applicable), an itemized expense list and resume.
How to Apply: There is no application form.
Deadline: None.
Amount: $1,000.
Number of Awards: Varies.

36 • Humane Studies Fellowships

Purpose: To award scholarships to students who are interested in the classical liberal/libertarian tradition of individual rights and market economies and wish to apply these principles in their work.
Eligibility: Applicants must be one of the following: undergraduates who will be juniors or seniors during the academic year of funding, graduate students who are in any field and at any stage before completion of the Ph.D., law students, MBA students or other professional students. The fellowships can be used for study in the US or abroad. Applicants must also be enrolled as full-time students at an accredited degree-granting institution.
How to Apply: Applications are available online.
Deadline: December 31.
Amount: Up to $12,000.
Number of Awards: Varies.

37 • Summer Graduate Research Fellowships

Purpose: To support graduate students who are interested in scholarly research in the classical liberal tradition.
Eligibility: Applicants must be graduate students in areas related to the classical liberal tradition and should be focusing on a discrete writing project. Selection is based on resume, GRE or LSAT scores

and graduate transcripts, writing sample and research proposal and bibliography for thesis chapter or publishable paper.

How to Apply: Applications are available online.
Deadline: February 15.
Amount: $3,000 + travel allowance.
Number of Awards: Varies.

Jack Kent Cooke Foundation

44325 Woodridge Parkway
Lansdowne, VA 20176
Phone: 800-498-6478
Fax: 703-723-8030
Email: jkc@jackkentcookefoundation.org
Website: http://www.jackkentcookefoundation.org

38 • Graduate Scholarship

Purpose: To help students with academic merit and financial need attend graduate school.

Eligibility: Applicants must be college seniors or recent graduates of an accredited U.S. college or university who plan to attend full-time graduate or professional programs for the first time. Applicants may not apply directly to the foundation but must be nominated by the Jack Kent Cooke Foundation faculty representatives at their institutions. The award is based on academic merit and unmet financial need.

How to Apply: Nomination forms are available online and by phone.
Deadline: May 1.
Amount: $50,000.
Number of Awards: 65.

39 • September 11th Scholarship

Purpose: To help spouses and dependents of those disabled or killed by the September 11 events.

Eligibility: Applicants must currently be enrolled at any two-year, four-year, technical or trade school in the United States; demonstrate financial need and be spouses or dependents of those disabled or killed by the September 11 events: United Airlines Flight 93, American Airlines Flight 77, American Airlines Flight 11, United Airlines Flight 175, World Trade Center, Pentagon or September and October 2001 anthrax attacks. Applications for summer funding must be postmarked by July 7, and applications for fall funding must be postmarked by October 13.

How to Apply: Applications are available online.
Deadline: July 7 and October 13.
Amount: $15,000.
Number of Awards: Varies.

40 • Undergraduate Transfer Scholarship

Purpose: To help community college students attend four-year universities.

Eligibility: Applicants must be students or recent alumni from accredited U.S. community colleges or two-year institutions who plan to pursue bachelor's degrees at four-year institutions. Applicants may not apply directly to the foundation but must be nominated by the Jack Kent Cooke Foundation faculty representatives at their institutions. The award is based on academic merit and unmet financial need.

How to Apply: Nomination forms are available online and by phone.
Deadline: February 1.
Amount: $30,000.
Number of Awards: 35.

Jack Kent Cooke Foundation Young Scholars Program

301 ACT Drive
P.O. Box 4030
Iowa City, IA 52243
Phone: 800-498-6478
Fax: 703-723-8030
Email: jkc@jackkentcookefoundation.org
Website: http://www.jackkentcookefoundation.org

41 • Young Scholars Program

Purpose: To help high-achieving students with financial need and provide them with educational opportunities throughout high school.

Eligibility: Applicants must have financial need, be in the 7th grade and plan to attend high school in the United States. Academic achievement and intelligence are important, and students must display strong academic records, academic awards and honors and a letter of recommendation. The award is also based on students' will to succeed, leadership and public service, critical thinking ability and participation in the arts and humanities. During two summers, recipients must participate in a Young Scholars Week and Young Scholars Reunion in Washington, DC.

How to Apply: Applications are available online and at regional talent centers.
Deadline: May 1.
Amount: Varies.
Number of Awards: 50.

Jaycees

Jaycee War Memorial Fund Scholarships
P.O. Box 7
Tulsa, OK 74102
Phone: 918-584-2481
Fax: 918-584-4422
Email: directorcommunications@usjaycees.org
Website: http://www.usjaycees.org

42 • Jaycees War Memorial Fund Scholarship

Purpose: To assist student leaders with strong academic performance.

Eligibility: Applicants must be U.S. citizens who demonstrate academic promise, leadership ability and financial need.

How to Apply: Applications are available by sending a self-addressed, stamped business-sized envelope and a $5 application fee. This scholarship has been included because it is legitimate. However, we still encourage students to apply for awards without fees.
Deadline: February 1.
Amount: $1,000.
Number of Awards: 25.

Josephine De Karman Fellowship Trust

P.O. Box 3389
San Dimas, CA 91773
Phone: 909-592-0607
Email: info@dekarman.org
Website: http://www.dekarman.org

43 • Josephine De Karman Fellowship

Purpose: To recognize students who demonstrate academic achievement.

Eligibility: Applicants must be undergraduate students entering their senior year or Ph.D. candidates nearing completion of their degree (all requirements except for the dissertation must be completed by January 31). Applicants may not be post-doctoral students. Special consideration is given to doctoral students in the humanities. The award is open to international students living in the U.S.
How to Apply: Applications are available online.
Deadline: January 31.
Amount: $16,000.
Number of Awards: 10.

Kaplan/Newsweek

888 7th Avenue, 22nd floor
New York, NY 10106
Phone: 800-526-2595
Email: classroom.service@newsweek.com
Website: http://www.kaplan.com

44 • "My Turn" Essay Competition

Purpose: To assist high school students who write a personal essay for the publication.
Eligibility: Applicants must be high school students planning to attend a college or university following high school who write a personal essay that shares an opinion or experience. Selection is based on criteria including creativity, organization and effectiveness.
How to Apply: Applications are available online.
Deadline: March 1.
Amount: $1,000-$5,000.
Number of Awards: 10.

Mensa Education & Research Foundation

1229 Corporate Drive West
Arlington, TX 76006-6103
Website: http://www.mensafoundation.org

45 • Mensa Education & Research Foundation Scholarship Program

Purpose: The purpose of the foundation is to "pursue excellence in the areas of intelligence."
Eligibility: Applicants must write an essay, which is used to determine the winners. Grades, academic achievement and financial need are not considered. Students do not need to be members of Mensa.
How to Apply: Application information is available online during the first week of September.
Deadline: January 15.
Amount: $60,000 in total awards.
Number of Awards: Varies.

National Ground Water Association

601 Dempsey Road
Westerville, OH 43081-8978
Phone: 800-551-7379
Fax: 614-898-7786
Email: ngwa@ngwa.org
Website: http://www.ngwa.org

46 • Len Assante Scholarship Fund

Eligibility: Despite being sponsored by a career association, students are not required to be studying any particular field.

Applicants must be high school graduates or college students with a minimum 2.5 GPA.
How to Apply: Applications are available by mail or e-mail.
Deadline: April 1.
Amount: Varies.
Number of Awards: Varies.

National Hook-Up of Black Women Inc.

1809 East 71st Street
Suite 205
Chicago, IL 60649
Phone: 773-667-7061
Fax: 773-667-7064
Email: nhbwdir@aol.com
Website: http://www.nhbwinc.com

47 • Dr. Arnita Young Boswell Scholarship

Purpose: To reward adult students for their academic achievement.
Eligibility: Applicants must be undergraduate or graduate continuing education students. Selection is based on academic accomplishments as well as involvement in school and community activities and an essay.
How to Apply: Applications are available by mail.
Deadline: April 30.
Amount: $1,000.
Number of Awards: Varies.

48 • Dr. Wynetta A. Frazier "Sister to Sister" Scholarship

Purpose: To assist women who are returning to school without the support of a spouse or family.
Eligibility: Applicants may have taken a break in their educations to seek employment, care for their children or because of financial burden.
How to Apply: Applications are available by mail.
Deadline: April.
Amount: $500.
Number of Awards: At least 2.

National Merit Scholarship Corporation

1560 Sherman Avenue, Suite 200
Evanston, IL 60201
Phone: 847-866-5100
Fax: 847-866-5113
Website: http://www.nationalmerit.org

49 • National Merit Scholarship Program and National Achievement Scholarship Program

Purpose: To provide scholarships through a merit-based academic competition.
Eligibility: Applicants must be enrolled full-time in high school, progressing normally toward completion and planning to enter college no later than the fall following completion of high school, be U.S. citizens or permanent legal residents in the process of becoming U.S. citizens and take the PSAT/NMSQT no later than the 11th grade. Participation in the program is based on performance on the exam.
How to Apply: Application is made by taking the PSAT/NMSQT test.
Deadline: Varies.
Amount: Varies.
Number of Awards: Varies.

National Security Agency (NSA)

9800 Savage Road, Suite 6779
Ft. George G. Meade, MD 20755-6779
Phone: 410-854-4725
Website: http://www.nsa.gov/careers/

50 • Stokes Educational Scholarship Program

Purpose: To recruit those with skills useful to the NSA, especially minority high school students.

Eligibility: Students must be seniors at the time of application, be U.S. citizens, have a 3.0 GPA, have a minimum ACT score of 25 or a minimum SAT score of 1600 and demonstrate leadership skills. Applicants must be planning to major in one of the following fields: computer science, electrical or computer engineering, languages, mathematics or intelligence analysis.

How to Apply: Applications are available online.
Deadline: November 30.
Amount: Tuition, fees, salary and summer employment.
Number of Awards: Varies.

Next Step Magazine

86 W. Main Street
Victor, NY 14565
Website: http://www.nextstepmagazine.com

51 • Ultimate Scholarship Giveaway

Purpose: A sweepstakes for scholarship prize money given out by a random drawing from applicants.

Eligibility: The drawing is open to residents of the U.S. or Canada (except for Puerto Rico and Quebec) who are at least 14 and currently in college or will be enrolled in college within the next two years.

How to Apply: Applications are available online.
Deadline: June 20.
Amount: $5,000.
Number of Awards: 1.

No-Addiction Scholarship Essay Campaign

4920 NW 165th Street
Miami, FL 33014
Phone: 800-327-3991
Email: info@no-ad.com
Website: http://www.solarcosmetics.com

52 • No-Addiction Campaign Essay Contest

Purpose: Solar Cosmetics believes in the importance of promoting personal and social responsibility.

Eligibility: Students must write a 300-word essay on why they have chosen to stay free of drugs and alcohol and what they are doing to promote this lifestyle in others.

How to Apply: Applications are available by phone or e-mail.
Deadline: April.
Amount: $500.
Number of Awards: 20.

Parent Answer Scholarship Sweepstakes-- $10,000

P.O. Box 9500
Wilkes-Barre, PA 18773-9500
Website: www.parentanswerservice.com

53 • Parent Answer Scholarship Sweepstakes

Purpose: To support the parents of undergraduate college students.

Eligibility: This $10,000 sweepstakes is open to all U.S. residents who are parents of undergraduate college students. Applicants must have children who are undergraduate students at a Title IV school. The children must be born in 1982 or later.

How to Apply: Applicants may enter the sweepstakes online or by mail.
Deadline: May 30.
Amount: $10,000.
Number of Awards: 1.

Paul and Daisy Soros

400 W. 59th Street
New York, NY 10019
Phone: 212-547-6926
Fax: 212-548-4623
Email: pdsoros_fellows@sorosny.org
Website: http://www.pdsoros.org

54 • Paul and Daisy Soros Fellowships for New Americans

Purpose: Named after Hungarian immigrants, the Paul and Daisy Soros Fellowships are designed to assist the graduate studies of immigrant children.

Eligibility: Applicants must be immigrants who are resident aliens, have been naturalized or are the children of two parents who have been naturalized. The potential winner of a fellowship must already have bachelor's degree or be a college senior and must not be over the age of 30 by the application deadline.

How to Apply: Applications are available online.
Deadline: November 1.
Amount: $20,000.
Number of Awards: 30.

QuestBridge

P.O. Box 20054
Stanford, CA 94309
Phone: 888-275-2054
Fax: 650-653-2516
Website: www.questbridge.org

55 • College Match Program

Purpose: To help low-income students who have academic achievement to find the right college, QuestBridge matches students with the colleges of their choice and provides scholarships.

Eligibility: Applicants should familiarize themselves with the participating colleges' requirements and will be required to answer essay questions. In addition to the application, students must send two teacher recommendations, one counselor recommendation, a transcript, SAT or ACT score reports and a copy of the family tax return. Selected applicants will be required to submit a list of colleges they want to attend and a CSS Profile to those colleges.

How to Apply: Applications are available online.
Deadline: October 1.
Amount: Varies.
Number of Awards: 75.

56 • College Prep Scholarship for High School Juniors

Purpose: To award high school juniors based on academic merit and financial need.

Eligibility: Applicants must submit essays and transcripts. Scholarship packages include one of the following: tuition and room and board for attending the summer school programs of Harvard, Stanford or Yale; SAT prep courses and materials or a computer. Assistance may also include expenses to visit colleges.

How to Apply: Applications are available online.

Deadline: May 15.

Amount: Varies.

Number of Awards: 500.

Rhodes Scholarship Trust

Attn.: Elliot F. Gerson
8229 Boone Boulevard, Suite 240
Vienna, VA 22182
Email: amsec@rhodesscholar.org
Website: http://www.rhodesscholar.org

57 • Rhodes Scholar

Purpose: To recognize qualities of young people that will contribute to the "world's fight."

Eligibility: Applicants must be U.S. citizens between the ages of 18 and 24 and have a bachelor's degree at the time of the award. The awards provides for two to three years of study at the University of Oxford including educational costs and other expenses. Selection is extremely competitive and is based on literary and scholastic achievements, athletic achievement and character.

How to Apply: Applications are available online.

Deadline: October.

Amount: Varies.

Number of Awards: 32.

Rotary International

One Rotary Center
1560 Sherman Avenue
Evanston, IL 60201
Phone: 847-866-3000
Fax: 847-328-8554
Email: scholarshipinquiries@rotaryintl.org
Website: http://www.rotary.org

58 • Cultural Ambassadorial Scholarships

Purpose: The scholarships aims to improve international understanding while encouraging friendly relations between people in different countries.

Eligibility: Students must have completed at least two years of college, including at least one year of college-level study of the focus language. Ideal candidates will have excellent leadership skills, demonstrate academic or vocational success, display a commitment to community service and be willing to fulfill their obligations to Rotary according to the terms of the scholarship. Applicants must be citizens of a country containing Rotary clubs, and applications can only be made through a local Rotary club. Rotarians, direct family members of Rotarians and employees or Rotary International or a Rotary district are not eligible for scholarships.

How to Apply: Applications are available online.

Deadline: Varies by Rotary district.

Amount: Varies.

Number of Awards: Varies.

Sallie Mae Fund, The

Scholarship America
One Scholarship Way
P.O. Box 297
Saint Peter, MN 56082
Phone: 507-931-1682
Website: http://www.thesalliemaefund.org

59 • Unmet Need Scholarship

Purpose: To assist students whose financial aid packages are not enough.

Eligibility: Applicants must have a minimum 2.5 GPA, family incomes of $30,000 or less and financial aid packages with unmet need of $1,000 or more. Applicants must also be accepted or enrolled as full-time undergraduate students at two- or four-year schools in the U.S. or Puerto Rico. The application must include a transcript, Student Aid Report and financial aid award letter from the school the student plans to attend.

How to Apply: Applications are available online.

Deadline: May 31.

Amount: $1,000-$3,800.

Number of Awards: Varies.

Scholarship Experts

Website: http://www.scholarshipexperts.com

60 • Scholarship Experts Scholarship for High School Students

Purpose: To assist high school students pursuing higher education.

Eligibility: Applicants must be students who are planning to graduate from high school in 2007, 2008 or 2009 and are least 13 years of age or older at the time of application.

How to Apply: Applications are available online.

Deadline: April 15.

Amount: $1,000.

Number of Awards: 5.

SuperCollege.com

Scholarship Dept. 673
3286 Oak Court
Belmont, CA 94002
Website: http://www.supercollege.com

61 • SuperCollege.com Student Scholarship

Purpose: Each year SuperCollege.com uses a portion of the proceeds from the sales of its books to award a scholarship to an outstanding high school or college student.

Eligibility: Applicants must be high school students, college undergraduates or graduate students, be U.S. citizens or legal residents and may study any major and attend or plan to attend any accredited college or university in the U.S. Selection is based on academic and extracurricular achievement and an essay.

How to Apply: Applications are only available online. Please do not call or write for an application.

Deadline: July 31.

Amount: $500-$2,500.

Number of Awards: Varies.

Talbots

Scholarship Management Services, Scholarship America
One Scholarship Way
P.O. Box 297
Saint Peter, MN 56082
Phone: 507-931-1682
Website: http://www.talbots.com

62 • Talbots Women's Scholarship Fund

Purpose: To provide scholarships for women returning to college.
Eligibility: Applicants must be female U.S. residents who have earned their high school diploma or GED at least 10 years ago and who are now enrolled or planning to attend undergraduate study at a two- or four-year college or university or vocational-technical school.
How to Apply: Applications are available online.
Deadline: January 15.
Amount: $1,000-$10,000.
Number of Awards: 55.

Telluride Association

217 West Avenue
Ithaca, NY 14850
Phone: 607-273-5011
Fax: 607-272-2667
Email: telluride@cornell.edu
Website: http://www.tellurideassociation.org

63 • Telluride Association Summer Programs

Purpose: Summer program to provide high school students with a college-level, intellectually enriching experience.
Eligibility: Applicants must be high school juniors. The association seeks applicants from a variety of socio-economic backgrounds and provides for their tuition and room and board during summer programs in New York, Texas and Michigan. Students are invited to apply either by receiving a score on the PSAT/NMSQT that is usually in the top 1 percent, or by nomination by a teacher or counselor.
How to Apply: Applications are sent to nominated students.
Deadline: January.
Amount: Varies.
Number of Awards: Varies.

Thomas J. Watson Foundation

810 7th Avenue, 31st Floor
New York, NY 10019
Phone: 212-245-8859
Fax: 212-245-8860
Email: tjw@watsonfellowship.org
Website: http://www.watsonfellowship.org

64 • Watson Travel Fellowship

Purpose: To award one-year grants for independent study and travel outside the U.S. to graduating college seniors.
Eligibility: Applicants must be nominated by participating colleges or universities and submit proposals for a project, personal statements, application forms, photos, transcripts and letters of recommendation. An interview with a representative may follow. Recipients must graduate before the fellowship can begin.

How to Apply: Applicants should contact the local Watson liaison for any local deadlines or additional information.
Deadline: Varies.
Amount: $35,000.
Number of Awards: 50.

U.S. Bank

U.S. Bancorp Center
800 Nicollet Mall
Minneapolis, MN 55402
Phone: 800-242-1200
Website: http://www.usbank.com/studentbanking

65 • U.S. Bank Internet Scholarship Program

Purpose: To support graduating high school seniors who plan to attend college.
Eligibility: Applicants must be high school seniors who plan to attend full-time an accredited two- or four-year college and be U.S. citizens or permanent residents. Recipients are selected through a random drawing.
How to Apply: Applications are only available online.
Deadline: February 28.
Amount: $1,000.
Number of Awards: Varies.

U.S. Department of State

Office of Academic Exchange Programs, Bureau of Educational and Cultural Affairs
U.S. Department of State, SA-44
301 4th Street SW, Room 234
Washington, DC 20547
Phone: 202-619-4360
Fax: 202-401-5914
Email: academic@state.gov
Website: http://exchanges.state.gov

66 • Fulbright Grants

Purpose: To increase the understanding between the people of the United States and the people of other countries.
Eligibility: Applicants must be graduate students, scholars or professionals. Funds are generally used to support students in university teaching, advanced research, graduate study or teaching in elementary and secondary schools.
How to Apply: Applications are available online.
Deadline: Varies.
Amount: Varies.
Number of Awards: 4,500.

USA Today

7950 Jones Branch Drive
McLean, VA 22108
Phone: 703-854-5890
Email: allstars@usatoday.com
Website: http://allstars.usatoday.com

67 • USA Today All-USA Academic Teams

Purpose: To recognize students who excel not only in scholarship but also in leadership roles on and off campus.
Eligibility: Full-time undergraduates at the sophomore level or higher at four-year institutions in the U.S. and its territories are

eligible for the college team. Community and junior college students in the U.S. and its territories are eligible for the two-year college team. Students graduating from a high school in the U.S. and its territories are eligible for the high school team. U.S. citizenship is not required. Special consideration is paid to students' original academic or intellectual product.

How to Apply: Nomination forms are available by telphone or email request.
Deadline: November 30.
Amount: $2,500.
Number of Awards: 20.

Vegetarian Resource Group

P.O. Box 1463
Baltimore, MD 21203
Phone: 410-366-8343
Email: vrg@vrg.org
Website: http://www.vrg.org

68 • VRG Scholarship

Purpose: To award high school seniors who promote vegetarianism.
Eligibility: Applicants must be graduating U.S. high school students who have promoted vegetarianism in their schools or communities. Vegetarians do not eat meat, fish or fowl. The award is based on compassion, courage and commitment to promoting a "peaceful world through a vegetarian diet or lifestyle." Applicants should submit transcripts and at least three recommendations.
How to Apply: Applications are available online, by mail, by phone or by email. A typed document containing the application's information will be accepted.
Deadline: February 20.
Amount: $5,000.
Number of Awards: 2.

Veterans of Foreign Wars

406 W. 34th Street
Kansas City, MO 64111
Phone: 816-968-1117
Fax: 816-968-1149
Email: info@vfw.org
Website: http://www.vfw.org

69 • Voice of Democracy Audio Essay Contests

Purpose: To encourage patriotism with students creating audio essays expressing their opinion on a patriotic theme.
Eligibility: Applicants must submit a three- to five-minute audio essay on tape or CD focused on a yearly theme. Students must be in the 9th to 12th grade in a public, private or parochial high school, home study program or overseas U.S. military school. Foreign exchange students are not eligible for the contest, and students who are age 20 or older also may not enter. Previous first place winners on the state level are ineligible.
How to Apply: Applications are available online but must be submitted to a local VFW post.
Deadline: November 1.
Amount: $1,000-$30,000.
Number of Awards: Varies.

Wachovia Education Finance

P.O. Box 13667
Sacramento, CA 95853
Phone: 877-689-0763
Website: https://educationloans.wachovia.com/web/gimmefive/

70 • Gimme Five Scholarship Sweepstakes

Purpose: To award high school seniors financial aid for their first year at college through a sweepstakes.
Eligibility: Applicants must be high school seniors in the U.S. planning to attend an accredited two or four-year college or trade school. Two awards are given, one on February 1 and one on October 1. Selection is based on random drawing and academic performance and financial need are not taken into consideration.
How to Apply: Applications are available online.
Deadline: October 1.
Amount: $5,000.
Number of Awards: 12.

Wal-Mart Foundation

c/o Scholarship Program Administrators
P.O. Box 22117
Nashville, TN 37202
Phone: 866-851-3372
Fax: 615-523-7100
Website: http://www.walmartfoundation.org

71 • Sam Walton Community Scholarship

Purpose: To support local communities and to help students achieve their educational dreams.
Eligibility: Applicants must be high school seniors. Selection is based on academic record, test scores, community and extracurricular involvement, work experience and financial need. Each Wal-Mart Store and Sam's Club awards up to two scholarships. Wal-Mart employees and the children of employees are not eligible.
How to Apply: Applications are only available at your local Wal-Mart Store or Sam's Club during the first week of December.
Deadline: February 1.
Amount: $1,000.
Number of Awards: 3,000.

Related Scholarships:

Japanese American Citizens League (JACL)

See #1001 · Japanese American Citizens League Entering Freshman Awards

Japanese American Citizens League (JACL)

See #1004 · Japanese American Citizens League Undergraduate Awards

Thurgood Marshall Scholarship Fund

See #1058 · Thurgood Marshall Scholarship Fund Scholarship

U.S. Pan Asian American Chamber of Commerce

See #1059 · Asian American Scholarship Fund

Financial Service Centers of America

See #571 · FiSCA Scholarship

Women's Sports Foundation

See #174 · Linda Riddle/SGMA Scholarship

Coca-Cola Scholars Foundation

See #567 · Coca-Cola Scholars Program

USA Funds

See #577 · USA Funds Access to Education Scholarships

Wendy's Restaurants

See #173 · Wendy's High School Heisman Award

National Beta Club

See #811 · National Beta Club Scholarship

National Honor Society

See #813 · National Honor Society Scholarship

Hispanic Heritage Awards Foundation

See #985 · Hispanic Heritage Youth Awards

Hispanic Scholarship Fund (HSF)

See #987 · College Scholarship Program

Japanese American Citizens League (JACL)

See #999 · Hagiwara Student Aid Award

Alexander Graham Bell Association

See #283 · AG Bell Scholarship Program

John F. Kennedy Library Foundation

See #1184 · John F. Kennedy Profile in Courage Essay Contest

NetAid Foundation

See #926 · Global Action Awards

Mirasol Center for Eating Disorder Recovery

See #1009 · Mirasol's You're Worth It! Scholarship Sweepstakes

Holland and Knight Charitable Foundation

See #1180 · Holocaust Remembrance Project Essay Contest

American Museum of Natural History

See #1118 · Young Naturalist Awards

Veterans of Foreign Wars

See #459 · Patriot's Pen Youth Essay Contest

Nuclear Age Peace Foundation

See #454 · Swackhamer Peace Essay Contest

CosmoGirl!

See #978 · CosmoGirl! Of The Year Award

Accounting/Finance

Also See Scholarships Listed Under:

Business/Management

Mathematics

American Institute Of Certified Public Accountants

American Institute of CPAs--Team 046
1211 Avenue of the Americas
New York, NY 10036-8775
Phone: 212-596-6224
Website: http://www.aicpa.org

72 • Accountemps/American Institute Of Certified Public Accountants Student Scholarship

Purpose: To provide financial assistance to students pursuing careers in business or accounting.

Eligibility: Applicants must be currently enrolled full-time undergraduate or graduate students at an accredited university, major in accounting, finance or information systems, have completed 30 semester or 45 quarter hours with six semester hours in accounting and be AICPA student affiliate members.

How to Apply: Applications are available online.

Deadline: April 1.

Amount: $2,500.

Number of Awards: 2.

Association of Certified Fraud Examiners

Scholarships Program Coordinator
The Gregor Building
716 West Avenue
Austin, TX 78701
Phone: 800-245-3321
Fax: 512-276-8187
Email: memberservices@acfe.com
Website: http://www.cfenet.com

73 • Ritchie-Jennings Memorial Scholarship

Purpose: To support the college education of accounting and criminal justice students who may become Certified Fraud Examiners in the future.

Eligibility: Applicants must be full-time undergraduate or graduate students with a declared major or minor in criminal justice or accounting. Applicants must submit three letters of recommendation, with at least one from a Certified Fraud Examiner or local CFE Chapter and must write an essay on why they deserve the scholarship and how fraud awareness will help their career.

How to Apply: Applications are available online.

Deadline: April 20.

Amount: $1,000.

Number of Awards: Varies.

Educational Foundation for Women in Accounting

P.O. Box 1925
Southeastern, PA 19399
Phone: 610-407-9229
Fax: 610-644-3713
Email: info@efwa.org
Website: http://www.efwa.org

74 • Laurel Fund

Purpose: To provide scholarships to women pursuing advanced degrees in accounting.

Eligibility: This award is available to women pursuing a Ph.D. in accounting. The awardees are selected based on scholarship, service and financial need.

How to Apply: Applications are available online.

Deadline: March 31.

Amount: $1,000-$5,000.

Number of Awards: Varies.

75 • Women in Need Scholarship

Purpose: This scholarship was established to provide financial assistance to female reentry students who are pursuing degrees in accounting.

Eligibility: Applicants must be female students pursuing a degree in accounting. This award is directed toward incoming, current or reentering juniors. Selection criteria include commitment to the study of accounting, accounting aptitude, established goals and financial need.

How to Apply: Applications are available online.

Deadline: April 15.

Amount: $2,000.

Number of Awards: 1.

76 • Women in Transition Scholarship

Purpose: This scholarship was established to provide financial assistance to female reentry students who are pursuing degrees in accounting.

Eligibility: Applicants must be female students pursuing a degree in accounting. The award is directed toward incoming, current or reentering freshmen. Selection criteria include commitment to the study of accounting, aptitude, and financial need.

How to Apply: Applications are available online.

Deadline: April 15.

Amount: $4,000.

Number of Awards: 1.

Institute of Management Accountants (IMA)

10 Paragon Drive
Montvale, NJ 07645-1760
Phone: 800-638-4427
Email: students@imanet.org
Website: http://www.imanet.org

77 • IMA Memorial Education Fund Scholarship

Purpose: To support students in fields related to management accounting.

Eligibility: Applicants must be full- and part-time undergraduate and graduate students, be IMA student members and declare which four- or five-year management accounting, financial management or information technology related program they plan to pursue as a career or list a related field. Candidates should submit applications, resumes, transcripts, two recommendations and statements. Advanced degree students must pass one part of the CMA/CFM certification.

How to Apply: Applications are available online.
Deadline: February 15.
Amount: $2,500.
Number of Awards: Varies.

78 • Stuart Cameron and Margaret McLeod Memorial Scholarship

Purpose: To help management accounting students.

Eligibility: Applicants must be full- and part-time undergraduate and graduate students, be IMA student members and declare which four- or five-year management accounting, financial management or information technology related program they plan to pursue as a career or list a related field. Candidates should submit applications, resumes, transcripts, two recommendations and statements. Advanced degree students must pass one part of the CMA/CFM certification.

How to Apply: Applications are available online.
Deadline: February 15.
Amount: $5,000.
Number of Awards: 1.

National Conference of CPA Practitioners NCCPAP Scholarship

Attention: Scholarship Committee
22 Jericho Turnpike, Suite 110
Mineola, NY 11501
Phone: 888-488-5400
Email: lanak.nccpap@verizon.net
Website: http://www.nccpap.org

79 • NCCPAP Scholarship

Purpose: To assist future certified public accountants.

Eligibility: Applicants must be graduating high school seniors with a minimum GPA of 3.3 planning to become certified public accountants. They must be full-time students applying to or accepted at a two- or four-year college.

How to Apply: Applications are available online.
Deadline: May 1.
Amount: $1,000.
Number of Awards: Varies.

National Society of Accountants Scholarship Program

Scholarship America
One Scholarship Way
P.O. Box 297
Saint Peter, MN 56082
Phone: 507-931-1682
Website: http://www.nsacct.org

80 • Charles Earp Memorial Scholarship

Purpose: To provide financial assistance to college students majoring in accounting. The Charles Earp Memorial Scholarship is awarded to the most outstanding applicant in the larger scholarship competition.

Eligibility: Applicants must be U.S. or Canadian citizens enrolled in an accredited college or university in the United States and have a GPA of 3.0 or better. Students in two-year and four-year programs are eligible. Scholarships are awarded on the basis of academics, leadership, honors, participation in school and community events, work experience, goals, unusual family or personal circumstances and an outside evaluation. Applicants must demonstrate financial need.

How to Apply: Applications are available online.
Deadline: March 10.
Amount: $700-$1,200+plaque.
Number of Awards: 1.

81 • NSA Scholarship Foundation

Purpose: To support students entering the accounting profession.

Eligibility: Applicants must be undergraduate students majoring in accounting with a minimum 3.0 GPA and be U.S. or Canadian citizens.

How to Apply: Applications are available online.
Deadline: March 10.
Amount: $500-$2,000.
Number of Awards: Varies.

Related Scholarships:

BI-LO Corporation

See #1528 • *BI-LO Minority Scholarship Program*

National Association of Black Accountants

See #1017 • *National Association of Black Accountants Scholarship Program*

Financial Markets Center

See #206 • *Henry B. Gonzalez Award*

Cargill

See #966 • *United Negro College Fund Cargill Scholarship-Internship Program*

Hispanic Scholarship Fund (HSF)

See #990 • *HSF/General Motors Scholarship*

Association of Government Accountants (AGA)

See #200 • *AGA Scholarships*

United Negro College Fund (UNCF)

See #1078 • *Citigroup Fellows Program*

Aerospace/Aviation

Also See Scholarships Listed Under:
Engineering
Mathematics

Air Traffic Control Association

Attn.: Scholarship Fund
1101 King Street, Suite 300
Alexandria, VA 22134
Phone: 703-299-2430
Fax: 703-299-2437
Email: info@atca.org
Website: http://www.atca.org

82 • Air Traffic Control Association Scholarship Program

Purpose: To assist students enrolled in aviation-related courses and full-time air traffic control employees and their children.

Eligibility: Applicants must be enrolled or accepted into an accredited college or university and have coursework leading to a bachelor's or graduate degree related to an aviation related career, be full-time aviation employees pursuing advanced study in air traffic control or aviation or be the children of air traffic control specialists.

How to Apply: Applications are available online.
Deadline: May 1.
Amount: $1,500-$2,500.
Number of Awards: Varies.

Aircraft Electronics Association

4217 S. Hocker
Independence, MO 64055
Phone: 816-373-6565
Fax: 816-478-3100
Email: info@aea.net
Website: http://www.aea.net

83 • Bud Glover Memorial Scholarship

Purpose: To support students who wish to pursue a career in avionics and aircraft repair.

Eligibility: Applicants must be high school seniors or college students who plan to or are attending an accredited school in an avionics or aircraft repair program.

How to Apply: Applications are available by contacting the organization for more information.
Deadline: February 15.
Amount: $1,000.
Number of Awards: 1.

84 • David Arver Memorial Scholarship

Purpose: To support students who wish to pursue a career in avionics or aircraft repair.

Eligibility: Applicants must be high school seniors or college students who plan to or are attending an accredited school in an avionics or aircraft repair program.

How to Apply: Applications are available by contacting the organization for more information.
Deadline: February 15.
Amount: $1,000.
Number of Awards: 1.

85 • Dutch and Ginger Arver Scholarship

Purpose: To support students who wish to pursue a career in avionics or aircraft repair.

Eligibility: Applicants must be high school seniors or college students who plan to or are attending an accredited school in avionics or aircraft repair.

How to Apply: Applications are available by contacting the organization for more information.
Deadline: February 15.
Amount: $1,000.
Number of Awards: 1.

86 • Garmin Scholarship

Purpose: To support students who wish to pursue a career in avionics and aircraft repair.

Eligibility: Applicants must be high school seniors or college students who plan to or are attending an accredited school in an avionics or aircraft repair program.

How to Apply: Applications are available online.
Deadline: February 15.
Amount: $2,000.
Number of Awards: 1.

87 • Johnny Davis Memorial Scholarship

Purpose: To support students of avionics and aircraft repair.

Eligibility: Applicants must be high school seniors or college students who plan to or are attending an accredited school in an avionics or aircraft repair program.

How to Apply: Applications are available by contacting the organization for more information.
Deadline: February 15.
Amount: $1,000.
Number of Awards: 1.

88 • Lee Tarbox Memorial Scholarship

Purpose: To support students of avionics and aircraft repair.

Eligibility: Applicants must be high school seniors or college students who plan to or are attending an accredited school in an avionics or aircraft repair program.

How to Apply: Applications are available by contacting the organization for more information.
Deadline: February 15.
Amount: $2,500.
Number of Awards: 1.

89 • Lowell Gaylor Memorial Scholarship

Purpose: To support students of avionics and aircraft repair.

Eligibility: Applicants must be high school seniors or college students who plan to or are attending an accredited school in an avionics or aircraft repair program.

How to Apply: Applications are available by contacting the organization for more information.
Deadline: February 15.
Amount: $1,000.
Number of Awards: 1.

90 • Mid-Continent Instrument Scholarship

Purpose: To support students who wish to pursue a career in avionics or aircraft repair.

Eligibility: Applicants must be high school seniors or college students who plan to or are attending an accredited school in an avionics or aircraft repair program.

How to Apply: Applications are available by contacting the organization for more information.
Deadline: February 15.
Amount: $1,000.
Number of Awards: 1.

American Association of Airport Executives

601 Madison Street
Alexandria, VA 22314
Phone: 703-824-0500
Fax: 703-820-1395
Email: member.services@aaae.org
Website: http://www.aaae.org

91 • AAAE Foundation Scholarship

Purpose: To support students of aviation.
Eligibility: Applicants must be enrolled in an aviation program with at least junior standing and at least a 3.0 GPA for a chance at 10 of the scholarships. Applicants must be pursuing any degree and be recommended by an active AAAE member for a chance at the remaining 15 scholarships.
How to Apply: Applicants should email the organization for more information.
Deadline: May 31.
Amount: $1,000.
Number of Awards: 25.

American Historical Association

400 A Street SE
Washington, DC 20003
Phone: 202-544-2422
Fax: 202-544-8307
Email: info@historians.org
Website: http://www.historians.org

92 • Fellowship in Aerospace History

Purpose: To provide funding for an academic research project related to aerospace history.
Eligibility: Applicants must possess a doctorate degree in history or a related field or be enrolled in a doctorate program (all coursework completed). One fellow will be appointed for one academic year. The fellow will be expected to write a report and present a paper or lecture on the research at the end of the term.
How to Apply: Applications are available online.
Deadline: March 1.
Amount: $20,000.
Number of Awards: 1.

American Institute of Aeronautics and Astronautics

1801 Alexander Bell Drive
Suite 500
Reston, VA 20191-4344
Phone: 800-639-AIAA
Fax: 703-264-7551
Email: stephenb@aiaa.org
Website: http://www.aiaa.org

93 • AIAA Foundation Undergraduate Scholarship Program

Purpose: AIAA advances the arts, sciences and technology of aeronautics and astronautics.
Eligibility: Applicants must be enrolled in an accredited college or university and have completed at least one semester or quarter of college work with a minimum 3.3 GPA. Applicants must plan to enter a career in science or engineering related to the technical activities of the AIAA. Selection is based on scholarship, career goals, recommendations and extracurricular activities.
How to Apply: Applications are available online.
Deadline: January 31.
Amount: $2,000-$2,500.
Number of Awards: 30.

AOPA Air Safety Foundation

421 Aviation Way
Frederick, MD 21701
Phone: 301-695-2000
Fax: 301-695-2375
Email: aopahq@aopa.org
Website: http://www.aopa.org

94 • Donald Burnside Memorial Scholarship

Purpose: To assist students in non-engineering aviation programs.
Eligibility: Applicants must be college juniors or seniors and have at least one semester or quarter to be completed, have a minimum 3.25 GPA and be enrolled in a baccalaureate level, non-engineering aviation degree program at a four-year institution. Applicants must also submit an essay on a topic provided on the website.
How to Apply: Applications are available online.
Deadline: March 31.
Amount: $1,000.
Number of Awards: 1.

95 • McAllister Memorial Scholarship

Purpose: To assist students in non-engineering aviation programs.
Eligibility: Applicants must be college juniors or seniors and have at least one semester or quarter to be completed, have a minimum 3.25 GPA and be enrolled in a baccalaureate level, non-engineering aviation degree program at a four-year institution. Applicants must also submit an essay on a topic posted on the website.
How to Apply: Applications are available online.
Deadline: March 31.
Amount: $1,000.
Number of Awards: 1.

EAA Aviation Center

P.O. Box 2683
Oshkosh, WI 54903
Phone: 877-806-8902
Fax: 920-426-6865
Email: scholarships@eaa.org
Website: http://www.youngeagles.org

96 • David Alan Quick Scholarship

Purpose: To support students in aerospace or aeronautical engineering.
Eligibility: Applicants must be in their junior or senior year at an accredited college or university pursuing a degree in aerospace or

aeronautical engineering. Applicants must be involved in school and community activities as well as aviation.

How to Apply: Applications are available online.

Deadline: March 30.

Amount: $1,000.

Number of Awards: 1.

97 • EAA Aviation Achievement Scholarship

Purpose: Presented by EAA to deserving students active in recreational aviation endeavors.

Eligibility: Applicants must be pursuing further aviation education or training. Applicants must also be involved in school and community activities as well as aviation. Applicants must pay a $5 application fee. This award has been included because it is from a legitimate organization. However, we encourage students to apply for scholarships without fees.

How to Apply: Applications are available online.

Deadline: March 30.

Amount: $500.

Number of Awards: 2.

98 • H.P. Milligan Aviation Scholarship

Purpose: To support excellence among individuals studying aviation.

Eligibility: Applicants must be enrolled in an accredited college, aviation academy or technical school pursuing a course of study focusing on aviation. Applicants must also be involved in school and community activities as well as aviation.

How to Apply: Applications are available online.

Deadline: March 30.

Amount: $1,000.

Number of Awards: 1.

99 • Hansen Scholarship

Purpose: To support excellence among individuals studying the technologies and the skills needed in the field of aviation.

Eligibility: Applicants must be enrolled in an accredited college or university pursuing a degree in aerospace engineering or aeronautical engineering and must be involved in school and community activities as well as aviation. Applicants must be in good academic standing. Financial need will be considered.

How to Apply: Applications are available online.

Deadline: March 30.

Amount: $1,000.

Number of Awards: 1.

100 • Herbert L. Cox Memorial Scholarship

Purpose: To support aviation students.

Eligibility: Applicants must be enrolled in an accredited college or university pursuing a course of study focusing on aviation and involved in school and community activities as well as aviation. Recipient of award must show need for financial support.

How to Apply: Applications are available online.

Deadline: March 30.

Amount: $500.

Number of Awards: 1.

101 • Payzer Scholarship

Purpose: To support students interested in technical careers.

Eligibility: Applicants must be accepted or enrolled in an accredited college or university with an emphasis on technical information and must intend to pursue a career in engineering, mathematics or the physical or biological sciences. Applicants must also be involved in school and community activities as well as aviation.

How to Apply: Applications are available online.

Deadline: March 30.

Amount: $5,000.

Number of Awards: 1.

National Air Transportation Foundation

Pioneers of Flight Scholarship Program, Attn.: Professor Gregory Schwab, Chair

Department of Aerospace Technology, TC 216

Indiana State University

Terre Haute, IN 47809

Email: aeschwab@isugw.indstate.edu

Website: http://www.nata.aero

102 • Pioneers of Flight

Purpose: To assist students pursuing general aviation as a career.

Eligibility: Applicants must be full-time students at an accredited four-year institution, be sophomores or juniors at the time of application and plan to pursue a career in aviation.

How to Apply: Applications are available online.

Deadline: Last Friday in December.

Amount: $1,000.

Number of Awards: 2.

National Air Transportation Foundation Meisinger Scholarship

4226 King Street

Alexandria, VA 22302

Phone: 703-845-9000

Fax: 703-845-8176

Website: http://www.nata.aero

103 • Dan L. Meisinger Sr. Memorial Learn to Fly Scholarship

Purpose: To provide an annual flight training scholarship.

Eligibility: Applicants must be enrolled in an aviation program with a B or better GPA and be a resident of Kansas, Missouri or Illinois. Students should be recommended by an aviation professional; independent applications are also considered.

How to Apply: Applications are available online.

Deadline: Last Friday in November.

Amount: $2,500.

Number of Awards: Varies.

University Aviation Association (UAA)

3410 Skyway Drive

Auburn, AL 36830

Phone: 334-844-2434

Fax: 334-844-2432

Website: http://www.uaa.aero

104 • Eugene S. Kropf Scholarship

Purpose: To support students studying an aviation-related curriculum.

Eligibility: Applicants must be U.S. citizens enrolled in an aviation-related curriculum at a UAA member college or university. Students must have a 3.0 GPA and write a 250-word paper on how they can improve aviation education.

How to Apply: Applications are available online.

Deadline: May 31.

Amount: $500.

Number of Awards: 1.

105 • Gary Kiteley Executive Director Scholarship

Purpose: To support aviation students at UAA institutions.
Eligibility: Applicants must be enrolled at a UAA member college or university in an aviation-related curriculum.
How to Apply: Contact the UAA for information.
Deadline: Varies.
Amount: $500.
Number of Awards: 1.

106 • Joseph Frasca Excellence in Aviation Scholarship

Purpose: To encourage students to reach the highest level of achievement in their aviation studies.
Eligibility: Applicants must be juniors or seniors enrolled at a UAA member college or university with at least a 3.0 GPA. Students must demonstrate excellence in all areas related to aviation and have FAA certification in either aviation maintenance or flight. Applicants must be a member of at least one aviation organization and be involved in aviation activities that demonstrate interest in and enthusiasm for aviation.
How to Apply: Applications are available online.
Deadline: April 9.
Amount: $1,000.
Number of Awards: 2.

Vertical Flight Foundation

217 N. Washington Street
Alexandria, VA 22314
Phone: 703-684-6777
Fax: 703-739-9279
Email: staff@vtol.org
Website: http://www.vtol.org

107 • Vertical Flight Foundation Engineering Scholarships

Purpose: The Vertical Flight Foundation was founded to support the education in rotorcraft and vertical-takeoff-and-landing aircraft engineering.
Eligibility: Applicants must be full-time students at accredited schools of engineering and submit a transcript with an academic endorsement from a professor or dean. Applicants need not be members of AHS.
How to Apply: Applications are available online.
Deadline: February 1.
Amount: $2,000-$4,000.
Number of Awards: Varies.

Related Scholarships:

Astronaut Scholarship Foundation

See #1128 • Astronaut Scholarship

Armed Forces Communications and Electronics Association

See #705 • AFCEA General Emmett Paige Scholarships

Armed Forces Communications and Electronics Association

See #253 • AFCEA General John A. Wickham Scholarships

Armed Forces Communications and Electronics Association

See #706 • AFCEA ROTC Scholarships

Armed Forces Communications and Electronics Association

See #254 • AFCEA Ralph W. Shrader Scholarships

Academia Resource Management

See #1110 • ARM Undergraduate Student Fellowships

Agriculture/Horticulture/ Animals

Also See Scholarships Listed Under:
Biological Sciences/Life Sciences
Forestry/Wildlife

American Foundation

3201 Frederick Avenue
St. Joseph, MO 64506
Phone: 816-383-5100
Fax: 816-233-9703
Email: angus@angus.org
Website: http://www.angusfoundation.org

108 • Angus Foundation Scholarship

Purpose: To provide scholarships to youth active in the Angus breed.

Eligibility: Applicants must have been members of the National Junior Angus Association and must be junior, regular or life members of the American Angus Association at the time of application. Applicants must be high school seniors or enrolled in a junior college, four-year college, or other accredited institution of post-secondary education in an undergraduate program and have a minimum 2.0 GPA. Students may not have reached their 25th birthday by January 1 of the year of application.

How to Apply: Applications are available online or by written request.

Deadline: May 1.

Amount: $1,000-$5,000.

Number of Awards: 52.

American Kennel Club

260 Madison Avenue
New York, NY 10016
Phone: 212-696-8200
Website: http://www.akc.org

109 • Junior Scholarship Program

Purpose: To assist students who are involved with AKC purebred dogs.

Eligibility: Applicants must be under age 18 with an AKC registered purebred dog. Selection is based on involvement with AKC registered dogs, academic achievement and financial need. The scholarship program awards a total of $150,000 annually.

How to Apply: Applications are available online.

Deadline: February 20.

Amount: Varies.

Number of Awards: Varies.

American Nursery and Landscape Association

Horticultural Research Institute
1000 Vermont Avenue NW
Suite 300
Washington, DC 20005
Phone: 202-789-5980 x3014
Fax: 202-789-1893
Email: tjodon@anla.org
Website: http://www.anla.org

110 • Carville M. Akehurst Memorial Scholarship

Purpose: To provide scholarships for undergraduate and graduate students who plan to pursue careers in horticulture.

Eligibility: Applicants must be enrolled full-time in a landscaping or horticultural program at a two- or four-year accredited institution and be residents of Maryland, Virginia or West Virginia.

How to Apply: Applications are available online.

Deadline: April 1.

Amount: $1,000.

Number of Awards: 1.

111 • Spring Meadow Nursery Scholarship

Purpose: To help students obtain a degree in horticulture.

Eligibility: Applicants must be enrolled full-time in an undergraduate or graduate landscape horticultural or related program at a two- or four-year accredited institution. Preference is given to those who plan to pursue a career in horticulture.

How to Apply: Applications are available online.

Deadline: April 1.

Amount: Varies.

Number of Awards: Varies.

112 • Timothy Bigelow and Palmer W. Bigelow, Jr. Scholarship

Purpose: To help students from New England who want to pursue a career in horticulture.

Eligibility: Applicants must be seniors in a two-year course and have finished the first year, juniors in a four-year course and have finished the first two years or be graduate students. Undergraduates must have a minimum 2.25 GPA and graduate students a minimum 3.0 GPA. Students must be from Connecticut, Maine, Massachusetts, New Hampshire, Rhode Island or Vermont.

How to Apply: Applications are available online.

Deadline: April 1.

Amount: $2,500.

Number of Awards: 3.

113 • Usrey Family Scholarship

Purpose: To help students who are seeking careers in horticulture.

Eligibility: Applicants must be in an undergraduate or graduate landscape horticulture program or related field at a two or four-year California state university or college. Applicants must also be current, full-time students, academically competitive and have a minimum 2.25 GPA and a minimum 2.7 GPA in the major.

How to Apply: Applications are available online.

Deadline: April 1.

Amount: Varies.

Number of Awards: Varies.

American Quarter Horse Foundation

Attn.: Scholarship Coordinator
2601 I-40 East
Amarillo, TX 79104
Phone: 806-378-5034
Fax: 806-376-1005
Email: lowens@aqha.org
Website: http://www.aqha.com

114 • American Quarter Horse Foundation Scholarship

Purpose: To encourage future Quarter Horse industry professionals.

Eligibility: Applicants must demonstrate involvement in equine-related activities and be members of American Quarter Horse Association (AQHA) or American Quarter Horse Youth Association (AQHYA) for up to three years, depending on the scholarship. Selection is based on financial need, academic achievement, equine involvement, references and career plans. A transcript and three references are required for all scholarships. All other requirements vary by scholarship.

How to Apply: Applications are available online.

Deadline: January 2.

Amount: $8,000.

Number of Awards: 30.

American Saddlebred Horse Association Foundation

4083 Iron Works Parkway
Lexington, KY 40511
Phone: 859-259-2742 x343
Fax: 859-259-1628
Website: http://www.saddlebred.com

115 • ASHA Youth Scholarships

Purpose: To help youths involved with Saddlebreds.

Eligibility: This award is based on academic excellence, financial need, extracurricular activities, community service, involvement with American Saddlebred horses and personal references. An interview may be part of the selection process. Applicants should write an essay about school experiences, special interests, hobbies and American Saddlebred Horse Association activities. Scholarships are given only to high school seniors or recent graduates.

How to Apply: Applications are available online.

Deadline: April 30.

Amount: $5,000.

Number of Awards: Varies.

American Society for Enology and Viticulture

P.O. Box 1855
Davis, CA 95617-1855
Phone: 530-753-3142
Fax: 530-753-3318
Email: society@asev.org
Website: http://www.asev.org

116 • ASEV Scholarships

Purpose: To support those seeking a degree in enology, viticulture or in a curriculum focusing on a science basic to the wine and grape industry.

Eligibility: Applicants must be undergraduate or graduate students enrolled in or accepted into a full-time accredited four-year university program, must reside in North America (Canada, Mexico or the U.S.) and must be at least juniors for the upcoming academic year. Undergraduate students must have a minimum 3.0 GPA, and graduate students must have a minimum 3.2 GPA. Applicants must be enrolled in a major or in a graduate group concentrating on enology or viticulture or in a curriculum with a focus on a science basic to the wine and grape industry. The application, transcripts and two letters of recommendation are required.

How to Apply: Applications are available online, by phone or by email.

Deadline: March 1.

Amount: Varies.

Number of Awards: Varies.

Appaloosa Horse Club

Appaloosa Youth Foundation Scholarship Committee
2720 W. Pullman Road
Moscow, ID 83843
Phone: 208-882-5578
Fax: 208-882-8150
Email: acaap@appaloosa.com
Website: http://www.appaloosa.com

117 • Appaloosa Youth Association Art Contest

Purpose: To allow students to showcase their artistic talents with Appaloosa-themed projects.

Eligibility: Applicants age 18 and under should submit drawings, paintings and hand-built ceramics or sculptures with the Appaloosa theme. There are two age divisions: 13 and under and 14 to 18. Awards are based on orginality, creativity and the theme.

How to Apply: Applications are available online.

Deadline: May 1.

Amount: $250.

Number of Awards: Varies.

118 • Appaloosa Youth Association Essay Contest

Purpose: To reward students for essays that demonstrate their love of the Appaloosa breed.

Eligibility: Applicants must be 18 and under and should submit entry forms and essays on the provided themes. There are two age divisions: 13 and under and 14 to 18. Awards are based on originality and accuracy.

How to Apply: Applications are available online.

Deadline: May 1.

Amount: $250.

Number of Awards: Varies.

119 • Appaloosa Youth Association Junior Journalist Contest

Purpose: To encourage students to become familiar with the Appaloosa industry.

Eligibility: Applicants must be current AYA members and aspiring writers between the ages of 14 and 18 who would like to report on news related to the AYA and the World Championship Appaloosa Youth Show. Applicants must submit an application and essay.

How to Apply: Applications are available online.

Deadline: April 1.

Amount: Varies.

Number of Awards: Varies.

120 • Appaloosa Youth Association Speech Contest

Purpose: To reward students for their speeches on Appaloosa.

Eligibility: Applicants should be 18 and under and can enter two divisions: a speech on a pre-determined topic or an impromptu speech. Age groups are 13 and under and 14 to 18. The speech is given at the World Championship Appaloosa Youth World Show.

How to Apply: Applications are available online.
Deadline: June 1.
Amount: $250.
Number of Awards: Varies.

121 • Larry Williams Photography and AYA Photo Contest

Purpose: To support students who express their love of the Appaloosa through photography.
Eligibility: Applicants must submit multiple photographs in three divisions: 13 and under, 14 to 18 and 4H/FFA youths 18 and under.
How to Apply: Applications are available online.
Deadline: May 1.
Amount: $150.
Number of Awards: 9.

122 • Youth Program

Purpose: To reward student members of the Appaloosa Youth Association or the Appaloosa Horse Club who are pursuing higher education.
Eligibility: Applicants must be members of the Appaloosa Youth Association or the Appaloosa Horse Club and must attend or plan to attend an institute of higher learning.
How to Apply: Applications are available online.
Deadline: June 10.
Amount: $1,000-$2,000.
Number of Awards: 9.

Floriculture Industry Research and Scholarship Trust

P.O. Box 280
East Lansing, MI 48826
Phone: 517-333-4617
Fax: 517-333-4494
Email: scholarship@firstinfloriculture.org
Website: http://www.firstinfloriculture.org

123 • FIRST Scholarship

Purpose: To promote the floriculture industry by assisting qualified students with education expenses.
Eligibility: Applicants must be high school senior, college undergraduate, vocational or graduate students pursuing a horticulture-related field. Applicants must also have a minimum 3.0 GPA or outstanding extracurricular activities and be U.S. citizens or residents or Canadian citizens.
How to Apply: Applications are available online.
Deadline: May 1.
Amount: $500-$2,000.
Number of Awards: 25.

Golf Course Superintendents Association of America Foundation

GCSAA Career Development Department
GCSAA Scholars Competition
1421 Research Park Drive
Lawrence, KS 66049
Phone: 800-472-7878
Email: infobox@gcsaa.org
Website: http://www.gcsaa.org

124 • GCSAA Scholars Program

Purpose: To recognize outstanding students who plan careers in golf course management or a related field.
Eligibility: Applicants must be GCSAA members who are enrolled in an undergraduate turf management program or related field and have completed their first year or 24 credit hours.
How to Apply: Applications are available by contacting Pam Smith, 800-472-7878 x3678.
Deadline: June 1.
Amount: $500-$6,000.
Number of Awards: Varies.

125 • GCSAA Student Essay Contest

Purpose: To support students pursuing degrees in golf course management.
Eligibility: Applicants must be undergraduate or graduate students pursuing degrees in turfgrass science, agronomy or any other golf course management-related field. Applicants must be members of GCSAA and write an essay on golf course management.
How to Apply: Applications are available by contacting Pam Smith, 800-472-7878 x3678.
Deadline: March 31.
Amount: Varies.
Number of Awards: Varies.

126 • Scotts Company Scholars Program

Purpose: To offer monetary assistance for postsecondary education to a students from diverse cultural and socioeconomic backgrounds.
Eligibility: Applicants must be graduating high school seniors or college freshmen, sophomores or juniors who have been accepted at a two-year or longer program and must be pursuing a career in the green industry.
How to Apply: Applications are available by contacting Pam Smith, 800-472-7878 x3678.
Deadline: March 1.
Amount: $500-$2,500.
Number of Awards: 7.

Harness Tracks of America

4640 E. Sunrise, Suite 200
Tucson, AZ 85718
Phone: 520-529-2525
Fax: 520-529-3235
Email: info@harnesstracks.com
Website: http://www.harnesstracks.com

127 • Harness Tracks of America Scholarship Fund

Purpose: To provide assistance to students who are involved in the harness racing industry.
Eligibility: Applicants must have a parent or parents involved in harness racing or must be active in the business. Applicants must also demonstrate active merit or financial need.
How to Apply: Applications are available by telephone.
Deadline: Varies.
Amount: $7,500.
Number of Awards: 6.

Humane Society of the United States

New England Regional Office
P.O. Box 619
Jacksonville, VT 05342
Phone: 802-368-2790
Fax: 802-368-2756
Email: nero@hsus.org
Website: http://www.hsus.org

128 • Shaw-Worth Memorial Scholarship

Purpose: To recognize a New England high school senior who has made a meaningful contribution to animal protection over a significant period of time.

Eligibility: Applicants must be high school seniors in a New England public, private, parochial or vocational school. Awards are based on the work the applicants have done on behalf of animals, such as inspiring leadership in animal protection organizations or presentations on humane topics. Neither scholastic standing nor financial need are considered. No application is required, only a narrative about the applicants' achievements in animal protection.

How to Apply: Submit materials to the address listed.
Deadline: March 15.
Amount: $1,500.
Number of Awards: 1.

Institute of Food Technologists (IFT)

525 W. Van Buren
Suite 1000
Chicago, IL 60607
Phone: 312-782-8424
Email: ejplummer@ift.org
Website: http://www.ift.org

129 • Freshman and Sophomore Scholarships

Purpose: To help young food scientists who plan to work in industry, government and academia.

Eligibility: Applicants for the freshman scholarships must be academically outstanding high school graduates or seniors who will enter college for the first time in an approved program in food science/technology. The deadline is February 15. Applicants for the sophomore scholarships must be academically outstanding college freshman with a minimum 2.5 GPA in an approved program in food science/technology. The deadline is March 1. All candidates must submit applications, transcripts and a recommendation.

How to Apply: Applications are available online.
Deadline: February 15 for freshmen and March 1 for sophomores.
Amount: $1,500.
Number of Awards: 46.

130 • Graduate Fellowships

Purpose: To award graduate students researching food science or technology.

Eligibility: Applicants should be graduate students pursuing an M.S. and/or Ph.D. at the time the fellowship becomes effective and should research an area of food science or technology. Applications, transcripts and three recommendation letters are required.

How to Apply: Applications are available online.
Deadline: February 1.
Amount: $5,000.
Number of Awards: Varies.

131 • Junior and Senior Scholarships

Purpose: To encourage undergraduate students in food science or technology.

Eligibility: Applicants must be college sophomores, juniors or seniors pursuing an approved program in food science or food technology. Applications, transcripts and a recommendation letter are required.

How to Apply: Applications are available online.
Deadline: February 1.
Amount: $2,500.
Number of Awards: 62.

National Council of Farmer Cooperatives

50 F Street NW
Suite 900
Washington, DC 20001
Phone: 202-626-8700
Fax: 202-626-8722
Website: http://www.ncfc.org

132 • W. Malcolm Harding Scholarship, Philip F. French Scholarship and Owen Hallberg Scholarship

Purpose: To aid students in the pursuit of education on farmer cooperative topics.

Eligibility: Applicants must be nominated by their college or university department or local cooperative, and have an interest in the cooperative form of business. In addition, four undergraduate awards of $200 each will be awarded to junior and senior students of a college or university, or second year students of junior colleges or technical institute. Papers must be submitted through a college or university instructor.

How to Apply: Applications will be mailed upon receipt of nomination forms.
Deadline: April 1 and June 1.
Amount: $200-$1,000.
Number of Awards: 7.

National Dairy Shrine

1224 Alton Darby Creek Road
Columbus, OH 43228
Phone: 614-878-5333
Fax: 614-870-2622
Email: shrine@cobaselect.com
Website: http://www.dairyshrine.org

133 • Dairy Student Recognition Program

Purpose: To recognize graduating seniors planning careers related to dairy-production agriculture.

Eligibility: Applicants must be high school seniors planning to enter the field of dairy-production agriculture.

How to Apply: Applications are available online.
Deadline: March 15.
Amount: $500-$1,500.
Number of Awards: 9.

134 • Klussendorf Scholarship

Purpose: To honor students in dairy husbandry fields.

Eligibility: Applicants must be first, second, or third year college students at two- or four-year universities, must major in a dairy husbandry field and plan to enter the dairy field.

How to Apply: Applications are available online.
Deadline: March 15.
Amount: $1,000.
Number of Awards: 2.

135 • Marshall E. McCullough Scholarship

Purpose: To support students who plan careers in agricultural-related communications.
Eligibility: Applicants must be high school seniors planning to enter a four-year university with intent to major in the dairy or animal sciences with a communications emphasis or agricultural journalism with a dairy or animal science emphasis.
How to Apply: Applications are available online.
Deadline: March 15.
Amount: Varies.
Number of Awards: 2.

136 • Milk Marketing Scholarship

Purpose: To encourage students to pursue careers in the marketing of dairy goods.
Eligibility: Applicants must be second, third, or fourth year college students at two- or four-year universities, have a minimum 2.5 GPA and major in dairy science, animal science, agricultural communications, agricultural education, general agriculture or food and nutrition.
How to Apply: Applications are available online.
Deadline: March 15.
Amount: $500-$1,000.
Number of Awards: 11.

National FFA Organization

P.O. Box 68960
6060 FFA Drive
Indianapolis, IN 46268-0960
Phone: 317-802-6060
Fax: 317-802-6061
Email: scholarships@ffa.org
Website: http://www.ffa.org

137 • National FFA College and Vocational/Technical School Scholarship Program

Purpose: The scholarship program supports FFA members and agriculture.
Eligibility: FFA awards more than $2 million in scholarships. The programs have various eligibility requirements and award amounts. Applicants must be U.S. citizens and high school seniors or current college students. For some awards, students must be FFA members.
How to Apply: Applications are available online or from your local FFA advisor.
Deadline: February 15.
Amount: Varies.
Number of Awards: Varies.

National Garden Clubs Inc.

4401 Magnolia Avenue
St. Louis, MO 63110
Phone: 314-776-7574
Fax: 314-776-5108
Email: headquarters@gardenclub.org
Website: http://www.gardenclub.org

138 • National Garden Clubs Scholarship

Purpose: To promote the study of horticulture and related fields.
Eligibility: Applicants must be full-time juniors, seniors, graduate students or sophomores applying for the junior year and major in one of the following fields: agriculture education, horticulture, floriculture, landscape design, botany, biology, plant pathology/science, forestry, agronomy, environmental concerns, economics, environmental conservation, city planning, wildlife science, habitat or forest/systems ecology, land management or related areas.
How to Apply: Applications are available online and must be mailed to the applicants' state Garden Club scholarship chairman.
Deadline: March 1.
Amount: $3,500.
Number of Awards: 34.

National Potato Council Women's Auxiliary

1300 L Street NW
Suite 910
Washington, DC 20005
Phone: 202-682-9456
Fax: 202-682-0333
Email: spudinfo@nationalpotatocouncil.org
Website: http://www.npcspud.com

139 • National Potato Council Women's Auxiliary Scholarship

Purpose: To assist the potato industry through education.
Eligibility: Applicants must be in potato-related areas of graduate study, be academically competent and have leadership abilities.
How to Apply: Applications are available online.
Deadline: July 1.
Amount: $2,000.
Number of Awards: 2.

Society for Range Management (SRM)

10030 W. 27th Avenue
Wheat Ridge, CO 80215-6601
Phone: 303-986-3309
Fax: 303-986-3892
Email: vskiff@rangelands.org
Website: http://www.rangelands.org

140 • Masonic-Range Science Scholarship

Purpose: To help a high school senior, college freshman or college sophomore majoring in range science or a closely related field.
Eligibility: Applicants must be sponsored by a member of the Society for Range Management (SRM), the National Association of Conservation Districts (NACD) or the Soil and Water Conservation Society (SWCS). Applicants must also submit an application form, transcript, SAT or ACT scores and two letters of reference.
How to Apply: Applications are available online.
Deadline: January 15.
Amount: Varies.
Number of Awards: Varies.

Related Scholarships:

American Society of Agricultural Engineers Foundation

See #357 · ASAE Student Engineer of the Year Scholarship

Society of Automotive Engineers

See #421 · Yanmar/SAE Scholarship

Association of Food and Drug Officials

See #643 · Association of Food and Drug Officials Scholarship Award

American Society of Agricultural Engineers Foundation

See #355 · Adams Scholarship Grant

American Society of Agricultural Engineers Foundation

See #356 · ASAE Foundation Scholarship

Harness Horse Youth Foundation

See #154 · Harness Racing Scholarship

Atlantic Salmon Federation

See #501 · ASF Olin Fellowships

American Orchid Society

See #175 · AOS Master's Scholarship Program

Intel Corporation and Science Service

See #1139 · International Science and Engineering Fair

Tree Research and Education Endowment Fund

See #504 · Robert Felix Memorial Scholarship

James F. Lincoln Arc Welding Foundation

See #1635 · Arc Welding Awards

Cargill

See #966 · United Negro College Fund Cargill Scholarship-Internship Program

Architecture/Landscape

Also See Scholarships Listed Under:
Agriculture/Horticulture/Animals

American Architectural Foundation

1799 New York Avenue NW
Washington, DC 20006
Phone: 202-626-7318
Fax: 202-626-7420
Email: info@archfoundation.org
Website: http://www.archfoundation.org

141 • AIA/AAF Minority/Disadvantaged Scholarship

Purpose: To provide scholarships for students who intend to study architecture and who could not otherwise afford to enter a degree-seeking program.

Eligibility: Applicants must be high school seniors or college freshmen who intend to study architecture in an NAAB-accredited program. Students must be nominated by a high school counselor, AIA component, architect or other person aware of student's aptitude.

How to Apply: Applications are available by email.
Deadline: January.
Amount: Up to $2,500.
Number of Awards: 20.

142 • American Architectural Foundation and Sir John Soane's Museum Foundation Traveling Fellowship

Purpose: To provide scholarships enabling graduate students to travel to England and to study the work of Sir John Soane (or Sir John Soane's Museum and its collections).

Eligibility: Applicants must be enrolled in graduate programs focusing on the history of art, architecture, decorative arts or interior design.

How to Apply: Applications are available online.
Deadline: March 1.
Amount: $5,000.
Number of Awards: 1.

143 • RTKL Traveling Fellowship

Purpose: To encourage travel outside the United States for students in pursuit of a professional archictecture degree.

Eligibility: Applicants must be in the second-to-last year of a BArch or MArch program and must complete travels before graduating. Travel pursuits should further the students' education.

How to Apply: Applications are available online.
Deadline: February 15.
Amount: $2,500.
Number of Awards: 1.

Illuminating Engineering Society of North America

1514 Gibbons Drive
Alameda, CA 94501
Phone: 510-864-0204
Fax: 510-864-8511
Email: mrcatisbac@aol.com
Website: http://www.iesna.org

144 • Robert E. Thunen Memorial Scholarships

Purpose: To help students who plan to pursue illumination as a career.

Eligibility: Applicants must be full-time junior, senior or graduate students in an accredited four-year college in Northern California, Nevada, Oregon or Washington who plan to pursue illumination as a career. The application, statement of purpose and at least three letters of recommendation are required. Students should review the IESNA Lighting Handbook to see the available fields of study.

How to Apply: Applications are available by mail and email.
Deadline: April 1.
Amount: $2,500.
Number of Awards: 2.

Landscape Architecture Foundation

818 18th Street NW
Suite 810
Washington, DC 20006
Email: rfigura@lafoundation.org
Website: http://www.laprofession.org

145 • Rain Bird Scholarship

Purpose: To recognize outstanding landscape architecture students.

Eligibility: Applicants must be college juniors or fourth- or fifth-year seniors, have a demonstrated commitment to the landscape architecture profession and exhibit financial need.

How to Apply: Applications are available by written request.
Deadline: Varies.
Amount: $1,000.
Number of Awards: 1.

146 • Raymond E. Page Scholarship

Purpose: To support landscape architecture students.

Eligibility: Applicants must study landscape architecture and submit a two-page essay describing their financial need and how they plan to use to award. Selection is based on essay and a letter of recommendation from a current professor.

How to Apply: Applications are available by written request.
Deadline: April.
Amount: $1,000.
Number of Awards: 1.

147 • William J. Locklin Scholarship

Purpose: To recognize the importance of 24-hour lighting in landscape design.

Eligibility: Applicants must submit an essay describing their design project as well as visual samples of it and a letter of recommendation from a professor.

How to Apply: Applications are available by written request.
Deadline: Varies.
Amount: $1,000.
Number of Awards: Varies.

Society of American Registered Architects

P.O. Box 280
Newport, TN 37822
Phone: 888-385-7272
Fax: 423-487-0365
Email: cathiemoscato@sara-national.org
Website: http://www.sara-national.org

148 • Student Design Competition

Purpose: To support architecture students.

Eligibility: Applicants may be attending accredited architectural schools, be undergraduate students in a Bachelor of Arts or a Bachelor of Science in an architecture program or be graduate students in a Master of Architecture program in pursuit of a first professional degree. Students must secure the sponsorship of a faculty member.

How to Apply: Applications are available online or by written request.

Deadline: September 1 for registration form.

Amount: $500-$6,000.

Number of Awards: 3.

Related Scholarships:

American Concrete Institute Student Fellowship Program

See #345 • ACI Student Fellowship Program

American Concrete Institute ACI-James Instruments Student Award

See #344 • ACI-James Instruments Student Award for Research on NDT of Concrete

American Planning Association

See #946 • APA Planning Fellowships

Scholastic

See #897 • Art Awards

Golf Course Superintendents Association of America Foundation

See #124 • GCSAA Scholars Program

Golf Course Superintendents Association of America Foundation

See #125 • GCSAA Student Essay Contest

Golf Course Superintendents Association of America Foundation

See #126 • Scotts Company Scholars Program

Hagley Museum and Library

See #1175 • Hagley-Winterthur Fellowships in Arts and Industries

Association for Women in Architecture

See #1220 • AWA Scholarships

National Garden Clubs Inc.

See #138 • National Garden Clubs Scholarship

Athletics/Outdoors

Also See Scholarships Listed Under:

Leadership

American Legion Baseball

700 N. Pennsylvania Street
Indianapolis, IN 46204
Fax: 317-630-1369
Email: baseball@legion.org
Website: http://www.baseball.legion.org

149 • American Legion Baseball Scholarship

Purpose: To award scholarships to members of American Legion-affiliated baseball teams.

Eligibility: Applicants must be graduating high school seniors and be nominated by a head coach or team manager. One player per department (state) will be selected. Nominations should be sent to the local Department Headquarters. Scholarships may be used to further education at any accredited college, university or other institution of higher education.

How to Apply: Applications are available online.
Deadline: July 15.
Amount: $1,000.
Number of Awards: 51.

American Water Ski Educational Foundation (AWSEF)

1251 Holy Cow Road
Polk City, FL 33868-8200
Phone: 863-324-2472
Email: info@waterskihalloffame.com
Website: http://www.waterskihalloffame.com

150 • AWSEF Scholarship

Purpose: To support those involved in USA WATER SKI.

Eligibility: Applicants must be full-time undergraduates at a two- or four-year college as incoming sophomores to incoming seniors. Applicants must also be active members of USA WATER SKI all divisions: AWSA-ABC-AKA-WSDA-NSSA-NCWSA-NCWSRA-USAWB-HYD. Students should submit applications, two reference letters, essays and transcripts.

How to Apply: Applications are available online.
Deadline: April 1.
Amount: $1,500.
Number of Awards: 6.

Dixie Boys Baseball

P.O. Box 8263
Dothan, AL 36304
Phone: 334-793-3331
Fax: 334-793-3331
Email: jjones29@sw.rr.com
Website: http://www.dixie.org

151 • Dixie Boys Baseball Scholarship Program

Purpose: To help high school seniors who have participated in a franchised Dixie Boys Baseball Inc. program.

Eligibility: Applicants must plan to pursue undergraduate studies at a college or university. An application, financial statement, two recommendation letters, proof of baseball participation, transcript and essay are required. Selection is based on class rankings, strong school and community leadership and financial need. Programs are located in Alabama, Arkansas, Florida, Georgia, Louisiana, Mississippi, North Carolina, South Carolina, Tennessee, Texas and Virginia.

How to Apply: Applications are available online.
Deadline: March 15.
Amount: $1,500.
Number of Awards: 11.

Dixie Youth Baseball

P.O. Box 877
Marshall, TX 75671
Phone: 903-927-2255
Email: dyb@dixie.org
Website: http://www.dixie.org

152 • Dixie Youth Scholarship Program

Purpose: To help high school seniors who have participated in a franchised Dixie Youth Baseball league.

Eligibility: Applicants must have been registered on a Dixie Youth Baseball team participating in a franchised Dixie Youth Baseball Inc. league prior to reaching age thirteen. Selection is based on financial need, scholastic record and citizenship. Programs are located in Alabama, Arkansas, Florida, Georgia, Louisiana, Mississippi, North Carolina, South Carolina, Tennessee, Texas and Virginia.

How to Apply: Contact your local league officials or a district, state or national director for an application, and applications are also available online.
Deadline: March 1.
Amount: $2,000.
Number of Awards: 60.

Eastern Surfing Association

P.O. Box 625
Virginia Beach, VA 23451
Phone: 757-233-1790
Fax: 757-233-1396
Email: info@surfesa.org
Website: http://www.surfesa.org

153 • Marsh Scholarship Fund

Purpose: To assist Eastern Surfing Association (ESA) student surfers.

Eligibility: Applicants must be current ESA members. Transcripts, a recommendation letter, purpose letters and applications are required. The award is based on academics and citizenship, not athletic ability.

How to Apply: Applications are available online and by email.
Deadline: May 15.
Amount: Varies.
Number of Awards: Varies.

Harness Horse Youth Foundation

16575 Carey Road
Westfield, IN 46074
Phone: 317-867-5877
Fax: 317-867-5896
Email: hhyfetaylor@iquest.net
Website: http://www.hhyf.org

154 • Harness Racing Scholarship

Purpose: To encourage the education of young people about harness racing.

Eligibility: Applicants must be pursuing a horse-related career, have financial need, demonstrate scholastic achievements and have experience with horses and harness racing. Applicants must also be at least a high school senior and under the age of 25.

How to Apply: Applications are available by mail.

Deadline: April 30.

Amount: Varies.

Number of Awards: Varies.

Ice Skating Institute of America (ISIA) Education Foundation

17120 N. Dallas Parkway, Suite 140
Dallas, TX 75248
Phone: 972-735-8800
Fax: 972-735-8815
Website: http://www.skateisi.com

155 • ISIA Education Foundation Scholarship

Purpose: To encourage skaters to make athletic and educational achievements.

Eligibility: Applicants must have completed at least three years of high school with a minimum 3.0 GPA during the last two years and enroll as full-time undergraduate students. Applicants must also have been members of the Ice Skating Institute (ISI) and have participated in the ISI Recreational Skater Program for at least four years, have participated in ISI competitions or classes within the last two years, and have completed 240 hours of verified service, with 120 hours volunteered. Applicants must also submit two evaluation forms and an essay of 500 words or less explaining why they should receive the award.

How to Apply: Applications are available online.

Deadline: March 1.

Amount: $4,000.

Number of Awards: 4.

National Amateur Baseball Federation

P.O. Box 705
Bowie, MD 20715
Phone: 301-464-5460
Fax: 301-352-0214
Email: nabf1914@aol.com
Website: http://www.nabf.com

156 • NABF Scholarship Program

Purpose: To support students who have been involved with the federation.

Eligibility: Applicants must be enrolled in an accredited college or university, must have participated in a federation event and must be sponsored by a member association. Selection is based on grades, financial need and previous awards.

How to Apply: Applications are available online.

Deadline: Varies.

Amount: Varies.

Number of Awards: Varies.

National Archery Association

One Olympic Plaza
Colorado Springs, CO 80909
Phone: 719-866-4576
Fax: 719-632-4733
Email: info@usarchery.org
Website: http://www.usarchery.org

157 • NAA College Scholarship

Purpose: To support student archers.

Eligibility: Applicants must be full-time students at two- or four-year institutions and compete in the NAA College Division. A minimum 2.50 GPA is required.

How to Apply: Applications are available online.

Deadline: December 31.

Amount: $500.

Number of Awards: 8.

National Association of Intercollegiate Athletics (NAIA)

NAIA Scholarships
23500 W. 105th Street
Olathe, KS 66061
Phone: 913-791-0044
Fax: 913-791-9555
Website: http://www.naia.org

158 • NAIA Scholarships

Purpose: To award scholarships to student-athletes attending NAIA member schools.

Eligibility: Applicants must be incoming freshmen at an NAIA member school and be nominated by a teammate, coach, counselor or teacher. Selection is based on respect, responsibility, integrity, servant leadership and sportsmanship.

How to Apply: Applications are available online.

Deadline: May 12.

Amount: $1,000.

Number of Awards: 5.

National Athletic Trainers' Association

National Athletic Trainer's Association Research and Education Foundation Inc.
2952 Stemmons Freeway
Dallas, TX 75247
Phone: 214-637-6282
Fax: 214-637-2206
Email: barbaran@nata.org
Website: http://www.nata.org

159 • NATA Scholarship

Purpose: To encourage study among athletic trainers.

Eligibility: Applicants must be at least a junior in college with a minimum 3.2 GPA, be sponsored by a certified athletic trainer and be a member of the NATA.

How to Apply: Applications are available online.
Deadline: February 10.
Amount: $2,000.
Number of Awards: 60.

National Bicycle League (NBL)

3958 Brown Park Drive
Suite D
Hilliard, OH 43026
Phone: 614-777-1625
Fax: 614-777-1680
Email: administration@nbl.org
Website: http://www.nbl.org

160 • Bob Warnicke Scholarship

Purpose: To help students who have participated in BMX racing events.
Eligibility: Applicants must be members, have a current NBL competition license or officials license and have participated in BMX racing events for at least a year. Students must also be high school graduates and plan to or currently attend a postsecondary institution full- or part-time.
How to Apply: Applications are available online, by mail or by phone.
Deadline: November 1.
Amount: Varies.
Number of Awards: Varies.

National Collegiate Athletic Association

700 W. Washington Street
P.O. Box 6222
Indianapolis, IN 46206
Phone: 317-917-6222
Fax: 317-917-6888
Email: ahightower@ncaa.org
Website: http://www.ncaa.org

161 • Ethnic Minority and Women's Enhancement Scholarship

Purpose: To assist minority and female students in intercollegiate athletics with postgraduate scholarships at the NCAA national office.
Eligibility: Applicants must be planning to attend a sports administration program and plan to pursue a career in intercollegiate athletics such as athletic administration, coaching or athletic training.
Deadline: Varies.
Amount: $6,000.
Number of Awards: 16.

162 • NCAA Postgraduate Scholarship

Purpose: To reward student athletes who perform well in both sports and academics.
Eligibility: Student athletes must show achievement in their last year of varsity-level intercollegiate athletics at an NCAA school. Applicants must be nominated by the faculty athletic representative or athletic director and be enrolling as a full- or part-time graduate student.
How to Apply: Applications are available online.
Deadline: December 12.
Amount: $7,500.
Number of Awards: Up to 174.

National Fluid Milk Processor Promotion Board

Scholar Athlete Milk Mustache of Year
P.O. Box 9249
Medford, NY 11763
Website: http://www.whymilk.com

163 • Scholar Athlete Milk Mustache of the Year Award (SAMMY)

Purpose: To reward outstanding student athletes.
Eligibility: Applicants must be legal residents of the 48 contiguous United States or the District of Columbia, high school seniors and participate in a high school or club sport. Applicants must describe in 75 words or less how drinking milk has been a part of their life and training regimen.
How to Apply: Applicants can be obtained online and only applications submitted online will be accepted.
Deadline: March 7.
Amount: Varies.
Number of Awards: Varies.

National Rifle Association

11250 Waples Mill Road
Fairfax, VA 22030
Phone: 703-267-1505
Website: http://www.nrahq.org

164 • NRA Outstanding Achievement Youth Award

Purpose: To recognize NRA Junior Members who actively participate in shooting sports.
Eligibility: Applicants must be NRA Junior Members (or Regular or Life Members under 18 years old) and have completed five core and five elective requirements. Core requirements are being current members of the NRA, attending and completing an NRA Basic Firearm Training Course, earning a rating in a shooting discipline and submitting an essay. Applicants must also complete five elective requirements from those listed on the website.
How to Apply: Applications are available online.
Deadline: Varies.
Amount: Varies.
Number of Awards: 1.

National Scholastic Surfing Association

P.O. Box 495
Huntington Beach, CA 92648
Phone: 714-378-0899
Fax: 714-964-5232
Email: jaragon@nssa.org
Website: http://www.nssa.org

165 • National Scholarship Program

Purpose: To assist NSSA members in their pursuit of post-high school education.
Eligibility: Applicants must be competitive student NSSA members and have a minimum 3.0 GPA in the current school year. Scholastic achievement, leadership, service, career goals and recommendations are considered.
How to Apply: Applications are available with organization membership.

Deadline: Varies.
Amount: Varies.
Number of Awards: Varies.

National Strength and Conditioning Association (NSCA) Foundation

1885 Bob Johnson Drive
Colorado Springs, CO 80906
Phone: 800-815-6826
Fax: 719-632-6367
Email: nsca@nsca-lift.org
Website: http://www.nsca-lift.org

166 • Challenge Scholarship

Purpose: To support NSCA members pursuing studies related to strength and conditioning.

Eligibility: Applicants must be NSCA members for one year before applying and be pursuing careers in strength and conditioning. Students must submit an essay detailing their course of study, career goals and financial need. Applications are evaluated based on grades, courses, experience, honors, recommendations and involvement in the community and with NSCA.

How to Apply: Applications are available with membership.
Deadline: March 15.
Amount: $1,000.
Number of Awards: Varies.

167 • GNC Nutritional Research Grant

Purpose: To fund nutrition-based research.

Eligibility: Applicants must be NSCA members for one year before applying and pursuing careers in strength and conditioning. Students must also plan a research project that falls within the mission of the NSCA and submit a proposal describing the rationale, purpose and methods of the planned research. Applications are evaluated based on grades, courses, experience, honors, recommendations and involvement in the community and with NSCA.

How to Apply: Applications are available with membership.
Deadline: March 15.
Amount: $2,500.
Number of Awards: 1.

168 • Graduate Research Grant - Master and Doctoral

Purpose: To support research in strength and conditioning.

Eligibility: Applicants must be master's or doctoral students and submit a proposal for a research project in the field of strength and conditioning that fulfills the mission of the NSCA. Students must be NSCA members for one year before applying and pursuing careers in strength and conditioning. Applications are evaluated based on grades, courses, experience, honors, recommendations and involvement in the community and with NSCA.

How to Apply: Applications are available with membership.
Deadline: March 15.
Amount: $2,500-$5,000.
Number of Awards: Varies.

169 • High School Scholarship

Purpose: To support high school students entering the strength and conditioning field.

Eligibility: Applicants must be high school seniors planning to graduate with a degree related to strength and conditioning with a current 3.0 GPA. Students must be NSCA members, although applicants may enroll at the time of application, and pursuing a career in strength and conditioning. Applications are evaluated based on grades, courses, experience, honors, recommendations and involvement in the community and with NSCA.

How to Apply: Applications are available by contacting the organization.
Deadline: March 15.
Amount: $1,000.
Number of Awards: 2.

170 • Undergraduate Research Grant

Purpose: To support undergraduate research in strength and conditioning.

Eligibility: Applicants must be undergraduate students planning to undertake a research project related to strength and conditioning that fits in with the mission of the NSCA. Students must submit a proposal with rationale, study methods and purpose and find a faculty advisor. Applicants must be NSCA members for one year before applying and be pursuing careers in strength and conditioning. Applications are evaluated based on grades, courses, experience, honors, recommendations and involvement in the community and with NSCA.

How to Apply: Applications are available with membership.
Deadline: March 15.
Amount: Up to $1,500.
Number of Awards: Varies.

Our World-Underwater Scholarship Society

6012 Perry Drive
Woodridge, IL 60517
Phone: 630-969-6690
Fax: 630-969-6690
Email: info@owuscholarship.org
Website: http://www.owuscholarship.org

171 • North American Rolex Scholarship

Purpose: To support students planning careers in underwater world or associated disciplines.

Eligibility: Applicants must be certified scuba divers with a minimum of 25 open-water dives, be academically excellent, not have earned graduate degrees and be at least 21 and have not yet reached their 25th birthday by March 1st of the scholarship year. Applicants must also pass a preliminary medical examination for diving fitness and pass a NOAA diving physical if selected.

How to Apply: Applications are available online.
Deadline: November 30.
Amount: $5,000.
Number of Awards: Varies.

Stonehouse Publishing Company

Scholarship Committee
1508 Leavenworth Street
Omaha, NE 68102
Phone: 800-949-7274
Fax: 402-344-3563
Email: pseina@stonehousegolf.com
Website: http://www.stonehousegolf.com

172 • Stonehouse Golf Youth Scholarship

Purpose: To recognize individuals who throughout their high school careers have shown outstanding academic and golf achievements.

Eligibility: Applicants must be seniors in high school, participate in at least two seasons on high school golf teams and have a minimum 3.5 GPA. Students must be intending to pursue a 2 or 4 year degree and must have participated with their school in the Stonehouse Golf Fundraiser.

How to Apply: Applications are available online.
Deadline: May 30.
Amount: $500.
Number of Awards: 20.

Wendy's Restaurants

c/o National Association of Secondary School Principals
1904 Association Drive
Reston, VA 20191
Phone: 800-205-6367
Email: dsa@principals.org
Website: http://www.wendyshighschoolheisman.com

173 • Wendy's High School Heisman Award

Purpose: To recognize scholarship, citizenship and athletic ability.
Eligibility: Applicants must be entering their high school senior year and participate in one of 32 officially sanctioned sports. Eligible students have a minimum 3.0 GPA. Selection is based on academic achievement, community service and athletic accomplishments.
How to Apply: Nomination forms are available online.
Deadline: October 1.
Amount: Varies.
Number of Awards: Varies.

Women's Sports Foundation

Eisenhower Park
East Meadow, NY 11554
Phone: 800-227-3988
Fax: 516-542-4716
Email: wosport@aol.com
Website: http://www.womenssportsfoundation.org

174 • Linda Riddle/SGMA Scholarship

Purpose: To help young women athletes with financial need to pursue their sports passion in addition to their college studies.
Eligibility: Applicants must be female high school student athletes with financial need. Selection is based on academic and athletic achievement.
How to Apply: Applications are available online.
Deadline: Varies.
Amount: $1,500.
Number of Awards: Varies.

Related Scholarships:

Outdoor Writers Association of America

See #248 • *Bodie McDowell Scholarship*

California Interscholastic Federation (CIF)

See #1233 • *California Interscholastic Federation (CIF) Scholar-Athlete of the Year*

High School Athletic Association

See #1305 • *Nissan Hawaii High School Hall of Honor*

American Quarter Horse Foundation

See #114 • *American Quarter Horse Foundation Scholarship*

Hispanic Heritage Awards Foundation

See #985 • *Hispanic Heritage Youth Awards*

Rhodes Scholarship Trust

See #57 • *Rhodes Scholar*

National Strength and Conditioning Association (NSCA) Foundation

See #682 • *Women's Scholarship*

National Strength and Conditioning Association (NSCA) Foundation

See #1030 • *Minority Scholarship*

Biological Sciences/Life Sciences

Also See Scholarships Listed Under:
Agriculture/Horticulture/Animals
Chemistry
Forestry/Wildlife
Medicine/Nursing/Health Profession

American Orchid Society

16700 AOS Lane
Delray Beach, FL 33446-4351
Phone: 561-404-2000
Fax: 561-404-2045
Email: theaos@aos.org
Website: http://www.aos.org

175 • AOS Master's Scholarship Program

Purpose: To provide a two-year scholarship for completing a master's thesis on orchid education, orchidology or a related topic.
Eligibility: Applicants must be enrolled in a master's program at an accredited institution. The thesis project must focus on orchid education, applied science or orchid biology. The scholarship is limited to two consecutive years.
How to Apply: Applications are available online.
Deadline: February 1.
Amount: $10,000.
Number of Awards: Varies.

American Ornithologists' Union

Avian Ecology Lab
Archbold Biological Station
123 Main Drive
Venus, FL 33960
Phone: 863-465-2571
Email: rbowman@archbold-station.org
Website: http://www.aou.org

176 • Research Award

Purpose: To provide research funding for members of the American Ornithologists Union.
Eligibility: Applicants must be members of the AOU and must submit proposals for research projects on avian biology, avian systematics, paleo-ornithology, biogeography, neotropical biology or ornithology.
How to Apply: The submission procedure and tips for writing a proposal are described on the website.
Deadline: February 1.
Amount: $1,800.
Number of Awards: 30.

American Physiological Society

Education Office
9650 Rockville Pike
Bethesda, MD 20814-3991
Phone: 301-634-7787
Fax: 301-634-7241
Email: education@the-aps.org
Website: http://www.the-aps.org

177 • David S. Bruce Awards for Excellence in Undergraduate Research

Purpose: To award undergraduate students for excellence in experimental biology research.
Eligibility: Applicants must be enrolled as an undergraduate at time of application and at time of meeting. Students must be first authors of the abstract and must be working with an APS member who will confirm the authorship. Applicants must submit a one-page paper discussing research and career plans and an abstract to be reviewed by a committee at the annual Experimental Biology meeting.
How to Apply: Applications are available online.
Deadline: October.
Amount: $500.
Number of Awards: Up to 4.

American Society of Ichthyologists and Herpetologists

Maureen Donnelly, Secretary
Department of Biological Sciences, Florida International University
11200 SW 8th Street
Miami, FL 33199
Phone: 305-348-1235
Fax: 305-348-1986
Email: asih@fiu.edu
Website: http://www.asih.org

178 • Gaige Fund Award

Purpose: To support young herpetologists.
Eligibility: Applicants must be members of ASIH and studying for an advanced degree. The award may be used for museum or laboratory study, travel, fieldwork, or other activities that will enhance their careers and their contributions to the science of herpetology. Both merit and need will be considered.
How to Apply: Applications are available by email or written request.
Deadline: March 1.
Amount: $400-$1,000.
Number of Awards: Varies.

179 • Raney Fund Award

Purpose: To support young ichthyologists.
Eligibility: Applicants should be members of ASIH and should be enrolled for an advanced degree, although those with developing careers may receive the award under exceptional circumstances. Awards may be used for museums or laboratory study, travel, fieldwork or other activities that will enhance their professional careers and their contributions to the science of ichthyology. Scholarships are awarded on the basis of merit and need.
How to Apply: Applications are available by email or written request.
Deadline: March 1.
Amount: $400-$1,000.
Number of Awards: Varies.

180 • Stoye and Storer Awards

Purpose: To recognize the best oral and poster presentations in categories related to ichthyology and herpetology.

Eligibility: Applicants must be the sole authors and presenters of their projects, be members of ASIH, be full-time students or have completed a thesis or dissertation defense during the previous 12 months. Presentations are judged by introduction, methods, data analysis and interpretation, conclusions, presentation and visual aids.

How to Apply: Applications are available by request.

Deadline: July.

Amount: Varies.

Number of Awards: Varies.

Association for Women in Science

1200 New York Avenue NW
Suite 650
Washington, DC 20005
Phone: 202-326-8940
Fax: 202-326-8960
Email: awis@awis.org
Website: http://www.awis.org

181 • Association for Women in Science College Scholarship

Purpose: To assist female students who plan to study science.

Eligibility: Applicants must be female high school seniors planning to study behavioral, life and physical sciences or engineering at an accredited college or university and must have a minimum 3.75 GPA and a minimum SAT score of 1200 or a minimum ACT score of 25. Selection is based on academic achievement, experience in research and commitment to a career in research or teaching, overcoming economic, social or other barriers and involvement in community activities.

How to Apply: Applications are available online.

Deadline: January 19.

Amount: Varies.

Number of Awards: 2-5.

Bat Conservation International

Scholarship Program
P.O. Box 162603
Austin, TX 78716
Phone: 512-327-9721
Fax: 512-327-9724
Email: grants@batcon.org
Website: http://www.batcon.org

182 • Student Research Scholarships

Purpose: To support students who will contribute to our knowledge about bats.

Eligibility: Applicants must be graduate students and submit a research proposal that addresses a specific area of bat conservation. The application form provides several potential research topics.

How to Apply: Applications are available online.

Deadline: December 15.

Amount: $1,000-$5,000.

Number of Awards: Varies.

Coleopterists Society

Anthony I. Cognato, Chair
Texas A & M University
College Station, TX 77845-2475
Phone: 979-458-0404
Email: a.cognato@tamu.edu
Website: http://www.coleopsoc.org

183 • Jean Theodore Lacordaire Prize

Purpose: To recognize the work of coleopterists.

Eligibility: Applicants must be graduate students whose papers are nominated for the competition. The papers must be about coleoptera (beetle) systematics or biology published in a journal or book. Self-nominations are not accepted.

How to Apply: Application materials are described online.

Deadline: August 1.

Amount: $300.

Number of Awards: Varies.

184 • Youth Incentive Award

Purpose: To recognize young people studying beetles.

Eligibility: Applicants should be coleopterists in grades 7-12 and submit individual proposals such as field collecting trips to conduct beetle species inventories or diversity studies, attending workshops or visiting entomology or natural history museums for training and projects on beetles, studying beetle biology, etc. Students are strongly encouraged to find an adult advisor (i.e., teacher, youth group leader, parent) to provide guidance in the proposal development, but the proposal must be written by the applicant. The Coleopterists Society can help establish contacts between applicants and professional coleopterists. The award is based on creativity, educational benefit to the applicant, scientific merit, feasibility and budget. There are two winners: one for grades 7-9 and one for grades 10-12.

How to Apply: Applications are available online.

Deadline: November 15.

Amount: Varies.

Number of Awards: 2.

Entomological Society of America

10001 Derekwood Lane
Suite 100
Lanham, MD 20706
Phone: 301-731-4535
Fax: 301-731-4538
Email: esa@entsoc.org
Website: http://www.entsoc.org

185 • John Henry Comstock Graduate Student Awards

Purpose: To encourage graduate students interested in entomology to attend the Annual Meeting of the Entomological Society of America.

Eligibility: Applicants must be graduate students and members of the ESA. Each ESA branch has its own eligibility requirements, so an interested student must contact their Branch Secretary-Treasurer for more information.

How to Apply: Applications are available online.

Deadline: September 1.

Amount: $100.

Number of Awards: 5.

186 • Normand R. Dubois Memorial Scholarship

Purpose: To encourage research by graduate students on the use of biologically based technologies to protect and preserve forests.

Eligibility: Applicants must be pursuing a master's or doctorate at an accredited university and propose research to advance knowledge of the best way to preserve forests using environmentally friendly and biologically based technologies.

How to Apply: Applications are available online.

Deadline: July 1.

Amount: $1,500.

Number of Awards: Varies.

187 • Stan Beck Fellowship

Purpose: To support college or graduate students in entomology.

Eligibility: Applicants must be undergraduate or graduate students in entomology who demonstrate need based on physical limitations, or economic, minority or environmental conditions.

How to Apply: Applications are available online.

Deadline: July 1.

Amount: Varies.

Number of Awards: 1.

188 • Undergraduate Scholarship

Purpose: To help students enter the field of entomology.

Eligibility: Applicants must have been enrolled in the previous fall as undergraduate students in entomology, zoology, biology or a related science at a college or university and must have accumulated a minimum of 30 credits at the time the award is presented in August. Students must have completed at least one course in entomology or a project in entomology.

How to Apply: Applications are available online.

Deadline: June 1.

Amount: Varies.

Number of Awards: 4.

Explorers Club

46 E. 70th Street
New York, NY 10021
Phone: 212-628-8383
Fax: 212-288-4449
Email: youth@explorers.org
Website: http://www.explorers.org

189 • Youth Activity Grant

Purpose: To provide grants for high school and college students to research the natural sciences through field research.

Eligibility: Applicants must provide a three-page explanation of their project, be high school or college students and be U.S. residents. The grants allow students to conduct field research in the natural sciences under the supervision of a qualified scientist or institution.

How to Apply: Applications are available online.

Deadline: Varies.

Amount: $500-$1,500.

Number of Awards: Varies.

Fannie and John Hertz Foundation

2456 Research Drive
Livermore, CA 94550-3850
Phone: 925-373-1642
Fax: 925-373-6329
Email: askhertz@hertzfoundation.org
Website: http://www.hertzfoundation.com

190 • Hertz Foundation's Graduate Fellowship Award

Purpose: To help graduate students in the applied physical and engineering sciences.

Eligibility: Applicants must be college seniors planning to pursue or graduate students currently pursuing a Ph.D. in the applied physical and engineering sciences or modern biology which applies the physical sciences. Successful applicants must attend one of the foundation's approved schools. The award is based on merit, creativity and potential for research.

How to Apply: Applications are available online, by phone or by email.

Deadline: October 28.

Amount: $33,000.

Number of Awards: Varies.

Herb Society of America

Attn.: Research Grant
9019 Kirtland Chardon Road
Kirtland, OH 44094
Phone: 440-256-0514
Fax: 440-256-0541
Email: herbs@herbsociety.org
Website: http://www.herbsociety.org

191 • HSA Research Grants

Purpose: To educate about herbs and contribute to the fields of horticulture, science, literature, history, art and/or economics.

Eligibility: Applicants must have a proposed program of scientific, academic or artistic investigation of herbal plants. Applicants must describe their research needs in 500 words or less and include a proposed budget with specific budget items listed. This grant may not be used in combination with funding from another source and may not be used to pay for salaries, tuition or private garden development.

How to Apply: Applications are available online or by written request.

Deadline: January 31.

Amount: Up to $5,000.

Number of Awards: Varies by year.

Huntington's Disease Society of America

505 Eighth Avenue, Suite 902
New York, NY 10018
Phone: 800-345-4372
Fax: 212-239-3430
Email: rgraze@hdsa.org
Website: http://www.hdsa.org

192 • Don King Student Fellowship

Purpose: To sponsor Huntington's Disease research.

Eligibility: Applicants must be current undergraduate life science or pre-medical students or first-year medical students attending accredited institutions in the United States where HDSA sponsors HD research. Recipients will conduct full-time research for 10 weeks. A letter of support and project plan are required. The award is based on academic achievement, scientific merit of the project and the relevancy to HD.

How to Apply: Applications are available by email, by mail or online.

Deadline: May 1.

Amount: $3,000.

Number of Awards: Varies.

Wilson Ornithological Society

Dr. Robert B. Payne
Museum of Zoology, University of Michigan
1109 Gedes Avenue
Ann Arbor, MI 48109
Email: rbpayne@umich.edu
Website: http://www.ummz.umich.edu/birds/wos

193 • George A. Hall / Harold F. Mayfield Award

Eligibility: Applicants must be independent researchers without access to funds available at colleges, universities, or government agencies, and must be non-professionals currently conducting avian research. Applicants must be willing to present their research results at an annual meeting of the Wilson Ornithological Society.
How to Apply: Applications are available online.
Deadline: January 15.
Amount: $1,000.
Number of Awards: 1.

194 • Louis Agassiz Fuertes Award

Purpose: To support ornitholigists' research.
Eligibility: Applicants must be students or young professionals doing avian research. Applicants must be willing to report their research results at an annual meeting of the Wilson Ornithological Society.
How to Apply: Applications are available online.
Deadline: January 15.
Amount: $2,500.
Number of Awards: 1.

195 • Paul A. Stewart Awards

Purpose: To promote bird research.
Eligibility: Applicants' proposals should, but are not required to, cover the area of the study of bird movements based on banding, using the analysis and recovery of banded birds, with an emphasis on economic ornithology. Applicants must be willing to present their research results at an annual meeting of the Wilson Ornithological Society.
How to Apply: Applications are available online.
Deadline: January 15.
Amount: $500.
Number of Awards: Up to 4.

Related Scholarships:

Massachusetts Office of Student Financial Assistance
See #1415 • CommonWealth Futures Grant Program

American Foundation
See #108 • Angus Foundation Scholarship

DuPont
See #1133 • DuPont Challenge Science Essay Award

Astronaut Scholarship Foundation
See #1128 • Astronaut Scholarship

EAA Aviation Center
See #101 • Payzer Scholarship

National Association of Water Companies
See #213 • National Association of Water Companies Scholarship

Microscopy Society of America
See #1144 • MSA Undergraduate Research Scholarship

Association for Women in Science
See #1127 • Association for Women in Science Predoctoral Awards

Intel Corporation and Science Service
See #1138 • Intel Science Talent Search

American Society of Agricultural Engineers Foundation
See #355 • Adams Scholarship Grant

Maryland Higher Education Commission
See #1402 • Science and Technology Scholarship

American Society of Agricultural Engineers Foundation
See #356 • ASAE Foundation Scholarship

American Society of Agricultural Engineers Foundation
See #357 • ASAE Student Engineer of the Year Scholarship

U.S. Department of Health and Human Services National Institutes of Health
See #691 • NIH Undergraduate Scholarship Program

Barry M. Goldwater Scholarship and Excellence in Education Foundation
See #391 • Barry M. Goldwater Scholarship and Excellence in Education Program

National Institutes of Health

See #674• *NIH Undergraduate Scholarship Program for Students from Disadvantaged Backgrounds*

National Wildlife Federation

See #503• *National Wildlife Federation Ecology Fellowship*

Tylenol

See #690• *Tylenol Scholarship*

Academia Resource Management

See #1110• *ARM Undergraduate Student Fellowships*

Department of Defense, American Society for Engineering Education

See #1132• *NDSEG Fellowship Program*

Davidson Institute for Talent Development

See #20• *Davidson Fellows Award*

National Garden Clubs Inc.

See #138• *National Garden Clubs Scholarship*

Neuroscience Nursing Foundation (NNF)

See #684• *NNF Scholarship Program*

Intel Corporation and Science Service

See #1139• *International Science and Engineering Fair*

National Consortium for Graduate Degrees for Minorities in Engineering and Science Inc. (GEM)

See #1026• *GEM Fellowship Program*

Society of Mexican American Engineers and Scientists Inc. (MAES)

See #1052• *MAES Scholarship Program*

Business/Management

Also See Scholarships Listed Under:

Accounting/Finance

Marketing

Leadership

All Student Loan Corporation

HS Scholarship Program
6701 Center Drive
Suite 500
Los Angeles, CA 90045-1547
Phone: 888-271-9721
Fax: 310-979-4714
Email: faoss@allstudentloan.org
Website: http://www.allstudentloan.org

196 • Allstudentloan.org College Scholarship Program for Business Students

Purpose: To reward members of business-related student organizations.

Eligibility: Applicants must be graduating high school seniors or post-secondary students who are active members of one of these vocational student organizations: Future Business Leaders of America-Phi Beta Lambda (FBLA-PBL), Business Professionals of America (BPA) or DECA for the current academic year. They must be enrolled in post-secondary institutions that participate in the Federal Family Education Loan Program.

How to Apply: Applications are available online.
Deadline: June 1.
Amount: $500.
Number of Awards: 4.

American Board of Funeral Service Education

Scholarship Committee
3432 Ashland Avenue, Suite U
St. Joseph, MO 64506
Phone: 816-233-3747
Fax: 816-233-3793
Email: exdir@abfse.org
Website: http://www.abfse.org

197 • National Scholarship Program

Purpose: To assist students enrolled in funeral service or mortuary science programs.

Eligibility: Applicants must have completed at least one semester or quarter of study in funeral service or mortuary science education at an accredited school and have at least one term remaining in their study. Selection is based on academic performance, financial need, references, extracurricular activities and required essays.

How to Apply: Applications are available online, from school financial aid offices or by written request.
Deadline: September 15.
Amount: $250-$500.
Number of Awards: Varies.

American Welding Society Foundation

550 NW LeJeune Road
Miami, FL 33126
Phone: 800-443-9353
Email: info@aws.org
Website: http://www.aws.org

198 • James A. Turner, Jr. Memorial Scholarship

Purpose: To aid those interested in a management career in welding store operations or distributorship.

Eligibility: Applicants must be full-time students pursuing a four-year bachelor's of business degree, plan to enter management careers in welding store operations or distributorship, be high school graduates at least 18 years of age and be employed a minimum of 10 hours per week at a welding distributorship. Preference is given to members of the American Welding Society.

How to Apply: Applications are available online.
Deadline: January 15.
Amount: $3,000.
Number of Awards: 1.

APICS-The Educational Society for Resource Management

5301 Shawnee Road
Alexandria, VA 22312
Phone: 800-444-2742
Fax: 703-354-8106
Email: service@apicshq.org
Website: http://www.apics.org

199 • Donald W. Fogarty International Student Paper Competition

Purpose: To aid students interested in operations management.

Eligibility: Applicants must be full- or part-time college students, undergraduate or graduate and submit a paper on a topic related to operations management.

How to Apply: Papers must be submitted to a local APICS chapter.
Deadline: May 15.
Amount: $100-$1,000.
Number of Awards: Varies.

Association of Government Accountants (AGA)

2208 Mount Vernon Avenue
Alexandria, VA 22301-1314
Phone: 800-242-7211
Email: rortiz@agacgfm.org
Website: http://www.agacgfm.org

200 • AGA Scholarships

Purpose: To support public financial management students.

Eligibility: Applicants for full-time or part-time scholarships must be an AGA member or family member (spouse, child or grandchild), and scholarships must be used for full-time or part-time undergraduate study in a financial management academic area such as accounting, auditing, budgeting, economics, finance, electronic data processing, information resources management or public administration. Essays and transcripts are required.

There are two categories for high school students/graduates and undergraduates/graduates. The Academic Scholarships are based on academic achievement and the student's potential for making a contribution to public financial management. A reference letter from an AGA member and from another professional such as a professor, guidance counselor or employer are required. Applicants to the Community Service Scholarships do not have to be AGA members, must be pursuing a degree in a financial management academic discipline and must be actively involved in community service projects. The awards are based on community service and accomplishments. A letter of recommendation from a community service organization and from another professional are required.

How to Apply: Applications are available online.
Deadline: March 31.
Amount: $1,000.
Number of Awards: 9.

Club Foundation

Joe Perdue Scholarship
1733 King Street
Alexandria, VA 22314
Phone: 703-739-9500
Fax: 703-739-0124
Email: schaverr@clubfoundation.org
Website: http://www.clubfoundation.org

201 • Joe Perdue Scholarship

Purpose: To support students pursuing careers in private club management.

Eligibility: Applicants must be pursuing managerial careers in the private club industry, have completed their freshman year of college, have a minimum 2.5 GPA and be enrolled full-time for the following year. An essay and letters of recommendation are also required.

How to Apply: Applications are available online.
Deadline: April 13.
Amount: $2,500.
Number of Awards: Varies.

Common Knowledge Scholarship Foundation

P.O. Box 290361
Davie, FL 33329-0361
Website: http://www.cksf.org

202 • National Business School Scholarship

Purpose: To reward high school students in grades 9-12 who are interested in attending business school.

Eligibility: Applicants must complete the free online registration and compete by taking a series of short multiple-choice quizzes online. Each week, the quiz will consist of 15 to 20 questions. Five hundred points are awarded for each correct answer, and one point is deducted for each second taken to complete each question. After rounds one and two, a percentage of the high scorers from each state advance to the next round. The winner is determined through a combination of time and accuracy in answering the questions.

How to Apply: Applicants must complete the free online registration and then answer questions.
Deadline: October 2.
Amount: $500.
Number of Awards: 1.

DECA Inc.

1908 Association Drive
Reston, VA 20191-1594
Phone: 703-860-5000
Fax: 703-860-4013
Email: Kathy_Onion@deca.org
Website: http://www.deca.org

203 • Harry A. Applegate Scholarship

Purpose: To reward current active members of DECA, the high school division or Delta Epsilon Chi, the college division of DECA.

Eligibility: Applicants must plan to be full-time students at a two-year or four-year program in marketing, entrepreneurship or management. This award is based on merit, not financial need, but applicants may include financial need statements for review. Applicants should submit transcripts, test scores, a statement of club participiation, proof of leadership outside DECA, three recommendation letters and proof of membership.

How to Apply: Applications are available online and should be submitted to state/provincial DECA advisors.
Deadline: Check with your state or provincial advisor about deadlines.
Amount: Varies.
Number of Awards: Varies.

Executive Women International (EWI)

515 South 700 East Suite 2A
Salt Lake City, UT 84102
Phone: 801-355-2800
Fax: 801-355-2852
Email: ewi@executivewomen.org
Website: http://www.executivewomen.org

204 • Adult Students in Scholastic Transition (ASIST)

Purpose: To assist adult students who face major life transitions.

Eligibility: Applicants may be single parents, individuals just entering the workforce or displaced workers.

How to Apply: Contact your local EWI chapter.
Deadline: Varies.
Amount: Varies.
Number of Awards: Varies.

205 • Executive Women International Scholarship Program

Purpose: To assist high school students in achieving their academic goals.

Eligibility: Applicants must be high school juniors who plan to pursue four-year degrees at accredited colleges or universities. Selection is based on application materials, communication skills, academic record, extracurricular activities and leadership.

How to Apply: Contact your local EWI chapter.
Deadline: Varies.
Amount: $500-$10,000.
Number of Awards: Varies.

Financial Markets Center

Gonzalez Award
P.O. Box 334
Philomont, VA 20131
Phone: 540-338-7754
Fax: 540-338-7757
Website: http://www.fmcenter.org

206 • Henry B. Gonzalez Award

Purpose: To promote institutional reforms that make the central bank more effective.

Eligibility: Applicants must submit a paper on the subject of central bank reform. Paper should be no longer than 15,000 words, not including footnotes, endnotes and references. Preference is given to clearly written entries accessible to a broad audience.

How to Apply: There is no official application form.
Deadline: Varies.
Amount: $2,500.
Number of Awards: Varies.

Funeral Service Foundation

13625 Bishop's Drive
Brookfield, WI 53005
Phone: 877-402-5900
Fax: 262-789-6977
Email: kbuenger@funeralservicefoundation.org
Website: http://www.funeralservicefoundation.org

207 • FSF Scholarship Program

Purpose: To provide financial assistance for higher education to those working in fields related to funeral service.

Eligibility: Applicants must be undergraduate students enrolled in funeral science programs.

How to Apply: Applications are available online.
Deadline: March.
Amount: Varies.
Number of Awards: Varies.

Institute of Internal Auditors

247 Maitland Avenue
Altamonte Springs, FL 32701-4201
Phone: 407-937-1100
Fax: 407-937-1101
Email: research@theiia.org
Website: http://www.theiia.org

208 • Esther R. Sawyer Scholarship Award

Purpose: To award internal auditing students.

Eligibility: Applicants should be accepted to or currently enrolled in a graduate program in internal auditing at an IIA-endorsed school or have taken internal auditing undergraduate courses at at an IIA-endorsed school and be enrolled in any graduate program in internal auditing or business. An original manuscript on a topic related to modern internal auditing is required. The award is based on the topic, value to the audit profession, originality and the quality of writing.

How to Apply: Application materials are described online.
Deadline: March 1.
Amount: $5,000.
Number of Awards: 1.

International Society of Logistics

Chairman, Scholarships Review Committee
Logistics Education Foundation
8100 Professional Place, Suite 111
Hyattsville, MD 20785
Phone: 301-459-8446
Fax: 301-459-1522
Email: solehq@sole.org
Website: http://www.sole.org

209 • Annual Logistics Scholarship Competition

Purpose: The organization is dedicated to upgrading the quality and availability of logistics education.

Eligibility: Applicants must be pursuing a bachelor's or master's degree in logistics or a logistics-related major and be full-time students with a full-time course load. Applicants' intention to pursue a logistics-related career, scholastic achievements and current and potential contributions to the logistics profession are considered.

How to Apply: Applications are available online.
Deadline: May 15.
Amount: $1,000.
Number of Awards: Varies.

James J. Hill Research Library

80 W. Fourth Street
Saint Paul, MN 55102
Phone: 651-265-5500
Email: manuscripts@jjhill.org
Website: http://www.jjhill.org

210 • James J. Hill Research Grants

Purpose: To assist scholars whose research requires them to use the business information manuscript collections at the Hill Library.

Eligibility: Applicants must be college or university professors, independent scholars, or Ph. D. candidates who are working on their dissertations. Applications must include a research proposal, projected budget and three letters of recommendation.

How to Apply: Applications are available by email, phone or online at http://www.jjhill.org/History/grant_program.html.
Deadline: November 1.
Amount: $2,000.
Number of Awards: Varies.

National Association of Insurance Women (NAIW) Education Foundation

5310 E. 31st Street
Tulsa, OK 74135
Phone: 918-622-1816
Fax: 918-622-1821
Email: foundation@naiwfoundation.org
Website: http://www.naiwfoundation.org

211 • College Scholarships

Purpose: To promote studies in the insurance industry.

Eligibility: Applicants must major or minor in insurance, risk management or actuarial science, be at least college sophomores, have completed or be currently enrolled in two insurance or risk management-related courses and have a minimum 3.0 GPA.

How to Apply: Applications are available online.
Deadline: March 1.
Amount: Varies.
Number of Awards: Varies.

212 • Professional Scholarships

Purpose: To promote excellence in the insurance industry by helping in the education of its employees.

Eligibility: Applicants must have been employed in the industry for at least two years and be studying to improve their skills.

How to Apply: Applications are available online.

Deadline: September 1, December 1, March 1.

Amount: Varies.

Number of Awards: Varies.

National Association of Water Companies

1725 K Street NW
Suite 200
Washington, DC 20006
Phone: 202-833-8383
Fax: 202-331-7442
Website: http://www.nawc.org

213 • National Association of Water Companies Scholarship

Purpose: To recognize scholastic achievement, leadership and initiative and to encourage students to pursue careers in the investor-owned water utility business.

Eligibility: Applicants must be graduating college seniors, college graduates or entering graduate students and attend a school located in California, Connecticut, Delaware, Florida, Indiana, Illinois, Maine, Massachusetts, Missouri, New Hampshire, New Jersey, New York, North Carolina, Ohio, Pennsylvania, Rhode Island, South Carolina or Vermont. Applicants must also study engineering, biology, chemistry, business administration or another field which may lead to a career in the investor-owned public water supply business.

How to Apply: Applications are available online.

Deadline: April 1.

Amount: $5,000.

Number of Awards: 1.

National Defense Transportation Association-Scott St. Louis Chapter

Attention: Scholarship Committee
P.O. Box 25486
Scott Air Force Base, IL 62225-0486
Website: http://www.ndtascottstlouis.org

214 • National Defense Transportation Association, St. Louis Area Chapter Scholarship

Purpose: To promote careers in business, transportation logistics and physical distribution.

Eligibility: Preference is given to students majoring in business, transportation logistics and physical distribution or a related field. High school students must live in Illinois or Missouri. College students must attend school in Colorado, Iowa, Illinois, Indiana, Kansas, Michigan, Minnesota, Missouri, Montana, North Dakota, Nebraska, South Dakota, Wisconsin or Wyoming.

How to Apply: Applications are available online.

Deadline: March 1.

Amount: $2,500.

Number of Awards: 6.

National Society of Hispanic MBAs

1303 Walnut Hill Lane Suite 100
Irving, TX 75038
Phone: 877-467-4622
Fax: 214-596-9325
Email: scholarships@nshmba.org
Website: http://www.nshmba.org

215 • National Society of Hispanic MBAs Scholarship

Purpose: To provide financial support to Hispanic students pursuing an MBA.

Eligibility: Applicants must be U.S. citizens or legal permanent residents of Hispanic heritage (defined as having at least one parent of full Hispanic heritage or both parents of half-Hispanic heritage). Students must be members of the NSHMBA, but they may enroll at a special application rate. Applicants must be enrolled or planning to enroll in master's programs in business or management at an accredited college or university. Scholarships are based on academic achievement, work experience, personal statement, community service, recommendations and financial need.

How to Apply: Applications are available online.

Deadline: June 12.

Amount: $1,500-$5,000.

Number of Awards: Varies.

Pacific Telecommunications Council (PTC)

Claudine Naruse
2454 S. Beretania Street, 3rd floor
Honolulu, HI 96826
Phone: 808-941-3789
Fax: 808-944-4874
Email: claudine@ptc.org
Website: http://www.ptc.org

216 • Pacific Telecommunications Essay Prize Contest

Purpose: To promote the development and use of telecommunications in the Pacific Hemisphere.

Eligibility: Applicants must be either working on a graduate degree or have obtained graduate level degrees within the last five years and write an essay on the topic provided.

How to Apply: Applications are available online.

Deadline: April 30.

Amount: $2,000.

Number of Awards: 3.

Related Scholarships:

Organization of Chinese Americans (OCA)

See #1037 · Lead Summer Program

Public Relations Student Society of America

See #596 · Betsy Plank/PRSSA Scholarship

Public Relations Student Society of America

See #597 · Gary Yoshimura Scholarship

Public Relations Student Society of America

See #599 · Professor Sidney Gross Memorial Award

National Association of Black Accountants

See #1017 · National Association of Black Accountants Scholarship Program

Women In Defense

See #565 · HORIZONS Foundation Scholarship

Institute for Humane Studies at George Mason University

See #37 · Summer Graduate Research Fellowships

BI-LO Corporation

See #1528 · BI-LO Minority Scholarship Program

American Society of Travel Agents (ASTA) Foundation Inc.

See #521 · Holland America Line-Westours Inc. Research Grant

American Society of Travel Agents (ASTA) Foundation Inc.

See #524 · Simmons Scholarship

American Society of Travel Agents (ASTA) Foundation Inc.

See #525 · Southern California Chapter/Pleasant Hawaiian Holidays Scholarship

American Society of Travel Agents (ASTA) Foundation Inc.

See #523 · Princess Cruises and Princess Tours Scholarship

American Society of Travel Agents (ASTA) Foundation Inc.

See #520 · Healy Scholarship

American Society of Travel Agents (ASTA) Foundation Inc.

See #522 · Joseph R. Stone Scholarship

American Society of Travel Agents (ASTA) Foundation Inc.

See #519 · Avis Scholarship

Hispanic College Fund

See #984 · Hispanic College Fund Scholarships

Delta Sigma Pi

See #769 · Undergraduate Scholarship

National Restaurant Association Educational Foundation

See #488 · Academic Scholarship For Undergraduate College Students

National Society of Professional Engineers

See #414 · Professional Engineers In Government (PEG)

Delta Sigma Pi

See #768 · Collegian of the Year

National Restaurant Association Educational Foundation

See #487 · Academic Scholarship for High School Seniors

Institute for Humane Studies at George Mason University

See #36 · Humane Studies Fellowships

National Urban League

See #1033 · Gillette/National Urban League Scholarship and Intern Program for Minority Students

Public Relations Student Society of America

See #598 · Lawrence G. Foster Award for Excellence in Public Relations

National Society of Accountants Scholarship Program

See #81 · NSA Scholarship Foundation

Bank of America

See #290 · Bank of America ADA Abilities Scholarship Program

Association of Certified Fraud Examiners

See #73 · Ritchie-Jennings Memorial Scholarship

National Tourism Foundation

See #528 · Travelers Conservation Foundation Sustainable Tourism Scholarship

American Society of Travel Agents (ASTA) Foundation Inc.

See #518 · American Express Travel Scholarship

National Association for the Advancement of Colored People

See #1012 · Earl Graves Scholarship

Aspen Institute

See #957 · William Randolph Hearst Endowed Scholarship for Minority Students

Golden Key National Honour Society

See #786 · Ford Motor Company Business and Leadership Scholarship

Institute of Management Accountants (IMA)

See #77 · IMA Memorial Education Fund Scholarship

Society of Satellite Professionals International (SSPI)

See #251 · SSPI Scholarship Program

National Association of Negro Business and Professional Women's Clubs Inc.

See #1025 · National Scholarship

United Negro College Fund (UNCF)

See #1078 · Citigroup Fellows Program

Hispanic Scholarship Fund (HSF)

See #990 · HSF/General Motors Scholarship

American Institute Of Certified Public Accountants

See #72 · Accountemps/American Institute Of Certified Public Accountants Student Scholarship

Casualty Actuarial Society/Society of Actuaries

See #967 · Actuarial Scholarships for Minority Students

Association for International Practical Training (AIPT)

See #526 · Jessica King Scholarship

Consortium for Graduate Study in Management

See #977 · Consortium Fellowship

Fund for American Studies

See #1173 · Fund for American Studies Internships

Golden Key National Honour Society

See #782 · Business Achievement Awards

German Marshall Fund of the United States

See #911 · Transatlantic Fellows Program

Hospitality Sales and Marketing Association International (HSMAI)

See #527 · HSMAI Foundation Scholarship

Hagley Museum and Library

See #1176 · Henry Belin du Pont Dissertation Fellowship

Institute of Management Accountants (IMA)

See #78 · Stuart Cameron and Margaret McLeod Memorial Scholarship

National Security Agency (NSA)

See #1189 · Pat Roberts Intelligence Scholars Program for Intelligence Analysts

National Security Agency (NSA)

See #246 · Pat Roberts Intelligence Scholars Program for Global Network Analysts

Cargill

See #966 · United Negro College Fund Cargill Scholarship-Internship Program

Chemistry

Also See Scholarships Listed Under:
Biological Sciences/Life Sciences
Engineering (Includes Chemical Eng.)
Medicine/Nursing/Health Professions
Sciences/Physical Sciences

American Institute of Chemical Engineers - (AIChE)

3 Park Avenue
New York, NY 10016
Phone: 212-591-7634
Fax: 212-591-8890
Email: awards@aiche.org
Website: http://www.aiche.org

217 • Donald F. and Mildred Topp Othmer Foundation

Purpose: To support AIChE student members.
Eligibility: Applicants must be members of an AIChE Student Chapter or Chemical Engineering Club. Applicants must be nominated by their student chapter advisors. Awards are presented on the basis of academic achievement and involvement in student chapter activities.
How to Apply: Applications are available online.
Deadline: May 7.
Amount: $1,000.
Number of Awards: 15.

218 • John J. McKetta Scholarship

Purpose: To support chemical engineering students.
Eligibility: Applicants must be chemical engineering incoming undergraduate juniors or seniors and be planning a career in the chemical engineering process industries. Applicants must also have a minimum 3.0 GPA and be attending an ABET accredited school in the U.S., Canada or Mexico. Selection is based on an essay outlining career goals, leadership in an AIChE student chapter or other university sponsored activity and letters of recommendation. Preference is given to members of AIChE.
How to Apply: Applications are available online.
Deadline: April 15.
Amount: $5,000.
Number of Awards: 1.

Electrochemical Society

65 S. Main Street, Building D
Pennington, NJ 08534-2839
Phone: 609-737-1902
Fax: 609-737-2743
Email: awards@electrochem.org
Website: http://www.electrochem.org

219 • Industrial Electrolysis and Electrochemical Engineering Division H.H. Dow Memorial Student Award

Purpose: To recognize young engineers and scientists in the fields of electrochemical engineering and applied electrochemistry.
Eligibility: Applicants must be accepted to or enrolled in a graduate program. The application requires transcripts, a description of the research project, a description of how the project relates to electrochemical engineering or applied electrochemistry, a biography, a resume or curriculum vitae and a letter of recommendation from the research supervisor. The award is based on academic performance, research and the recommendation.
How to Apply: Application materials are described online.
Deadline: September 15.
Amount: $1,000.
Number of Awards: Varies.

220 • SemiZone E-Learning Fellowships

Purpose: To provide training for ECS members.
Eligibility: Applicants should be Electrochemical Society (ECS) student members, ECS members who are currently unemployed or in job transition, ECS members who are full-time employees of academic and other non-profit institutions, retired professionals or industry members under the age of 30 and interested in SemiZone distance-learning courses.
How to Apply: Contact the organization for application information.
Deadline: Varies.
Amount: $1,000.
Number of Awards: 3.

221 • Student Poster Session Awards

Purpose: To award students for work related to fields of interest to ECS.
Eligibility: Applicants must be pursuing degrees at any college or university and prepare an abstract on work performed. The applicants must also prepare a poster to present at the society meeting where they will be judged. Two awards are in the categories of electrochemical science and technology and solid-state science and technology.
How to Apply: Application materials are described online.
Deadline: Varies.
Amount: $250.
Number of Awards: 2.

Iota Sigma Pi (ISP)

Dr. Joanne Bedlek-Anslow, MAL Coordinator
Camden High School, Science
1022 Ehrenclou Drive
Camden, SC 29020
Website: http://www.iotasigmapi.info

222 • Members-at-Large Reentry Award

Purpose: To recognize potential achievement in chemistry and related fields for a woman undergraduate or graduate student who has been absent from academia for at least three years.
Eligibility: Applicants must be female undergraduate or graduate students at an accredited four-year institution and be nominated by a faculty member or an Iota Sigma Pi member.
How to Apply: Application information is available online.
Deadline: March 20.
Amount: $1,000.
Number of Awards: 1.

Iota Sigma Pi (ISP) ND

Professor Kathryn A. Thomasson, Iota Sigma Pi Director for
Student Awards
University of North Dakota, Department of Chemistry
P.O. Box 9024
Grand Forks, ND 58202-9024
Phone: 701-777-3199
Fax: 701-777-2331
Email: kthomasson@chem.und.edu
Website: http://www.iotasigmapi.info

223 • Gladys Anderson Emerson Scholarship

Purpose: To award achievement in the fields of chemistry and
biochemistry by women.

Eligibility: Applicants must have attained junior status at an
accredited college or university, be female and be nominated by a
member of Iota Sigma Pi.

How to Apply: Applications are available online.

Deadline: February 15.

Amount: $2,000.

Number of Awards: 1.

224 • Undergraduate Award for Excellence in Chemistry

Purpose: To award female undergraduate students for excellence
in the field of chemistry study.

Eligibility: Applicants must be female senior chemistry students
at an accredited four-year college or university and be nominated
by a member of the faculty.

How to Apply: Applications are available online.

Deadline: February 15.

Amount: $500.

Number of Awards: 1.

Related Scholarships:

American Chemical Society

See #935 • American Chemical Society Scholars Program

Maryland Higher Education Commission

See #1402 • Science and Technology Scholarship

Society of Plastics Engineers

*See #424 • American Plastics Council (APC)/SPE Plastics
Environmental Division Scholarship*

Society of Plastics Engineers

See #426 • Polymer Modifiers and Additives Division Scholarships

Society of Plastics Engineers

See #428 • Ted Neward Scholarship

Society of Plastics Engineers

*See #430 • Thermoset Division/James I. MacKenzie Memorial
Scholarship*

American Council of Independent Laboratories

See #1111 • ACIL Scholarship

American Meteorological Society

See #1115 • AMS/Industry/Government Graduate Fellowships

National Association for Surface Finishing

*See #1145 • American Electroplaters and Surface Finishers Society
Scholarship*

Astronaut Scholarship Foundation

See #1128 • Astronaut Scholarship

National Association of Water Companies

See #213 • National Association of Water Companies Scholarship

American Institute of Chemical Engineers - (AICHE)

See #351 • National Student Design Competition

American Institute of Chemical Engineers - (AICHE)

See #943 • Minority Scholarship Awards for College Students

American Institute of Chemical Engineers - (AICHE)

*See #942 • Minority Affairs Committee Award for Outstanding
Scholastic Achievement*

American Institute of Chemical Engineers - (AICHE)

See #944 • Minority Scholarship Awards for Incoming College Freshmen

National Urban League

See #1031 • American Chemical Society Minority Scholars Program

Intel Corporation and Science Service

See #1138 • Intel Science Talent Search

Siemens Foundation

See #1149 • Siemens Westinghouse Competition in Math, Science and Technology

Society of Plastics Engineers

See #425 • Composites Division/Harold Giles Scholarship

Society of Plastics Engineers

See #427 • SPE General Scholarships

Society of Plastics Engineers

See #429 • Thermoforming Division Memorial Scholarships

Society of Plastics Engineers

See #431 • Vinyl Plastics Division Scholarship

National Association for the Advancement of Colored People

See #1016 • Willems Scholarship

American Water Works Association

See #375 • Larson Aquatic Research Support (LARS)

Cargill

See #966 • United Negro College Fund Cargill Scholarship-Internship Program

Academia Resource Management

See #1110 • ARM Undergraduate Student Fellowships

Department of Defense, American Society for Engineering Education

See #1132 • NDSEG Fellowship Program

Davidson Institute for Talent Development

See #20 • Davidson Fellows Award

Communications

Also See Scholarships Listed Under:
English/Writing
Journalism/Broadcasting

American Radio Relay League Foundation

225 Main Street
Newington, CT 06111
Phone: 860-594-0200
Email: foundation@arrl.org
Website: http://www.arrl.org

225 • ARRL Scholarship Honoring Senator Barry Goldwater, K7UGA

Purpose: To assist ham radio operators in furthering their educations.

Eligibility: Applicants must have at least a novice ham radio license, be studying for a bachelor's or graduate degree and attend a regionally-accredited institute.

How to Apply: Applications are available online.
Deadline: February 1.
Amount: $5,000.
Number of Awards: 1.

226 • Charles Clarke Cordle Memorial Scholarship

Purpose: To assist ham radio operators in furthering their educations.

Eligibility: Applicants must have any class of ham radio license, have a minimum 2.5 GPA and be residents of and attend school in Georgia or Alabama.

How to Apply: Applications are available online.
Deadline: February 1.
Amount: $1,000.
Number of Awards: 1.

227 • Charles N. Fisher Memorial Scholarship

Purpose: To assist ham radio operators in furthering their educations.

Eligibility: Applicants must have any class of ham radio license, be residents of the ARRL Southwestern Division (Arizona, Los Angeles, Orange County, San Diego or Santa Barbara), attend a regionally-accredited college or university and study electronics, communications or a related field.

How to Apply: Applications are available online.
Deadline: February 1.
Amount: $1,000.
Number of Awards: 1.

228 • Chicago FM Club Scholarships

Purpose: To assist ham radio operators in furthering their educations.

Eligibility: Applicants must have at least a technician ham radio license, be residents of the FCC Ninth Call District (Illinois, Indiana, Wisconsin) and be students at an accredited post-secondary two- or four-year college or trade school.

How to Apply: Applications are available online.
Deadline: February 1.
Amount: $500.
Number of Awards: Varies.

229 • Donald Riebhoff Memorial Scholarship

Purpose: To assist ham radio operators in furthering their educations.

Eligibility: Applicants must have at least a technician ham radio license, be undergraduate or graduate students in international studies at an accredited post-secondary institution and be members of ARRL.

How to Apply: Applications are available online.
Deadline: February 1.
Amount: $1,000.
Number of Awards: 1.

230 • Dr. James L. Lawson Memorial Scholarship

Purpose: To assist ham radio operators in furthering their educations.

Eligibility: Applicants must have at least a general ham radio license, be residents of and attend post-secondary institutions in the New England states (Connecticut, Maine, Massachusetts, New Hampshire, Rhode Island or Vermont) or New York state and be pursuing a bachelor's or graduate degree in electronics, communications or a related field.

How to Apply: Applications are available online.
Deadline: February 1.
Amount: $500.
Number of Awards: 1.

231 • Earl I. Anderson Scholarship

Purpose: To assist ham radio operators with furthering their educations.

Eligibility: Applicants must have some form of ham radio operating license, be residents of Florida, Illinois, Indiana or Michigan, major in electronic engineering or a related technical field and be ARRL members.

How to Apply: Applications are available online.
Deadline: February 1.
Amount: $1,250.
Number of Awards: 3.

232 • Edmond A. Metzger Scholarship

Purpose: To assist ham radio operators in furthering their educations.

Eligibility: Applicants must have at least a novice ham radio license, be undergraduate or graduate students in electrical engineering, be residents of and attend schools in the ARRL Central Division (Illinois, Indiana, Wisconsin) and be members of ARRL.

How to Apply: Applications are available online.
Deadline: February 1.
Amount: $500.
Number of Awards: 1.

233 • Francis Walton Memorial Scholarship

Purpose: To assist ham radio operators in furthering their educations.

Eligibility: Applicants must have at least five words per minute certification, be residents of the ARRL Central Division (Illinois, Indiana, Wisconsin) and pursue a bachelor's or graduate degree at a regionally-accredited institution.

How to Apply: Applications are available online.
Deadline: February 1.
Amount: $500.
Number of Awards: Varies.

234 • Fred R. McDaniel Memorial Scholarship

Purpose: To assist ham radio operators in furthering their educations.

Eligibility: Applicants must have at least a general ham radio license, be residents of and attend a post-secondary institution in the FCC Fifth Call District (Texas, Oklahoma, Arkansas, Louisiana, Mississippi or New Mexico) and be studying for a bachelor's or graduate degree in electronics, communications or a related field. Preference is given to applicants with a 3.0 GPA or higher.

How to Apply: Applications are available online.

Deadline: February 1.

Amount: $500.

Number of Awards: 1.

235 • General Fund Scholarships

Purpose: To assist ham radio operators in furthering their educations.

Eligibility: Applicants must have any level of ham radio license.

How to Apply: Applications are available online.

Deadline: February 1.

Amount: $1,000.

Number of Awards: Varies.

236 • K2TEO Martin J. Green, Sr. Memorial Scholarship

Purpose: To assist ham radio operators in furthering their educations.

Eligibility: Applicants must have at least a general ham radio license. Preference is given to student hams from ham families.

How to Apply: Applications are available online.

Deadline: February 1.

Amount: $1,000.

Number of Awards: 1.

237 • L. Phil Wicker Scholarship

Purpose: To assist ham radio operators in furthering their educations.

Eligibility: Applicants must have at least a general ham radio license, be residents of and attending school in the ARRL Roanoke Division (North Carolina, South Carolina, Virginia, West Virginia) and be undergraduate or graduate students in electronics, communications or another related field.

How to Apply: Applications are available online.

Deadline: February 1.

Amount: $1,000.

Number of Awards: 1.

238 • Mary Lou Brown Scholarship

Purpose: To assist ham radio operators with furthering their educations.

Eligibility: Applicants must have at least a general ham radio license, be residents of the ARRL Northwest Division (Alaska, Idaho, Montana, Oregon or Washington), be working for a bachelor's or graduate degree, have a minimum 3.0 GPA and have demonstrated interest in promoting the Amateur Radio Service.

How to Apply: Applications are available online.

Deadline: February 1.

Amount: $2,500.

Number of Awards: Varies.

239 • New England FEMARA Scholarships

Purpose: To assist ham radio operators in furthering their educations.

Eligibility: Applicants must have at least a technician ham radio license and be residents of the New England States (Connecticut, Maine, Massachusetts, New Hampshire, Rhode Island, Vermont).

How to Apply: Applications are available online.

Deadline: February 1.

Amount: $1,000.

Number of Awards: Varies.

240 • Paul and Helen L. Grauer Scholarship

Purpose: To assist ham radio operators in furthering their educations.

Eligibility: Applicants must have at least a novice ham radio license, be residents and attend school in the ARRL Midwest Division (Iowa, Kansas, Missouri, Nebraska) and be undergraduate or graduate students in electronics, communications or another related field.

How to Apply: Applications are available online.

Deadline: February 1.

Amount: $1,000.

Number of Awards: 1.

241 • PHD ARA Scholarship

Purpose: To assist ham radio operators in furthering their educations.

Eligibility: Applicants must have any class of ham radio license, be residents of the ARRL Midwest Division (Iowa, Kansas, Missouri, Nebraska) and be studying journalism, computer science or electronic engineering. Applicants may also be the children of deceased amateur radio operators.

How to Apply: Applications are available online.

Deadline: February 1.

Amount: $1,000.

Number of Awards: 1.

242 • Tom and Judith Comstock Scholarship

Purpose: To assist ham radio operators in furthering their educations.

Eligibility: Applicants must have any class of ham radio license, be residents of Texas or Oklahoma and be high school seniors accepted at a two- or four-year college or university.

How to Apply: Applications are available online.

Deadline: February 1.

Amount: $1,000.

Number of Awards: 1.

Charles and Lucille King Family Foundation

366 Madison Avenue
10th Floor
New York, NY 10017
Phone: 212-682-2913
Email: info@kingfoundation.org
Website: http://www.kingfoundation.org

243 • Charles & Lucille King Family Foundation Scholarship

Purpose: To assist film and television students.

Eligibility: Applicants must be undergraduate juniors or seniors and demonstrate academic ability, financial need and professional potential. Applicants must also major in film and television.

How to Apply: Applications are available online or by written request between September 1 and April 1.

Deadline: April 15.

Amount: $5,000.

Number of Awards: Varies.

Electronic Document Systems Foundation

608 Silver Spur Road, Suite 280
Rolling Hills Estates, CA 90274
Phone: 310-265-5510
Fax: 310-265-5588
Email: info@edsf.org.
Website: http://www.edsf.org

244 • Electronic Document Systems Foundation Scholarship Awards

Purpose: To support students interested in pursuing careers in document management and communication.

Eligibility: Applicants must be full-time students interested in a career in the preparation, production or distribution of documents. Possible areas of study include marketing, graphic arts, e-commerce, imaging science, printing, web authoring, electronic publishing, computer science, telecommunications or business. For most scholarships, applicants must be junior, senior or graduate students; however opportunities exist for students at all levels, including those attending two-year colleges. Specific scholarships are available for U.S. and Canadian citizens.

How to Apply: Applications are available online.
Deadline: May 15.
Amount: $250-$5,000.
Number of Awards: Varies.

National Association of Broadcasters

1771 N Street NW
Washington, DC 20036
Phone: 202-429-5300
Fax: 202-429-4199
Email: kfox@nab.org
Website: http://www.nab.org

245 • Grants for Research in Broadcasting

Purpose: To support academic research on economic, business, policy and social issues important to policy makers and station managers in the network broadcast industry.

Eligibility: Applicants may be academic faculty, graduate students or undergraduate seniors. Research issues may include the economic and social dynamics of digital TV multicasting, broadcasting's public service role during natural disasters, adoption of HD radio, impact of new regulations, analysis of audience response to digital broadcasting, impact of new technologies, consumer media habits, effectiveness of local news programs, trends in audience measurement technologies, commercial advertising effectiveness, impact of non-response on media research, training future broadcasters and the importance of television and radio advertising on local and national economies.

How to Apply: Applications are available online.
Deadline: Varies.
Amount: Varies.
Number of Awards: 4-6.

National Security Agency (NSA)

9800 Savage Road, Suite 6779
Ft. George G. Meade, MD 20755-6779
Phone: 410-854-4725
Website: http://www.nsa.gov/careers/

246 • Pat Roberts Intelligence Scholars Program for Global Network Analysts

Purpose: To support students who plan to work in global network analysis after graduation.

Eligibility: Applicants must be college sophomores or juniors pursuing one of the following fields related to global network analysis: technical studies (computer science major with a minor in political science or international relations); topical studies (telecommunications and information systems networks, terrorism, proliferation or related sciences, international banking and finance) or disciplines (technical intelligence analysis, information assurance, network and telecommunications). Recipients are expected to become full-time employees of NSA's Global Network Analysis Intern Program after graduation. One- and two-year scholarships are offered.

How to Apply: Applications are available online.
Deadline: November 30.
Amount: Up to $25,000 per year.
Number of Awards: Varies.

Optimist International

4494 Lindell Boulevard
St. Louis, MO 63108
Phone: 314-371-6000
Fax: 314-371-6006
Email: programs@optimist.org
Website: http://www.optimist.org

247 • Optimist International Oratorical Contest

Purpose: To reward students based on their oratorical performance.

Eligibility: Applicants must be students in the U.S., Canada or Caribbean under the age of 16 as of December 31st of the entry year. Selection is based on an oratorical contest.

How to Apply: Contact your local Optimist Club.
Deadline: June 15.
Amount: $500-$1,500.
Number of Awards: Varies.

Outdoor Writers Association of America

121 Hickory Street
Suite 1
Missoula, MT 59801
Phone: 406-728-7434
Fax: 406-728-7445
Website: http://www.owaa.org

248 • Bodie McDowell Scholarship

Purpose: To support students in outdoor communications fields.

Eligibility: Applicants must be students of outdoor communications fields including print, film, art or broadcasting and must be either undergraduate students entering their junior or senior year or graduate students. The school must be registered with OWAA as a scholarship program participant.

How to Apply: Applicants are available through your college.
Deadline: February 28.
Amount: $2,500-$3,500.
Number of Awards: 3 or more.

Society for Technical Communication

901 N. Stuart Street, Suite 904
Arlington, VA 22203
Phone: 703-522-4114
Email: stc@stc.org
Website: http://www.stc.org

249 • Distinguished Service Award for Students

Purpose: To assist students who are pursuing degrees in an area of technical communication.

Eligibility: Applicants must be full-time undergraduate or graduate students who have completed at least one year of post-secondary education and who have at least one full year of academic work remaining to complete their degree programs. Applicants must also be in the field of communication of information about technical subjects.

How to Apply: Applications are available by written request.
Deadline: November 30.
Amount: $1,000.
Number of Awards: 7.

Society of Broadcast Engineers

9102 N. Meridian Street
Suite 150
Indianapolis, IN 46260
Phone: 317-846-9000
Fax: 317-846-9120
Email: mclappe@sbe.org
Website: http://www.sbe.org

250 • Youth Scholarship

Purpose: To help students who plan to pursue a career in the technical aspects of broadcasting.

Eligibility: Applicants must be graduating high school seniors who plan to enroll in a technical school, college or university and should pursue studies leading to a career in broadcasting engineering or a related field. Preference is given to members of SBE, but any student may apply. Applicants should submit applications, transcripts, biographies and statements. Recipients must write a paper about broadcast engineering.

How to Apply: Applications are available online.
Deadline: July 1.
Amount: $3,000.
Number of Awards: Varies.

Society of Satellite Professionals International (SSPI)

Tamara Bond
55 Broad Street
14th Floor
New York , NY 10004
Phone: 212-809-5199
Fax: 212-825-0075
Email: rbell@sspi.org
Website: http://www.sspi.org

251 • SSPI Scholarship Program

Purpose: To help high school and university graduates with undergraduate and post-graduate study in satellite-related disciplines.

Eligibility: Applicants must be high school seniors, undergraduate or graduate students who are members of SSPI (membership is free) studying satellite-related technologies, policies or applications. Some scholarships have requirements such as interests, financial need, residency, gender, race or GPA. The award is based on commitment to education and careers in the satellite fields, academic and leadership achievement, potential for contribution to the satellite communications industry and a scientific, engineering, research, business or creative submission.

How to Apply: Applications are available online.
Deadline: April 30.
Amount: $5,000.
Number of Awards: Varies.

Tag and Label Manufacturers Institute Inc.

40 Shuman Boulevard, Suite 295
Naperville, IL 60563
Phone: 630-357-9222
Fax: 630-357-0192
Website: http://www.tlmi.com

252 • TLMI Four Year Colleges/Full-Time Students Scholarship

Purpose: To assist upper-level students planning to pursue a career in tag and label manufacturing.

Eligibility: Applicants must demonstrate an interest in the tag and label manufacturing industry while taking appropriate courses at an accredited four-year college. They must be full-time sophomores or juniors with a GPA of at least 3.0. Applicants must submit a personal statement and three letters of recommendation attesting to their character.

How to Apply: Applications are available online and by phone.
Deadline: March 31.
Amount: $5,000.
Number of Awards: 6.

Related Scholarships:

Armed Forces Communications and Electronics Association

See #254 · AFCEA Ralph W. Shrader Scholarships

National Speakers Association

See #450 · Earl Nightengale Scholarship

National Speakers Association

See #449 · Cavett Robert Scholarship

National Dairy Shrine

See #136 · Milk Marketing Scholarship

BI-LO Corporation

See #1528 · BI-LO Minority Scholarship Program

Graphic Arts Information Network

See #507 · Print and Graphics Scholarship

National Speakers Association

See #451 · Nido Qubein Scholarship

Institute for Humane Studies at George Mason University

See #535 · Young Communicators Fellowships

Public Relations Student Society of America

See #1045 · Multicultural Affairs Scholarship Program

National Speakers Association

See #448 · Bill Gove Scholarship

Hispanic Heritage Awards Foundation

See #985 · Hispanic Heritage Youth Awards

Pacific Telecommunications Council (PTC)

See #216 · Pacific Telecommunications Essay Prize Contest

Optimist International

See #310 · Optimist International Communications Contest

Rolling Stone

See #554 · Rolling Stone Annual College Journalism Competition

California Chicano News Media Association

See #1223 · Frank del Olmo Memorial Scholarship

California Chicano News Media Association

See #1222 · CCNMA Scholarships

Golden Key National Honour Society

See #790 · Literary Achievement Awards

German Marshall Fund of the United States

See #911 · Transatlantic Fellows Program

International Foodservice Editorial Council (IFEC)

See #486 · IFEC Scholarships Award

Journalism Education Association

See #537 · Student Journalist Impact Award

Journalism Education Association Future Teacher Scholarship

See #333 · Future Teacher Scholarship

National Security Agency (NSA)

See #1189 · Pat Roberts Intelligence Scholars Program for Intelligence Analysts

National Association of Negro Business and Professional Women's Clubs Inc.

See #1024 · Julianne Malveaux Scholarship

Common Knowledge Scholarship Foundation

See #594 · Public Relations Scholarship

California Chicano News Media Association

See #1224 · Joel Garcia Memorial Scholarship

Fund for American Studies

See #1173 · Fund for American Studies Internships

Computer and Information Science

Also See Scholarships Listed Under:
Engineering
Mathematics
Sciences/Physical Sciences

Armed Forces Communications and Electronics Association

4400 Fair Lakes Court
Fairfax, VA 22033
Phone: 800-336-4583
Fax: 703-631-4693
Email: scholarship@afcea.org
Website: http://www.afcea.org

253 • AFCEA General John A. Wickham Scholarships

Purpose: Monetary assistance for college is awarded to sophomores and juniors who are studying electrical, computer, chemical or aerospace engineering, computer science, physics or mathematics.

Eligibility: Applicants must be full-time college sophomores or juniors in accredited four-year U.S. colleges or universities, be U.S. citizens, be working toward a degree in electrical, computer, chemical or aerospace engineering, computer science, physics or mathematics and have a minimum 3.5 GPA. Applicants do not need to be affiliated with the U.S. military.

How to Apply: Applications are available online.
Deadline: May 1.
Amount: $2,000.
Number of Awards: Varies.

254 • AFCEA Ralph W. Shrader Scholarships

Purpose: Monetary assistance is awarded to graduate students studying electrical, computer, chemical or aerospace engineering, mathematics, physics, computer science, computer technology, electronics, communications technology or engineering or information management systems.

Eligibility: Applicants must be U.S. citizens, full-time postgraduate students working toward a master's degree in electrical, computer, chemical or aerospace engineering, mathematics, physics, computer science, computer technology, electronics, communications technology, communications engineering or information management at an accredited U.S. university. Primary consideration will be given for demonstrated excellence. Applicants do not need to be affiliated with the U.S. military.

How to Apply: Applications are available online.
Deadline: February 1.
Amount: $3,000.
Number of Awards: Varies.

Association of Old Crows

1000 N. Payne Street
Suite 300
Alexandria, VA 22314-1652
Phone: 703-549-1600
Fax: 703-549-2589
Email: richetti@crows.org
Website: http://www.myaoc.org

255 • AOC Scholarships

Purpose: To encourage students interested in strong defense capability emphasizing electronic warfare and information operations.

Eligibility: Applicants should consult their AOC chapters for scholarship guidelines.

How to Apply: Applications are available online.
Deadline: December 1.
Amount: Varies.
Number of Awards: Varies.

Datatel

4375 Fair Lakes Court
Fairfax, VA 22033
Phone: 800-328-2835
Email: scholars@datatel.com
Website: http://www.datatel.com

256 • Nancy Goodhue Lynch Scholarship

Purpose: Datatel has created scholarship programs as part of its commitment to higher education and also to give back to its clients.

Eligibility: Applicants must be undergraduate students majoring in an information technology field and attending a Datatel Client college or university. Students must include a personal statement about why they have chosen to study an information technology field, the impact of technology on their futures and the importance of the scholarship.

How to Apply: Applications are available online.
Deadline: January 31.
Amount: $2,500.
Number of Awards: 2.

Healthcare Information and Management Systems Society

230 E. Ohio Street, Suite 500
Chicago, IL 60611-3269
Phone: 312-664-4467
Fax: 312-664-6143
Website: http://www.himss.org

257 • HIMSS Foundation Scholarship

Purpose: To provide scholarships based on academic achievement and leadership in the field of healthcare information and management systems.

Eligibility: Applicants must be members of HIMSS and study healthcare information and management systems. Scholarships are also available from individual chapters listed on the HIMSS website.

Deadline: Varies.
Amount: Varies.
Number of Awards: 7.

Institute of Electrical and Electronics Engineers History Center

445 Hoes Lane
Piscataway, NJ 08854
Phone: 732-562-3860

Email: supportieee@ieee.org
Website: http://www.ieee.org/history_center

258 • IEEE Presidents' Scholarship

Purpose: To award a student for a project relevant to electrical engineering, electronics engineering, computer science or other IEEE fields of interest.

Eligibility: Applicants must be high school students planning to study engineering or engineering-related fields and must compete in the Intel ISEF competitions beginning at the state/local level and advance to the international competition.

How to Apply: Contact the organization for more information.
Deadline: Varies.
Amount: $10,000.
Number of Awards: Varies.

Microsoft Corporation

One Microsoft Way
Redmond, WA 98052-8303
Phone: 800-642-7676
Fax: 425-936-7329
Email: scholars@microsoft.com
Website: http://www.microsoft.com/college/

259 • Microsoft Tuition Scholarships

Purpose: Offering more than a half-million dollars in scholarships, Microsoft is looking for undergraduates who display an interest in the software industry and are committed to leadership.

Eligibility: Applicants must be in a full-time undergraduate program related to computer science. Recipients will have to complete salaried internships in Redmond, Washington. There are special scholarships for women, minorities and disabled students.

How to Apply: Application requirements are online.
Deadline: January 15.
Amount: Varies.
Number of Awards: Varies.

Related Scholarships:

Intel Corporation and Science Service

See #1138 • Intel Science Talent Search

Siemens Foundation

See #1149 • Siemens Westinghouse Competition in Math, Science and Technology

Armed Forces Communications and Electronics Association

See #707 • AFCEA Sgt Jeannette L. Winters, USMC Memorial Scholarship

Armed Forces Communications and Electronics Association

See #705 • AFCEA General Emmett Paige Scholarships

Armed Forces Communications and Electronics Association

See #706 • AFCEA ROTC Scholarships

Massachusetts Office of Student Financial Assistance

See #1415 • CommonWealth Futures Grant Program

Astronaut Scholarship Foundation

See #1128 • Astronaut Scholarship

Hispanic College Fund

See #984 • Hispanic College Fund Scholarships

Women In Defense

See #565 • HORIZONS Foundation Scholarship

Bank of America

See #290 • Bank of America ADA Abilities Scholarship Program

Society for Imaging Science and Technology

See #417 • Raymond Davis Scholarship

Academia Resource Management

See #1110 • ARM Undergraduate Student Fellowships

Association of Government Accountants (AGA)

See #200 • AGA Scholarships

Golden Key National Honour Society

See #785 • Engineering/Technology Achievement Awards

National Security Agency (NSA)

See #1189 • Pat Roberts Intelligence Scholars Program for Intelligence Analysts

National Security Agency (NSA)

See #246 • Pat Roberts Intelligence Scholars Program for Global Network Analysts

National Security Agency (NSA)

See #50 • Stokes Educational Scholarship Program

Intel Corporation and Science Service

See #1139 • International Science and Engineering Fair

United Negro College Fund (UNCF)

See #1078 • Citigroup Fellows Program

Davidson Institute for Talent Development

See #20 • Davidson Fellows Award

Cargill

See #966 • United Negro College Fund Cargill Scholarship-Internship Program

Construction Trades

Also See Scholarships Listed Under:
Vocational/Technical

Associated Builders and Contractors

Trimmer Education Foundation
4250 N. Fairfax Drive
9th Floor
Arlington, VA 22203
Phone: 703-812-2000
Email: studentchapters@abc.org
Website: http://www.abc.org

260 • Trimmer Foundation Student Scholarships

Purpose: To assist students in construction-related degree programs.
Eligibility: Applicants must be enrolled in a construction-related program and must be current active members in the student chapter program or be employed by an ABC firm.
How to Apply: Applications are available by email request.
Deadline: Late May/early June.
Amount: Up to $1,000.
Number of Awards: Varies.

Associated General Contractors of America

333 John Carlyle Street
Suite 200
Alexandria, VA 22314
Phone: 703-837-5342
Fax: 703-837-5402
Email: sladef@agc.org
Website: http://www.agc.org

261 • AGC Graduate Scholarships

Purpose: Monetary assistance is awarded to college seniors pursuing graduate degrees that will lead to careers in construction or civil engineering.
Eligibility: Applicants must be college seniors enrolled in an undergraduate construction or civil engineering degree program or college graduates with a degree in construction or civil engineering. Applicants must also be enrolled or planning to enroll full-time in a graduate level construction or civil engineering degree program.
How to Apply: Applications are available online.
Deadline: November 1.
Amount: $7,500.
Number of Awards: 2.

262 • AGC Undergraduate Scholarships

Purpose: Monetary assistance is awarded to students pursuing studies that lead to a career in construction or civil engineering.
Eligibility: Successful candidates are sophomores and junior enrolled in or planning to enroll in ABET- or ACCE-accredited construction or civil engineering programs at four- or five-year colleges.

How to Apply: Applications are available online.
Deadline: November 1.
Amount: $2,000.
Number of Awards: Varies.

National Association of Women in Construction Founders' Scholarship Foundation

327 S. Adams Street
Fort Worth, TX 76104
Phone: 800-552-3506
Fax: 817-877-0324
Email: nawic@nawic.org
Website: http://www.nawic.org

263 • Undergraduate Scholarship and Construction Crafts Scholarship

Purpose: To offer financial aid to women pursuing construction-related degrees.
Eligibility: Applicants must be currently enrolled in a construction-related degree program as full-time students, have at least one term of study remaining in a course of study leading to a degree or an associate degree in a construction-related field, desire a career in a construction-related field and have a minimum 3.0 GPA.
How to Apply: Applications are available online.
Deadline: February 1.
Amount: $500-$2,000.
Number of Awards: Varies.

Plumbing-Heating-Cooling Contractors–National Association

P.O. Box 6808
Falls Church, VA 22040
Phone: 800-533-7694
Fax: 703-237-7442
Email: naphcc@naphcc.org
Website: http://www.phccweb.org

264 • Delta Faucet Company Scholarships

Purpose: To elevate the technical and business competence of the plumbing-heating-cooling (p-h-c) industry by awarding scholarships to students who are enrolled in a p-h-c-related major.
Eligibility: Applicants must be students who currently are or will be enrolled in a p-h-c-related major at an accredited four-year college or university or two-year technical college, community college or trade school. Applicants must be sponsored by an active member of Plumbing-Heating-Cooling Contractors National Association who has maintained that status for at least the two-year period prior to the date of the application.
How to Apply: Applications are available online or by email or phone.
Deadline: June 1.
Amount: $2,500.
Number of Awards: 6.

265 • PHCC Educational Foundation Scholarship

Purpose: To elevate the technical and business competence of the plumbing-heating-cooling (p-h-c) industry by awarding scholarships to students who are enrolled in a p-h-c-related major.

Eligibility: Applicants must be students who currently are or will be enrolled in a p-h-c-related major at an accredited four-year college or university or two-year technical college, community college or trade school. Applicants must be sponsored by an active member of Plumbing-Heating-Cooling Contractors-National Association who has maintained that status for at least the two-year period prior to the date of the application.
How to Apply: Applications are available online or by email.
Deadline: May 1.
Amount: $1,500-$3,000.
Number of Awards: 5.

Related Scholarships:

American Fire Sprinkler Association

See #6 • American Fire Sprinkler Association Scholarship Program

Society of Automotive Engineers

See #421 • Yanmar/SAE Scholarship

Culinary Arts

Also See Scholarships Listed Under:
Food Services
Hospitality/Travel/Tourism

American Academy of Chefs

180 Center Place Way
St. Augustine, FL 32095
Phone: 800-624-9458
Fax: 904-825-4758
Email: educate@acfchefs.net
Website: http://www.acfchefs.org

266 • Chain des Rotisseurs Scholarship

Purpose: To assist students attending culinary programs.
Eligibility: Applicants must be enrolled full-time in an accredited post-secondary school of culinary arts or AAC-approved post-secondary culinary training program, be excellent students and have completed at least one grading period. Selection is based on application, financial need, references and transcript.
How to Apply: Applications are available online.
Deadline: December 1.
Amount: $1,000.
Number of Awards: 25.

267 • Chair's Scholarship

Purpose: To assist students attending culinary programs.
Eligibility: Applicants must be enrolled full-time in two- or four-year culinary programs, be excellent students, have completed at least one grading period and plan to become either chefs or pastry chefs. Selection is based on application, references, financial need and transcript.
How to Apply: Applications are available online.
Deadline: July 1.
Amount: $1,000.
Number of Awards: 5.

National Restaurant Association Educational Foundation

175 W. Jackson Boulevard
Suite 1500
Chicago, IL 60604
Phone: 800-765-2122
Fax: 312-715-1010
Email: info@nraef.org
Website: http://www.nraef.org/scholarships/

268 • ProStart National Certificate of Achievement Scholarship

Purpose: To support students who have been recognized in the HBA/ProStart School-to-Career Initiative.
Eligibility: Applicants must have received the ProStart national Certificate of Achievement from participation in the HBA/ProStart School-to-Career Initiative. Applicants must also submit a copy of the National Restaurant Association Educational Foundation's ProStart National Certificate of Achievement, GPA and acceptance into a culinary and/or restaurant/foodservice management related program.
How to Apply: Applications are available online.
Deadline: July.
Amount: $2,000.
Number of Awards: Varies.

Related Scholarships:

Golden Gate Restaurant Association

See #484• Golden Gate Restaurant Association Scholarship

International Food Service Executives Association

See #485• IFSEA Worthy Goal Scholarship

National Restaurant Association Educational Foundation

See #487• Academic Scholarship for High School Seniors

National Restaurant Association Educational Foundation

See #488• Academic Scholarship For Undergraduate College Students

International Foodservice Editorial Council (IFEC)

See #486• IFEC Scholarships Award

Dentistry

Also See Scholarships Listed Under:
Medicine/Nursing/Health Professions

American Association of Women Dentists

216 W. Jackson Boulevard
Suite 625
Chicago, IL 60606
Phone: 800-920-2293
Email: nfo@womendentists.org
Website: http://www.womendentists.org

269 • Student Scholarships

Purpose: To support women in dentistry.

Eligibility: Applicants must be sophomore or juniors in dental school, demonstrate financial need and be members of the American Association of Women Dentists.

How to Apply: Applications are online.

Deadline: August 1.

Amount: $2,000.

Number of Awards: Varies.

American Dental Association Foundation

211 E. Chicago Avenue
Chicago, IL 60611
Phone: 312-440-2763
Fax: 312-440-3526
Email: famularor@ada.org
Website: http://www.ada.org

270 • Allied Dental Health Scholarships

Purpose: To encourage students to pursue careers in dental hygiene, dental assisting, dentistry and dental laboratory technology.

Eligibility: Applicants must be either in their final year of study in an accredited dental hygiene program, entering students in an accredited dental assisting program or in their final year of study in an accredited dental laboratory technician program. Selection is based on minimum financial need of $1,000, academic achievement, a biographical sketch and references. A minimum 3.0 GPA is required. Only two scholarship applications per school are allowed, so schools may set their own in-school application deadlines that are earlier.

How to Apply: Applications are available from dental school officials.

Deadline: October 16.

Amount: $1,000.

Number of Awards: 30.

271 • Dental Student Scholarship

Purpose: To encourage students to pursue careers in dental hygiene, dental assisting, dentistry and dental laboratory technology.

Eligibility: Applicants must be full-time entering second-year students in an accredited dental program and demonstrate a minimum financial need of $2,500. Selection is based on financial need, academic achievement, biographical sketch and references. A minimum 3.0 GPA is required. Only two scholarship applications are allowed per school, so schools may set their own in-school application deadlines that are earlier.

How to Apply: Applications are available from dental school officials.

Deadline: October 16.

Amount: Up to $2,500.

Number of Awards: 25.

272 • Minority Dental Student Scholarship

Purpose: To encourage minority students to pursue careers in dental hygiene, dental assisting, dentistry and dental laboratory technology.

Eligibility: Applicants must be African American, Hispanic or Native American full-time students entering their second year in an accredited dental program and must demonstrate a minimum financial need of $2,500. Selection is based on financial need, academic achievement, biographical sketch and references. A minimum 3.0 GPA is required. Only two scholarship applications per school are allowed, so schools may set their own in-school application deadlines that are earlier.

How to Apply: Applications are available from dental school officials.

Deadline: October 16.

Amount: Up to $2,500.

Number of Awards: 25.

American Dental Hygenists' Association (ADHA) Institute for Oral Health

444 N. Michigan Avenue
Suite 3400
Chicago, IL 60611
Phone: 800-735-4916
Email: institute@adha.net
Website: http://www.adha.org/institute

273 • ADHA Institute Scholarship Program

Purpose: To assist students pursuing a career in dental hygiene.

Eligibility: Applicants should be enrolled full-time (unless applying for a part-time scholarship) in an accredited dental hygiene program in the U.S., be finishing their first year and have a minimum 3.0 GPA. Undergraduate students should be active members of the Student American Dental Hygienists' Association or the American Dental Hygienists Association. Graduate students should be active members of the Student American Dental Hygienists' Association or the American Dental Hygienists Association, have a valid dental hygiene license and a bachelor's degree. There should be financial need of at least $1,500, with the exception of the merit-based scholarships.

How to Apply: Applications are available online.

Deadline: June 30.

Amount: $1,000-$2,000.

Number of Awards: Varies.

274 • Cadbury Adams Community Outreach Scholarships

Purpose: To reward students committed to improving oral health in their communities.

Eligibility: Applicants must have completed one year in an accredited dental hygiene program and demonstrate financial need of at least $1,500. They must also demonstrate through an essay a commitment to improving oral health in their communities. Applicants must be active SADHA or ADHA members and submit a goals statement.

How to Apply: Applications are available online.

Deadline: May 1.

Amount: $1,500.
Number of Awards: Varies.

275 • Colgate "Bright Smiles, Bright Futures" Minority Scholarships

Purpose: To support members of groups underrepresented in dental hygiene programs.

Eligibility: Applicants must have completed one year of an accredited dental hygiene curriculum and be a member of a group that is underrepresented in the field of dental hygiene. Examples of eligible groups include African-American, Hispanic, Asian, Native American and male students. Applicants must also demonstrate financial need of at least $1,500, be active members of SADHA or ADHA and submit a goals statement.

How to Apply: Applications are available online.
Deadline: May 1.
Amount: $1,250.
Number of Awards: Varies.

276 • Dr. Alfred C. Fones Scholarship

Purpose: To provide support to dental hygiene educators.

Eligibility: Applicants must be undergraduate or graduate students planning to become a teacher of dental hygienists and submit a goals statement. They must also be active members of SADHA or ADHA and demonstrate financial need of at least $1,500.

How to Apply: Applications are available online.
Deadline: May 1.
Amount: $1,500.
Number of Awards: 1.

277 • Dr. Harold Hillenbrand Scholarship

Purpose: To support outstanding dental hygiene students.

Eligibility: Applicants must have completed one year of an accredited dental hygiene program with a GPA of at least 3.5. They must demonstrate excellence in both academics and clinical performance. Applicants must also demonstrate financial need of at least $1,500, be active members of SADHA or ADHA and submit a goals statement.

How to Apply: Applications are available online.
Deadline: May 1.
Amount: $1,500.
Number of Awards: 1.

278 • Irene E. Newman Scholarship

Purpose: To support students interested in public health or community dental health.

Eligibility: Applicants must be undergraduate or graduate students interested in public health or community dental health. They must also demonstrate financial need of at least $1,500, submit a goals statement and be active members of SADHA or ADHA.

How to Apply: Applications are available online.
Deadline: May 1.
Amount: $1,500.
Number of Awards: 1.

279 • Margaret E. Swanson Scholarship

Purpose: To provide support to dental hygiene students who show leadership potential.

Eligibility: Applicants must have completed one year of an accredited dental hygiene program, pursuing a certificate or associates degree in the field. They must show evidence of organizational leadership potential. Applicants must also demonstrate financial need of at least $1,500, be active members of SADHA or ADHA and submit a goals statement.

How to Apply: Applications are available online.

Deadline: May 1.
Amount: $1,500.
Number of Awards: 1.

280 • Marsh Affinity Group Services Scholarships

Purpose: To provide support to successful dental hygiene students.

Eligibility: Applicants must have completed one year of an accredited dental hygiene program and have a GPA between 3.0 and 3.5. They must demonstrate financial need of at least $1,500, submit a goals statement and be active members of SADHA or ADHA.

How to Apply: Applications are available online.
Deadline: May 1.
Amount: $1,000.
Number of Awards: Varies.

281 • Oral-B Laboratories Dental Hygiene Scholarships

Purpose: To provide support to dental hygiene students who are committed to academic excellence, research and education.

Eligibility: Applicants must be pursuing a baccalaureate degree in dental hygiene with a GPA of at least 3.5 and show dedication to professional excellence, scholarship, quality research and dental hygiene education. They must demonstrate financial need of at least $1,500, be active members of SADHA or ADHA and submit a goals statement.

How to Apply: Applications are available online.
Deadline: May 1.
Amount: $1,000.
Number of Awards: Varies.

282 • Pfizer Inc. Scholarships

Purpose: To support excellent dental hygiene students.

Eligibility: Applicants must have completed one year in an accredited dental hygiene program with a GPA of 3.5 or higher. They must also demonstrate financial need of at least $1,500, submit a goals statement and be active members of SADHA or ADHA.

How to Apply: Applications are available online.
Deadline: May 1.
Amount: $1,500.
Number of Awards: Varies.

Related Scholarships:

Maryland Higher Education Commission

See #1397 • Graduate and Professional Scholarship Program

New York State Higher Education Services Corporation

See #1484 • Regents Health Care Opportunity Scholarships

Howard Hughes Medical Institute

See #663 • Research Training Fellowships for Medical Students (Medical Fellows Program)

National Health Service Corps

See #673 • NHSC Scholarship

Disability / Illness

Also See Scholarships Listed Under:
Academics/General

Alexander Graham Bell Association

Manager, AG Bell Financial Aid and Scholarship Programs
3417 Volta Place NW
Washington, DC 20007
Phone: 202-337-5220
Fax: 202-337-8314
Email: info@agbell.org
Website: http://www.agbell.org

283 • AG Bell Scholarship Program

Purpose: To recognize students with moderate to profound hearing loss who have academically excelled.

Eligibility: Applicants must have moderate to profound hearing loss since birth or before learning to speak with a hearing loss of 60 dB or greater. Students must use spoken communication as their primary means of communicating and be enrolled in an accredited mainstream university. The TTY phone number is 202-337-5221.

How to Apply: Applications are available online.

Deadline: March 1.

Amount: $500-$5,000.

Number of Awards: Varies.

American Academy of Allergy, Asthma and Immunology

555 E. Wells Street
Suite 1100
Milwaukee, WI 53202-3823
Phone: 414-272-6071
Email: info@aaaai.org
Website: http://www.aaaai.org

284 • Award of Excellence Asthma Scholarship Program

Purpose: The AAAAI provides college scholarships to graduating high school seniors with asthma to recognize their achievements in a wide variety of areas, including academic and extracurricular.

Eligibility: Applicants must be asthmatic students who will attend college or an accredited technical school within three years of graduating from high school.

How to Apply: Applications are available online.

Deadline: January 7.

Amount: $1,000.

Number of Awards: 23.

American Council of the Blind

Scholarship Program
1155 15th Street NW
Suite 1004
Washington, DC 20005
Phone: 202-467-5081
Website: http://www.acb.org

285 • American Council of the Blind Scholarships

Purpose: To reward outstanding blind students.

Eligibility: Students must be legally blind in both eyes and admitted full-time to a post-secondary academic or vocational program. A minimum GPA of 3.3 is required, except in extenuating circumstances. Students who work full-time and attend school part-time may apply for the John Hebner Memorial Scholarship. Scholarship recipients are expected to attend a national convention if they are over 18.

How to Apply: Applications are available online and by phone.

Deadline: March 1.

Amount: Varies.

Number of Awards: Over two dozen.

American Foundation for the Blind

11 Penn Plaza
Suite 300
New York, NY 10001
Phone: 800-232-5463
Fax: 212-502-7771
Email: afbinfo@afb.net
Website: http://www.afb.org

286 • Ferdinand Torres Scholarship

Purpose: The foundation addresses the issues of literacy, independent living, employment and access for visually impaired Americans.

Eligibility: Applicants must be full-time, post-secondary students with proof of legal blindness. Students must reside in the U.S. and provide evidence of economic need. Preference is given to applicants living in the New York metropolitan area and new immigrants to the U.S.

How to Apply: Applications are available online.

Deadline: March 31.

Amount: $1,500.

Number of Awards: 1.

287 • Karen D. Carsel Memorial Scholarship

Purpose: The foundation addresses the issues of literacy, independent living, employment and access for visually impaired Americans.

Eligibility: Applicants must be full-time graduate students who are legally blind and can present evidence of financial need. Students must submit two letters of recommendation and a typed statement describing educational and personal goals, work experience, extracurricular activities and how the scholarship funds will be used.

How to Apply: Applications are available online.

Deadline: March 31.

Amount: $500.

Number of Awards: 1.

Association for Education and Rehabilitation of the Blind and Visually Impaired

1703 N. Beauregard Street
Suite 440
Alexandria, VA 22311
Phone: 877-493-2708
Fax: 703-671-6391
Website: http://www.aerbvi.org

288 • William and Dorothy Ferrell Scholarship

Purpose: To assist visually-impaired students who plan to assist others who are visually impaired.

Eligibility: Applicants must be legally blind, with a vision of 20/200 or less in the best eye or 20 degrees or less in the visual field. Applicants must also study in college or a similar institution and must be in the field of services for the blind or visually impaired. Scholarships are only awarded in the even numbered years.

How to Apply: Applications are available online or by phone request.

Deadline: March 15.

Amount: Varies.

Number of Awards: 2.

Autism Society of America

7910 Woodmont Avenue, Suite 300
Bethesda, MD 20814-3067
Phone: 800-328-8476
Email: chapters@autism-society.org
Website: http://www.autism-society.org

289 • Eden Services Charles H. Hoens, Jr., Scholars Program

Purpose: To assist an autistic student in completing a post-secondary program.

Eligibility: Applicants must have autism and be accepted into an accredited post-secondary educational or vocational program. Nominations must be made by members of the ASA.

How to Apply: Applications are available online.

Deadline: March 14.

Amount: $1,000.

Number of Awards: 1.

Bank of America

P.O. Box 1465
Taylors, SC 29687
Phone: 864-268-3363
Fax: 864-268-7160
Email: cfsainc@earthlink.net
Website: http://www.scholarshipprograms.org

290 • Bank of America ADA Abilities Scholarship Program

Purpose: To provide aid for students with disabilities.

Eligibility: Applicants must be disabled and be high school seniors, high school graduates, or college students with a minimum 3.0 GPA. Applicants must pursue finance, business or computer systems and plan a career with a banking institution. Applicants must have permanent residence in Arizona, Arkansas, California, Florida, Georgia, Idaho, Illinois, Iowa, Kansas, Maryland, Missouri, Nevada, New Mexico, North Carolina, Oklahoma, Oregon, South Carolina, Tennessee, Texas, Virginia, Washington or the District of Columbia and be U.S. citizens.

How to Apply: Applications are available online.

Deadline: February 15.

Amount: Varies.

Number of Awards: Varies.

Chair Scholars

16101 Carencia Lane
Odessa, FL 33556
Phone: 813-920-2737
Email: info@chairscholars.org
Website: http://www.chairscholars.org

291 • Chair Scholars Scholarship

Purpose: To allow financially disadvantaged, physically challenged students a chance to obtain a college education.

Eligibility: Applicants must be significantly physically challenged (although not necessarily in a wheelchair), demonstrate severe financial need (such that they could not attend college without financial aid), and have at least a B+ average in previous scholastic work. Applicants must also be under age 21 and be high school seniors or college freshmen with previous community contributions.

How to Apply: Applications are available online.

Deadline: March 1.

Amount: $3,000-$5,000.

Number of Awards: 10.

Christian Record Services

Melisa Welch
4444 S. 52nd Street
Lincoln, NE 68516-1302
Phone: 402-488-0981
Fax: 402-488-7582
Email: info@christianrecord.org
Website: http://www.christianrecord.org

292 • CRS Scholarship

Purpose: To assist legally blind youths in obtaining a college education.

Eligibility: Applicants must be legally blind and intend to attend undergraduate institutions to gain independence and self sufficiency. Applicants should submit application forms and character reference forms.

How to Apply: Applications are available online.

Deadline: April 1.

Amount: $500.

Number of Awards: 10.

Cystic Fibrosis Scholarship Foundation

1555 Sherman Avenue #116
Evanston, IL 60201
Phone: 847-328-0127
Fax: 847-328-0127
Email: mkbcfsf@aol.com
Website: http://www.cfscholarship.org

293 • Cystic Fibrosis Foundation Scholarship

Purpose: To aid to students with cystic fibrosis.

Eligibility: Applicants must be high school seniors or college undergraduates who have cystic fibrosis. Recipients are chosen on the basis of academic achievement, leadership skills and financial need.

How to Apply: Applications are available online.

Deadline: March 8.

Amount: $1,000.

Number of Awards: Varies.

EAR Foundation

P.O. Box 330867
Nashville, TN 37203
Phone: 800-545-HEAR
Fax: 615-627-2728
Email: info@earfoundation.org
Website: http://www.earfoundation.org

294 • Minnie Pearl Scholarship

Purpose: To help integrate hearing impaired persons into mainstream society through education.

Eligibility: Applicants must be high school seniors with a minimum 3.0 GPA and be accepted to, but not attend, a college, university or technical school and be planning to attend full-time. Applicants must also be U.S. citizens, be mainstreamed hearing impaired students and have significant bilateral hearing impairment.

How to Apply: Applications are available online.
Deadline: February 15.
Amount: $2,000.
Number of Awards: 14.

Ethel Louise Armstrong Foundation

2460 N. Lake Avenue, PMB #128
Altadena, CA 91001
Phone: 626-398-8840
Email: executivedirector@ela.org
Website: http://www.ela.org

295 • Ethel Louise Armstrong Foundation Scholarship

Purpose: To promote the inclusion of people with disabilities and to expand the opportunities of female graduate students with disabilities.

Eligibility: Applicants must be female with a physical disability, active in a disability organization, currently enrolled in or applying to a graduate school in the U.S. and willing to work with the foundation on future research work.

How to Apply: Applications are available online.
Deadline: June 1.
Amount: $500-$2,000.
Number of Awards: Varies.

Foundation for Exceptional Children

1110 N. Glebe Road
Suite 300
Arlington, VA 22201
Phone: 800-224-6830
Email: yesican@cec.sped.org
Website: http://www.cec.sped.org

296 • Sara Conlon Memorial Scholarship

Purpose: To help disabled students who major in special education.

Eligibility: Applicants must be enrolled in two- or four-year undergraduate college programs or vocational, technical or fine arts training programs. Students should submit the application form, transcript, three letters of recommendation, goals statement, statement verifying disability and statement verifying financial need.

How to Apply: Applications are available online.
Deadline: February 1.
Amount: $500.
Number of Awards: 1.

297 • Stanley E. Jackson Scholarship Awards

Purpose: To honor the memory of Mr. Stanley E. Jackson through the provision of funds to disabled students.

Eligibility: Applicants must be U.S. citizens who are enrolling for the first time in full-time post-secondary education or training in the coming year. The scholarship is composed of four awards, and different recipients are selected for each category. For Award #1, applicants must be disabled. For Award #2, applicants must be disabled and be a member of a minority ethnic group such as African American, Native American, Hispanic or Asian American. For Award #3, applicants must be disabled and must demonstrate a gift or talent in general intellectual ability, specific academic aptitude, creativity, leadership or the visual or performing arts. For Award #4, applicants must be disabled, be a member of a minority ethnic group and display ability in one of the fields mentioned in Award #3.

How to Apply: Applications are available online.
Deadline: February 1.
Amount: $500.
Number of Awards: 4-10.

Hemophilia Resources of America

Attn.: Scholarships 4
45 Route 46 East, Suite 609
P.O. Box 2011
Pine Brook, NJ 07058
Phone: 973-276-0254
Fax: 973-276-0998
Email: mscudiery@hrahemo.com
Website: http://www.hrahemo.com

298 • Hemophilia Resources of America

Purpose: To provide financial assistance to individuals living with hemophilia or von Willebrand disease, or their children.

Eligibility: Applicants must have either hemophilia or von Willebrand disease or be the child of an individual with one of these two diseases. Applicants must also demonstrate financial need, as well as a record of academic excellence and community service.

How to Apply: Applications are available online or by calling 800-549-2654.
Deadline: May 15.
Amount: $1,000.
Number of Awards: 20.

Immune Deficiency Foundation

40 W. Chesapeake Avenue
Suite 308
Towson, MD 21204
Phone: 800-296-4433
Email: idf@primaryimmune.org
Website: http://www.primaryimmune.org

299 • Immune Deficiency Foundation Scholarship

Purpose: To provide financial assistance to undergraduate students afflicted with a primary immune deficiency disease.

Eligibility: Applicant must have been admitted or must currently be enrolled in an accredited college or university as an undergraduate student. Applicants must also have demonstrated financial need and a record of community involvement.

How to Apply: Applications are available online, by email or by telephone.

Deadline: March 31.
Amount: $750-$1,000.
Number of Awards: Varies.

Lighthouse International

111 E. 59th Street
New York, NY 10022
Phone: 212-821-9200
Fax: 212-821-9707
Email: info@lighthouse.org
Website: http://www.lighthouse.org

300 • Career Incentive Award

Purpose: To assist blind or partially-sighted collegiate or college-bound students.
Eligibility: Applicants must be blind or have low vision capabilities in one of four categories: college-bound high school student, undergraduate college student, undergraduate student returning to college at least 10 years after high school or graduate student.
How to Apply: Applications are available by phone, fax or email to kboyle@lighthouse.org.
Deadline: March 31.
Amount: $5,000.
Number of Awards: 4.

Lilly Reintegration Programs

PMB 327
310 Busse Highway
Park Ridge, IL 60068
Phone: 800-809-8202
Email: lillyscholarships@reintegration.com
Website: http://www.reintegration.com

301 • Lilly Reintegration Scholarship

Purpose: To provide aid to students with schizophrenia or similar disorders who are seeking to advance themselves academically and vocationally.
Eligibility: Applicants must have been diagnosed with schizophrenia, schizophreniform, schizoaffective disorder or bipolar disorder, be undergoing medical treatment for their disease(s) and be involved in other rehabilitative efforts, such as working part-time or volunteering with a civic organization.
How to Apply: Applications are available online or by phone, mail or email.
Deadline: February 15.
Amount: Varies.
Number of Awards: Varies.

National Association of the Deaf

8630 Fenton Street, Suite 820
Silver Spring, MD 20910
Phone: 301-587-1789
Fax: 301-587-1791
Email: nadinfo@nad.org
Website: http://www.nad.org

302 • William C. Stokoe Scholarship

Purpose: To increase the number of deaf social scientists who research sign language or the deaf community.
Eligibility: Applicants must be deaf students who have graduated from a four-year college program and are pursuing graduate studies in fields relating to sign language or the deaf community. Deaf grad students who are developing a special project on one of those topics are also eligible. Selection is based on a plan for a special project relating to deafness and academic record.
How to Apply: Applications are available by written request.
Deadline: March 15.
Amount: $2,000.
Number of Awards: 1.

National Center for Learning Disabilities

381 Park Avenue South, Suite 1401
New York, NY 10016
Phone: 212-545-7510
Fax: 212-545-9665
Email: afscholarship@ncld.org
Website: http://www.ncld.org

303 • Anne Ford Scholarship Program

Purpose: To provide financial assistance to students with learning disabilities who plan to pursue undergraduate degrees.
Eligibility: Applicants must be U.S. citizens who are academically successful in public or private secondary schools and with an identified learning disability. Financial need is considered.
How to Apply: Applications are available online.
Deadline: December 31.
Amount: $10,000.
Number of Awards: 1.

National Federation of Music Clubs (NC)

Norma Bibb
3211 "A" Clarendon Drive
Springfield, IL 62704
Email: norbibb@insightbb.com
Website: http://www.nfmc-music.org

304 • NFMC Hinda Honigman Award for the Blind

Purpose: To support blind instrumentalists or vocalists.
Eligibility: Applicants must be between the ages of 16 and 25, be an instrumentalist or vocalist and submit an affidavit from an ophthalmologist stating that they are blind. Applicants must also be affiliated with the National Federation of Music Clubs.
How to Apply: Applications are available online.
Deadline: February 1.
Amount: $350-$650.
Number of Awards: 2.

National Federation of the Blind

Ms. Peggy Elliott
805 Fifth Avenue
Grinnell, IA 50112
Phone: 641-236-3366
Email: nfb@nfb.org
Website: http://www.nfb.org

305 • Educator of Tomorrow Award

Eligibility: Applicants must be legally blind, full-time post-secondary students pursuing a career in education at any level. Academic excellence, financial need and community service involvement will be considered. Applicants must submit a personal letter, letters of recommendation, transcripts, a letter from a

Federation state president or designee and test score reports for high school seniors.

How to Apply: Applications are available online.
Deadline: March 31.
Amount: $3,000.
Number of Awards: 1.

306 • National Federation of the Blind Scholarship

Purpose: The National Federation of the Blind offers a number of scholarships to exceptional blind scholars.

Eligibility: Applicants must be legally blind and pursue a full-time postsecondary study in the following semester in the U.S. One scholarship may be given to a part-time student. There are no additional restrictions for most of the scholarships. However, a few require study in certain fields and the Michael and Marie Marucci Scholarship requires competence in a foreign language. Awards are based on academic excellence, community service and financial need.

How to Apply: Applications are available online.
Deadline: March 31.
Amount: $3,000-$12,000.
Number of Awards: 30.

National Fraternal Society of the Deaf

1118 S. Sixth Street
Springfield, IL 62703
Phone: 217-789-7429
Fax: 217-789-7489
Email: thefrat@nfsd.com
Website: http://www.nfsd.com

307 • Deaf Scholarship

Purpose: To award scholarships to members of the NFSD.

Eligibility: Applicants must be members of the NFSD for one full year and be in a post-secondary program or preparing to enter one as a full-time student.

How to Apply: Requests for applications are available online.
Deadline: Varies.
Amount: $1,000.
Number of Awards: 1.

National PKU News

6869 Woodlawn Avenue NE #116
Seattle, WA 98115-5469
Email: schuett@pkunews.org
Website: http://www.pkunews.org

308 • Robert Guthrie PKU Scholarship and Awards

Purpose: In honor of the doctor who created the newborn screening test for PKU, the scholarship gives support to bright students living with PKU.

Eligibility: Students must have PKU, follow the diet and attend an accredited school. Financial need is considered along with academic excellence.

How to Apply: Applications are available by mail.
Deadline: November 1.
Amount: Varies.
Number of Awards: Varies.

NuFACTOR

41093 County Center Drive
Temecula, CA 92591
Phone: 800-323-6832
Fax: 951-296-2565
Website: http://www.kelleycom.com

309 • Eric Dostie Memorial College Scholarship

Purpose: To assist students who suffer from hemophilia or related bleeding disorder, as well as their immediate families.

Eligibility: Applicants must be individuals with hemophilia or related to said individuals, enrolled full-time in an accredited college or university and demonstrate academic achievement, financial need and a history of community service.

How to Apply: Applications are available after November 1 by telephone or mail.
Deadline: March 1.
Amount: $1,000.
Number of Awards: 10.

Optimist International

4494 Lindell Boulevard
St. Louis, MO 63108
Phone: 314-371-6000
Fax: 314-371-6006
Email: programs@optimist.org
Website: http://www.optimist.org

310 • Optimist International Communications Contest

Purpose: To reward students based on their communications performance.

Eligibility: Applicants must be students up to grade 12 in the U.S. and Canada, to CEGEP in Quebec and to grade 13 in the Caribbean who are recognized by their schools as deaf or hard of hearing.

How to Apply: Contact your local Optimist Club.
Deadline: September.
Amount: $1,500.
Number of Awards: Varies.

Orange County Community Foundation

30 Corporate Park, Suite 410
Irvine, CA 92606
Phone: 949-553-4202
Fax: 949-553-4211
Email: rho@oc-cf.org
Website: http://www.oc-cf.org

311 • Michael A. Hunter Memorial Scholarship Fund

Purpose: To support those who have been affected by leukemia as they pursue an education.

Eligibility: Applicants must be high school seniors or current college students who are leukemia patients and/or are the children of non-surviving leukemia patients. Applicants must be full-time students with a GPA of at least 3.0 and demonstrate financial need. They must submit an essay describing how leukemia has impacted their life, a doctor's note verifying the leukemia diagnosis and two letters of recommendation.

How to Apply: Applications are available online.
Deadline: February 28.
Amount: $5,000.
Number of Awards: 2.

P. Buckley Moss Society

20 Stoneridge Drive, Suite 102
Waynesboro, VA 22980
Phone: 540-943-5678
Fax: 540-949-8408
Email: society@mosssociety.org
Website: http://www.mosssociety.org

312 • Ann And Matt Harbison Scholarship

Purpose: This scholarship recognizes the persistence and dedication to academic or extracurricular pursuits of students with a learning disability.
Eligibility: Applicants must be nominated by a P. Buckley Moss Society member, have a language-related learning difference and pursue a post-secondary education.
How to Apply: Applications are available online.
Deadline: March 31.
Amount: $1,000.
Number of Awards: 1.

Patient Advocate Foundation

Ruth Anne Reed, Vice President of Special Programs
700 Thimble Shoals Boulevard
Suite 200
Newport News, VA 23606
Phone: 800-532-5274
Fax: 757-873-8999
Email: help@patientadvocate.org
Website: http://www.patientadvocate.org

313 • Scholarships for Survivors

Purpose: This group of scholarships seeks to assist students whose educations have been delayed due to life-threatening illness.
Eligibility: Eligible students must be survivors of life-threatening diseases. If awarded a scholarship, the student must maintain a 3.0 GPA, be enrolled full time, and perform 20 hours of community service each year.
How to Apply: Applications are available online.
Deadline: May 1.
Amount: $5,000.
Number of Awards: 8.

Pfizer Epilepsy Scholarship Award

c/o The Eden Communications Group
515 Valley Street
Suite 200
Maplewood, NJ 07040
Phone: 800-292-7373
Email: czoppi@edencomgroup.com
Website: http://www.epilepsy-scholarship.com

314 • Pfizer Epilepsy Scholarship

Purpose: To recognize outstanding students who demonstrate how they have overcome the challenge of epilepsy in their lives.
Eligibility: Applicants must be high school seniors or college undergraduates currently under a physician's care for epilepsy,

demonstrate achievement in academic and extracurricular activities and submit verification of academic status and two letters of recommendation. Selection is made by a panel of judges composed of opinion leaders in the fields of medicine and education.
How to Apply: Applications are available online.
Deadline: March 1.
Amount: $3,000.
Number of Awards: 16.

Recording for the Blind and Dyslexic

20 Roszel Road
Princeton, NJ 08540
Phone: 866-RFBD-585
Fax: 609-520-7990
Email: custserv@rfbd.org
Website: http://www.rfbd.org

315 • Marion Huber Learning Through Listening Awards

Purpose: To assist learning-disabled high school seniors.
Eligibility: Applicants must demonstrate leadership skills, scholarship and a desire to help others and attend a two- or four-year college or vocational school. Students must have a specific learning disability and be registered with RFB&D for at least one year prior to the application deadline.
How to Apply: Applications are available online.
Deadline: February 20.
Amount: $2,000-$6,000.
Number of Awards: 9.

316 • Mary P. Oenslanger Scholastic Achievement Awards

Purpose: Assistance for graduate study is awarded to blind college senior students who have shown leadership skills, scholarship and a desire to help others.
Eligibility: Applicants must be legally blind, have been registered with RFB&D for at least one year prior to the application deadline and hold a bachelor's degree from an accredited U.S. college or university.
How to Apply: Applications are available online.
Deadline: February 20.
Amount: $1,000-$6,000.
Number of Awards: 9.

Sertoma International

1912 E. Meyer Boulevard
Kansas City, MO 64132
Phone: 816-333-8300
Fax: 816-333-4320
Email: infosertoma@sertoma.org
Website: http://www.sertoma.org

317 • Sertoma Hearing Impaired Scholarship

Purpose: The organization's focus is to concentrate on communicative disorders.
Eligibility: Applicants must be entering or continuing as full-time undergraduates in the U.S. or Canada, show proof that they have a clinically significant (40dB) bilateral hearing loss and have a minimum 3.2 GPA for all high school and college courses.
How to Apply: Applications are available online.
Deadline: May 1.
Amount: $1,000.
Number of Awards: Varies.

Spina Bifida Association of America

4590 MacArthur Boulevard NW
Suite 250
Washington, DC 20017
Phone: 800-621-3141
Fax: 202-944-3295
Email: sbaa@sbaa.org
Website: http://www.sbaa.org

318 • SBAA Four-Year Scholarship

Purpose: To create opportunities for high school students with spina bifida to attend a four-year college that is otherwise outside of the applicants' financial reach.

Eligibility: Applicants must have spina bifida with a statement of disability from a physician, be high school juniors or entering seniors at the time of application and show financial need by submitting the Free Application for Federal Student Aid (FAFSA). Awards are based on academic record, financial need, work history, community service, leadership and commitment to personal goals.

How to Apply: Applications are available online.
Deadline: March 1.
Amount: Up to $5,000.
Number of Awards: Varies.

TPA Scholarship Trust for the Deaf and Near Deaf

3755 Lindell Boulevard
St. Louis, MO 63108
Phone: 314-371-0533
Fax: 314-371-0537
Email: support@tpahq.org
Website: http://www.travelersprotectiveasn.com

319 • TPA Scholarship Trust for the Deaf and Near Deaf

Purpose: To provide financial aid to children and adults who are deaf or hearing impaired and who need assistance in obtaining mechanical devices, treatment or specialized education.

Eligibility: Applicants must suffer from deafness or hearing impairment.

How to Apply: Applications are available by written request.
Deadline: March 1.
Amount: Varies.
Number of Awards: Varies.

VSA Arts

818 Connecticut Avenue NW
Suite 600
Washington, DC 20006
Phone: 800-933-8721
Fax: 202-429-0868
Email: info@vsarts.org
Website: http://www.vsarts.org

320 • Young Soloists Awards

Purpose: To award promising young musicians with disabilities with scholarship funds and a chance to perform in Washington, DC, at the John F. Kennedy Center for the Performing Arts.

Eligibility: Applicants must be instrumentalists or vocalists no older than 25 years of age and have physical or mental disabilities that limit one or more of their major life activities. Applicants need to include audio or videocassette recordings of three musical selections along with a one-page biography explaining why they feel they should be selected for the award. Awards are based on technique, tone, intonation, rhythm and interpretation from the taped performances.

How to Apply: Applications are available online.
Deadline: November 1.
Amount: Varies.
Number of Awards: 2.

Education/Teaching

Also See Scholarships Listed Under:
Academics/General
English/Writing
Public Administration/Social Work
Public Service/Community Service

American Council of Learned Societies (ACLS)

633 Third Avenue
New York, NY 10017-6795
Phone: 212-697-1505
Fax: 212-949-8058
Email: sfisher@acls.org
Website: http://www.acls.org

321 • ACLS Digital Innovation Fellowships
Purpose: To support humanities scholars who work on digital projects.
Eligibility: Applicants must be scholars in the humanities fields and have Ph.D. degrees. An application, a proposal, a project plan, a budget plan, a bibliography, a publications list, three reference letters and one institutional statement are required. In addition to the stipend, there are also funds for project costs. The fellowship should last an academic year.
How to Apply: Applications are available online.
Deadline: November 10.
Amount: $55,000.
Number of Awards: 5.

322 • ACLS Fellowships
Purpose: To support a scholar in the study of humanities.
Eligibility: Applicants must have a Ph.D. degree and at least a three year period since their last supported research. An application, a proposal, bibliography, publications list and two reference letters are required. The award levels are based on the position of the applicant: professor and equivalent, associate professor and equivalent and assistant professor and equivalent. The ACLS fellowships include ACLS/SSRC/NEH International and Area Studies Fellowships and ACLS/New York Public Library Fellowships.
How to Apply: Applications are available online.
Deadline: September 28.
Amount: $50,000.
Number of Awards: Varies.

323 • Charles A. Ryskamp Research Fellowships
Purpose: To support scholars researching the humanities field.
Eligibility: The fellowships are for advanced assistant professors and untenured associate professors. By the application deadline, the applicants should have finished their institution's last reappointment review before tenure review, and their tenure review is not finished. The applicants should have a Ph.D. or equivalent and be in a tenure-track position at degree-granting U.S. institutions during the fellowship. Previous supported research leaves do not affect eligibility. The application process involves the application, proposal, bibliography, publications list and four reference letters.

How to Apply: Applications are available online.
Deadline: September 28.
Amount: $64,000.
Number of Awards: 12.

324 • Frederick Burkhardt Residential Fellowships for Recently Tenured Scholars
Purpose: To support scholars researching in the humanities field.
Eligibility: Applicants must be recently tenured humanists and must be employed in tenured positions at U.S. degree-granting institutions during the fellowship. An application, a proposal, a bibliography, a publications list, three reference letters and one institutional statement are required. Previous supported research leaves does not affect eligibility.
How to Apply: Applications are available online.
Deadline: September 28.
Amount: $75,000.
Number of Awards: 11.

American Montessori Society

281 Park Avenue South
New York, NY 10010
Phone: 212-358-1250
Fax: 212-358-1256
Email: info@amshq.org
Website: http://www.amshq.org

325 • Teacher Education Scholarship Fund
Purpose: To support future Montessori teachers.
Eligibility: Applicants must be accepted into but not yet attending an AMS teacher education program. Financial need, the applicant's personal statement and letters of recommendation are considered.
How to Apply: Applications are available online.
Deadline: May 1.
Amount: Tuition.
Number of Awards: Varies.

American Orff-Schulwerk Association (AOSA)

P.O. Box 391089
Cleveland, OH 44139-8089
Phone: 440-543-5366
Email: info@aosa.org
Website: http://www.aosa.org

326 • Shields-Gillespie Scholarship
Purpose: To assist pre-K and kindergarten teachers with program funding, including instruments and training.
Eligibility: Applicants must be a member of AOSA. Applicants must be U.S. citizens or have lived in the United States for the past five years. Programs should focus on music/movement learning.
How to Apply: Applications are available online for AOSA members.
Deadline: Varies.
Amount: Varies.
Number of Awards: Varies.

Common Knowledge Scholarship Foundation

P.O. Box 290361
Davie, FL 33329-0361
Website: http://www.cksf.org

327 • Future Teacher of America Scholarship-- High School

Purpose: To help high school students interested in teaching.
Eligibility: Applicants must be in grades 9-12 and should be interested in teaching or education as a career. Students first register for free at the website. On specified dates, there is a multiple-choice, online quiz competition that tests the student's knowledge in subjects related to teaching: math, language arts, science, history and common knowledge, with some questions from the sponsor's website. Applicants receive 500 points for each correct answer and lose one point for each second taken to complete a question. The person with the most points at the end is the scholarship winner.
How to Apply: Applicants may register online.
Deadline: December 4.
Amount: $250.
Number of Awards: 2.

International Order of Alhambra

4200 Leeds Avenue
Baltimore, MD 21229
Phone: 410-242-0660
Fax: 410-536-5729
Email: hq@orderalhambra.org
Website: http://www.orderalhambra.org

328 • International Order of Alhambra Scholarship

Purpose: To provide financial assistance to undergraduate students who wish to become special education teachers or to those who give care to the permanently disabled.
Eligibility: One of the purposes of the organization is to provide assistance, education and residences to the developmentally disabled.
How to Apply: Contact the organization for more information.
Deadline: Varies.
Amount: Varies.
Number of Awards: Varies.

International Technology Education Association

Foundation for Technology Education
1914 Association Drive, Suite 201
Reston, VA 20191
Phone: 703-860-2100
Fax: 703-860-0353
Email: bmongold@iteaconnect.org
Website: http://www.iteaconnect.org

329 • Litherland Scholarship

Purpose: To provide scholarships for undergraduate students pursuing a career in teaching technology.
Eligibility: Applicants must be members of ITEA, be full-time undergraduate students majoring in technology education teacher preparation and have a minimum 2.5 GPA.
How to Apply: Application information is available online.
Deadline: December 1.
Amount: $1,000.
Number of Awards: Varies.

330 • Maley Teacher Scholarship

Purpose: To support technology education teachers.
Eligibility: Applicants must be members of ITEA and plan to pursue or continue graduate study. Candidates must provide their plans for graduate study, description of need, college transcript and three recommendation letters.
How to Apply: Application information is available online.
Deadline: December 1.
Amount: $1,000.
Number of Awards: Varies.

331 • TSA-Sponsored ITEA Scholarship

Purpose: To provide scholarships for TSA students who plan to pursue a career in teaching technology to students in grades K-12.
Eligibility: Applicants must be TSA members and have participated in a local chapter for at least two years; served as a TSA officer at the local, state, or national level for at least one academic year and attended at least one TSA state or national conference.
How to Apply: Application information is available online.
Deadline: December 31.
Amount: $500.
Number of Awards: 1.

332 • Undergraduate Scholarship

Purpose: To support undergraduate students majoring in technology education teacher preparation.
Eligibility: Applicants must be members of ITEA, be full-time undergraduate students and have a minimum 2.5 GPA.
How to Apply: Application information is available online.
Deadline: December 1.
Amount: $1,000.
Number of Awards: 1.

Journalism Education Association Future Teacher Scholarship

Kansas State University
103 Kedzie Hall
Manhattan, KS 66506
Phone: 330-672-8297
Email: cbowen@kent.edu
Website: http://www.jea.org

333 • Future Teacher Scholarship

Purpose: To provide scholarships for upper-level or master's students who intend to teach scholastic journalism.
Eligibility: Applicants must be education majors focusing on learning to teach scholastic journalism at the secondary school level.
How to Apply: Application information is available online.
Deadline: October 1.
Amount: $1,000.
Number of Awards: Up to 3.

National Association for Gifted Children

1707 L Street NW
Suite 550
Washington, DC 20036
Phone: 202-785-4268
Fax: 202-785-4248
Email: nagc@nagc.org
Website: http://www.nagc.org

334 • A. Harry Passow Classroom Teacher Scholarship

Purpose: To award excellent teachers of gifted students of grades K-12.

Eligibility: Applicants must be teachers of gifted students of grades K-12 and be continuing their education. Applicants must also have been members of NAGC for at least one year. Selection is based on commitment to teaching as shown by reviews from students, parents, principal and peers and admission into a graduate or certification program in gifted education.

How to Apply: Applications are available online.
Deadline: April 1.
Amount: $2,000.
Number of Awards: Varies.

National Council for Geographic Education

Jacksonville State University
206-A Martin Hall
700 Pelham Road North
Jacksonville, AL 36265-1602
Phone: 256-782-5293
Fax: 256-782-5336
Email: ncge@ncge.org
Website: http://www.ncge.org

335 • Women in Geographic Education Scholarship

Purpose: To aid undergraduate or graduate women planning careers in geographic education.

Eligibility: Applicants must be enrolled in a program leading to a career in geographic education, submit an essay on the provided topic and have an overall GPA of 3.0 and a geography GPA of 3.5. The winner receives an additional $300 travel stipend if she attends the NCGE Annual Meeting.

How to Apply: Applications are available online.
Deadline: March 15.
Amount: $300.
Number of Awards: 1.

National Council of Teachers of English

1111 W. Kenyon Road
Urbana, IL 61801
Phone: 877-369-6283
Fax: 217-328-9645
Email: pyw@ncte.org
Website: http://www.ncte.org

336 • Achievement Award

Purpose: To recognize outstanding student writers.

Eligibility: Applicants must be current high school juniors who will graduate the following school year, and they must be nominated for the award by their high school English department. Nominees must provide two writing samples: one timed response to a prompt written under the supervision of a teacher and one sample of their best work.

How to Apply: Applications are available online. However, students must be nominated by their high school English departments.
Deadline: February 2.
Amount: Certificate of commendation.
Number of Awards: Up to 876.

National Federation of Music Clubs (FL)

Mrs. Ralph Suggs
327 E. Ridge Village Drive
Miami, FL 33157
Phone: 317-638-4003
Fax: 317-638-0503
Email: rose331s@bellsouth.net
Website: http://www.nfmc-music.org

337 • NFMC Gretchen E. Van Roy Music Education Scholarship

Purpose: To support students majoring in music education.

Eligibility: Applicants must be college juniors majoring in music education and must be affiliated with the National Federation of Music Clubs. There is no application fee to apply.

How to Apply: Applications are available online.
Deadline: April 1.
Amount: $1,000.
Number of Awards: 1.

National Federation of Music Clubs (Music Education)

Lee Meyer
8101 Club Court Circle
Austin, TX 78759
Phone: 512-345-5072
Website: http://www.nfmc-music.org

338 • NFMC Myrtle Mehan/Hazel Morgan Music Education Scholarship

Purpose: To assist students who plan to work in music education.

Eligibility: Applicants must be college sophomores, juniors or seniors majoring in music education at a college or university. A $5 entry fee and recommendations must be submitted in addition to the application. Applicants must be members of the National Federation of Music Clubs. This award was included because it is from a legitimate organization. However, students are encouraged to apply for scholarships without a fee.

How to Apply: Applications are available online.
Deadline: April 1.
Amount: $750.
Number of Awards: 1.

Pi Lambda Theta

P.O. Box 6626
Bloomington, IN 47407
Phone: 800-487-3411
Fax: 812-339-3462
Email: office@pilambda.org
Website: http://www.pilambda.org

339 • Distinguished Student Scholar Award

Purpose: To recognize education majors with leadership potential and a dedication to education.

Eligibility: Applicants must be education majors of at least sophomore level who demonstrate leadership skills and a strong dedication to education. They must be nominated for the scholarship by an instructor or supervisor. Applicants must have a GPA of at least 3.5 and demonstrate significant contributions to local or national education efforts. This scholarship is only available in odd years.

How to Apply: Applications are available online.
Deadline: February 10 of odd years.
Amount: $500.
Number of Awards: 1.

340 • Tobin Sorenson Physical Education Scholarship

Purpose: To support future K-12 physical education teachers.

Eligibility: Applicants must be pursuing a career as a physical education teacher, adapted physical education teacher, coach, recreational therapist, dance therapist or related profession at the K-12 level. They must be at least college sophomores with a GPA of 3.5 or higher. Applicants must also demonstrate leadership abilities and involvement in extracurricular activities related to their chosen profession. This scholarship is only awarded in odd years.

How to Apply: Applications are available online.
Deadline: February 10 of odd years.
Amount: $1,000.
Number of Awards: 1.

Society of Physics Students

One Physics Ellipse
College Park, MD 20740
Phone: 301-209-3007
Fax: 301-209-0839
Email: sps@aip.org
Website: http://www.spsnational.org

341 • SPS Future Teacher Scholarship

Purpose: To provide scholarships to physics majors who are participating in a teacher education program and who intend to pursue a career in physics education.

Eligibility: Applicants must be members of SPS and intend to pursue a career in teaching physics. Students must be undergraduate physics majors, at least in their junior year of study at the time of application.

How to Apply: Applications are available online or from chapter advisors.
Deadline: February 15.
Amount: $2,000.
Number of Awards: 1.

Veterans of Foreign Wars

406 W. 34th Street
Kansas City, MO 64111
Phone: 816-968-1117
Fax: 816-968-1149
Email: info@vfw.org
Website: http://www.vfw.org

342 • Teacher of the Year Award

Purpose: To salute the nation's top elementary, junior high and high school teachers who educate their students about citizenship and American history and traditions.

Eligibility: Applicants must be current classroom teachers who teach at least half of the school day in a classroom environment, grades K-12. Previous winners from the state or national levels are not eligible. Fellow teachers, supervisors or other interested individuals who are not related to the nominee may send in nominations; no self-nominations will be accepted.

How to Apply: Applications are available online but initial nominations must be sent to the local VFW office. Visit the website for more information.
Deadline: November 1.
Amount: $1,000.
Number of Awards: 3.

Zeta Phi Beta Sorority Inc. National Educational Foundation

1734 New Hampshire Avenue NW
Washington, DC 20009
Email: ihq@zphib1920.org
Website: http://www.zphib1920.org

343 • Isabel M. Herson Scholarship in Education

Purpose: To support education students.

Eligibility: Applicants must be current or future full-time undergraduate or graduate education students. They must submit three letters of recommendation, transcripts and a personal essay.

How to Apply: Applications are available online or by sending a self-addressed, stamped envelope.
Deadline: February 1.
Amount: $500-$1,000.
Number of Awards: 1.

Related Scholarships:

New Hampshire Postsecondary Education Commission

See #1463 • Workforce Incentive Program

Maryland Higher Education Commission

See #1393 • Child Care Provider Scholarship

Mississippi Office of Student Financial Aid

See #1438 • Critical Needs Teacher Program

Mississippi Office of Student Financial Aid

See #1442 • William Winter Teacher Scholarship

American Federation of Teachers

See #1595 • Robert G. Porter Scholars Program

Elie Wiesel Foundation for Humanity

See #443 • Prize in Ethics Essay Contest

Council for Exceptional Children

See #980 • Student CEC/Black Caucus Scholarship

Society of Automotive Engineers

See #418 • Doctoral Scholars Forgivable Loan Program

National Association for the Advancement of Colored People

See #1015 • Sutton Scholarship

Horace Mann Insurance Companies

See #800 • Horace Mann Scholarship

Council for Exceptional Children

See #979 • Student CEC Ethnic Diversity Scholarship

U.S. Department of State

See #66 • Fulbright Grants

Truman Scholarship Foundation

See #931 • Truman Scholar

Massachusetts Office of Student Financial Assistance

See #1420 • Tomorrow's Teachers Scholarship Program

National Dairy Shrine

See #136 • Milk Marketing Scholarship

Association for Women in Science

See #181 • Association for Women in Science College Scholarship

Golden Key National Honour Society

See #784 • Education Achievement Awards

Foundation for Exceptional Children

See #296 • Sara Conlon Memorial Scholarship

Brown Foundation Scholarship Program

See #962 • Brown Foundation Scholarships

Engineering

Also See Scholarships Listed Under:
Aerospace/Aviation
Computer and Information Science
Sciences/Physical Sciences

American Concrete Institute ACI-James Instruments Student Award

F. Dirk Heidbrink
Wiss Janney, Elstner Associates, Inc
330 Pfingsten Road
Northbrook, IL 60062
Phone: 248-848-3700
Fax: 248-848-3701
Email: fheidbrink@wje.com
Website: http://www.aci-int.org

344 • ACI-James Instruments Student Award for Research on NDT of Concrete

Purpose: To recognize outstanding research in the area of concrete and concrete materials using NDT methods.
Eligibility: Applicants must submit an original research paper on a topic related to the nondestructive testing (NDT) of concrete. The research must have been done by applicants while enrolled either as an undergraduate or a graduate student in an accredited institution of higher education.
How to Apply: There is no application form. Papers must be submitted by mail.
Deadline: December 5.
Amount: $800.
Number of Awards: 1.

American Concrete Institute Student Fellowship Program

38800 Country Club Drive
Farmington Hills, MI 48331
Phone: 248-848-3700
Fax: 248-848-3701
Email: scholarships@concrete.org
Website: http://www.concrete.org

345 • ACI Student Fellowship Program

Purpose: To encourage careers in the concrete field.
Eligibility: Applicants must be full-time undergraduate or graduate students nominated by a faculty member who is also a member of the ACI. Students must be studying engineering, construction management or another relevant field. Applicants may live anywhere in the world, but actual study must take place in the U.S. or Canada. Finalists for a fellowship must attend an ACI convention for an interview. In addition to the monetary award, the scholarship also includes conference fees, mentoring and a potential internship.
How to Apply: Applicants must be nominated by ACI-member faculty in order to receive an application.
Deadline: November 15.
Amount: $10,000.
Number of Awards: Varies.

American Congress on Surveying and Mapping (ACSM)

6 Montgomery Village Avenue
Suite 403
Gaithersburg, MD 20879
Phone: 240-632-9716
Fax: 240-632-1321
Website: http://www.acsm.net

346 • ACSM - AAGS - NSPS Scholarships

Purpose: To award excellent surveying and mapping students.
Eligibility: There are several different types of awards. The first is for students enrolled in two-year degree programs in surveying technology. The second is for students enrolled in or accepted to a graduate program in geodetic surveying or geodesy. The third is for students enrolled in four-year degree programs in surveying (or in related areas such as geomatics or surveying engineering). The last type is for students enrolled in a two-year or four-year surveying (and closely related) degree program, either full or part-time. All awards are based on academic record, statement, recommendation letters and professional activities.
How to Apply: Applications are available online.
Deadline: December 1.
Amount: $500-$5,000.
Number of Awards: Varies.

American Ground Water Trust

16 Centre Street
Concord, NH 03301
Phone: 603-228-5444
Fax: 603-228-6557
Website: http://www.agwt.org

347 • Amtrol Inc. Scholarship

Purpose: To provide scholarships for high school seniors to pursue a career in a ground water-related field.
Eligibility: Applicants must be high school seniors with intentions to pursue a career in ground water management or a related field. Students must be entering their freshman year at a four-year accredited institution. Prior research or experience with the field is required.
How to Apply: Applications are available online.
Deadline: June 1.
Amount: Up to $2,000.
Number of Awards: Varies.

348 • Baroid Scholarship

Purpose: To support high school seniors intending to pursue a career in a ground water-related field.
Eligibility: Applicants must be high school seniors entering an accredited four-year college or university and intending to pursue a career in a ground water-related field.
How to Apply: Applications are available online.
Deadline: June 1.
Amount: Up to $2,000.
Number of Awards: Varies.

349 • Ben Everson Scholarship

Purpose: To provide scholarships to high school seniors pursuing a career in a ground water-related field.
Eligibility: Applicants must be high school seniors entering a four-year accredited institution and intending to pursue a career in a ground water-related field.

How to Apply: Applications are available online.
Deadline: June 1.
Amount: $2,500.
Number of Awards: 1.

350 • Thomas M. Stetson Scholarship

Purpose: To provide scholarships for high school seniors pursuing careers in a ground water-related field.

Eligibility: Applicants must be high school seniors with intentions to pursue a career in ground water-related field. Applicants must attend a college or university located west of the Mississippi River.

How to Apply: Applications are available online.
Deadline: June 1.
Amount: $1,000.
Number of Awards: 1.

American Institute of Chemical Engineers - (AIChE)

3 Park Avenue
New York, NY 10016
Phone: 212-591-7634
Fax: 212-591-8890
Email: awards@aiche.org
Website: http://www.aiche.org

351 • National Student Design Competition

Purpose: To test chemical engineering students' skills in calculation and evaluation of technical data and economic factors.

Eligibility: Applicants must be members of an AIChE student chapter.

How to Apply: Applications are available online.
Deadline: June 4.
Amount: $200-$500.
Number of Awards: 3.

American Society for Nondestructive Testing

1711 Arlingate Lane
P.O. Box 28518
Columbus, OH 43228
Phone: 800-222-2768
Fax: 614-274-6899
Email: sthomas@asnt.org
Website: http://www.asnt.org

352 • ASNT Fellowship

Purpose: To fund research in nondestructive testing.

Eligibility: The award is given to an educational institution accredited by ABET to fund research in nondestructive testing (NDT) at the postgraduate level. One proposal per faculty member will be considered annually. Applicants should submit research proposal, program of study, description of facilities, budget, background on faculty advisor and background on graduate student.

How to Apply: Applications are available online.
Deadline: October 15.
Amount: $15,000.
Number of Awards: Varies.

353 • Engineering Undergraduate Award

Purpose: To support students studying nondestructive testing.

Eligibility: Applicants must be undergraduate students enrolled in an engineering program of an accredited university and specialize in nondestructive testing (NDT). A nominating letter, transcript, three letters of recommendation and an essay describing the role of NDT/NDE in their career are required.

How to Apply: Applications are available online.
Deadline: December 15.
Amount: $3,000.
Number of Awards: Varies.

354 • Robert B. Oliver ASNT Scholarship

Purpose: To support students in nondestructive testing.

Eligibility: Applicants must be undergraduate students enrolled in an engineering program of an accredited university and specialize in nondestructive testing (NDT). A nominating letter, transcript, three letters of recommendation and an essay describing the role of NDT/NDE in their career are required. The award is based on creativity, content, format and readability and the student's involvement in a research project.

How to Apply: Applications are available online.
Deadline: February 15.
Amount: $2,500.
Number of Awards: Varies.

American Society of Agricultural Engineers Foundation

Administrator
Scholarship Fund
2950 Niles Road
St. Joseph, MI 49085
Phone: 269-429-0300
Fax: 269-429-3852
Website: http://www.asae.org

355 • Adams Scholarship Grant

Purpose: To aid undergraduate students with an interest in agricultural machinery product design and development.

Eligibility: Applicants must be biological or agricultural engineering majors in eligible accredited programs in the U.S. or Canada. Applicants must also have completed at least one year of undergraduate study and have at least one year of undergraduate study remaining, have a minimum 2.5 GPA, have an interest in agricultural machinery product design and development and demonstrate financial need.

How to Apply: Application is by formal letter.
Deadline: March 15.
Amount: $1,000.
Number of Awards: 1.

356 • ASAE Foundation Scholarship

Eligibility: Applicants must be student members of ASAE, have completed at least one year of undergraduate study and have at least one year of undergraduate study remaining, major in agricultural or biological engineering at an eligible accredited degree program in the U.S. or Canada, have a minimum 2.5 GPA and demonstrate financial need.

How to Apply: Application is by formal letter.
Deadline: March 15.
Amount: $1,000.
Number of Awards: 1.

357 • ASAE Student Engineer of the Year Scholarship

Purpose: To award outstanding agricultural or biological engineering undergraduate students in the U.S. or Canada.

Eligibility: Applicants must be biological or agricultural engineering students and have completed at least one year of undergraduate study with at least one year of undergraduate study remaining. Applicants must also be enrolled in an eligible accredited engineering program and have a minimum 3.0 GPA. Selection is based on academic performance, character, student membership in ASAE, activities, leadership, paper and some financial need.

How to Apply: Applications are available online.
Deadline: March 15.
Amount: $1,000.
Number of Awards: 1.

American Society of Certified Engineering Technicians (ASCET)

P.O. Box 1536
Brandon, MS 39043
Phone: 601-824-8991
Email: general-manager@ascet.org
Website: http://www.ascet.org

358 • Joseph C. Johnson Memorial Grant

Purpose: To support engineering technology students.
Eligibility: Applicants must have a minimum 3.0 GPA, be U.S. citizens or legal residents of the country in which they are currently living, be either a student, certified, regular, registered or associate member of the American Society of Certified Engineering Technicians (ASCET) and be full- or part-time students in an engineering technology program. Students in a two-year program should apply in the first year to receive the grant for their second year. Students in a four-year program who apply in the third year may receive the grant for their fourth year. Applicants must show financial need and submit three letters of recommendation.

How to Apply: Applications are available online.
Deadline: April 1.
Amount: $750.
Number of Awards: 1.

359 • Joseph M. Parish Memorial Grant

Purpose: To help engineering technology students.
Eligibility: Applicants must have a minimum 3.0 GPA, be U.S. citizens or legal residents of the country in which they are currently living, be student members of the American Society of Certified Engineering Technicians (ASCET) and be full-time students in an engineering technology program. Applicants in a two-year program should apply in the first year to receive the grant for their second year. Students in a four-year program who apply in the third year may receive the grant for their fourth year. Applicants must show financial need. Students pursuing a BS degree in engineering are not eligible for this grant.

How to Apply: Applications are available online.
Deadline: April 1.
Amount: $500.
Number of Awards: 1.

360 • Small Cash Grant Program

Purpose: To help engineering technology students.
Eligibility: Applicants must be a student, certified, regular, registered or associate member of the American Society of Certified Engineering Technicians (ASCET) or be high school seniors in the last five months of the academic year who will be enrolled in an engineering technology curriculum no later than six months following the selection for the award. Students must have passing grades in their present curriculum and submit transcripts and a recommendation letter.

How to Apply: Applications are available online.
Deadline: April 1.
Amount: $100.
Number of Awards: Varies.

American Society of Heating, Refrigerating and Air-Conditioning Engineers Inc.

Lois Benedict
Scholarship Administrator, ASHRAE Inc.
1791 Tullie Circle NE
Atlanta, GA 30329
Phone: 404-636-8400
Fax: 404-321-5478
Email: benedict@ashrae.org
Website: http://www.ashrae.org

361 • ASHRAE Scholarship Program

Purpose: To encourage heating, ventilating, air conditioning and refrigeration education.
Eligibility: Applicants must be full-time undergraduates majoring in engineering or engineering technology or graduate students in a related course of study approved by the Accreditation Board for Engineering and Technology (ABET) or another accrediting agency recognized by ASHRAE with a minimum 3.0 GPA. Selection is based on financial need, leadership, character and potential contribution to the heating, ventilating, air conditioning or refrigeration profession. Applicants must also submit recommendations from instructors.

How to Apply: Applications are available online.
Deadline: December 1.
Amount: Varies.
Number of Awards: Varies.

American Society of Mechanical Engineers

Three Park Avenue
New York, NY 10016
Phone: 800-843-2763
Fax: 973-882-1717
Email: infocentral@asme.org
Website: http://www.asme.org

362 • ASME Foundation Scholarships

Purpose: To support mechanical engineering students.
Eligibility: Applicants must be ASME student members in good standing and enrolled in an ABET-accredited (or equivalent) program of study. Eligible candidates must be in their sophomore, junior or senior years.

How to Apply: Applications are available online.
Deadline: March 15.
Amount: $1,500.
Number of Awards: 15.

363 • F.W. Beichley Scholarship

Purpose: To support mechanical engineering students.
Eligibility: Applicants must be ASME student members enrolled in an eligible accredited mechanical engineering baccalaureate program. Selection is based on leadership, scholastic ability, potential contribution to the mechanical engineering profession and financial need. The scholarship is only applicable for study in the junior or senior year.

How to Apply: Applications are available online.
Deadline: March 15.
Amount: $2,000.
Number of Awards: 1.

364 • Frank and Dorothy Miller ASME Auxiliary Scholarships

Purpose: To support mechanical engineering students.

Eligibility: Applicants must be ASME student members, be enrolled in an eligible accredited mechanical engineering baccalaureate program, be North American residents and U.S. citizens and demonstrate character and integrity.

How to Apply: Applications are available online.

Deadline: March 15.

Amount: $1,500.

Number of Awards: 2.

365 • Garland Duncan Scholarships

Purpose: To support mechanical engineering students.

Eligibility: Applicants must be ASME student members, be enrolled in an eligible accredited mechanical engineering baccalaureate program, have strong academic performance and be college juniors or seniors. Selection is based on character, integrity, leadership, scholastic ability, potential contribution to the mechanical engineering profession and financial need.

How to Apply: Applications are available online.

Deadline: March 15.

Amount: $3,500.

Number of Awards: 2.

366 • John and Elsa Gracik Scholarships

Purpose: To support mechanical engineering students.

Eligibility: Applicants must be ASME student members, enrolled in an eligible accredited mechanical engineering baccalaureate program and be U.S. citizens. Selection is based on scholastic ability, financial need, character, leadership and potential contribution to the mechanical engineering profession.

How to Apply: Applications are available online.

Deadline: March 15.

Amount: $1,500.

Number of Awards: 18.

367 • Kenneth Andrew Roe Scholarship

Purpose: To support students who are studying mechanical engineering.

Eligibility: Applicants must be ASME student members, be enrolled in an ABET accredited mechanical engineering baccalaureate program, be North American residents and be U.S. citizens. Applicants must also be juniors or seniors in college with strong academic performance, character and integrity.

How to Apply: Applications are available online.

Deadline: March 15.

Amount: $10,000.

Number of Awards: 1.

368 • Melvin R. Green Scholarships

Purpose: To support mechanical engineering students.

Eligibility: Applicants must have outstanding character and integrity, be ASME student members, be enrolled in an eligible accredited mechanical engineering baccalaureate program, be college juniors or seniors and have strong academic performance.

How to Apply: Applications are available online.

Deadline: March 15.

Amount: $3,500.

Number of Awards: 3.

369 • Robert F. Sammataro Pressure Vessel Piping Division Scholarship

Purpose: To support mechanical engineering students.

Eligibility: Applicants must be ASME student members and be enrolled in an eligible accredited mechanical engineering baccalaureate program. Applicants must demonstrate a special interest in pressure vessels and piping.

How to Apply: Applications are available online.

Deadline: March 15.

Amount: $1,000.

Number of Awards: 1.

American Society of Naval Engineers

1452 Duke Street
Alexandria, VA 22314
Phone: 703-836-6727
Fax: 703-836-7491
Email: dwoodbury@navalengineers.org
Website: http://www.navalengineers.org

370 • ASNE Scholarship Program

Purpose: To encourage college students to enter the field of naval engineering and to provide support to naval engineers pursuing advanced education.

Eligibility: Applications must be for the last year of a full-time or co-op undergraduate program or for one year of full-time graduate study for a designated engineering or physical science degree at an accredited school. Applicants must be U.S. citizens pursuing careers in naval engineering. Graduate student applicants must be members of ASNE. An applicant's academic record, work history, professional promise and interest, extracurricular activities and recommendations are considered. Financial need may be considered.

How to Apply: Applications are available online or by written request.

Deadline: February 15.

Amount: $2,500-$3,500.

Number of Awards: Varies by year.

American Society of Safety Engineers

1800 E. Oakton Street
Des Plaines, IL 60018
Phone: 847-699-2929
Fax: 847-768-3434
Email: customerservice@asse.org
Website: http://www.asse.org

371 • Liberty Mutual Safety Research Fellowship Program

Purpose: To award research fellowships to promote safety research.

Eligibility: Applicants must be U.S. citizens and either have their Ph.D. or be working toward a master's or Ph.D. Preference is given to applicants working within an ABET-accredited safety program. The selection committee prefers applied safety/health research with a broad appeal and gives special consideration to ASSE members. Recipients must spend four to six weeks during the summer at the Liberty Mutual Research Center, in Hopkinton, MA, and write an article on their research or an outline for a grant proposal to continue the research.

How to Apply: Applications are available online.
Deadline: March 1.
Amount: Up to $9,500 stipend.
Number of Awards: 2.

American Water Works Association

6666 W. Quincy Avenue
Denver, CO 80235-3098
Phone: 303-347-6201
Fax: 303-795-7603
Email: swheeler@awwa.org
Website: http://www.awwa.org

372 • Abel Wolman Fellowship

Purpose: To support doctoral students pursuing advanced training and research in the field of water supply and treatment.

Eligibility: Applicants must obtain a Ph.D. within two years of the award, must be citizens of the U.S., Canada or Mexico and should submit applications, transcripts, GRE scores, three recommendation letters, course of study and description of the dissertation research study and how it pertains to water supply and treatment. The award is based on academics, the connection between the research and water supply and treatment and the applicant's research skills.

How to Apply: Applications are available online.
Deadline: January 15.
Amount: $20,000.
Number of Awards: 1.

373 • Academic Achievement Award

Purpose: To recognize contributions to the field of public water supply.

Eligibility: Master's theses and doctoral dissertations that are relevant to the water supply industry are eligible. Unbound manuscripts must be the work of a single author and be submitted during the competition year in which they were submitted for the degree. Students may major in any area as long as the research is directly related to the drinking water supply industry. In addition to the application, students must submit a one-page abstract of the manuscript and a letter of endorsement from the major professor or department chair. The doctoral dissertation awards are $3,000 and $1,500. The master's thesis awards are $3,000 and $1,500.

How to Apply: Applications are available online.
Deadline: October 1.
Amount: $3,000.
Number of Awards: 4.

374 • Holly Cornell Scholarship

Purpose: To support female and/or minority master's students pursuing advanced training in the field of water supply and treatment.

Eligibility: Applicants must be females and/or minorities who have been accepted to or are current master's degree students in engineering. Applications, transcripts, GRE scores, three recommendation letters, statements and course of study are required. The award is based on academics and leadership.

How to Apply: Applications are available online.
Deadline: January 15.
Amount: $5,000.
Number of Awards: 1.

375 • Larson Aquatic Research Support (LARS)

Purpose: To support doctoral and master's students interested in careers in the fields of corrosion control, treatment and distribution of domestic and industrial water supplies, aquatic chemistry and/or environmental chemistry.

Eligibility: Applicants must pursue an advanced (master's or doctoral) degree at an institution of higher education located in Canada, Guam, Puerto Rico, Mexico or the U.S. Applications, resumes, transcripts, GRE scores, three recommendation letters and a course of study are required. Master's students also must submit a statement of educational plans and career objectives or a research plan. Ph.D. students must submit research plans. The master's grant is $5,000, and the doctoral grant is $7,000. The award is based on academics and leadership.

How to Apply: Applications are available online.
Deadline: January 15.
Amount: $7,000.
Number of Awards: 2.

376 • Thomas R. Camp Scholarship

Purpose: To support students conducting applied research in the drinking water field.

Eligibility: Applicants must pursue graduate degrees at an institution of higher education in Canada, Guam, Puerto Rico, Mexico or the U.S. This is awarded to doctoral students in even years and master's students in odd years. Applicants must submit applications, resumes, transcripts, GRE scores, three recommendation letters, statements and research plans. The award is based on academics and leadership.

How to Apply: Applications are available online.
Deadline: January 15.
Amount: $5,000.
Number of Awards: 1.

ASM International Foundation

9639 Kinsman Road
Materials Park, OH 44073-0002
Phone: 440-338-5151
Fax: 440-338-4634
Email: crhayes@asminternational.org
Website: http://www.asminternational.org

377 • ASM Foundation Scholarship Awards

Purpose: To support undergraduates studying metallurgy or materials science engineering.

Eligibility: Applicants must be student members of ASM International, major in metallurgy or materials science engineering and be juniors or seniors at a North American university that has a bachelor's degree program in science and engineering. Applications, personal statements, transcripts, two recommendation forms and photographs are required. The award is based on academics, interest in the metallurgy/materials engineering field and character.

How to Apply: Applications are available online.
Deadline: May 1.
Amount: $1,000.
Number of Awards: 12.

378 • ASM Foundation Technical and Community College Scholarship Awards

Purpose: To support community college students in engineering fields.

Eligibility: Applicants must be student members who are majoring in metallurgy or materials science engineering at technical or community colleges, are training to be technicians in various engineering fields and have completed at least one year of college. Applications, personal statements, transcripts, two recommendation

forms and photographs are required. The award is based on academics, interest in the metallurgy/materials engineering field and character.
How to Apply: Applications are available online.
Deadline: May 1.
Amount: $500.
Number of Awards: 10.

379 • ASM Outstanding Scholars Awards
Purpose: To recognize distinguished scholars in metallurgy or materials science engineering.
Eligibility: Applicants must be student members of ASM International, major in metallurgy or materials science engineering and be juniors or seniors at a North American university that has a bachelor's degree program in science and engineering. Applications, personal statements, transcripts, two recommendation forms and photographs are required. The award is based on academics, interest in the metallurgy/materials engineering field and personal character.
How to Apply: Applications are available online.
Deadline: May 1.
Amount: $2,000.
Number of Awards: 3.

380 • George A. Roberts Scholarships
Purpose: To help students interested in the metallurgy or materials engineering field.
Eligibility: Applicants must be student members of ASM International, plan to major in metallurgy or materials science engineering and be juniors or seniors at a North American university that has a bachelor's degree program in science and engineering. Applications, personal statements, transcripts, two recommendation forms, photographs and financial aid officers' contact information are required. The award is based on academics, interest in the field, character and financial need.
How to Apply: Applications are available online.
Deadline: May 1.
Amount: $6,000.
Number of Awards: 7.

381 • Nicholas J. Grant Scholarship
Purpose: To recognize students who have excelled in scholarship, leadership and service.
Eligibility: Applicants must be student members of ASM International, major in metallurgy or materials science engineering and be juniors or seniors at a North American university that has a bachelor's degree program in science and engineering. Applications, personal statements, transcripts, two recommendation forms, photographs and financial aid officers' contact information are required. The award is based on academics, interest in the metallurgy/materials engineering field, character and financial need. The scholarship provides one year of full tuition.
How to Apply: Applications are available online.
Deadline: May 1.
Amount: Varies.
Number of Awards: Varies.

382 • William Park Woodside Founder's Scholarship
Purpose: To support students who follow the spirit of ASM International.
Eligibility: Applicants must be student members of ASM International, major in metallurgy or materials science engineering and be juniors or seniors at a North American university that has a bachelor's degree program in science and engineering.

Applications, personal statements, transcripts, two recommendation forms, photographs and financial aid officers' contact information are required. The award is based on academics, interest in the metallurgy/materials engineering field, character and financial need. The award is for one year of full tuition up to $10,000.
How to Apply: Applications are available online.
Deadline: May 1.
Amount: $10,000.
Number of Awards: Varies.

Association of Engineering Geologists Foundation Marliave Fund
Paul Santi, Department of Geology and Geological Engineering
Colorado School of Mines
Berthoud Hall
Golden, CO 80401
Phone: 303-273-3108
Email: psanti@mines.edu
Website: http://www.aegfoundation.org

383 • Marliave Fund
Purpose: To reward outstanding students in engineering geology and geological engineering.
Eligibility: Applicants must be seniors or graduate students in a college or university program directly applicable to geological engineering and be members of the Association of Engineering Geologists.
How to Apply: Applications are available online or by written request.
Deadline: April 15.
Amount: Varies.
Number of Awards: Varies.

Association of Engineering Geologists Foundation Tilford Fund
NRT Scholarship Committee
70 Forest Lane
Placitas, NM 87043
Website: http://www.aegfoundation.org

384 • Tilford Fund
Purpose: To provide financial assistance for field studies in engineering geology.
Eligibility: Applicants must be members of the Association of Engineering Geologists who are college or graduate students. Applicants are chosen on the basis of scholarship, ability, participation and potential for contributions to the profession.
How to Apply: Applications are available online.
Deadline: February 16.
Amount: Varies.
Number of Awards: Varies.

Association of State Dam Safety Officials
450 Old Vine Street
2nd Floor
Lexington, KY 40507
Phone: 859-257-5140
Fax: 859-323-1958
Email: info@damsafety.org
Website: http://www.damsafety.org

385 • ASDSO Dam Safety Scholarships

Purpose: To increase awareness of careers in dam safety.

Eligibility: Applicants must be full-time seniors in an accredited civil engineering program or a related field and show an interest in a career related to dam design, construction or operation. Students must have a minimum 2.5 GPA for the first two years of college, be recommended by their academic advisor and write an essay on what ASDSO is and why dam safety is important. Financial need is considered.

How to Apply: Applications are available online.

Deadline: March 31.

Amount: Up to $5,000.

Number of Awards: Varies.

Automotive Hall of Fame

Award and Scholarship Programs
21400 Oakwood Boulevard
Dearborn, MI 48124
Phone: 313-240-4000
Fax: 313-240-8641
Website: http://www.automotivehalloffame.org

386 • Automotive Hall of Fame Scholarships

Purpose: To assist students interested in automotive careers.

Eligibility: Applicants must be interested in automotive careers. Other requirements vary depending on the specific scholarship.

How to Apply: Applications are available online or by sending a self-addressed, stamped envelope.

Deadline: May 30.

Amount: Varies.

Number of Awards: Varies.

AVS (American Vacuum Society)

120 Wall Street, 32nd Floor
New York, NY 10005-3993
Phone: 212-248-0200
Fax: 212-248-0245
Email: angela@avs.org
Website: http://www.avs.org

387 • Dorothy M. and Earl S. Hoffman Award

Purpose: To recognize excellence in continuing graduate studies in the sciences and technologies related to AVS.

Eligibility: Applicants must be graduate students in an accredited academic institution. An application, summary of research, letters of recommendation and transcript are required. The award is based on achievement in research and academic record. The top five student nominees are invited to present talks on their research to the trustees at the international symposium. The trustees then select one recipient for the Dorothy M. and Earl S. Hoffman Award. The award covers travel expenses to the symposium.

How to Apply: Applications are available online.

Deadline: March 31.

Amount: $1,500.

Number of Awards: 3.

388 • Graduate Research Award (GRA)

Purpose: To support graduate studies in the sciences and technologies related to the AVS.

Eligibility: Applicants must be graduate students in an accredited academic institution. Awards are based on research and academic record. The awards cover travel expenses to the international symposium. Applicants should submit applications, recommendation letters, research summaries and transcripts.

How to Apply: Applications are available online.

Deadline: March 31.

Amount: $1,000.

Number of Awards: 10.

389 • Nellie Yeoh Whetten Award

Purpose: To support women in graduate studies in the sciences and technologies related to AVS.

Eligibility: Applicants must be female graduate students in an accredited academic institution and must send an application, report on candidate form, two letters of recommendation and college and graduate school transcripts.

How to Apply: Applications are available online.

Deadline: March 31.

Amount: $1,500.

Number of Awards: 3.

390 • Russell and Sigurd Varian Award

Purpose: To support continuing graduate studies in the sciences and technologies related to AVS.

Eligibility: Applicants must be graduate students in an accredited academic institution. Five finalists are invited to present talks on their research to the trustees at the international symposium. The trustees then select one of the top three students to receive the award, which also covers travel expenses. Applicants should submit applications, research summaries, letters of recommendations and transcripts.

How to Apply: Applications are available online.

Deadline: March 31.

Amount: $1,500.

Number of Awards: 3.

Barry M. Goldwater Scholarship and Excellence in Education Foundation

6225 Brandon Avenue, Suite 315
Springfield, VA 22150
Phone: 703-756-6012
Fax: 703-756-6015
Email: goldwater@act.org
Website: http://www.act.org/goldwater/

391 • Barry M. Goldwater Scholarship and Excellence in Education Program

Purpose: To assist college students who pursue studies that lead to careers as scientists, mathematicians and engineers.

Eligibility: Applicants must be full-time college sophomores or juniors, U.S. citizens or resident aliens, have a minimum "B" GPA and be in the upper fourth of their class. Award must be used during the junior or senior year of college. Selection is based on potential and intent to pursue careers in mathematics, the natural sciences or engineering.

How to Apply: Institutions nominate college sophomores or juniors. Applicants may not apply directly to the foundation.

Deadline: February 1.

Amount: $7,500.

Number of Awards: Up to 300.

Black and Veatch

11401 Lamar Avenue
Overland Park, KS 66211
Phone: 913-458-2000
Fax: 913-458-2934
Website: http://www.bv.com

392 • Black and Veatch Scholarships

Purpose: To assist students at select universities, technical schools and engineering colleges.

Eligibility: Black and Veatch is an engineering, consulting and construction company that specializes in infrastructure development in energy, water, information and government markets. For information on eligibility, please contact the endowment or financial aid office at your university, engineering college or technical school.

How to Apply: Contact the financial aid office for application information.

Deadline: Varies.

Amount: Varies.

Number of Awards: Varies.

Desk and Derrick Educational Trust

5153 E 51st Street, Suite 107
Tulsa, OK 74135
Phone: 918-622-1749
Fax: 918-622-1675
Email: adotulsa@swbell.net
Website: http://www.addc.org

393 • ADDC Education Trust Scholarship

Purpose: To promote studies in the energy industry.

Eligibility: Applicants must be U.S. or Canadian citizens, have completed two years of undergraduate study, have a minimum 3.0 GPA and demonstrate financial need. Students must be pursuing a degree in a field related to the petroleum, energy or allied industries and plan to work full-time in the petroleum, energy or allied industry or research alternative fuels such as coal, electric, solar, wind hydroelectric, nuclear or ethanol.

How to Apply: Applications are available online.

Deadline: April 1.

Amount: Varies.

Number of Awards: Varies.

Electrochemical Society

65 S. Main Street, Building D
Pennington, NJ 08534-2839
Phone: 609-737-1902
Fax: 609-737-2743
Email: awards@electrochem.org
Website: http://www.electrochem.org

394 • Battery Division Student Research Award

Purpose: To recognize young engineers and scientists in the field of electrochemical power sources.

Eligibility: Applicants must be accepted or enrolled in a college or university and must submit transcripts, an outline of the proposed research project, a description of how the project is related to the field of electrochemical power sources, a record of achievements in industrial work and a letter of recommendation from the research supervisor. Awards are based on academic performance, past research, proposed research and the recommendation.

How to Apply: Application materials are described online.

Deadline: March 15.

Amount: $1,000.

Number of Awards: Varies.

395 • Industrial Electrolysis and Electrochemical Engineering Engineering Division Student Achievement Awards

Purpose: To recognize young engineers and scientists in electrochemical engineering and to encourage the recipients to enter careers in the field.

Eligibility: Applicants must be accepted by or enrolled in a college or university and propose a research project. The application must include transcripts, research outline, statement describing how the project relates to electrochemical engineering, record of industrial work and letter of recommendation from the research supervisor. The award is based on academic performance, research and the recommendation.

How to Apply: Application materials are described online.

Deadline: September 15.

Amount: $1,000.

Number of Awards: Varies.

Institute of Industrial Engineers (IIE)

3577 Parkway Lane
Suite 200
Norcross, GA 30092
Phone: 800-494-0460
Fax: 770-441-3295
Email: bcameron@iienet.org
Website: http://www.iienet.org/studentcenter

396 • A.O. Putnam Memorial Scholarship

Purpose: To help undergraduate Institute members who plan to pursue careers in management consulting.

Eligibility: Applicants must be undergraduate students enrolled in a college in the United States, Canada or Mexico with an accredited industrial engineering program, major in industrial engineering and be active members. Preference is given to students who plan to work in management consulting. Students may not apply directly for this scholarship and must be nominated. The award is based on academic ability, character, leadership, potential service to the industrial engineering profession and financial need.

How to Apply: Nomination forms are available online.

Deadline: February 15.

Amount: $600.

Number of Awards: 1.

397 • Benjamin Willard Niebel Scholarship

Purpose: To award students majoring in industrial engineering.

Eligibility: Applicants must be full-time undergraduate or graduate students enrolled in a college in the United States, Canada or Mexico with an accredited industrial engineering program, major in industrial engineering and be active members. Students may not apply directly for this scholarship and must be nominated. The award is based on academic ability, character, leadership, potential service to the industrial engineering profession and financial need.

How to Apply: Nomination forms are available online.

Deadline: February 15.

Amount: $1,000.

Number of Awards: 1.

398 • C.B. Gambrell Undergraduate Scholarship

Purpose: To help undergraduate industrial engineering students from the U.S.

Eligibility: Applicants must be full-time undergraduate students who have completed their freshman year in an accredited industrial engineering program, major in industrial engineering and be active members. Students may not apply directly for this scholarship and must be nominated. The award is based on academic ability, character, leadership, potential service to the industrial engineering profession and financial need.

How to Apply: Nomination forms are available online.

Deadline: February 15.

Amount: $600.

Number of Awards: 1.

399 • Dwight D. Gardner Scholarship

Purpose: To award undergraduate members.

Eligibility: Applicants must be undergraduate students enrolled in a college in the United States, Canada or Mexico with an accredited industrial engineering program, major in industrial engineering and be active members. Students may not apply directly for this scholarship and must be nominated. The award is based on academic ability, character, leadership, potential service to the industrial engineering profession and financial need.

How to Apply: Nomination forms are available online.

Deadline: February 15.

Amount: $1,000.

Number of Awards: 2.

400 • E.J. Sierieja Memorial Fellowship

Purpose: To award graduate students pursuing advanced studies in the area of transportation.

Eligibility: Applicants must be full-time graduate students, majoring in transportation and active members. Students may not apply directly for this scholarship and must be nominated. The award is based on academic ability, character, leadership, potential service to the industrial engineering profession and financial need. Preference is given to students focusing on rail transportation.

How to Apply: Nomination forms are available online.

Deadline: February 15.

Amount: $600.

Number of Awards: 1.

401 • Gilbreth Memorial Fellowship

Purpose: To support graduate student Institute members.

Eligibility: Applicants must be graduate students at an institution in the United States, Canada or Mexico, majoring in industrial engineering or its equivalent and active members. Students may not apply directly for this scholarship and must be nominated. The award is based on academic ability, character, leadership, potential service to the industrial engineering profession and financial need.

How to Apply: Nomination forms are available online.

Deadline: February 15.

Amount: $1,000.

Number of Awards: 2.

402 • IIE Council of Fellows Undergraduate Scholarship

Purpose: To support undergraduate student members.

Eligibility: Applicants must be full-time undergraduate students enrolled in a college in the United States, Canada or Mexico with an accredited industrial engineering program, major in industrial engineering and be active members. Students may apply directly for this scholarship and do not need to be nominated. The award is based on academic ability, character, leadership, potential service to the industrial engineering profession and financial need.

How to Apply: Applications are available online.

Deadline: February 15.

Amount: $1,000.

Number of Awards: 2.

403 • John L. Imhoff Scholarship

Purpose: To award a student who has contributed to the development of the industrial engineering profession through international understanding.

Eligibility: Applicants must be pursuing a B.S., master's or doctorate degree in an accredited IE program and have at least two years of school remaining. Students may not apply directly for this scholarship and must be nominated. An essay describing the candidate's international contributions to industrial engineering and three references are required. IIE membership is not required.

How to Apply: More information is available online.

Deadline: February 15.

Amount: $1,000.

Number of Awards: 1.

404 • John S.W. Fargher Scholarship

Purpose: To award graduate students in industrial engineering who have demonstrated leadership.

Eligibility: Applicants must be full-time graduate students with at least one full year left who are enrolled in a college in the United States with an accredited industrial engineering program. Candidates must also major in industrial engineering or engineering management and be active members who have demonstrated leadership in industrial engineering-related activities. Students may not apply directly for this scholarship and must be nominated.

How to Apply: More information is available online.

Deadline: September 11.

Amount: $1,000.

Number of Awards: 1.

405 • Lisa Zaken Award For Excellence

Purpose: To award excellence in scholarly activities and leadership related to the industrial engineering profession on campus

Eligibility: Applicants must be undergraduate or graduate students with at least one year remaining, major in industrial engineering and be active members who have been leaders in IIE. Students may not apply directly for this scholarship and must be nominated. The award is based on academic ability and leadership related to industrial engineering.

How to Apply: Nomination forms are available online.

Deadline: February 15.

Amount: $600.

Number of Awards: 1.

406 • Marvin Mundel Memorial Scholarship

Purpose: To assist undergraduate engineering students with an interest in work measurement and methods engineering.

Eligibility: Applicants must be full-time undergraduate students enrolled in a college in the United States, Canada or Mexico with an accredited industrial engineering program, major in industrial engineering and be active members. Students may not apply directly for this scholarship and must be nominated. The award is based on academic ability, character, leadership, potential service to the industrial engineering profession and financial need. Preference is given to students with a demonstrated interest in work measurement and methods engineering.

How to Apply: Nomination forms are available online.
Deadline: February 15.
Amount: $600.
Number of Awards: 1.

407 • United Parcel Service Scholarship for Female Students

Purpose: To help female undergraduate engineering students.
Eligibility: Applicants must be full-time female students at an institution in the United States, Canada or Mexico with an accredited industrial engineering program, majoring in industrial engineering or its equivalent and active members. Students may not apply directly for this scholarship and must be nominated. The award is based on academic ability, character, leadership, potential service to the industrial engineering profession and financial need.
How to Apply: Nomination forms are available online.
Deadline: February 15.
Amount: $4,000.
Number of Awards: 1.

International Society for Optical Engineering

P.O. Box 10
Bellingham, WA 98227
Phone: 360-676-3290
Fax: 360-647-1445
Email: education@spie.org
Website: http://www.spie.org

408 • Michael Kidger Memorial Scholarship

Purpose: To support students in the optical design field.
Eligibility: Applicants must be in the optical design field and must have one year remaining of their studies. Students must submit a summary of their academic background and interest in optical design and two letters of recommendation.
How to Apply: Applications are available online.
Deadline: March 31.
Amount: Varies.
Number of Awards: 1.

League of United Latin American Citizens

2000 L Street NW
Suite #610
Washington, DC 20036
Phone: 202-833-6130
Email: lnescaward@aol.com
Website: http://www.lulac.org

409 • GM Fund

Purpose: To aid minority engineering students with completing college.
Eligibility: Applicants must be minority full-time college students and must major in courses leading to an engineering career. Selection is based on academics, engineering skills, writing ability, extracurricular activities and community service.
How to Apply: Applications are available online.
Deadline: July 15.
Amount: $2,000.
Number of Awards: 20.

National Association of Minority Engineering Program Administrators

1133 W. Morse Boulevard
Suite 201
Winter Park, FL 32789
Phone: 407-647-8839
Fax: 407-629-2502
Email: namepa@namepa.org
Website: http://www.namepa.org

410 • NAMEPA Scholarship Program

Purpose: To support minority students to become engineers.
Eligibility: Applicants must be admitted at a college or university as an engineering major with a minimum 3.0 GPA and minimum ACT score of 25 or minimum SAT score of 1000. Applicants must attend a NAMEPA member institution. Transfer students are also eligible. Selection is based on coursework in high school, course distribution, activities, a one-page narrative and recommendations.
How to Apply: Applications are available online.
Deadline: March 30.
Amount: $1,000.
Number of Awards: Varies.

National Inventors Hall of Fame

221 S. Broadway
Akron, OH 44308
Phone: 330-849-6887
Email: collegiate@invent.org
Website: http://www.invent.org

411 • Collegiate Inventors Competition

Purpose: To encourage college students in science, engineering, mathematics, technology and creative invention and to stimulate interest in technology and economic leadership.
Eligibility: Applicants must have been full-time college or university students during part of the 12-month period prior to the entry date. Up to four students may work as a team, and at least one student must meet the full-time criteria. Judging is based on originality and inventiveness, as well as the invention's potential value to society.
How to Apply: Applications are available online.
Deadline: June 1.
Amount: $5,000-$50,000.
Number of Awards: 6.

National Society of Professional Engineers

1420 King Street
Alexandria, VA 22314
Phone: 703-684-2884
Fax: 703-836-4875
Email: egarcia@nspe.org
Website: http://www.nspe.org

412 • Auxiliary Scholarships

Purpose: To aid female students who want to major in engineering.
Eligibility: Applicants must be female high school seniors planning to study engineering. Applicants must be U.S. citizens. Selection is based only on achievement.
How to Apply: Applications are available online.
Deadline: December 2.
Amount: $1,000.
Number of Awards: 1.

413 • Paul H. Robbins, P.E., Honorary Scholarship

Purpose: To aid students in engineering.

Eligibility: Applicants must be members of NSPE, current engineering undergraduate students (junior year only) and enrolled in ABET-accredited engineering programs that participate in the NSPE Professional Engineers in Education (PEE) Sustaining University Program (SUP).

How to Apply: Applications are available online.

Deadline: May 16.

Amount: $10,000.

Number of Awards: 1.

414 • Professional Engineers In Government (PEG)

Purpose: To aid students in engineering.

Eligibility: Applicants must be graduate students pursuing an MBA, master's degree in public administration or master's degree in engineering management and must also be engineering interns or licensed professional engineers. Selection is based on undergraduate GPA, GRE or GMAT score, professional activities, community activities, essay and membership. Preference is given to government employees.

How to Apply: Applications are available online.

Deadline: March 15.

Amount: $2,500.

Number of Awards: 1.

415 • Professional Engineers In Industry (PEI) Scholarship

Purpose: To aid students in engineering.

Eligibility: Applicants must be undergraduate sophomores, juniors or seniors or graduate students with a minimum 2.5 GPA who are sponsored by a NSPE/PEI member and enrolled in an accredited engineering program. Preference is given to relatives or dependents of NSPE members.

How to Apply: Applications are available online.

Deadline: June 1.

Amount: $2,500.

Number of Awards: 1.

416 • Virginia D. Henry Memorial Scholarship

Purpose: To aid students in engineering.

Eligibility: Applicants must be female, high school seniors and study engineering at a college or university accredited by the Engineering Accreditation Commission. Selection is based only on achievement.

How to Apply: Applications are available online.

Deadline: December 2.

Amount: $1,000.

Number of Awards: 1.

Society for Imaging Science and Technology

7003 Kilworth Lane
Springfield, VA 22151
Phone: 703-642-9090
Fax: 703-642-9094
Email: info@imaging.org
Website: http://www.imaging.org

417 • Raymond Davis Scholarship

Purpose: To support students who are studying imaging science and technology.

Eligibility: Applicants must be full-time graduate or undergraduate students studying photographic or imaging engineering or science who have completed or will complete two academic years of college before the term of the scholarship.

How to Apply: Applications are available online.

Deadline: December 15.

Amount: $1,000.

Number of Awards: Varies.

Society of Automotive Engineers

400 Commonwealth Drive
Warrendale, PA 15096
Phone: 724-776-4841
Fax: 724-776-5760
Email: connie@sae.org
Website: http://www.sae.org

418 • Doctoral Scholars Forgivable Loan Program

Purpose: To provide funding to assist promising engineering graduate students to pursue careers in teaching at the college level.

Eligibility: Applicants must hold an undergraduate degree from an engineering program and have been admitted to a doctoral program with the purpose of teaching engineering at the college level. Selection is based on scholastic achievement, desire to teach, interest in mobility technology and support of the SAE Collegiate Chapter Faculty advisor.

How to Apply: Applications are available online.

Deadline: April 1.

Amount: $5,000.

Number of Awards: 2.

419 • Long-Term Member Sponsored Scholarship

Purpose: This scholarship recognizes outstanding SAE student members who actively support SAE and its activities.

Eligibility: Applicants must be college juniors and student members of SAE, major in engineering and actively support SAE and its programs. The scholarship will be awarded purely on the basis of the student's support for SAE and its programs.

How to Apply: Applications are available online.

Deadline: April 1.

Amount: $1,000.

Number of Awards: Varies.

420 • SAE Engineering Scholarships

Purpose: To offer a number of scholarships to qualified students who are interested in the study of engineering and related sciences.

Eligibility: Applicants must be high school seniors and intend to enroll in an engineering or related science program and meet minimum grade point averages and SAT/ACT scores. There are several corporate sponsored scholarships available.

How to Apply: Applications are available online.

Deadline: December 1.

Amount: $1,000-$10,000.

Number of Awards: Varies.

421 • Yanmar/SAE Scholarship

Purpose: This scholarship is sponsored by the SAE Foundation and the Yanmar Diesel America Corporation.

Eligibility: Applicants must be entering their senior year of undergraduate engineering or enrolled in a postgraduate engineering or related science program. Applicants must also pursue a course of study or research related to the conservation of energy in transportation, agriculture and construction and power generation.

How to Apply: Applications are available online.

Deadline: April 1.

Amount: $1,000.

Number of Awards: 1.

Society of Exploration Geophysicists

Scholarship Committee
SEG Foundation
P.O. Box 702740
Tulsa, OK 74170
Phone: 918-497-5574
Fax: 918-497-5565
Email: students@seg.org
Website: http://students.seg.org

422 • SEG Scholarship

Purpose: To fund individuals who are involved or interested in the field of geophysics.

Eligibility: Applicants must intend to pursue a career in exploration geophysics. Applicants must also be one of the following: A high school student with above average grades planning to enter college the next fall term, an undergraduate whose grades are above average, or a graduate student pursuing a career in exploration geophysics in operations, teaching or research.

How to Apply: Applications are available online or by written request.

Deadline: March 1.

Amount: $500-$12,000.

Number of Awards: Varies.

Society of Naval Architects and Marine Engineers

601 Pavonia Avenue
Jersey City, NJ 07306
Phone: 201-798-4800
Fax: 201-798-4975
Email: efaustino@sname.org
Website: http://www.sname.org

423 • Society of Naval Architects and Marine Engineers Undergraduate Scholarships

Purpose: To assist college juniors and seniors who are studying marine industry fields.

Eligibility: Applicants must be U.S. or Canadian college juniors and seniors who are members of the SNAME and are working towards degrees in naval architecture, marine engineering, ocean engineering or marine industry related areas fields.

How to Apply: Applications are available by email.

Deadline: Varies.

Amount: $2,000.

Number of Awards: Varies.

Society of Plastics Engineers

14 Fairfield Drive
P.O. Box 403
Brookfield, CT 06804
Phone: 203-775-0471
Fax: 203-775-8490
Email: info@4spe.org
Website: http://www.4spe.org

424 • American Plastics Council (APC)/SPE Plastics Environmental Division Scholarship

Purpose: To aid students who have an interest in the plastics industry.

Eligibility: Applicants must have an interest in the plastics industry, major in or take courses leading to a career in the plastics industry and be in good academic standing. Financial need is considered.

How to Apply: Applications are available online.

Deadline: January 15.

Amount: $2,500.

Number of Awards: 1.

425 • Composites Division/Harold Giles Scholarship

Purpose: To aid undergraduate and graduate students who have an interest in the plastics industry.

Eligibility: Applicants must have an interest in the plastics industry, major in or take courses leading to a career in the plastics industry and be in good academic standing. Financial need is considered.

How to Apply: Applications are available online.

Deadline: January 15.

Amount: $1,000.

Number of Awards: 1.

426 • Polymer Modifiers and Additives Division Scholarships

Purpose: To aid students who have an interest in the plastics industry.

Eligibility: Applicants must have an interest in the plastics industry, major in or take courses leading to a career in the plastics industry and be in good academic standing. Financial need is considered.

How to Apply: Applications are available online.

Deadline: January 15.

Amount: $4,000.

Number of Awards: 4.

427 • SPE General Scholarships

Purpose: To aid students who have demonstrated or expressed an interest in the plastics industry.

Eligibility: Applicants must have a demonstrated or expressed interest in the plastics industry and be majoring in or taking courses that would lead to a career in the plastics industry. Applicants must be in good academic standing. Financial need is considered for most scholarships.

How to Apply: Applications are available online.

Deadline: January 15.

Amount: Up to $4,000.

Number of Awards: 10-12.

428 • Ted Neward Scholarship

Purpose: To aid students who have an interest in the plastics industry.

Eligibility: Applicants must be U.S. citizens, have an interest in the plastics industry, major in or take courses leading to a career in the plastics industry and be in good academic standing. Financial need is considered.

How to Apply: Applications are available online.
Deadline: January 15.
Amount: $3,000.
Number of Awards: 2.

429 • Thermoforming Division Memorial Scholarships

Purpose: To aid students who have an interest in the plastics industry.

Eligibility: Applicants must have a 3.0 GPA and an interest in the plastics industry, major in or take courses leading to a career in the plastics industry and be in good academic standing. Applicants must have experience in the thermoforming industry, such as courses taken, research conducted or jobs held.

How to Apply: Applications are available online.
Deadline: January 15.
Amount: $5,000.
Number of Awards: 2.

430 • Thermoset Division/James I. MacKenzie Memorial Scholarship

Purpose: To aid students who have an interest in the plastics industry and have experience in the thermoset industry.

Eligibility: Applicants must have an interest in the plastics industry and major in or take courses leading to a career in the plastics industry. Applicants must also have experience in the thermoset industry, such as courses taken, research conducted or jobs held.

How to Apply: Applications are available online.
Deadline: January 15.
Amount: $2,000.
Number of Awards: 1-2.

431 • Vinyl Plastics Division Scholarship

Purpose: To aid students who plan to enter the vinyl plastics industry.

Eligibility: Applicants must be undergraduate students pursuing a career in the plastics industry and be in good academic standing. Preference is given to applicants with experience in the vinyl industry. Financial need is considered.

How to Apply: Applications are available online.
Deadline: January 15.
Amount: $1,000.
Number of Awards: 1.

Transportation Clubs International Scholarships

Attn.: Bill Blair
Zimmer Worldwide Logistics
15710 JFK Boulevard
Houston, TX 77032
Phone: 877-858-8627
Email: bblair@zimmerworldwide.com
Website: http://www.transportationclubsinternational.com

432 • Charlotte Woods Memorial Scholarship

Purpose: To support students who want to enter the transportation industry.

Eligibility: Applicants must be enrolled in an accredited institution of higher learning in a vocational or degree program in the fields of transportation logistics or traffic management and must be TCI members or dependents of members. The awards are based upon scholastic ability, potential, professional interest and character. Financial need is also considered.

How to Apply: Applications are available online.
Deadline: April 30.
Amount: $1,000.
Number of Awards: 1.

433 • Denny Lydic Scholarship

Purpose: To support students in the field of transportation.

Eligibility: Applicants must be enrolled in an accredited institution of higher learning in a vocational or degree program in the fields of transportation, logistics or traffic management. The awards are based upon scholastic ability, potential, professional interest and character. Financial need is also considered.

How to Apply: Applications are available online.
Deadline: April 30.
Amount: $500.
Number of Awards: 1.

434 • Hooper Memorial Scholarship

Purpose: To support students who want to enter the transportation industry.

Eligibility: Applicants must be enrolled in an accredited institution of higher learning in a vocational or degree program in the fields of transportation logistics or traffic management. The awards are based upon scholastic ability, potential, professional interest and character. Financial need is also considered.

How to Apply: Applications are available online.
Deadline: April 30.
Amount: $1,500.
Number of Awards: 1.

Related Scholarships:

National Urban League

See #1031 • American Chemical Society Minority Scholars Program

American Institute of Chemical Engineers - (AICHE)

See #217 • Donald F. and Mildred Topp Othmer Foundation

American Institute of Chemical Engineers - (AICHE)

See #942 • Minority Affairs Committee Award for Outstanding Scholastic Achievement

American Institute of Chemical Engineers - (AICHE)

See #943 • Minority Scholarship Awards for College Students

American Institute of Chemical Engineers - (AICHE)

See #944 • Minority Scholarship Awards for Incoming College Freshmen

Associated General Contractors of America

See #261 • AGC Graduate Scholarships

National Urban League

See #1033 · Gillette/National Urban League Scholarship and Intern Program for Minority Students

Association for Women in Science

See #181 · Association for Women in Science College Scholarship

Armed Forces Communications and Electronics Association

See #253 · AFCEA General John A. Wickham Scholarships

EAA Aviation Center

See #96 · David Alan Quick Scholarship

EAA Aviation Center

See #99 · Hansen Scholarship

Vertical Flight Foundation

See #107 · Vertical Flight Foundation Engineering Scholarships

International Society for Optical Engineering

See #1140 · SPIE Student Scholarships

Massachusetts Office of Student Financial Assistance

See #1415 · CommonWealth Futures Grant Program

National Association for Surface Finishing

See #1145 · American Electroplaters and Surface Finishers Society Scholarship

American Nuclear Society

See #1120 · ANS Undergraduate Scholarship

American Public Transportation Foundation

See #910 · APTF Transit Hall of Fame Scholarship Award

American Radio Relay League Foundation

See #230 · Dr. James L. Lawson Memorial Scholarship

American Institute of Chemical Engineers - (AICHE)

See #218 · John J. McKetta Scholarship

American Institute of Aeronautics and Astronautics

See #93 · AIAA Foundation Undergraduate Scholarship Program

American Nuclear Society

See #1121 · John and Muriel Landis Scholarship

American Nuclear Society

See #1119 · ANS Graduate Scholarship

American Radio Relay League Foundation

See #231 · Earl I. Anderson Scholarship

American Radio Relay League Foundation

See #232 · Edmond A. Metzger Scholarship

American Radio Relay League Foundation

See #234 · Fred R. McDaniel Memorial Scholarship

Astronaut Scholarship Foundation

See #1128 · Astronaut Scholarship

Environmental Protection Agency

See #502 · National Network for Environmental Management Studies Fellowship Program

Tau Beta Pi Association

See #825 · Tau Beta Pi Scholarships

Women In Defense

See #565 · HORIZONS Foundation Scholarship

Association for Women in Science

See #1127 · Association for Women in Science Predoctoral Awards

Hispanic College Fund

See #984 · Hispanic College Fund Scholarships

Triangle Education Foundation

See #830 · Rust Scholarship

EAA Aviation Center

See #101 · Payzer Scholarship

National Association of Water Companies

See #213 · National Association of Water Companies Scholarship

Armed Forces Communications and Electronics Association

See #707 · AFCEA Sgt Jeannette L. Winters, USMC Memorial Scholarship

Armed Forces Communications and Electronics Association

See #705 · AFCEA General Emmett Paige Scholarships

Armed Forces Communications and Electronics Association

See #706 · AFCEA ROTC Scholarships

Armed Forces Communications and Electronics Association

See #254 · AFCEA Ralph W. Shrader Scholarships

Iron and Steel Society

See #1142 · ISS Scholarship Foundation

Intel Corporation and Science Service

See #1138 · Intel Science Talent Search

Siemens Foundation

See #1149 · Siemens Westinghouse Competition in Math, Science and Technology

Associated General Contractors of America

See #262 · AGC Undergraduate Scholarships

American Indian Science and Engineering Society

See #940 · General Motors Engineering Scholarship

Academia Resource Management

See #1110 · ARM Undergraduate Student Fellowships

Davidson Institute for Talent Development

See #20 · Davidson Fellows Award

Electrochemical Society

See #219 · Industrial Electrolysis and Electrochemical Engineering Division H.H. Dow Memorial Student Award

Electrochemical Society

See #1134 · Corrosion Division Morris Cohen Graduate Student Award

Electrochemical Society

See #220 · SemiZone E-Learning Fellowships

Electrochemical Society

See #221 · Student Poster Session Awards

Golden Key National Honour Society

See #787 · Ford Motor Company Engineering and Leadership Scholarship

Illuminating Engineering Society of North America

See #144 · Robert E. Thunen Memorial Scholarships

Institute of Industrial Engineers (IIE)

See #996 · United Parcel Service Scholarship for Minority Students

Society of Broadcast Engineers

See #250 · Youth Scholarship

Society of Mexican American Engineers and Scientists Inc. (MAES)

See #1052 · MAES Scholarship Program

Cargill

See #966 · United Negro College Fund Cargill Scholarship-Internship Program

National Association for the Advancement of Colored People

See #1016 · Willems Scholarship

American Indian Science and Engineering Society

See #938 · Bureau of Reclamation Scholarship and Internship

Association for Women in Architecture

See #1220 · AWA Scholarships

Department of Defense, American Society for Engineering Education

See #1132 · NDSEG Fellowship Program

Fannie and John Hertz Foundation

See #190 · Hertz Foundation's Graduate Fellowship Award

National Consortium for Graduate Degrees for Minorities in Engineering and Science Inc. (GEM)

See #1026 · GEM Fellowship Program

Golden Key National Honour Society

See #785 · Engineering/Technology Achievement Awards

Institute of Electrical and Electronics Engineers History Center

See #258 · IEEE Presidents' Scholarship

American Congress on Surveying and Mapping (ACSM)

See #1157 · CaGIS Scholarships

Society of Satellite Professionals International (SSPI)

See #251 · SSPI Scholarship Program

National Security Agency (NSA)

See #50 · Stokes Educational Scholarship Program

Hispanic Scholarship Fund (HSF)

See #990 · HSF/General Motors Scholarship

English/Writing

Also See Scholarships Listed Under:
Academics/General
Education/Teaching
Communications
Journalism/Broadcasting
Library Science

Actors Theatre of Louisville

National Ten Minute Play Contest
316 W. Main Street
Louisville, KY 40202-4218
Phone: 502-584-1265
Website: http://www.actorstheatre.org

435 • National Ten Minute Play Contest

Purpose: To identify emerging playwrights.
Eligibility: Each playwright may only submit one script no more than 10 pages in length that has not been previously submitted.
How to Apply: No application is necessary.
Deadline: December 1.
Amount: $1,000.
Number of Awards: Varies.

America's Intercultural Magazine (AIM)

P.O. Box 1174
Maywood, IL 60153
Phone: 708-344-4414
Email: apiladoone@aol.com
Website: http://www.aimmagazine.org

436 • AIM Short Story Contest

Purpose: AIM Magazine's purpose is to purge racism from society through writing.
Eligibility: This contest seeks compelling stories with lasting social significance to prove that people from different racial and ethnic backgrounds are more alike than different. Stories are limited to 4,000 words.
How to Apply: No application form is necessary.
Deadline: August 15.
Amount: $100.
Number of Awards: 1.

Ayn Rand Institute (ARI)

Atlas Shrugged Essay Contest, Dept. W
P.O. Box 57044
Irvine, CA 92619
Phone: 949-222-6550
Fax: 949-222-6558
Email: essay@aynrand.org
Website: http://www.aynrand.org

437 • Anthem Essay Contest

Purpose: To honor high school students who distinguish themselves in their understanding of Ayn Rand's novel Anthem.
Eligibility: Applicants must be high school freshmen or sophomores who submit a 600-1200 word essay that will be judged on both style and content, with an emphasis on writing that is clear, articulate and logically organized. Winning essays must demonstrate an outstanding grasp of the philosophic meaning of Anthem.
How to Apply: Application request information is available online.
Deadline: March 18.
Amount: $30-$2,000.
Number of Awards: 229.

438 • Atlas Shrugged Essay Contest

Purpose: To honor college students who distinguish themselves in their understanding of Ayn Rand's novel Atlas Shrugged.
Eligibility: Applicants must be full-time college students who submit a 1,000-1,200 word essay which will be judged on both style and content, with an emphasis on writing that is clear, articulate and logically organized. Winning essays must demonstrate an outstanding grasp of the philosophic meaning of Atlas Shrugged.
How to Apply: Application request information is available online.
Deadline: September 16.
Amount: $50-$5,000.
Number of Awards: 49.

439 • Fountainhead Essay Contest

Purpose: To honor high school students who distinguish themselves in their understanding of Ayn Rand's novel Fountainhead.
Eligibility: Applicants must be high school juniors or seniors who submit a 600-1,600 word essay which will be judged on both style and content, with an emphasis on writing that is clear, articulate and logically organized. Winning essays must demonstrate an outstanding grasp of the philosophic and psychological meaning of the Fountainhead.
How to Apply: Application request information is available online.
Deadline: April 15.
Amount: $50-$10,000.
Number of Awards: 244.

Choate, Hall and Stewart

Two International Place
Boston, MA 02110
Phone: 617-248-5253
Email: amylowell@choate.com
Website: http://www.amylowell.org

440 • Amy Lowell Poetry Travelling Scholarship

Purpose: To support travel abroad for American-born poets.
Eligibility: Applicants should submit applications, curriculum vitae and poetry samples. Recipients should not accept another scholarship during the scholarship year, must travel outside North America and should have three poems by the end of scholarship year.
How to Apply: Applications are available online.
Deadline: October 15.
Amount: $47,000.
Number of Awards: 1.

Council for the Advancement of Science Writing (CASW)

P.O. Box 910
Hedgesville, WV 25427
Phone: 304-754-5077
Email: diane@nasw.org
Website: http://www.casw.org

441 • Taylor/Blakeslee University Fellowships

Purpose: To help graduate students in science writing.
Eligibility: Applicants must be U.S. citizens who are enrolled in U.S. graduate-level science writing programs.
How to Apply: Contact the organization for more information.
Deadline: Varies.
Amount: $2,000.
Number of Awards: Varies.

Diet-Live Poets Society

P.O. Box 8841
Turnersville, NJ 08012
Website: http://www.geocities.com/diet-lps

442 • National High School Poetry Contest/ Easterday Poetry Award

Purpose: To provide a venue for young poets to be recognized.
Eligibility: Applicants must be U.S. high school students. Submitted poems must be 20 lines or less, in English, unpublished and not simultaneously submitted to any other competition. Applicants may only submit one poem during any 90-day span and must include a self-addressed, stamped envelope with each mailed entry, or applicants may submit their poems online.
How to Apply: There is no application form.
Deadline: October 31 and March 31.
Amount: $100-$1,000 + publication.
Number of Awards: 12.

Elie Wiesel Foundation for Humanity

555 Madison Avenue, 20th Floor
New York, NY 10022
Phone: 212-490-7777
Fax: 212-490-6006
Email: info@eliewieselfoundation.org
Website: http://www.eliewieselfoundation.org

443 • Prize in Ethics Essay Contest

Purpose: To promote the thought and discussion of ethics and their place in education.
Eligibility: Applicants must be registered full-time juniors and seniors at accredited colleges and universities in the U.S. Students must write an essay dealing with ethics and have a faculty sponsor review their essay and sign the entry form.
How to Apply: Applications are available online.
Deadline: December 3.
Amount: $500-$5,000.
Number of Awards: 5.

Guideposts Magazine

Young Writers Contest
16 East 34 Street
New York, NY 10016
Website: http://www.guidepostsmag.com

444 • Young Writers Contest

Purpose: To recognize talented high school writers.
Eligibility: Applicants must be either high school juniors or seniors, or international students of similar criteria. Applicants must write a first-person story about a significant personal experience, in English. Story must be must be typed, double spaced, with a maximum of 1,200 words.
How to Apply: There is no application form.
Deadline: November 24.
Amount: $1,000-$10,000.
Number of Awards: 20.

International Reading Association

The Jeanne S. Chall Research Fellowship
Division of Research and Policy
800 Barksdale Road, P.O. Box 8139
Newark, DE 19714
Phone: 302-731-1600
Fax: 302-731-1057
Website: http://www.reading.org

445 • Jeanne S. Chall Research Fellowship

Purpose: To support dissertation research in reading.
Eligibility: Applicants must be doctoral students planning or beginning their dissertation on one of the following topics in the field of reading: beginning reading, readability, reading difficulty, stages of reading development, the relation of vocabulary to reading and diagnosing and teaching adults with limited reading ability. Applicants must also be members of the International Reading Association.
How to Apply: Applications are available online.
Deadline: January 15.
Amount: $6,000.
Number of Awards: 1.

L. Ron Hubbard

P.O. Box 1630
Los Angeles, CA 90078
Email: contests@authorservicesinc.com
Website: http://www.writersofthefuture.com

446 • Writers of the Future

Purpose: To discover deserving amateur aspiring writers.
Eligibility: Applicants must not have professionally published more than three short stories, one novelette or a novel and must submit an original English work of prose.
How to Apply: There is no application form.
Deadline: December 31, May 31, June 30, September 30.
Amount: $500-$4,000.
Number of Awards: 3 awards are given quarterly with a grand prize awarded annually.

National Federation of State Poetry Societies

NFSPS College/University-Level Competition
N. Colwell Snell
P.O. Box 520698
Salt Lake City, UT 84152
Phone: 801-484-3113
Email: SBSenior@juno.com
Website: http://www.nfsps.com

447 • Edna Meudt Memorial Award and the Florence Kahn Memorial Award

Purpose: To recognize the importance of poetry on the nation's culture.

Eligibility: Applicants can be college students at any level.

How to Apply: Applications are available online.

Deadline: February 1.

Amount: $500.

Number of Awards: 2.

National Speakers Association

1500 S. Priest Drive
Tempe, AZ 85281
Phone: 480-968-2552
Fax: 480-968-0911
Website: http://www.nsaspeaker.org

448 • Bill Gove Scholarship

Purpose: To encourage study in the field of professional speaking.

Eligibility: Applicants must be full-time students majoring or minoring in speech. Selection is based on application, essay, recommendation and college transcript.

How to Apply: Applications are available online or by written request.

Deadline: June 1.

Amount: $1,000.

Number of Awards: 1.

449 • Cavett Robert Scholarship

Purpose: To encourage study in the field of professional speaking.

Eligibility: Applicants must be full-time students majoring or minoring in speech. Selection is based on application, essay, recommendation and college transcript.

How to Apply: Applications are available online or by written request.

Deadline: June 1.

Amount: $1,000.

Number of Awards: 1.

450 • Earl Nightengale Scholarship

Purpose: To encourage study in the field of professional speaking.

Eligibility: Applicants must be full-time students majoring or minoring in speech. Selection is based on application, essay, recommendation and college transcript.

How to Apply: Applications are available online or by written request.

Deadline: June 1.

Amount: $1,000-$12,500.

Number of Awards: 4.

451 • Nido Qubein Scholarship

Purpose: To encourage study in the field of professional speaking.

Eligibility: Applicants must be full-time students majoring or minoring in speech. Selection is based on application, essay, recommendation and college transcript.

How to Apply: Applications are available online or by written request.

Deadline: June 1.

Amount: $1,000.

Number of Awards: 1.

National Writers Association Foundation

10940 S. Parker Road #508
Parker, CO 80134
Phone: 303-841-0246
Fax: 303-841-2607
Email: contests@nationalwriters.com
Website: http://www.nationalwriters.com

452 • National Writers Association Foundation Scholarship

Purpose: To assist future writers with their education.

Eligibility: Scholarships are awarded solely on a merit basis. Applicants interested in pursuing further education in writing are given preference. Scholarship applications are reviewed from October 1 to December 31 annually.

How to Apply: Applications are available online.

Deadline: Varies.

Amount: $1,000.

Number of Awards: 1.

Nuclear Age Peace Foundation

1187 Coast Village Road
PMB 121, Suite 1
Santa Barbara, CA 93108-2794
Phone: 805-965-3443
Fax: 805-568-0466
Website: http://www.wagingpeace.org

453 • Barbara Mandigo Kelly Peace Poetry Awards

Purpose: To have poets of all ages write about world peace.

Eligibility: Adult applicants must send a $15 fee for up to three poems. There is no fee for youth applicants. Applicants must send unpublished poems in English and should send copies, not the originals as they can't be returned.

How to Apply: Send poems to mailing address or fax number.

Deadline: July 1.

Amount: $200-$1,000.

Number of Awards: 3.

454 • Swackhamer Peace Essay Contest

Purpose: To encourage high school students to write an essay on world peace.

Eligibility: Students must be in any high school in the world and write an essay up to 1,200 words on the provided topic. Selection is based on analysis of the subject matter, originality, development of point of view, insight, clarity of expression, organization and grammar.

How to Apply: Applications are available online.

Deadline: June 1.

Amount: $500-$1,500.

Number of Awards: 3.

Optimist International

4494 Lindell Boulevard
St. Louis, MO 63108
Phone: 314-371-6000
Fax: 314-371-6006
Email: programs@optimist.org
Website: http://www.optimist.org

455 • Optimist International Essay Contest

Purpose: To reward students based on their essay-writing skills.

Eligibility: Applicants must be under 19 years of age as of December 31 of the current school year and application must be made through a local Optimist Club. The essay topic is, "I want to make a difference because..." Applicants compete at the club, district and international level. District winners receive a $650 scholarship, and three international winners receive prizes up to $6,000. Scoring is based on organization, vocabulary and style, grammar and punctuation, neatness and adherence to the contest rules.

How to Apply: Contact your local Optimist Club.

Deadline: February 28.

Amount: $650-$6,000.

Number of Awards: Varies.

Penguin Group (USA)

Academic Marketing Department
Signet Classic Student Scholarship
375 Hudson Street
New York, NY 10014
Website: http://us.penguingroup.com/static/html/services-academic/essayhome.html

456 • Signet Classic Student Scholarship Essay Contest

Purpose: To reward high school students for their essays on literature.

Eligibility: Applicants must be high school juniors or seniors or equivalent home schooled students and write an essay on one of four selected topics based on a piece of literature. Each English teacher may only submit one junior and one senior essay. Selection is based on style, content, grammar and originality.

How to Apply: English teachers submit entries.

Deadline: April 15.

Amount: $1,000.

Number of Awards: 5.

Scholastic

557 Broadway
New York, NY 10012
Phone: 212-343-6493
Email: a&wgeneralinfo@scholastic.com
Website: http://www.scholastic.com/artandwritingawards

457 • Writing Awards

Purpose: To reward creative young people in the U.S.

Eligibility: Applicants must be in grades 7 through 12 in U.S. or Canadian schools and must submit writing pieces or portfolios in one of the following categories: dramatic script, humor, journalism, novel writing, personal essay/memoir, poetry, science fiction/fantasy, short story, short short story or general writing portfolio.

How to Apply: Applications are available online.

Deadline: Varies based on location.

Amount: $100-$5,000.

Number of Awards: 300 awards, 8 scholarships.

United Nations Association of the United States of America

801 Second Avenue, 2nd Floor
New York, NY 10017
Phone: 212-907-1300
Fax: 212-682-9185
Email: unahq@unausa.org
Website: http://www.unausa.org

458 • National High School Essay Contest

Purpose: To encourage thought on issues of international importance.

Eligibility: Applicants must submit an essay of no more than 1,500 words on a designated topic. The contest is open to all students in grades 9 to 12. Applicants must submit essays to a local chapter for the first level of judging.

How to Apply: Applications are available from UNA-USA chapters.

Deadline: January 3.

Amount: $750-$3,000 + trip to UN Headquarters.

Number of Awards: 3.

Veterans of Foreign Wars

406 W. 34th Street
Kansas City, MO 64111
Phone: 816-968-1117
Fax: 816-968-1149
Email: info@vfw.org
Website: http://www.vfw.org

459 • Patriot's Pen Youth Essay Contest

Purpose: To give students in grades 6 through 8 an opportunity to write essays that express their views on democracy.

Eligibility: Applicants must be enrolled as a 6th, 7th or 8th grader in a public, private or parochial school in the U.S., its territories or possessions. Home-schooled students and dependents of U.S. military or civilian personnel in overseas schools may also apply. Foreign exchange students and former applicants who placed in the national finals are ineligible. Students must submit essays based on an annual theme to their local VFW posts. If an essay is picked to advance, the entry is judged at the District (regional) level, then the Department (state) level and finally at the National level. Essays are judged 30 percent on knowledge of the theme, 35 percent on development of the theme and 35 percent on clarity.

How to Apply: Applications are available online or by contacting the local VFW office. Entries must be turned into the local VFW office. Contact information for these offices can be found online or by calling the VFW National Programs headquarters at 816-968-1117.

Deadline: November 1.

Amount: Up to $10,000.

Number of Awards: Varies.

Related Scholarships:

Organization of Chinese Americans (OCA)
See #1039 • OCA-KFC National Essay Contest

SuperCollege.com
See #61 • SuperCollege.com Student Scholarship

Minnesota Higher Education Services Office
See #1433 • Minnesota Academic Excellence Scholarship

EF Educational Tours
See #24 • Global Citizen Awards

Random House Inc. Creative Writing Competition
See #1490 • Random House Inc. Creative Writing Competition

Hispanic Heritage Awards Foundation
See #985 • Hispanic Heritage Youth Awards

John F. Kennedy Library Foundation
See #1184 • John F. Kennedy Profile in Courage Essay Contest

A&E Television Network
See #1 • A&E Essay Contests

Elder & Leemaur Publishers
See #25 • Student Authors

American Atheists
See #1090 • Life Members' Scholarship

California Teachers Association (CTA)
See #1245 • CTA César E. Chávez Memorial Education Awards Program

National Association of Negro Business and Professional Women's Clubs Inc.
See #1024 • Julianne Malveaux Scholarship

Kaplun Foundation
See #1101 • Moris J. and Betty Kaplun Scholarship

No-Addiction Scholarship Essay Campaign
See #52 • No-Addiction Campaign Essay Contest

Mensa Education & Research Foundation
See #45 • Mensa Education & Research Foundation Scholarship Program

Veterans of Foreign Wars
See #69 • Voice of Democracy Audio Essay Contests

Elder & Leemaur Publishers
See #27 • Young Authors Head Start Program

Elder & Leemaur Publishers
See #26 • University Writing Scholarship

Davidson Institute for Talent Development
See #20 • Davidson Fellows Award

American Atheists
See #934 • Chinn Scholarship

Golden Key National Honour Society
See #790 • Literary Achievement Awards

Huntington Library, Art Collections and Botanical Gardens
See #1181 • Huntington Fellowships

Huntington Library, Art Collections and Botanical Gardens
See #1182 • Huntington-British Academy Fellowships for Study in Great Britain

Huntington Library, Art Collections and Botanical Gardens
See #1183 • W.M. Keck Foundation Fellowships for Young Scholars

Holland and Knight Charitable Foundation
See #1180 • Holocaust Remembrance Project Essay Contest

American Museum of Natural History
See #1118 • Young Naturalist Awards

Ethnic and Area Studies

Also See Scholarships Listed Under:
Foreign Language
Social Science/History

American Hellenic Education Progressive Association

1909 Q Street NW
Suite 500
Washington, DC 20009
Phone: 202-232-6300
Fax: 202-232-2140
Email: ahepa@ahepa.org
Website: http://www.ahepa.org

460 • National and District Scholarships

Purpose: To support projects furthering the goals of AHEPA: studies concerning Hellenism, Hellenic culture or Greek-American life.

Eligibility: Applicants must be high school seniors, college students, post-graduate students or adult students.

How to Apply: Applications are available online.

Deadline: June 1.

Amount: Up to $5,000.

Number of Awards: Varies.

American Institute for Contemporary German Studies (AICGS)

DAAD
871 UN Plaza
New York, NY 10017
Phone: 212-758-3223
Fax: 212-755-5780
Email: daadny@daad.org
Website: http://www.daad.org

461 • German Studies Research Grant

Purpose: To encourage the research of cultural, political, historical, economic and social aspects of modern and contemporary German affairs.

Eligibility: Applicants must be junior or senior undergraduates pursuing a German studies major or minor, or master's degree students or Ph.D. candidates in the humanities or social sciences who are working on a certificate in German studies at U.S. or Canadian institutions of higher education or a dissertation on modern German topic, respectively. Applicants must be nominated by their department and must have completed two years of college German and a minimum of three courses in German studies (literature, history, politics or other fields).

How to Apply: Applications are available online.

Deadline: May 1 and November 1.

Amount: $1,500-$2,500.

Number of Awards: Varies.

American Institute for Contemporary German Studies - (AICGS)

1755 Massachusetts Avenue NW
Suite 700
Washington, DC 20036
Phone: 202-332-9312
Fax: 202-265-9531
Email: kverclas@aicgs.org
Website: http://www.aicgs.org

462 • DAAD/AICGS Research Fellowship Program

Purpose: To encourage the research of modern and contemporary postwar Germany.

Eligibility: Applicants must be Ph.D. candidates, recent Ph.D.s or junior faculty who hold U.S. or German citizenship. The grant provides summer residency at AICGS.

How to Apply: Applications are available by mail.

Deadline: September 30.

Amount: $4,600.

Number of Awards: 1-2.

American Institute for Foreign Study

AIFS College Division
River Plaza
9 W. Broad Street
Stamford, CT 06902
Phone: 800-727-2437
Email: college.info@aifs.com
Website: http://www.aifsabroad.com

463 • International Scholarships

Purpose: To promote international understanding through study abroad.

Eligibility: Applicants must be currently enrolled college undergraduates with a minimum 3.0 GPA who show leadership potential and are involved in extra-curricular activities centered on multicultural or international issues. Applicants must submit a 1,000-word essay on how study abroad will change their lives.

How to Apply: Applications are available online.

Deadline: April 15 for fall semester, October 15 for spring semester.

Amount: $1,000.

Number of Awards: Up to 100.

American Sephardi Federation

15 W. 16th Street
New York, New York 10011
Phone: 212-294-8350
Fax: 212-294-8348
Website: http://www.americansephardifederation.org

464 • Broome and Allen Boys Camp and Scholarship Fund

Purpose: To help those of Sephardic origin or those working in Sephardic studies.

Eligibility: Applicants must be undergraduate or graduate students or those doing research projects. Two letters of recommendation, a family tax return, and transcripts are required. Applicants do not have to be United States citizens or living in the United States but they should be conducting their research in the United States.

How to Apply: Applications are available online.
Deadline: May 15.
Amount: Varies.
Number of Awards: Varies.

American-Scandinavian Foundation

58 Park Avenue
New York, NY 10016
Phone: 212-879-9779
Fax: 212-686-2115
Email: info@amscan.org
Website: http://www.amscan.org

465 • Academic Fellowships and Grants

Purpose: To encourage research projects related to Scandinavia.
Eligibility: Applicants must have completed their undergraduate educations and have a research or study project requiring a stay in Scandinavia. Some language proficiency is required.
How to Apply: Applications are available online and by written request.
Deadline: November 1.
Amount: $4,000-$20,000.
Number of Awards: Varies.

Appalachian Studies Association Carl A. Ross Student Paper Award

William Schumann
Emory and Henry College
P.O. Box 947
Emory, VA 24327
Phone: 304-696-2904
Fax: 276-944-6170
Website: http://www.appalachianstudies.org

466 • Carl A. Ross Student Paper Award

Purpose: To promote Appalachian studies.
Eligibility: Applicants must submit a 20- to 30-page research paper on an Appalachian studies topic. Selections will be made from two categories: middle/high school and undergraduate/graduate.
How to Apply: Submission of research paper is the application.
Deadline: December 9.
Amount: $100.
Number of Awards: 2.

Association of Teachers of Japanese

Bridging Project Clearinghouse
Campus Box 279
240 Humanities Building, University of Colorado
Boulder, CO 80309
Phone: 303-492-5487
Fax: 303-492-5856
Email: atj@colorado.edu
Website: http://www.colorado.edu/ealld/atj

467 • Bridging Scholarships for Study in Japan

Purpose: To assist students with travel and living expenses while studying in Japan.
Eligibility: Applicants must be undergraduates, U.S. citizens or permanent residents and be enrolled in a U.S. college. Students must submit a letter of recommendation and an essay on their interest in studying in Japan.

How to Apply: Applications are available online.
Deadline: October 5.
Amount: $2,500-$4,000.
Number of Awards: 100.

Clan MacBean Foundation

441 Wadsworth Boulevard, Suite 213
Denver, CO 80226
Website: http://www.clanmacbean.net

468 • Clan MacBean Foundation Grant Program

Purpose: To provide financial assistance to those studying Scottish culture.
Eligibility: Applicants must be graduating high school seniors with a course of study related directly to Scottish culture. If pursuing a project, applicants must pick a project that reflects direct involvement in the preservation or enhancement of Scottish culture.
How to Apply: Applications are available by written request.
Deadline: Varies.
Amount: Varies.
Number of Awards: Varies.

Council on International Educational Exchange

7 Custom House Street, 3rd Floor
Portland, ME 04101
Phone: 800-40-STUDY
Fax: 207-553-7699
Email: scholarships@ciee.org
Website: http://www.ciee.org

469 • Council on International Educational Exchange (CIEE) Scholarships

Purpose: To make the study abroad program available to a wider audience and to provide assistance to CIEE Study Center (CSC) members who have demonstrated academic talent and financial need in order to study abroad.
Eligibility: Applicants must be applicants to the CIEE Study Center (CSC) at member institutions (list available online). Financial need is strongly considered along with other materials from the study abroad application.
How to Apply: Applications are available online.
Deadline: Varies.
Amount: $500-$1,000.
Number of Awards: Varies.

Irish-American Cultural Institute (IACI)

An Foras Cultúir Gael – Mheiriceánach
1 Lackawanna Place
Morristown, NJ 07960
Phone: 973-605-1991
Fax: 973-605-8875
Email: irishwaynj@aol.com
Website: http://www.iaci-usa.org

470 • IACI/NUI Visiting Fellowship in Irish Studies

Purpose: To award fellowships to Irish studies scholars to spend one semester at the University of Ireland-Galway.

Eligibility: Applicants must provide a description of how the fellowship will be used and a curriculum vitae with a list of publications.

How to Apply: Application is available online.

Deadline: December 31.

Amount: $13,000.

Number of Awards: Varies.

Kosciuszko Foundation

15 E. 65th Street
New York, NY 10021
Phone: 212-734-2130
Fax: 212-628-4552
Email: addy@thekf.org
Website: http://www.kosciuszkofoundation.org

471 • Graduate and Postgraduate Study and Research in Poland

Purpose: To allow American graduate students and university faculty members to conduct research at universities in Poland.

Eligibility: Applicants must be U.S. citizens or permanent residents and be graduate students or university faculty members. Applicants must also possess a level of Polish language proficiency appropriate for their proposed research projects. Selection is based on academic excellence and motivation for pursuing research in Poland. Host institutions must fall under the jurisdiction of the Polish Ministry of National Education.

How to Apply: Applications are available online.

Deadline: January 15.

Amount: Stipend.

Number of Awards: Varies.

472 • Metchie J.E. Budka Award

Purpose: To honor works that contribute significantly to the knowledge and understanding of Polish literature, Polish history and Polish-American relations.

Eligibility: Applicants may be either graduate students who are working in the fields of Polish literature, Polish history, or Polish-American relations at American colleges and universities, or postdoctoral candidates who received their Ph.D. degrees for work in these fields and who apply during or at the close of the first three years of their postdoctoral careers in the field.

How to Apply: Applications are available online.

Deadline: Third Wednesday in July.

Amount: $1,500.

Number of Awards: 1.

473 • Tuition Scholarship Program

Purpose: To provide funding to qualified students for full-time graduate studies in the United States and several graduate programs in Poland.

Eligibility: Applicants must be U.S. citizens or permanent residents of Polish descent, be undergraduate seniors or graduate students and have a minimum 3.0 GPA. U.S. citizens who are majoring in Polish studies are also eligible. Selection is based on academic performance, achievements, motivation, interest in Polish subjects or involvement in the Polish community and financial need.

How to Apply: Applications are available online.

Deadline: January 15.

Amount: $1,000-$7,000.

Number of Awards: Varies.

474 • Year Abroad Program

Purpose: To allow an American student to study and live in Poland for a year or a semester.

Eligibility: Applicants must be U.S. citizens or permanent residents, be current undergraduate sophomores, juniors, seniors or graduate students and have a minimum 3.0 GPA. Selection is based on academic excellence, motivation for pursuing Polish studies and interest in Polish subjects or involvement in Polish American communities.

How to Apply: Applications are available online.

Deadline: January 15.

Amount: Tuition waiver and stipend.

Number of Awards: Varies.

Rotary International

One Rotary Center
1560 Sherman Avenue
Evanston, IL 60201
Phone: 847-866-3000
Fax: 847-328-8554
Email: scholarshipinquiries@rotaryintl.org
Website: http://www.rotary.org

475 • Rotary International Ambassadorial Scholarship Program

Purpose: To further international understanding and friendly relations among people of different countries.

Eligibility: Applicants must be citizens of a country in which there are Rotary clubs and have completed at least two years of college-level coursework or equivalent professional experience before starting their scholarship studies. Initial applications are made through local clubs. Students must be proficient in the language of the proposed host country.

How to Apply: Applications are available through your local Rotary club or online.

Deadline: As early as March for club deadlines.

Amount: Varies.

Number of Awards: Varies.

Sons of Norway

1455 W. Lake Street
Minneapolis, MN 55408
Phone: 800-945-8851
Fax: 612-827-0658
Website: http://www.sofn.com

476 • General Heritage and Culture Grants

Purpose: To preserve Norwegian heritage.

Eligibility: Applicants may be individuals, groups, or organizations dedicated to the preservation of Norwegian heritage. Selection is based on applicants' record or activities and adherence to the goals and objectives of the Sons of Norway Foundation.

How to Apply: Applications are available online.

Deadline: April 1.

Amount: Up to $3,000.

Number of Awards: Varies.

477 • King Olav V Norwegian-American Heritage Fund

Purpose: To promote educational exchange between Norway and North America.

Eligibility: Applicants must be Americans, 18 years or older, who would like to further their interest in Norwegian heritage or in modern Norway at an institution of higher learning. The fund also welcomes applications from Norwegians who desire to further their studies in North America. Selection is based on grade point average, participation in school and community activities, work experience, education and career goals, and personal and school references.

How to Apply: Applications are available online.

Deadline: March 1.

Amount: $250-$3,000.

Number of Awards: Varies.

478 • Scholarships to Oslo International Summer School

Purpose: To give financial support to students who attend Oslo International Summer School.

Eligibility: Applicants who are admitted to Oslo International Summer School and who are Sons of Norway members or children or grandchildren of current members are eligible. Selection is based on financial need, essay, GPA and letters of recommendation. Extra consideration is given to students who are members of Sons of Norway.

How to Apply: Applications are available online.

Deadline: March 1.

Amount: $1,500.

Number of Awards: 2.

Related Scholarships:

General Commission on Archives and History, The United Methodist Church

See #1098 • Racial/Ethnic History Research Grant

American Institute for Foreign Study

See #941 • Minority Scholarships

U.S. Department of State

See #66 • Fulbright Grants

National Italian American Foundation

See #497 • National Italian American Foundation Scholarship

Council on International Educational Exchange

See #493 • Department of Education Scholarship for Programs in China

America's Intercultural Magazine (AIM)

See #436 • AIM Short Story Contest

Institute of International Education

See #495 • National Security Education Program David L. Boren Undergraduate Scholarships

National Security Agency (NSA)

See #1189 • Pat Roberts Intelligence Scholars Program for Intelligence Analysts

Golden Key National Honour Society

See #792 • Study Abroad Scholarships

German Marshall Fund of the United States

See #29 • Marshall Memorial Fellowship

Food Services

Also See Scholarships Listed Under:
Culinary Arts
Hospitality/Travel/Tourism

Association for Food and Drug Officials

2550 Kingston Road
Suite 311
York, PA 17402
Phone: 717-757-2888
Fax: 717-755-8089
Email: afdo@afdo.org
Website: http://www.afdo.org

479 • Association for Food and Drug Officials Scholarship Fund

Purpose: To encourage studies in food, drugs or consumer product safety.

Eligibility: Students must be in their third or fourth year of college, have achieved a 3.0 grade point average during the first two years of undergraduate study and pursue a degree in research, regulatory work, quality control or teaching as it relates to food, drugs or consumer product safety.

How to Apply: Applications are available online.
Deadline: February 1.
Amount: $1,500.
Number of Awards: Varies.

Child Nutrition Foundation

Scholarship Committee
700 S. Washington Street, Suite 300
Alexandria, VA 22314
Phone: 800-877-8822
Website: http://www.schoolnutrition.org

480 • CNF Professional Growth Scholarship

Purpose: To support the continuing education of School Nutrition Association members.

Eligibility: Applicants must be members of the School Nutrition Association for at least one year who are enrolled in an undergraduate or graduate program in a school foodservice related field.

How to Apply: Applications are available online.
Deadline: April 15.
Amount: Tuition, fees and books.
Number of Awards: Varies.

481 • GED Jump Start Scholarship

Purpose: To support School Nutrition Association members in earning a GED.

Eligibility: Applicants must be School Nutrition Association members who do not currently have a GED or high school diploma and plan on earning a GED within a year of receiving the scholarship.

How to Apply: Applications are available online.
Deadline: Applications are accepted throughout the year.
Amount: $200.
Number of Awards: Approximately 20.

482 • Nancy Curry Scholarship

Purpose: To support students wishing to enter the school foodservice industry.

Eligibility: Applicants or the parents of applicants must be School Nutrition Association members for at least one year and be enrolled in a school foodservice-related program at an educational institution.

How to Apply: Applications are available online.
Deadline: April 15.
Amount: Tuition, fees and books.
Number of Awards: 1.

483 • Schwan's Food Service Scholarship

Purpose: To support those entering the school foodservice industry.

Eligibility: Applicants or parents of applicants must be School Nutrition Association members for at least one year and be pursuing a field of study related to school foodservice.

How to Apply: Applications are available online.
Deadline: April 15.
Amount: Tuition, fees and books.
Number of Awards: Varies.

Golden Gate Restaurant Association

Scholarship Foundation
120 Montgomery Street, Suite 1280
San Francisco, CA 94104
Phone: 415-781-5348
Fax: 415-781-3925
Email: ggra@ggra.org
Website: http://www.ggra.org

484 • Golden Gate Restaurant Association Scholarship

Purpose: To provide scholarships for college students who wish to pursue a career in the restaurant/food service industry.

Eligibility: Applicants must be California residents at time of application submission and pursue a major in food service.

How to Apply: Applications are available online or by mail.
Deadline: March 31.
Amount: Up to $5,000.
Number of Awards: Varies.

International Food Service Executives Association

Joseph Quagliano
8824 Stancrest Drive
Las Vegas, NV 89134
Phone: 502-589-3602
Website: http://www.ifsea.com

485 • IFSEA Worthy Goal Scholarship

Purpose: To help students receive food service management training beyond the high school level.

Eligibility: Applicants must be enrolled or accepted at a college as a full-time student in a food service related major. Students must provide a financial statement, personal statement, list of work experience and professional activities, transcripts, recommendations and a statement describing how the scholarship would help them reach their goals.

How to Apply: Applications are available online.
Deadline: February 1.
Amount: $500-$1,000.
Number of Awards: Varies.

International Foodservice Editorial Council (IFEC)

P.O. Box 491
Hyde Park, NY 12538
Phone: 845-229-6973
Email: ifec@aol.com
Website: http://www.ifec-is-us.com

486 • IFEC Scholarships Award

Purpose: To assist students interested in foodservice combined with communication arts.
Eligibility: Applicants must be enrolled at a post-secondary, degree-granting educational institution and must demonstrate training, skill and interest in the foodservice industry and communication arts. Eligible majors from foodservice and communications areas include culinary arts, hotel/restaurant/hospitality management, dietetics, nutrition, food science/technology, journalism, public relations, mass communication, English, broadcast journalism, marketing, photography, graphic arts and related studies.
How to Apply: Applications are available online.
Deadline: March 15.
Amount: Varies.
Number of Awards: Varies.

National Restaurant Association Educational Foundation

175 W. Jackson Boulevard
Suite 1500
Chicago, IL 60604
Phone: 800-765-2122
Fax: 312-715-1010
Email: info@nraef.org
Website: http://www.nraef.org/scholarships/

487 • Academic Scholarship for High School Seniors

Purpose: To support students majoring in food services.
Eligibility: Applicants must have been accepted into an accredited restaurant or food service related program, have had at least 250 hours of restaurant or food service-related work experience, submit a letter of recommendation and have a minimum 2.75 GPA.
How to Apply: Applications are available online.
Deadline: April 22.
Amount: $2,000.
Number of Awards: Varies.

488 • Academic Scholarship For Undergraduate College Students

Purpose: To assist restaurant and food service students.
Eligibility: Applicants must be currently majoring in a restaurant or foodservice program and submit a transcript, proof of restaurant or foodservice-related work experience of a minimum of 750 hours and a letter of recommendation.
How to Apply: Applications are available online.
Deadline: November 19 and April 8.
Amount: $2,000.
Number of Awards: Varies.

Related Scholarships:

BI-LO Corporation

See #1528 • BI-LO Minority Scholarship Program

National Restaurant Association Educational Foundation

See #268 • ProStart National Certificate of Achievement Scholarship

Foreign Language

Also See Scholarships Listed Under:
Ethnic and Area Studies

American Foundation for Translation and Interpretation

Columbia Plaza, Suite 101
350 E. Michigan Avenue
Kalamazoo, MI 49007
Phone: 269-387-3212
Fax: 269-387-6333
Email: peter.krawutschke@wmich.edu
Website: http://www.afti.org

489 • JTG Scholarship in Scientific and Technical Translation or Interpretation

Purpose: To encourage scientific and technical translation and interpretation.

Eligibility: Applicants must be undergraduate or graduate students enrolled in or planning to enroll in a program in scientific and technical translation or in interpretation. Applicants must have completed at least one year of college with a 3.0 GPA and a 3.5 GPA in related courses and preferably have at least one year of study left in their program. Applications are judged on demonstrated achievement in the field, academic record, recommendations and an essay detailing the candidate's interest and goals in the field of translation or interpretation.

How to Apply: Applications are available online, by email and by mail.

Deadline: June 1.

Amount: $2,500.

Number of Awards: 1.

American School of Classical Studies at Athens

6-8 Charlton Street
Princeton, NJ 08540
Phone: 609-683-0800
Fax: 609-683-0800
Email: ascsa@ascsa.org
Website: http://www.ascsa.edu.gr

490 • Fellowships for Regular Program

Purpose: The institution is devoted to allowing American students to study the language, literature, art, history, archaeology and philosophy of Greece and the Greek world.

Eligibility: Applicants must take exams in Greek language, history and either literature or art and archaeology. Students must be able to read French, German, ancient Greek and Latin with an ability to also read modern Greek and Italian considered helpful. Applicants must be graduate students who are preparing for an advanced degree in classical and ancient Mediterranean studies or a related field. Preference is given to current graduate students, but highly qualified applicants with bachelor's degrees will be considered.

How to Apply: Applications are available online.

Deadline: March 15.

Amount: $10,000.

Number of Awards: 13.

American Translators Association

225 Reinekers Lane
Suite 590
Alexandria, VA 22314
Phone: 703-683-6100
Fax: 703-683-6122
Email: ata@atanet.org
Website: http://www.atanet.org

491 • Student Translation Award

Purpose: To encourage translation projects by students.

Eligibility: Applicants must be graduate or undergraduate students, or group of students attending an accredited U.S. college or university. The project should have post-grant results such as a publication, conference presentation or teaching material. Computer-assisted translations, dissertations and theses are not eligible, and students who are already published translators are not eligible. Translations must be from a foreign language into English. Preference is given to students who have been or are currently enrolled in translator training programs. There is a limit of one entry per student. Applicants should submit entry forms, statements of purpose, letter of recommendation, translation sample with corresponding source-language text, proof of permission to publish from copyright holder, and sample outline or other material demonstrating the nature of the work (if the project is not a translation).

How to Apply: Applications are available online.

Deadline: April 17.

Amount: $500.

Number of Awards: 1.

American-Scandinavian Foundation

58 Park Avenue
New York, NY 10016
Phone: 212-879-9779
Fax: 212-686-2115
Email: info@amscan.org
Website: http://www.amscan.org

492 • Translation Prize

Purpose: To encourage the English translation of Scandinavian literature.

Eligibility: The award is given to the best English translation of poetry, fiction, drama or literary prose written by a Scandinavian author in Danish, Finnish, Icelandic, Norwegian or Swedish after 1800. Translations may not previously have been published in the English language.

How to Apply: There is no application form. Please see website for submission details.

Deadline: June 1.

Amount: $1,000-$2,000.

Number of Awards: 2.

Council on International Educational Exchange

7 Custom House Street, 3rd Floor
Portland, ME 04101
Phone: 800-40-STUDY
Fax: 207-553-7699
Email: scholarships@ciee.org
Website: http://www.ciee.org

493 • Department of Education Scholarship for Programs in China

Purpose: To assist students who are participating in the Chinese language programs offered by the Council Study Centers.

Eligibility: Applicants must participate in the Council Study Centers Chinese language programs at Beijing, Shanghai, Nanjing, or Taipei, have completed two years of college level Mandarin Chinese, be a U.S. citizen or U.S. permanent resident, be a junior, senior, or graduate student who plans to teach modern foreign languages or area studies, demonstrate high merit, and show an interest in pursuing post-graduate work related to Chinese studies. Financial need is recommended but not required.

How to Apply: Applications are available online.
Deadline: Varies.
Amount: Varies.
Number of Awards: Varies.

FALCON Program

Department of Asian Studies, Cornell University
338 Rockefeller Hall
Ithaca, NY 14853
Phone: 607-255-6457
Fax: 607-255-1345
Email: falcon@cornell.edu
Website: http://lrc.cornell.edu/falcon/

494 • FALCON - Full Year Asian Language CONcentration

Purpose: To provide scholarships for undergraduate and graduate students seeking intensive, long-term instruction in Chinese and Japanese.

Eligibility: The program is conducted at Cornell University, and students receive Cornell credits.

How to Apply: Applications are available online.
Deadline: Varies.
Amount: Varies.
Number of Awards: Varies.

Institute of International Education

1400 K Street NW
Washington, DC 20005
Phone: 800-618-NSEP
Fax: 202-326-7835
Email: nsep@iie.org
Website: http://www.iie.org/nsep

495 • National Security Education Program David L. Boren Undergraduate Scholarships

Purpose: To provide an opportunity for undergraduate students to study abroad in countries vital to future American security interests.

Eligibility: Applicants must prove that they have a serious interest in pursuing academic study in a foreign country. Applicants must also be well-versed in foreign languages and be willing to commit up to a year living overseas.

How to Apply: Applications are available online.
Deadline: Varies.
Amount: $2,500-$6,000.
Number of Awards: Varies.

Klingon Language Institute

P.O. Box 634
Flourtown, PA 19031
Website: http://www.kli.org/scholarship

496 • KOR Memorial Scholarship

Purpose: To encourage language study.

Eligibility: Applicants must be full-time undergraduate or graduate students pursuing a degree in the field of language study. They must be nominated by the chair, head or dean of their department. Nominating faculty must submit a nominating letter, two additional faculty letters of recommendation and a personal statement and resume from the nominee. Knowledge of Klingon is not required.

How to Apply: There is no application form.
Deadline: June 1.
Amount: $500.
Number of Awards: 1.

National Italian American Foundation

1860 19th Street NW
Washington, DC 20009
Phone: 202-387-0600
Fax: 202-387-0800
Email: scholarships@niaf.org
Website: http://www.niaf.org

497 • National Italian American Foundation Scholarship

Purpose: To support Italian American students and students of any ethnic background studying Italian language or studies.

Eligibility: Applicants must either be Italian American students who demonstrate outstanding academic achievement or be students from any ethnic background majoring or minoring in Italian language, Italian studies, Italian American studies or a related field and demonstrate outstanding academic achievement. Applicants must also plan to be or currently be enrolled in an accredited institution of higher education, have a minimum 3.25 GPA and be U.S. citizens or permanent residents.

How to Apply: Applications are available online.
Deadline: April 30.
Amount: $2,000-$5,000.
Number of Awards: Varies.

National Junior Classical League

1122 Oak Street North
Fargo, ND 58102
Phone: 513-529-7741
Fax: 513-529-7742
Email: administrator@njcl.org
Website: http://www.njcl.org

498 • NJCL Scholarships

Purpose: To support students studying the classics.

Eligibility: Applicants must be NJCL members in good standing, entering college the upcoming year, and studying the classics. Special consideration is given to those planning to teach Latin, Greek or classical humanities. Selection is based on financial need, JCL service, academics and recommendations.

How to Apply: Applications are available online or by written request.

Deadline: May 1.
Amount: $1000-$2,000.
Number of Awards: 8.

National Latin Exam

University of Mary Washington
1301 College Avenue
Fredericksburg, VA 22401
Phone: 888-378-7721
Email: nle@umw.edu
Website: http://www.nle.org

499 • National Latin Exam Scholarship

Purpose: To reward students for their Latin proficiency.
Eligibility: Applicants must be gold medal winners in Latin III-IV Prose, III-IV Poetry or Latin V-VI on the National Latin Exam. Applicants must be high school seniors who agree to take at least one year of Latin or classical Greek in college. A classics in translation course does not count. An additional post-graduate scholarship is available for those intending to teach Latin and/or Greek at the elementary, intermediate or high school level.
How to Apply: Applications are mailed to eligible students. Renewal applications are available online.
Deadline: September 15.
Amount: $1,000.
Number of Awards: 21.

National Security Agency (NSA)

9800 Savage Road, Suite 6779
Ft. George G. Meade, MD 20755-6779
Phone: 410-854-4725
Website: http://www.nsa.gov/careers/

500 • Pat Roberts Intelligence Scholars Program for Language Analysts

Purpose: To support students who plan to work in language analysis after graduation.
Eligibility: Applicants must be within two years of completing a master's or doctorate degree in a language or language-related field. Recipients are expected to enter the NSA Language Analysis New Hire Program after graduation.
How to Apply: Applications are available online.
Deadline: October 30.
Amount: Up to $25,000 per year.
Number of Awards: Varies.

Related Scholarships:

Council on International Educational Exchange

See #469 • Council on International Educational Exchange (CIEE) Scholarships

Rotary International

See #475 • Rotary International Ambassadorial Scholarship Program

New Hampshire Postsecondary Education Commission

See #1463 • Workforce Incentive Program

Association of Teachers of Japanese

See #467 • Bridging Scholarships for Study in Japan

Rotary International

See #58 • Cultural Ambassadorial Scholarships

Golden Key National Honour Society

See #792 • Study Abroad Scholarships

National Security Agency (NSA)

See #1189 • Pat Roberts Intelligence Scholars Program for Intelligence Analysts

National Security Agency (NSA)

See #50 • Stokes Educational Scholarship Program

Forestry/Wildlife

Also See Scholarships Listed Under:

Agriculture/Horticulture/Animals

Biological Sciences/Life Sciences

Atlantic Salmon Federation

P.O. Box 807
Calais, ME 04619-0807
Phone: 506-529-1033
Fax: 506-529-4438
Email: asfweb@nbnet.nb.ca
Website: http://www.asf.ca

501 • ASF Olin Fellowships

Purpose: To help fund projects that focus on solving problems in Atlantic salmon biology, management and conservation.

Eligibility: Applicants must be studying or actively engaged in salmon management or research. The award is open to U.S. and Canadian applicants.

How to Apply: Applications are available by mail.

Deadline: March 15.

Amount: $1,000-$3,000.

Number of Awards: Varies.

Environmental Protection Agency

NNEMS Fellowship Program
Tetra Tech EM Inc.
1881 Campus Commons Drive, Suite 200
Reston, VA 20191
Phone: 800-358-8769
Email: steve.michener@ttemi.com
Website: http://www.epa.gov/enviroed/students.html

502 • National Network for Environmental Management Studies Fellowship Program

Purpose: To provide students with research opportunities, to increase public awareness of environmental issues and to encourage students to pursue careers in environmental protection.

Eligibility: Applicants must be undergraduate or graduate students, be U.S. citizens or legal residents, be enrolled in an academic program directly related to pollution control, have a minimum 3.0 GPA, have completed four courses relating to the environmental field and submit a research project proposal.

How to Apply: Applications are available online.

Deadline: January.

Amount: Stipend during research.

Number of Awards: Varies.

National Wildlife Federation

11100 Wildlife Center Drive
Reston, VA 20190-5362
Phone: 800-822-9919
Website: http://www.nwf.org

503 • National Wildlife Federation Ecology Fellowship

Purpose: The fellowship program provides funding for campus ecology projects.

Eligibility: Applicants must create a plan for a campus ecology program, working with a project advisor and verifier. All Campus Ecology fellows are required to attend a training program.

How to Apply: Applications are available online.

Deadline: December 19.

Amount: Up to $1,200.

Number of Awards: Varies.

Tree Research and Education Endowment Fund

711 E. Roosevelt Road
Wheaton, IL 60172
Phone: 630-221-8127
Fax: 630-690-0702
Email: treefund@treefund.org
Website: http://www.treefund.org

504 • Robert Felix Memorial Scholarship

Purpose: To help undergraduate and technical college students pursuing careers in commercial arboriculture.

Eligibility: Applicants should be undergraduate or technical college students entering the second year of a two-year program or entering the third or fourth year of a four-year program, plan to pursue a career in commercial arboriculture and be student members of the International Society of Arboriculture. An advisor referral, two letters of recommendation, letter of intent from applicant and application forms are required.

How to Apply: Applications are available online.

Deadline: May 1.

Amount: $3,000.

Number of Awards: 4.

Related Scholarships:

American Ornithologists' Union

See #176 · Research Award

Louisiana Office of Student Financial Assistance

See #1374 · Rockefeller Wildlife Scholarship

National Safety Council

See #676 · Campus Safety Health And Environmental Management Association Scholarship

Association for Women in Science

See #181 · Association for Women in Science College Scholarship

Wilson Ornithological Society

See #193 · George A. Hall / Harold F. Mayfield Award

Wilson Ornithological Society

See #195 · Paul A. Stewart Awards

U.S. Fish and Wildlife Service

See #902 · Federal Junior Duck Stamp Program and Scholarship Competition

Intertribal Timber Council

See #997 · Truman D. Picard Scholarship

Bat Conservation International

See #182 · Student Research Scholarships

Entomological Society of America

See #186 · Normand R. Dubois Memorial Scholarship

Wilson Ornithological Society

See #194 · Louis Agassiz Fuertes Award

National Garden Clubs Inc.

See #138 · National Garden Clubs Scholarship

Society for Range Management (SRM)

See #140 · Masonic-Range Science Scholarship

Graphic Arts

Also See Scholarships Listed Under:
Performing Arts/Music/Drama/Visual Arts

Armed Forces Communications and Electronics Association

4400 Fair Lakes Court
Fairfax, VA 22033
Phone: 800-336-4583
Fax: 703-631-4693
Email: scholarship@afcea.org
Website: http://www.afcea.org

505 • Computer Graphic Design Scholarships

Purpose: Monetary assistance is awarded to full-time graduate or undergraduate students majoring in computer graphic design or related fields.

Eligibility: Applicants must be full-time students working toward an undergraduate or graduate degree in computer graphic design or a related field at an accredited U.S. college or university, be U.S. citizens, and be at least college sophomores. Selection is based on a single sample of digital artwork. Applicants do not need to be affiliated with the military.

How to Apply: Applications are available online.
Deadline: October 15.
Amount: $2,000.
Number of Awards: Varies.

Flexographic Technical Association

900 Marconi Avenue
Ronkonkoma, NY 11779
Phone: 631-737-6020
Fax: 631-737-6813
Email: education@flexography.org
Website: http://www.flexography.org

506 • FFTA Scholarship Competition

Purpose: To advance the state of the flexographic industry.

Eligibility: Applicants must demonstrate interest in a career in flexography and must be high school seniors with plans to attend a post-secondary institution or be presently enrolled at a post-secondary institution offering a course of study in flexography. Applicants must exhibit exemplary performance in their studies, particularly in the area of graphic communications and must have a minimum 3.0 GPA.

How to Apply: Applications are available online.
Deadline: February 11.
Amount: $2,000.
Number of Awards: 19.

Graphic Arts Information Network

Print and Graphics Scholarship Foundation
Scholarship Competition
200 Deer Run Road
Sewickley, PA 15143
Phone: 412-741-6860
Fax: 412-741-2311
Email: pgsf@gatf.org
Website: http://www.gain.org

507 • Print and Graphics Scholarship

Purpose: To provide financial assistance for postsecondary education to students interested in graphic communications careers.

Eligibility: Applicants must be high school seniors or high school graduates who have not started college yet, or college students enrolled in a two- or four-year college program. Applicants must be full-time students, be interested in a career in graphic communications and able to maintain a 3.0 GPA.

How to Apply: Applications are available online.
Deadline: March 1 for high school.
Amount: $1,000-$1,500.
Number of Awards: 300.

Imation Corporation

Attn.: Community Affairs Manager
1 Imation Place
Oakdale, MN 55128
Phone: 888-466-3456
Fax: 888-704-4200
Email: CAS@imation.com
Website: http://www.imation.com

508 • Imation Computer Arts Scholarship Program

Purpose: To promote the use of technology in arts education and encourage innovation among high school students.

Eligibility: Applicants must attend high school, be home-schooled in the U.S., or attend school on U.S. military bases and must be nominated to the national competition by their schools. Selection is based on quality and creativity of the submitted artwork.

How to Apply: Applications are available online.
Deadline: December.
Amount: $1,000.
Number of Awards: 25.

International Housewares Association

6400 Shafer Court, Suite 650
Rosemont, IL 60018
Phone: 847-292-4200
Fax: 847-292-4211
Website: http://www.housewares.org

509 • Student Design Competition

Purpose: To honor and encourage young, up-and-coming designers to enter careers in the housewares industry.

Eligibility: Applicants must be enrolled as an undergraduate or graduate student at an IDSA-affiliated college or university.

How to Apply: Applications are available online.
Deadline: December 19.
Amount: Varies.
Number of Awards: Varies.

International Library of Photography

3600 Crondall Lane
Suite 101-3111
Owings Mills, MD 21117
Website: http://www.picture.com

510 • Free Photo Contest

Purpose: To award cash prizes to amateur photographers.

Eligibility: All amateur photographers are eligible. Various photos are considered for publication by the International Library of Photography.

How to Apply: Applications are available online.

Deadline: Ongoing.

Amount: $1,000-$10,000.

Number of Awards: Varies.

Lions Club International

300 W. 22nd Street
Oak Brook, IL 60523-8842
Website: http://www.lionsclubs.org

511 • Lions International Peace Poster Contest

Purpose: To award creative youngsters with cash prizes for outstanding poster designs.

Eligibility: Students must be 11, 12 or 13 years old as of the deadline and must be sponsored by their local Lions club. Entries will be judged at the local, district, multiple district and international levels. Posters will be evaluated on originality, artistic merit and expression of the assigned theme, "Celebrate Peace."

How to Apply: Applicants must be sponsored by the local Lions club.

Deadline: November 15.

Amount: $500-$2,500.

Number of Awards: 24.

Rhythm and Hues Studios

5404 Jandy Place
Attn.: Scholarship
Los Angeles, CA 90066
Phone: 310-448-7500
Fax: 310-448-7600
Email: scholarship@rhythm.com
Website: http://www.rhythm.com

512 • Computer Graphics Scholarship

Purpose: To encourage and reward student artists in the computer graphics field.

Eligibility: Applicants must be full-time undergraduate or graduate students within six months of the deadline. Awards are given in computer modeling, computer character animation and digital cinematography.

How to Apply: Applications are available online.

Deadline: June 15.

Amount: $1,000.

Number of Awards: 1 computer modeling, 1 computer character animation, 3 digital cinematography.

Troy Studios

Loomis , CA
Email: support@animoids.com
Website: http://www.animoids.com

513 • Animoids 3D Animation Contest

Purpose: To support students interested in graphic design.

Eligibility: Applicants may be anyone who creates animated characters, props, movie sets and movie scenes using ANIMOIDS. The judges recommend that entries have sound, action and a good story and that applicants use creativity. Employees of Troy Studios may not enter.

How to Apply: Get software from the site and send the finished product back to the site.

Deadline: May 31 and November 30.

Amount: $500.

Number of Awards: 2.

Related Scholarships:

Scholastic

See #897 • Art Awards

Hospitality/Travel/Tourism

Also See Scholarships Listed Under:
Business/Management

American Hotel and Lodging Educational Foundation (AH&LEF)

1201 New York Avenue NW
Suite 600
Washington, DC 20005-3931
Phone: 202-289-3188
Fax: 202-289-3199
Email: chammond@ahlef.org
Website: http://www.ahlef.org

514 • American Express Scholarship Competition

Purpose: To provide financial assistance to students pursuing a degree in hospitality management.

Eligibility: Applicants must be enrolled in an accredited undergraduate program resulting in a degree in hospitality management. Students or their parents must be employed in the lodging industry by an American Hotel & Lodging Association member facility.

How to Apply: Applications are available online.

Deadline: June 15.

Amount: Up to $2,000.

Number of Awards: Varies.

515 • Ecolab Scholarship Competition

Purpose: To provide scholarships for students who intend to earn a degree in hospitality management.

Eligibility: Applicants must be enrolled or intend to enroll full-time in a two- or four-year U.S. college or university.

How to Apply: Applications are available online.

Deadline: June 15.

Amount: Up to $2,000.

Number of Awards: Varies.

516 • Lodging Management Program (LMP)

Purpose: To recognize high school students who have completed the two-year LMP curriculum and who have intent to pursue a career in hospitality management.

Eligibility: Applicants must be graduating seniors who have completed the two-year LMP high school program. Students must be employed in the lodging industry or have applied to a post-secondary hospitality institution.

How to Apply: Applications are available online.

Deadline: April 15.

Amount: $1,000.

Number of Awards: Varies.

517 • Steven Hymans Extended Stay Scholarship

Purpose: To provide scholarships to help educate students on the needs of extended stay visitors in the lodging industry.

Eligibility: Applicants must be undergraduate students who have experience working at an extended stay facility and must pursue a career in that segment of the lodging industry.

How to Apply: Applications are available online.

Deadline: June 15.

Amount: Up to $2,000.

Number of Awards: Varies.

American Society of Travel Agents (ASTA) Foundation Inc.

1101 King Street
Suite 200
Alexandria, VA 22314
Phone: 703-739-2782
Fax: 703-684-8319
Email: scholarship@astahq.com
Website: http://www.astanet.com

518 • American Express Travel Scholarship

Purpose: To encourage the growth and development of the future travel and tourism work force.

Eligibility: Applicants must be enrolled in a travel and tourism program in either a two- or four-year college or university or proprietary travel school, have a minimum 2.5 GPA and write a 500-word paper detailing their plans in travel and tourism and their views of the travel industry's future. Applicants must be a resident, citizen or legal alien of the U.S. or Canada.

How to Apply: Applications are available online.

Deadline: August 16.

Amount: Varies.

Number of Awards: 1.

519 • Avis Scholarship

Purpose: To promote management skills in current travel professionals.

Eligibility: Applicants must have two years of full-time travel industry experience or an undergraduate degree in travel/tourism and submit proof of current employment in the travel industry. Students must be enrolled in a minimum of two courses per semester in an accredited undergraduate or graduate level program in business, have a minimum 3.0 GPA and write a brief essay (500-750 words) explaining how the degree program relates to their future career in the travel industry. Applicants must also be a resident, citizen or legal alien of the United States or Canada.

How to Apply: Applications are available online.

Deadline: August 16.

Amount: $2,000.

Number of Awards: 1.

520 • Healy Scholarship

Purpose: To encourage study in the field of travel and tourism.

Eligibility: Applicants must be admitted to or enrolled in a four-year college or university, be enrolled in travel and tourism classes, have a minimum 2.5 GPA and write a 500-word paper suggesting improvements in the travel industry. Applicants must be residents, citizens or legal aliens of the U.S. or Canada.

How to Apply: Applications are available online.

Deadline: August 16.

Amount: $2,000.

Number of Awards: 1.

521 • Holland America Line-Westours Inc. Research Grant

Purpose: To fund research projects in the travel and tourism field.

Eligibility: Applicants must be enrolled at a travel school, community or junior college, college or university with proof of enrollment in travel courses, have a minimum 2.5 GPA and be residents, citizens or legal aliens of the U.S. or Canada. Research proposals must be based on one of five areas listed on the website. Funds are awarded based on proposals submitted by students which include an abstract/summary on the intended topic of research, purpose of study, methodology, cost of research, objectives and timeline. This may be a school, class or individual project.

How to Apply: Applications are available online.
Deadline: August 16.
Amount: Varies.
Number of Awards: 2.

522 • Joseph R. Stone Scholarship

Purpose: To aid students whose parents work in the travel industry.

Eligibility: Applicants must be undergraduates at a four year college or university, have a minimum 2.5 GPA, provide proof that one parent is employed in the travel industry and submit a 500-word paper on their goals. Applicants must be a resident, citizen or legal alien of the U.S. or Canada.

How to Apply: Applications are available online.
Deadline: August 16.
Amount: $2,400.
Number of Awards: 3.

523 • Princess Cruises and Princess Tours Scholarship

Purpose: To encourage study in the field of travel and tourism.

Eligibility: Applicants must be admitted or enrolled in a travel and tourism curriculum at a two- or four-year college or university or proprietary travel school, have a minimum 2.5 GPA and write a 300-word paper on the two features cruise ships will need to offer passengers in the next 10 years. Applicants must be a resident, citizen, or legal alien of the United States or Canada.

How to Apply: Applications are available online.
Deadline: August 16.
Amount: $2,000.
Number of Awards: 2.

524 • Simmons Scholarship

Purpose: To aid graduate study in travel and tourism.

Eligibility: Applicants must have a minimum 2.5 GPA, be residents, citizens or legal aliens of the U.S. or Canada and be graduate students pursuing master's or doctorate degrees with an emphasis in travel and tourism. Applicants must also submit a travel and tourism-related paper or thesis.

How to Apply: Applications are available online.
Deadline: August 16.
Amount: $2,000.
Number of Awards: Up to 2.

525 • Southern California Chapter/Pleasant Hawaiian Holidays Scholarship

Purpose: To encourage students to enter the profession of travel and tourism.

Eligibility: Applicants must be enrolled in a four-year college or university and be enrolled in travel and tourism classes, have a minimum 2.5 GPA and write a 500-word paper entitled, "My Goals in the Travel Industry." Students should also include why they should be selected and must be U.S. citizens. One winner from the Southern California area and one winner from anywhere in the U.S. will be chosen.

How to Apply: Applications are available online.
Deadline: August 16.
Amount: $2,500.
Number of Awards: 2.

Association for International Practical Training (AIPT)

10400 Little Patuxent Parkway
Suite 250
Columbia, MD 21044-3519
Phone: 410-997-2200
Fax: 410-992-3924
Email: aipt@aipt.org
Website: http://www.aipt.org

526 • Jessica King Scholarship

Purpose: To help students in the international hospitality field.

Eligibility: Applicants must be between 18 and 35 years old, have a degree in the hospitality industry or be currently employed for at least one year in the hospitality industry and be fluent in the host country's language. Applicants must also have been offered an overseas position and be participating in an AIPT-sponsored program. The scholarship is based on merit.

How to Apply: Applications are available by email.
Deadline: June 1.
Amount: $1,000.
Number of Awards: Varies.

Hospitality Sales and Marketing Association International (HSMAI)

8201 Greensboro Drive, Suite 300
McLean, VA 22102
Phone: 703-610-9024
Fax: 703-610-9005
Email: info@hsmai.org
Website: http://www.hsmai.org

527 • HSMAI Foundation Scholarship

Purpose: To assist students pursuing a career in hospitality sales and marketing.

Eligibility: For the $2,000 scholarships, applicants must be full-time undergraduate or graduate students pursuing a career in hospitality sales and marketing. For the $500 scholarships, applicants must be part-time associate's, bachelor's or graduate students pursuing a career in hospitality sales and marketing.

How to Apply: Applications are available online.
Deadline: May 31.
Amount: $500-$2,000.
Number of Awards: 4.

National Tourism Foundation

Attn.: Scholarships
546 E. Main Street
Lexington, KY 40508
Phone: 800-682-8886
Fax: 859-226-4437
Email: ray@nftonline.com
Website: http://www.ntfonline.com

528 • Travelers Conservation Foundation Sustainable Tourism Scholarship

Purpose: To provide funds for students pursuing a degree in tourism.

Eligibility: Applicants must be a part or full-time graduate student in good standing pursuing a degree in tourism. Applicants will be required to supply an essay along with the application.

How to Apply: Applications are available online.

Deadline: May 10.

Amount: $500.

Number of Awards: Varies.

Related Scholarships:

AAA

See #3 • Travel High School Challenge

International Foodservice Editorial Council (IFEC)

See #486 • IFEC Scholarships Award

Journalism/Broadcasting

Also See Scholarships Listed Under:

Communications

Broadcast Education Association

1771 North Street NW
Washington, DC 20036
Phone: 888-380-7222
Email: beainfo@beaweb.org
Website: http://www.beaweb.org

529 • Broadcast Education Association Scholarship Program

Purpose: To honor broadcasters and the broadcast industry.

Eligibility: Applicants must be college juniors or seniors or graduate students at BEA member universities, students pursuing freshman and sophomore instruction only or students who have already completed BEA two-year programs at a four-year college.

How to Apply: Applications are available online.

Deadline: September 15.

Amount: Varies.

Number of Awards: Varies.

Dow Jones Newspaper Fund

P.O. Box 300
Princeton, NJ 08543-0300
Phone: 609-452-2820
Fax: 609-520-5804
Email: newsfund@wsj.dowjones.com
Website: http://djnewspaperfund.dowjones.com

530 • DJNF Summer Internships

Purpose: To assist student journalists.

Eligibility: Applicants must be college students interested in pursuing journalism careers and paid summer internships. The three programs have their own requirements. Applicants to the Newspaper Copy Editing Program and the Sports Copy Editing Program must be juniors, seniors or graduate students and must take copy editing exams and seminars. Candidates must submit the application form, a resume, a list of courses and grades and a 500-word essay. Applicants for the Business Reporting Internship Program must be minority college sophomores and juniors who are African American, Hispanic, Asian American/Pacific Islander or American Indian/Alaskan Native. Candidates should submit application forms, resumes, three to five recent clips, a list of courses and grades and 500-word essays. They must also take the business reporting tests.

How to Apply: Applications are available online.

Deadline: November 1.

Amount: $1,000.

Number of Awards: Varies.

Fisher Communications Inc.

100 4th Avenue N.
Suite 440
Seattle, WA 98109
Phone: 206-404-7000
Email: info@fsci.com
Website: http://www.fsci.com

531 • Fisher Broadcasting Scholarships for Minorities

Purpose: To attract minority students into careers in broadcasting.

Eligibility: Applicants must be college sophomores enrolled in a broadcast, marketing or journalism curriculum at a college or vocational-technical school, be of non-white origin, and have a minimum 2.5 GPA. Residents outside of Washington, Oregon, Idaho, Montana and must apply scholarship funds to colleges in those states. Residents of those states may apply scholarship awards to out-of-state schools.

How to Apply: Applications are available online.
Deadline: April 30.
Amount: Varies.
Number of Awards: Varies.

Freedom Forum

1101 Wilson Boulevard
Arlington, VA 22209
Phone: 703-284-2814
Fax: 703-284-3529
Email: freespirit@freedomforum.org
Website: http://www.freedomforum.org/freespirit

532 • Al Neuharth Free Spirit Scholarship and Conference Program

Purpose: To provide assistance to students who meet the criteria of being a "free spirit."

Eligibility: Applicants must be high school seniors who plan to pursue a career in journalism and who are "free spirits," defined as those who "dream, dare and do."

How to Apply: Applications are available online.
Deadline: October 15.
Amount: $1,000-$50,000.
Number of Awards: 102.

Institute for Humane Studies at George Mason University

3301 N. Fairfax Drive
Suite 440
Arlington, VA 22201
Phone: 800-697-8799
Fax: 703-993-4890
Email: ihs@gmu.edu
Website: http://www.theihs.org

533 • Felix Morley Journalism Competition

Purpose: To support young writers whose work demonstrates an appreciation of classical liberal principles.

Eligibility: Applicants must be young writers who are 25 years or younger and full-time students. Applicants must submit three to five articles, editorials, opinion pieces, essays or reviews published in student newspapers or other periodicals. Submissions are judged on the basis of writing ability, potential to succeed and appreciation of liberty.

How to Apply: Applications are available online.
Deadline: December 1.
Amount: $250-$2,500.
Number of Awards: 6.

534 • IHS Journalism Internships

Purpose: To offer students reporting experience.

Eligibility: Applicants must be current college students, graduates, graduate students or professional students and demonstrate interest in journalism and an understanding of the principles of a free society.

How to Apply: Applications are available online.
Deadline: January 30.
Amount: $1,500 + internship, travel and lodging expenses.
Number of Awards: Varies.

535 • Young Communicators Fellowships

Purpose: To help students pursue careers that involve the communication of ideas.

Eligibility: Applicants must be college juniors or seniors, graduate students or recent graduates, have a clearly demonstrated interest in the classical liberal tradition of individual rights and market economies and pursue careers in journalism, film, writing (fiction or nonfiction), publishing or market-oriented public policy. Applicants must also have arranged or applied for an internship, training program or other short-term opportunity related to the intended career. Applicants must submit a written proposal, cover letter, resume, writing sample and two references.

How to Apply: There is no application form.
Deadline: March 15 for summer positions or 10 weeks in advance for others.
Amount: $2,500 and housing and travel assistance up to $2,500.
Number of Awards: Varies.

John Bayliss Radio

P.O. Box 51126
Pacific Grove, CA 93950
Phone: 831-655-5229
Website: http://www.baylissfoundation.org

536 • John Bayliss Radio Scholarship

Purpose: To promote interest in the broadcasting industry.

Eligibility: Applicants must be college juniors, seniors or graduate students majoring in broadcast communications who have a minimum 3.0 GPA.

How to Apply: Applications are available online.
Deadline: Varies.
Amount: Varies.
Number of Awards: Varies.

Journalism Education Association

Kansas State University
103 Kedzie Hall
Manhattan, KS 66506
Phone: 785-532-5532
Email: jea@spub.ksu.edu
Website: http://www.jea.org

537 • Student Journalist Impact Award

Purpose: To award scholarships to secondary school students who have made a difference in their own lives, the lives of others or their community or school through journalism.

Eligibility: Applicants must have a teacher who is a member of JEA. Submitted works must have been published within the past two years.

How to Apply: Applications are available online.

Deadline: March 1.

Amount: $1,000.

Number of Awards: 1.

National Institute for Labor Relations Research (NILRR)

William B. Ruggles Scholarship Selection Committee
5211 Port Royal Road, Suite 510
Springfield, VA 22151
Phone: 703-321-9606
Fax: 703-321-7342
Email: research@nilrr.org
Website: http://www.nilrr.org

538 • William B. Ruggles Right to Work Scholarship

Purpose: To support student who are dedicated to high journalistic standards.

Eligibility: Applicants must be undergraduate or graduate students majoring in journalism and demonstrate an understanding of the principles of voluntary unionism and the economic and social problems of compulsory unionism.

How to Apply: Applications are available online.

Deadline: December 31.

Amount: $2,000.

Number of Awards: 1.

National Press Photographers Foundation

Fay Blackburn
The Columbian
P.O. Box 180
Vancouver, WA 98666
Phone: 360-759-8027
Email: fay.blackburn@columbian.com
Website: http://www.nppa.org

539 • Reid Blackburn Scholarship

Purpose: To support photojournalism students.

Eligibility: Applicants must have completed one year at a full-time four-year college or university, provide a portfolio, demonstrate financial need and must have courses in photojournalism and have at least half a year of undergraduate study left. Applicants can apply to as many NPPA scholarships as desired, but only one award will be granted.

How to Apply: Applications are available online.

Deadline: March 1.

Amount: Varies.

Number of Awards: Varies.

National Press Photographers Foundation (NPPA)

3200 Croasdaile Drive
Suite 306
Durham, NC 27705
Phone: 919-383-7246
Fax: 919-383-7261
Email: jourdlr@showme.missouri.edu
Website: http://www.nppa.org

540 • Bob East Scholarship

Purpose: To encourage newcomers in photojournalism.

Eligibility: Applicants must be either in their first 3.5 years of undergraduate studies or planning to attend graduate school.

How to Apply: Applications are available online.

Deadline: March 1.

Amount: $2,000.

Number of Awards: 1.

541 • College Photographer of the Year

Purpose: To award outstanding student work in photojournalism and provide a forum for student photographers to gauge their skills.

Eligibility: Applicants must be currently enrolled in a full-time four-year college or university, provide a portfolio and demonstrate financial need. Applicants can apply to as many NPPA scholarships as desired, but only one award will be granted.

How to Apply: Applications are available by written or email request.

Deadline: October 1.

Amount: $500-$1,000.

Number of Awards: 2.

542 • Kit C. King Graduate Scholarship Fund

Purpose: To support photojournalism students.

Eligibility: Applicants must provide a portfolio, be pursuing an advanced degree in journalism with an emphasis in photojournalism and demonstrate financial need. Applicants can apply to as many NPPA scholarships as desired, but only one award will be granted.

How to Apply: Applications are available online.

Deadline: March 1.

Amount: $1,000.

Number of Awards: 1.

543 • NPPF Television News Scholarship

Purpose: To support students with television news photojournalism potential but with little opportunity and great need.

Eligibility: Applicants must be full-time juniors or seniors at a four-year college or university, provide a portfolio and demonstrate financial need. Applicants must also have courses in photojournalism and continue in this program towards a bachelor's degree. Applicants can apply to as many NPPA scholarships as desired, but only one award will be granted.

How to Apply: Applications are available online.

Deadline: March 1.

Amount: $1,000.

Number of Awards: Varies.

544 • Still Photographer Scholarship

Purpose: To honor the profession of photojournalism.

Eligibility: Applicants must have completed one year in a full-time four-year college or university with courses in photojournalism, provide a portfolio and demonstrate financial need. Applicants can apply to as many NPPA scholarships as desired, but only one award will be granted.

How to Apply: Applications are available online.
Deadline: March 1.
Amount: $2,000.
Number of Awards: Varies.

Overseas Press Club Foundation

40 W. 45 Street
New York, NY 10036
Phone: 212-626-9220
Fax: 212-626-9210
Email: foundation@opcofamerica.org
Website: http://www.opcofamerica.org

545 • Overseas Press Club Foundation Scholarships

Purpose: To encourage undergraduate and graduate students attending American colleges and universities to pursue careers as foreign correspondents.
Eligibility: Scholarships are open to undergraduate and graduate students with an interest in a career as a foreign correspondent. Eligible students must be attending American colleges or universities.
How to Apply: Applications are available online.
Deadline: December 1.
Amount: $2,000.
Number of Awards: 11.

Quill and Scroll Society

University of Iowa School of Journalism and Mass Communications
100 Adler Journalism Building E346
Iowa City, IA 52242
Phone: 319-335-3457
Fax: 319-335-3989
Email: quill-scroll@uiowa.edu
Website: http://www.uiowa.edu/~quill-sc/

546 • Edward J. Nell Memorial Scholarships in Journalism

Purpose: To aid high school journalists seeking to improve their skills and techniques.
Eligibility: Applicants to the Nell Scholarship must have been national winners in the Yearbook Excellence Contest or the International Writing/Photography Contest.
How to Apply: Applications are available by written request.
Deadline: May 10.
Amount: $500-$1,000.
Number of Awards: 9-10.

Radio and Television News Directors Association

1600 K Street NW
Suite 700
Washington, DC 20006
Phone: 202-659-6510
Fax: 202-223-4007
Email: rtnda@rtnda.org
Website: http://www.rtnda.org

547 • Abe Schechter Graduate Scholarship

Purpose: To honor professional achievements in electronic journalism.
Eligibility: Applicants must be full-time or incoming graduate students. Applicants may be enrolled in any major as long as their career intent is television or radio news. Applicants may only apply for one RTNDA scholarship.
How to Apply: Applications are available online.
Deadline: May 3.
Amount: $2,000.
Number of Awards: Varies.

548 • Carole Simpson Scholarship

Purpose: To honor professional achievements in electronic journalism.
Eligibility: Applicants must be full-time college sophomores or higher with at least one full academic year remaining. Applicants may be enrolled in any major as long as their career intent is television or radio news. Applicants may only apply for one RTNDA scholarship. Preference is given to students of color.
How to Apply: Applications are available online.
Deadline: May 3.
Amount: $2,000.
Number of Awards: 1.

549 • Ed Bradley Scholarship

Purpose: To honor professional achievements in electronic journalism.
Eligibility: Applicants must be full-time college sophomores or higher with at least one full academic year remaining. Applicants may be enrolled in any major as long as their career intent is television or radio news. Applicants may only apply for one RTNDA scholarship. Preference will be given to undergraduate students of color.
How to Apply: Applications are available online.
Deadline: May 3.
Amount: $10,000.
Number of Awards: 1.

550 • Ken Kashiwahara Scholarship

Purpose: To honor professional achievements in electronic journalism.
Eligibility: Applicants must be full-time college sophomores or higher with at least one full academic year remaining. Applicants may be enrolled in any major as long as their career intent is television or radio news. Applicants may only apply for one RTNDA scholarship. Preference is given to students of color.
How to Apply: Applications are available online.
Deadline: May 3.
Amount: $2,500.
Number of Awards: 1.

551 • Lou and Carole Prato Sports Reporting Scholarship

Purpose: To provide monetary assistance to a student pursuing a career as a sports reporter for radio or television.
Eligibility: Applicants must be full-time college sophomores or higher with at least one full academic year remaining. Applicants may be enrolled in any major but must have a career goal of becoming a sports reporter for television or radio. Applicants may only apply for one RTNDA scholarship.
How to Apply: Applications are available online.
Deadline: May 3.
Amount: $1,000.
Number of Awards: 1.

552 • Mike Reynolds Scholarship

Purpose: To honor professional achievements in electronic journalism.

Eligibility: Applicants must be full-time college sophomores or higher with at least one full academic year remaining. Applicants may be enrolled in any major as long as their career intent is television or radio news. Applicants may only apply for one RTNDA scholarship. Preference is given to students who demonstrate financial need by describing media-related jobs held and contributions made to funding their own education.

How to Apply: Applications are available online.

Deadline: May 3.

Amount: $1,000.

Number of Awards: 1.

553 • Undergraduate Scholarships

Purpose: To honor professional achievements in electronic journalism.

Eligibility: Applicants must be full-time college sophomores or higher with at least one full academic year remaining. Applicants may be enrolled in any major as long as their career intent is television or radio news. Applicants may only apply for one RTNDA scholarship.

How to Apply: Applications are available online.

Deadline: May 3.

Amount: Varies.

Number of Awards: Varies.

Rolling Stone

College Journalism Competition
1290 Avenue of the Americas, 2nd Floor
New York, NY 10104
Website: http://www.rollingstone.com

554 • Rolling Stone Annual College Journalism Competition

Purpose: To reward outstanding college journalism in the fields of entertainment reporting, feature writing and essays and criticism.

Eligibility: Awards are available in the categories of entertainment reporting, feature writing and essays and criticism. Applicants must submit a piece published between June 1 and May 30 of the current school year in a college student newspaper or magazine. Applicants must have been full- or part-time students at the time the entries were published. Only one entry is allowed per category, but students may submit to more than one category. Each entry must be submitted separately with a completed entry form, and the submitted piece must be a tearsheet from the magazine or newspaper with the date of publication shown.

How to Apply: Applications are available online.

Deadline: June 15.

Amount: $2,500.

Number of Awards: 3.

Scripps Howard Foundation

Top Ten Scholarship
P.O. Box 5380
Cincinnati, OH 45201
Phone: 513-977-3035
Fax: 513-977-3800
Email: vlmartin@scripps.com
Website: http://www.scripps.com

555 • Scripps Howard Top Ten Scholarship

Purpose: To recognize the top journalism students in the country.

Eligibility: Applicants are nominated by their college and must be full-time college students entering their junior or senior year and studying journalism. Selection is based on academic achievement, commitment to a career journalism and essay.

How to Apply: Applications are available by request.

Deadline: Varies.

Amount: $10,000.

Number of Awards: 10.

Related Scholarships:

Asian American Journalists Association

See #956 • National AAJA General Scholarship Awards

LinTV

See #1007 • Minority Scholarship and Training Program

National Association of Hispanic Journalists

See #1020 • NAHJ Scholarships

National Association of Hispanic Journalists

See #1021 • Newhouse Scholarship Program

Native American Journalists Association

See #1034 • NAJA Scholarship Fund

National Dairy Shrine

See #135 • Marshall E. McCullough Scholarship

Outdoor Writers Association of America

See #248 • Bodie McDowell Scholarship

Scholastic

See #457 • Writing Awards

Asian American Journalists Association

See #954 • AAJA Newhouse National Scholarship And Internship Awards

Asian American Journalists Association

See #955 • Mary Moy Quan Ing Memorial Scholarship

National Association of Black Journalists

See #1018 • National Association of Black Journalists Scholarship Program

National Association of Hispanic Journalists

See #1019 • *Maria Elena Salinas Scholarship Program*

United Methodist Church

See #1108 • *Leonard M. Perryman Communications Scholarship for Ethnic Minority Students*

Academy of Television Arts and Sciences Foundation

See #833 • *College Television Awards*

Hispanic Heritage Awards Foundation

See #985 • *Hispanic Heritage Youth Awards*

Arab American Institute Foundation

See #949 • *Al Muammar Scholarships for Journalism*

California Chicano News Media Association

See #1224 • *Joel Garcia Memorial Scholarship*

Fund for American Studies

See #1173 • *Fund for American Studies Internships*

California Chicano News Media Association

See #1223 • *Frank del Olmo Memorial Scholarship*

California Chicano News Media Association

See #1222 • *CCNMA Scholarships*

Golden Key National Honour Society

See #790 • *Literary Achievement Awards*

German Marshall Fund of the United States

See #911 • *Transatlantic Fellows Program*

Journalism Education Association Future Teacher Scholarship

See #333 • *Future Teacher Scholarship*

National Association of Broadcasters

See #245 • *Grants for Research in Broadcasting*

National Association of Negro Business and Professional Women's Clubs Inc.

See #1024 • *Julianne Malveaux Scholarship*

Law

Also See Scholarships Listed Under:

Leadership

American Bar Association

321 North Clark Street
Chicago, IL 60610
Phone: 312-988-5000
Email: abalsd@abanet.org
Website: http://www.abanet.org/lsd/

556 • ABA Essay and Writing Competitions

Purpose: To support and recognize achievement among law students.

Eligibility: The ABA sponsors a variety of essay and writing competitions for law students. Each is centered on a specific legal topic. Topics include: affordable housing and community, community development law, law and aging, antitrust, business law, criminal justice, dispute resolution, entertainment and sports law, family law, health care, labor and employment, liability, education, public contracts, real estate, tort and insurance and children.

How to Apply: Applications and specific deadlines for each competition are available online.

Deadline: Varies.

Amount: $1,000-$5,000.

Number of Awards: Varies.

557 • Legal Opportunity Scholarship Fund

Purpose: To encourage members of underrepresented ethnic groups to enter the legal profession.

Eligibility: Applicants must be members of a racial and/or ethnic minority that has been underrepresented in the legal profession. Applicants must be entering, first-year law students, demonstrate financial need and show participation in community service activities. Applicants who have not yet been accepted by a law school may also apply.

How to Apply: Applications are available online.

Deadline: February 22.

Amount: $5,000.

Number of Awards: 20.

BAR/BRI Bar Review

ABA Scholarship Committee
111 W. Jackson Boulevard
Chicago, IL 60604
Email: abalsd@abanet.org
Website: http://www.abanet.org/lsd/

558 • American Bar Association-Bar/Bri Scholarships

Purpose: To defer the cost of study for graduating law students who must take the BAR/Bri exam.

Eligibility: Applicants must be ABA Law Student Division members who will be December or May graduates and will use the award toward their BAR/BRI tuition. Scholarships will vary in amount depending upon the applicant's financial condition and the size of the applicant pool.

How to Apply: Applications are available online.

Deadline: October 31 or February 1.

Amount: Varies.

Number of Awards: Varies.

Federal Circuit Bar Association

1620 I Street NW
Suite 900
Washington, DC 20006
Phone: 202-466-3923
Fax: 202-833-1061
Website: http://www.fedcirbar.org

559 • Giles Sutherland Rich Memorial Scholarship

Purpose: To support promising law students who demonstrate financial need.

Eligibility: Applicants must be undergraduate or graduate law students who demonstrate academic ability and financial need. They must submit a one-page statement describing their financial need, their interest in law and their qualifications for the award. Applicants must also submit transcripts and a curriculum vitae.

How to Apply: There is no application form.

Deadline: April 30.

Amount: $10,000.

Number of Awards: 1.

560 • William S. Bullinger Scholarship

Purpose: To support financially needy but academically promising law students.

Eligibility: Applicants must be undergraduate or graduate law student who demonstrate financial need and academic promise. They must submit a one-page statement describing their financial circumstances, their interest in law and their qualifications for the scholarship along with transcripts and a curriculum vitae. Applicants will be considered for the William S. Bullinger Scholarship when applying for the Giles Sutherland Rich Memorial Scholarship.

How to Apply: There is no application form.

Deadline: April 30.

Amount: $5,000.

Number of Awards: Varies.

Fredrikson and Byron, P.A.

200 S. Sixth Street
Suite 4000
Minneapolis, MN 55402-1425
Phone: 612-492-7000
Fax: 612-492-7077
Email: market@fredlaw.com
Website: http://www.fredlaw.com

561 • Minority Scholarship Program

Purpose: To provide opportunities for law students from diverse backgrounds.

Eligibility: In addition to the financial award, scholarship winners are also invited to serve as summer associates at the firm.

Deadline: Varies.

Amount: $5,000.

Number of Awards: 2.

National Court Reporters Association

8224 Old Courthouse Road
Vienna, VA 22182-3808
Phone: 800-272-6272
Email: dgaede@ncrahq.org
Website: http://www.ncraonline.org

562 • Council on Approved Student Education's Scholarship Fund

Purpose: To support the reporting profession.

Eligibility: Applicants must be in good academic standing at an approved court-reporting program, be members of the NCRA, write 140 to 180 words per minute and submit a two-page essay with references.

How to Apply: Applications are available by email.
Deadline: April 1.
Amount: $500-$1,500.
Number of Awards: 3.

Pride Law Fund

P.O. Box 2602
San Francisco, CA 94104
Email: info@pridelawfund.org
Website: http://www.pridelawfund.org

563 • Thomas H. Steel Fellowship Fund

Purpose: To support a law students with a project that serves the lesbian, gay, bisexual and transgendered community.

Eligibility: Applicants must be students in their last year of law school or lawyers within three years of graduating from law school. The award is based on the quality and scope of the project, proposal, public service activities, and relation to the LGBT community. Applicants should submit applications, resumes, project descriptions, two reference letters, budget, timetable and law school transcript.

How to Apply: Applications are available online.
Deadline: December 31.
Amount: $25,000-$35,000.
Number of Awards: 1.

Unitarian Universalist Association

25 Beacon Street
Boston, MA 02108
Phone: 617-742-2100
Email: info@uua.org
Website: http://www.uua.org

564 • Otto M. Stanfield Legal Scholarship

Purpose: To help Unitarian Universalist students entering or attending law school.

Eligibility: Applicants should be planning to attend or currently attending law school at the graduate level. The award is based on activity with Unitarian Universalism and financial need. Applicants should submit transcripts and recommendations.

How to Apply: Applications are available online.
Deadline: February 15.
Amount: Varies.
Number of Awards: Varies.

Women In Defense

HORIZONS Foundation
c/o National Defense Industrial Association
2111 Wilson Boulevard, Suite 400
Arlington, VA 22201
Phone: 703-247-2552
Fax: 703-527-6945
Email: jcasey@ndia.org
Website: http://wid.ndia.org

565 • HORIZONS Foundation Scholarship

Purpose: To encourage women to pursue careers related to the national security interests of the United States and to provide development opportunities to women already working in national security fields.

Eligibility: Applicants must be full- or part-time female students at an accredited university or college and must have reached at least junior level status. Applicants must also demonstrate an interest in a career related to national security and defense, have a minimum GPA of 3.25 and demonstrate financial need. Preference is given to students in security studies, military history, government relations, engineering, computer science, physics, mathematics, business, law, international relations, political science, or economics.

How to Apply: Applications are available online.
Deadline: November 1 and July 1.
Amount: Varies.
Number of Awards: Varies.

Related Scholarships:

Japanese American Citizens League (JACL)

See #1003 • Japanese American Citizens League Law Scholarships

American Legion Auxiliary, Department of California

See #1212 • American Legion Auxiliary, Department of California $1,000 Scholarships

Institute for Humane Studies at George Mason University

See #36 • Humane Studies Fellowships

Maryland Higher Education Commission

See #1397 • Graduate and Professional Scholarship Program

American Legion Auxiliary, Department of California

See #1213 • American Legion Auxiliary, Department of California $2,000 Scholarships

Institute for Humane Studies at George Mason University

See #37 • Summer Graduate Research Fellowships

American Association of Law Libraries

See #582 • John R. Johnson Memorial Scholarship Endowment

American Association of Law Libraries

See #581 • *James F. Connolly LexisNexis Academic and Library Solutions Scholarship*

National Association of Blacks in Criminal Justice

See #724 • *Jonathan Jasper Wright Award*

American Association of Law Libraries

See #578 • *AALL Educational Scholarships*

American Association of Law Libraries

See #579 • *George A. Strait Minority Scholarship*

American Association of Law Libraries

See #580 • *Institute for Court Management Scholarship*

National Association of Blacks in Criminal Justice

See #726 • *Medger Evers Award*

National Association of Blacks in Criminal Justice

See #725 • *Mary Church Terrell Award*

National Association of Blacks in Criminal Justice

See #727 • *William L. Hastie Award*

Leadership

Also See Scholarships Listed Under:
Academics/General
Public Service/Community Service
Public Administration/Social Work

Campus Compact

P.O. Box 1975
Brown University
Providence, RI 02912
Phone: 401-867-3950
Email: campus@compact.org
Website: http://www.compact.org

566 • Frank Newman Leadership Award

Purpose: To provide scholarships and opportunities for civic mentoring to students with financial need.

Eligibility: Emphasis is on students who have demonstrated leadership abilities and significant interest in civic responsibility. Students must attend Campus Compact member institutions and be nominated by the Campus Compact member president.

How to Apply: Nominations must be made by the Campus Compact member president.

Deadline: Varies.

Amount: Varies.

Number of Awards: Varies.

Coca-Cola Scholars Foundation

P.O. Box 442
Atlanta, GA 30301
Phone: 800-306-2653
Email: questions@coca-colascholars.org
Website: http://www.coca-colascholars.org

567 • Coca-Cola Scholars Program

Purpose: Begun in 1986 to celebrate the Coca-Cola Centennial, the program is designed to contribute to the nation's future and to assist a wide range of students.

Eligibility: Applicants must be high school seniors in the U.S. and must use the awards at an accredited U.S. college or university. Selection is based on character, personal merit and commitment. Merit is shown through leadership, academic achievement, and motivation to serve and succeed.

How to Apply: Applications are available online.

Deadline: October 31.

Amount: $4,000-$20,000.

Number of Awards: 250.

Comcast

1500 Market Street
Philadelphia, PA 19102
Website: http://www.comcast.com

568 • Leaders and Achievers Scholarship Program

Purpose: To provide one-time scholarship awards of $1,000 each to graduating high school seniors. Emphasis is on students who take leadership roles in school and community service and improvement.

Eligibility: Students must have a minimum 2.8 GPA, be nominated by their high school principal and attend school in a Comcast community. See the website for a list of eligible communities by state. Comcast employees, their families or other Comcast affiliates are not eligible to apply.

How to Apply: Applicants must be nominated by their high school principal.

Deadline: February 10.

Amount: $1,000.

Number of Awards: 1,300.

Discover Card

c/o American Association of School Administrators
801 N. Quincy Street
Suite 700
Arlington, VA 22203
Phone: 703-528-0700
Fax: 703-841-1543
Email: tributeaward@aasa.org
Website: http://www.discoverfinancial.com

569 • Discover Card Tribute Award Scholarships

Purpose: To recognize high school juniors for their accomplishments beyond academics.

Eligibility: Applicants must be high school juniors at an accredited U.S. high school and have a minimum cumulative 2.75 GPA for their 9th and 10th grades. Applicants must also show accomplishments in three of the four following areas: Special Talents, Leadership, Obstacles Overcome and Community Service.

How to Apply: Requests for applications are available online.

Deadline: January.

Amount: $2,500-$25,000.

Number of Awards: Varies.

Do Something

24-32 Union Square East
4th Floor
New York, NY 10003
Phone: 212-254-2390
Website: http://www.dosomething.org

570 • BRICK Award

Purpose: To award scholarships and community grants to young social entrepreneurs who make a measurable difference in their communities.

Eligibility: Young community leaders up to age 25 may apply. Emphasis on those who take a leadership role in creating a positive, lasting impact on the community. Focus areas include health, environment and community building.

How to Apply: Applications are available online.

Deadline: October 25.

Amount: Up to $25,000.

Number of Awards: 9.

Financial Service Centers of America

Attn.: FiSCA Scholarship Program
Court Plaza South, East Wing
21 Main Street, 1st Floor, P.O. Box 647
Hackensack, NJ 07602
Phone: 201-487-0412
Fax: 201-487-3954
Email: info@fisca.org
Website: http://www.fisca.org

571 • FiSCA Scholarship

Purpose: To help collegebound high school seniors from areas served by FiSCA centers.
Eligibility: Applicants must be high school seniors. Selection is based on leadership, academic achievement and financial need.
How to Apply: Applications are available online.
Deadline: June 15.
Amount: $2,000.
Number of Awards: 2.

Herff Jones

c/o National Association of Secondary School Principals
1904 Association Drive
Reston, VA 20191
Phone: 800-253-7746
Email: carrollw@principals.org.
Website: http://www.principals.org/awards/

572 • Principal's Leadership Award

Purpose: To recognize students for their leadership.
Eligibility: Applicants must be seniors and nominated by their high school principal. Each principal can nominate one student leader from the senior class. Application packets are mailed each fall to every secondary school.
How to Apply: Nomination forms are available online.
Deadline: December 3.
Amount: $1,000.
Number of Awards: 150.

Ladies Auxiliary VFW

406 W. 34th Street
Kansas City, MO 64111
Phone: 816-561-8655
Fax: 816-931-4753
Email: info@ladiesauxvfw.com
Website: http://www.ladiesauxvfw.com

573 • National Junior Girls Scholarships

Purpose: To award Junior Girls who excel academically, are actively involved in Junior Girls and demonstrate leadership at school.
Eligibility: Applicants must be Junior Girls ages 13 to 16 and members of a Ladies Auxiliary VFW Junior Girls Unit. Applicants must also submit letters of recommendation, transcript and list of activities.
How to Apply: Applications are available online.
Deadline: March 12.
Amount: $100-$10,000.
Number of Awards: Varies.

National Association for Campus Activities

13 Harbison Way
Columbia, SC 29212-3401
Phone: 803-732-6222
Fax: 803-749-1047
Email: info@naca.org
Website: http://www.naca.org

574 • Scholarships for Student Leaders

Purpose: The NACA foundation is committed to developing professionals in the field of campus activities.
Eligibility: Students must hold a significant campus leadership position, have made significant contributions to their campus communities and have demonstrated leadership skills and abilities.
How to Apply: Applications are available online.
Deadline: November 1.
Amount: Varies.
Number of Awards: Varies.

575 • Tese Caldarelli Memorial Scholarship

Purpose: To provide financial assistance to student leaders.
Eligibility: Students must hold a significant campus leadership position and demonstrate significant leadership skills and abilities. Students must also be making significant contributions through on- or off-campus volunteering.
How to Apply: Applications are available online.
Deadline: November 1.
Amount: Varies.
Number of Awards: Varies.

Penguin Group (USA)

Academic Marketing Department
Signet Classic Student Scholarship
375 Hudson Street
New York, NY 10014
Website: http://us.penguingroup.com/static/html/services-academic/essayhome.html

576 • Phillips Foundation Ronald Reagan Future Leaders Program

Purpose: To recognize students who demonstrate leadership on behalf of freedom, American values and constitutional principles.
Eligibility: Applicants must be enrolled full-time at any accredited, four-year degree-granting institution in the U.S. or its territories. Applicants may apply for a Ronald Reagan Future Leaders Program grant during their sophomore or junior year. Selection is based on merit and financial need.
How to Apply: Applications are available online.
Deadline: January 15.
Amount: $1,000-7,500.
Number of Awards: Varies.

USA Funds

Scholarship Management Services, CSFA
1505 Riverview Road
St. Peter, MN 56082
Phone: 888-537-4180
Email: scholarship@usafunds.org
Website: http://www.usafunds.org

577 • USA Funds Access to Education Scholarships

Purpose: To assist students in achieving their higher education goals.

Eligibility: This is a need-based scholarship program with aid for full-time and half-time students. Applicants must be high school seniors or other individuals who plan to enroll or are enrolled in full- or half-time undergraduate or graduate coursework at an accredited two- or four-year college, university or vocational or technical school. Students must be U.S. citizens or eligible noncitizens and must have an adjusted gross family income of $35,000 or less. Selection is based on academic performance, leadership, activities, work experience and career and educational goals.

How to Apply: Applications are available online.

Deadline: March.

Amount: Varies.

Number of Awards: Varies.

Related Scholarships:

National Merit Scholarship Corporation

See #49 • National Merit Scholarship Program and National Achievement Scholarship Program

Elks National Foundation (IL)

See #28 • Most Valuable Student Scholarships

Wal-Mart Foundation

See #71 • Sam Walton Community Scholarship

SuperCollege.com

See #61 • SuperCollege.com Student Scholarship

Target Department Stores

See #929 • Target All-Around Scholarships for Students

Hispanic Heritage Awards Foundation

See #985 • Hispanic Heritage Youth Awards

Hispanic Outlook Magazine

See #986 • Hispanic Outlook Scholarship

Humane Society of the United States

See #128 • Shaw-Worth Memorial Scholarship

Rotary International

See #58 • Cultural Ambassadorial Scholarships

Campus Compact

See #916 • Howard R. Swearer Student Humanitarian Award

National Association for Campus Activities

See #924 • Markley Scholarship

Golden Key National Honour Society

See #791 • Student Leader Award

German Marshall Fund of the United States

See #29 • Marshall Memorial Fellowship

National Association for Campus Activities

See #1201 • Lori Rhett Memorial Scholarship

ArtCarved Class Rings

See #9 • ArtCarved Get Cash for College Scholarship

NetAid Foundation

See #926 • Global Action Awards

Library Science

Also See Scholarships Listed Under:
English/Writing

American Association of Law Libraries

53 W. Jackson Boulevard
Suite 940
Chicago, IL 60604
Phone: 312-939-4764
Fax: 312-431-1097
Email: scholarships@aall.org
Website: http://www.aallnet.org

578 • AALL Educational Scholarships

Purpose: To encourage students to pursue careers as law librarians.
Eligibility: There are five levels of awards: 1. Library Degree for Law School Graduates, awarded to a law school graduate with law library experience pursuing a degree at an accredited library school. 2. Library School Graduates Attending Law School, awarded to a library school graduate pursuing a degree at an accredited law school who has law library experience and no more than 36 semester credit hours left before obtaining the law degree. 3. Library Degree for Non-Law School Graduates, awarded to a college graduate with law library experience who is seeking a degree involving law librarianship courses at an accredited library school. 4. Library School Graduates Seeking A Non-Law Degree, awarded to library school graduates who are seeking degrees in fields other than law. 5. Law Librarians in Continuing Education Courses, awarded to law librarians with a degree from an accredited library or law school who are continuing their education. Preference is given to AALL members, but a non-member can apply. All applicants must intend to have careers as law librarians. There must be financial need for awards 1-4.
How to Apply: Applications are available online, by mail with a self-addressed, stamped envelope, by fax, by phone or by email.
Deadline: April 1.
Amount: Varies.
Number of Awards: Varies.

579 • George A. Strait Minority Scholarship

Purpose: To encourage minorities to enter careers as law librarians.
Eligibility: Applicants must be a member of a minority group as defined by U.S. government rules, degree candidates in an accredited library or law school, and intend to pursue a career as law librarians. Law library experience is preferred. Applicants must also have financial need and have at least one quarter or semester left after the scholarship is given.
How to Apply: Applications are available online, by mail with a self-addressed, stamped envelope, by fax, by phone or by email.
Deadline: April 1.
Amount: Varies.
Number of Awards: Varies.

580 • Institute for Court Management Scholarship

Purpose: To support education at the Institute for Court Management.
Eligibility: Applicants must belong to the AALL and be a member of the State, Court & County Law Libraries Special Interest Section. Applicants should submit a resume, a registration form and a statement explaining why they want to continue their education with the Institute for Court Management and the seminar or conference they want to attend.
How to Apply: Applications are available online.
Deadline: April 1.
Amount: $1,700.
Number of Awards: 2.

581 • James F. Connolly LexisNexis Academic and Library Solutions Scholarship

Purpose: To support a librarian interested in becoming a law librarian.
Eligibility: Preference will be given to librarians who are interested in government documents. Applicants must be library school graduates with experience working in a law library who intend to obtain a degree at an accredited law school and have careers as law librarians. Applicants should have no more than 36 semester credit hours left before qualifying for the degree and should have financial need.
How to Apply: Applications are available online, by mail with a self-addressed, stamped envelope, by fax, by phone and by email.
Deadline: April 1.
Amount: $3,000.
Number of Awards: 1.

582 • John R. Johnson Memorial Scholarship Endowment

Purpose: To encourage current and future law librarians in memory of John Johnson, a prominent law librarian.
Eligibility: Applicants who apply for any of the AALL Educational Scholarships become automatically eligible to receive this award. No separate application is necessary. Applicants must intend to have careers as law librarians. Preference is given to AALL members, but a non-member may apply.
How to Apply: Applications are available online, by mail with a self-addressed, stamped envelope, by fax, by phone or by email.
Deadline: April 1.
Amount: Varies.
Number of Awards: Varies.

Association for Library Service to Children

50 E. Huron Street
Chicago, IL 60611
Phone: 800-545-2433
Fax: 312-944-7671
Email: alsc@ala.org
Website: http://www.ala.org/alsc

583 • Bound to Stay Bound Books Scholarship

Purpose: To support students pursuing their MLS degrees.
Eligibility: Applicants must intend to pursue an MLS or advanced degree, plan to work in children's librarianship and be U.S. or

Canadian citizens. Selection is based on academic excellence, leadership and a desire to work with children in any type of library.

How to Apply: Applications are available online.
Deadline: March 1.
Amount: $6,500.
Number of Awards: 4.

584 • Frederic G. Melcher Scholarship

Purpose: To support students who want to become children's librarians.

Eligibility: Applicants must intend to pursue an MLS degree, plan to work in children's librarianship and be U.S. or Canadian citizens. Selection is based on academic excellence, leadership and desire to work with children in any type of library.

How to Apply: Applications are available online.
Deadline: March 1.
Amount: $6,000.
Number of Awards: 2.

California Library Association

717 20th Street, Suite 200
Sacramento, CA 95814
Phone: 916-447-8541
Fax: 916-447-8394
Email: info@cla-net.org
Website: http://www.cla-net.org

585 • Begun Scholarship

Purpose: To assist California library or information sciences graduate students at California schools.

Eligibility: Applicants must be California graduate students attending an American Library Association accredited school and have completed core coursework toward a master's of library and science or information studies degree. Recipients must also plan to become a children's or young adult librarian in a California public library and to join the California Library Association if not already a member.

How to Apply: Applications are available online.
Deadline: July 15.
Amount: $3,000.
Number of Awards: 1.

586 • CLA Reference Services Press Fellowship

Purpose: To support college seniors and graduates pursuing master's degrees in library science.

Eligibility: Applicants must either be California residents enrolled in a master's program at an American Library Association-approved library school in any state or residents of any state enrolled in an ALA-approved library school master's program in California. Recipients are expected to pursue a career in reference or information service librarianship and take at least three classes about reference or information service.

How to Apply: Applications are available online.
Deadline: June 15.
Amount: $3,000.
Number of Awards: 1.

587 • CLA Scholarship for Minority Students in Memory of Edna Yelland

Purpose: To assist minority California graduate students who are pursuing degrees in library or information science.

Eligibility: Applicants must be California residents, be American Indian, African American, Mexican American, Latino, Asian

American, Pacific Islander or Filipino and be accepted into or enrolled in an American Library Association accredited state library school. Based on financial need, and an interview is required.

How to Apply: Applications are available online.
Deadline: May 31.
Amount: $2,500.
Number of Awards: 3.

California School Library Association

1001 26th Street
Sacramento, CA 95816
Phone: 916-447-2684
Fax: 916-447-2695
Email: csla@pacbell.net
Website: http://www.schoolibrary.org

588 • Above and Beyond Scholarship

Purpose: To support library media teachers pursuing advanced degrees or National Board Certification.

Eligibility: Applicants must be professional members of the California School Library Association and California residents intending to continue working in California in the school library profession after completing their additional education. Students must submit a 500-word essay describing their professional goals and how an advanced degree or certification applies to those goals and three letters of recommendation.

How to Apply: Applications are available online.
Deadline: June 30.
Amount: $1,000.
Number of Awards: 1.

Medical Library Association

65 E. Wacker Place
Suite 1900
Chicago, IL 60601
Phone: 312-419-9094
Email: spectrum@ala.org
Website: http://www.mlanet.org

589 • MLA Scholarship

Purpose: To aid a student with finishing their education at an ALA-accredited library school.

Eligibility: Applicants must be either entering or less than half-way through an accredited graduate school program in a field relevant to library science and be U.S. or Canadian citizens or permanent residents.

How to Apply: Applications are available online.
Deadline: December 1.
Amount: $5,000.
Number of Awards: 1.

590 • MLA Scholarship for Minority Students

Purpose: To aid minority students entering or currently attending graduate library school.

Eligibility: Applicants must be African-American, Hispanic, Asian, Native American or Pacific Islander and entering or currently attending an accredited library school. Applicants must also be citizens or permanent residents of the United States or Canada.

How to Apply: Applications are available online.
Deadline: December 1.
Amount: $5,000.
Number of Awards: 1.

591 • MLA/NLM Spectrum Scholarship

Purpose: To aid minority students in becoming health sciences information professionals.

Eligibility: Applicants must be African American, Hispanic, Asian, Native American or Pacific Islander students attending accredited library schools who are studying fields relevant to library science and who plan to enter the health sciences information field.

How to Apply: Applications are available by written request.

Deadline: March 1.

Amount: Varies.

Number of Awards: Varies.

Special Libraries Association

331 S. Patrick Street
Alexandria, VA 22314
Phone: 703-647-4900
Fax: 703-647-4901
Email: sla@sla.org
Website: http://www.sla.org

592 • Affirmative Action Scholarship

Purpose: To support minority students who show an interest in special librarianship.

Eligibility: Applicants must be college seniors or graduates who are members of a minority group admitted by a recognized library school or information science program and demonstrate financial need. Preference is given to SLA members and those who show an interest in special library work. Applicants must submit an essay on their contribution to special librarianship.

How to Apply: Applications are available online.

Deadline: October 31.

Amount: $6,000.

Number of Awards: 1.

593 • SLA Scholarship

Purpose: To support students who wish to pursue careers in special librarianship.

Eligibility: Applicants must be college graduates or college seniors with an interest in special librarianship who are admitted by a recognized library school or information science program and demonstrate financial need. Preference is given to SLA members and those who show an interest in special library work.

How to Apply: Applications are available online.

Deadline: October 31.

Amount: $6,000.

Number of Awards: 3.

Related Scholarships:

National Security Agency (NSA)

See #1189 • Pat Roberts Intelligence Scholars Program for Intelligence Analysts

Marketing

Also See Scholarships Listed Under:
Business/Management

Common Knowledge Scholarship Foundation

P.O. Box 290361
Davie, FL 33329-0361
Website: http://www.cksf.org

594 • Public Relations Scholarship

Purpose: To reward college students majoring in public relations, journalism, advertising or communications.
Eligibility: Applicants must complete the free online registration. This scholarship contest has two rounds: Round one is a short, multiple choice online quiz based on questions from college-level public relations courses. The top 20 students progress to Round two. Participants in Round two submit articles on one of three topics. Articles can be no more than two pages and are judged on creativity, accuracy and spelling/punctuation/correct use of Associated Press style. There are first, second and third places. Second and third place winners receive $50 gift certificates.
How to Apply: Applicants must complete the free online registration.
Deadline: Feburary 4.
Amount: $250.
Number of Awards: 3.

DECA Inc.

1908 Association Drive
Reston, VA 20191-1594
Phone: 703-860-5000
Fax: 703-860-4013
Email: Kathy_Onion@deca.org
Website: http://www.deca.org

595 • Coca-Cola USA Scholarship

Purpose: To reward DECA members who are committed to leadership and community service.
Eligibility: Applicants must be active DECA members showing leadership, scholastic ability and community involvement. They must be planning to attend a 2-year or 4-year school to study marketing, business or marketing education.
How to Apply: Applications are available from DECA advisors.
Deadline: February 17.
Amount: $1,000.
Number of Awards: Up to 6.

Public Relations Student Society of America

33 Maiden Lane
11th Floor
New York, NY 10038
Phone: 212-460-1474
Fax: 212-995-0757
Email: prssa@prsa.org
Website: http://www.prssa.org

596 • Betsy Plank/PRSSA Scholarship

Purpose: To assist public relations students.
Eligibility: Applicants must be PRSSA members enrolled in an undergraduate public relations program and be college juniors or seniors. One eligible student may be nominated from each PRSSA chapter. Selection is based on academic achievement, leadership, experience and commitment to public relations. Applicants need to include a 300-word statement of committment to public relations.
How to Apply: Applications are available online.
Deadline: June 4.
Amount: Varies.
Number of Awards: 3.

597 • Gary Yoshimura Scholarship

Purpose: To assist public relations students.
Eligibility: Applicants must be PRSSA members with a minimum 3.0 GPA in the pursuit of higher education in the public relations field. Applicants must submit an essay on personal or professional challenges and a statement on financial need.
How to Apply: Applications are available online.
Deadline: January 16.
Amount: $2,400.
Number of Awards: 1.

598 • Lawrence G. Foster Award for Excellence in Public Relations

Purpose: To assist public relations students.
Eligibility: Applicants must be undergraduate students majoring in public relations who are committed to careers in public relations. Applicants must submit an essay on what excellence in public relations is and how they plan to achieve excellence in their own careers.
How to Apply: Applications are available online.
Deadline: June 4.
Amount: $1,500.
Number of Awards: 1.

599 • Professor Sidney Gross Memorial Award

Purpose: To assist public relations undergraduate students.
Eligibility: Applicants must be undergraduate students who demonstrate superior understanding of ethical principles in public relations. Applicants need to write a response to a given scenario and must be members of the PRSSA.
How to Apply: Applications are available online.
Deadline: April 16.
Amount: $1,000.
Number of Awards: Varies.

Related Scholarships:

Public Relations Student Society of America

See #1045 · Multicultural Affairs Scholarship Program

National Dairy Shrine

See #136 · Milk Marketing Scholarship

BI-LO Corporation

See #1528 · BI-LO Minority Scholarship Program

American Society of Travel Agents (ASTA) Foundation Inc.

See #522 · Joseph R. Stone Scholarship

American Society of Travel Agents (ASTA) Foundation Inc.

See #523 · Princess Cruises and Princess Tours Scholarship

American Society of Travel Agents (ASTA) Foundation Inc.

See #521 · Holland America Line-Westours Inc. Research Grant

American Society of Travel Agents (ASTA) Foundation Inc.

See #524 · Simmons Scholarship

American Society of Travel Agents (ASTA) Foundation Inc.

See #518 · American Express Travel Scholarship

American Society of Travel Agents (ASTA) Foundation Inc.

See #519 · Avis Scholarship

APICS-The Educational Society for Resource Management

See #199 · Donald W. Fogarty International Student Paper Competition

National Tourism Foundation

See #528 · Travelers Conservation Foundation Sustainable Tourism Scholarship

Women In Defense

See #565 · HORIZONS Foundation Scholarship

Fisher Communications Inc.

See #531 · Fisher Broadcasting Scholarships for Minorities

Executive Women International (EWI)

See #205 · Executive Women International Scholarship Program

Golden Key National Honour Society

See #782 · Business Achievement Awards

German Marshall Fund of the United States

See #911 · Transatlantic Fellows Program

Hospitality Sales and Marketing Association International (HSMAI)

See #527 · HSMAI Foundation Scholarship

Golden Key National Honour Society

See #786 · Ford Motor Company Business and Leadership Scholarship

International Foodservice Editorial Council (IFEC)

See #486 · IFEC Scholarships Award

National Association of Negro Business and Professional Women's Clubs Inc.

See #1025 · National Scholarship

DECA Inc.

See #203 · Harry A. Applegate Scholarship

Mathematics

Also See Scholarships Listed Under:
Accounting/Finance
Computer And Information Science
Aerospace/Aviation
Sciences/Physical Sciences

Actuarial Foundation

475 North Martingale Road
Suite 600
Schaumburg, IL 60173
Phone: 847-706-3600
Fax: 847-706-3599
Email: scholarships@actfnd.org
Website: http://www.aerf.org

600 • John Culver Wooddy Scholarships

Purpose: To assist students who plan to become actuaries.
Eligibility: Applicants must be undergraduate students who will receive their degrees by August 31 of the year following the application deadline. Students must be in the top quartile and have completed a minimum of one actuarial examination. A recommendation from a professor is required. Only one applicant per school is permitted. Preference is given to applicants who have demonstrated leadership ability in extracurricular activities.
How to Apply: Applications are available online.
Deadline: June 23.
Amount: $2,000.
Number of Awards: Varies.

American Mathematical Society

Dr. Martha J. Siegel, MAA Secretary
Mathematics Department, Towson University
Stephens Hall 302, 8000 York Road
Towson, MD 21252
Phone: 410-704-2980
Email: siegel@towson.edu
Website: http://www.ams.org

601 • Frank and Brennie Morgan Prize for Outstanding Research in Mathematics by an Undergraduate Student

Purpose: Awarded to an undergraduate student (or students who have collaborated) for research in the field of mathematics.
Eligibility: Applicants must be undergraduate students at colleges or universities in the United States or its possessions, Canada and Mexico. Students must be nominated.
How to Apply: Nomination information is available by email. Questions should be directed to Dr. Martha J. Siegel at the address above. Nominations and submissions should be sent to: Morgan Prize Committee, c/o Robert J. Daverman, American Mathematical Society, 312D Ayres Hall, University of Tennessee, Knoxville, TN 37996.
Deadline: Varies.
Amount: $1,000-$2,000.
Number of Awards: 1.

American Statistical Association

Dr. Amita Manatunga, Gertrude Cox Scholarship Committee Chair
Department of Biostatistics, Emory University
1518 Clifton Road NE #374
Atlanta, GA 30322
Phone: 404-727-1309
Fax: 404-727-1370
Email: amanatu@sph.emory.edu
Website: http://www.amstat.org

602 • Gertrude Cox Scholarship For Women In Statistics

Purpose: To encourage women to pursue education for careers in statistics.
Eligibility: Applicants must be women who are full-time students in a graduate-level statistics programs.
How to Apply: Applications are available online.
Deadline: April 1.
Amount: $1,000.
Number of Awards: Varies.

Association for Women in Mathematics

4114 Computer and Space Sciences Building
University of Maryland
College Park, MD 20742
Phone: 301-405-7892
Fax: 301-314-9074
Email: awm@math.umd.edu
Website: http://www.awm-math.org

603 • Alice T. Schafer Prize

Purpose: To support female students who are studying mathematics.
Eligibility: Nominees must be female college undergraduates and either be U.S. citizens or have a school address in the U.S. Selection is based on performance in advanced mathematics courses and special programs, interest in mathematics, ability to conduct independent work and performance in mathematical competitions at the local or national level.
How to Apply: Applicants must be nominated.
Deadline: October 1.
Amount: Varies.
Number of Awards: 1-2.

604 • AWM Biographies Contest

Purpose: To increase awareness of women's contributions to the mathematical sciences.
Eligibility: Applicants must interview a woman working in a mathematical career and write an essay based on the interview. Applicants may be from the sixth grade to graduate students.
How to Apply: Applications are available online.
Deadline: October 29.
Amount: Varies.
Number of Awards: Varies.

D.W. Simpson and Company

1800 Larchmont Avenue
Chicago, IL 60613
Phone: 800-837-8338
Fax: 312-951-8386
Email: actuaries@dwsimpson.com
Website: http://www.dwsimpson.com/scholar.html

605 • D.W. Simpson Actuarial Science Scholarship

Purpose: To assist college students interested in an actuarial science career.

Eligibility: Eligible students must be college seniors majoring in actuarial science who are eligible to work in the U.S. and have taken and passed a minimum of one actuarial examination.

How to Apply: Applications are available online.

Deadline: April 30 and October 31.

Amount: $1,000.

Number of Awards: 2.

Related Scholarships:

Armed Forces Communications and Electronics Association

See #707 • *AFCEA Sgt Jeannette L. Winters, USMC Memorial Scholarship*

Armed Forces Communications and Electronics Association

See #705 • *AFCEA General Emmett Paige Scholarships*

Armed Forces Communications and Electronics Association

See #706 • *AFCEA ROTC Scholarships*

Massachusetts Office of Student Financial Assistance

See #1415 • *CommonWealth Futures Grant Program*

Minnesota Higher Education Services Office

See #1433 • *Minnesota Academic Excellence Scholarship*

Casualty Actuarial Society/Society of Actuaries

See #967 • *Actuarial Scholarships for Minority Students*

Astronaut Scholarship Foundation

See #1128 • *Astronaut Scholarship*

Barry M. Goldwater Scholarship and Excellence in Education Foundation

See #391 • *Barry M. Goldwater Scholarship and Excellence in Education Program*

Women In Defense

See #565 • *HORIZONS Foundation Scholarship*

EAA Aviation Center

See #101 • *Payzer Scholarship*

National Inventors Hall of Fame

See #411 • *Collegiate Inventors Competition*

Armed Forces Communications and Electronics Association

See #253 • *AFCEA General John A. Wickham Scholarships*

Armed Forces Communications and Electronics Association

See #254 • *AFCEA Ralph W. Shrader Scholarships*

Intel Corporation and Science Service

See #1138 • *Intel Science Talent Search*

Siemens Foundation

See #1149 • *Siemens Westinghouse Competition in Math, Science and Technology*

Hispanic Heritage Awards Foundation

See #985 • *Hispanic Heritage Youth Awards*

Department of Defense, American Society for Engineering Education

See #1132 • *NDSEG Fellowship Program*

Davidson Institute for Talent Development

See #20 • *Davidson Fellows Award*

National Security Agency (NSA)

See #50 • *Stokes Educational Scholarship Program*

National Association for the Advancement of Colored People

See #1016 • *Willems Scholarship*

Medicine/Nursing/Health Professions

Also See Scholarships Listed Under:
Biological Sciences/Life Sciences
Chemistry
Dentistry

AMBUCS

P.O. Box 5127
High Point, NC 27262
Phone: 800-838-1845
Fax: 336-852-6830
Email: janiceb@ambucs.org
Website: http://www.ambucs.com

606 • AMBUCS Scholars

Purpose: To provide more opportunities for the disabled by encouraging students to become therapists.

Eligibility: Applicants must be undergraduate juniors or seniors or graduate students pursuing their master's or doctoral degrees and must have been accepted into an accredited program in physical therapy, occupational therapy, speech language pathology or hearing audiology. Assistant programs are ineligible. Selection is based on financial need, U.S. citizenship, community service, academic achievement, character and career plans.

How to Apply: Applications are available online.
Deadline: April 15.
Amount: $500-$6,000.
Number of Awards: Varies.

American Alliance for Health, Physical Education, Recreation and Dance

1900 Association Drive
Reston, VA 20191
Phone: 800-213-7193
Email: dcallis@aahperd.org
Website: http://www.aahperd.org

607 • Ruth Abernathy Presidential Scholarship

Purpose: To honor deserving students in the areas of heath, physical education, recreation and dance.

Eligibility: Applicants must be members of the American Alliance for Health, Physical Education, Recreation and Dance (AAHPERD), but they may join when applying and must major in health, physical education, recreation or dance. Undergraduate applicants must have a minimum 3.5 GPA and have junior or senior status when applying. Graduate applicants must have a minimum 3.5 GPA and have completed one semester of full-time study. Selection is based on scholastic achievement, leadership, community service and character.

How to Apply: Applications are available online in the spring.
Deadline: October 15.
Amount: $1,000-$1,500.
Number of Awards: 5.

American Association for Health Education

1900 Association Drive
Reston, VA 20191
Phone: 703-476-3437
Fax: 703-476-6638
Email: aahe@aahperd.org
Website: http://www.aahperd.org/aahe

608 • Bill Kane Scholarship, Undergraduate

Purpose: To support health education students.

Eligibility: Applicants must be full-time undergraduate health majors in their sophomore, junior or senior years. They must have a GPA of at least 3.25 and write an essay about what they hope to accomplish as a health educator.

How to Apply: Applications are available online.
Deadline: November 15.
Amount: $1,000.
Number of Awards: 1.

American Association for Respiratory Care

9425 N. MacArthur Boulevard
Suite 100
Irving, TX 75063-4706
Phone: 972-243-2272
Fax: 972-484-2720
Email: info@aarc.org
Website: http://www.aarc.org

609 • Jimmy A. Young Memorial Education Recognition Award

Purpose: To recognize outstanding minority students in respiratory care education programs.

Eligibility: Applicants must be enrolled in an accredited respiratory care education program and have a minimum 3.0 GPA. Students must submit an original paper on respiratory care. Preference is given to minority students.

How to Apply: Applications are available online.
Deadline: June 19.
Amount: Up to $1,000.
Number of Awards: 1.

610 • Morton B. Duggan, Jr. Memorial Education Recognition Award

Purpose: To recognize outstanding students in respiratory care education programs.

Eligibility: Applicants must be enrolled in an accredited respiratory care education program and have a minimum 3.0 GPA. Students must submit an original paper on respiratory care. Preference is given to residents of Georgia and South Carolina.

How to Apply: Applications are available online.
Deadline: June 19.
Amount: Up to $1,000.
Number of Awards: 1.

611 • NBRC/AMP Gareth B. Gish, MS, RRT Memorial and William F. Miller, MD Postgraduate Education Recognition Awards

Purpose: To aid qualified respiratory therapists in pursuing advanced degrees.

Eligibility: Applicants must have been accepted into an advanced degree program of a fully accredited school. Application must be accompanied by an original essay describing how the award will aid in achieving an advanced degree and future goals in health care. A minimum 3.0 GPA is required.

How to Apply: Applications are available online.
Deadline: June 30.
Amount: Up to $1,500.
Number of Awards: 2.

612 • NBRC/AMP William W. Burgin, Jr. MD and Robert M. Lawrence, MD Education Recognition Awards

Purpose: To recognize outstanding students in respiratory care education programs.

Eligibility: Applicants must be enrolled in an accredited respiratory care education program as a second-year student pursuing an associate's degree or as a junior or senior pursuing a bachelor's degree. In addition to an original paper dealing with respiratory care, applicants must submit an original essay describing how this award will help them reach their degrees and their future goals in the field of health care.

How to Apply: Applications are available online.
Deadline: June 19.
Amount: Up to $2,500.
Number of Awards: 2.

American Association of Colleges of Nursing

One Dupont Circle NW
Suite 350
Washington, DC 20036
Phone: 202-463-6930
Fax: 202-785-8320
Email: lspicer@aacn.nche.edu
Website: http://www.aacn.nche.edu

613 • AfterCollege/AACN Nursing Scholarship Fund

Purpose: To assist students pursuing careers in nursing.

Eligibility: Applicants must be enrolled in a bachelor's, master's or doctoral program in nursing and have a minimum 3.25 GPA.

How to Apply: Applications are available online. There are four deadlines: January 31, April 30, July 31 and October 31. Winners are announced within 60 days of each deadline.
Deadline: Varies.
Amount: $2,500.
Number of Awards: 4.

614 • Lydia's Professional Uniform/AACN Excellence in Academics Nursing Scholarship

Purpose: To support undergraduate nursing students.

Eligibility: Applicants must be full-time nursing students in their junior year of a bachelor of science (BSN) program with a minimum 3.5 GPA. The application form and an essay about their career aspirations and financial need are required.

How to Apply: Applications are available online and may be returned by fax or email.
Deadline: August 1 and November 1.
Amount: $2,500.
Number of Awards: 2.

American Association of Critical-Care Nurses

101 Columbia
Aliso Viejo, CA 92656
Phone: 800-899-2226
Fax: 949-362-2020
Email: info@aacn.org
Website: http://www.aacn.org

615 • AACN Educational Advancement Scholarship

Purpose: To advance critical care nursing and promote nursing professionalism.

Eligibility: Applicants must be AACN members in good standing with active RN licenses, have a minimum 3.0 GPA, be junior status or higher, be currently working in critical care or have worked in critical care for one full year in the last three years and be currently enrolled in a nursing program accredited by the State Board of Nursing in their state.

How to Apply: Applications are available online.
Deadline: April 1.
Amount: $1,500.
Number of Awards: Varies.

American Association of Medical Assistants' Endowment

20 North Wacker Drive
Suite 1575
Chicago, IL 60606
Phone: 800-228-2262
Email: info@aama-ntl.org
Website: http://www.aama-ntl.org

616 • FA Davis Student Award

Purpose: To reward aspiring medical assistants for ad design.

Eligibility: Applicants must be enrolled in and have finished a quarter or a semester at an accredited postsecondary medical assisting program. Students must create one ad that supports the medical assisting profession, the CMA credential and the AAMA. The ad must have a slogan, body copy and a call to action and can be designed using any medium.

How to Apply: Applications are available online.
Deadline: July 1.
Amount: $1,000.
Number of Awards: 1.

American Association of Occupational Health Nurses (AAOHN) Foundation

2920 Brandywine Road
Suite 100
Atlanta, GA 30341
Phone: 770-455-7757
Fax: 770-455-7271
Email: ann@aaohn.org
Website: http://www.aaohn.org

617 • Academic Study Award

Purpose: To provide further education for occupational and environmental health professionals.

Eligibility: Applicants must be registered nurses enrolled full- or part-time in a nationally accredited school of nursing baccalaureate program with an interest in occupational and environmental health

or be registered nurses enrolled full- or part-time in a graduate program that has application to occupational and environmental health. Applicants should submit a narrative and letters of recommendation.
How to Apply: Applications are available online.
Deadline: December 1.
Amount: $3,500.
Number of Awards: 4.

618 • Continuing Education Award

Purpose: To support the continuing education of occupational and environmental health professionals.

Eligibility: Applicants must be employed in the field of occupational and environmental health nursing and demonstrate an interest in occupational and environmental health. A narrative, a letter of support from the employer and material describing the continuing education activity are required. This scholarship is for continuing education activities not tuition for an academic program.

How to Apply: Applications are available online.
Deadline: December 1.
Amount: $1,500.
Number of Awards: 13.

619 • Leadership Development Award

Purpose: To reward volunteer leadership development in occupational and environmental health nursing.

Eligibility: Applicants must work in the field of occupational and environmental health nursing and demonstrate an interest in occupational and environmental health. The funds may be used for leadership development activity/program registration, travel and/or associated travel-related expenses. Applicants must submit a narrative and letter of support from their employer.

How to Apply: Applications are available online.
Deadline: August 1.
Amount: $1,500.
Number of Awards: 3.

American Dietetic Association Foundation

120 South Riverside Plaza
Suite 2000
Chicago, IL 60606-6995
Phone: 800-877-1600
Email: education@eatright.org
Website: http://www.eatright.org

620 • ADAF Student Scholarship

Purpose: To encourage students in a dietetic program.

Eligibility: Applicants should be American Dietetic Association members and enrolled in their junior or senior year of a baccalaureate or coordinated program in dietetics or the second year of study in a dietetic technician program, a dietetic internship program or a graduate program. One application form is used for all ADAF scholarships.

How to Apply: Applications are available online.
Deadline: February.
Amount: Varies.
Number of Awards: Varies.

American Federation for Aging Research (AFAR)

70 West 40th Street, 11th Floor
New York, NY 10018
Phone: 212-703-9977
Fax: 212-997-0330
Email: grants@afar.org
Website: http://www.afar.org

621 • Medical Student Summer Research Training in Aging Program

Purpose: To support early medical students who demonstrate an interest in geriatric medicine or age-related research with an opportunity to serve under top experts in the field.

Eligibility: Applicants must be osteopathic or allopathic students who have completed at least one year of medical school at a U.S. institution. Students must have a faculty sponsor from their home institution. The program lasts 8 to 12 weeks, and monthly stipends are provided.

How to Apply: Applications are available online.
Deadline: February 7.
Amount: Up to $5,193.
Number of Awards: 120.

American Health Information Management Association

Foundation of Research and Education in Health Information Management
233 N. Michigan Avenue, 21st Floor
Chicago, IL 60601-5800
Phone: 312-233-1168
Fax: 312-233-1090
Email: fore@ahima.org
Website: http://www.ahima.org

622 • Merit Scholarships and Educational Loans

Purpose: To provide merit scholarships to undergraduate students pursuing degrees in health information administration or health information technology.

Eligibility: Applicants must be members of AHIMA, have at least one semester remaining in their course of study and be taking at least six hours per semester in pursuit of the degree. Scholarships are also available for HIM professionals pursuing graduate degrees in the health information field, and loans are also available.

How to Apply: Applications are available online.
Deadline: April 28.
Amount: Up to $5,000.
Number of Awards: Varies.

American Legion

Attn.: Americanism and Children and Youth Division
P.O. Box 1055
Indianapolis, IN 46206
Phone: 317-630-1249
Fax: 317-630-1369
Email: acy@legion.org
Website: http://www.legion.org

623 • Eight and Forty Lung and Respiratory Nursing Scholarship Fund

Purpose: To assist registered nurses.

Eligibility: Applicants must plan to be employed full-time in hospitals, clinics or health departments in a position related to lung and respiratory control.

How to Apply: Applications are available by written request.

Deadline: May 15.

Amount: $2,500.

Number of Awards: Varies.

American Medical Technologists

10700 W. Higgins Road
Rosemont, IL 60018
Phone: 800-275-1268
Fax: 847-823-0458
Website: http://www.amt1.com

624 • AMT Student Scholarship

Purpose: To provide financial assistance to students interested in medical technology careers.

Eligibility: Applicants must be high school graduates or current seniors planning to attend an accredited institution to pursue an American Medical Technologists-certified career, which includes medical laboratory technology, medical assisting, dental assisting, phlebotomy and office laboratory technician.

How to Apply: Applications are available online.

Deadline: April 1.

Amount: $500.

Number of Awards: 5.

American Medical Women's Association

211 N. Union Street, Suite 100
Alexandria, VA 22314
Website: http://www.amwa-doc.org

625 • Wilhelm-Frankowski Scholarship

Purpose: To recognize women in the medical community and to encourage medical pursuits for young women.

Eligibility: The award is meant to support students who contribute to their medical communities.

How to Apply: Contact the organization for more information.

Deadline: Varies.

Amount: Varies.

Number of Awards: Varies.

American Nurses Association (ANA)

8515 Georgia Avenue, Suite 400
Attn.: Janet Jackson, Program Manager
Silver Spring, MD 20910-3492
Phone: 301-628-5247
Fax: 301-628-5349
Website: http://www.nursingworld.org

626 • Clinical Research Pre-Doctoral Fellowship

Purpose: To provide stipends and tuition assistance to nurses studying minority psychiatric-mental health and substance abuse.

Eligibility: Applicants must be members of the ANA, have their master's degree and plan to pursue doctoral degrees. Fellowships may last from three to five years.

How to Apply: Applications available online.

Deadline: March 1.

Amount: Varies.

Number of Awards: Varies.

American Psychological Foundation

750 First Street NE
Washington, DC 20002
Phone: 800-374-2721
Website: http://www.apa.org

627 • Henry Hecaen and Manfred Meier Neuropsychology Scholarships

Eligibility: Applicants must demonstrate need and demonstrate potential for a promising career in the field of neuropsychology. Applicants should also submit a letter that documents their scholarly and research accomplishments, financial need and how the award will be used.

How to Apply: There is no official application.

Deadline: June 1.

Amount: $2,500.

Number of Awards: 2.

American Radiological Nurses Association

7794 Grow Drive
Pensacola, FL 32514
Phone: 866-486-2762
Fax: 850-484-8762
Email: arna@puetzamc.com
Website: http://www.arna.net

628 • Dorothy Budnek Memorial Scholarship

Purpose: To help ARNA members continue their nursing education.

Eligibility: Applicants must be active members of the American Radiological Nurses Association for three years, have a current nursing license and be enrolled in an approved academic program. Students should submit the application, a statement of purpose, two recommendation letters, a transcript which shows a minimum 2.5 GPA, a statement of financial support and a copy of the nursing license.

How to Apply: Applications are available online.

Deadline: December 1.

Amount: $600.

Number of Awards: 1.

American Society for Clinical Laboratory Science

6701 Democracy Boulevard, Suite 300
Bethesda, MD 20817
Phone: 301-657-2768
Fax: 301-657-2909
Email: ascls@ascls.org
Website: http://www.ascls.org

629 • Alpha Mu Tau Fraternity Scholarships

Purpose: To support new professionals in the clinical laboratory sciences.

Eligibility: Applicants must be undergraduate students entering or in their last year of study in an NAACLS-accredited program in Clinical Laboratory Science/Medical Technology or Clinical

Laboratory Technician/Medical Laboratory Technician. Applicants must be a U.S. citizen or a permanent resident of the U.S.
How to Apply: Applications are available online.
Deadline: April 1.
Amount: Up to $1,500.
Number of Awards: Varies.

630 • ASCLS Student Award

Purpose: To reward outstanding student case studies and research papers.
Eligibility: Applicants must be current ASCLS members. For research papers, they must have been enrolled in a NAACLS-accredited CLS/CLT program at the time the research was conducted. For case studies, they must be currently attending a NAACLS-accredited CLS/CLT program. Case studies must represent actual patient cases.
How to Apply: Applications are available online.
Deadline: May 1.
Amount: $500 for case studies and travel expenses for research papers.
Number of Awards: 1 for research papers and 1 for case studies.

631 • Dade-Behring/Coordinating Council on the Clinical Laboratory Workforce Scholarship

Purpose: To assist students in the second year of a Clinical Laboratory Technician (CLT/MLT) program.
Eligibility: Applicants must be currently enrolled in a NAACLS-accredited Clinical Laboratory Technician (CLT/MLT) program and planning to complete their final year of study by the end of the following August. Applicants must have a GPA of at least 2.5.
How to Apply: Applications are available online.
Deadline: October 1.
Amount: $1,000.
Number of Awards: 50.

American Society of Extra-Corporeal Technology (AmSECT)

2209 Dickens Road
P.O. Box 11086
Richmond, VA 23230-1086
Phone: 804-565-6363
Fax: 804-282-0090
Email: patelpump@sbcglobal.net
Website: http://www.amsect.org

632 • Michael Dunaway Scholarship

Purpose: To support those studying perfusion.
Eligibility: Applicants must be current student members of AmSECT, be in a CAAHEP accredited perfusion education program, have finished 25 percent of the coursework, have a minimum 2.75 GPA and submit an application, essay and a transcript.
How to Apply: Applications are available online.
Deadline: December 15.
Amount: $1,000.
Number of Awards: Varies.

633 • AmSECT Scholarship

Purpose: To support academic achievement in the study of cardiovascular perfusion.
Eligibility: Applicants must be current student members of AmSECT, be in a CAAHEP-accredited perfusion education program, have finished 25 percent of the coursework, have a minimum 2.75 GPA and submit an application, essay and a transcript.
How to Apply: Applications are available online.
Deadline: December 15.
Amount: $1,000.
Number of Awards: Varies.

634 • James P. Dearing Scholarship

Purpose: To support perfusion education.
Eligibility: Applicants must be current student members of AmSECT, be in a CAAHEP accredited perfusion education program, have finished 25 percent of the coursework, have a minimum 2.75 GPA and submit an application, essay and transcript.
How to Apply: Applications are available online.
Deadline: December 15.
Amount: $2,000.
Number of Awards: Varies.

635 • Jerry W. Richmond Memorial Scholarship

Purpose: To support perfusion education.
Eligibility: Applicants must be current student members of AmSECT, be in a CAAHEP accredited perfusion education program, have finished 25 percent of the coursework, have a minimum 2.75 GPA and submit an application, essay and transcript.
How to Apply: Applications are available online.
Deadline: December 15.
Amount: $1,000.
Number of Awards: Varies.

636 • Mary Gibbon Scholarship

Purpose: To support perfusion education.
Eligibility: Applicants must be current student members of AmSECT, be in a CAAHEP accredited perfusion education program, have finished 50 percent of the coursework, have a minimum 2.5 GPA and submit an application, essay and transcript.
How to Apply: Applications are available online.
Deadline: December 15.
Amount: $2,500.
Number of Awards: Varies.

637 • Perfusion Student Scholarship

Purpose: To support perfusion education.
Eligibility: Applicants must be current student members of AmSECT, be in a CAAHEP accredited perfusion education program, have finished 25 percent of the coursework, have a minimum 2.75 GPA and submit an application, essay and transcript.
How to Apply: Applications are available online.
Deadline: December 15.
Amount: $1,000.
Number of Awards: Varies.

638 • Pioneer in Perfusion Scholarship

Purpose: To support perfusion education.
Eligibility: Applicants must be current student members of AmSECT, be in a CAAHEP accredited perfusion education program, have finished 25 percent of the coursework, have a minimum 2.75 GPA and submit an application, essay and transcript.

How to Apply: Applications are available online.
Deadline: December 15.
Amount: $1,500.
Number of Awards: Varies.

639 • Presidential Scholarship

Purpose: To support students in studying perfusion.

Eligibility: Applicants must be current student members of AmSECT, be in a CAAHEP accredited perfusion education program, have finished 25 percent of the coursework, have a minimum 2.75 GPA and submit an application, essay and transcript.

How to Apply: Applications are available online.
Deadline: December 15.
Amount: $1,000.
Number of Awards: Varies.

American Speech-Language-Hearing Foundation

10801 Rockville Pike
Rockville, MD 20852
Phone: 800-498-2071 x4314
Email: foundation@asha.org
Website: http://www.ashfoundation.org

640 • Graduate Student Scholarship

Purpose: To support graduate students in communication sciences and disorders.

Eligibility: Applicants must be full-time graduate students in U.S. communication sciences and disorders programs. Master's degree candidates must be in programs accredited by the Council on Academic Accreditation for Audiology and Speech Pathology, but doctoral programs do not have to be accredited. Transcripts, an essay, a reference form and a statement of good standing are required.

How to Apply: Applications are available online.
Deadline: January 13.
Amount: $4,000.
Number of Awards: Varies.

641 • International Student Scholarship

Purpose: To support an international graduate student in communication sciences and disorders.

Eligibility: Applicants must be full-time students in the U.S. Master's degree candidates must be in programs accredited by the Council on Academic Accreditation for Audiology and Speech Pathology, but doctoral programs do not have to be accredited. The applicants should submit transcripts, an essay and a reference form.

How to Apply: Applications are available online.
Deadline: January 13.
Amount: $4,000.
Number of Awards: 1.

642 • Minority Student Scholarship

Purpose: To support a minority graduate student in communication sciences and disorders.

Eligibility: Applicants should be full-time minority graduate students. Master's degree candidates must be in programs accredited by the Council on Academic Accreditation for Audiology and Speech Pathology, but doctoral programs do not have to be accredited. Transcripts, an essay and a reference form are required.

How to Apply: Applications are available online.
Deadline: January 13.
Amount: $4,000.
Number of Awards: 1.

Association of Food and Drug Officials

2550 Kingston Road
Suite 311
York, PA 17402
Phone: 717-757-2888
Fax: 717-755-8089
Email: afdo@afdo.org
Website: http://www.afdo.org

643 • Association of Food and Drug Officials Scholarship Award

Purpose: To support college students who are studying food, drug or consumer product safety.

Eligibility: Applicants must be in their third or fourth year of college at an accredited institution and demonstrate a desire to work in a career of research, regulatory work, quality control or teaching in an area related to food, drug or consumer product safety. Applicants must also have demonstrated leadership capabilities, a minimum 3.0 GPA and submit two letters of recommendation from faculty.

How to Apply: Applications are available online.
Deadline: February 1.
Amount: $1,500.
Number of Awards: 2.

Association of Perioperative Registered Nurses

2170 S. Parker Road
Suite 300
Denver, CO 80231
Phone: 800-755-2676
Email: sstokes@aorn.org
Website: http://www.aorn.org

644 • AORN Foundation Scholarship Program

Purpose: To encourage the education of nurses and future nurses.

Eligibility: Applicants must be current nursing students or AORN members accepted to an accredited program and have a minimum 3.0 GPA. Applicants must also demonstrate financial need.

How to Apply: Applications are available online.
Deadline: June 1.
Amount: $500-$4,000.
Number of Awards: Varies.

Association of Rehabilitation Nurses

4700 W. Lake Avenue
Glenview, IL 60025
Phone: 800-229-7530
Fax: 888-458-0456
Email: gelliott@connect2amc.com
Website: http://www.rehabnurse.org

645 • BSN Scholarship

Purpose: To help nurses pursuing a bachelor's of science in nursing.

Eligibility: Applicants must be members of and involved in ARN, enrolled in a bachelor's of science in nursing (BSN) program, have completed at least one course, be currently practicing rehabilitation nursing and have a minimum of two years' experience in rehabilitation nursing. Applications, transcripts, a summary of professional and educational goals and achievements and two recommendation letters are required. Applications should be submitted by fax or email.

How to Apply: Applications are available online.
Deadline: June 1.
Amount: $1,000.
Number of Awards: Varies.

Association of Surgical Technologists

6 W. Dry Creek Circle
Littleton, CO 80120
Phone: 800- 637-7433
Fax: 303-694-9169
Email: kfrey@ast.org
Website: http://www.ast.org

646 • ARC-ST Scholarships

Purpose: To support the continuing education of surgical technology students.

Eligibility: Applicants should be AST members in CAAHEP-accredited surgical technology programs. Applications, transcripts, a minimum 3.0 GPA, essays and recommendation letters are required.

How to Apply: Applications are available online.
Deadline: April 1.
Amount: $1,000.
Number of Awards: 1.

647 • AST National Honor Society Scholarship

Purpose: To help members of the AST National Honor Society.

Eligibility: Applicants must be members of the AST National Honor Society, plan to attend or currently attend a CAAHEP-accredited surgical assisting program and have a minimum 3.0 GPA. The award is given after the completion of one semester of classes.

How to Apply: Applications are available online.
Deadline: September 1.
Amount: $1,000.
Number of Awards: Varies.

648 • Foundation for Surgical Technology Advanced Education/Medical Mission Scholarship

Purpose: To help practitioners with continuing education or medical missionary work.

Eligibility: Applicants must be active AST members, document the educational program or mission program and provide two recommendation letters.

How to Apply: Applications are available online.
Deadline: Varies.
Amount: Varies.
Number of Awards: Varies.

649 • Foundation for Surgical Technology Student Scholarship

Purpose: To help surgical technology students in CAAHEP-accredited surgical technology programs.

Eligibility: Applicants must be currently enrolled in a surgical technology program accredited by the Commission on Accreditation of Allied Health Education Programs (CAAHEP). Applicants must also demonstrate academic achievement and financial need. Applications, transcripts and an instructor evaluation are required.

How to Apply: Applications are available online.
Deadline: April 1.
Amount: Varies.
Number of Awards: Varies.

650 • Thompson Delmar Learning Student Scholarship

Purpose: To support surgical technology students.

Eligibility: The award is based on academic achievement and writing skills. Applicants must plan to attend or currently attend a CAAHEP-accredited program. Applications and progress reports are required.

How to Apply: Applications are available online.
Deadline: April 1.
Amount: $1,000.
Number of Awards: 1.

Autism Society of America

7910 Woodmont Avenue, Suite 300
Bethesda, MD 20814-3067
Phone: 800-328-8476
Email: chapters@autism-society.org
Website: http://www.autism-society.org

651 • Collins Scholarship

Purpose: To fund graduate and post-doctoral study in the prevention and cure of of autism.

Eligibility: ASA members must submit nominations, and preference is given to students who are ASA members. Accomplishments must have been achieved within the previous year.

How to Apply: Applications available online.
Deadline: March 14.
Amount: $1,000.
Number of Awards: 1.

California Nurses Association

2000 Franklin Street
Oakland, CA 94612
Phone: 510-273-2200
Email: execoffice@calnurses.org
Website: http://www.calnurse.org

652 • Sandra R. Spaulding Memorial Scholarship

Purpose: To support diversity in nursing both in terms of ethnicity and socio-economic background.

Eligibility: Students must be accepted to an accredited second-year ADN degree program at least half-time and plan to complete the program within two years. References, financial need, professional vision and direction and participation in nursing and health-related organizations are considered.

How to Apply: Applications are available online.
Deadline: July 1.
Amount: Varies.
Number of Awards: Varies.

Common Knowledge Scholarship Foundation

P.O. Box 290361
Davie, FL 33329-0361
Website: http://www.cksf.org

653 • National Nursing Scholarship - College

Purpose: To reward nursing students based on their knowledge.
Eligibility: Applicants must complete the free online registration and compete by taking a series of short multiple-choice online quizzes about nursing. Each week, the quiz will have 15 to 25 questions. The winner is determined through a combination of time and accuracy in answering the questions.
How to Apply: Applicants must complete the free online registration and then answer questions.
Deadline: March 11.
Amount: $500.
Number of Awards: 1.

654 • National Nursing Scholarship - High School

Purpose: To reward high school students interested in a career in nursing.
Eligibility: Applicants must compete by taking a series of short multiple-choice online quizzes about nursing. Each week, the quiz will consist of 15 to 25 questions. The winner is determined through a combination of time and accuracy in answering the questions.
How to Apply: Applicants must complete the free online registration and then answer questions.
Deadline: February 11.
Amount: $500.
Number of Awards: 1.

Crohn's and Colitis Foundation of America Inc.

386 Park Avenue South
17th floor
New York, NY 10016
Phone: 800-932-2423
Email: info@ccfa.org
Website: http://www.ccfa.org

655 • Student Research Fellowship Award

Purpose: To stimulate interest in research careers in inflammatory bowel disease by providing salary support for research projects.
Eligibility: Applicants must be undergraduate, graduate or medical students not yet engaged in thesis research. Students must attend an accredited North American school and conduct their research with a mentor. The planned research project must last at least 10 weeks and must be relevant to IBD.
How to Apply: Applications are available online.
Deadline: March 15.
Amount: $2,500.
Number of Awards: Up to 16.

DeMolay Foundation

10200 NW Ambassador Drive
Kansas City, MO 64153
Phone: 800-336-6529
Fax: 816-891-9062
Email: demolay@demolay.org
Website: http://www.demolay.org

656 • Grotto Scholarships

Purpose: To assist medical students.
Eligibility: Applicants must be enrolled in a dental, medical or pre-medical program at an accredited institution but do not need to be active members of DeMolay. Students should complete an application and submit it to the DeMolay Service and Leadership Center.
How to Apply: Applications are available online.
Deadline: April 1.
Amount: $1,500.
Number of Awards: 4.

Emergency Nurses Association

915 Lee Street
Des Plaines, IL 60016
Phone: 847-460-4100
Fax: 847-460-4004
Email: foundation@ena.org
Website: http://www.ena.org

657 • ENA Foundation Undergraduate Scholarship

Purpose: To promote research and education in emergency care.
Eligibility: Applicants must be nurses pursuing baccalaureate degrees in nursing and must have been ENA members for at least 12 months before applying. Selection is based on application, statement of goals, references and transcript.
How to Apply: Applications are available online.
Deadline: June 1.
Amount: $2,000-$5,000.
Number of Awards: 7.

658 • Karen O'Neil Endowed Advanced Nursing Practice Scholarship

Purpose: To promote advanced degrees in emergency nursing.
Eligibility: Applicants must be nurses pursuing an advanced degree and must have been ENA members for at least 12 months before applying.
How to Apply: Applications are available online.
Deadline: June 1.
Amount: $3,000.
Number of Awards: 1.

659 • Medtronic Physio-Control Advanced Nursing Practice Scholarship

Purpose: Monetary assistance for an advanced degree is awarded to an emergency nurse. Priority is given to those pursuing careers in cardiac nursing.
Eligibility: Applicants must be nurses pursuing advanced clinical practice degrees to become clinical nurse specialists or nurse practitioners. Preference is given to applicants focusing on cardiac nursing. Applicants must have been ENA members for at least 12 months before applying.

How to Apply: Applications are available online.
Deadline: June 1.
Amount: $3,000.
Number of Awards: 1.

Epilepsy Foundation

8301 Professional Place
Landover, MD 20785
Phone: 800-332-1000
Email: researchwebsupport@efa.org
Website: http://www.epilepsyfoundation.org

660 • Behavioral Sciences Student Fellowship

Purpose: To encourage students to pursue careers in epilepsy research or practice settings.
Eligibility: Applicants must be undergraduate or graduate students in the behavioral sciences, have an epilepsy-related study, have a qualified mentor who can supervise the project and have an interest in careers in epilepsy research or practice settings. The project must be in the U.S. and should not be for dissertation research. The award is based on the quality of the project, relevance to epilepsy, interest in epilepsy, and the quality of the proposed lab or facility. Applicants must submit three recommendation letters, statement of intent, biographical sketch and research plan.
How to Apply: Application materials are described online.
Deadline: March 1.
Amount: $3,000.
Number of Awards: Varies.

661 • Health Sciences Student Fellowship

Purpose: To encourage students to pursue careers in epilepsy in either research or practice settings.
Eligibility: Applicants must be enrolled in medical school, a doctoral program or other graduate program; have an epilepsy-related study; have a qualified mentor who can supervise the project and have access to a lab or clinic to conduct the project. The project must be in the U.S. and should not be for dissertation research. The award is based on the quality of the project, relevance of the project to epilepsy, applicant's interest in epilepsy, applicant's qualifications and the quality of the lab or clinic. Applicants should submit three recommendation letters, statement of intent, biographical sketch and research plan.
How to Apply: Applications are available online.
Deadline: March 1.
Amount: $3,000.
Number of Awards: Varies.

Foundation for Surgical Technology

6 West Dry Creek Circle
Suite 200
Littleton, CO 80120
Phone: 800-637-7433
Fax: 888-627-8018
Website: http://www.ffst.org

662 • Surgical Technology Scholarships

Purpose: To offer assistance to those who seek a career in surgical technology.
Eligibility: Applicants must be currently enrolled in a surgical technology program accredited by the Commission of Accreditation of Allied Health Education Programs. Both academic ability and financial need must be demonstrated.

How to Apply: Applications are available online.
Deadline: April 1.
Amount: Varies.
Number of Awards: Varies.

Howard Hughes Medical Institute

4000 Jones Bridge Road
Chevy Chase, MD 20815-6789
Phone: 800-448-4882
Fax: 301-215-8888
Email: fellows@hhmi.org
Website: http://www.hhmi.org

663 • Research Training Fellowships for Medical Students (Medical Fellows Program)

Purpose: To support a year of full-time biomedical research training for medical and dental students.
Eligibility: Applicants must be enrolled in a U.S. medical school or dental school, and the fellowship research may be conducted at an academic or nonprofit institution in the United States or abroad if the fellow's mentor is affiliated with a U.S. institution. The research should focus on biological processes or disease mechanisms. The fellowship is based on the applicant's ability, potential research career as a physician/scientist and training. Applicants must submit research plans, personal statements, letters of reference, transcripts and MCAT or DAT scores.
How to Apply: Applications are available online.
Deadline: January 11.
Amount: $25,000.
Number of Awards: Up to 60.

Howard Hughes Medical Institute Research Scholars

1 Cloister Court, Building 60
Bethesda, MD 20814-1460
Phone: 800-424-9924
Email: research_scholars@hhmi.org
Website: http://www.hhmi.org/research/cloister/

664 • HHMI-NIH Research Scholars (Cloister Program)

Purpose: To award fellowships to medical students.
Eligibility: Applicants must be enrolled in a U.S. medical school or dental school but not in M.D./Ph.D., D.D.S./Ph.D. or Ph.D. programs or have an M.D. or Ph.D. in lab-based biological sciences. Recipients will conduct research at the National Institutes of Health in Bethesda, MD. Research experience is not required. Applicants should submit research areas of interest, personal statements, professional activities, awards, publications (optional), letters of reference, undergraduate and medical or dental school transcripts and MCAT or DAT scores.
How to Apply: Applications are available online.
Deadline: January 10.
Amount: $25,000.
Number of Awards: Varies.

Huntington's Disease Society of America

505 Eighth Avenue, Suite 902
New York, NY 10018
Phone: 800-345-4372
Fax: 212-239-3430

Email: rgraze@hdsa.org
Website: http://www.hdsa.org

665 • HDSA Research Fellowships

Purpose: To help postdoctoral researchers in the early stages of their careers.

Eligibility: Applicants must have M.D. or Ph.D. degrees and work on clinical or basic research projects related to Huntington's Disease. Candidates should submit a research and training plan summary, budget, biography and letter of support.

How to Apply: Applications are available online.

Deadline: May 1.

Amount: $40,000.

Number of Awards: Varies.

International Order of the King's Daughters and Sons

Director
P.O. Box 1040
Chautauqua, NY 14722
Website: http://www.iokds.org

666 • Health Careers Scholarship

Purpose: To assist students interested in pursuing health careers.

Eligibility: Applicants must be full-time students pursuing a career in medicine, dentistry, nursing, pharmacy, physical or occupational therapy or medical technologies. R.N. students and those pursuing an M.D. or D.D.S must have completed at least one year of schooling at an accredited institution. All others must be entering at least their third year of school. Pre-med students are not eligible. Applicants must be U.S. or Canadian citizens.

How to Apply: Applications are available by sending a self-addressed, stamped legal size envelope.

Deadline: April 1.

Amount: $1,000.

Number of Awards: Varies.

National Association of Pediatric Nurse Practitioners (NAPNAP)

20 Brace Road
Suite 200
Cherry Hill, NJ 08034-2634
Phone: 856-857-9700
Fax: 856-857-1600
Email: info@napnap.org
Website: http://www.napnap.org

667 • McNeil Rural Health Scholarship

Purpose: To improve pediatric health care provided by pediatric nurse practitioners.

Eligibility: Applicants must be enrolled in a full-time master's degree PNP program, plan to work in a rural area for two years after graduating, be a registered nurse with one year of pediatrics experience (other experience may be considered), have financial need and be a NAPNAP member. An application and RN license are required.

How to Apply: Applications are available online.

Deadline: June 30.

Amount: $20,000.

Number of Awards: Varies.

National Black Nurses Association

8630 Fenton Street
Suite 330
Silver Spring, MD 20910
Phone: 301-589-3200
Fax: 301-589-3223
Email: NBNA@erols.com
Website: http://www.nbna.org

668 • Annual NBNA Scholarships

Purpose: To promote excellence in education and in continuing education programs for African American nurses and allied health professionals.

Eligibility: Applicants must be currently enrolled in a nursing program and be in good academic standing, be members of the NBNA, be members of a local chapter and have at least a full year of school remaining. Applicants must submit with their application a five page written essay, references, an official transcript and evidence of participation in student nurse activities and involvement in the African American Community.

How to Apply: Applications are available online.

Deadline: April 15.

Amount: $500-$2,000.

Number of Awards: Varies.

National Community Pharmacists Association

NCPA Foundation
100 Daingerfield Road
Alexandria, VA 22314
Phone: 703-683-8200
Fax: 703-683-3619
Email: info@ncpanet.org
Website: http://www.ncpanet.org

669 • NCPA Foundation Presidential Scholarship

Purpose: To support students who plan to enter the pharmaceutical field.

Eligibility: Applicants must be student members of NCPA and enrolled in a U.S. school or college of pharmacy full-time. Selection is based on academic achievement and leadership.

How to Apply: Applications are available online.

Deadline: March 1.

Amount: $2,000.

Number of Awards: Varies.

National Environmental Health Association and the American Academy of Sanitarians

NEHA/AAS Scholarship
Scholarship Coordinator
720 S. Colorado Boulevard, Suite 970
Denver, CO 80246
Phone: 303-756-9090
Fax: 303-691-9490
Email: cdimmitt@neha.org
Website: http://www.neha.org

670 • NEHA/AAS Scholarship Awards

Purpose: To support students planning careers in environmental health.

Eligibility: Applicants must be either undergraduate or graduate students. The undergraduate scholarships are to be used during the junior or senior year at an Environmental Health Accreditation Council (EHAC) or NEHA member school. The graduate scholarship is available to applicants who are enrolled in a graduate program of studies in environmental health sciences and/or public health.

How to Apply: Applications are available online.
Deadline: February 1.
Amount: Varies.
Number of Awards: Varies.

National Federation of Music Clubs Bullock and Robertson Awards

Anita Louise Steele
Gilden School of Music
Ohio University
Athens, OH 45701
Phone: 740-593-4249
Fax: 317-638-0503
Email: steelea@ohio.edu
Website: http://www.nfmc-music.org

671 • NFMC Dorothy Dann Bullock Music Therapy Award and the NFMC Ruth B. Robertson Music Therapy Award

Purpose: To assist students who plan to enter careers in music therapy.

Eligibility: Applicants must be college students majoring in Music Therapy in schools approved by the National Association of Music Therapists and AMTA. Selection is based on musical talent, skills and training, with an emphasis on piano ability in accompanying and sight reading. Self-reliance, leadership, ability to work with groups and dedication to Music Therapy as a career are also considered. Applicants must be members of the National Federation of Music Clubs.

How to Apply: Applications are available online.
Deadline: March 1.
Amount: $750-$1,000.
Number of Awards: Varies.

National Gerontological Nursing Association (NGNA)

7794 Grow Drive
Pensacola, FL 32514-7072
Phone: 800-723-0560
Fax: 850-484-8762
Website: http://www.ngna.org

672 • Mary Opal Wolanin Scholarship

Purpose: To award gerontology and geriatric nursing undergraduate and graduate students.

Eligibility: For the undergraduate scholarship, applicants must be full- or part-time nursing students in an accredited U.S. school of nursing and must plan to work in a gerontology or geriatric setting. For the graduate scholarship, applicants must be nursing students with a major in gerontology or geriatric nursing at an accredited U.S. nursing program and carry a minimum of six credits. Applicants

must submit two recommendation letters, transcripts, professional/educational statements and financial statements.

How to Apply: Applications are available online.
Deadline: June 1.
Amount: $1,500.
Number of Awards: 2.

National Health Service Corps

U.S. Department of Health and Human Services
200 Independence Avenue SW
Washington, DC 20201
Phone: 800-638-0824
Email: nhsc@hrsa.gov
Website: http://nhsc.bhpr.hrsa.gov

673 • NHSC Scholarship

Purpose: To aid students committed to providing health care in communities of great need.

Eligibility: Applicants must be enrolled or accepted into allopathic or osteopathic medical schools, family nurse practitioner programs, nurse-midwifery programs, physician assistant programs or dental school. Upon completion of training, scholars must choose practice sites in federally designated health professional shortage areas for one year for each year of support received.

How to Apply: Applications are available by telephone request.
Deadline: March.
Amount: Award covers tuition and fees.
Number of Awards: Varies.

National Institutes of Health

Office of Loan Repayment and Scholarship
2 Center Drive
MSC 0230
Bethesda, MD 20892-0230
Phone: 800-528-7689
Fax: 301-480-3123
Email: ugsp@nih.gov
Website: http://www.ugsp.nih.gov

674 • NIH Undergraduate Scholarship Program for Students from Disadvantaged Backgrounds

Purpose: To develop new health-related researchers and to give disadvantaged students research opportunities that they might not have otherwise.

Eligibility: Applicants must be planning a career in biomedical, behavioral or social science health-related research, have financial need, have a minimum 3.5 GPA or be within the top 5 percent of their class and attend an accredited school. For every year that students receive the scholarship, they must attend a summer training program and work for one year at the NIH.

How to Apply: Applications are available online.
Deadline: February 28.
Amount: Up to $20,000.
Number of Awards: Up to 15.

National Medical Fellowships Inc.

5 Hanover Square
15th Floor
New York, NY 10004
Phone: 212-483-8880

Email: info@nmfonline.org
Website: http://www.nmfonline.org

675 • Need-Based Scholarship Program

Purpose: To help first- and second-year minority medical students.

Eligibility: Applicants must be African American, Mexican American, Native American, Alaska Native, Native Hawaiian or mainland Puerto Rican students accepted by accredited U.S. medical schools for M.D. or D.O. degrees. Select programs are open to third-year students. Applications, transcripts, recommendation letters and financial documents are required.

How to Apply: Applications are available online, by mail and from the medical schools.

Deadline: June 30.

Amount: $10,000.

Number of Awards: Varies.

National Safety Council

Scholarship Committee
CSHEMA Division, National Safety Council
1121 Spring Lake Drive
Itasca, IL 60143
Phone: 630-775-2227
Fax: 630-285-1315
Email: info@nsc.org
Website: http://www.nsc.org

676 • Campus Safety Health And Environmental Management Association Scholarship

Purpose: To encourage the study of safety.

Eligibility: Applicants must be full-time undergraduate or graduate students with at least one year left in their degree program. Applicants must also write an essay about health, safety or environmental issues relevant to the university or college campus.

How to Apply: Applications are available online.

Deadline: March 31.

Amount: $2,000.

Number of Awards: 1.

National Society Daughters of the American Revolution

1776 D Street NW
Washington, DC 20006
Phone: 202-628-1776
Website: http://www.dar.org

677 • Alice W. Rooke Scholarship And Irene And Daisy MacGregor Memorial Scholarship

Purpose: To assist students in becoming medical doctors.

Eligibility: Applicants must be accepted into or enrolled in a graduate course of study to become a medical doctor. Those pursuing study in psychiatric nursing at the graduate level at a medical school may also apply to the Irene and Daisy MacGregor Memorial Scholarship. Preference is given to females.

How to Apply: Applications are available by written request.

Deadline: April 15.

Amount: $5,000.

Number of Awards: 2.

678 • Caroline E. Holt Nursing Scholarship

Purpose: To support students who are studying to become nurses.

Eligibility: Applicants must demonstrate financial need and attend a school of nursing.

How to Apply: Applications are available by written request.

Deadline: February 15 and August 15.

Amount: $500.

Number of Awards: 1.

679 • Madeline Pickett (Halbert) Cogswell Nursing Scholarship

Purpose: To support nursing students.

Eligibility: Applicants must desire to attend or be attending an accredited school of nursing. Applicants must be members, descendents of members or eligible for membership in NSDAR. Applicants must put their DAR Member Number on the Application.

How to Apply: Applications are available by written request.

Deadline: February 15 and August 15.

Amount: $500.

Number of Awards: 1.

680 • Mildred Nutting Nursing Scholarship

Purpose: To support students who are studying to become nurses.

Eligibility: Applicants must have been accepted or are currently enrolled in an accredited school of nursing. Preference will be given to candidates from the greater Lowell, MA area.

How to Apply: Applications are available by written request.

Deadline: February 15 and August 15.

Amount: $500.

Number of Awards: 1.

681 • Occupational/Physical Therapy Scholarship

Purpose: To support students who are studying occupational or physical therapy.

Eligibility: Applicants must have financial need and have been accepted or are attending an accredited school of occupational or physical therapy (including art or music therapy).

How to Apply: Applications are available by written request.

Deadline: February 15 and August 15.

Amount: $500.

Number of Awards: 1.

National Strength and Conditioning Association (NSCA) Foundation

1885 Bob Johnson Drive
Colorado Springs, CO 80906
Phone: 800-815-6826
Fax: 719-632-6367
Email: nsca@nsca-lift.org
Website: http://www.nsca-lift.org

682 • Women's Scholarship

Purpose: To encourage women to enter the field of strength and conditioning.

Eligibility: Applicants should be women age 17 and older who have been accepted by an accredited institution for a graduate degree in strength and conditioning. Applicants must be NSCA members and plan to pursue careers in strength and conditioning. A cover letter

of application, application form, resume, transcript, three letters of recommendation and essay are required. The award is based on grades, strength and conditioning experience, NSCA involvement, awards, community involvement, essay and recommendations.
How to Apply: Application materials are described online.
Deadline: March 15.
Amount: $1,000.
Number of Awards: 2.

National Student Nurses' Association

45 Main Street
Suite 606
Brooklyn, NY 11201
Phone: 718-210-0705
Fax: 718-210-0710
Email: nsna@nsna.org
Website: http://www.nsna.org

683 • National Student Nurses' Association Scholarship

Purpose: To promote interest in the nursing field.
Eligibility: Applicants must be currently enrolled in a state-approved school of nursing or pre-nursing in associate degree, baccalaureate, diploma, doctorate or master's programs.
How to Apply: Applications are available online.
Deadline: January 20.
Amount: $1,000-$2,000.
Number of Awards: Varies.

Neuroscience Nursing Foundation (NNF)

4700 W. Lake Avenue
Glenview, IL 60025
Phone: 888-557-2266
Email: info@aann.org
Website: http://www.aann.org

684 • NNF Scholarship Program

Purpose: To promote excellence in neuroscience nursing.
Eligibility: Applicants must be registered nurses pursuing undergraduate or graduate studies to enter a career in neuroscience nursing. In addition to the application, applicants must submit resumes, transcripts and RN license.
How to Apply: Applications are available online.
Deadline: January 15.
Amount: $1,500.
Number of Awards: Varies.

Oncology Nursing Society

ONS Foundation
125 Enterprise Drive
Pittsburgh, PA 15275
Phone: 412-921-7373
Website: http://www.ons.org

685 • Bachelor's Scholarships

Purpose: To improve oncology nursing by assisting RNs in furthering their education.
Eligibility: Applicants must have a current license to practice as an RN, demonstrate an interest in and commitment to oncology nursing or be currently enrolled in an undergraduate nursing degree

program in a school of nursing recognized by the National League for Nursing or the Commission on Collegiate Nursing Education.
How to Apply: Applications are available online or by email request.
Deadline: February 1.
Amount: $2,000.
Number of Awards: Varies.

Pacers Foundation

125 S. Pennsylvania Street
Indianapolis, IN 46204
Phone: 317-917-2864
Fax: 317-917-2599
Email: foundation@pacers.com
Website: http://www.nba.com/pacers/news/Foundation_Index. html

686 • Linda Craig Memorial Scholarship Presented by St. Vincent Sports Medicine

Purpose: To support students interested in sports medicine, physical therapy and related fields.
Eligibility: Applicants must U.S. citizens who have completed at least four semesters of an undergraduate program majoring in medicine, sports medicine, physical therapy or a related area. They must have a GPA of at least 3.0 and demonstrate outstanding character, integrity and leadership. Applicants may not have received a full scholarship from any other organization.
How to Apply: Applications are available online.
Deadline: July 1.
Amount: Varies.
Number of Awards: Varies.

Physician Assistant Foundation

PA Foundation Scholarship Committee
950 North Washington Street
Alexandria, VA 22314
Phone: 703-836-2272
Fax: 703-684-1924
Email: aapa@aapa.org
Website: http://www.aapa.org

687 • Physician Assistant Foundation Scholarship

Purpose: To support physician assistants.
Eligibility: Applicants must be AAPA members and currently enrolled in the professional phase of a PA training program at an ARC-PA-accredited physician assistant program. Applicants are judged on the basis of financial need, community and professional involvement, goals, and academic performance.
How to Apply: Applications are available online.
Deadline: February 1.
Amount: Varies.
Number of Awards: Varies.

Sertoma International

1912 E. Meyer Boulevard
Kansas City, MO 64132
Phone: 816-333-8300
Fax: 816-333-4320
Email: infosertoma@sertoma.org
Website: http://www.sertoma.org

#688 • Sertoma Communicative Disorders Scholarship

Purpose: To fund graduate students of audiology and speech-language pathology in the U.S., Canada or Mexico.

Eligibility: Applicants must be citizens and/or permanent residents of the U.S. and its territories, Canada or Mexico. Applicants must also be full-time students accepted into a graduate level program in speech language pathology and/or audiology at a college in the U.S. or Canada recognized by ASHA's Council and have a minimum 3.2 overall GPA in all undergraduate and graduate-level courses.

How to Apply: Applications are available online.

Deadline: March 30.

Amount: $2,500.

Number of Awards: 30.

Society of Nuclear Medicine

Development Office
1850 Samuel Morse Drive
Reston, VA 20190
Phone: 703-708-9000
Email: grantinfo@snm.org
Website: http://www.snm.org

#689 • Paul Cole Scholarship Award

Purpose: To promote excellence in healthcare through the support of education and research in nuclear medicine.

Eligibility: Applicants must have a minimum 2.5 GPA, be college undergraduates and be in the nuclear medicine field.

How to Apply: Applications are available online.

Deadline: October 15.

Amount: $1,000.

Number of Awards: 24.

Tylenol

Phone: 877-895-3665
Website: http://tylenolscholarship.com

#690 • Tylenol Scholarship

Purpose: Each year Tylenol gives away $250,000 in scholarships to college and graduate students pursuing careers in healthcare.

Eligibility: Applicants must major or intend to major in a healthcare-related area.

How to Apply: Applications are available online.

Deadline: September 15.

Amount: $1,000-$5,000.

Number of Awards: 120.

U.S. Department of Health and Human Services National Institutes of Health

2 Center Drive
Room 2E30
MSC 0230
Bethesda, MD 20892
Phone: 800-528-7689
Fax: 301-480-3123
Email: ugsp@nih.gov
Website: http://www.ugsp.nih.gov

#691 • NIH Undergraduate Scholarship Program

Purpose: To offer competitive scholarships to students who are committed to careers in biomedical, behavioral and social science health-related research.

Eligibility: Applicants must be enrolled or accepted for enrollment as full-time students at an accredited undergraduate institution, have an underprivileged background and have a minimum 3.5 GPA or be within the top 5 percent of their class. Applicants must also show a commitment to pursuing careers in biomedical, behavioral and social science research at the NIH.

How to Apply: Applications are available online.

Deadline: February 28.

Amount: $20,000.

Number of Awards: 15.

United States Public Health Service

Health Resources and Services Administration
5600 Fishers Lane
Rockville, MD 20857
Website: http://bhpr.hrsa.gov/dsa

#692 • Health Resources and Services Administration-Bureau of Health Professions Scholarships for Disadvantaged Students

Purpose: To support students from disadvantaged backgrounds who are pursuing health-related careers.

Eligibility: Applicants must be full-time students, be from a disadvantaged background, demonstrate financial need and be studying in a health field, including medicine, nursing, veterinary medicine, dentistry, pharmacy and others. They must be U.S. citizens, nationals or permanent residents. All other criteria are set by individual schools.

How to Apply: Applications are available from participating schools.

Deadline: Varies.

Amount: Up to the full cost of schooling plus living allowance.

Number of Awards: Varies.

Related Scholarships:

American Legion Auxiliary, Department of California

See #1217 • Past Presidents' Parley Nursing Scholarships

New Hampshire Postsecondary Education Commission

See #1463 • Workforce Incentive Program

Maryland Higher Education Commission

See #1397 • Graduate and Professional Scholarship Program

American Dental Association Foundation

See #271 • Dental Student Scholarship

American Dental Association Foundation

See #270 • Allied Dental Health Scholarships

American Dental Association Foundation

See #272 • Minority Dental Student Scholarship

American Federation of Teachers

See #1595 • Robert G. Porter Scholars Program

Presbyterian Church (USA)

See #1104 • Grant Programs for Medical Studies

New York State Higher Education Services Corporation

See #1484 • Regents Health Care Opportunity Scholarships

Maryland Higher Education Commission

See #1404 • State Nursing Scholarship

Medical Library Association

See #589 • MLA Scholarship

Association for Food and Drug Officials

See #479 • Association for Food and Drug Officials Scholarship Fund

American Physiological Society

See #177 • David S. Bruce Awards for Excellence in Undergraduate Research

Healthcare Information and Management Systems Society

See #257 • HIMSS Foundation Scholarship

Huntington's Disease Society of America

See #192 • Don King Student Fellowship

National Association of Hispanic Nurses

See #1022 • Juanita Robles-Lopez

Medical Library Association

See #591 • MLA/NLM Spectrum Scholarship

American Physiological Society

See #945 • Explorations Summer Research Fellowships

American Physiological Society

See #1123 • Undergraduate Student Summer Research Fellowships

National Medical Fellowships Inc. California Community Service Scholarship

See #1248 • California Community Service Scholarship Program

National Association of Hispanic Nurses

See #1023 • NAHN Scholarship

Military/Police/Fire

Also See Scholarships Listed Under:
Leadership

1st Marine Division Association Inc.

410 Pier View Way
Oceanside, CA 92054
Phone: 877-967-8561
Fax: 760-967-8567
Email: oldbreed@sbcglobal.net
Website: http://www.1stmarinedivisionassociation.org

693 • 1st Marine Division Association Scholarship

Purpose: To provide financial aid to undergraduate students who are the dependents of deceased or disabled veterans of the 1st Marine Division.

Eligibility: Applicants must be dependents of honorably discharged veterans of the 1st Marine Division or units attached to or supporting the Division who are now deceased or totally and permanently disabled for any reason. Applicants must attend an accredited university as full-time undergraduate students.

How to Apply: Applications are available online.
Deadline: Varies.
Amount: Up to $1,500.
Number of Awards: Varies.

25th Infantry Division Association (TIDA)

P.O. Box 7
Flourtown, PA 19031
Website: http://www.25thida.com

694 • Education Memorial Scholarship Awards / George and Rosemary Murray Scholarship Award

Purpose: To aid in the education of the members of the 25th Infantry Division Association or the children and grandchildren of active and former members of the association.

Eligibility: Applicants must be high school seniors who are the child or grandchild of an active association member, the child of a former member who died during combat with the Division or an active member who will be discharged before the end of the award year. Selection is based on future plans, school activities, interests, financial status and academic achievement.

How to Apply: Applications are available throughout the year in Tropic Lightning Flashes, the quarterly newsletter of the 25th Infantry Division Association.
Deadline: April 1.
Amount: Up to $1,500.
Number of Awards: Varies.

Aerospace Education Foundation

1501 Lee Highway
Arlington, VA 22209
Phone: 800-291-8480
Fax: 703-247-5853
Email: aefstaff@aef.org
Website: http://www.afa.org

695 • Air Force Spouse Scholarship

Purpose: This scholarship provides aid to Air Force spouses who plan to pursue associate's, bachelor's or graduate degrees.

Eligibility: Applicants must be the spouses of members of the Air Force Active Duty, Air National Guard or Air Force Reserve and attend a college or university in the current academic year. However, spouses who are themselves Air Force members or in ROTC are not eligible.

How to Apply: Applications are available online.
Deadline: January 30.
Amount: $1,000.
Number of Awards: 30.

Air Force Aid Society Inc.

Education Assistance Department
241 18th Street S., Suite 202
Arlington, VA 22202
Phone: 800-429-9475
Fax: 703-607-3022
Website: http://www.afas.org

696 • General Henry H. Arnold Education Grant Program

Purpose: To help Air Force members and their families realize their academic goals.

Eligibility: Applicants must be the dependent sons and daughters of Air Force members, spouses of active duty members or surviving spouses of Air Force members who died while on active duty or in retired status. They must also be high school graduates enrolled or accepted as full-time undergraduates for the following school year and maintain a minimum 2.0 GPA.

How to Apply: Applications are available online.
Deadline: March 9.
Amount: $2,000.
Number of Awards: Varies.

Air Force Reserve Officer Training Corps

AFROTC Admissions
551 E. Maxwell Boulevard
Maxwell AFB, AL 36112-5917
Phone: 866-423-7682
Fax: 334-953-6167
Website: http://www.afrotc.com

697 • Air Force ROTC College Scholarship

Purpose: To help students with financial need who are also interested in joining the Air Force pay for college.

Eligibility: Applicants must pass the physical fitness assessment and demonstrate academic achievement or outstanding leadership skills. There are three types of award: one that pays full tuition, most fees and for books, one that pays tuition up to $15,000, most fees and for books and one that pays full tuition at a college or university that costs less than $9,000 per year. In return for the scholarship, recipients must serve in the Air Force.

How to Apply: Applications are available online.
Deadline: December 1.
Amount: Varies.
Number of Awards: Varies.

American Criminal Justice Association

P.O. Box 601047
Sacramento, CA 95860
Phone: 916-484-6553
Fax: 916-488-2227
Email: acjalae@aol.com
Website: http://www.acjalae.org

698 • ACJA/Lambda Alpha Epsilon Scholarship

Purpose: To assist criminal justice students.

Eligibility: Applicants must be undergraduate or graduate students who are studying criminal justice. Students must be ACJA/LAE members, but they may submit a membership form at the time of application. Applicants must have completed at least two semesters or three quarters of their education while earning at least a 3.0 GPA.

How to Apply: Applications are available online and by written request.

Deadline: December 31.

Amount: $100-$400.

Number of Awards: Varies.

699 • Student Paper Competition

Purpose: To encourage scholarship in criminal justice students.

Eligibility: Applicants must be student members of the American Criminal Justice Association-Lambda Alpha Epsilon and submit an original paper on criminology, law enforcement, juvenile justice, courts, corrections, prevention, planning and evaluation or career development and education in the field of criminal justice. Students may apply for membership along with their paper submission.

How to Apply: Applications are available online and by written request.

Deadline: January 31.

Amount: $50-$150.

Number of Awards: Varies.

American Legion Auxiliary

777 North Meridian Street
Third Floor
Indianapolis, IN 46204-1420
Phone: 317-955-3845
Fax: 317-955-3884
Email: alahq@legion-aux.org
Website: http://www.legion-aux.org

700 • National President Scholarship

Purpose: To support students who are the children of veterans who served in the Armed Forces with the American Legion.

Eligibility: Applicants must complete 50 hours of volunteer service and be the sons or daughters of veterans who served in the Armed Forces during eligibility dates for membership in the American Legion. Awards are based on character, essay, application, leadership, financial need and scholarship.

How to Apply: Applications are available online.

Deadline: March 1.

Amount: $1,000-$2,500.

Number of Awards: 10.

701 • National President's Scholarship

Purpose: To award scholarships to children of veterans who served in the Armed Forces.

Eligibility: Applicants must be the daughters or sons of veterans who served in the Armed Forces for membership in The American Legion, be high school seniors and complete 50 hours of community service. Selection is based on character, application/essay, scholastic achievement, leadership and financial need.

How to Apply: Applications are available online.

Deadline: March 10.

Amount: $2,000-$2,500.

Number of Awards: 2 per Division.

American Military Retirees Association

5436 Peru Street
Suite 1
Plattsburg, NY 12901
Phone: 800-424-2969
Fax: 518-324-5204
Email: info@amra1973.org
Website: http://www.amra1973.org

702 • Sergeant Major Douglas R. Drum Memorial Scholarship Fund

Purpose: To provide funds for members of the AMRA or their dependents, children or grandchildren for tuition, room and board or books.

Eligibility: Applicants must be current members of the AMRA or the dependent, child or grandchild of a current member.

How to Apply: Applications are available online.

Deadline: August 2.

Amount: Varies.

Number of Awards: Varies.

American Society of Criminology Gene Carte Student Paper Competition

Nancy Rodriguez
Department of Criminology and Criminal Justice, Arizona State University West
4701 W. Thunderbird Road
Glendale, AZ 85306
Phone: 602-543-6601
Fax: 602-543-6658
Email: nancy.rodriguez@asu.edu
Website: http://www.asc41.com

703 • Gene Carte Student Paper Competition

Purpose: To recognize outstanding student works in criminology.

Eligibility: Applicants must be full-time undergraduate or graduate students. The writing competition requires applicants to write on a topic directly related to criminology and must be accompanied by a letter signed by the dean or department chair. Other paper formatting requirements are listed on the website. The first place winner also receives a travel award.

How to Apply: There is no application form.

Deadline: April 15.

Amount: $200-$500.

Number of Awards: 3.

Anchor Scholarship Foundation

P.O. Box 9535
Norfolk, VA 23505
Phone: 757-374-3769
Email: admin@anchorscholarship.com
Website: http://www.anchorscholarship.com

704 • Anchor Scholarship Foundation Scholarship

Purpose: To assist the dependents of current and former members of the Naval Surface Forces, Atlantic and Naval Surface Forces, Pacific.

Eligibility: Applicants must be high school seniors or college students planning to attend or currently attending an accredited, four-year college or university full-time. Applicants must also be dependents of service members who are on active duty or retired and have served a minimum of six years in a unit under the administrative control of Commander, Naval Surface Forces, U.S. Atlantic Fleet or U.S. Pacific Fleet. The award is based on academics, extracurricular activities, character, all-around ability and financial need.

How to Apply: Applications are available online.
Deadline: March 15.
Amount: Varies.
Number of Awards: 35.

Armed Forces Communications and Electronics Association

4400 Fair Lakes Court
Fairfax, VA 22033
Phone: 800-336-4583
Fax: 703-631-4693
Email: scholarship@afcea.org
Website: http://www.afcea.org

705 • AFCEA General Emmett Paige Scholarships

Purpose: To offer scholarships to members of the armed forces.
Eligibility: Applicants must be on active duty in the uniformed military services, honorably discharged veterans or their spouses or dependents who are full-time students in an accredited four-year U.S. college or university. Applicants must also be U.S. citizens, majoring in electrical, computer, chemical or aerospace engineering, computer science, physics or mathematics and have a minimum 3.4 GPA. Veterans may apply for the scholarship as college freshmen. All others must apply as college sophomores or juniors.
How to Apply: Applications are available online.
Deadline: March 1.
Amount: $2,000.
Number of Awards: Varies.

706 • AFCEA ROTC Scholarships

Purpose: To assist ROTC sophomores or juniors who are majoring in aerospace engineering, electronics, computer science, computer engineering, physics or mathematics.
Eligibility: Applicants must major in electrical or aerospace engineering, electronics, computer science, computer engineering, physics or mathematics at an accredited U.S. four-year college or university. Applicants must also be enrolled full-time as college sophomores or juniors and be nominated by professors of military science, naval science or aerospace studies. Applicants must be U.S. citizens enrolled in ROTC, have good moral character, demonstrate

academic excellence and the potential to serve as an officer in the U.S. Armed Forces and have financial need.
How to Apply: Applications are available online.
Deadline: April 1.
Amount: $2,000.
Number of Awards: Varies.

707 • AFCEA Sgt Jeannette L. Winters, USMC Memorial Scholarship

Purpose: To support active duty Marine Corps members or veterans.
Eligibility: Applicants must be on active duty in the U.S. Marine Corps or honorably discharged veterans of the U.S. Marine Corps. Applicants must also be current undergraduate sophomores, juniors or seniors attending an accredited U.S. college or university majoring in electrical, aerospace or computer engineering, computer science, physics or mathematics with a minimum 3.4 GPA.
How to Apply: Applications are available online.
Deadline: September 15.
Amount: $2,000.
Number of Awards: 1.

Army Emergency Relief (AER)

200 Stovall Street Rm. 5N13
Alexandria, VA 22332
Phone: 703-428-0035
Fax: 703-325-7183
Email: education@aerhq.org
Website: http://www.aerhq.org

708 • MG James Ursano Scholarship Fund

Purpose: To assist the children of Army families with their undergraduate education, vocational training and service academy education.
Eligibility: Applicants must be dependent children of Army soldiers who are unmarried and under the age of 22. Students must also be registered with the Defense Eligibility Enrollment Reporting System, have a minimum 2.0 GPA and be enrolled and accepted or pending acceptance as full-time students in post-secondary educational institutions. Awards are based primarily on financial need.
How to Apply: Applications are available online and by mail.
Deadline: March 1.
Amount: Varies.
Number of Awards: Varies.

Blinded Veterans Association (BVA)

477 H Street, NW
Washington, DC 20001-2694
Phone: 202-371-8880
Email: bva@bva.org
Website: http://www.bva.org

709 • Kathern F. Gruber Scholarship Program

Purpose: To assist the spouses and children of blinded veterans with their higher-learning goals.
Eligibility: Applicants must be the spouses or children of a blind veteran and be accepted or enrolled at an accredited, higher learning institution.
How to Apply: Contact the BVA for application materials.
Deadline: April.
Amount: $1,000-$2,000.
Number of Awards: 4.

Chief of Naval Education and Training/ NROTC

Phone: 800-NAV-ROTC
Website: https://www.nrotc.navy.mil

710 • NROTC Scholarship Program

Purpose: To prepare young men and women for leadership roles in the Navy and Marine Corps.

Eligibility: Applicants must be U.S. citizens who are at least 17 years old as of September 1 of their first year of college, no older than 23 on June 30 of that first year and must be younger than 27 at the time of anticipated graduation. Students must attend an NROTC college and have no moral or personal convictions against military service. Those interested in the Navy program, including Nurse-option, must have an SAT critical reading score of 530 and a math score of 520 or an ACT score of 22 in English and 22 in math. For the Marine Corps option, students must have an SAT composite score of 1000 or an ACT composite score of 22. Applicants must also meet all Navy or Marine Corps physical standards.

How to Apply: Applications are available online. Contact information for regional offices is available online.

Deadline: January 31.

Amount: Full tuition and fees, books, uniforms and monthly stipend.

Number of Awards: Varies.

Daughters of the Cincinnati

National Headquarters
122 E. 58th Street
New York, NY 10022
Phone: 212-319-6915
Website: http://fdncenter.org/grantmaker/cincinnati/

711 • Daughters of the Cincinnati Scholarship

Purpose: To support daughters of Armed Services commissioned officers.

Eligibility: Applicants must be daughters of career officers in the United States Army, Navy, Air Force, Coast Guard or Marine Corps (active, retired or deceased). Daughters of reserve officers or enlisted personnel cannot apply. Applicants must also be high school seniors.

How to Apply: Applications are available by mailing the organization your parent's rank and branch of service and enclosing a self-addressed, stamped envelope.

Deadline: March 15.

Amount: $1,000-$3,000.

Number of Awards: Varies.

Dolphin Scholarship Foundation

5040 Virginia Beach Boulevard
Suite 104A
Virginia Beach, VA 23462
Phone: 757-671-3200
Fax: 757-671-3330
Email: dsfscholars@exis.net
Website: http://www.dolphinscholarship.org

712 • Dolphin Scholarship

Purpose: To assist the children of navy submariners or members.

Eligibility: Applicants must be the unmarried children or stepchildren of navy submariners or navy members who have served in submarine support activities and must be under 24 years old at the time of the application deadline. The parents must have been part of the Submarine Force for at least eight years, have served in submarine activities for at least 10 years or died on active duty while in the Submarine Force. Applicants must attend an accredited four-year college, working for a bachelor's degree.

How to Apply: Applications are available online.

Deadline: March 15.

Amount: $3,000.

Number of Awards: 25.

Explosive Ordnance Disposal (EOD) Memorial Committee

P.O. Box 594
Niceville, FL 32588
Phone: 850-729-2401
Fax: 850-729-2401
Email: admin@eodmemorial.org
Website: http://www.eodmemorial.org

713 • EOD Memorial Scholarship

Purpose: To support those connected to Explosive Ordnance Disposal (EOD) technicians.

Eligibility: Applicants must be accepted or enrolled as full-time undergraduates in a U.S. accredited two-year, four-year, or vocational school. Students must also be the family member of an active duty, guard/reserve, retired or deceased EOD technician. The award is based on academic achievement, community involvement and financial need. Applicants should submit the Free Application for Federal Student Aid form.

How to Apply: Applications are available online.

Deadline: March 1.

Amount: Varies.

Number of Awards: Varies.

Foundation of the First Cavalry Division Association

Alumni Of The First Team
302 North Main Street
Copperas Cove, TX 76522
Phone: 254-547-6537
Email: firstcav@1cda.org
Website: http://www.1cda.org/

714 • First Cavalry Division Association Scholarship

Purpose: To assist the children of 1st Cavalry troopers who have become disabled or who died while serving in the Division.

Eligibility: Applicants must be First Cavalry Division troopers who have become totally disabled while serving in the division or active duty members, their spouses or children or the spouses or children of troopers who died while in service.

How to Apply: Applications are available by request.

Deadline: Varies.

Amount: $1,000.

Number of Awards: Varies.

Fraternal Order of Eagles

1623 Gateway Circle S.
Grove City, OH 43123
Phone: 614-883-2200
Fax: 614-883-2201
Email: assistance@foe.com
Website: http://www.foe.com

715 • Fraternal Order of Eagles Memorial Foundation

Purpose: To provide financial support for post-secondary education to the children of Eagles.

Eligibility: Applicants must be the children of Eagles who lost their lives while serving in the military or in the commission of their daily employment. Applicants must have a 2.0 minimum GPA.

How to Apply: Eligible juniors in high school will be sent a form requesting post high school plans, and eligible seniors will be mailed the scholarship application form.

Deadline: Varies.

Amount: Up to $6,000.

Number of Awards: Varies.

Headquarters

U.S. Army Cadet Command
55 Patch Road
Fort Monroe, VA 23651
Email: atccps@monroe.army.mil
Website: http://www.rotc.monroe.army.mil

716 • Army ROTC Four-Year Scholarship Program

Purpose: To bolster the ranks of the Army, Army Reserve and Army National Guard by providing monetary assistance to eligible student candidates.

Eligibility: Applicants must be U.S. citizens and high school seniors, graduates or college freshmen with at least four years of college remaining who wish to attend one of 600 colleges and earn a commission. Recipients must serve in the Army for four to eight years after graduation.

How to Apply: Applications are available online.

Deadline: November 15.

Amount: Varies.

Number of Awards: Varies.

717 • Army ROTC Green To Gold Scholarship Program

Purpose: To provide scholarship funds for Army enlisted soldiers.

Eligibility: Applicants must be active duty enlisted members of the Army who wish to complete their baccalaureate degree requirements and obtain a commission. Recipients are required to serve in the U.S. Army.

How to Apply: Applications are available online.

Deadline: Varies.

Amount: Varies.

Number of Awards: Varies.

Imagine America Foundation

1101 Connecticut Avenue NW
Suite 901
Washington, DC 20036

Phone: 202-336-6724
Fax: 202-408-8102
Email: kerryt@career.org
Website: http://www.imagine-america.org

718 • Military Award Program (MAP)

Purpose: To help those who have served in the military with their education and make the transition from military to civilian life.

Eligibility: Applicants must be active duty members or honorably discharged veterans of a United States military service branch, have financial need and plan to attend one of the 500 participating career colleges. There is a list of career colleges on the website. Before applying, the applicant selects a career college and program of study. The application is sent electronically to the career college, and the career college notifies the applicant if an award is available.

How to Apply: Applications are available online.

Deadline: June 30.

Amount: $1,000.

Number of Awards: Varies.

International Association of Fire Chiefs Foundation

4025 Fair Ridge Drive
Fairfax, VA 22033-2868
Phone: 571-344-5410
Email: iafcfoun@msn.com
Website: http://www.iafcf.org

719 • IAFC Foundation Scholarship

Purpose: To assist students in fire sciences or related academic programs.

Eligibility: Applicants must be active members with a minimum of three years volunteer work, two years paid work or a combination of paid and volunteer work of three years with a state, county, provincial, municipal, community, industrial or federal fire department who will use the scholarship at an accredited institution of higher education. Students must submit application forms, statements, a list of credits and a transcript. Preference is given to those demonstrating need, desire and initiative.

How to Apply: Applications are available online.

Deadline: August 1.

Amount: $4,000.

Number of Awards: Varies.

International Military Community Executives Association (IMCEA)

1530 Dunwoody Village
Parkway Suite 203
Atlanta, GA 30338
Phone: 770-396-2101
Fax: 770-396-2198
Email: imcea@imcea.com
Website: http://www.imcea.com

720 • IMCEA Scholarships

Purpose: To provide scholarships for high school students and military welfare and recreation professionals seeking to further their educations.

Eligibility: High school or college applicants must be children of IMCEA members. Candidates must provide information about their activities, honors and awards and submit an essay on the provided topic.

How to Apply: Applications are available online.
Deadline: Varies.
Amount: Varies.
Number of Awards: Varies.

Marine Corps Scholarship Foundation

P.O. Box 3008
Princeton, NJ 08543
Phone: 800-292-7777
Fax: 609-452-2259
Email: mcsf@marine-scholars.org
Website: http://www.marine-scholars.org

721 • Marine Corps Scholarship Foundation Scholarship

Purpose: To provide financial assistance to sons and daughters of U.S. Marines and children of former Marines in their pursuit of higher education.
Eligibility: Applicants must be children of one of the following: an active duty or reserve U. S. Marine, a U.S. Marine who has received an Honorable Discharge, Medical Discharge or was killed while serving in the U.S. Marine Corps, an active duty or reserve U.S. Navy Corpsman who is serving, or has served, with the U.S. Marine Corps, a U.S. Navy Corpsman who has served with the U.S. Marine Corps and has received an Honorable Discharge, Medical Discharge or was killed while serving in the U.S. Navy. Applicants can also be grandchildren of one of the following: A U.S. Marine who served with the 4th Marine Division during World War II and is/was a member of their association, a U.S. Marine who served with the 6th Marine Division during World War II and is/was a member of their association. Applicants must be either high school graduates or undergraduate students.
How to Apply: Applications are available online.
Deadline: April 1.
Amount: Varies.
Number of Awards: Varies.

Military Order of the Purple Heart

MOPH National Headquarters
5413-B Backlick Road
Attn.: Scholarship Committee
Springfield, VA 22151
Phone: 703-642-5360
Fax: 703-642-1841
Email: info@purpleheart.org
Website: http://www.purpleheart.org

722 • Military Order of the Purple Heart Scholarship

Purpose: To recognize outstanding achievement.
Eligibility: Applicants must be the children or grandchildren of a Purple Heart recipient or of a member in good standing with the organization. Applicants must also be U.S. citizens, be high school graduates, have a 3.5 minimum GPA and be enrolled in a full-time program in a college. Applicants must write a 150-word essay on why they wish to attend college.
How to Apply: Applications are available online.
Deadline: March 31.
Amount: $1,750.
Number of Awards: Varies.

Montgomery GI Bill - Active Duty

Veterans Benefits Administration
Phone: 888-442-4551
Website: http://www.gibill.va.gov

723 • Montgomery GI Bill - Active Duty

Purpose: To provide educational benefits to veterans.
Eligibility: Applicants must have an Honorable Discharge and high school diploma and meet other service requirements. The bill provides up to 36 months of educational benefits to veterans for college, technical or vocational courses, correspondence courses, apprenticeship/job training or flight training.
How to Apply: Applications are available online.
Deadline: None.
Amount: Varies.
Number of Awards: Varies.

National Association of Blacks in Criminal Justice

North Carolina Central University
P.O. Box 19788
Durham, NC 27707
Phone: 919-683-1801
Fax: 919-683-1903
Email: office@nabcj.org
Website: http://www.nabcj.org

724 • Jonathan Jasper Wright Award

Purpose: To award regional and national leadership in the field of criminal justice.
Eligibility: Award recipients will be involved in affecting policy change. Nominator should be a member of NABCJ.
How to Apply: Nomination applications are available online.
Deadline: May 1.
Amount: Varies.
Number of Awards: Varies.

725 • Mary Church Terrell Award

Purpose: To award activism for positive change in criminal justice on city and state levels.
Eligibility: Nominator should be a member of NABCJ. Awarded to an individual who has initiated relationships with churches, courts, councils and assemblies.
How to Apply: Nomination applications are available online.
Deadline: May 1.
Amount: Varies.
Number of Awards: Varies.

726 • Medger Evers Award

Purpose: To award efforts to ensure that all people, including those in institutions, receive equal justice under the law.
Eligibility: This award honors the slain civil rights leader. Nominator should be a member of NABCJ.
How to Apply: Nomination applications are available online.
Deadline: May 1.
Amount: Varies.
Number of Awards: Varies.

727 • William L. Hastie Award

Purpose: To award demonstrations of national leadership in criminal justice and the pursuit of policy change within the field.
Eligibility: The award honors the first African American appointed to the bench in 1937 by President Franklin Roosevelt. Nominator should be a member of NABCJ.

How to Apply: Nomination applications are available online.
Deadline: May 1.
Amount: Varies.
Number of Awards: Varies.

National Black Police Association

NBPA Scholarship Award
3251 Mt. Pleasant Street NW
Washington, DC 20010
Phone: 202-986-2070
Fax: 202-986-0410
Email: nbpanatofc@worldnet.att.net
Website: http://www.blackpolice.org

728 • Alphonso Deal Scholarship Award

Purpose: To support students who plan careers in law enforcement.
Eligibility: Applicants must be collegebound high school seniors planning to study law enforcement who are U.S. citizens and are recommended by their high school principal, counselor or teacher.
How to Apply: Applications are available online.
Deadline: June 1.
Amount: Varies.
Number of Awards: Varies.

Naval Academy Women's Club

P.O. Box 826
Annapolis, MD 21404-0826
Email: navyscholars@aol.com
Website: http://www.usna.edu/WomensClub/

729 • Naval Academy Women's Club Scholarship

Purpose: To help military dependants, dependents of employees of the Naval Academy Complex, dependents of current NAWC Board Members and current members of NAWC.
Eligibility: Applicants must be high school seniors or graduates and plan to or currently attend full-time a two- or four-year undergraduate college or university, visual or performing arts school or vocational-technical school. Students must also be dependents less than 23 years old of current or past members of the U.S. Armed Forces stationed at the Naval Academy Complex, dependents less than 23 years old of civilian staff or faculty members who are currently employed, retired or deceased after full-time employment at the Naval Academy Complex, dependents less than 23 years old of a current NAWC Board Member or current regular members of NAWC for at least one year. The award is merit-based.
How to Apply: Applications are available online.
Deadline: March 31.
Amount: Varies.
Number of Awards: Varies.

Naval Special Warfare Foundation

P.O. Box 5965
Virginia Beach, VA 23471
Phone: 757-363-7490
Email: info@nswfoundation.org
Website: http://www.nswfoundation.org

730 • UDT-SEAL Scholarship

Purpose: To assist the dependents of UDT-SEAL Association members.
Eligibility: Students must be single dependents of a UDT-SEAL Association member who has served in or is serving in the U.S. Armed Forces and the Naval Special Warfare community. Selection is based on academic achievement, a written essay and extracurricular involvement.
How to Apply: Applications are available by contacting the NWSF.
Deadline: First quarter of the year.
Amount: Varies.
Number of Awards: Varies.

Navy League Foundation

2300 Wilson Boulevard
Arlington, VA 22201
Phone: 800-356-5760
Fax: 703-528-2333
Email: lhuycke@navyleague.org
Website: http://www.navyleague.org

731 • Navy League Endowed Scholarships

Purpose: To help military dependents attend college
Eligibility: Applicants must be dependents or direct descendants of an active, reserve, retired or honorably discharged member of the U.S. Navy, Coast Guard, U.S.-Flag Merchant Marine, Marine Corps or U.S. Naval Sea Cadet Corps; be high school seniors or the equivalent and enter an accredited college or university. Students should submit a list of scholastic and extracurricular activities, transcripts, no more than two recommendations, SAT or ACT scores, FAFSA information, proof of qualifying sea service duty and personal statement. There are various scholarships available.
How to Apply: Applications are available online.
Deadline: March 1.
Amount: $10,000.
Number of Awards: 22.

Navy Supply Corps Foundation Inc.

1425 Prince Avenue
Athens, GA 30606
Phone: 706-354-4111
Website: http://www.usnscf.com

732 • Navy Supply Corps Foundation Scholarship

Purpose: To provide financial aid for undergraduate studies to family members of Foundation members and enlisted Navy personnel, including reservists and retirees.
Eligibility: Applicants must be family members of a member of the Navy Supply Corps Foundation or an enlisted member, meaning active duty, reservist or retired. Awards are based on character, leadership, academic performance and financial need.
How to Apply: Applications are available online.
Deadline: April 1.
Amount: Varies.
Number of Awards: 56.

Navy-Marine Corps Relief Society

875 North Randolph Street Suite 225
Arlington, VA 22203
Phone: 703-696-4960
Fax: 703-696-0144
Email: education@hq.nmcrs.org
Website: http://www.nmcrs.org

733 • Admiral Mike Boorda Scholarship Program

Purpose: To help eligible Navy and Marine Corps members.
Eligibility: Applicants must be enrolled or planning to enroll as full-time undergraduate students at an eligible post-secondary, technical or vocational institution. Applicants must have a minimum 2.0 GPA and be active duty servicemembers accepted to the Enlisted Commissioning Program, the Marine Enlisted Commissioning Education Program or the Medical Enlisted Commissioning Program.
How to Apply: Applications are available online.
Deadline: May 1.
Amount: Varies.
Number of Awards: Varies.

734 • VADM E. P. Travers Scholarship And Loan Program

Purpose: To aid Navy and Marine Corps families.
Eligibility: Applicants must be enrolled or planning to enroll as full-time undergraduate students at an eligible post-secondary, technical or vocational institution. Applicants must also have a minimum 2.0 GPA and be unmarried dependent sons or daughters of active duty or retired Navy or Marine Corps service members or spouses of active duty Navy or Marine Corps service members.
How to Apply: Applications are available online.
Deadline: March 1.
Amount: $2,000.
Number of Awards: Varies.

Non-Commissioned Officers Association

10635 IH 35 N
San Antonio, TX 78233
Phone: 800-662-2620
Email: membsvc@ncoausa.org
Website: http://www.ncoausa.org

735 • Non-Commissioned Officers Association Scholarships

Purpose: The scholarships are given to help the children and spouses of members of the Non-Commissioned Officers Association.
Eligibility: Students must be children or spouses of members of the Non-Commissioned Officers Association. Children must be under 25 to receive the scholarship.
How to Apply: Applications are available online.
Deadline: March 31.
Amount: $900-$1,000.
Number of Awards: 16.

Reserve Officers Association of the U.S.

Ms. Chandra Oliphant
One Constitution Avenue NE
Washington, DC 20002
Phone: 202-479-2200
Fax: 202-479-0416
Email: coliphant@roa.org
Website: http://www.roa.org

736 • Henry J. Reilly Memorial Scholarship

Purpose: To help Reserve Officers Association members and their families.
Eligibility: Applicants must have registered for the draft and be members of the ROA or be the children or grandchildren of members.
How to Apply: Contact the ROA offices for application information.
Deadline: April.
Amount: $500.
Number of Awards: Varies.

Retired Officers Association (TROA)

201 N. Washington Street
Alexandria, VA 22314
Phone: 800-245-8762
Email: edassist@troa.org
Website: http://www.troa.org

737 • TROA Scholarship

Purpose: To award scholarships to children of military families.
Eligibility: Applicants must have a minimum 3.0 GPA, be under the age of 24 and be the children of a member of the uniformed services. Children of enlisted personnel are also eligible for the scholarship. Recipients are selected on the basis of scholastic ability, potential, character, leadership and financial need. Students accepting a military academy appointment are not eligible for the grants, but recipients who join the armed forces during college may have their maximum age for eligibility raised by as much as five years.
How to Apply: Applications are available online.
Deadline: March 1.
Amount: $3,000.
Number of Awards: 25.

Seabee Memorial Scholarship Association

P.O. Box 6574
Silver Spring, MD 20916
Phone: 301-570-2850
Email: smsa@erols.com
Website: http://www.seabee.org

738 • Seabee Memorial Scholarship

Purpose: To provide scholarships for sons, daughters and grandchildren of Seabees, both past and present, active, reserve or retired.
Eligibility: Applicants must be sons, daughters, step-children or grandchildren of Regular, Reserve, Retired or deceased officers or enlisted members who have served or are now serving with the Naval Construction Force or Naval Civil Engineer Corps, or who have served but have been honorably discharged. Scholarships are for bachelor's degrees.

How to Apply: Applications are available online or by written request.
Deadline: April 15.
Amount: $2,200.
Number of Awards: 89.

Seafarers International Union of North America

Ms. Kathleen Eno, Assistant Administrator
Seafarers Health and Benefits Plan-Scholarship Program
5201 Auth Way
Camp Springs, MD 20746
Phone: 301-899-0675
Fax: 301-899-7355
Website: http://www.seafarers.org

739 • Charlie Logan Scholarship Program for Seamen

Purpose: To offer scholarships to members of the SIU.
Eligibility: Applicants must be active seamen who are high school graduates or its equivalent, are eligible to receive Seafarers Plan benefits and have credit for two years (730 days) of employment with an employer who is obligated to make contributions to the Seafarers' Plan on the employee's behalf prior to the date of application. Recipients may attend any U.S. accredited institution (college or trade school). Selection is based on high school equivalency scores or secondary school records, college transcripts, if any, SAT/ACT scores, references on character or personality and autobiography.
How to Apply: Applications are available by written request.
Deadline: April 15.
Amount: $3,000-$5,000.
Number of Awards: 3.

Tailhook Association

The Tailhook Educational Foundation
9696 Businesspark Avenue
San Diego, CA 92131
Phone: 800-322-4665
Email: thookassn@aol.com
Website: http://www.tailhook.org

740 • Tailhook Educational Foundation Scholarship

Purpose: To assist the members of and the children of the members of the United States Navy carrier aviation.
Eligibility: Applicants must be high school graduates who are accepted at an undergraduate institution and are the natural or adopted children of current or former Naval Aviators, Naval Flight Officers or Naval Aircrewmen. Applicants may also be individuals or children of individuals who are serving or have served on board a U.S. Navy Aircraft Carrier in the ship's company or the air wing. Educational and extracurricular achievements, merit and citizenship will be considered.
How to Apply: Applications are available online.
Deadline: March 15.
Amount: Varies.
Number of Awards: Varies.

Tet '68

P.O. Box 31885
Richmond, VA 23294
Website: http://www.tet68.org

741 • Tet '68 Scholarship

Purpose: To provide scholarship opportunities for the children or stepchildren of Vietnam War veterans.
Eligibility: Applicants must be high school seniors who are the children or stepchildren of a Vietnam veteran and must complete a 500-word or less essay on the topic, "What is Freedom?"
How to Apply: Details about what to include in the application packet are available online.
Deadline: March 31.
Amount: $1,000.
Number of Awards: Varies.

Third Marine Division Association

MFySgt. James G. Kyser, USMC (Ret)
15727 Vista Drive
Dumfries, VA 22025
Email: scholarship@caltrap.org
Website: http://www.caltrap.com

742 • Memorial Scholarship Fund

Purpose: To assist veterans and their families.
Eligibility: Applicants must be the children of Marines (Corpsman or other) who served with the Third Marine Division or in support of the Division at any time and who have been members of the Third Marine Division Association for at least two years. Applicants must be 16-23 and unmarried dependents. Applicants must attend school in the U.S. or Canada.
How to Apply: Applications are available by written request after September 1.
Deadline: April 15.
Amount: Varies.
Number of Awards: Varies.

Related Scholarships:

American Legion Auxiliary, Department of California

See #1213 · American Legion Auxiliary, Department of California $2,000 Scholarships

American Legion Auxiliary, Department of California

See #1214 · American Legion Auxiliary, Department of California $500 Scholarships

American Legion Auxiliary, Department of California

See #1216 · Past Department Presidents' Junior Scholarship Award

American Legion, Department of Michigan

See #1422 · Guy M. Wilson Scholarship

American Society of Criminology

See #948 · American Society of Criminology Fellowships for Ethnic Minorities

Women In Defense

See #565 · HORIZONS Foundation Scholarship

American Legion, Department of Michigan

See #1424 · William D. and Jewell Brewer Scholarship

Association of Certified Fraud Examiners

See #73 · Ritchie-Jennings Memorial Scholarship

American Legion Auxiliary, Department of California

See #1212 · American Legion Auxiliary, Department of California $1,000 Scholarships

American Legion Auxiliary, Department of California

See #1215 · Continuing/Re-entry Students Scholarship

American Legion Auxiliary, Department of California

See #1217 · Past Presidents' Parley Nursing Scholarships

American Fire Sprinkler Association

See #6 · American Fire Sprinkler Association Scholarship Program

American Society of Naval Engineers

See #370 · ASNE Scholarship Program

Veterans of Foreign Wars

See #459 · Patriot's Pen Youth Essay Contest

Organizations/Clubs/Employers

Also See Scholarships Listed Under:

Unions

American Foreign Service Association (AFSA)

2101 East Street NW
Washington, DC 20037
Phone: 202-944-5504
Fax: 202-338-6820
Email: dec@afsa.org
Website: http://www.afsa.org

743 • AFSA Financial Aid Scholarships

Purpose: To provide financial aid to university students who are the children or dependents of Foreign Service employees.

Eligibility: Applicants must be dependents of U.S. government Foreign Service employees with a minimum 2.0 GPA. Students must attend or plan to attend full-time an undergraduate U.S. college, university, community college, art school, conservatory or other post-secondary institution. Applicants must submit applications, transcripts and financial need reports. Recipients must complete their undergraduate degree within four years and must demonstrate financial need.

How to Apply: Applications are available after November 1.
Deadline: February 6.
Amount: $1,000-$3,500.
Number of Awards: 55.

744 • AFSA/AAFSW Merit Award

Purpose: To recognize the academic and artistic achievements of high school seniors who are the children or dependents of Foreign Service employees.

Eligibility: Applicants must be dependents of U.S. government Foreign Service employees who are members of AFSA or AAFSW. Students must be high school seniors with a minimum 2.0 GPA. Applicants can also submit an art entry under the categories of visual arts, musical arts, drama, dance or creative writing. Awards are based on GPA, SAT scores, a two-page essay, letters of recommendation and extra-curricular activities.

How to Apply: Applications are available online after November 1.
Deadline: February 6.
Amount: $250-$1,500.
Number of Awards: 25.

American Legion

Attn.: Americanism and Children and Youth Division
P.O. Box 1055
Indianapolis, IN 46206
Phone: 317-630-1249
Fax: 317-630-1369
Email: acy@legion.org
Website: http://www.legion.org

745 • American Legion Eagle Scout of the Year

Purpose: To provide scholarships for Eagle Scouts.

Eligibility: Applicants must be registered, active members of a Boy Scout Troop, Varsity Scout Team or Venturing crew chartered to an American Legion Post or Auxiliary or Scouts who are the sons or grandsons of Legionnaires or Auxiliary Members. Applicants must receive the Eagle Scout Award, be active members of their religious institutions, receiving the appropriate Boy Scouts religious emblem, demonstrate citizenship, be at least 15 years old and be high school students.

How to Apply: Applications are available online.
Deadline: March 1.
Amount: $2,500-$10,000.
Number of Awards: 4.

American Legion Auxiliary

777 North Meridian Street
Third Floor
Indianapolis, IN 46204-1420
Phone: 317-955-3845
Fax: 317-955-3884
Email: alahq@legion-aux.org
Website: http://www.legion-aux.org

746 • Girl Scout Achievement Award

Purpose: To reward Girl Scout Gold Award winners.

Eligibility: Applicants must be Cadet or Senior Girl Scouts who have received the Girls Scout Gold Award, be active members of their religious institution and have received the appropriate religious emblem, and demonstrate citizenship. Applicants must submit four letters of recommendation from Religious Institution, school, community and scouting.

How to Apply: Applications are available online.
Deadline: February 11.
Amount: Varies.
Number of Awards: Varies.

AMVETS Auxiliary

4647 Forbes Boulevard
Lanham, MD 20706
Phone: 301-459-6255
Website: http://www.amvetsaux.org

747 • AMVETS National Ladies Auxiliary Scholarship

Purpose: To promote educational opportunities for students interested in or involved with a national service organization.

Eligibility: Applicants must be the child or grandchild of a current member of the AMVETS Ladies Auxiliary.

How to Apply: Applications are available by mail.
Deadline: June 1.
Amount: $500-$1,000.
Number of Awards: 12.

ARA Scholarship Foundation Inc.

ARA Scholarship Advisor
109 Defiant Way
Grass Valley, CA 95945
Phone: 703-385-1001
Email: arascholar@sbcglobal.net
Website: http://www.a-r-a.org

748 • ARA Scholarship

Purpose: To support the children of Automotive Recyclers Association (ARA) members.

Eligibility: Applicants must be high school seniors and/or planning to attend college full-time and have earned a minimum 3.0 GPA in their last educational program. Applicants must also be the children of employees of a Direct Member of ARA who were hired at least one year prior to March 15 of the application year. Scholarships are based on academic merit, not financial need.

How to Apply: Applications are available online and by email request.

Deadline: March 15.

Amount: Varies.

Number of Awards: Varies.

Arby's Foundation/Big Brothers Big Sisters Of America

230 North 13th Street
Philadelphia, PA 19107-1538
Phone: 215-567-7000
Website: http://www.bbbsa.org

749 • Arby's-Big Brothers Big Sisters Scholarship Award

Purpose: To aid Little Brothers or Little Sisters in the Big Brothers/Big Sisters program.

Eligibility: Applicants must be a Little Brother or Little Sister in a Big Brothers/Big Sisters program. Selection is based on community involvement, academic and extracurricular achievement and financial need.

How to Apply: Applications are available online.

Deadline: March 15.

Amount: $1,000-$5,000.

Number of Awards: 12.

Armstrong Foundation

2500 Columbia Avenue
Lancaster, PA 17603
Phone: 717-396-5536
Fax: 717-396-6124
Email: foundation@armstrongfoundation.com
Website: http://www.armstrongfoundation.com

750 • Armstrong Achievement Scholarships

Purpose: The Armstrong Foundation awards four-year awards for college to children of employees and retirees of Armstrong and its subsidiaries.

Eligibility: Applicants must be sons or daughters of full-time or retired employees of Armstrong or its subsidiaries. Eligible students must also meet all requirements for participation in the Merit Program as sponsored by the National Merit Scholarship Corporation.

How to Apply: Applications are available online.

Deadline: January 27.

Amount: $2,000.

Number of Awards: Varies.

Association for Women in Sports Media

P.O. Box 601557
Dallas, TX 75360
Email: awsmintern@hotmail.com
Website: http://www.awsmonline.org

751 • Women in Sports Media Scholarship/Internship Program

Purpose: To encourage females interested in sports media careers.

Eligibility: Applicants must be female students working full-time toward a graduate or undergraduate degree with the goal of becoming a sports writer, editor, broadcaster or public relations representative. Applicants must submit a resume, an essay on a memorable experience in sports or sports media, three references, two letters of recommendation and up to five samples of their work. Application fee is waived for AWSM members.

How to Apply: Applications are available online.

Deadline: October 20.

Amount: $1,000-$2,000+internship pay and expenses for convention attendance.

Number of Awards: Varies.

Aviation Boatswain Mates Association (ABMA)

Scholarship Chairman
Lanny Vines
144 CR 1515
Alba, TX 75410
Email: secretary@abma-usn.org
Website: http://www.abma-usn.org

752 • Isabella M. Gillen Memorial Scholarship Fund

Purpose: To support family members of ABMA.

Eligibility: Applicants must be the spouses or dependent children of ABMA members who have paid dues for at least two years. In addition to the application, applicants must write a letter stating their professional goals and how they plan to reach them.

How to Apply: Applications are available online.

Deadline: June 1.

Amount: $2,500.

Number of Awards: 1.

Boy Scouts of America, Eagle Scout Service

1325 W. Walnut Hill Lane
P.O. Box 152079
Irving, TX 75015-2079
Phone: 972-580-2000
Website: http://www.scouting.org

753 • Elks' Eagle Scout Scholarship

Purpose: To support Boy Scouts who have achieved Eagle Scout rank.

Eligibility: Applicants must be registered Boy Scouts with an Eagle rank, have a minimum SAT score of 1090 and/or an ACT score of 26, be high school seniors and demonstrate financial need.

How to Apply: Applications are available from the local Scout Council Service Center and online.

Deadline: February 28.

Amount: $1,000-2,000.

Number of Awards: 8.

754 • Mable and Lawrence S. Cooke Scholarship

Purpose: To provide scholarship funds for college students who have earned the rank of Eagle Scout in the Boy Scouts of America.

Eligibility: Applicants must enroll as full-time college students at a four-year, non-military college or university and have achieved the rank of Eagle Scout in the Boy Scouts program.

Deadline: February 28.

Amount: $5,000-$12,000.

Number of Awards: 5.

755 • National Eagle Scout Scholarship

Purpose: To support Jewish Boy Scouts who have received their Eagle Scout award based on their commitment to scouting ideals and community and religious service.

Eligibility: Applicants must be seniors in high school and active members of the Boy Scouts or Varsity Scouts who have received the Eagle Scout award. In addition, applicants must be an active member of a synagogue or have received the Ner Tamid or Etz Chaim religious emblem.

How to Apply: Applications are available online.

Deadline: February 28.

Amount: $500-$1,000.

Number of Awards: Varies.

Boys and Girls Clubs of America

1275 Peachtree Street NE
Atlanta, GA 30309
Phone: 404-487-5700
Email: info@bgca.org
Website: http://www.bgca.org

756 • Boys and Girls Clubs of America National Youth of the Year Award

Purpose: To reward club members who demonstrate good academic performance, perform services for both their club and community and who are active in both family and spiritual life.

Eligibility: Applicants must be a member of a BGCA and be selected by their local club to compete for the regional and national scholarships.

How to Apply: Contact your local club for more information.

Deadline: Varies.

Amount: $5,000-$10,000.

Number of Awards: Varies.

California Teachers Association (CTA)

CTA Human Rights Department
P.O. Box 921
Burlingame, CA 94011-0921
Phone: 650-697-1400
Fax: 650-552-5001
Website: http://www.cta.org

757 • CTA Scholarship for Dependent Children

Purpose: To support the children of CTA members.

Eligibility: Students must be the dependents of active, retired or deceased California Teachers Association members. Applicants must have a 3.5 high school GPA or high academic achievement in college, although there is the opportunity to explain any extenuating circumstances affecting grades. Scholarships are based on a personal statement, school and community activities and letters of recommendation.

How to Apply: Applications are available online.

Deadline: January 27.

Amount: $2,000.

Number of Awards: 25.

758 • CTA Scholarship for Members

Purpose: To support CTA members as they further their education.

Eligibility: Applicants must be current active members of the California Teachers Association who are attending college. Their coursework must show high academic achievement, although they may explain any extenuating circumstances affecting their grades. Scholarships are awarded based on a personal statement, school and community activities and letters of recommendation.

How to Apply: Applications are available online.

Deadline: January 27.

Amount: $2,000.

Number of Awards: 5.

759 • L. Gordon Bittle Memorial Scholarship for Student CTA (SCTA)

Purpose: To support members of the Student California Teachers Association.

Eligibility: Applicants must be planning to work in public education and have a minimum 3.5 high school GPA or show high academic achievement in college coursework, explaining any special circumstances affecting their grades. Scholarships are based on a personal statement, school and community activities and letters of recommendation.

How to Apply: Applications are available online.

Deadline: January 27.

Amount: $2,000.

Number of Awards: 3.

760 • Martin Luther King, Jr. Memorial Scholarship

Purpose: To encourage ethnic minority students to become teachers and support the continuing education of ethnic minority teachers.

Eligibility: Applicants must be African American, American Indian/Alaska Native, Asian/Pacific Islander or Hispanic students pursuing a teaching-related career in public education. Candidates must also be active members of the California Teachers Association or Student California Teachers Association or the dependents of an active, retired-life or deceased California Teachers Association member.

How to Apply: Applications are available online.

Deadline: March 15.

Amount: Varies.

Number of Awards: Varies.

Circle K International

3636 Woodview Trace
Indianapolis, IN 46268
Website: http://www.circlek.org

761 • Cunat Visionary Scholarship

Purpose: This scholarship, provided by Kiwanis International Past President Brian Cunat and Miki Cunat, was established to recognize Kiwanis members who aspire to make a difference in people's lives and create a better world for all.

Eligibility: Applicants must be either college-attending Circle K International members or graduating Key Club members.
How to Apply: Applications are available online.
Deadline: April 15.
Amount: $2,500.
Number of Awards: 2.

762 • Himmel Scholarship

Purpose: This scholarship is in memory of Harry S. Himmel, deceased President Emeritus of the Kiwanis International Foundation. Recipients should demonstrate dedication and leadership within the organization.
Eligibility: Applicants must be Key Club or Circle K members who appear on the international roster, are currently enrolled in college or are college-bound and have completed 100 service hours with the organization. Key Club members must have also held an elected officer position within the organization.
How to Apply: Applications are available online.
Deadline: February 13.
Amount: $500.
Number of Awards: 2.

763 • J. Walker Field Endowed Scholarship

Purpose: The scholarship is in memory of J. Walker Field, a former Kiwanis governor and dedicated Circle K supporter who allowed no obstacle to stand between him and his Circle K'ers. The recipient should demonstrate similar commitment to the organization.
Eligibility: Applicants must be Circle K members who appear on the international roster, are currently enrolled in college and have completed 100 service hours with the organization.
How to Apply: Applications are available online.
Deadline: February 13.
Amount: $1,000.
Number of Awards: 1.

Civitan

Civitan International Foundation
P.O. Box 130744
Birmingham, AL 35213-0744
Phone: 205-591-8910
Fax: 205-592-6307
Email: civitan@civitan.org
Website: http://www.civitan.org

764 • Shropshire Scholarship

Purpose: The Shropshire Scholarship assists deserving Civitan members who will pursue careers that further the ideals of Civitan International, such as working toward world peace and unity, fighting for justice and building better citizenship.
Eligibility: Applicants must be Civitans or a Civitan's immediate family member, have been Civitan or Junior Civitan members for at least two years, be enrolled in a college or university and pursue careers which help further the ideals of Civitan International.
How to Apply: Applications are available online.
Deadline: January 31.
Amount: Up to $1,000.
Number of Awards: Varies.

Clara Abbott Foundation

1505 White Oak Drive
Waukegan, IL 60085
Phone: 866-754-1333
Fax: 847-938-6511
Website: http://clara.abbott.com

765 • Clara Abbott Foundation Educational Grant Program

Purpose: To help children of eligible Abbott employees and retirees worldwide receive a college-level education by providing scholarships on the basis of financial need.
Eligibility: Applicants must be full- or part-time students at an accredited college, university, community college, vocational school or trade school. Applicants must also be 29 years of age or younger, be the children or dependents of retirees or full-time/part-time employees of Abbott Laboratories and be residents of the United States or Puerto Rico. Scholarships are awarded according to financial need. Applicants may first apply as high school seniors.
How to Apply: Applications are available online.
Deadline: December 15.
Amount: Varies.
Number of Awards: Varies.

Council for Exceptional Children

1110 North Glebe Road
Suite 300
Arlington, VA 22201
Phone: 888-232-7733
Fax: 703-264-9494
Email: fec@cec.sped.org
Website: http://www.cec.sped.org

766 • Student CEC Graduation Awards

Purpose: To provide financial aid to student members transitioning to professional membership status in the Council for Exceptional Children.
Eligibility: Applicants must be undergraduate or graduate students enrolled at an accredited college or university graduating in the academic year the award is given. Applicants must be members of the Student CEC with a minimum 3.0 GPA. Selection is based on an essay, GPA, letters of recommendation and extracurricular activities.
How to Apply: Applications are available online.
Deadline: November 5.
Amount: $350.
Number of Awards: 2.

Delta Gamma Foundation

3250 Riverside Drive
P.O. Box 21397
Columbus, OH 43221
Phone: 614-481-8169
Fax: 614-481-0133
Email: scholarshipapply@deltagamma.org
Website: http://www.deltagamma.org

767 • Delta Gamma Foundation Scholarship

Purpose: To support student members.
Eligibility: Applicants must be initiated members of Delta Gamma, have maintained a 3.0 GPA and have completed three semesters or five quarters of college coursework. Applicants should also be active participants in chapter, campus and community leadership activities. Awards are based on academic achievement and participation in activities.
How to Apply: Applications are available online.
Deadline: February 1.
Amount: $1,000.
Number of Awards: Varies.

Delta Sigma Pi

330 S. Campus Avenue
Oxford, OH 45056
Phone: 513-523-1907
Fax: 513-523-7292
Email: centraloffice@dspnet.org
Website: http://www.dspnet.org

768 • Collegian of the Year

Purpose: To honor the most outstanding collegian member of Delta Sigma Pi who exemplifies the ideals of the organization.

Eligibility: Nominees must be members in good standing and be nominated by their chapter by October 15. Demonstrated Fraternity involvement, demonstrated college/university and/or community involvement, demonstrated pursuit of professional development and scholastic average will all be considered along with other desirable characteristics like moral character and professional attitude.

How to Apply: Applications are available online.
Deadline: November 15.
Amount: $3,000.
Number of Awards: 1.

769 • Undergraduate Scholarship

Purpose: To assist student members.

Eligibility: Applicants must be members in good standing of Delta Sigma Pi with at least one semester or quarter of undergraduate studies remaining. Applicants are judged on scholastic achievement, financial need, fraternal service, service activities, letters of recommendation and overall presentation of required materials.

How to Apply: Applications are available online.
Deadline: June 30.
Amount: $500-$1,250.
Number of Awards: 10.

Drug, Chemical, and Allied Trades Association (DCAT)

One Washington Boulevard, Suite 7
Robbinsville, NJ 8520
Phone: 800-640-3228
Fax: 609-448-1944
Email: gdeaner@dcat.org
Website: http://www.dcat.org

770 • Drug, Chemical and Allied Trades Association (DCAT) Scholarship

Purpose: To benefit the children of DCAT member employees.

Eligibility: Applicants must be high school seniors with a parent employed by a DCAT member company, which are companies that manufacture, distribute or provide services to the pharmaceutical, chemical, nutritional and related industries. Based on leadership, academic achievement and ability to support a point of view.

How to Apply: Applications are available online in mid-October.
Deadline: February 7.
Amount: $10,000 over four years.
Number of Awards: 5.

Duke Energy Corporation

526 S. Church Street
Charlotte, NC 28202-1904
Phone: 704-594-6200
Email: contactus@duke-energy.com
Website: http://www.duke-energy.com

771 • Duke Energy Scholars

Purpose: To support the children of Duke Energy employees and retirees.

Eligibility: Applicants should be children of Duke Energy employees and retirees who are undergraduates at accredited, two-year technical schools or community colleges or four-year colleges or universities in the U.S. and Canada. The awards are based on academics, references, community service and financial need.
How to Apply: Contact the company for more information.
Deadline: Varies.
Amount: $5,000.
Number of Awards: 15.

Elks National Foundation (IL)

2750 N. Lakeview Avenue
Chicago, IL 60614
Phone: 773-755-4732
Fax: 773-755-4733
Email: scholarship@elks.org
Website: http://www.elks.org

772 • Emergency Educational Fund Grants

Purpose: To assist children of deceased and incapacitated Elks.

Eligibility: Applicants must be the children of deceased or incapacitated Elks who were/are members in good standing, unmarried, under 23 years old and full-time undergraduate students at a U.S. school. Applicants must also demonstrate financial need and investigate all other sources of financial aid before submitting an application.

How to Apply: Applications are available from the local Elks Lodge or by phone or e-mail request.
Deadline: December 31.
Amount: Up to $4,000.
Number of Awards: Varies.

773 • Gold Award Scholarship

Purpose: To support Girl Scouts who have achieved the Gold Award.

Eligibility: Applicants must have achieved the Gold Award, the highest in Girl Scouting and be graduating high school seniors. Selection is based on academics, activities, leadership, individual interests and community involvement.

How to Apply: Applications are available from Girl Scout Councils.
Deadline: Varies depending on individual Girl Scout Councils.
Amount: $1,500.
Number of Awards: 8.

774 • Legacy Award

Purpose: To assist the descendants of Elk members.

Eligibility: Applicants must be children or grandchildren (including step-children/grandchildren and legal wards) of Elk members in good standing and be high school seniors planning to attend accredited U.S. postsecondary institutions (with the exception of some non-U.S. Elks Lodges). Applicants must also take or have taken the SAT or ACT. The selection committee will evaluate applicants on the core values of knowledge, charity, community, and integrity. Financial need is not a consideration.

How to Apply: Applications are available from local Elks Lodges, online or by written request.

Deadline: January 14.

Amount: $1,000.

Number of Awards: Up to 500.

Federal Employee Education and Assistance Fund

8441 W. Bowles Avenue
Suite 200
Littleton, CO 80123
Phone: 303-933-7580
Fax: 303-933-7587
Website: http://www.feea.org

775 • FEEA Scholarship

Purpose: The FEEA scholarship program aids postal employees and their family members.

Eligibility: Applicants must be current civilian federal and postal employees with three years of service or their children or spouses. Applicants must also be enrolled or plan to enroll in an accredited post secondary school, have a minimum 3.0 GPA and may be high school seniors, college students or graduate students.

How to Apply: Applications are available online or by sending a self-addressed and stamped envelope.

Deadline: March.

Amount: $300-$1,500.

Number of Awards: Varies.

Federation of American Consumers and Travelers (FACT)

P.O. Box 104
318 Hillsboro Avenue
Edwardsville, IL 62025
Phone: 800-872-3228
Email: cservice@fact-org.org
Website: http://www.fact-org.org

776 • Continuing Education Scholarships

Purpose: To help FACT members and their families.

Eligibility: Applicants must be FACT members or their immediate families in the following categories: current high school seniors, students already in college, graduated from high school four or more years ago or planning to attend a trade or technical school.

How to Apply: Contact the organization for more information.

Deadline: Varies.

Amount: $10,000.

Number of Awards: Varies.

Fleet Reserve Association

FRA Scholarship Administrator
125 N. West Street
Alexandria, VA 22314
Phone: 800-372-1924
Website: http://www.fra.org

777 • Fleet Reserve Association Scholarship

Purpose: To provide financial support for post-secondary education to FRA members and their dependents and grandchildren.

Eligibility: Applicants must be either FRA members or the dependents or grandchildren of an FRA member who is in good standing or was in good standing at time of death. Applicants are judged on the basis of leadership skills, financial need, academic record and character.

How to Apply: Applications are available online.

Deadline: April 15.

Amount: Varies.

Number of Awards: Varies.

778 • Oliver and Esther R. Howard Scholarship

Purpose: To provide financial aid to the dependent children of FRA members or LA FRA members.

Eligibility: Applicants must be the dependent children of members of either the Fleet Reserve Association or the Ladies' Auxiliary of the Fleet Reserve Association who are in good standing. This scholarship is alternated between male and female recipients each year (males - odd years) (females - even years). Recipients must be high school seniors or college undergraduates pursuing undergraduate degrees and are selected on the basis of academic record, financial need, leadership skills and character.

How to Apply: Applications are available online.

Deadline: April 15.

Amount: Varies.

Number of Awards: Varies.

779 • Schuyler S. Pyle Award

Purpose: To support members of the FRA, their spouses and their dependent children or grandchildren.

Eligibility: Applicants must be members of the FRA in good standing, or the spouse or dependent children/grandchildren of a member who is in good standing or was in good standing at time of death. Recipients are determined on the basis of academic record, leadership skills, character and financial need.

How to Apply: Applications are available online.

Deadline: April 15.

Amount: Varies.

Number of Awards: Varies.

780 • Stanley A. Doran Memorial Scholarship

Purpose: To provide financial aid to the dependents of FRA members.

Eligibility: Applicants must be the dependent children of a member in good standing of the FRA or a member who was in good standing at time of death. Recipients are selected on the basis of academic achievement, leadership skills, financial need and character.

How to Apply: Applications are available online.

Deadline: April 15.

Amount: Varies.

Number of Awards: Varies.

Girls Inc.

120 Wall Street
New York, NY 10005
Phone: 800-374-4475
Website: http://www.girlsinc.org

781 • National Scholars and Awards Program

Purpose: To support young members of Girls Incorporated.

Eligibility: Applicants must be young women who are in their junior or senior year of high school and members of a Girls Incorporated affiliate.

How to Apply: Applications are available by written request.

Deadline: Varies.

Amount: Varies.

Number of Awards: Varies.

Golden Key National Honour Society

Scholarship Program Administrators
Golden Key Scholarships/Awards
P.O. Box 23737
Nashville, TN 37202-3737
Phone: 800-377-2401
Email: scholarships@goldenkey.org
Website: http://www.goldenkey.org

782 • Business Achievement Awards

Purpose: To support Golden Key members who are studying business.

Eligibility: Applicants must be undergraduate, graduate or post-graduate members who are currently attending classes in a degree-granting program. The award is based on academic achievement and a business-related paper or report.

How to Apply: Applications are available online.

Deadline: March 1.

Amount: $500-$1,000.

Number of Awards: 2.

783 • Community Service Award

Purpose: To support a Golden Key member who has served the community.

Eligibility: Applicants must be undergraduate or graduate Golden Key members who were enrolled during the previous academic year. Selection is based on the impact of the community service. Applicants must provide an essay of up to 500 words describing the community service project, recommendation letters and list of extracurricular activities.

How to Apply: Applications are available online.

Deadline: February 15.

Amount: $250.

Number of Awards: 1.

784 • Education Achievement Awards

Purpose: To support members studying education.

Eligibility: Applicants must be undergraduate, graduate or post-graduate Golden Key members who are taking classes in a degree-granting program. Selection is based on academic achievement and education-related paper or report.

How to Apply: Applications are available online.

Deadline: March 1.

Amount: $500-$1,000.

Number of Awards: 2.

785 • Engineering/Technology Achievement Awards

Purpose: To support members who are studying engineering or technology.

Eligibility: Applicants must be undergraduate, graduate or post-graduate members who are taking classes in a degree-granting program. Selection is based on academic achievement and engineering-related paper or report.

How to Apply: Applications are available online.

Deadline: March 1.

Amount: $500-$1,000.

Number of Awards: 2.

786 • Ford Motor Company Business and Leadership Scholarship

Purpose: To provide opportunities for undergraduate and graduate students majoring in business.

Eligibility: Applicants must be Golden Key members and must be majoring in business. The award is based on academic achievement, leadership, Golden Key involvement and extracurricular activities.

How to Apply: Applications are available online.

Deadline: March 1.

Amount: $10,000.

Number of Awards: 1.

787 • Ford Motor Company Engineering and Leadership Scholarship

Purpose: To provide opportunities for undergraduate and graduate students majoring in engineering.

Eligibility: Applicants must be Golden Key members and must be majoring in engineering. Award is based on academic achievement, leadership, Golden Key involvement and extracurricular activities.

How to Apply: Applications are available online.

Deadline: March 1.

Amount: $10,000.

Number of Awards: 1.

788 • GEICO Life Scholarship

Purpose: To support undergraduate students who balance family, career or other life commitments with pursuing a degree.

Eligibility: Applicants must be members of Golden Key, be enrolled in a baccalaureate program and have completed at least 12 hours at the time of application. The award is based on academic achievement, extracurricular activities and family and/or career commitments.

How to Apply: Applications are available online.

Deadline: April 1.

Amount: $1,000.

Number of Awards: 10.

789 • Golden Key Graduate Scholar Award

Purpose: To support Golden Key members' graduate studies at accredited universities in the U.S. or abroad.

Eligibility: Applicant must be a Golden Key member. Selection is based on academic achievement, involvement in Golden Key and extracurricular activities.

How to Apply: Applications are available online.

Deadline: January 20.

Amount: $10,000.

Number of Awards: 12.

790 • Literary Achievement Awards

Purpose: To support members who demonstrate literary talents.

Eligibility: Applicants must be undergraduate, graduate or post-graduate members who are taking classes in a degree-granting program. Selection is based on an original composition. One winner is selected in each of four categories: fiction, non-fiction, poetry and news writing.

How to Apply: Applications are available online.
Deadline: April 1.
Amount: $1,000.
Number of Awards: 4.

791 • Student Leader Award

Purpose: To support student members who have demonstrated leadership.

Eligibility: Applicants must be currently or previously involved in Golden Key and be currently enrolled in an undergraduate or graduate program at an accredited college or university. There are awards for both U.S. and international students. U.S. applicants must submit an application form, personal statement, description of Golden Key involvement, list of activities, recommendation letter and transcript.

How to Apply: Applications are available online.
Deadline: June 1.
Amount: $500.
Number of Awards: 10.

792 • Study Abroad Scholarships

Purpose: To assist members who study abroad.

Eligibility: Applicants must be undergraduate members who plan to be or are currently enrolled in a study abroad program. Selection is based on academic achievement and relevance of the study abroad program to the applicants' major.

How to Apply: Applications are available online.
Deadline: April 15 and October 20.
Amount: $1,000.
Number of Awards: 10.

793 • Undergraduate Research Grants

Purpose: To assist members in their thesis research or in presenting their research at a professional conference.

Eligibility: Applicants must be undergraduate student members. Selection is based on academic achievement and the quality of the research.

How to Apply: Applications are available online.
Deadline: April 15 and October 20.
Amount: $500.
Number of Awards: 10.

794 • Visual and Performing Arts Achievement Awards

Purpose: To assist members who are talented in the visual and performing arts.

Eligibility: Applicants must be undergraduate, graduate or post-graduate members who are currently taking classes at a degree-granting program. Selection is based on the work submitted. For the visual arts, students must submit a slide or slides of their artwork. For the performing arts, students must submit a videotape or DVD of a performance up to 10 minutes. The competition categories are: painting, drawing, photography, sculpture, computer-generated art/graphic design/illustration, mixed media, instrumental performance, vocal performance and dance.

How to Apply: Applications are available online.
Deadline: April 1.
Amount: $500.
Number of Awards: 9.

Golf Course Superintendents Association of America Foundation

GCSAA Career Development Department
GCSAA Scholars Competition
1421 Research Park Drive
Lawrence, KS 66049
Phone: 800-472-7878
Email: infobox@gcsaa.org
Website: http://www.gcsaa.org

795 • GCSAA Legacy Awards

Purpose: To support the children and grandchildren of GCSAA members.

Eligibility: The applicants' parents or grandparents must have been GCSAA members for five or more consecutive years. Applicants must also be full-time college students or high school seniors already accepted into a postsecondary school.

How to Apply: Applications are available by contacting Pam Smith, 800-472-7878, x3678.
Deadline: April 15.
Amount: $1,500.
Number of Awards: Varies.

Grange Insurance Association

Scholarship Committee
P.O. Box 21089
Seattle, WA 98111-3089
Phone: 800-247-2643
Website: http://www.grange.com

796 • Grange Insurance Group Scholarship

Purpose: To help those associated with Grange Insurance Group.

Eligibility: Applicants must be current Grange Insurance Group (GIG) policyholders (or children or grandchildren of GIG policyholders) in California, Colorado, Idaho, Oregon, Washington or Wyoming; Grange members (or children or grandchildren of Grange members) or children or grandchildren of current GIG employees and residents in California, Colorado, Idaho, Oregon, Washington and Wyoming. Applicants can apply for scholarships in either academic or vocational studies. Three of the awards will be for students wishing to pursue vocational studies and 22 will be for academic studies. The top scoring student in each category receives $1,500 and each additional winner receives $1000. Scholarships may be used toward a certificate or degree in a recognized profession or vocation, including community colleges, business colleges and technical institutes, as well as institutions offering an academic degree program. Vocational scholarships are intended for use at community colleges, technical or business schools or other institutions that offer vocational training which does not lead to a two- or four-year academic degree. Selection is based on academic achievement and essays.

How to Apply: Applications are available online.
Deadline: April 15.
Amount: $1,500.
Number of Awards: 25.

Guy and Gloria Muto Memorial Scholarship Foundation Inc.

P.O. Box 60159
Sacramento, CA 95860
Email: ggmuto@aol.com
Website: http://www.ggmuto.org

797 • Guy and Gloria Muto Memorial Scholarship

Purpose: To provide scholarships for pool and spa industry employees and their immediate families.

Eligibility: Applicants or their immediate family must have been employed full-time in the pool and spa industry for at least one year. Students must have the endorsement of an officer of a chapter of a recognized pool and spa association. Scholarships may be used for college, graduate school, trade school or vocational education.

How to Apply: Applications are available online.

Deadline: May 31.

Amount: Varies.

Number of Awards: Varies.

Honor Society of Phi Kappa Phi

P.O. Box 16000
Louisiana State University
Baton Rouge, LA 70893-6000
Phone: 800-804-9880 x13
Email: awards@phikappaphi.org
Website: http://www.phikappaphi.org

798 • Literacy Grants

Purpose: To award grants to Phi Kappa Phi members and chapters to offer literacy programs.

Eligibility: The project leader must be a member of Phi Kappa Phi. Previous winners have provided books and book bags to literacy programs, organized literacy fairs and conducted research on literacy.

How to Apply: Applications are available online.

Deadline: February 1.

Amount: Up to $2,500.

Number of Awards: Varies.

799 • Phi Kappa Phi Fellowship

Purpose: To provide fellowships for Phi Kappa Phi members entering their first year of graduate or professional studies.

Eligibility: Applicants may enter any professional or graduate field and must not have completed one full term of graduate study. Selection is based on academic achievement, service, leadership, letters of recommendation, personal statement and career goals.

How to Apply: Applications are available online.

Deadline: February 1.

Amount: $5,000.

Number of Awards: 60.

Horace Mann Insurance Companies

1 Horace Mann Plaza
Springfield, IL 62715
Phone: 800-999-1030
Website: http://www.horacemann.com

800 • Horace Mann Scholarship

Purpose: To help the families of public school teachers.

Eligibility: Applicants must be high school seniors whose parents are U.S. public or private education employees and have at least a "B" average and a minimum ACT score of 23 or SAT score of 1100. Students are asked to submit an essay, transcript, list of activities and honors and two letters of recommendation.

How to Apply: Applications are available online.

Deadline: February 12.

Amount: $1,000-$10,000.

Number of Awards: 26.

Imagine America Foundation

1101 Connecticut Avenue NW
Suite 901
Washington, DC 20036
Phone: 202-336-6724
Fax: 202-408-8102
Email: kerryt@career.org
Website: http://www.imagine-america.org

801 • Imagine America II

Purpose: To help Imagine America scholarship recipients.

Eligibility: Students do not apply for these scholarships and must be nominated by a participating career college. Applicants must also be adult students currently attending career colleges in the United States and Puerto Rico, have been an Imagine America (high school) scholarship recipient, have a 95 percent or higher attendance record and obtain a written recommendation.

How to Apply: Nomination forms are available online.

Deadline: May 31.

Amount: Varies.

Number of Awards: Varies.

International Order of the Golden Rule

Education Department
P.O. Box 28689
St. Louis, MO 631461189
Phone: 800-637-8030
Fax: 314-209-7213
Email: jgabbert@ogr.org
Website: http://www.ogr.org

802 • Awards of Excellence Scholarship Program

Purpose: To provide aid for students in mortuary science and who intend to pursue a career in the funeral service profession.

Eligibility: Applicants must be currently enrolled in a mortuary science school and have a minimum 3.0 GPA. The award is based on community service, honors, grades and potential contributions to the funeral service profession.

How to Apply: Applications are available online or by email.

Deadline: October 1.

Amount: $500-$2,500.

Number of Awards: 3.

803 • Koven L. Brown Scholarship Program

Purpose: To assist mortuary science students with financial need.

Eligibility: Applicants must be studying mortuary science and have a minimum 3.0 GPA. The award is based on community service, honors, grades and potential contributions to the funeral service profession.

How to Apply: Applications are available online.
Deadline: October 1.
Amount: Varies.
Number of Awards: Varies.

Jewish War Veterans of the USA

1811 R Street NW
Washington, DC 20009
Phone: 202-265-6280
Fax: 202-234-5662
Email: jwv@jwv.org
Website: http://www.jwv.org

804 • Bernard Rotberg Memorial Scholarship Fund

Purpose: To provide scholarships for descendents of members of the Jewish War Veterans of the USA.

Eligibility: Applicants must be a direct descendent of a JWV member in good standing. Candidates must also have been accepted to an accredited college, university or nursing school, be in the upper 25 percent of their class and be active in activities at school and within the Jewish community.

How to Apply: Applications are available online and should be submitted by the applicant's school to the department commander in the local post.

Deadline: May 3.
Amount: $1,000.
Number of Awards: 1.

805 • JWV Grant

Purpose: To provide scholarships for descendents of members of the Jewish War Veterans of the USA.

Eligibility: Applicants must be direct descendents of a JWV member in good standing. Candidates must also have been accepted to an accredited college, university or nursing school, be in the upper 25 percent of their class and be active in activities at school and within the Jewish community.

How to Apply: Applications are available online and should be submitted by the applicant's school to the department commander in the local post.

Deadline: May 3.
Amount: $500.
Number of Awards: 1.

806 • Louis S. Silvey Grant

Purpose: To provide scholarships for descendents of members of the Jewish War Veterans of the USA.

Eligibility: Applicants must be direct descendents of a JWV member in good standing. Candidates must also have been accepted to an accredited college, university or nursing school, be in the upper 25 percent of their class and be active in activities at school and within the Jewish community.

How to Apply: Applications are available online and should be submitted by the applicant's school to the department commander in the local post.

Deadline: May 3.
Amount: $750.
Number of Awards: 1.

Kappa Alpha Theta Foundation

Attn.: Undergraduate Scholarship Application
8740 Founders Road
Indianapolis, IN 46268

Phone: 888-526-1870 x119
Fax: 317-876-1925
Email: cthoennes@kappaalphatheta.org
Website: http://www.kappaalphatheta.org

807 • Foundation Scholarship Program

Purpose: To provide merit-based scholarships for undergraduate, graduate and alumna Kappa Alpha Theta members.

Eligibility: The award is based on academics, fraternity activities, campus and community activities and references.

How to Apply: Applications are available online.
Deadline: February 1.
Amount: Varies.
Number of Awards: Varies.

Knights of Columbus

Department of Scholarships
P.O. Box 1670
New Haven, CT 06507
Phone: 203-752-4000
Email: info@kofc.org
Website: http://www.kofc.org

808 • Fourth Degree Pro Deo and Pro Patria Scholarships

Purpose: To provide aid to members or the children of members of the Knights of Columbus.

Eligibility: Applicants must be members or the children of current or deceased members of the Knights of Columbus or, in some cases, be members of the Columbian Squires. Applicants must be entering their freshmen year at a U.S. Catholic college.

How to Apply: Applications are available by mail.
Deadline: March 1.
Amount: $1,500.
Number of Awards: 62.

809 • John W McDevitt (Fourth Degree) Scholarship Fund

Purpose: To provide financial assistance to college students who are Knights of Columbus members or family members of a member.

Eligibility: Applicants must be a Knights of Columbus member, or the wife, widow or child of a member in good standing. New applicants must also be entering their freshman year at a Catholic college or university.

How to Apply: Applications are available by mail.
Deadline: March 1.
Amount: $1,500.
Number of Awards: Varies.

NASA Federal Credit Union

P.O. Box 1910
Bowie, MD 20717
Phone: 888-627-2328
Fax: 301-249-0799
Email: support@nasafcu.com
Website: http://www.nasafcu.com

810 • Mitchell-Beall Scholarship

Purpose: To assist younger members of the NASA FCU to further their educations.

Eligibility: Applicants must be current members of the NASA FCU, high school seniors under the age of 21 and have a minimum 2.0 GPA.

How to Apply: Applications are available online.
Deadline: February 10.
Amount: $3,000-$7,000.
Number of Awards: Varies.

National Beta Club

151 Beta Club Way
Spartanburg, SC 29306
Phone: 800-845-8281
Fax: 864-542-9300
Email: jburnett@betaclub.org
Website: http://www.betaclub.org

811 • National Beta Club Scholarship

Purpose: To award outstanding Beta Club members.
Eligibility: Applicants must be active National Beta Club members who are registered with the national headquarters by June 3 of the application year, high school seniors and nominated by their chapters. Awards are based on factors including academic excellence, leadership, character and school and community service.
How to Apply: Applications are available from your Beta Club sponsor.
Deadline: December 10.
Amount: $1,000-$15,000.
Number of Awards: 208.

National Exchange Club

3050 Central Avenue
Toledo, OH 43606
Phone: 800-924-2643
Fax: 419-535-1989
Email: info@nationalexchangeclub.org
Website: http://www.nationalexchangeclub.com

812 • Youth of the Year Award

Purpose: To recognize students who excel in academics, leadership and community service.
Eligibility: Applicants are chosen by their local Exchange Clubs. The process begins with Youth of the Month Awards. At the end of the year, a Youth of the Year nominee is selected from Youth of the Month winners. Applicants are judged based on participation in activities, community service, special achievements/awards, grades and a required essay. To be eligible to win, applicants must be able to attend national convention to accept the award.
How to Apply: Applications are available online.
Deadline: Varies.
Amount: $10,000.
Number of Awards: 1.

National Honor Society

c/o National Association of Secondary School Principals
1904 Association Drive
Reston, VA 20191
Phone: 703-860-0200
Fax: 703-476-5432
Email: nhs@nhs.us
Website: http://www.nhs.us

813 • National Honor Society Scholarship

Purpose: To recognize NHS members.
Eligibility: Each high school chapter may nominate two senior members. Nominees must demonstrate character, scholarship, service and leadership.
How to Apply: Nomination forms are available from your local NHS chapter adviser.
Deadline: January 21.
Amount: $1,000.
Number of Awards: 200.

National Independent Automobile Dealers Association

2521 Brown Boulevard
Arlington, TX 76006-5203
Phone: 817-640-3838
Fax: 817-649-5866
Email: rachel@niada.com
Website: http://www.niada.com

814 • NIADA Scholarship

Purpose: To support high school seniors with academic achievement and ties to NIADA members.
Eligibility: Applicants must be the son, daughter or grandchild of a NIADA member, have an excellent high school academic record and have high SAT or ACT scores. Applications, transcripts, test scores and a maximum of five recommendation letters are required.
How to Apply: Applications are available online and should be submitted to the state association.
Deadline: January 31.
Amount: $2,500.
Number of Awards: 4.

National Society Daughters of the American Revolution

1776 D Street NW
Washington, DC 20006
Phone: 202-628-1776
Website: http://www.dar.org

815 • Lillian And Arthur Dunn Scholarship

Purpose: To assist the children of members with their education.
Eligibility: Applicants must be sons or daughters of current women members of NSDAR, must be U.S. citizens and plan to attend an accredited U.S. college or university.
How to Apply: Applications are available by written request.
Deadline: February 15.
Amount: $2,000.
Number of Awards: 1.

National Society of the Sons of the American Revolution

1000 S. Fourth Street
Louisville, KY 40203
Phone: 502-589-1776
Email: contests@sar.org
Website: http://www.sar.org

816 • Eagle Scout Scholarship

Purpose: To reward exceptional students who have reached the status of Eagle Scout.

Eligibility: Applicants must have reached Eagle Scout status, must currently be registered in an active unit and can't have reached their 19th birthday during the year of application. Applicants can apply multiple years as long as they are under the age limit, but the maximum award amount is $8,000. Applicants usually apply at the chapter level. Applicants will be required to submit an essay and four-generation ancestor chart with their application.

How to Apply: Applications are available online.
Deadline: December 31.
Amount: $2,000-$4,000.
Number of Awards: 3.

National Strength and Conditioning Association (NSCA) Foundation

1885 Bob Johnson Drive
Colorado Springs, CO 80906
Phone: 800-815-6826
Fax: 719-632-6367
Email: nsca@nsca-lift.org
Website: http://www.nsca-lift.org

817 • Power Systems Professional Scholarship

Purpose: To support students interested in becoming strength and conditioning coaches.

Eligibility: Applicants must be undergraduate or graduate students and be working under a coach in the school's athletic department. Applicants must be members of the National Strength and Conditioning Association for one year prior to applying for a scholarship. Applications must include a resume, transcript, personal essay and letter from the head strength coach. The application must also be submitted by the head strength coach.

How to Apply: Applications are available online.
Deadline: March 15.
Amount: $1,000.
Number of Awards: 1.

NATSO Foundation

Heather Mooney
c/o Bill Moon Scholarship Committee
60 Main Street
Farmington, CT 06032
Phone: 703-549-2100
Fax: 703-684-9667
Website: http://www.natsofoundation.org

818 • Bill Moon Scholarship

Purpose: To assist Truck Stop Operators industry employees and their families.

Eligibility: Applicants must be Truck Stop Operators industry employees or their family members and must submit applications, essays, recommendation letters, transcripts and financial information. The award is based on academic merit, financial need, community activities and essays.

How to Apply: Applications are available online.
Deadline: April 14.
Amount: Varies.
Number of Awards: 12.

Phi Sigma Kappa International Headquarters

2925 E. 96th Street
Indianapolis, IN 46240
Phone: 317-573-5420
Fax: 317-573-5430
Website: http://www.phisigmakappa.org

819 • Terrill Graduate Fellowship

Purpose: To award money to graduating senior and alumni members entering graduate school or members already enrolled in graduate school.

Eligibility: Applicants must graduate from college by August of the year during which they apply, plan to begin graduate or professional study during the next academic year and have a minimum B GPA for all undergraduate work. Scholarships are awarded based on scholastic performance.

How to Apply: Applications are available online.
Deadline: January 31.
Amount: $3,000.
Number of Awards: 1.

820 • Wenderoth Undergraduate Scholarship

Purpose: To give financial aid to college sophomore and junior members.

Eligibility: Applicants must be sophomores or juniors in college for the year that the scholarship will apply to, have completed two semesters or three quarters of study and have a minimum B GPA. Scholarships are awarded on the basis of academic accomplishments and essays.

How to Apply: Applications are available online.
Deadline: January 31.
Amount: $1,750-$4,000.
Number of Awards: 4.

Sigma Alpha Epsilon (SAE)

Dave Sandell
Sigma Alpha Epsilon Foundation Scholarships
1856 Sheridan Road
Evanston, IL 60201
Phone: 800-233-1856 x234
Fax: 847-475-2250
Email: dsandell@sae.net
Website: http://www.sae.net

821 • Jones-Laurence Award for Scholastic Achievement

Purpose: To improve scholarship among active Sigma Alpha Epsilon members.

Eligibility: Applicants must be brothers of Sigma Alpha Epsilon in good standing and either must have junior standing or higher or must be pursuing full-time graduate study. This award is merit-based, with an emphasis on combining academic excellence, leadership, service and campus involvement. Applicants are nominated by their chapters and have a minimum 3.9 GPA.

How to Apply: Contact the coordinator of educational programs and services.
Deadline: April 28.
Amount: $1,000-$3,000.
Number of Awards: 2.

Sons of Norway

1455 W. Lake Street
Minneapolis, MN 55408
Phone: 800-945-8851
Fax: 612-827-0658
Website: http://www.sofn.com

822 • Astrid G. Cates Scholarship Fund and the Myrtle Beinhauer Scholarship

Purpose: To support the members and children and grandchildren of members of the Sons of Norway.

Eligibility: Applicants must have a certificate of completion from high school and be enrolled in post-secondary training or education (college, vocational school or trade school), and be current members of Sons of Norway or the children or grandchildren of current Sons of Norway members in Sons of Norway districts 1-6. Applicants must also have strong financial need. Selection is based on degree of financial need, a statement of education and career goals, applicants' grade-point averages, a letter of recommendation and applicants' extracurricular involvements.

How to Apply: Applications are available online.
Deadline: March 1.
Amount: $500-$3,000.
Number of Awards: 2.

Subway Restaurants

Susan Lee
Center for Scholarship Administration, Subway Scholarship Fund
P.O. Box 1465
Taylors, SC 29687
Phone: 864-268-3363
Fax: 864-268-7160
Email: susanjlee@bellsouth.net
Website: http://www.subway.com

823 • Subway Scholarship Fund

Purpose: To provide scholarships for Subway employees.

Eligibility: Applicants must be either high school seniors or full-time college students and must be Subway employees who work a minimum of 15 hours a week and have worked at least 6 months prior to January 1. Academic achievement, scholarship performance, scholastic aptitude, essays and letters of recommendation will be considered.

How to Apply: Applications are available online at www.scholarshipprograms.org starting December 1.
Deadline: February 27.
Amount: $1,000.
Number of Awards: Varies.

Tall Clubs International

6770 River Terrace Drive
Franklin, WI 53132
Phone: 888-468-2552
Email: info@tcifoundation.org
Website: http://www.tall.org

824 • Tall Club International Kae Sumner Einfeldt Scholarship

Purpose: To support students of tall stature.

Eligibility: Applicants must be high school seniors or college students under the age of 21 attending or planning to attend a two- or four-year institution of higher learning. Female applicants must meet the height requirement of 5'10" and male applicants must meet the requirement of 6'2". Applicants must live within the geographic area of a participating club.

How to Apply: Applications are available online.
Deadline: Varies.
Amount: Varies.
Number of Awards: Varies.

Tau Beta Pi Association

Attn.: D. Stephen Pierre Jr., P.E.
Alabama Power Company
150 Joseph Street, P.O. Box 2247
Mobile, AL 36652
Phone: 251-694-2512
Email: fellowships@tbp.org
Website: http://www.tbp.org

825 • Tau Beta Pi Scholarships

Purpose: To assist members who are studying engineering.

Eligibility: Applicants must be undergraduate members of Tau Beta Pi and be juniors at the time of application who are planning to remain in or return to school for a senior year of full-time study in engineering.

How to Apply: Applications are available online.
Deadline: March 1.
Amount: $2,000.
Number of Awards: Up to 40.

Tire Association of North America

Michelin/TIA Scholarship Program
P.O. Box 1465
Taylors, SC 29687
Phone: 864-268-3363
Email: sallyking@bellsouth.net
Website: http://www.tireindustry.org

826 • Michelin/TIA Scholarship Program

Purpose: To offer financial assistance to children of full-time TIA employees and part-time TIA employees.

Eligibility: Applicants must be part-time employees or dependent children of full-time employees of the Tire Industry Association. Applicants must also be seniors in high school with a minimum 3.0 GPA and be pursuing further education at an accredited two-year or four-year school. Academic achievement, scholarship performance, scholastic aptitude, essays and leadership skills will all be considered.

How to Apply: Applications are available online.
Deadline: March 31.
Amount: $1,250-$2,500.
Number of Awards: 3.

Tri Delta

Delta Delta Delta Foundation
2331 Brookhollow Plaza Drive
Arlington, TX 76006
Phone: 817-633-8001
Email: info@trideltaeo.org
Website: http://www.tridelta.org

827 • Tri Delta Graduate Scholarship

Purpose: To offer scholarships to graduate student members.

Eligibility: The Mary Margaret Hafter Fellowship, Luella Akins Key Scholarship, Second Century Graduate Scholarship, Margaret Stafford Memorial Scholarship and Sarah Shinn Marshall Scholarship may be awarded to Tri Delta members who are admitted or current graduate students. Applicants to the Durning Sisters Scholarship must be unmarried Tri Delta members who have completed at least 12 graduate credits and who will be continuing graduate study during the year in which the award is given. There is usually one winner for each award.

How to Apply: Applications are available online.

Deadline: January 30.

Amount: $3,000.

Number of Awards: Varies.

828 • Tri Delta Undergraduate Scholarship

Purpose: To offer scholarships to undergraduate members.

Eligibility: Applicants must be sophomores or juniors in good standing with the organization.

How to Apply: Applications are available online.

Deadline: January 30.

Amount: $500-$1,500.

Number of Awards: 50.

Triangle Education Foundation

Chairman, Scholarship and Loan Committee
120 S. Center Street
Plainfield, IN 46168
Phone: 317-837-9640
Fax: 317-837-9642
Website: http://www.triangle.org

829 • Mortin Scholarship

Purpose: To help deserving active members of Triangle Fraternity in completing their education.

Eligibility: Applicants must be active members of the Triangle Fraternity, enrolled in a course of study leading to a degree. Applicants must have at least a 3.0 GPA, have completed at least two full academic years of school and be undergraduates in the year following their application. Selection is based on financial need, grades and participation in campus and Triangle activities.

How to Apply: Applications are available online.

Deadline: February 15.

Amount: $2,500.

Number of Awards: 1.

830 • Rust Scholarship

Purpose: To help deserving active members of Triangle Fraternity in completing their education.

Eligibility: Applicants must be active members of the Triangle Fraternity who have completed at least two full academic years of school and will be undergraduates in the school year following their application. Selection is based on financial need, grades and participation in campus and Triangle activities. Preference is given to applicants in engineering and the hard sciences. Applicants must have at least a 3.0 GPA.

How to Apply: Applications are available online.

Deadline: February 15.

Amount: $3,500.

Number of Awards: 1.

Tuition Exchange

1743 Connecticut Avenue NW
Washington, DC 20009
Phone: 202-518-0135
Email: info@tuitionexchange.org
Website: http://www.tuitionexchange.org

831 • Tuition Exchange Scholarships

Purpose: To assist the children or other family members of the faculty and staff at participating colleges and universities to encourage employment of parents and guardians in higher education.

Eligibility: Eligibility varies by institution. Applicants must be family members of the home institution where they are applying. However specific details about employment status, years of service or other requirements are determined solely by the home institution.

How to Apply: Applications are available from the liaison officer at the home institution.

Deadline: Varies.

Amount: Varies.

Number of Awards: Varies.

Veterans of Foreign Wars

406 W. 34th Street
Kansas City, MO 64111
Phone: 816-968-1117
Fax: 816-968-1149
Email: info@vfw.org
Website: http://www.vfw.org

832 • Outstanding Scouts Awards

Purpose: To recognize outstanding Boy Scouts and support the common bonds between the Boy Scouts of America and the VFW: belief in God, respect for others, honesty and patriotism.

Eligibility: Applicants must be nominated as the top Scout by a VFW organization.

How to Apply: Applications are available online.

Deadline: March 1.

Amount: $1,000-$5,000.

Number of Awards: 3.

Related Scholarships:

Gamma Theta Upsilon

See #1174 • Gamma Theta Upsilon-Geographical Honor Society

Sigma Alpha Iota Philanthropies

See #898 • Undergraduate Scholarships

Association of Engineering Geologists Foundation Marliave Fund

See #383 • Marliave Fund

Society of Automotive Engineers

See #419 • Long-Term Member Sponsored Scholarship

American Society of Mechanical Engineers

See #368 • Melvin R. Green Scholarships

American Society of Mechanical Engineers

See #365 • Garland Duncan Scholarships

American Society of Mechanical Engineers

See #363 • F.W. Beichley Scholarship

American Society of Mechanical Engineers

See #366 • John and Elsa Gracik Scholarships

Public Relations Student Society of America

See #599 • Professor Sidney Gross Memorial Award

Costume Society of America (CSA)

See #853 • Stella Blum Research Grant

Air Traffic Control Association

See #82 • Air Traffic Control Association Scholarship Program

Appaloosa Horse Club

See #122 • Youth Program

Golf Course Superintendents Association of America Foundation

See #124 • GCSAA Scholars Program

Golf Course Superintendents Association of America Foundation

See #125 • GCSAA Student Essay Contest

Golf Course Superintendents Association of America Foundation

See #126 • Scotts Company Scholars Program

DECA Inc.

See #595 • Coca-Cola USA Scholarship

Public Relations Student Society of America

See #596 • Betsy Plank/PRSSA Scholarship

Emergency Nurses Association

See #657 • ENA Foundation Undergraduate Scholarship

Emergency Nurses Association

See #659 • Medtronic Physio-Control Advanced Nursing Practice Scholarship

American Alliance for Health, Physical Education, Recreation and Dance

See #607 • Ruth Abernathy Presidential Scholarship

American Criminal Justice Association

See #699 • Student Paper Competition

American Radio Relay League Foundation

See #231 • Earl I. Anderson Scholarship

American Foundation

See #108 • Angus Foundation Scholarship

American Guild of Organists

See #836 • National Young Artists Competition in Organ Performance

Ladies Auxiliary VFW

See #573 • National Junior Girls Scholarships

National Federation of Music Clubs Bullock and Robertson Awards

See #671 • NFMC Dorothy Dann Bullock Music Therapy Award and the NFMC Ruth B. Robertson Music Therapy Award

National Rifle Association

See #164 • NRA Outstanding Achievement Youth Award

National Society of Professional Engineers

See #415 • Professional Engineers In Industry (PEI) Scholarship

American Society of Mechanical Engineers

See #367 • Kenneth Andrew Roe Scholarship

American Society of Mechanical Engineers

See #364 • Frank and Dorothy Miller ASME Auxiliary Scholarships

American Society of Mechanical Engineers

See #362 · *ASME Foundation Scholarships*

American Society of Mechanical Engineers

See #369 · *Robert F. Sammataro Pressure Vessel Piping Division Scholarship*

American Ornithologists' Union

See #176 · *Research Award*

American Society of Ichthyologists and Herpetologists

See #179 · *Raney Fund Award*

Entomological Society of America

See #185 · *John Henry Comstock Graduate Student Awards*

American Institute of Chemical Engineers - (AICHE)

See #217 · *Donald F. and Mildred Topp Othmer Foundation*

American Institute of Chemical Engineers - (AICHE)

See #351 · *National Student Design Competition*

Association of Engineering Geologists Foundation Tilford Fund

See #384 · *Tilford Fund*

National Society of Professional Engineers

See #413 · *Paul H. Robbins, P.E., Honorary Scholarship*

Public Relations Student Society of America

See #597 · *Gary Yoshimura Scholarship*

Public Relations Student Society of America

See #598 · *Lawrence G. Foster Award for Excellence in Public Relations*

Emergency Nurses Association

See #658 · *Karen O'Neil Endowed Advanced Nursing Practice Scholarship*

National Black Nurses Association

See #668 · *Annual NBNA Scholarships*

National Society Daughters of the American Revolution

See #679 · *Madeline Pickett (Halbert) Cogswell Nursing Scholarship*

Physician Assistant Foundation

See #687 · *Physician Assistant Foundation Scholarship*

Navy Supply Corps Foundation Inc.

See #732 · *Navy Supply Corps Foundation Scholarship*

National Federation of Music Clubs (NY)

See #882 · *Victor Herbert ASCAP Young Composers Awards and The NFMC Marion Richter American Music Composition Award*

National Federation of Music Clubs (Coral Gables, FL)

See #881 · *Thelma A. Robinson Award in Ballet*

National Federation of Music Clubs Stillman-Kelley Award

See #886 · *Stillman-Kelley Awards*

National Federation of Music Clubs Junior Composers Award

See #884 · *Junior Composers Award*

National Federation of Music Clubs (AR)

See #880 · *NFMC Wendell Irish Viola Award*

National Federation of Music Clubs (Miami, FL)

See #883 · *NFMC Claire Ulrich Whitehurst (Flanagan) Piano Award*

National Federation of Music Clubs Wiegand Award

See #887 · *NFMC Elizabeth Grieger Wiegand Sacred Music of the Faiths Award*

National Federation of Music Clubs Olson Awards

See #885 · *NFMC Lynn Freeman Olson Composition Awards*

Sinfonia Foundation

See #899 · *Sinfonia Foundation Scholarship*

American Society of Ichthyologists and Herpetologists

See #178 · *Gaige Fund Award*

American Society of Ichthyologists and Herpetologists

See #180 · *Stoye and Storer Awards*

American Institute of Chemical Engineers - (AICHE)

See #218 · *John J. McKetta Scholarship*

American Society of Agricultural Engineers Foundation

See #356 · *ASAE Foundation Scholarship*

American Society of Agricultural Engineers Foundation

See #357 · *ASAE Student Engineer of the Year Scholarship*

American Society of Naval Engineers

See #370 · *ASNE Scholarship Program*

American Health Information Management Association

See #622 · *Merit Scholarships and Educational Loans*

National Bicycle League (NBL)

See #160 · *Bob Warnicke Scholarship*

Child Nutrition Foundation

See #480 · *CNF Professional Growth Scholarship*

Child Nutrition Foundation

See #482 · *Nancy Curry Scholarship*

Pi Sigma Alpha

See #1195 · *Pi Sigma Alpha Washington Internship Scholarships*

Child Nutrition Foundation

See #481 · *GED Jump Start Scholarship*

International Military Community Executives Association (IMCEA)

See #720 · *IMCEA Scholarships*

National Scholastic Surfing Association

See #165 · *National Scholarship Program*

Child Nutrition Foundation

See #483 · *Schwan's Food Service Scholarship*

Performing Arts/Music/Drama/ Visual Arts

Also See Scholarships Listed Under:
English/Writing
Graphic Arts

Academy of Television Arts and Sciences Foundation

5220 Lankershim Boulevard
North Hollywood, CA 91601
Phone: 818-754-2830
Fax: 818-761-2827
Email: collegeawards@emmys.org
Website: http://www.emmys.org

833 • College Television Awards

Purpose: To award college student film or video producers.
Eligibility: Applicants must produce an original film or video in one of the following categories: drama, comedy, music, documentary, news, magazine show, traditional or computer-generated animation or children's programming. Applicants must have no professional experience as a producer, director, camera operator, lighting or sound technician or production manager. Applicants must also be full-time students who have produced their video for course credit at an American college or university from September 1 of the previous year to December 15.
How to Apply: Applications are available online from September 1 to December 15 annually and are also sent to college film and television departments.
Deadline: December 15.
Amount: $500-$4,000.
Number of Awards: Varies.

Actors' Fund of America/Actors' Work Program

729 Seventh Avenue
11th Floor
New York, NY 10019
Phone: 800-221-7303
Fax: 212-921-4295
Email: info@actorsfund.org
Website: http://www.actorsfund.org

834 • Actors' Work Program

Purpose: To assist members of the entertainment industry with finding sideline work and pursuing new careers.
Eligibility: Applicants must be members in good standing of an entertainment industry union and have a referral from the Fund's social service department or other organization able to document entertainment industry work.
How to Apply: Applicants must attend an Actors' Work Program Orientation to learn more about the program.
Deadline: Varies.
Amount: Varies.
Number of Awards: Varies.

American Council of Learned Societies (ACLS)

633 Third Avenue
New York, NY 10017-6795
Phone: 212-697-1505
Fax: 212-949-8058
Email: sfisher@acls.org
Website: http://www.acls.org

835 • Henry Luce Foundation/ACLS Dissertation Fellowships in American Art

Purpose: To support Ph.D. candidates working on art history dissertations.
Eligibility: Applicants must be Ph.D. candidates in an art history department in the U.S. who are working on dissertations about American visual arts history. All the Ph.D. requirements should be met except the dissertation before taking the fellowship. Applicants should submit an application, a proposal, a bibliography, illustrations (optional), a publications list (optional), three reference letters and an official transcript of graduate record. The fellowship lasts for a year.
How to Apply: Applications are available online.
Deadline: November 10.
Amount: $22,500.
Number of Awards: 10.

American Guild of Organists

475 Riverside Drive
Suite 1260
New York, NY 10115
Phone: 212-870-2310
Fax: 212-870-2163
Email: info@agohq.org
Website: http://www.agohq.org

836 • National Young Artists Competition in Organ Performance

Purpose: To support student organists.
Eligibility: Applicants must be between 22 and 32 years old. The preliminary round includes a tape recording of a solo organ performance. This competition is open to members of the American Guild of Organists or the Royal Canadian College of Organists. There is a registration fee. This award has been included because it is from a legitimate organization. However, students are encouraged to apply for scholarships without a fee.
How to Apply: Applications are available online and by written request.
Deadline: April 18.
Amount: $500-$2,000.
Number of Awards: 4.

837 • Regional Competition for Young Organists

Purpose: To support student organists.
Eligibility: Applicants do not need to be members of the American Guild of Organists. This competition is for organists under 23 years of age. There is a registration fee for the chapter competition, which is the first level. This award has been included because it is from a legitimate organization. However, students are encouraged to apply for scholarships without a fee.
How to Apply: Applications are available by written request.

Deadline: January 15.
Amount: $500-$1,000.
Number of Awards: 2.

American Recorder Society

1129 Ruth Drive
St. Louis, MO 63122-1019
Phone: 800-491-9588
Fax: 314-966-4649
Email: recorder@americanrecorder.org
Website: http://www.americanrecorder.org

838 • ARS Recorder Workshop Scholarships

Purpose: To support workshop attendance by recording players.
Eligibility: Applicants should apply at least two months before funds are needed and must submit an application, essay and letter of recommendation.
How to Apply: Applications are available online.
Deadline: April 15.
Amount: Varies.
Number of Awards: Varies.

American Sheep Industry Association

Box 175
Lavina, MT 59046
Phone: 406-636-2731
Fax: 406-636-2731
Website: http://www.sheepusa.org

839 • National Make It Yourself With Wool Competition

Purpose: To encourage creativity in sewing, knitting and crocheting with the use of wool fabrics and yarns as applicants construct and model handmade garments.
Eligibility: The four divisions of competition are: preteens (12 and under), juniors (13-16), seniors (17-24) and adults (25+). Garments must be made of 100 percent wool or wool-blend specialty fiber yarn or fabric. The body of the garment including back, front and sleeves must be made of wool or wool-blend fabric. The trims, facings, linings, interfacings and underlinings may be made of other fabrics. Entrants must make and model their own garment.
How to Apply: Applications are available by mail.
Deadline: November 15.
Amount: Varies.
Number of Awards: $1,000-$2,000.

American Society of Interior Designers (ASID) Educational Foundation Inc.

608 Massachusetts Avenue NE
Washington, DC 20002-6006
Phone: 202-546-3480
Fax: 202-546-3240
Website: http://www.asid.org

840 • Joel Polsky Academic Achievement Award

Purpose: To recognize an interior design student's project.
Eligibility: Applicants must be undergraduate or graduate students in interior design and should submit entry forms and projects such as research papers or doctoral and master's theses that focus on interior design topics. The projects are judged on content, breadth of material, coverage of the topic, innovative subject matter, bibliography and references. The society may exhibit any entry for two years.
How to Apply: Applications are available online.
Deadline: May 15.
Amount: $1,000.
Number of Awards: 1.

841 • Mabelle Wilhelmina Boldt Scholarship

Purpose: To help interior designers continue their education.
Eligibility: Applicants must be enrolled in or have applied for admission to a graduate-level interior design program at a degree-granting institution. Students must have been active designers for at least five years before returning to graduate school. The scholarship is based on academic and creative accomplishment. Applicants must submit undergraduate transcripts, a statement and a letter of recommendation. Preference is given to students with a focus on design research. ASID may publish some of the research.
How to Apply: Applications are available online.
Deadline: May 15.
Amount: $2,000.
Number of Awards: 1.

American String Teachers Association (ASTA) with National School Orchestra Association

4153 Chain Bridge Road
Fairfax, VA 22030
Phone: 703-279-2113
Fax: 703-279-2114
Email: asta@astaweb.com
Website: http://www.astaweb.com

842 • Urban Outreach Grants

Purpose: To help economically disadvantaged urban school children study stringed instruments.
Eligibility: Applicants must be economically disadvantaged urban school children through grade 12 who want to study stringed instruments. There are two projects, individual and group. Funds given by the Urban Outreach Program must be matched by state and/or local sources. Project coordinator(s) must be active members of ASTA. Applicants should submit an application signed by the state chapter president, project description and proposed budget.
How to Apply: Applications are available online.
Deadline: April 1.
Amount: $500.
Number of Awards: Varies.

American Theatre Organ Society

Carlton B. Smith, Director
2175 N. Irwin Street
Indianapolis, IN 46219
Phone: 317-356-1240
Fax: 317-322-9379
Email: smith@atos.org
Website: http://www.atos.org

843 • American Theatre Organ Society Scholarships

Purpose: To provide students with an opportunity to study with professional theatre organ teachers or to further their organ performance education in college.

Eligibility: Applicants must be between the ages of 13 and 27 as of July 1 and either working toward college organ performance degrees or be studying with professional organ instructors. Students' names must be submitted by their present organ instructor or the school's music department head. An essay is also required.
How to Apply: Applications are available online.
Deadline: April 15.
Amount: Up to $1,000.
Number of Awards: Varies.

ASCAP Foundation

One Lincoln Plaza
New York, NY 10023
Phone: 212-621-6219
Website: http://www.ascapfoundation.org

844 • Morton Gould Young Composer Award

Purpose: To encourage young composers early in their careers.
Eligibility: Applicants must be composers who have not turned 30 before January 1 of the current year. They must be U.S. citizens or permanent residents or enrolled students with a student visa. Applicants must submit an original composition.
How to Apply: Applications are available online.
Deadline: March 1.
Amount: Varies.
Number of Awards: Varies.

845 • Young Jazz Composer Award

Purpose: To recognize the talent of young jazz composers.
Eligibility: Applicants must be under the age of 30 and U.S. citizens or permanent residents. They must submit one original composition, including a score and performance, if possible.
How to Apply: Applications are available online.
Deadline: December 1.
Amount: Varies.
Number of Awards: Varies.

Associated Male Choruses of America

Robert H. Torborg, Scholarship Chair
P.O. Box 342
Cold Spring, MN 56320
Phone: 320-685-3848
Email: scholarship@amcofa.net
Website: http://www.amcofa.net

846 • AMCA Music Scholarship

Purpose: To promote the study of chorus and music studies in college.
Eligibility: Applicants must be full-time students obtaining their bachelor's degree in a music-related field (with preference given to voice or choral concentrations) and be sponsored by a chorus of the Associated Male Choruses of America. Applicants must submit references and a personal letter.
How to Apply: Applications are available online or by contacting your local AMCA chorus.
Deadline: March 1.
Amount: Varies.
Number of Awards: Varies.

Beem Foundation for the Advancement of Music

309 E. Hillcrest Boulevard, Suite 350
Inglewood, CA 900301
Phone: 301-677-6793
Fax: 310-677-6664
Email: info@beemfoundation.org
Website: http://www.beemfoundation.com

847 • BEEM Foundation Scholarships

Purpose: To support winners of an annual music competition.
Eligibility: Applicants must be vocal or instrumental music students under the age of 25 and must perform in the annual Scholarship and Showcase Competition at the Los Angeles Center for Enriched Studies.
How to Apply: Applications are available online.
Deadline: May 2.
Amount: Varies.
Number of Awards: Varies.

BMI Foundation Inc.

320 W. 57th Street
New York, NY 10019
Phone: 212-586-2000
Email: info@bmifoundation.org
Website: http://www.bmifoundation.org

848 • John Lennon Scholarship Competition

Purpose: Established in 1997 by Yoko Ono in conjunction with the BMI Foundation, the John Lennon Scholarship recognizes the talent of young songwriters.
Eligibility: Applicants must be age 15 to 25 and write an original song to be reviewed by a prestigious panel of judges. Entries are to be submitted by music schools, universities, youth orchestras and the Music Educators National Conference (MENC).
How to Apply: Please see the website for a full list of eligible organizations that may submit entries.
Deadline: January 26.
Amount: $5,000-$10,000.
Number of Awards: 3.

BMI Foundation Pete Carpenter Fellowship

Ms. Linda Livingston, Director
8730 Sunset Boulevard, 3rd Floor West
Los Angeles, CA 90069
Email: carpenterfellowship@bmifoundation.org
Website: http://www.bmifoundation.org

849 • Pete Carpenter Fellowship for Aspiring Film Composers

Purpose: Established by the BMI Foundation and Mr. Carpenter's family, colleagues and friends to honor the late co-composer of television themes and scores.
Eligibility: Applicants must be under the age of 35 and submit an original one- to three- minute composition or part of a score that they consider appropriate as the theme of a film or series with the application. The winner can work for one month in Los Angeles on a day-to-day basis with distinguished theatrical film and television composers and receives a $2,000 stipend for travel and expenses.
How to Apply: Applications are available online.

Deadline: January 27.
Amount: $2,000.
Number of Awards: 1.

Career Transition for Dancers

Caroline and Theodore Newhouse Center for Dancers
165 W. 46th Street, Suite 701
The Actors' Equity Building
New York, NY 10036
Phone: 212-764-0172
Fax: 212-764-0343
Email: info@careertransition.org
Website: http://www.careertransition.org

850 • Caroline H. Newhouse Scholarship Fund

Purpose: To provide educational grants for dancers seeking second careers.
Eligibility: Applicants must provide documentation of 100 weeks or more of paid employment as a dance performer in the U.S. over at least seven years. For work not performed under union jurisdiction, applicants must also provide documentation of total gross earnings of at least $56,000. Choreographers and dance teachers are not eligible for this program.
How to Apply: Applicants must call to confirm their eligibility.
Deadline: Varies.
Amount: Up to $2,000.
Number of Awards: Varies.

Chopin Foundation of the United States

1440 79th Street Causeway
Suite 117
Miami, FL 33141
Phone: 305-868-0624
Fax: 305-865-5150
Email: info@chopin.org
Website: http://www.chopin.org

851 • Scholarship Program for Young Pianists

Purpose: To support pianists to prepare and qualify for the American National Chopin Piano Competition.
Eligibility: The program is available to any qualified American pianists age 14 to 17 who are enrolled in secondary or undergraduate institutions as full-time students. Applicants also must study music and major in piano.
How to Apply: Applications are available online.
Deadline: February 15.
Amount: $1,000.
Number of Awards: Up to 10.

Christophers

12 E. 48th Street
New York, NY 10017
Website: http://www.christophers.org

852 • Poster Contest for High School Students

Purpose: To reward students for interpreting a given theme through poster art.
Eligibility: Entrants must be high school students. Students must work individually to create posters of original content. Posters are judged by a panel based on overall impact, expression of the year's theme, artistic merit and originality.
How to Apply: Applications are available online.

Deadline: January 23.
Amount: $250-$1,000.
Number of Awards: 8.

Costume Society of America (CSA)

Ann Wass
5903 60th Avenue
Riverdale, MD 20737
Phone: 800-272-9447
Fax: 908-359-7619
Email: national.office@costumesocietyamerica.com
Website: http://www.costumesocietyamerica.com

853 • Stella Blum Research Grant

Purpose: To support a CSA student member working in the field of North American costume.
Eligibility: Applicants must be accepted into an undergraduate or graduate degree program at an accredited university for the time during which the grant would apply, conduct a research project in the area of North American costume and be members of the Costume Society of America (CSA) in good standing. Applications are judged according to significance of topic, feasibility, time frame, methodology, bibliography, budget, applicants' qualifications and how the research might further the field of costumes.
How to Apply: Applications are available by email or phone.
Deadline: May 1.
Amount: $2,000 plus a travel component of up to $500 to attend National Symposium.
Number of Awards: 1.

Donna Reed Foundation for the Performing Arts

1305 Broadway
Denison, IA 51442
Phone: 712-263-3334
Fax: 712-263-8026
Email: info@donnareed.org
Website: http://www.donnareed.org

854 • Donna Reed Performing Arts Scholarships - National Scholarship

Purpose: To recognize students who demonstrate excellence and a high level of interest in the performing arts.
Eligibility: Applicants must graduate or have graduated from high school between September 1 and August 31 of the award year. Applicants must be registered as full-time students in the Donna Reed Performing Arts Workshop Program. Finalists must take part in a live competition at the workshop. Available categories are acting and musical theater, with each category requiring a separate audition tape. Two of the available scholarships are set aside for Iowa residents.
How to Apply: Applications are available online.
Deadline: June 1.
Amount: $500-$1,000.
Number of Awards: 8.

Educational Theatre Association

2343 Auburn Avenue
Cincinnati, OH 45219
Phone: 513-421-3900
Website: http://www.edta.org

855 • Thespian Scholarships

Purpose: To support student thespians.

Eligibility: Applicants must be seniors in high school, active members of the International Thespian Society and planning to major or minor in communicative arts. An audition or tech portfolio is required.

How to Apply: Applications are available online.

Deadline: May 15.

Amount: $1,500-$4,500.

Number of Awards: Varies.

Elizabeth Greenshields Foundation

1814 Sherbrooke Street West Suite #1
Montreal
Quebec, Canada H3H 1E4
Phone: 514-937-9225
Fax: 514-937-0141
Website: http://www.calarts.edu

856 • Elizabeth Greenshields Foundation Grants

Purpose: To promote an appreciation of painting, drawing, sculpture and the graphic arts by supporting art students, artists or sculptors.

Eligibility: Applicants must have already started or completed training at an established school of art and/or demonstrated, through past work and future plans, a commitment to make art a lifetime career. Applicants must be in the early stages of their careers working in painting, drawing, printmaking or sculpture. Abstract work will not be considered.

How to Apply: Applications are available by phone or written request.

Deadline: None.

Amount: $10,000 CDN.

Number of Awards: Varies.

Forest Roberts Theatre at Northern Michigan University

1401 Presque Isle Avenue
Marquette, MI 49855
Phone: 906-227-2553
Email: bowersr1@chartermi.net
Website: http://www.nmu.edu/theatre/

857 • Mildred and Albert Panowski Playwriting Award

Purpose: To provide students and faculty the opportunity produce an original work on the university stage.

Eligibility: This award is available to any playwright, and entries must be original, full-length productions.

How to Apply: There is no application form. The play is the application.

Deadline: November.

Amount: $2,000.

Number of Awards: 1.

Fort Collins Symphony

FCSO Young Artist Competition
P.O. Box 1963
Fort Collins, CO 80522
Phone: 970-482-4823
Fax: 970-482-4858
Email: note@fcsymphony.org
Website: http://www.fcsymphony.org

858 • Annual Young Artist Competition

Purpose: To support student pianists.

Eligibility: Contestants must be under age 25 or younger and must compete in piano or orchestral performance.

How to Apply: Applications are available online.

Deadline: January 12.

Amount: $300-$6,000.

Number of Awards: 6.

859 • Junior Competition

Purpose: To reward student pianists.

Eligibility: Applicants must be between 12 and 18 and perform one movement of a standard, published solo concerto or similar work. The competition is limited to the first 20 applicants and 2 alternates in each division.

How to Apply: Applications are available online.

Deadline: January 12.

Amount: $300-$500.

Number of Awards: 2.

Gina Bachauer International Piano Foundation

138 W. Broadway, Suite 220
Salt Lake City, UT 84101
Phone: 801-297-4250
Fax: 801-521-9202
Email: info@bachauer.com
Website: http://www.bachauer.com

860 • 2008 Junior Competition

Purpose: To reward top piano prodigies, ages 11 to 13.

Eligibility: Applicants must be between the ages of 11 and 13 for this competition that occurs in 2008 in Salt Lake City.

How to Apply: Applications are available online.

Deadline: Varies.

Amount: Up to $20,000.

Number of Awards: Varies.

Glenn Miller Birthplace Society

107 East Main Street
P.O. Box 61
Clarinda, IA 51632
Phone: 712-542-2461
Fax: 712-542-2461
Email: gmbs@heartland.net
Website: http://www.glennmiller.org

861 • Glenn Miller Scholarship Competition

Purpose: To honor Glenn Miller by recognizing future musical leaders.

Eligibility: Applicants may apply as instrumentalists or vocalists. They must be high school seniors or college freshmen who plan to focus on music in their future lives. Applicants must submit an audition CD or tape in addition to an application form. High school seniors may reapply as college freshmen as long as they weren't first-place winners the previous year.

How to Apply: Applications are available online.

Deadline: March 15.
Amount: $1,000-$3,000.
Number of Awards: 6.

Gravure Education Foundation

1200-A Scottsville Road
Rochester, NY 14624
Phone: 315-589-8879
Fax: 585-436-7689
Email: lwshatch@gaa.org
Website: http://www.gaa.org

862 • Corporate Leadership Scholarships

Purpose: To provide scholarships to undergraduate and graduate students pursuing degrees in printing or graphic arts.
Eligibility: Applicants must be enrolled full-time at a GEF Learning Resource Center at Arizona State University, California Polytechnic State University, Clemson University, Murray State, Rochester Institute of Technology, University of Wisconsin - Stout or Western Michigan University. Students must major in printing, graphic arts or graphic communications and be a sophomore, junior or senior at the time the scholarship is awarded.
How to Apply: Applications are available online.
Deadline: May 31.
Amount: $1,500.
Number of Awards: 6.

863 • GEF Resource Center Scholarships

Purpose: To award scholarships to undergraduate and graduate students majoring in printing, graphic arts or graphic communications.
Eligibility: Applicants must be enrolled at one of the following GEF Learning Resource Centers: Arizona State University, California Polytechnic State University, Clemson University, Murray State University, Rochester Institute of Technology, University of Wisconsin - Stout or Western Michigan University.
How to Apply: Applications are available online.
Deadline: May 31.
Amount: Varies.
Number of Awards: Varies.

864 • Gravure Catalog and Insert Council Scholarship

Purpose: To support undergraduate students to help them enter the printing industry.
Eligibility: Applicants must major in printing, graphic arts or graphic communications and be at least a junior at the time the scholarship is awarded. Applicants should be interested in promoting gravure as the preferred method in high-quality printing.
How to Apply: Applications are available online.
Deadline: May 31.
Amount: Varies.
Number of Awards: Varies.

865 • Hallmark Graphic Arts Scholarship

Purpose: To provide a scholarship to an undergraduate student in printing or graphic arts who exhibits leadership through involvement in clubs, associations, sports, community involvement or volunteering.
Eligibility: Applicants must be enrolled full-time at a GEF Learning Resource Center at Arizona State University, California Polytechnic State University, Clemson University, Murray State, Rochester Institute of Technology, University of Wisconsin - Stout or Western Michigan University. Students must major in printing, graphic arts or graphic communications and be a junior or senior at the time the scholarship is awarded.
How to Apply: Applications are available online.
Deadline: May 31.
Amount: Up to $1,500.
Number of Awards: 1.

866 • Werner B. Thiele Memorial Scholarship

Purpose: To award scholarships to college juniors and seniors majoring in printing, graphic arts or graphic communications.
Eligibility: Applicants must be enrolled full-time at one of the GEF Learning Resource Centers: Arizona State University, California Polytechnic State University, Clemson University, Murray State, Rochester Institute of Technology, University of Wisconsin - Stout or Western Michigan University.
How to Apply: Applications are available online or by mail.
Deadline: May 31.
Amount: $1,250.
Number of Awards: 2.

HAPCO Music Foundation Inc.

P.O. Box 784581
Winter Garden, FL 34778
Phone: 407-877-2262
Fax: 407-654-0308
Email: info@hapcopromo.org
Website: http://www.hapcopromo.org

867 • HAPCO Music Scholarship

Purpose: To encourage students to pursue their interest in music while attending college.
Eligibility: Applicants must be accepted at a college or university. They may major in any area but must participate in a music organization at their school. Students must have at least a 3.0 GPA, have taken a set of required core credits and earn a score of 970 on the SAT or 20 on the ACT. Home-schooled students must earn a score or 1070 on the SAT or 23 on the ACT unless they can provide proof of the college-preparatory credits. Applicants must include a letter of recommendation, a high school transcript, a photo and an essay on their future educational goals.
How to Apply: Applications are available online.
Deadline: December 31.
Amount: $250-$1,000.
Number of Awards: Varies.

Houston Symphony

Education Department
615 Louisiana Street
Suite 102
Houston, TX 77002
Phone: 713-224-7575
Email: office@houstonsymphony.org
Website: http://www.houstonsymphony.org

868 • Houston Symphony Ima Hogg National Young Artist Competition

Purpose: To honor the memory of Ima Hogg, a co-founder of the Houston Symphony.
Eligibility: Applicants must submit a $25 non-refundable application fee with a tape of a non-concerto repertoire and be U.S. citizens or currently enrolled in college. This award is listed because it is from a legitimate organization. However, students are encouraged to apply for scholarships without a registration fee.

How to Apply: Applications are available online.
Deadline: February 15.
Amount: $1,000-$5,000.
Number of Awards: 3.

Industrial Designers Society of America

45195 Business Court
Suite 250
Dulles, VA 20166
Phone: 703-707-6000
Fax: 703-787-8501
Email: idsa@idsa.org
Website: http://www.idsa.org

869 • IDSA Undergraduate Scholarships

Purpose: To help industrial design students in their final year of schooling.
Eligibility: Applicants must be full-time students enrolled in an IDSA-listed program in their next-to-last year of the program, have a minimum 3.0 GPA, be members of an IDSA Student Chapter and be U.S. citizens or residents. Applicants must submit a letter of intent, 20 visual examples of their work and a transcript. Awards are based solely on the excellence of the submitted works.
How to Apply: Applications are available online.
Deadline: May 2.
Amount: Varies.
Number of Awards: 2.

Institute for Humane Studies at George Mason University

3301 N. Fairfax Drive
Suite 440
Arlington, VA 22201
Phone: 800-697-8799
Fax: 703-993-4890
Email: ihs@gmu.edu
Website: http://www.theihs.org

870 • Film and Fiction Scholarships

Purpose: To support promising young filmmakers and writers with an interest in classical liberal ideas and their contemporary application.
Eligibility: Applicants must be pursuing a Master of Fine Arts (M.F.A.) degree in filmmaking, fiction writing or playwriting. Applicants must also have a demonstrated interest in classical liberal ideas and must show their commitment to their profession through desire, motivation and creative ability.
How to Apply: Applications are available online.
Deadline: January 15.
Amount: Up to $10,000.
Number of Awards: Varies.

International Trumpet Guild

John Irish, Department of Music
Angelo State University
ASU Station #10906
San Angelo, TX 76909
Email: confscholarships@trumpetguild.org
Website: http://www.trumpetguild.org

871 • International Trumpet Guild Conference Scholarship

Purpose: To improve the artistic level of trumpet players.
Eligibility: Applicants must be students and record audition songs onto a tape or CD. There are different age group categories, and each category has its own performance requirements. Applicants must be ITG members.
How to Apply: Applications are available online.
Deadline: February 15.
Amount: $200 + conference registration fee.
Number of Awards: Varies.

John F. and Anna Lee Stacey Scholarship Fund

1700 N.E. 63rd Street
Oklahoma City, OK 73111
Phone: 405-478-2250
Fax: 405-478-4714
Website: http://www.cowboyhalloffame.org

872 • Stacey Scholarship Fund

Purpose: To educate young men and women who aim to enter the art profession.
Eligibility: Applicants must be between the ages of 18 and 35 and must submit not more than 10 35mm slides of their painting or drawing work for judging along with a letter outlining the applicant's ambitions and plans. Letters of recommendation will also be taken into account during selection.
How to Apply: Applications are available online.
Deadline: February 1.
Amount: Up to $10,000.
Number of Awards: Varies.

Kosciuszko Foundation

15 E. 65th Street
New York, NY 10021
Phone: 212-734-2130
Fax: 212-628-4552
Email: addy@thekf.org
Website: http://www.kosciuszkofoundation.org

873 • Chopin Piano Competition

Purpose: To encourage young pianists to continue their studies and to perform Polish composers' works.
Eligibility: Applicants must be U.S. citizens or permanent residents or international full-time students with valid student visas and must be between the ages of 16 and 22. Applicants are required to prepare a repertoire of works by designated composers.
How to Apply: Applications are available online.
Deadline: February 20.
Amount: Varies.
Number of Awards: Varies.

Kosciuszko Foundation Sembrich Voice Competition

15 E. 65th Street
New York, NY 10021
Phone: 212-734-2130
Fax: 212-628-4552
Email: culture@thekf.org
Website: http://www.kosciuszkofoundation.org

874 • Marcella Sembrich Voice Competition

Purpose: In honor of Polish soprano Marcella Sembrich, monetary awards are given to singers to encourage study of the repertoire of Polish composers.

Eligibility: Applicants must be singers preparing for professional careers who are U.S. citizens or international full-time students with valid student visas and who are between 18 and 35 years old.

How to Apply: Applications are available online.

Deadline: Varies.

Amount: $500-$1,000.

Number of Awards: 3.

Kurt Weill Foundation for Music

7 E. 20th Street
3rd Floor
New York, NY 10003
Phone: 212-505-5240
Fax: 212-353-9663
Email: kwfinfo@dwf.org
Website: http://www.kwf.org

875 • Lotte Lenya Competition for Singers

Purpose: To recognize excellence in music theater performance.

Eligibility: Applicants must be between 18 and 32 years old and attend a regional competition, performing four selections. Finalists will be chosen, based on vocal beauty and technique, interpretation, acting, repertoire variety and presence.

How to Apply: Applications are available online.

Deadline: January 10.

Amount: $1,000-$7,500.

Number of Awards: Varies.

L. Ron Hubbard

P.O. Box 1630
Los Angeles, CA 90078
Email: contests@authorservicesinc.com
Website: http://www.writersofthefuture.com

876 • Illustrators of the Future

Purpose: To discover deserving amateur aspiring illustrators.

Eligibility: Applicants must not have published more than three black-and-white story illustrations or more than one color painting in national media. Applicants must also submit three original illustrations done in a black-and-white medium in three different themes.

How to Apply: There is no application form.

Deadline: December 31, May 31, June 30, September 30.

Amount: $500-$4,000.

Number of Awards: 3 awards are given quarterly with a grand prize awarded annually.

Ladies Auxiliary VFW

406 W. 34th Street
Kansas City, MO 64111
Phone: 816-561-8655
Fax: 816-931-4753
Email: info@ladiesauxvfw.com
Website: http://www.ladiesauxvfw.com

877 • Young American Creative Patriotic Art Awards Program

Purpose: To encourage patriotic art.

Eligibility: Applicants must be high school students in the same state as the sponsoring Ladies Auxiliary. They must submit one piece of patriotic art on paper or canvas. Art must have been completed during the current school year and must be accompanied by a teacher's signature. Applicants must participate in a local Auxiliary competition before advancing to the national level.

How to Apply: Applications are available online.

Deadline: March 31.

Amount: $2,500-$10,000.

Number of Awards: 3.

Mill Mountain Theatre

Literary Coordinator
One Market Square SE
Roanoke, VA 24011
Phone: 540-342-5749
Email: outreach@millmountain.org
Website: http://www.millmountain.org

878 • MMT New Play Competition

Purpose: To promote play-writing.

Eligibility: Applicants must submit an act that should be 25 to 35 minutes long. The script must be agent-submitted or accompanied by a professional letter of recommendation by a director or literary manager. Film or TV scripts, translations or adaptations are not accepted. Plays that have received developmental workshops or musicals accompanied by a demo tape or CD are accepted.

How to Apply: There is no official application.

Deadline: January 1.

Amount: $1,000.

Number of Awards: Varies.

National Coalition Against Censorship (NCAC)

275 Seventh Avenue
15th Floor
New York, NY 10001
Phone: 212-807-6222
Fax: 212-807-6245
Email: ncac@ncac.org
Website: http://www.ncac.org

879 • Youth Free Expression Network Film Contest

Purpose: To reward students who create films on war and free speech.

Eligibility: Awards are given for the top three films addressing the topic "War and (Free) Speech: Can They Co-exist?" Entries must be four minutes or less and may include documentary, animation, experimental and/or music. Winners will receive cash stipends and will be flown to New York for a gala awards ceremony. Applicants must be age 19 and under.

How to Apply: Applications are available online.

Deadline: August 14.

Amount: Up to $1,000.

Number of Awards: 3.

National Federation of Music Clubs (AR)

Dr. George Keck
421 Cherry Street
Arkadelphia, AR 71923
Phone: 317-638-4003
Fax: 317-638-0503
Email: keckg@obu.edu
Website: http://www.nfmc-music.org

880 • NFMC Wendell Irish Viola Award

Purpose: To recognize musically talented students.

Eligibility: Applicants must be between the ages of 12 and 18 and must be Individual Junior Special members or Active Junior Club members of the National Federation of Music Clubs. Applicants must enter in their state of residence by submitting a taped performance.

How to Apply: Applications are available online.
Deadline: February 1.
Amount: $1,000.
Number of Awards: 4.

National Federation of Music Clubs (Coral Gables, FL)

Anne Cruxent
5530 Lajeune Road
Coral Gables, FL 33146
Phone: 317-638-4003
Fax: 317-638-0503
Email: acruxent@bellsouth.net
Website: http://www.nfmc-music.org

881 • Thelma A. Robinson Award in Ballet

Purpose: To support students who are ballet dancers.

Eligibility: Applicants must be between the ages of 13 and 16. There is no entry fee, but applicants must be members of the NFMC.

How to Apply: Applications are available online.
Deadline: October 1.
Amount: $2,000.
Number of Awards: 1.

National Federation of Music Clubs (NY)

Wilmot Irish
600 Warren Road, #3-2A
Ithaca, NY 14850
Phone: 317-638-4003
Fax: 317-638-0503
Email: wwi1@cornell.edu
Website: http://www.nfmc-music.org

882 • Victor Herbert ASCAP Young Composers Awards and The NFMC Marion Richter American Music Composition Award

Purpose: To support young musicians and composers.

Eligibility: Applicants must be between the ages of 18 and 25 for the Victor Herbert award, and a college junior majoring in Composition for the Richter award. These awards are for original musical compositions in the categories of Sonata, Chorus work, Piano solo and Vocal solo with accompaniment. Entry fees range from $5-10 per manuscript. Applicants must be affiliated with the National Federation of Music Clubs. This award is listed because it is from a legitimate organization. However, students are encouraged to apply for scholarships without fees.

How to Apply: Applications are available online.
Deadline: March 1.
Amount: $50-$1,250.
Number of Awards: 6.

National Federation of Music Clubs (Miami, FL)

Claier-Frances Whitehurst
3360 SW 18th Street
Miami, FL 33145
Phone: 317-638-4003
Fax: 317-638-0503
Email: info@nfmc-music.org
Website: http://www.nfmc-music.org

883 • NFMC Claire Ulrich Whitehurst (Flanagan) Piano Award

Purpose: To support young piano players.

Eligibility: Applicants must be high school sophomores, juniors or seniors, and members of the National Federation of Music Clubs and must submit taped piano solo performances.

How to Apply: Applications are available online.
Deadline: February 1.
Amount: $750.
Number of Awards: 1.

National Federation of Music Clubs Junior Composers Award

Jan Hill
1503 Wellington Road
Homewood, AL 35209
Phone: 317-638-4003
Fax: 317-638-0503
Email: info@nfmc-music.org
Website: http://www.nfmc-music.org

884 • Junior Composers Award

Purpose: To support young composers.

Eligibility: Applicants must be between the ages of 16 and 18, and be members of the National Federation of Music Clubs. Selection is based on content and musicianship.

How to Apply: Applications are available online.
Deadline: February 1.
Amount: $50-$200.
Number of Awards: 9.

National Federation of Music Clubs Olson Awards

James Schnars
6550 Shoreline Drive
Suite 7505
St. Petersburg, FL 33708
Phone: 317-638-4003
Fax: 317-638-0503
Email: info@nfmc-music.org
Website: http://www.nfmc-music.org

885 • NFMC Lynn Freeman Olson Composition Awards

Purpose: To support student composers.

Eligibility: Applicants must be at least in grade 7 and no older than age 25. Three awards are given, one for each category: intermediate (grades 7 to 9), high school (grades 10 to 12), and advanced (high school graduates through age 25). Applicants must be members of the National Federation of Music Clubs and must submit an original piano composition to be judged.

How to Apply: Applications are available online.

Deadline: March 1.

Amount: $1,500.

Number of Awards: 1.

National Federation of Music Clubs Stillman-Kelley Award

Sue Breuer
4404 Travis Country
Circle B4
Austin, TX 78735
Phone: 512-892-5633
Website: http://www.nfmc-music.org

886 • Stillman-Kelley Awards

Purpose: To support young musicians and composers.

Eligibility: Applicants must be instrumentalists under the age of 17 and be members of the National Federation of Music Clubs. This award rotates by region with the Northeastern and Southeastern regions in even years and Central and Western regions in odd years.

How to Apply: Applications are available online.

Deadline: February 1.

Amount: $500-$1,000.

Number of Awards: 2.

National Federation of Music Clubs Wiegand Award

Justine Macurdy
#73 Tall Oaks Court
Stamford, CT 06903
Phone: 317-638-4003
Fax: 317-638-0503
Email: info@nfmc-music.org
Website: http://www.nfmc-music.org

887 • NFMC Elizabeth Grieger Wiegand Sacred Music of the Faiths Award

Purpose: To support students majoring in church music.

Eligibility: Applicants must be between 16 and 25 years old and a member of the National Federation of Music Clubs. Applicants must submit with application a $5 entry fee and a tape. This contest is open for choral conducting, piano, organ or voice for students majoring in church music. This award is listed because it is from a legitimate organization. However, students are encouraged to apply for scholarships without fees.

How to Apply: Applications are available online.

Deadline: March 1.

Amount: $750.

Number of Awards: 1.

National Foundation for Advancement in the Arts

444 Brickell Avenue
P-14
Miami, FL 33131
Phone: 800-970-ARTS
Fax: 305-377-1149
Email: info@nfaa.org
Website: http://www.nfaa.org

888 • Arts Recognition and Talent Search Scholarships

Purpose: To reward talented young individuals in the arts.

Eligibility: Applicants must be either high school seniors or 17 or 18 years old by December 1 of the year of application. Applicants must be U.S. citizens or permanent residents. Those applying in the discipline of music or jazz may be registered aliens.

How to Apply: Applications are available online.

Deadline: October 1.

Amount: $100-$10,000.

Number of Awards: Varies.

National Guild of Community Schools of the Arts

Carissa Reddick, YCA Coordinator
The Hartt School Community Division
200 Bloomfield Avenue
West Hartford, CT 06117
Phone: 860-768-7768
Email: youngcomp@hartford.edu
Website: http://www.nationalguild.org

889 • Young Composers Award

Purpose: To honor talented young composers.

Eligibility: Applicants must be residents of the U.S. or Canada, be between the ages of 13 and 18 and be enrolled in a public or private secondary school, in a recognized musical institution or study music privately with an established teacher.

How to Apply: Applications are available online.

Deadline: April.

Amount: $250-$1,000.

Number of Awards: 4.

National Opera Association

Vocal Competition
P.O. Box 60869
Canyon, TX 60869
Phone: 806-651-2857
Email: rhansen@mail.wtamu.edu
Website: http://www.noa.org

890 • Constance Eberhardt Memorial Award, AIMS Graz Experience Scholarship and Banff Center School of Fine Arts Scholarship

Purpose: To provide financial support for young opera singers.

Eligibility: Applicants must be enrolled in undergraduate or graduate programs, or the equivalent, be between the ages of 18 and 24 and applicants' teachers must be members of the National Opera Association. Selection is based on a recording of two arias for preliminary hearings and a live audition of four arias for the final judging.

How to Apply: Applications are available online.
Deadline: October 15.
Amount: $250-$1,000.
Number of Awards: 5.

National Sculpture Society

237 Park Avenue
Ground Floor
New York, NY 10017
Phone: 212-764-5645
Email: nss1893@aol.com
Website: http://www.nationalsculpture.org

891 • National Sculpture Society Scholarship

Purpose: To award scholarships to students of figurative or representative sculpture.
Eligibility: Applicants must provide brief biographies and an explanation of their background in sculpture and photographs of their sculpture work and demonstrate financial need.
How to Apply: Applications are available online.
Deadline: April 30.
Amount: $1,000.
Number of Awards: Varies.

Nicholl Fellowships in Screenwriting

Academy of Motion Picture Arts and Sciences
1313 N. Vine Street
Hollywood, CA 90028
Phone: 310-247-3010
Email: nicholl@oscars.org
Website: http://www.oscars.org

892 • Don and Gee Nicholl Fellowships in Screenwriting

Purpose: To identify and support talented new screenwriters.
Eligibility: Competition is based on an original, feature-film screenplay written by a sole author or a collaboration of two writers. Applicants may not have earned more than $5,000 as professional screenwriters or won a screenwriting scholarship that includes a "first look" clause, may not be members or employees of the Academy of Motion Picture Arts and Sciences or their immediate families and may not hold other fellowships. An application fee of $30 is required. This award is listed because it is from a legitimate organization. However, students are encouraged to apply for scholarships without fees.
How to Apply: Applications are available online and by mail or email request from January through late April.
Deadline: May 1.
Amount: $30,000.
Number of Awards: Up to 5.

893 • Student Academy Awards

Purpose: To support student filmmakers with no previous professional experience who are enrolled as full-time students.
Eligibility: Applicants must be full-time students at an accredited U.S. college, university, film school or art school. Films must be made as a part of a school curriculum in the categories of alternative, animation, documentary or narrative. Entries must have been completed after April 1 of the previous year. In case of graduation or other departure from a program, a film may be submitted up to one year from that date. All entries must be submitted on DVD-R format. Selection is based on originality, entertainment, production quality and resourcefulness.
How to Apply: Applications are available online.
Deadline: April 3.
Amount: $2,000-$5,000.
Number of Awards: 3 per category.

Omaha Symphony Guild

c/o Susan Woodford
9925 Broadmoor
Omaha, NE 68114
Phone: 402-342-3836
Fax: 402-342-3819
Email: bertese@aol.com
Website: http://www.omahasymphony.org

894 • Omaha Symphony Guild International New Music Competition

Purpose: Created in 1978, the Omaha Symphony Guild International New Music Competition offers not only a monetary award to amateur composers but also the opportunity to hear their contemporary classical work performed by a professional orchestra, the Omaha Symphony.
Eligibility: The New Music Competition is open to any composer over the age of 25. The entry must not have been published or performed previously and must not exceed 20 minutes in length. Compositions intended for small ensembles do not qualify for submission.
How to Apply: Applications and further submission rules are available online.
Deadline: April 15.
Amount: $3,000.
Number of Awards: 1.

Princess Grace Awards

150 E. 58th Street
21st Floor
New York, NY 10155
Phone: 212-317-1470
Fax: 212-317-1473
Email: pgfusa@pgfusa.com
Website: http://www.pgfusa.com

895 • Princess Grace Awards

Purpose: To assist emerging young artists in theater, dance and film to realize their career goals.
Eligibility: Applicants must submit an example of their work in the category in the category in which they apply: theatre, dance, film or playwriting. Theatre and dance applicants require the sponsorship of a professional company or school, one nominee per institution. Awards are based on the artistic quality of the artist's work, potential for future excellence and activities.
How to Apply: Applications are available online.
Deadline: Varies.
Amount: Varies.
Number of Awards: Varies.

San Angelo Symphony

Sorantin Award
P.O. Box 5922
San Angelo, TX 76902
Phone: 915-658-5877
Fax: 915-653-1045
Email: receptionist@sanangelosymphony.org
Website: http://www.sanangelosymphony.org

896 • Sorantin Competition

Purpose: To promote musical performances.

Eligibility: There are four divisions of the competition: Piano, Vocal, Strings and Instrumental. A winner and a runner-up are selected in each division, and an overall winner is selected to perform with the San Angelo Symphony and receive an extra $2,000. Applicants under strings, instrumentalists and pianists cannot have reached their 28th birthday by November 21. Vocalists cannot have reached their 31st birthday by November 21.

How to Apply: Applications are available online.

Deadline: October 4.

Amount: $500-$2,000.

Number of Awards: Varies.

Scholastic

557 Broadway
New York, NY 10012
Phone: 212-343-6493
Email: a&wgeneralinfo@scholastic.com
Website: http://www.scholastic.com/artandwritingawards

897 • Art Awards

Purpose: To reward America's best student artists.

Eligibility: Applicants must be in grades 7 through 12 in American or Canadian schools and must submit artwork in one of the following categories: architecture and environmental design, ceramics and glass, computer graphics, drawing, graphic design, jewelry and metalsmithing, mixed media, painting, photography, printmaking, product design, sculpture, textile and fiber design, video and film, art portfolio or photography portfolio.

How to Apply: Applications are available online.

Deadline: Varies by location.

Amount: $250-$5,000.

Number of Awards: 600 awards, 16 scholarships.

Sigma Alpha Iota Philanthropies

Director, Undergraduate Scholarships
One Tunnel Road
Asheville, NC 28805
Phone: 828-251-0606
Fax: 828-251-0644
Email: saiphxalum@joetapscott.com
Website: http://www.sai-national.org

898 • Undergraduate Scholarships

Purpose: To assist members of the Sigma Alpha Iota organization who have shown financial need, and at the same time have demonstrated outstanding leadership abilities, musical talent and scholastic achievement.

Eligibility: Applicants must be members of the Sigma Alpha Iota organization who have demonstrated financial need.

How to Apply: Chapter must download application from website to nominate applicants.

Deadline: March 15.

Amount: $1,000.

Number of Awards: 15.

Sinfonia Foundation

Scholarship Committee
10600 Old State Road
Evansville, IN 47711
Phone: 800-473-2649
Email: lyrecrest@sinfonia.org
Website: http://www.sinfoniafoundation.org

899 • Sinfonia Foundation Scholarship

Purpose: To assist the collegiate members and chapters of Sinfonia.

Eligibility: Applicants must have a minimum 3.3 GPA, be in college for at least two semesters with good academic standing and submit references and an essay on, "Sinfonia-What it means to me."

How to Apply: Applications are available online.

Deadline: May 1.

Amount: $500.

Number of Awards: 4.

Thelonious Monk Institute of Jazz

5225 Wisconsin Avenue NW
Suite 605
Washington, DC 20015
Phone: 202-364-7272
Email: lebrown@tmonkinst.org
Website: http://www.monkinstitute.com

900 • Thelonious Monk International Jazz Composers Competition

Purpose: To support student jazz composers.

Eligibility: Applicants must be composers who have not had their jazz compositions recorded on a major label or recorded by a major jazz artist. The composition must contain a minimum of one voice and one instrument. There is a $35 application fee. This award is listed because it is from a legitimate organization. However, students are encouraged to apply for scholarships without fees.

How to Apply: Applications are available online.

Deadline: July 1.

Amount: $10,000.

Number of Awards: 1.

901 • Thelonious Monk International Jazz Saxophone Competition

Purpose: To assist students who wish to pursue careers in jazz performance.

Eligibility: Applicants must be saxophonists who plan to pursue jazz performance as a career, be under 36 years of age and have never recorded as a leader on a major label. Selection is based on the audio tape presentation, resume and application form. There is an application fee. This award is listed because it is from a legitimate organization. However, students are encouraged to apply for scholarships without fees.

How to Apply: Applications are available online.
Deadline: November 1.
Amount: Varies.
Number of Awards: Varies.

U.S. Fish and Wildlife Service

Federal Duck Stamp Office
4401 N. Fairfax Drive
MBSP-4070
Arlington, VA 22203
Phone: 877-887-5508
Email: duckstamps@fws.gov
Website: http://duckstamps.fws.gov/

902 • Federal Junior Duck Stamp Program and Scholarship Competition

Purpose: To introduce children to an important part of the natural world.
Eligibility: Applicants must be in kindergarten to 12th grade and submit a 9- by 12-inch original artwork picturing one of several duck species. The first place national winner receives a $5,000 cash award and a free trip to Washington, D.C. Applicants must submit their artwork to their state or local department.
How to Apply: Applications are available online.
Deadline: March 15.
Amount: $100-$5,000.
Number of Awards: 100.

VSA Arts

818 Connecticut Avenue NW
Suite 600
Washington, DC 20006
Phone: 800-933-8721
Fax: 202-429-0868
Email: info@vsarts.org
Website: http://www.vsarts.org

903 • Playwright Discovery Award

Purpose: To award promising young writers with scholarship funds and a chance to have one of their scripts professionally produced at the John F. Kennedy Center for the Performing Arts.
Eligibility: Applicants must be students in grades 6-12. Applicants are to create an original one-act script of less than 40 pages that documents the experience of living with a disability. Applicants themselves need not be disabled, but the script must address the issue. Selected scripts will be performed for middle school, high school, and adult audiences. First and second place winners will have their plays performed at the JFK Performing Arts Center.
How to Apply: Applications are available online.
Deadline: April 15.
Amount: $1,000 + Washington D.C. trip.
Number of Awards: 2.

WAMSO–Minnesota Orchestra Volunteer Association

1111 Nicollet Mall
Minneapolis, MN 55403-2477
Phone: 612-371-5654
Fax: 612-371-7176
Email: wamso@mnorch.org
Website: http://www.wamso.org

904 • Young Artist Competition

Purpose: To award outstanding young musicians with cash prizes, performance engagements and opportunities to attend music-based programs during the summer.
Eligibility: Applicants must play an instrument that also holds a permanent chair in the Minnesota Orchestra and be residents of or currently be enrolled in school in one of the following states: Illinois, Indiana, Iowa, Kansas, Michigan, Minnesota, Missouri, Nebraska, North Dakota, South Dakota, Wisconsin or Manitoba or Ontario (Canada). The preliminary round of the competition is judged by CD submission. The semifinal and final rounds require live performances. An entry fee of $75 applies. Repertoire requirements are outlined in the application. This award is listed because it is from a legitimate organization. However, students are encouraged to apply for scholarships without fees.
How to Apply: Applications are available online.
Deadline: September 11.
Amount: $1,000-$5,000.
Number of Awards: 9.

Women Band Directors International

Diane Gorzycki
WBDI Scholarship Chair
7424 Whistlestop Drive
Austin, TX 78749
Email: dgorzycki@austin.rr.com
Website: http://www.womenbanddirectors.org

905 • Women Band Directors International College Scholarships

Purpose: To support future female band directors.
Eligibility: Applicants must be studying instrumental music with the intention of becoming a band director. One scholarship will be available to all-level college and graduate students, while the other three are designated for undergraduate upperclassmen.
How to Apply: Applications are available online.
Deadline: December 1.
Amount: $300.
Number of Awards: 4.

Worldstudio Foundation

200 Varick Street
Suite 507
New York, NY 10014
Phone: 212-807-1990
Fax: 212-807-1799
Email: scholarshipcoordinator@worldstudio.org
Website: http://www.worldstudio.org

906 • Worldstudio Foundation Scholarship Program

Purpose: To support art and design students who need financial assistance.

Eligibility: Applicants must be full-time undergraduate or graduate students of fine or commercial art, design or architecture. They must have a GPA of at least 2.0 and demonstrate financial need. Applicants must be U.S. citizens or permanent residents. Minority students will be given special consideration.

How to Apply: Applications are available online.

Deadline: April 13.

Amount: Varies.

Number of Awards: Varies.

Related Scholarships:

Japanese American Citizens League (JACL)

See #1000 • Japanese American Citizens League Creative and Performing Arts Awards

Armed Forces Communications and Electronics Association

See #505 • Computer Graphic Design Scholarships

National Federation of Music Clubs Bullock and Robertson Awards

See #671 • NFMC Dorothy Dann Bullock Music Therapy Award and the NFMC Ruth B. Robertson Music Therapy Award

Graphic Arts Information Network

See #507 • Print and Graphics Scholarship

Scholastic

See #457 • Writing Awards

Screen Actors Guild Foundation

See #1621 • John L. Dales Scholarship Fund

Minnesota Higher Education Services Office

See #1433 • Minnesota Academic Excellence Scholarship

American Foreign Service Association (AFSA)

See #744 • AFSA/AAFSW Merit Award

Charles and Lucille King Family Foundation

See #243 • Charles & Lucille King Family Foundation Scholarship

American Federation of Television and Radio Artists

See #1597 • AFTRA/Heller Memorial Foundation Scholarships

American Alliance for Health, Physical Education, Recreation and Dance

See #607 • Ruth Abernathy Presidential Scholarship

Rhythm and Hues Studios

See #512 • Computer Graphics Scholarship

VSA Arts

See #903 • Playwright Discovery Award

National Press Photographers Foundation (NPPA)

See #541 • College Photographer of the Year

National Press Photographers Foundation (NPPA)

See #540 • Bob East Scholarship

National Press Photographers Foundation (NPPA)

See #543 • NPPF Television News Scholarship

Institute for Humane Studies at George Mason University

See #535 • Young Communicators Fellowships

VSA Arts

See #320 • Young Soloists Awards

Random House Inc. Creative Writing Competition

See #1491 • World of Expressions Scholarship - Music

National Press Photographers Foundation

See #539 • Reid Blackburn Scholarship

National Press Photographers Foundation (NPPA)

See #542 • Kit C. King Graduate Scholarship Fund

National Press Photographers Foundation (NPPA)

See #544 • Still Photographer Scholarship

National Federation of Music Clubs (NC)

See #304 • NFMC Hinda Honigman Award for the Blind

Imation Corporation

See #508 • Imation Computer Arts Scholarship Program

Flexographic Technical Association

See #506 • FFTA Scholarship Competition

Outdoor Writers Association of America

See #248 • Bodie McDowell Scholarship

National Federation of Music Clubs (Music Education)

See #338 · NFMC Myrtle Mehan/Hazel Morgan Music Education Scholarship

Hispanic Heritage Awards Foundation

See #985 · Hispanic Heritage Youth Awards

National Federation of Music Clubs (FL)

See #337 · NFMC Gretchen E. Van Roy Music Education Scholarship

AAA

See #2 · AAA Traffic Safety Poster Program

American Architectural Foundation

See #142 · American Architectural Foundation and Sir John Soane's Museum Foundation Traveling Fellowship

Association for Women in Architecture

See #1220 · AWA Scholarships

Davidson Institute for Talent Development

See #20 · Davidson Fellows Award

Huntington Library, Art Collections and Botanical Gardens

See #1181 · Huntington Fellowships

Huntington Library, Art Collections and Botanical Gardens

See #1182 · Huntington-British Academy Fellowships for Study in Great Britain

International Foodservice Editorial Council (IFEC)

See #486 · IFEC Scholarships Award

James F. Lincoln Arc Welding Foundation

See #1635 · Arc Welding Awards

Henkel Consumer Adhesives

See #32 · Stuck at Prom Scholarship

Fellowship of United Methodists in Music and Worship Arts

See #1096 · Fellowship of United Methodists in Music and Worship Arts Scholarship

Golden Key National Honour Society

See #794 · Visual and Performing Arts Achievement Awards

Hagley Museum and Library

See #1175 · Hagley-Winterthur Fellowships in Arts and Industries

Unitarian Universalist Association

See #1106 · Stanfield and D'Orlando Art Scholarship

Psychology

Also See Scholarships Listed Under:
Social Science/History

American Psychological Foundation

750 First Street NE
Washington, DC 20002
Phone: 800-374-2721
Website: http://www.apa.org

907 • APF/COGDOP Graduate Research Scholarships

Eligibility: Applicants must attend a school whose psychology department is a member in good standing of Council of Graduate Departments of Psychology (COGDOP). Applicants are nominated by their schools' departments with no more than three nominees at each school.
How to Apply: Applicants must be nominated.
Deadline: May 28.
Amount: $1,000-$3,000.
Number of Awards: Up to 13.

908 • APF/TOPSS Scholars Competition

Eligibility: Applicants must be high school students who have been or are presently enrolled in a psychology course and must write an essay answering a question from the APA. A Teachers of Psychology in Secondary Schools (TOPSS) member must sponsor all candidates, and each school may submit no more than ten papers.
How to Apply: There is no official application.
Deadline: February 16.
Amount: $1,000.
Number of Awards: 3.

Parapsychology Foundation

P.O. Box 1562
New York, NY 10021
Phone: 212-628-1550
Fax: 212-628-1559
Email: office@parapsychology.org
Website: http://www.parapsychology.org

909 • Eileen J. Garrett Scholarship

Purpose: To aid a student attending an accredited school in the academic study of parapsychology.
Eligibility: Applicants must be college undergraduates or graduate students and include a sample of writings on parapsychology, three references and application form.
How to Apply: Applications are available online or by written request.
Deadline: July 15.
Amount: $3,000.
Number of Awards: 1.

Related Scholarships:

American Psychological Foundation

See #627• Henry Hecaen and Manfred Meier Neuropsychology Scholarships

Epilepsy Foundation

See #660• Behavioral Sciences Student Fellowship

Public Administration/Social Work

Also See Scholarships Listed Under:

Leadership

Education/Teaching

Public Service/Community Service

American Public Transportation Foundation

1666 K Street NW
Suite 1100
Washington, DC 20006
Phone: 202-496-4800
Fax: 202-496-4321
Email: info@apta.com
Website: http://www.apta.com

910 • APTF Transit Hall of Fame Scholarship Award

Purpose: To encourage students to enter the transit field.

Eligibility: Applicants must be enrolled in an accredited undergraduate or graduate institution, have a minimum 3.0 GPA, be employed by or demonstrate an interest in entering the public transportation industry and be nominated by a member organization of American Public Transportation Association (APTA) with which recipients must participate in an internship. Selection is based on this, as well as academic achievement, essay, financial need and extracurricular and leadership activities. There is also a $500 award for the best application essay.

How to Apply: Applications are available from your local APTA member organization or by email.

Deadline: June 16.

Amount: At least $2,500.

Number of Awards: 7.

German Marshall Fund of the United States

1744 R Street NW
Washington, DC 20009
Phone: 202-745-3950
Fax: 202-265-1662
Email: info@gmfus.org
Website: http://www.gmfus.org

911 • Transatlantic Fellows Program

Purpose: To research topics of foreign policy, international security, trade and economic development and immigration.

Eligibility: Fellowships are by invitation from GMF and are issued to senior policy-practitioners, journalists, academics and businesspeople. Fellows work in residence in Washington, DC and Brussels, Belgium.

How to Apply: Contact John K. Glenn at the organization for more information.

Deadline: Varies.

Amount: Varies.

Number of Awards: Varies.

Institute for Humane Studies at George Mason University

3301 N. Fairfax Drive
Suite 440
Arlington, VA 22201
Phone: 800-697-8799
Fax: 703-993-4890
Email: ihs@gmu.edu
Website: http://www.theihs.org

912 • Charles G. Koch Summer Fellow Program

Purpose: To encourage the understanding of market-based solutions to social and economic problems, especially through public policy.

Eligibility: Applicants must be current college students, graduates, graduate students or professional students and have a demonstrated interest in public policy issues and in learning how a market-based approach might help solve social and economic problems.

How to Apply: Applications are available online.

Deadline: February 15.

Amount: $1,500 and internship.

Number of Awards: 40.

William Randolph Hearst Foundation

90 New Montgomery Street, Suite 1212
San Francisco, CA 94105
Phone: 800-841-7048
Fax: 415-243-0760
Email: USSYP@hearstfdn.org
Website: http://www.hearstfdn.org/ussyp/

913 • United States Senate Youth Program

Purpose: To expose students to their government in action.

Eligibility: Applicants must be high school juniors or seniors in an elected position at school or in civic or educational offices. Award winners must attend an educational program in Washington, DC.

How to Apply: Contact your school principal, counselor or state-level education administrator.

Deadline: Varies.

Amount: $5,000.

Number of Awards: 104.

Related Scholarships:

National Society of Professional Engineers

See #414 · Professional Engineers In Government (PEG)

Harry S. Truman Library Institute for National and International Affairs

See #1178 · Harry S. Truman Undergraduate Student Grant

Institute for Humane Studies at George Mason University

See #535 · Young Communicators Fellowships

Women In Defense

See #565 · HORIZONS Foundation Scholarship

Truman Scholarship Foundation

See #931 · Truman Scholar

Fund for American Studies

See #1173 · Fund for American Studies Internships

German Marshall Fund of the United States

See #918 · Transatlantic Community Foundation Fellowship

John F. Kennedy Library Foundation

See #1184 · John F. Kennedy Profile in Courage Essay Contest

United Nations Association of the United States of America

See #458 · National High School Essay Contest

Association of Government Accountants (AGA)

See #200 · AGA Scholarships

National Association of Negro Business and Professional Women's Clubs Inc.

See #1024 · Julianne Malveaux Scholarship

Public Service/Community Service

Also See Scholarships Listed Under:
Academics/General
Leadership
Education/Teaching

American Red Cross

National Headquarters
2025 E Street NW
Washington, DC 20006
Phone: 202-303-4498
Website: http://www.redcross.org

914 • Navin Narayan Scholarship

Purpose: The scholarship is named after Navin Narayan, a former youth volunteer with the Red Cross who died from cancer at the age of 23. In his honor, the Red Cross awards this scholarship to youth volunteers who have made significant humanitarian contributions to the organization and who have also achieved academic excellence in high school.

Eligibility: Applicants must plan to attend a four-year college or university and have volunteered a minimum of two years with the Red Cross.

Deadline: Varies.
Amount: $2,500.
Number of Awards: 1.

Bonner Foundation

10 Mercer Street
Princeton, NJ 08540
Phone: 609-924-6663
Fax: 609-683-4626
Email: info@bonner.org
Website: http://www.bonner.org

915 • Bonner Scholarship

Purpose: To award four-year community service scholarships to students planning to attend one of 27 participating colleges.

Eligibility: Students must complete annual service requirements as stipulated by the organization. Awards are geared toward students demonstrating significant financial need. Scholarship recipients are named Bonner Scholars.

How to Apply: Contact the admission office at each participating school to request an application.
Deadline: Varies.
Amount: Varies.
Number of Awards: 1,500.

Campus Compact

P.O. Box 1975
Brown University
Providence, RI 02912
Phone: 401-867-3950
Email: campus@compact.org
Website: http://www.compact.org

916 • Howard R. Swearer Student Humanitarian Award

Purpose: Awards granted to college students for use in strengthening or maintaining a service program/project. Emphasis is on college students who work to improve their communities while encouraging others to do the same.

Eligibility: Applicants must be undergraduate students attending institutions that are Campus Compact members and must be nominated by the Campus Compact member president. Students of any class year are eligible.

How to Apply: Nominations must be made by the Campus Compact member president.
Deadline: February.
Amount: Varies.
Number of Awards: 5.

Freedom from Religion Foundation

P.O. Box 750
Madison, WI 53701
Phone: 608-256-5800
Email: info@ffrf.org
Website: http://www.ffrf.org

917 • Student Activist Awards

Purpose: To assist high school and college student activists.
Eligibility: Selection is based on activism for freethought or separation of church and state.
How to Apply: Contact the organization for more information.
Deadline: Varies.
Amount: $1,000.
Number of Awards: Varies.

German Marshall Fund of the United States

1744 R Street NW
Washington, DC 20009
Phone: 202-745-3950
Fax: 202-265-1662
Email: info@gmfus.org
Website: http://www.gmfus.org

918 • Transatlantic Community Foundation Fellowship

Purpose: To provide fellowships for community foundation staff to exchange experiences with European colleagues.

Eligibility: The fellowships provide a two-week program including roundtrip airfare, a daily stipend and reimbursement for car rental expenses.

How to Apply: Contact the organization for application information.
Deadline: Varies.
Amount: Varies.
Number of Awards: 5.

Grandmothers for Peace International

Wiedner and Vandercook MSF
c/o Leal Portis, President
301 Redbud Way
Nevada, CA 95949
Phone: 530-265-3887
Email: portis.leal@gmail.com
Website: http://www.grandmothersforpeace.org

919 • Barbara Wiedner and Dorothy Vandercook Memorial Peace Scholarship

Purpose: To reward students who have exhibited their commitment to peace and justice through volunteer work and have plans to help create a more peaceful and just world.

Eligibility: Applicants must be high school seniors or college freshmen and provide an autobiography of activities relating to nuclear disarmament, conflict resolution or community service and describe their plans for contributing to a healthy planet. Applicants must also provide information on community activities and include two letters of recommendation.

How to Apply: Applications are available online.

Deadline: March 1.

Amount: $250-$500.

Number of Awards: Varies.

Hitachi Foundation

1215 17th Street NW
Washington, DC 20036
Phone: 202-457-0588
Fax: 202-296-1098
Website: http://www.hitachifoundation.org

920 • Yoshiyama Award

Purpose: To recognize exemplary service and community involvement.

Eligibility: Applicants must be graduating high school seniors in the U.S. and U.S. territories, demonstrate outstanding community service and have shown leadership, self-motivation, creativity, dedication and commitment to the community. Applicants service should impact a socially, economically or culturally isolated area. Applicants must also be nominated by someone familiar with their service; family members may not nominate their relatives, and students may not nominate themselves.

How to Apply: Applicants must be nominated.

Deadline: April 1.

Amount: $5,000 over two years.

Number of Awards: 10.

Kiwanis International

Key Club International
Youth Funds Specialist
Phone: 800-549-2647
Website: http://www.kiwanis.org

921 • Kiwanis International Foundation Scholarships

Purpose: To recognize Key Club members for their outstanding service and leadership.

Eligibility: Applicants must be high school seniors who have been active, dues-paying Key Club members in good standing for two years or more. Students must plan to attend a post-secondary institution and have a 3.0 GPA or "B" average. A high school transcript is required. Applications must be submitted to the Key Club district administrator.

How to Apply: Applications are available online. More information is available from Key Club districts, which are listed online.

Deadline: Varies.

Amount: Typically $1,000, but can vary by Key Club district.

Number of Awards: 1-10 per Key Club district.

Kohls Corporation

N56 W17000 Ridgewood Drive
Menomonee Falls, WI 53051
Phone: 262-703-7000
Fax: 262 703-7115
Email: community.relations@kohls.com
Website: http://www.kohlscorporation.com

922 • Kohl's Kids Who Care Scholarship

Purpose: To recognize young people who volunteer in their communities.

Eligibility: Applicants must be nominated by parents, educators or community members. There are two categories: one for kids ages 6-12 and another for ages 13-18.

How to Apply: Applications are available online and at Kohl's stores.

Deadline: March 15.

Amount: Varies.

Number of Awards: Varies.

Massachusetts Electric Company

Samuel Huntington Fund
Attn.: Amy F. Stacy
25 Research Drive
Westborough, MA 01582
Phone: 508-389-3390
Email: amy.stacy@us.ngrid.com
Website: http://www.nationalgridus.com

923 • Samuel Huntington Public Service Award

Purpose: To provide money for graduating college seniors to pursue public service anywhere in the world.

Eligibility: Applicants must be graduating college seniors.

How to Apply: Applications are available online.

Deadline: February 15.

Amount: $10,000.

Number of Awards: 1-3.

National Association for Campus Activities

13 Harbison Way
Columbia, SC 29212-3401
Phone: 803-732-6222
Fax: 803-749-1047
Email: info@naca.org
Website: http://www.naca.org

924 • Markley Scholarship

Purpose: To support undergraduate and graduate students who have made exceptional contributions in the field of student activities. The focus is on involvement with NACA Central, along with contributions to other activities-based organizations.

Eligibility: Applicants must attend a college/university in the former NACA South Central Region (AR, LA, NM, OK, TX); must be enrolled as juniors, seniors or graduate students at a four-year institution or as sophomores at a two-year institution and must have a minimum 2.5 GPA.

How to Apply: Applications are available online.

Deadline: September 1.

Amount: Varies.

Number of Awards: 2.

National Grid

25 Research Drive
Westborough, MA 01582
Phone: 508-389-2000
Website: http://www.nationalgridus.com

925 • Samuel Huntington Public Service Award

Purpose: To assist students who wish to perform one year of humanitarian service immediately upon graduation.

Eligibility: Applicants must be graduating college seniors, and must intend to perform one year of public service in the U.S. or abroad. The service may be individual work or through charitable, religious, educational, governmental or other public service organizations.

How to Apply: Applications are available online.
Deadline: February 15.
Amount: $10,000.
Number of Awards: 1.

NetAid Foundation

75 Broad Street, Suite 2410
New York, NY 10004
Phone: 212-537-0500
Fax: 212-537-0501
Email: gaa@netaid.org
Website: http://www.netaid.org

926 • Global Action Awards

Purpose: To support high school students who have helped the poor at home or abroad.

Eligibility: Applicants must be in high school, live in the U.S. and have led projects on issues such as hunger, HIV/AIDS or education in developing countries.

How to Apply: Applications are available online.
Deadline: November 30.
Amount: $5,000.
Number of Awards: Varies.

Prudential Spirit of Community Awards

751 Broad Street, 16th Floor
Newark, NJ 07102
Phone: 888-450-9961
Email: spirit@principals.org
Website: http://www.prudential.com/community

927 • Prudential Spirit of Community Award

Purpose: To recognize students for their self-initiated community service.

Eligibility: Applicants must be middle and high school students in the U.S. or Puerto Rico and involved in volunteer work that was completed during the year prior to date of application.

How to Apply: Applications are available online.
Deadline: October 29.
Amount: $1,000-$5,000.
Number of Awards: 104.

Soroptimist International

1709 Spruce Street
Philadelphia, PA 19103
Phone: 215-893-9000
Fax: 215-893-5200
Email: siahq@soroptimist.org
Website: http://www.soroptimist.org

928 • Violet Richardson Award

Purpose: To recognize young women who contribute to the community through volunteer efforts.

Eligibility: Applicants must be young women between the ages of 14 and 17 who make outstanding contributions to volunteer efforts. Efforts that benefit women or girls are of particular interest. This award is administered by local, participating Soroptimist clubs and is not available in all communities.

How to Apply: Contact your local Soroptimist club.
Deadline: Varies.
Amount: Varies.
Number of Awards: Varies.

Target Department Stores

Citizens' Scholarship Foundation of America Inc.
1505 Riverview Road
P.O. Box 480
St. Peter, MN 56082
Phone: 612-696-6098
Website: http://www.target.com

929 • Target All-Around Scholarships for Students

Purpose: To recognize outstanding community service among students.

Eligibility: Applicants must be high school seniors, high school graduates or current college students and legal U.S. residents age 24 or under. In addition, applicants must enroll in a full-time undergraduate course of study no later than the fall term of the school year at an accredited two-or four-year college, university or vocational-technical school in the U.S.

How to Apply: Applications are available online.
Deadline: November 1.
Amount: $1,000.
Number of Awards: 600.

Toyota

Scholarship and Recognition Programs
Educational Testing Service
P.O. Box 6730
Princeton, NJ 08541
Phone: 609-771-7878
Fax: 609-734-5410
Website: http://www.toyota.com/about/community/education/

930 • Toyota Community Scholars

Purpose: To recognize students for their academic achievement and community involvement.

Eligibility: Applicants must be high school seniors with at least at 3.0 GPA, be nominated by their high school, and be involved in community service.

How to Apply: Contact your high school guidance counselor.
Deadline: December.
Amount: $10,000-$20,000.
Number of Awards: 100.

Truman Scholarship Foundation

712 Jackson Place NW
Washington, DC 20006
Phone: 202-395-4831
Fax: 202-395-6995
Email: office@truman.gov
Website: http://www.truman.gov

931 • Truman Scholar
Purpose: To provide college junior leaders who plan to pursue careers in government, non-profits, education or other public service with financial support for graduate study and leadership training.
Eligibility: Applicants must be juniors, attending an accredited U.S. college or university and be nominated by the institution. Students may not apply directly. Applicants must be U.S. citizens or U.S. nationals, complete an application and write a policy recommendation.
How to Apply: See your school's Truman Faculty Representative or contact the foundation.
Deadline: February 7.
Amount: $30,000.
Number of Awards: 70-75.

Related Scholarships:

Japanese American Citizens League (JACL)
See #1001 • Japanese American Citizens League Entering Freshman Awards

Japanese American Citizens League (JACL)
See #1004 • Japanese American Citizens League Undergraduate Awards

Thurgood Marshall Scholarship Fund
See #1058 • Thurgood Marshall Scholarship Fund Scholarship

Wal-Mart Foundation
See #71 • Sam Walton Community Scholarship

Coca-Cola Scholars Foundation
See #567 • Coca-Cola Scholars Program

Discover Card
See #569 • Discover Card Tribute Award Scholarships

Wendy's Restaurants
See #173 • Wendy's High School Heisman Award

SuperCollege.com
See #61 • SuperCollege.com Student Scholarship

Elks National Foundation (IL)
See #773 • Gold Award Scholarship

National Honor Society
See #813 • National Honor Society Scholarship

National Society of the Sons of the American Revolution
See #816 • Eagle Scout Scholarship

William Randolph Hearst Foundation
See #913 • United States Senate Youth Program

Hispanic Heritage Awards Foundation
See #985 • Hispanic Heritage Youth Awards

Horatio Alger Association
See #34 • Horatio Alger Association Scholarship Program

ArtCarved Class Rings
See #9 • ArtCarved Get Cash for College Scholarship

Do Something
See #570 • BRICK Award

Congressional Hispanic Caucus Institute Inc.
See #976 • CHCI Scholarship Award

Rotary International
See #58 • Cultural Ambassadorial Scholarships

Comcast
See #568 • Leaders and Achievers Scholarship Program

Campus Compact
See #566 • Frank Newman Leadership Award

Aspen Institute
See #957 • William Randolph Hearst Endowed Scholarship for Minority Students

Imagine America Foundation
See #1633 • Imagine America scholarship

Race/Ethnicity/Gender/Family Status

Also See Scholarships Listed Under:
Academics/General

America's Junior Miss

P.O. Box 2786
Mobile, AL 36652
Phone: 251-438-3621
Fax: 251-431-0063
Email: lynne@ajm.org
Website: http://www.ajm.org

932 • America's Junior Miss Scholarship Program

Purpose: To provide scholarship opportunities and encourage personal development for high school girls through a competitive pageant stressing academics and talent as well as poise and fitness.

Eligibility: Teen girls are selected from state competitions to participate in a national pageant. Contestants are judged on a combination of scholastics, personal interview, talent, fitness and poise. Applicants should be a high school student at least in their sophomore year.

How to Apply: Applications are available from the local Junior Miss Program offices. A list of local contacts is available online.

Deadline: Varies.

Amount: Varies.

Number of Awards: Varies.

American Association of University Women (AAUW) Educational Foundation

Dept. 60
301 ACT Drive
Iowa City, IA 52243-4030
Phone: 319-337-1716 x60
Fax: 202-872-1425
Email: aauw@act.org
Website: http://www.aauw.org

933 • AAUW Educational Foundation Career Development Grants

Purpose: To support college-educated women who need additional training to advance their careers, re-enter the workforce or change careers.

Eligibility: Applicants must be U.S. citizens, hold a bachelor's degree, have earned their last degree on or before June 30, 2001 and enroll in courses at a regionally-accredited program related to their professional development, including two- and four-year colleges, technical schools and distance learning programs. Special preference is given to women of color, AAUW members and women pursuing their first advanced degree or credentials in a nontraditional field.

How to Apply: Applications are available online from August 1-December 15.

Deadline: December 15.

Amount: $2,000-$8,000.

Number of Awards: Varies.

American Atheists

P.O. Box 5733
Parsippany, NJ 07054
Phone: 908-276-7300
Fax: 908-276-7402
Website: http://www.atheists.org

934 • Chinn Scholarship

Purpose: To support gay or lesbian Atheist students.

Eligibility: Applicants must be high school seniors or college students who are Atheists, have a minimum 2.5 GPA and be student activists. The award is based on the level of activism and requires a 500- to 1,000-word essay. In addition to the scholarship, the winner will receive a free trip to the American Atheists National Convention.

How to Apply: Applications are available online.

Deadline: January 31.

Amount: $1,000.

Number of Awards: 1.

American Chemical Society

1155 16th Street NW
Washington, DC 20036
Phone: 800-227-5558
Fax: 202-872-6067
Email: scholars@acs.org
Website: http://www.chemistry.org

935 • American Chemical Society Scholars Program

Purpose: To encourage minority students to pursue careers in the sciences and to help them acquire the skills necessary for success in these fields.

Eligibility: Applicants must be African American, Hispanic/Latino or American Indian and graduating high school seniors or college freshmen, sophomores or juniors enrolled full-time at an accredited institution. Students must major in chemistry, biochemistry, chemical engineering or a chemically-related science and plan to work in a chemistry-related field. Those entering pre-med programs or pursuing pharmacy degrees are not eligible. A minimum GPA of 3.0 or "B" or better with high academic achievement in chemistry or science is required. Students must also demonstrate financial need through the Free Application for Federal Student Aid (FAFSA).

How to Apply: Applications are available online.

Deadline: March 1.

Amount: Up to $3,000.

Number of Awards: Varies.

American Geological Institute

4220 King Street
Alexandria, VA 22302
Phone: 703-379-2480
Fax: 703-379-7563
Website: http://www.agiweb.org

936 • American Geological Institute Minority Scholarship

Purpose: To increase the number of minority students in the geosciences by providing financial awards and mentorship.

Eligibility: Applicants must be black, Latino or Native American (American Indian, Eskimo, Hawaiian or Samoan) and full-time students with demonstrable financial need who are currently majoring in geoscience at the undergraduate or graduate level.

How to Apply: Applications available online.

Deadline: March 10.

Amount: Varies.

Number of Awards: Varies.

American Indian Science and Engineering Society

P.O. Box 9828
Albuquerque, NM 87119-9828
Phone: 505-765-1052
Fax: 505-765-5608
Website: http://www.aises.org

937 • A.T. Anderson Memorial Scholarship

Purpose: To provide scholarships for Native American and Alaskan Native students majoring in science, engineering, medicine, natural resources, math and technology.

Eligibility: Applicants must be full-time undergraduate or graduate students at an accredited college or university. Applicants must also be members of a Native American tribe or Alaskan Native and members of AISES.

How to Apply: Applications are available online.

Deadline: June 15.

Amount: $1,000-$2,000.

Number of Awards: Varies.

938 • Bureau of Reclamation Scholarship and Internship

Purpose: To provide scholarships for Native American and Alaskan Native students seeking bachelor's degrees in science or engineering, related to water resources and/or the environment.

Eligibility: Applicants must be enrolled full-time at an accredited college or university, seeking a degree in science or engineering, related to water resources and/or the environment. Students must belong to a federally recognized Indian tribe and must be members of AISES. Recipients must complete an eight- to ten-week internship with the Bureau of Reclamation.

How to Apply: Applications are available online.

Deadline: June 15.

Amount: $5,000 per year.

Number of Awards: Varies.

939 • Burlington Northern Santa Fe (BNSF) Foundation Scholarship

Purpose: To provide a four-year scholarship for an American Indian student attending an accredited four-year college or university in a state where Burlington Northern Santa Fe operates.

Eligibility: Applicants must reside in one of the following states: Arizona, California, Colorado, Kansas, Minnesota, Montana, New Mexico, North Dakota, Oklahoma, Oregon, South Dakota or Washington. Applicants must also major in one of the following areas: business, engineering, math, medicine/health administration, natural/physical sciences, technology or education and belong to AISES.

How to Apply: Applications are available online.

Deadline: April 15.

Amount: $2,500 per year.

Number of Awards: Varies.

940 • General Motors Engineering Scholarship

Purpose: To provide scholarships for members of AISES who are American Indian or Alaskan Native and who are pursuing undergraduate or graduate degrees in engineering.

Eligibility: Applicants must be full-time undergraduate or graduate students at an accredited college or university, members of an American Indian tribe or Alaskan Native and members of AISES. Preference is given to those majoring in electrical, industrial or mechanical engineering.

How to Apply: Applications are available online.

Deadline: June 15.

Amount: $3,000.

Number of Awards: Varies.

American Institute for Foreign Study

AIFS College Division
River Plaza
9 W. Broad Street
Stamford, CT 06902
Phone: 800-727-2437
Email: college.info@aifs.com
Website: http://www.aifsabroad.com

941 • Minority Scholarships

Purpose: To help increase the participation of ethnic minority college students in study abroad programs.

Eligibility: Applicants must be African-Americans, Asian-Americans, Native-Americans, Hispanic-Americans or Pacific Islanders who are currently enrolled as undergraduates at a U.S. institution. Applicants must also meet the admission requirements of the AIFS program selected, demonstrate financial need, have a minimum 3.0 GPA and be involved in community or extra-curricular activities focused on multicultural or international issues.

How to Apply: Applications are available online.

Deadline: April 15 and October 15.

Amount: Full tuition or $2,000.

Number of Awards: Varies.

American Institute of Chemical Engineers - (AIChE)

3 Park Avenue
New York, NY 10016
Phone: 212-591-7634
Fax: 212-591-8890
Email: awards@aiche.org
Website: http://www.aiche.org

942 • Minority Affairs Committee Award for Outstanding Scholastic Achievement

Purpose: Recognizes outstanding achievements by a chemical engineering student who serves as a role model for minority students.

Eligibility: Applicants must be ethnic minorities, major in chemical engineering and be undergraduate or graduate students.

How to Apply: Applications are available online or by telephone or written request.

Deadline: April 15.

Amount: $1,500.

Number of Awards: 1.

943 • Minority Scholarship Awards for College Students

Purpose: To offer financial aid to minority students in chemical engineering.

Eligibility: Applicants must be AIChE national student members, undergraduates in chemical engineering, and members of a minority group (i.e., African American, Hispanic, Native American or Alaskan Native) that is underrepresented in chemical engineering. Selection is based on academic record, participation in AIChE student and professional activities, career objectives and financial need.

How to Apply: Applications are available online or by telephone or written request.

Deadline: May 15.

Amount: $1,000.

Number of Awards: 10.

944 • Minority Scholarship Awards for Incoming College Freshmen

Purpose: To offer financial aid to minority students in chemical engineering.

Eligibility: Applicants must be members of a minority group (i.e. African American, Hispanic, Native American or Alaskan Native) that is underrepresented in chemical engineering. Applicants must also be high school graduates during the academic year of application and plan to enroll in a four-year college or university. Applicants are encouraged to major in science or engineering. Selection is also based on academic record, reason for choosing science or engineering, work or activities and financial need.

How to Apply: Applications are available online or by telephone or written request.

Deadline: May 15.

Amount: $1,000.

Number of Awards: 10.

American Physiological Society

Education Office
9650 Rockville Pike
Bethesda, MD 20814-3991
Phone: 301-634-7787
Fax: 301-634-7241
Email: education@the-aps.org
Website: http://www.the-aps.org

945 • Explorations Summer Research Fellowships

Purpose: To support undergraduate Native American students in summer research programs focusing on biomedical research and physiology.

Eligibility: Applicants must be Native American undergraduate students with little or no research experience in life sciences or physiology not including coursework. Students have the opportunity to participate in a major scientific meeting.

How to Apply: Applications are available online.

Deadline: February 3.

Amount: Up to $4,000, plus living and travel expenses.

Number of Awards: Varies.

American Planning Association

122 S. Michigan Avenue
Suite 1600
Chicago, IL 60603
Phone: 312-431-9100
Fax: 312-431-9985
Website: http://www.planning.org

946 • APA Planning Fellowships

Purpose: To foster increased minority interest in the study of urban planning at the graduate level.

Eligibility: Applicants must be African American, Hispanic American or Native American, be U.S. citizens and demonstrate financial need. Applicants must also be students enrolled or accepted for enrollment in a graduate planning program that has been accredited by the Planning Accreditation Board. Selection is based on personal background statement, academic performance, letters of recommendation, financial need and geographic diversity. Applicants must be first or second-year graduate students.

How to Apply: Applications are available online.

Deadline: May 15.

Amount: Varies.

Number of Awards: Varies.

American Society for Clinical Laboratory Science

6701 Democracy Boulevard, Suite 300
Bethesda, MD 20817
Phone: 301-657-2768
Fax: 301-657-2909
Email: ascls@ascls.org
Website: http://www.ascls.org

947 • Forum for Concerns of Minorities Scholarship

Purpose: To assist minority students in becoming clinical laboratory scientists and clinical laboratory technicians.

Eligibility: Applicants must be minority students accepted to an NAACLS-accredited Clinical Laboratory Science/Medical Technology program or a Clinical Laboratory Technician/Medical Laboratory Technician program. They must also demonstrate financial need.

How to Apply: Applications are available online.

Deadline: April 1.

Amount: Varies.

Number of Awards: 2.

American Society of Criminology

1314 Kinnear Road
Suite 212
Columbus, OH 43212
Phone: 614-292-9207
Fax: 614-292-6767
Email: asc41@infinet.com
Website: http://www.asc41.com

948 • American Society of Criminology Fellowships for Ethnic Minorities

Purpose: To encourage minorities to study criminology or criminal justice.

Eligibility: Applicants must be African American, Asian American, Latino or Native American. Recipients must have been accepted

into a doctoral studies program. Selection is based on curriculum vitae, college transcripts, financial need, references and letter describing career plans, experiences and interest in criminology.
How to Apply: Applications are available by written request.
Deadline: March 1.
Amount: $6,000.
Number of Awards: 3.

Arab American Institute Foundation

1600 K Street NW
Suite 600
Washington, DC 20006
Phone: 202-429-9210
Email: saltaf@aaiusa.org
Website: http://www.aaiusa.org

949 • Al Muammar Scholarships for Journalism
Purpose: To support Arab American journalism majors.
Eligibility: Applicants must be full-time Arab American college students majoring in journalism at an accredited U.S. college or university or college seniors who have been accepted to a graduate journalism school. Students must have a demonstrated commitment to print or broadcast journalism and to pursuing journalism as a career. The applicants' sensitivity to Arab American issues, social advocacy and community involvement are seriously considered, as well as financial need and academic achievement.
How to Apply: Applications are available online.
Deadline: February 15.
Amount: $5,000.
Number of Awards: 4.

Armenian Educational Foundation Inc.

600 W. Broadway
Suite 130
Glendale, CA 91204
Phone: 818-242-4154
Email: aef@aefweb.org
Website: http://www.aefweb.org

950 • Richard R. Tufenkian Memorial Scholarship
Purpose: To support Armenian undergraduate students.
Eligibility: Applicants must be full-time undergraduate students of Armenian descent at U.S. universities, have a minimum 3.0 GPA, demonstrate financial need and be involved in the Armenian community. Tax returns, transcripts, two reference letters, essays and applications are required.
How to Apply: Applications are available online.
Deadline: July 30.
Amount: $2,000.
Number of Awards: 5.

Armenian General Benevolent Union (AGBU)

55 E. 59th Street, 7th Floor
New York, NY 10022-1112
Phone: 212-319-6383
Fax: 212-319-6507
Email: scholarship@agbu.org
Website: http://www.agbu.org

951 • AGBU Scholarship Program
Purpose: To help students of Armenian descent.
Eligibility: Applicants should be international full-time students or high school seniors of Armenian descent who attend academic institutions and graduate programs. Applications, two recommendation letters, transcripts, college acceptance letters, financial award letters, resumes and photographs are required.
How to Apply: Applications are available online.
Deadline: May 15.
Amount: Varies.
Number of Awards: Varies.

Armenian Relief Society Of North America Inc.

80 Bigelow Avenue
Watertown, MA 02472
Phone: 617-926-5892
Fax: 617-926-4855
Email: ars1910@aol.com
Website: http://www.ars1910.org

952 • Armenian Relief Society Undergraduate Scholarship
Purpose: To provide merit and need-based scholarships for students of Armenian ancestry.
Eligibility: Applicants must be of Armenian ancestry and not related to the ARS Central Executive or Eremian Scholarship Committee members. Specific requirements may vary by region.
How to Apply: Applications are available by mail.
Deadline: Varies.
Amount: Varies.
Number of Awards: Varies.

Armenian Students' Association of America

333 Atlantic Avenue
Warwick, RI 02888
Phone: 401-461-6114
Email: asa@asainc.org
Website: http://www.asainc.org

953 • ASA Scholarships
Purpose: To provide scholarships for students of Armenian descent.
Eligibility: Applicants must be college sophomores or beyond in the year of application and be of Armenian descent.
How to Apply: Request forms for applications are available online.
Deadline: March 15.
Amount: Varies.
Number of Awards: Varies.

Asian American Journalists Association

1182 Market Street
Suite 230
San Francisco, CA 94102
Phone: 415-346-2051
Fax: 415-346-6343
Email: lilac@aaja.org
Website: http://www.aaja.org

954 • AAJA Newhouse National Scholarship And Internship Awards

Purpose: Offers monetary assistance to print journalism college students from historically underrepresented Asian Pacific American groups.

Eligibility: The AAJA encourages students from historically underrepresented Asian Pacific American groups, including Vietnamese, Cambodians, Hmong and other Southeast Asians, South Asians and Pacific Islanders to apply. Applicants must demonstrate a commitment to the field of journalism, sensitivity to Asian American issues as demonstrated by community involvement, journalistic ability, scholastic ability and financial need. Applicants may be high school seniors, college students or graduate students.

How to Apply: Applications are available online.
Deadline: April.
Amount: $5,000.
Number of Awards: Varies.

955 • Mary Moy Quan Ing Memorial Scholarship

Purpose: Monetary assistance is awarded to a high school senior pursuing college studies that lead to a journalism career.

Eligibility: Applicants must be high school seniors intending to major in journalism. Applicants must also demonstrate a commitment to the field of journalism, sensitivity to Asian American issues as demonstrated by community involvement, journalistic ability, scholastic ability and financial need.

How to Apply: Applications are available online.
Deadline: April.
Amount: $1,500.
Number of Awards: 1.

956 • National AAJA General Scholarship Awards

Purpose: Monetary assistance is awarded to students pursuing studies that lead to careers in print, broadcast or photo journalism.

Eligibility: Applicants must demonstrate a commitment to the field of journalism, sensitivity to Asian American issues demonstrated by community involvement, journalistic ability, scholastic ability and financial need. Applicants may be high school seniors, college students or graduate students.

How to Apply: Applications are available online.
Deadline: April.
Amount: $2,000.
Number of Awards: Varies.

Aspen Institute

Nonprofit Sector Research Fund
Attn.: John Russell, Program Coordinator
One Dupont Circle, Suite 700
Washington, DC 20036
Phone: 202-736-5800
Fax: 202-293-0525
Email: hearstinfo@aspeninstitute.org
Website: http://www.nonprofitresearch.org

957 • William Randolph Hearst Endowed Scholarship for Minority Students

Purpose: To provide fellowships for minority students interested in philanthropy, volunteerism and the nonprofit sector.

Eligibility: Applicants must be undergraduate or graduate students belonging to a minority group. Hearst fellows work as interns at the Fund, providing assistance with research and outreach programs. Awards are based on academic excellence and financial need.

How to Apply: Application information is available online.
Deadline: March 15, July 15, December 15.
Amount: Up to $5,000.
Number of Awards: Varies.

Association of Sikh Professionals

2917 Oak Brook Hills Road
Oak Brook, IL 60523
Email: contact@sikhprofessionals.org
Website: http://www.sikhprofessionals.org

958 • Sikh Education Aid Fund

Purpose: To recognize Sikh students for academic achievement.

Eligibility: Applicants must be accepted by or attend an accredited U.S. institution. Recipients are usually high school seniors or college students. Financial documents, a photo, copies of recent transcripts, essays and names and addresses of five Sikhs in the community are required. Financial need is the most important criteria, but academic ability and involvement in Sikh activities is also considered. Candidates may be interviewed.

How to Apply: Applications are available online.
Deadline: June 1.
Amount: $2,500.
Number of Awards: Varies.

Association On American Indian Affairs

Lisa Wyzlic, Scholarship Coordinator
966 Hungerford Drive, Suite 12-B
Rockville, MD 20850
Phone: 240-314-7155
Fax: 240-314-7159
Website: http://www.indian-affairs.org

959 • Adolph Van Pelt Scholarship

Purpose: To assist American Indian students based on merit and financial need.

Eligibility: Applicants must be full-time students and provide proof of tribal enrollment, a Certificate of Indian Blood (showing 1/4 Indian blood) and an essay on educational goals.

How to Apply: Applications are available online.
Deadline: July 20.
Amount: $500-$800.
Number of Awards: Varies.

960 • Association on American Indian Affairs Displaced Homemaker Scholarship

Purpose: To provide financial assistance toward child care, transportation, living expenses or educational costs for men and women who would be unable to attend college due to family responsibilities.

Eligibility: Applicants must be full-time students able to prove financial need, proof of tribal enrollment and Certificate of Indian Blood (showing 1/4 Indian blood).

How to Apply: Applications are available online.
Deadline: July 20.
Amount: $1,000.
Number of Awards: Varies.

961 • Sequoyah Graduate Fellowships for American Indian and Alaskan Natives

Purpose: To provide graduate fellowships for students of American Indian and Alaskan Native heritage.

Eligibility: Applicants must be full-time students who can provide proof of tribal enrollment, a Certificate of Indian Blood (showing 1/4 Indian blood) and an essay on educational goals.

How to Apply: Applications are available online.

Deadline: July 20.

Amount: $1,500.

Number of Awards: Varies.

Brown Foundation Scholarship Program

P.O. Box 4862
Topeka, KS 66604
Phone: 785-235-3939
Fax: 785-235-1001
Email: brownfound@juno.com
Website: http://www.brownvboard.org/foundatn/sclrbroc.htm

962 • Brown Foundation Scholarships

Purpose: To help minority students who are either high school seniors or college juniors who want to teach.

Eligibility: High school seniors should have a demonstrated desire to enter a teacher education program through volunteer experience, work experience, and/or references and should plan to enroll in college at least half-time. The high school senior scholarship is $300 for the freshman year. College juniors must be accepted to a teacher education program and attend at least half-time. The college award is $500 per year for two academic years. Selection for both awards is based on GPA, school, community and extracurricular activities, career plans and goals in education, essays and two recommendations.

How to Apply: Applications are available from high school counselors, from departments of education at participating colleges, from the Brown Foundation and online.

Deadline: April 1.

Amount: $300-$500.

Number of Awards: 2.

Bureau of Indian Affairs

1849 C Street NW
Washington, DC 20240
Phone: 202-208-6123
Fax: 202-208-3312
Website: http://www.oiep.bia.edu

963 • Higher Education Grant

Purpose: To assist American Indian and Alaska Native students obtaining their undergraduate degrees.

Eligibility: Applicants must be members of a tribe or at least one-quarter degree Indian blood descendents of members of an American Indian tribe, be accepted into a college or another similar institution that provides an associate's or bachelor's degrees and show financial need.

How to Apply: Applications are available through tribes.

Deadline: Varies.

Amount: Varies.

Number of Awards: Varies.

Business and Professional Association Foundation

Career Advancement Scholarship Program
P.O. Box 4030
Iowa City, IA 52243-4030
Phone: 800-525-3729
Fax: 202-861-0298
Email: bpwfoundation@act.org
Website: http://www.bpwusa.org

964 • Career Advancement Scholarship

Purpose: To support disadvantaged women who wish to advance in their career or enter the workforce.

Eligibility: Applicants must be female U.S. citizens who are at least 25, demonstrate financial need, have clear career plans, be officially accepted in an accredited institution in the United States, Puerto Rico or the Virgin Islands and graduate within 12 to 24 months of the grant.

How to Apply: Applications are available online.

Deadline: April 15.

Amount: $1,000-$2,000.

Number of Awards: between 50 and 100.

CAP Charitable Foundation

Ron Brown Scholar Program
1160 Pepsi Place
Suite 206
Charlottesville, VA 22901
Phone: 434-964-1588
Fax: 434-964-1589
Email: franh@ronbrown.org
Website: http://www.ronbrown.org

965 • Ron Brown Scholar Program

Purpose: To award scholarships to academically talented, highly motivated African American high school seniors.

Eligibility: Applicants must be African American collegebound high school seniors. Selection is based on academic promise, leadership, communication skills, school and community involvement and financial need.

How to Apply: Applications are available online.

Deadline: January 9.

Amount: $10,000.

Number of Awards: Varies.

Cargill

The College Fund/UNCF
8260 Willow Oaks Corporate Drive
Fairfax, VA 22031-4511
Phone: 952-742-7874
Website: http://www.cargill.com/commun/grantmk.htm

966 • United Negro College Fund Cargill Scholarship-Internship Program

Purpose: To help minority students majoring in engineering, information technology, finance or science.

Eligibility: Applicants must be African American, American Indian, Asian American, Hispanic American or other minority students at a UNCF institution or one of the Cargill-specified schools. Students must also be rising freshmen, sophomores or juniors majoring in engineering (chemical, mechanical), information technology (MIS, computer science), accounting/finance or science (chemistry, biochemistry food science, microbiology and agricultural and animal science), show financial need and be able to work in the U.S. Applicants should submit transcripts, resumes, recommendation letters and essays and may need to do a phone interview. Recipients may participate in a summer internship at selected Cargill locations throughout the United States.

How to Apply: Applications are available online.
Deadline: February 28.
Amount: $5,000.
Number of Awards: 6.

Casualty Actuarial Society/Society of Actuaries

475 N, Martingale Road, Suite 600
Schaumburg, IL 60173-2226
Phone: 847-706-3501
Fax: 847-706-3599
Email: kwiener@soa.org
Website: http://www.beanactuary.org

967 • Actuarial Scholarships for Minority Students

Purpose: To provide scholarships at the undergraduate or graduate level for minority students who are interested in pursuing actuarial careers.

Eligibility: This award is available to the following groups interested in an actuarial career: African American, Hispanic and Native North American. Applicants must be admitted to a college or university offering either a program in actuarial science or courses that will serve to prepare the student for an actuarial career. In addition, applicants must have taken either the SAT or ACT. They should submit applications, two nomination forms, student aid reports, proof of college expenses, transcripts and test scores.

How to Apply: Applications are available online.
Deadline: January 17.
Amount: Varies.
Number of Awards: Varies.

Catching the Dream

Attn.: Scholarship Affairs Office
8200 Mountain Road NE
Suite 203
Albuquerque, NM 87110
Phone: 505-262-2351
Email: nscholarsh@aol.com
Website: http://www.catchingthedream.org

968 • MESBEC Program

Purpose: To provide scholarships to high-achieving American Indians in the fields of math, engineering, science, business, education and computers.

Eligibility: Applicants must be 1/4 or more degree American Indian, enrolled in a tribe and attend or plan to attend college full-time. Students must apply to all other sources of funding at the same time they apply for this scholarship. Selection is based on grades, SAT or ACT scores, work experience, leadership, clear goals, commitment to the American Indian community and the potential to improve the lives of American Indian people.

How to Apply: Applications are available online.
Deadline: March 15, April 15 and September 15.
Amount: $500-$5,000.
Number of Awards: Varies.

969 • Native American Leadership Education Program

Purpose: To increase the number of American Indian teachers in American Indian schools.

Eligibility: Applicants must be at least 1/4 degree American Indian, enrolled in a tribe and current paraprofessionals in an American Indian school who are attending or plan to attend college full-time studying education, counseling or school administration. Students are required to apply for all other sources of funding at the same time as applying for this scholarship. Scholarships are based on grades, ACT or SAT scores, work experience, leadership, commitment to the American Indian community, goals and potential to improve the lives of American Indian people.

How to Apply: Applications are available online.
Deadline: March 15, April 15 and September 15.
Amount: $500-$5,000.
Number of Awards: Varies.

970 • Tribal Business Management Program

Purpose: To support American Indian students majoring in business, finance, management, economics, banking, hotel management and related fields who plan to work in economic development for tribes.

Eligibility: Applicants must be 1/4 or more degree American Indian, enrolled in a U.S. tribe and attending or planning to attend college full-time. Candidates are required to apply for all other forms of funding in addition to applying for this scholarship. Scholarships are based on grades, SAT or ACT scores, work experience, leadership, commitment to the tribe, personal goals and potential to improve the lives of American Indian people.

How to Apply: Applications are available online.
Deadline: March 15, April 15 and September 15.
Amount: $500-$5,000.
Number of Awards: Varies.

Center for Native American Studies

Berger Scholarship Selection Committee
P.O. Box 172340 / 2-179 Wilson Hall
Bozeman, MT 59717-2340
Phone: 406-994-3881
Email: zna7001@montana.edu
Website: http://www.montana.edu/wwwnas/

971 • Memorial Scholarships for American Indian Students

Purpose: To promote academic excellence among American Indians.

Eligibility: Applicants must be freshmen, transfer students from a tribally-controlled community college or graduate students who are enrolled members of a federally-recognized tribe or a member of the Little Shell Band of Chippewa Crees. Candidates must be graduates of an accredited high school or tribally-controlled community college.

How to Apply: Applications are available online, by phone and by email.
Deadline: March 3.
Amount: $1,000.
Number of Awards: Varies.

Cherokee Nation

Cherokee Nation Undergraduate Scholarship Programs
Attn.: Higher Education
P.O. Box 948
Tahlequah, OK 74465
Phone: 918-456-0671
Email: highereducation@cherokee.org
Website: http://www.cherokee.org

972 • Cherokee Nation PELL Scholarship
Purpose: To support students who are Cherokee Nation Tribal Members.
Eligibility: Applicants must be high school senior Cherokee Nation tribal members planning to attend an institution of higher education.
How to Apply: Applications are available online.
Deadline: June 17.
Amount: Varies.
Number of Awards: Varies.

Chickasaw Nation Education Foundation

P.O. Box 1726
Ad, OK 74821
Phone: 580-421-9031
Website: http://www.chickasaw.net

973 • Chickasaw Nation Education Foundation Program
Purpose: To assist Chickasaw students who demonstrate academic excellence, community service, dedication to learning and a commitment to Native Americans.
Eligibility: Applicants must be full-time Chickasaw students. Other eligibility requirements vary by scholarship.
How to Apply: Applications are available online.
Deadline: June 1.
Amount: Varies.
Number of Awards: 29.

CIRI Foundation

3600 San Jeronimo Drive
Suite 256
Anchorage, AK 99508
Phone: 800-764-3382
Fax: 907-263-5588
Email: tcf@thecirifoundation.org
Website: http://www.thecirifoundation.org

974 • Foundation Scholarships
Purpose: To provide financial aid for Alaska Natives.
Eligibility: Applicants must be qualified Alaska Native beneficiaries who plan to attend or are currently attending undergraduate or graduate institutions. There are a number of awards based on field of study or career goal.
How to Apply: Applications are available online.
Deadline: Varies.
Amount: $500-$18,000.
Number of Awards: Varies.

Citizen Potawatomi Nation

1601 S. Gordon Cooper
Shawnee, OK 74801
Phone: 405-275-3121
Email: hownikan@potawatomi.org
Website: http://www.potawatomi.org

975 • Citizen Potawatomi Nation Tribal Scholarship
Purpose: To provide financial assistance to tribal members who are studying in undergraduate or graduate programs, vocational technical career courses or other accredited educational programs.
Eligibility: Applicants must be tribal members who maintain a GPA of 2.0 and meet requirements for financial aid.
How to Apply: Applications are available online.
Deadline: August 15.
Amount: Varies.
Number of Awards: Varies.

Congressional Hispanic Caucus Institute Inc.

911 2nd Street NE
Washington, DC 20002
Phone: 202-543-1771
Email: shernandez@chci.org
Website: http://www.chci.org

976 • CHCI Scholarship Award
Purpose: To award Latino students for public service activities in their communities.
Eligibility: Applicants must be Latinos who have actively participated in public service; be accepted as full-time students into an accredited community college, four-year university or a graduate/professional program; demonstrate financial need and have good writing skills. Students should submit applications, resumes, essays, Student Aid Reports, two recommendation letters, transcripts and a self-addressed stamped postcard to be notified when application is received.
How to Apply: Applications are available online.
Deadline: March 1.
Amount: $5,000.
Number of Awards: Varies.

Consortium for Graduate Study in Management

5585 Pershing
Suite 240
St. Louis, MO 63112-4621
Phone: 314-877-5500
Email: frontdesk@cgsm.org
Website: http://www.cgsm.org

977 • Consortium Fellowship
Purpose: To support graduate business students at member schools.
Eligibility: Applicants must be African Americans, Hispanic Americans or Native Americans and U.S. citizens and U.S. permanent residents of other races and ethnicities who fulfill the Consortium's mission. Applicants must have a bachelor's degree, and the degree may be in any academic discipline from an accredited institution recognized by Consortium member

schools. The fellowship supports full-time graduate business studies at member schools only. Applicants must submit two references, transcripts, copies of GMAT scores and application fees. All applicants must also interview with a Consortium representative.
How to Apply: Applications are available online.
Deadline: January 15.
Amount: Varies.
Number of Awards: Varies.

CosmoGirl!

300 W. 57th Street
20th Floor
New York, NY 10019
Email: cgoftheyear@cosmogirl.com
Website: http://www.cosmogirl.com

978 • CosmoGirl! Of The Year Award

Purpose: To recognize girls and young women who have made contributions to the world.
Eligibility: Applicants must be age 11 to 25 and send an essay of up to 500 words about how they are a CosmoGirl along with a photo of themselves. Only females from the U.S. and Canada may enter. In addition to the monetary prize, the winner receives a trip to New York City to the awards ceremony.
How to Apply: Applications are available online. Applications may be sent by postal mail or through an email instead of an online application. Applicants who are 11 and 12 must enter by postal mail.
Deadline: July 26.
Amount: $10,000.
Number of Awards: 1.

Council for Exceptional Children

1110 North Glebe Road
Suite 300
Arlington, VA 22201
Phone: 888-232-7733
Fax: 703-264-9494
Email: fec@cec.sped.org
Website: http://www.cec.sped.org

979 • Student CEC Ethnic Diversity Scholarship

Purpose: To recognize a student CEC member from an ethnically diverse background who is currently pursuing a degree in special education.
Eligibility: Applicants must be U.S. or Canadian citizens, junior, senior or graduate students enrolled in an accredited college or university, members of an ethnically diverse group and pursuing a degree in special education. Students must be student CEC members in good standing with a minimum 2.5 GPA. Applicants must also submit a list of their Student CEC activities and/or other involvement with those with disabilities and a short autobiography focusing on their interest in special education.
How to Apply: Applications are available online.
Deadline: November 5.
Amount: $500.
Number of Awards: 1.

980 • Student CEC/Black Caucus Scholarship

Purpose: To recognize an African American student who is a student CEC member and pursuing a degree in special education.
Eligibility: Applicants must be African American and junior, senior or graduate students enrolled in an accredited college or university

and be U.S. or Canadian citizens. Applicants must also be student CEC members in good standing and majoring in special education with a minimum 2.5 GPA. Applicants must submit a list of their Student CEC activities and/or other involvement with programs for those with disabilities and a short autobiography focusing on their interest in special education.
How to Apply: Applications are available online.
Deadline: November 5.
Amount: $500.
Number of Awards: 1.

Gates Foundation

P.O. Box 10500
Fairfax, VA 22031
Phone: 877-690-4677
Website: http://www.gmsp.org

981 • Gates Millennium Scholars Program

Purpose: To provide outstanding minority students with opportunities to complete their undergraduate college educations.
Eligibility: Applicants must be African American, American Indian/Alaska Native, Asian Pacific Islander American or Hispanic American students with a minimum 3.3 GPA, enter an accredited college or university and have significant financial need. Applicants must also be eligible for federal Pell Grants.
How to Apply: Students are nominated by teachers, principals or other education professionals. Nomination materials are available online.
Deadline: January.
Amount: Varies.
Number of Awards: 1000.

Hebrew Immigrant Aid Society

333 Seventh Avenue, 16th Floor
New York, NY 10001-5004
Phone: 212-613-1358
Fax: 212-967-4483
Email: scholarship@hias.org
Website: http://www.hias.org

982 • HIAS Scholarship

Purpose: To award scholarships to Jewish immigrant students.
Eligibility: Applicants must have completed one year of high school or college in the United States and have arrived in the United States after January 1, 1992. Selection is based on academic achievement, financial need and service within the Jewish community.
How to Apply: Applications are available online.
Deadline: March 15.
Amount: Varies.
Number of Awards: Varies.

Hellenic Times Scholarship Fund

823 Eleventh Avenue
Attn.: Nick Katsoris
New York, NY 10019
Fax: 212-977-3662
Email: htsfund@aol.com
Website: http://www.htsfund.org

983 • Hellenic Times Scholarship

Purpose: To financially help Greek American students.

Eligibility: Applicants must be undergraduate or graduate students of Greek descent between the ages of 17 and 25 and may not win any other full scholarships. Applicants must submit transcripts and may be required to submit tax returns.

How to Apply: Applications are available online.

Deadline: January 16.

Amount: Varies.

Number of Awards: Varies.

Hispanic College Fund

1301 K Street NW
Suite 450-A
Washington, DC 20005
Phone: 800-644-4223
Fax: 202-296-3774
Email: hcf-info@hispanicfund.org
Website: http://www.hispanicfund.org

984 • Hispanic College Fund Scholarships

Purpose: To develop future Hispanic business leaders by aiding students who have demonstrated excellence and potential.

Eligibility: Applicants must be Hispanic students applying to or enrolled at a college or university in the U.S. or Puerto Rico. Applicants must be U.S. citizens or permanent residents, plan to attend school full-time during the next academic year and have a minimum 3.0 GPA. Selection is based on academics and financial need. Some specific awards have additional eligibility requirements.

How to Apply: Applications are available online.

Deadline: April 15.

Amount: Varies.

Number of Awards: Varies.

Hispanic Heritage Awards Foundation

2600 Virginia Avenue NW
Suite 406
Washington, DC 20037
Phone: 202-861-9797
Fax: 202-861-9799
Email: contact@hispanicheritageawards.org
Website: http://www.hispanicawards.org

985 • Hispanic Heritage Youth Awards

Purpose: To promote Hispanic excellence and recognize the contributions of Hispanic American youth.

Eligibility: Applicants must be high school seniors who are U.S. citizens or permanent residents, reside in Chicago, Denver, Dallas, Los Angeles, Miami, New York City, Philadelphia, Phoenix, San Antonio, San Diego, San Jose and Washington DC and have Hispanic parentage (Hispanic parentage can be one parent of Mexican, Central American, Cuban, Puerto Rican, South American, Spanish or Caribbean Hispanic descent). Selection criteria include achievement in the applicant's discipline, involvement in community, ability to overcome adversity and character. The disciplines are: Academic Excellence, Sports, the Arts, Literature/Journalism, Mathematics, Leadership/Community Service and Science and Technology.

How to Apply: Applications are available by request.

Deadline: February.

Amount: $2,000-$5,000.

Number of Awards: Varies.

Hispanic Outlook Magazine

Scholarship Fund
210 Route 4 East
Suite 310
Paramus, NJ 07652
Website: http://www.hispanicoutlook.com

986 • Hispanic Outlook Scholarship

Eligibility: Applicants must be high school seniors who are Hispanic.

How to Apply: Applications are available by sending a self-addressed, stamped envelope to the organization.

Deadline: May 1.

Amount: Varies.

Number of Awards: 2.

Hispanic Scholarship Fund (HSF)

55 Second Street
Suite 1500
San Francisco, CA 94105
Phone: 877-473-4636
Fax: 415-808-2302
Email: scholar1@hsf.net
Website: http://www.hsf.net

987 • College Scholarship Program

Purpose: To advance the college education of Hispanic Americans. Over the past 25 years, HSF has awarded more than 68,000 scholarships.

Eligibility: Applicants must be of Hispanic heritage (one parent must be fully Hispanic or both parents must be half Hispanic), be U.S. citizens or permanent residents, and be eligible to apply and receive Title IV funds. Selection is based on academic achievement, letter of recommendation, personal statement and financial need.

How to Apply: Applications are available online.

Deadline: August.

Amount: Varies.

Number of Awards: Varies.

988 • Community College Transfer Scholarship Program

Purpose: To support students of Hispanic heritage who plan to transfer from a community college program to a four-year college or university.

Eligibility: Applicants must be of Hispanic heritage (one parent fully Hispanic or each parent half-Hispanic) and be a part-time or full-time community college student with a minimum 3.0 GPA. Applicants must plan to transfer to a four-year college or university the following academic year.

How to Apply: Applications are available online.

Deadline: January 2.

Amount: $1,000-$2,500.

Number of Awards: Varies.

989 • High School Scholarship Program

Purpose: To assist high school students of Hispanic descent with college expenses. Over the past 25 years, HSF has provided more than 68,000 scholarships.

Eligibility: Applicants must be of Hispanic heritage (one parent fully Hispanic or each parent half Hispanic) and graduating high school seniors with a minimum 3.0 GPA. Students must have definite plans to attend a college or university the following fall semester after graduation.

How to Apply: Applications are available online.
Deadline: December 15.
Amount: $1,000-$2,500.
Number of Awards: Varies.

990 • HSF/General Motors Scholarship

Purpose: To help Latinos pursuing degrees in engineering and business.

Eligibility: Applicants must be of Hispanic heritage, enrolled full-time at a four-year U.S. accredited college or university in the U.S., Puerto Rico or U.S. Virgin Islands and major in engineering (electrical, industrial, manufacturing or mechanical) or business (accounting, business administration, economics or finance). Applicants or their families must have ethnic backgrounds from Spain, Mexico, Guatemala, Honduras, El Salvador, Costa Rica, Nicaragua, Panama, Colombia, Venezuela, Ecuador, Peru, Argentina, Chile, Bolivia, Uruguay, Paraguay, Brazil, Cuba, Puerto Rico or the Dominican Republic. However, students from Belize, Guyana, Suriname and French Guiana are ineligible. Semifinalists must complete the GM online assessment.

How to Apply: Applications are available online.
Deadline: June 30.
Amount: $2,500.
Number of Awards: Varies.

Hopi Tribe Grants and Scholarship Program

P.O. Box 123
Kykotsmovi , AZ 86039
Phone: 800-762-9630
Fax: 928-734-9575
Email: info@hopi.nsn.us
Website: http://www.hopi.nsn.us

991 • Hopi Scholarship

Purpose: To help Hopi students with academic achievement.

Eligibility: Applicants must be enrolled members of the Hopi tribe, be high school graduates or have earned a GED, have been accepted to a regionally accredited college and plan to attend full-time and have completed the Free Application for Federal Student Aid. Students must be in top 10 percent of their high school class or score 930 on the SAT or 21 on the ACT as entering freshmen; have a minimum 3.0 GPA as undergraduates or have a minimum 3.2 GPA as graduate, post graduate or professional degree students. Applications, statements of goals, financial needs analysis, proof of Hopi enrollment and transcripts are required.

How to Apply: Applications are available by mail.
Deadline: Varies.
Amount: Varies.
Number of Awards: Varies.

992 • Private High School Scholarship

Purpose: To help Hopi students who plan to attend an accredited private high school.

Eligibility: Applicants must be enrolled members of the Hopi tribe and should submit applications, statements of goals, financial needs analysis, proof of Hopi enrollment and transcripts.

How to Apply: Applications are available by mail.
Deadline: Varies.
Amount: Varies.
Number of Awards: Varies.

993 • Standardized Test Fee Scholarship

Purpose: To help Hopi students who are required to take an entrance exams or career certification tests.

Eligibility: Applicants must be enrolled members of the Hopi tribe, be high school graduates or have earned a GED, have been accepted to and plan to attend full-time a regionally accredited college and have completed the Free Application for Federal Student Aid. Applications, statements of goals, financial needs analysis, proof of Hopi enrollment and transcripts are required. The award provides assistance with the Graduate Record Exam, Law School Admission Test, Arizona Teachers Proficiency Exam, Bar Exam and others. Applications should be submitted 30 days before the test date.

How to Apply: Applications are available by mail.
Deadline: Varies.
Amount: Varies.
Number of Awards: Varies.

994 • Tuition and Book Scholarship

Purpose: To assist Hopi students pursuing post-secondary education.

Eligibility: Applicants should be pursuing post-secondary education because of personal growth, career enhancement or change, continuing education, as part-time students or as students without financial need. Students must be enrolled members of the Hopi tribe, be high school graduates or GED recipients and have been accepted to regionally accredited colleges. Applicants should submit applications, statements of goals, proof of Hopi enrollment and transcripts.

How to Apply: Applications are available by mail.
Deadline: Varies.
Amount: Varies.
Number of Awards: Varies.

Horizons Foundation

870 Market Street
Suite 728
San Francisco, CA 94102
Phone: 415-398-2333
Fax: 415-398-4733
Email: jdorf@horizonsfoundation.org
Website: http://www.horizonsfoundation.org

995 • GAPA's George Choy Memorial Scholarship

Purpose: To assist Bay Area gay, lesbian, bisexual and transgender Asian and Pacific Islander graduating high school students.

Eligibility: Applicants should have at least 25 percent Asian/ Pacific Islander ancestry, plan to attend or currently attend a post-secondary institution as a freshman or sophomore and reside in one of the nine Bay Area counties (Alameda, Contra Costa, Marin, San Francisco, San Mateo, Santa Clara, Napa, Sonoma or Solano). Preference is given to those who are lesbian, gay, bisexual or transgender or who are involved in the LGBT community.

How to Apply: Applications are available by phone.
Deadline: Varies.
Amount: $1,000.
Number of Awards: Varies.

Institute of Industrial Engineers (IIE)

3577 Parkway Lane
Suite 200
Norcross, GA 30092
Phone: 800-494-0460
Fax: 770-441-3295
Email: bcameron@iienet.org
Website: http://www.iienet.org/studentcenter

996 • United Parcel Service Scholarship for Minority Students

Purpose: To help minority undergraduate students in industrial engineering.

Eligibility: Applicants must be full-time undergraduate minority students enrolled in a college in the United States, Canada or Mexico with an accredited industrial engineering program, major in industrial engineering and be active members. Students may not apply directly for this scholarship and must be nominated. The award is based on academic ability, character, leadership, potential service to the industrial engineering profession and financial need.

How to Apply: Nomination forms are available online.
Deadline: February 15.
Amount: $4,000.
Number of Awards: 1.

Intertribal Timber Council

Attn.: Education Committee
1112 NE 21st Avenue
Portland, OR 97232
Phone: 503-282-4296
Fax: 503-282-1274
Email: itc1@teleport.com
Website: http://www.itcnet.org

997 • Truman D. Picard Scholarship

Purpose: To promote the field of natural resources.

Eligibility: Applicants must be high school seniors or college students and must pursue the natural resources field. Applicants must submit a resume, letters of reference, validated enrollment in Tribe/Native Alaska Corporation, letter about interest in natural resources, education, academics and financial need.

How to Apply: There is no official application form.
Deadline: January 30.
Amount: $1,200-$1,800.
Number of Awards: Varies.

Jackie Robinson Foundation

3 W. 35th Street
11th Floor
New York, NY 10001
Phone: 212-290-8600
Fax: 212-290-8081
Email: general@jackierobinson.org
Website: http://www.jackierobinson.org

998 • Jackie Robinson Scholarship

Purpose: To help minority students who have shown leadership skills in their communities.

Eligibility: Applicants must be minority high school seniors with demonstrated financial need and academic achievement and who have already been accepted to a four-year college or university.

How to Apply: Applications are available online, by email to requests@jackierobinson.org or by mail.
Deadline: April 1.
Amount: $6,000.
Number of Awards: Varies.

Japanese American Citizens League (JACL)

National Scholarship Awards
1765 Sutter Street
San Francisco, CA 94115
Phone: 415-921-5225
Email: jacl@jacl.org
Website: http://www.jacl.org

999 • Hagiwara Student Aid Award

Purpose: To aid students who otherwise would have to delay or terminate their education due to lack of financing.

Eligibility: Applicants must be National JACL members and must be attending a college, university, trade school, business school or any other institution of higher learning. A personal statement, letter of recommendation, academic performance, work experience and community involvement are considered.

How to Apply: Applications are available online.
Deadline: April 1.
Amount: Varies.
Number of Awards: Varies.

1000 • Japanese American Citizens League Creative and Performing Arts Awards

Purpose: To recognize and encourage performing arts and creative projects among JACL members.

Eligibility: Applicants must be National JACL members and must be attending a college, university, trade school, business school or any other institution of higher learning. A personal statement, letter of recommendation, academic performance, work experience and community involvement are considered. Professional artists are not allowed.

How to Apply: Applications are available online.
Deadline: April 1.
Amount: Varies.
Number of Awards: 2.

1001 • Japanese American Citizens League Entering Freshman Awards

Purpose: To recognize and encourage education as a key to greater opportunities among JACL members.

Eligibility: Applicants must be National JACL members and must be planning to attend a college, university, trade school, business school, or any other institution of higher learning at the undergraduate level. A personal statement, letter of recommendation, academic performance, work experience, and community involvement will all be considered.

How to Apply: Applications are available through local JACL chapters, regional offices, National JACL Headquarters and website.
Deadline: March 1.
Amount: Varies.
Number of Awards: 11.

1002 • Japanese American Citizens League Graduate Awards

Purpose: To provide monetary assistance for graduate studies to JACL members.

Eligibility: Applicants must be National JACL members and must attend a college or university at the graduate level. A personal statement, letter of recommendation, academic performance, work experience and community involvement are considered.

How to Apply: Applications are available online.

Deadline: April 1.

Amount: Varies.

Number of Awards: 8.

1003 • Japanese American Citizens League Law Scholarships

Purpose: To assist JACL members who are law students.

Eligibility: Applicants must be National JACL members and must be studying law at a college or university. A personal statement, letter of recommendation, academic performance, work experience, and community involvement will all be considered.

How to Apply: Applications are available online.

Deadline: April 1.

Amount: Varies.

Number of Awards: 2.

1004 • Japanese American Citizens League Undergraduate Awards

Purpose: To recognize and encourage education as a key to greater opportunities among JACL members.

Eligibility: Applicants must be National JACL members and must be attending a college, university, trade school, business school, or any other institution of higher learning at the undergraduate level. A personal statement, letter of recommendation, academic performance, work experience, and community involvement will all be considered.

How to Apply: Applications are available through local JACL chapters, regional offices, National JACL Headquarters and website.

Deadline: April 1.

Amount: Varies.

Number of Awards: 10.

Jeannette Rankin Foundation

P.O. Box 6653
Athens, GA 30604
Phone: 706-208-1211
Fax: 706-208-1211
Email: info@rankinfoundation.org
Website: http://www.rankinfoundation.org

1005 • Jeannette Rankin Foundation Award

Purpose: To support the education of low-income women 35 years or older.

Eligibility: Applicants must be women 35 years of age or older, plan to obtain an undergraduate or vocational education, and meet maximum household income guidelines.

How to Apply: Applications are available online or by sending a self-addressed and stamped envelope to the foundation.

Deadline: March 1.

Amount: $2,000.

Number of Awards: Varies.

League of United Latin American Citizens

2000 L Street NW
Suite #610
Washington, DC 20036
Phone: 202-833-6130
Email: lnescaward@aol.com
Website: http://www.lulac.org

1006 • LULAC National Scholarship Fund

Purpose: To aid Hispanic students attending colleges and universities.

Eligibility: Applicants must have applied to or be enrolled in a college, university or graduate school. Eligible candidates cannot be related to scholarship committee members, the Council President or contributors to the Council funds. Since applications must be sent from local LULAC Councils, students without LULAC Councils in their states are ineligible.

How to Apply: Applications are available online.

Deadline: March 31.

Amount: $250-$2,000.

Number of Awards: Varies.

LinTV

8 Elm Street
New Haven, CT 06510
Phone: 203-784-8958
Email: Gail.Brekke@lintv.com
Website: http://www.lintv.com

1007 • Minority Scholarship and Training Program

Purpose: To help educate outstanding minority students who plan to enter the television broadcast field.

Eligibility: Applicants must have a minimum 3.0 GPA, major in journalism or a related broadcast field at an accredited university or college, be college sophomores, be U.S. citizens and of non-white origin.

How to Apply: Applications are available online.

Deadline: March 15.

Amount: $20,000.

Number of Awards: Varies.

Margaret Mcnamara Memorial Fund

1818 H Street NW, MSN H2-204
Washington, DC 20433
Phone: 202-473-8751
Fax: 202 522-3142
Email: familynetwork@worldbank.org
Website: http://www.worldbank.org/yournet

1008 • Margaret Mcnamara Memorial Fund Fellowships

Purpose: To provide financial assistance to women from developing countries who are currently studying to earn a college degree in the U.S.

Eligibility: Applicants must be from an eligible nation, have a record of community service in their country and be U.S. or Canadian residents at the time of application, while intending to return to their country of origin with two years. Individuals under the age of 25 and relatives of World Bank employees are not eligible.

How to Apply: Applications are available online.
Deadline: February 10.
Amount: $11,000.
Number of Awards: 6.

Mirasol Center for Eating Disorder Recovery

7650 E. Broadway Boulevard
Suite 303
Tucson, AZ 85710
Phone: 888-520-1700
Fax: 520-546-3205
Email: information@mirasol.net
Website: http://www.mirasolteen.com

1009 • Mirasol's You're Worth It! Scholarship Sweepstakes

Purpose: To help girls 15 and above with their educations.
Eligibility: Applicants must be females enrolled at a two- or four-year accredited U.S. high school, college or university and sign up to receive the monthly newsletter "The Sunflower."
How to Apply: Applications are available online.
Deadline: October 31.
Amount: $3,000.
Number of Awards: 3.

National Association for Campus Activities

13 Harbison Way
Columbia, SC 29212-3401
Phone: 803-732-6222
Fax: 803-749-1047
Email: info@naca.org
Website: http://www.naca.org

1010 • Multicultural Scholarship Program

Purpose: To increase participation in campus activities by ethnic minority students by making conferences and other events more affordable.
Eligibility: Applicants must be African American, Latino(a), Native American, Asian American or Pacific Islander students who are involved in campus activities. Students must demonstrate financial need and commit to at least one year of further involvement in campus activities after receiving the scholarship. NACA membership is not required. Scholarship recipients must submit a report after attending the event describing how it helped their professional development.
How to Apply: Applications are available online.
Deadline: May 1.
Amount: Varies.
Number of Awards: 4.

National Association for the Advancement of Colored People

The United Negro College Fund
Scholarships and Grants Administration
8260 Willow Oaks Corporate Drive
Fairfax, VA 22031
Phone: 703-205-3400
Website: http://www.naacp.org

1011 • Agnes Jones Scholarship

Purpose: To reward NAACP members with financial need.
Eligibility: Students must be members of the NAACP, U.S. citizens and attending an accredited U.S. college. Undergraduates must attend college full-time, while graduates may be full- or part-time students. High school seniors and undergraduates must have a minimum 2.5 GPA while graduate students must have a minimum 3.0 GPA. Applicants must demonstrate financial need according to the formula in the application form.
How to Apply: Applications are available online.
Deadline: Last Friday in March.
Amount: $1,500-$2,500.
Number of Awards: Varies.

1012 • Earl Graves Scholarship

Purpose: The NAACP created its scholarships to promote equal opportunity in education.
Eligibility: Applicants must be junior or senior business majors or accepted into a business master's or doctoral program at an accredited U.S. college or university, in the top 20 percent of their class and attend school full-time.
How to Apply: Applications are available online and by written request.
Deadline: The last Friday in the month of March.
Amount: $5,000.
Number of Awards: Varies.

1013 • Louis Stokes Scholarship

Purpose: To promote equal opportunity in education.
Eligibility: Applicants must be incoming freshman at an accredited Historically Black College or University in the U.S., must major in engineering, computer science or science and demonstrate financial need. Membership in the NAACP is not required, but highly recommended.
How to Apply: Applications are available online and by mail.
Deadline: The last Friday in the month of March.
Amount: $2,000.
Number of Awards: Varies.

1014 • Roy Wilkins Scholarship

Purpose: The NAACP created its scholarships to promote equal opportunity in education.
Eligibility: Students must be entering college freshmen at an accredited U.S. college and be full-time students. Membership in the NAACP is not required, but highly recommended.
How to Apply: Applications are available online or by mail.
Deadline: The last Friday in the month of March.
Amount: $1,000.
Number of Awards: Varies.

1015 • Sutton Scholarship

Purpose: To support African Americans entering the field of education.
Eligibility: Applicants must be education majors at an accredited college and U.S. citizens. Undergraduates must be full-time students with a GPA of 2.5, while graduates may be full- or part-time students and must maintain a GPA of 3.0. NAACP membership is not required but is highly desirable.
How to Apply: Applications are available online.
Deadline: Last Friday in March.
Amount: $1,000-$2,000.
Number of Awards: Varies.

1016 • Willems Scholarship

Purpose: To encourage African-American males in scientific and technical fields.

Eligibility: Students must be males majoring in engineering, chemistry, physics or mathematical sciences. Applicants must be U.S. citizens attending an accredited U.S. school. Undergraduates must be full-time students with a 2.5 GPA. Graduate students may be full- or part-time students and must maintain a 3.0 GPA. Students must display financial need according to the chart included in the application materials. Membership in the NAACP is not required but preferred.

How to Apply: Applications are available online.

Deadline: Last Friday in March.

Amount: $2,000-$3,000.

Number of Awards: Varies.

National Association of Black Accountants

7249-A Hanover Parkway
Greenbelt, MD 20770
Phone: 301-474-NABA
Fax: 301-474-3114
Website: http://www.nabainc.org

1017 • National Association of Black Accountants Scholarship Program

Purpose: To support African Americans and other minorities in the accounting and finance professions.

Eligibility: Applicants must be ethnic minorities currently enrolled as full-time undergraduates in accounting, finance or business or as graduate students in a Master's of Accountancy program. Applicants must also be NABA members and have a minimum 2.5 GPA.

How to Apply: Applications are available online.

Deadline: December 31.

Amount: $500-$6,000.

Number of Awards: Varies.

National Association of Black Journalists

Scholarship Program
8701-A Adelphi Road
Adelphi, MD 20783
Phone: 301-445-7100
Fax: 301-445-7101
Email: warren@nabj.org
Website: http://www.nabj.org

1018 • National Association of Black Journalists Scholarship Program

Purpose: To support African American students who are planning to pursue careers in journalism.

Eligibility: Applicants must be African American high school seniors, college students or graduate students who plan to pursue careers in journalism and who are journalism majors or in staff positions on the school newspaper or campus television, radio or website.

How to Apply: Applications are available online.

Deadline: Varies.

Amount: Varies.

Number of Awards: Varies.

National Association of Hispanic Journalists

Scholarship Committee
1000 National Press Building
Washington, DC 20045
Phone: 202-662-7145
Fax: 202-662-7144
Email: ntita@nahj.org
Website: http://www.nahj.org

1019 • Maria Elena Salinas Scholarship Program

Purpose: To support Spanish speaking students who plan to become broadcast journalists.

Eligibility: Applicants must be high school seniors, undergraduates or first-year graduate students who plan to pursue careers in journalism in Spanish-language television or radio. The award includes an opportunity to intern with the news division of Univision or an affiliate. Applicants must write an essay in Spanish outlining their career goals and provide Spanish-language samples of their work.

How to Apply: Applications are available online.

Deadline: Last Friday in January.

Amount: $5,000.

Number of Awards: 2.

1020 • NAHJ Scholarships

Purpose: To support Hispanic students who plan to enter the journalism field.

Eligibility: Applicants must be high school seniors, college undergraduate or graduate students majoring in print, photo, online or broadcast journalism.

How to Apply: Applications are available online.

Deadline: Last Friday in January.

Amount: Varies.

Number of Awards: Varies.

1021 • Newhouse Scholarship Program

Purpose: To support Hispanic students who plan to enter the journalism field.

Eligibility: Applicants must be current college sophomores. Recipients are required to intern at a Newhouse newspaper the summer following their junior year. The program provides a stipend to attend NAHJ's annual convention.

How to Apply: Applications are available online.

Deadline: Last Friday in January.

Amount: $5,000.

Number of Awards: Varies.

National Association of Hispanic Nurses

Attn.: Maria Castro, NAHN Awards and Scholarship Committee Chair
1501 Sixteenth Street NW
Washington, DC 20036
Phone: 202-387-2477
Fax: 202-483-7183
Email: info@thehispanicnurses.org
Website: http://www.thehispanicnurses.org

1022 • Juanita Robles-Lopez

Purpose: To support graduate students enrolled in a maternal-child nursing program.

Eligibility: Students must be members of NAHN, although they may apply for membership at the time of application. Selection is based on an essay describing the maternal-child needs in Hispanic communities and the applicant's potential leadership in this field, recommendations, academic achievement and application form.

How to Apply: Applications are available online or by mail.

Deadline: April 14.

Amount: $2,000.

Number of Awards: 1.

1023 • NAHN Scholarship

Purpose: To aid Hispanic nursing students who demonstrate the potential to make contributions to the nursing profession and who will act as positive role models for other nursing students.

Eligibility: Applicants must be members of the NAHN and be enrolled in a diploma, associate, baccalaureate, graduate or practical/vocational nursing program.

How to Apply: Applications are available online or by mail.

Deadline: April 14.

Amount: $1,000.

Number of Awards: Varies.

National Association of Negro Business and Professional Women's Clubs Inc.

1806 New Hampshire Avenue NW
Washington, DC 20009-3298
Phone: 202-483-4206
Email: info@nanbpwc.org
Website: http://www.nanbpwc.org

1024 • Julianne Malveaux Scholarship

Purpose: To award scholarships to college students majoring in journalism, economics or a related field.

Eligibility: Applicants must be enrolled as sophomores or juniors at an accredited college or university and have a minimum 3.0 GPA. Students may major in related fields such as public policy or creative writing.

How to Apply: Applications are available online.

Deadline: April 30.

Amount: $1,000.

Number of Awards: Varies.

1025 • National Scholarship

Purpose: To award scholarships to aspiring business and professional college or university students.

Eligibility: Applicants must be graduating high school seniors and have a minimum 3.0 GPA. Students must submit a transcript, an application form, two letters of recommendation and an essay that is at least 300 words on "Why is education important to me?"

How to Apply: Applications are available online.

Deadline: March 1.

Amount: Up to $1,000.

Number of Awards: Varies.

National Consortium for Graduate Degrees for Minorities in Engineering and Science Inc. (GEM)

GEM Consortium
P.O. Box 537
Notre Dame, IN 46556
Phone: 574-631-7771
Fax: 574-287-1486
Website: http://www.gemfellowship.org

1026 • GEM Fellowship Program

Purpose: To provide fellowships for minority students pursuing graduate degrees in engineering, physical science or natural science.

Eligibility: Applicants must be college sophomore, junior or senior or graduate student majors in engineering, physical science or natural science and be members of one of the following minority groups: African American, Native American or Puerto Rican, Latino or other Hispanic American.

How to Apply: Applications are available online.

Deadline: November 1.

Amount: Varies.

Number of Awards: Varies.

National Foster Parent Association

7512 Stanich Avenue #6
Gig Harbor, WA 98335
Phone: 800-557-5238
Fax: 253-853-4001
Email: Info@NFPAinc.org
Website: http://www.nfpainc.org

1027 • National Foster Parent Association Vocational/Job Training Scholarship

Purpose: To support foster youth in furthering their education through technical or vocational programs.

Eligibility: Applicants must be foster children at least 17 years old planning to enroll in vocational, job training or correspondence courses, including the GED.

How to Apply: Applications are available online.

Deadline: March 31.

Amount: $1,000.

Number of Awards: 5.

National Society Daughters of the American Revolution

1776 D Street NW
Washington, DC 20006
Phone: 202-628-1776
Website: http://www.dar.org

1028 • American Indian Scholarship

Purpose: To assist Native American students.

Eligibility: Applicants must be Native Americans with papers proving Native American blood, have a minimum 2.75 GPA and demonstrate financial need and academic achievement. Preference is given to undergraduate students.

How to Apply: Applications are available by written request.

Deadline: April 1 and October 1.

Amount: $500.

Number of Awards: Varies.

1029 • Frances Crawford Marvin American Indian Scholarship

Purpose: To assist Native American students.

Eligibility: Applicants must be Native Americans able to prove Native American blood, demonstrate financial need and academic achievement, be enrolled full-time at a college or university and have a minimum 3.0 GPA.

How to Apply: Applications are available by written request.
Deadline: February 1.
Amount: Varies.
Number of Awards: Varies.

National Strength and Conditioning Association (NSCA) Foundation

1885 Bob Johnson Drive
Colorado Springs, CO 80906
Phone: 800-815-6826
Fax: 719-632-6367
Email: nsca@nsca-lift.org
Website: http://www.nsca-lift.org

1030 • Minority Scholarship

Purpose: To encourage minorities to enter the field of strength and conditioning.
Eligibility: Applicants must be African American, Hispanic, Asian American or Native American students working toward a graduate degree related to strength and conditioning. Students must be NSCA members for one year before applying and be pursuing careers in strength and conditioning. Applications are evaluated based on grades, courses, experience, honors, recommendations and involvement in the community and with NSCA.
How to Apply: Applications are available with membership.
Deadline: March 15.
Amount: $1,000.
Number of Awards: 2.

National Urban League

120 Wall Street
New York, NY 10005
Phone: 888-839-0467
Email: info@nul.org
Website: http://www.nul.org

1031 • American Chemical Society Minority Scholars Program

Purpose: To aid minority students with a strong interest in chemistry.
Eligibility: Applicants must be high school seniors planning to attend college, college students who are currently pursuing or planning to pursue full-time study in a chemically related field, community college graduates and transfer students who plan to attain a baccalaureate degree in chemistry, biochemistry, chemical engineering or a chemically related field, or community college freshmen majoring in a two-year chemical technology program.
How to Apply: Applications are available by request.
Deadline: February 15.
Amount: Varies.
Number of Awards: 200.

1032 • Campaign For African American Achievement Scholarship Program

Purpose: To recognize young people who exhibit potential for success at the highest levels and provide them with financial aid in their higher education.
Eligibility: Applicants must be African American high school seniors. Selection is based on academic and personal achievement, community service and leadership.

How to Apply: Applications are available online.
Deadline: January 15.
Amount: Varies.
Number of Awards: Varies.

1033 • Gillette/National Urban League Scholarship and Intern Program for Minority Students

Purpose: To recognize outstanding undergraduates majoring in engineering and business fields.
Eligibility: Applicants must be African American undergraduate juniors studying engineering, marketing, manufacturing operations, finance, business administration or human resource management or related fields. Applicants must be in the top 25 percent of their class and must show proof of work experience, extracurricular activities, leadership skills and volunteer work.
How to Apply: Applications are available by request.
Deadline: January 15.
Amount: $5,000.
Number of Awards: Varies.

Native American Journalists Association

555 Dakota Street
Al Neuharth Media Center
Vermillion, SD 57069
Phone: 605-677-5282
Fax: 866-694-4262
Email: info@naja.com
Website: http://www.naja.com

1034 • NAJA Scholarship Fund

Purpose: To assist Native American students pursuing journalism degrees.
Eligibility: Applicants must be current members of NAJA.
How to Apply: Applications are available online.
Deadline: May 15.
Amount: $1,000-$3,000.
Number of Awards: Varies.

Office of Navajo Nation Scholarship and Financial Assistance

Website: http://www.onnsfa.org

1035 • Chief Manuelito Scholarship Program

Purpose: The scholarship was created to help high-achieving Navajo students.
Eligibility: Students must be enrolled members of the Navajo nation, submit a Certificate of Indian Blood, attend a regionally-accredited school and complete a FAFSA form. Students must also complete a Navajo Government course (available online).
How to Apply: Applications are available online and must be submitted to your agency, which is listed online.
Deadline: Varies by term.
Amount: $5,000.
Number of Awards: Varies.

Order Sons of Italy in America (OSIA)

219 East Street NE
Washington, DC 20002
Phone: 202-547-5106
Fax: 202-546-8168

Email: scholarships@osia.org
Website: http://www.osia.org

1036 • National Leadership Grant

Purpose: To provide awards to college students of Italian descent.

Eligibility: Applicants must be enrolled in an undergraduate or graduate program at a four-year university and of Italian descent. Applicants must submit official transcripts, test scores, letters of recommendation and an essay. Awards are given based on academic merit.

How to Apply: Applications are available online.
Deadline: February 28.
Amount: Varies.
Number of Awards: Varies.

Organization of Chinese Americans (OCA)

1001 Connecticut Avenue NW
Suite 601
Washington, DC 20036
Phone: 202-223-5500
Fax: 202-296-0540
Email: oca@ocanatl.org
Website: http://www.ocanatl.org

1037 • Lead Summer Program

Purpose: To invite African American, Asian American, Hispanic American and Native American high school students to participate in summer institutes at graduate business schools and support them through college and beyond.

Eligibility: Applicants must be high school juniors, have a B or better academic average, a combined score of at least 100 on the PSAT, 1000 on the SAT, or 22 on the ACT and demonstrate leadership.

How to Apply: Applications are available online.
Deadline: Varies.
Amount: Varies.
Number of Awards: Varies.

1038 • OCA Avon College Scholarship

Purpose: To support Asian Pacific American women.

Eligibility: Applicants must be Asian Pacific American women entering their first year of college, demonstrate financial need and have a minimum 3.0 GPA.

How to Apply: Applications are available online.
Deadline: May 1.
Amount: $2,000.
Number of Awards: 15.

1039 • OCA-KFC National Essay Contest

Purpose: To support Asian Pacific American students.

Eligibility: Applicants must be Asian Pacific American students in the ninth through twelfth grade and submit an essay. Employees of the KFC Corporations and their family members may NOT apply. Selection is based on content, organization and development, grammar and mechanics and style.

How to Apply: Applications are available online or by written request.
Deadline: June 5.
Amount: $300-$1,000.
Number of Awards: 3.

1040 • OCA/UPS Gold Mountain Scholarship

Purpose: To support first generation Asian American students.

Eligibility: Applicants must be Asian Pacific Americans who intend to begin college in the fall of the year of application and must demonstrate significant financial need. Applicants must also be the first in their family to attend college and have a minimum 3.0 GPA.

How to Apply: Applications are available online or by written request.
Deadline: May 1.
Amount: $2,000.
Number of Awards: 12.

Parents without Partners

1650 S. Dixie Highway, Suite 510
Boca Raton, FL 33432
Phone: 561-391-8833
Fax: 561-395-8557
Website: http://www.parentswithoutpartners.org

1041 • Parents without Partners International Scholarship Program

Purpose: To aid children raised by single parents.

Eligibility: Applicants should be the dependent children of Parents without Partners members and be no more than 25 years old. Students must be seniors applying to a college or trade school or current undergraduates.

How to Apply: Applications are available with membership in the organization.
Deadline: March 15.
Amount: $250-$500.
Number of Awards: Up to 10.

PEO International Peace Scholarship Fund

3700 Grand Avenue
Des Moines, Iowa 50312
Phone: 515-255-3153
Fax: 515-255-3820
Website: http://www.peointernational.org

1042 • PEO International Peace Scholarship

Purpose: Women from countries other than the U.S. or Canada are assisted in their graduate studies within North America.

Eligibility: Applicants must be female, attend a North American graduate school or Cottey College and be from a country other than the U.S. or Canada.

How to Apply: Applicants must first submit an eligibility form, available online. If found eligible, students will be mailed application materials.
Deadline: January 31.
Amount: $6,000.
Number of Awards: Varies.

Polish National Alliance

Educational Department
6100 Cicero Avenue
Chicago, IL 60646
Phone: 800-621-3723
Email: pna@pna-znp.org
Website: http://www.pna-znp.org

1043 • Polish National Alliance Scholarship

Purpose: To assist members of the Polish National Alliance with their undergraduate studies.

Eligibility: Applicants must be college sophomores, juniors or seniors and have been paying members in good standing with the Polish National Association for at least three years. If the applicant has been in good standing with the PNA for at least two years, his or her parents must have been paying PNA members for at least five years.

How to Apply: Applications are available by email at mary. srodon@pna-znp.org.

Deadline: April 15.

Amount: Varies.

Number of Awards: Varies.

Presbyterian Church (USA)

100 Witherspoon Street
Louisville, KY 40202
Phone: 888-728-7228 x5776
Email: fcook@ctr.pcusa.org
Website: http://www.pcusa.org

1044 • Native American Education Grant

Purpose: To aid Alaska Natives and Native Americans pursuing full-time post-secondary education.

Eligibility: Applicants must be U.S. Citizens who are high school graduates or G.E.D. recipients and demonstrate financial need. Applicants must present proof of tribal membership, and preference will be given to members of the Presbyterian Church and students who have already completed at least one semester of work at an accredited post-secondary institution.

How to Apply: Applications are available online or by phone request.

Deadline: June 1.

Amount: $200-$2,500.

Number of Awards: Varies.

Public Relations Student Society of America

33 Maiden Lane
11th Floor
New York, NY 10038
Phone: 212-460-1474
Fax: 212-995-0757
Email: prssa@prsa.org
Website: http://www.prssa.org

1045 • Multicultural Affairs Scholarship Program

Purpose: To assist minority communications majors.

Eligibility: Applicants must be of African American, Hispanic, Asian, Native American, Alaskan Native or Pacific Islander ancestry, be at least college juniors studying communications in an undergraduate program and have a minimum 3.0 GPA. Applicants are required to submit a typed, double-spaced essay no more than three pages in length about workplace diversity or a similar topic.

How to Apply: Applications are available online.

Deadline: April 16.

Amount: $1,500.

Number of Awards: 2.

Sallie Mae Fund

12061 Bluemont Way
Reston, VA 20190
Website: http://www.thesalliemaefund.org

1046 • American Dream Scholarship

Purpose: To support African-American students based on academic merit and financial need.

Eligibility: Applicants must have financial need, meet Pell Grant eligibility criteria and intend to be enrolled full-time at two- or four-year schools.

How to Apply: Applications are available online.

Deadline: April 15.

Amount: $500-$5,000.

Number of Awards: Varies.

1047 • Community College Transfer Scholarships

Purpose: To help Hispanic students attending community college attend a four-year college.

Eligibility: Applicants must be Hispanic, apply for federal financial aid and be part-time or full-time community college students. Applicants must also intend to be full-time students at a four-year college.

How to Apply: Applications are available online.

Deadline: February 1.

Amount: $1,000-$2,500.

Number of Awards: Varies.

1048 • First in My Family Scholarship

Purpose: To award Hispanic students who are the first in their family to go to college based on academic merit and financial need.

Eligibility: Applicants must be Hispanic full-time undergraduate students studying in the U.S. or Puerto Rico and have financial need. Qualified applicants need to write an essay and send a recommendation letter, financial verification form, transcript and proof of citizenship.

How to Apply: Applications are available online.

Deadline: April 15.

Amount: $500-$5,000.

Number of Awards: Varies.

1049 • Writers of Passage Scholarship

Purpose: To support students attending black colleges or universities.

Eligibility: Applicants must be enrolled as full-time undergraduate students at a black institution of higher learning, have financial need and apply for federal student aid. Applicants must also send an essay about how they have overcome difficulties, an application, a transcript and a copy of the Student Aid Report. The colleges of the winners also receive $20,000 grants.

How to Apply: Applications are available online.

Deadline: March 3.

Amount: $5,000.

Number of Awards: Varies.

Slovenian Women's Union of America

Mary Turvey, SWUA Scholarship Director
52 Oakridge Drive
Marquette, MI 49855
Email: mturvey@aol.com
Website: http://www.swua.org

1050 • Continuing Education Award

Purpose: To promote Slovenian culture.

Eligibility: Applicants must be returning to an accredited college in the fall as full- or part-time students and must have been a member of the SWUA for at least three years or an active participant. Students must include a photograph, resume, FAFSA, income tax return and a letter of recommendation from their SWU branch president or secretary. The awards committee considers life goals and involvement in school, church and community.

How to Apply: Applications are available online and from SWUA branch secretaries.

Deadline: March 1.

Amount: $500.

Number of Awards: Varies.

1051 • Slovenian Women's Union of America Scholarship Program

Purpose: To promote Slovenian culture.

Eligibility: Students must be high school seniors or current college students at an accredited school. Applicants must have been members of the SWUA for at least three years. High school senior applications must include a photo, FAFSA, a letter of recommendation from high school principal or teacher, brief autobiography, including personal and educational goals, a high school transcript including SAT and ACT scores, a letter of recommendation from an SWUA branch officer and a financial statement from their parents. College student applications must include a photo, FAFSA, a brief autobiography including personal and educational goals, letters of recommendation from a college professor/instructor and an SWUA branch officer, and grade transcripts from the last two semesters. The committee considers life goals, scholastic achievement, financial need and involvement in school, church and community.

How to Apply: Applications are available online and from SWUA branch secretaries.

Deadline: March 1.

Amount: $1,000-$2,000.

Number of Awards: Varies.

Society of Mexican American Engineers and Scientists Inc. (MAES)

711 W. Bay Area Boulevard
Suite #206
Webster, TX 77598-4051
Phone: 281-557-3677
Fax: 281-557-3757
Email: execdir@maes-natl.org
Website: http://www.maes-natl.org

1052 • MAES Scholarship Program

Purpose: To assist Hispanic students in the fields of science and engineering.

Eligibility: Applicants must be current Hispanic MAES student members who are full-time undergraduate and graduate students in an accredited U.S. college or university majoring in science or engineering. Community college applicants must be enrolled in majors that are transferable to a four-year institution offering bachelor's degrees. There are various scholarships in the program. Some sponsors require students to be U.S. citizens or permanent residents. Awards are based on financial need, academic achievement, personal qualities, strengths and leadership abilities. Applicants should submit applications, financial information, recommendations and transcripts.

How to Apply: Applications are available online.

Deadline: October 6.

Amount: $3,000.

Number of Awards: 5.

Soroptimist International

1709 Spruce Street
Philadelphia, PA 19103
Phone: 215-893-9000
Fax: 215-893-5200
Email: siahq@soroptimist.org
Website: http://www.soroptimist.org

1053 • Women's Opportunity Awards Program

Purpose: To assist women entering or re-entering the workforce with educational and skills training support.

Eligibility: Applicants must be attending or been accepted by a vocational/skills training program or an undergraduate degree program. Applicants must be the women heads of household who provide the primary source of financial support for their families and demonstrate financial need. Applicants must submit their application to the appropriate regional office.

How to Apply: Applications are available online.

Deadline: December 1.

Amount: Varies.

Number of Awards: 31.

Spinsters Ink

P.O. Box 242
Midway, FL 32343
Phone: 800-301-6860
Email: info@spinstersink.com
Website: http://www.spinsters-ink.com

1054 • Spinsters Ink Young Feminist Scholarship

Purpose: To award female students who write an essay about feminism.

Eligibility: Applicants must be female high school seniors who write about the topic, "What Feminism Means to Me." Winning scholars are also invited to a week-long writers' retreat.

How to Apply: Application information is available online.

Deadline: December 31.

Amount: $1,000.

Number of Awards: 1.

St. Andrew's Society of Washington, DC

Charity and Education Committee
P.O. Box 372
Glen Echo, MD 20812
Email: secretary@saintandrewsociety.com
Website: http://www.saintandrewsociety.com

1055 • Donald Malcolm MacArthur Scholarship

Purpose: To encourage foster study between the U.S. and Scotland, monies are awarded to third and fourth year college students and full-time graduate students who are either Scots wishing to study in the U.S., or U.S. students intending to study in Scotland.

Eligibility: Eligible U.S. candidates must live or attend school within a 200 mile radius of Washington, D.C. and be of Scottish descent.

How to Apply: Applications are available online.
Deadline: April 30.
Amount: $2,500.
Number of Awards: Varies.

Swiss Benevolent Society of New York

Scholarship Committee
500 Fifth Avenue, Room 1800
New York, NY 10110
Website: http://www.swissbenevolentny.com

1056 • Medicus Student Exchange

Purpose: To provide need and merit-based scholarships for students from Swiss-American backgrounds.

Eligibility: Applicants or one of their parents must be a Swiss national. The Medicus grant for study in Switzerland is only open to U.S. residents and is a need-based award. Applicants must be college juniors or seniors or graduate-level students accepted to a Swiss university or the Federal Institute of Technology.

How to Apply: Applications are available online.
Deadline: January 31.
Amount: Varies.
Number of Awards: Varies.

Third Wave Foundation

25 E. 21st Street
Fourth Floor
New York, NY 10010
Phone: 212-228-8311
Fax: 212-780-9181
Email: info@thirdwavefoundation.org
Website: http://www.thirdwavefoundation.org

1057 • Third Wave Foundation Scholarship Program

Purpose: To provide resources to support the cutting-edge work of young women activists.

Eligibility: Applicants must be full-time or part-time students under the age of 30 who are enrolled in or have been accepted to a college, must show financial need and must be female or transgender. Applicants must be involved with activist work.

How to Apply: Applications are available online.
Deadline: April 1 and October 1.
Amount: $500-$5,000.
Number of Awards: Varies.

Thurgood Marshall Scholarship Fund

80 Maiden Lane
Suite 2204
New York, NY 10038
Phone: 212-573-8888
Fax: 212-573-8497
Email: studentinfo@tmsf.org
Website: http://www.thurgoodmarshallfund.org

1058 • Thurgood Marshall Scholarship Fund Scholarship

Purpose: To provide support to the nation's 45 historically Black public colleges and universities by offering merit-based scholarships.

Eligibility: Applicants must be currently enrolled or planning to enroll as full-time students at one of the 45 TMSF member schools, have a minimum 3.0 high school GPA and have a minimum SAT score of 1100 or ACT score of 25. Applicants must demonstrate a commitment to academic excellence and community service and show financial need. Winners need to maintain a 3.0 GPA for the duration of the scholarship. Applicants must submit a head shot photograph, letters of recommendation, essay, and resume.

How to Apply: Applications are available through the member schools.
Deadline: Varies.
Amount: Varies.
Number of Awards: Varies.

U.S. Pan Asian American Chamber of Commerce

1329 18th Street NW
Washington, DC 20036
Phone: 202-296-5221
Fax: 202-296-5225
Email: administrator@uspaacc.com
Website: http://www.uspaacc.com

1059 • Asian American Scholarship Fund

Purpose: To support the higher education goals of Asian American students.

Eligibility: Applicants must be U.S. citizens or permanent residents and Asian American high school seniors who will pursue post-secondary educations at an accredited institution in the U.S. Selection is based on academic achievement, leadership in extracurricular activities, community service and financial need. Minimum 3.3 GPA required.

How to Apply: Applications are available online.
Deadline: March 8.
Amount: $5,000.
Number of Awards: 1.

1060 • Bernadette Wong-Yu Scholarship

Purpose: To support the higher education goals of Asian American students.

Eligibility: Applicants must be U.S. citizens or permanent residents and be students of Asian or Pacific Heritage planning to enroll or currently enrolled in post-secondary education at an accredited institution in the U.S. or China. Selection is based on academic excellence, community service involvement and financial need. Minimum 3.3 GPA and Chinese Language or Chinese Studies major required. Applicants must be able to attend the Excellence Awards and Scholarships Dinner during the CelebrAsian Annual Conference (in May).

How to Apply: Applications are available online.
Deadline: February 28.
Amount: Up to $3,000.
Number of Awards: 1.

1061 • Bruce Lee Scholarship

Purpose: To support the higher education goals of Asian American students.

Eligibility: Applicants must be U.S. citizens or permanent residents and be high school seniors of Asian or Pacific Heritage who will pursue post-secondary educations at an accredited institution in the U.S. Selection is based on character, the ability to persevere over adversity, academic excellence with at least a 3.0 GPA, community service involvement and financial need. Applicants must be able to attend the Excellence Awards and Scholarships Dinner during the CelebrAsian Annual Conference (in May).

How to Apply: Applications are available online.

Deadline: February 28.

Amount: $5,000.

Number of Awards: 1.

1062 • Cary C. and Debra Y.C. Wu Scholarship

Purpose: To support the higher education goals of Asian American students.

Eligibility: Applicants must be U.S. citizens or permanent residents and be high school seniors of Asian or Pacific Heritage who will pursue post-secondary educations at an accredited institution in the U.S. Selection is based on academic excellence, leadership in extracurricular activities, community service involvement and financial need. Minimum 3.5 GPA required. Applicants must be able to attend the Excellence Awards and Scholarships Dinner during the CelebrAsian Annual Conference (in May).

How to Apply: Applications are available online.

Deadline: February 28.

Amount: Up to $5,000.

Number of Awards: 1.

1063 • Drs. Poh Shien and Judy Young Scholarship

Purpose: To support the higher education goals of Asian American students.

Eligibility: Applicants must be U.S. citizens or permanent residents and be high school seniors of Asian or Pacific Heritage who will pursue post-secondary educations at an accredited institution in the U.S. Selection is based on academic excellence, leadership in extracurricular activities, community service involvement and financial need. Minimum 3.5 GPA required. Applicants must be able to attend the Excellence Awards and Scholarships Dinner during the CelebrAsian Annual Conference (in May).

How to Apply: Applications are available online.

Deadline: February 28.

Amount: Up to $4,000.

Number of Awards: 1.

1064 • Jackie Chan Scholarship

Purpose: To support the higher education goals of Asian American students.

Eligibility: Applicants must be U.S. citizens or permanent residents and be high school seniors of Asian or Pacific Heritage who will pursue post-secondary educations at an accredited institution in the U.S. Selection is based on academic excellence, leadership in extracurricular activities, community service involvement and financial need. Minimum 3.3 GPA required. Applicants must be able to attend the Excellence Awards and Scholarships Dinner during the CelebrAsian Annual Conference (in May).

How to Apply: Applications are available online.

Deadline: February 28.

Amount: Up to $8,000.

Number of Awards: 2.

1065 • Ruth Mu-Lan Chu and James S.C. Chao Scholarship

Purpose: To support the higher education goals of Asian American students.

Eligibility: Applicants must be female U.S. citizens or permanent residents and be high school seniors of Asian or Pacific Heritage who will pursue post-secondary educations at an accredited institution in the U.S. Selection is based on academic excellence, community service involvement and financial need. Minimum 3.5

GPA required. Applicants must be able to attend the Excellence Awards and Scholarships Dinner during the CelebrAsian Annual Conference (in May).

How to Apply: Applications are available online.

Deadline: February 28.

Amount: Up to $5,000.

Number of Awards: 1.

1066 • Telamon Scholarship

Purpose: To support the higher education goals of Asian American students.

Eligibility: Applicants must be U.S. citizens or permanent residents and be high school seniors of Asian or Pacific Heritage who will pursue post-secondary educations at an accredited institution in the U.S. Selection is based on academic excellence, leadership in extracurricular activities, community service involvement and financial need. Minimum 3.5 GPA required. Applicants must be able to attend the Excellence Awards and Scholarships Dinner during the CelebrAsian Annual Conference (in May).

How to Apply: Applications are available online.

Deadline: February 28.

Amount: Up to $3,500.

Number of Awards: 1.

United Negro College Fund (UNCF)

8260 Willow Oaks Corporate Drive
P.O. Box 10444
Fairfax, VA 22031-8044
Phone: 800-331-2244
Website: http://www.uncf.org

1067 • Abercrombie and Fitch Scholarship Program

Purpose: To help African Americans who are enrolled in a UNCF member college or university or any other accredited four-year college or university.

Eligibility: Applicants must have a minimum 3.0 GPA, complete the Free Application for Federal Student Aid (FAFSA) and have unmet financial need that is verified by the college or university financial aid office. UNCF students are encouraged to complete the UNCF General Scholarship application to be matched with scholarships for which they meet the criteria. The scholarship is renewable as long as the recipient meets the eligibility requirements.

How to Apply: Applications are available online.

Deadline: October 13.

Amount: $3,000.

Number of Awards: 22.

1068 • Alliance Data Scholarship

Purpose: To assist African-American students who are enrolled at a UNCF institution.

Eligibility: Applicants must have a minimum 3.0 GPA, complete the Free Application for Federal Student Aid (FAFSA) and have unmet financial need that is verified by the college or university financial aid office. UNCF students are encouraged to complete the UNCF General Scholarship application to be matched with scholarships for which they meet the criteria.

How to Apply: Applications are available online.

Deadline: Varies.

Amount: $5,000.

Number of Awards: 1.

1069 • American Hotel Management Foundation Scholarship

Purpose: To promote the study of hotel management.

Eligibility: Applicants must be major in hotel management at United Negro College Fund (UNCF) member colleges and universities. Students must also have a minimum 2.5 GPA, complete the Free Application for Federal Student Aid (FAFSA) and have unmet financial need that is verified by the college or university financial aid office. UNCF students are encouraged to complete the UNCF General Scholarship application to be matched with scholarships for which they meet the criteria.

How to Apply: Applications are available online.

Deadline: Varies.

Amount: $1,500.

Number of Awards: 1.

1070 • Amtrak Travel Scholarship

Purpose: To assist African-American students with their college-related travel expenses.

Eligibility: Applicants must be enrolled at one of the following schools: Bennett College for Women, Bethune-Cookman College, Claflin University, Clark Atlanta University, Dillard University, Edward Waters College, Johnson C. Smith University, Lane College, LeMoyne-Owen College, Morehouse College, Philander Smith College, Shaw University, Spelman College, Tougaloo College, Virginia Union University, Wiley College, Xavier University, Howard University or Hampton University. Selected students will be given the opportunity to travel to any destination serviced by Amtrak.

How to Apply: Applications are available online.

Deadline: October 30.

Amount: $750.

Number of Awards: 185.

1071 • Berbeco Senior Research Fellowship

Purpose: To encourage African Americans to conduct independent research internationally.

Eligibility: Applicants must be college juniors who attend United Negro College Fund (UNCF) member colleges or universities. The need-based award is for students to work on their senior thesis or research projects outside the U.S. during the summer between their junior and senior years.

How to Apply: Applications are available online.

Deadline: December 12.

Amount: Varies.

Number of Awards: Varies.

1072 • Best Buy Scholarship Program

Purpose: To help African Americans majoring in business- and computer science-related fields.

Eligibility: There are two programs, one for employees and one for non-employees. Employee awards are $2,500 while non-employee awards are $5,000. To qualify for the employee program, applicants must have worked for six consecutive months at Best Buy. For both programs, applicants must be undergraduates at United Negro College Fund (UNCF) member colleges or universities or Florida A&M University and must demonstrate financial need. Students must major in business, finance, accounting, marketing, communications, computer science or advertising. A transcript, resume, two recommendation letters and essay are required.

How to Apply: Applications are available online.

Deadline: November 5.

Amount: $5,000.

Number of Awards: Varies.

1073 • Burton G. Bettingen Foundation Scholarship

Purpose: To support higher education among African-American students.

Eligibility: Applicants must attend United Negro College Fund (UNCF) member colleges and universities, have a minimum 2.5 GPA, complete the Free Application for Federal Student Aid (FAFSA) and have unmet financial need that is verified by the college or university financial aid office. UNCF students are encouraged to complete the UNCF General Scholarship application to be matched with scholarships for which they meet the criteria.

How to Apply: Applications are available online.

Deadline: Varies.

Amount: Varies.

Number of Awards: Varies.

1074 • C-SPAN Scholarship Program

Purpose: To assist African-American students in communications- and social science-related fields.

Eligibility: Applicants must be sophomores or juniors at United Negro College Fund (UNCF) member colleges and universities and must major in radio/television/film, communications, journalism, political science, English or history. This program also offers a paid summer internship.

How to Apply: Applications are available online.

Deadline: March 28.

Amount: $2,000.

Number of Awards: 1.

1075 • Cardinal Health Scholarship

Purpose: To reward African Americans who are leaders outside of college.

Eligibility: Applicants must be rising sophomores or juniors at any four-year accredited undergraduate college majoring in accounting/finance, computer science, business, information systems/technology, marketing purchasing/operations, operations management, engineering or chemistry or in their first or second year of majoring in pharmacy. Applicants must have a minimum 3.0 GPA and show leadership experience outside of college.

How to Apply: Applications are available online.

Deadline: October 30.

Amount: $5,000.

Number of Awards: Varies.

1076 • CDM Scholarship/Internship

Purpose: To support African Americans studying engineering, science or construction disciplines.

Eligibility: Applicants must be undergraduates majoring in engineering, science or construction fields, such as chemical, civil, electrical, environmental, geotechnical, geology/hydrogeology, geography, GIS, mechanical, mining and structural or must be planning to pursue a master's degree in one of these disciplines at United Negro College Fund (UNCF) member colleges and universities. A minimum 3.0 GPA is required. There is also an internship as a part of the program.

How to Apply: Applications are available online.

Deadline: April 6.

Amount: $6,000.

Number of Awards: 6.

1077 • Chrysler Corporation Scholarship

Purpose: To help African Americans attending United Negro College Fund (UNCF) member colleges and universities.

Eligibility: Applicants must have a minimum 2.5 GPA, complete the Free Application for Federal Student Aid (FAFSA) and have unmet financial need that is verified by the college or university financial aid office. UNCF students are encouraged to complete the UNCF General Scholarship application to be matched with scholarships for which they meet the criteria.

How to Apply: Applications are available online.
Deadline: Varies.
Amount: $3,900.
Number of Awards: 10.

1078 • Citigroup Fellows Program

Purpose: To assist sophomores at United Negro College Fund (UNCF) member colleges and universities who plan to pursue business careers.

Eligibility: Applicants must major in business, finance, economics, accounting, information systems, computer science/MIS, computer science, banking, business-related, information technology, business (sales interest), computer engineering, management or management information systems. The program also provides access to Citigroup professionals as mentors and professional development conferences.

How to Apply: Applications are available online.
Deadline: April 1.
Amount: $6,400.
Number of Awards: Varies.

1079 • Colgate-Palmolive Company/UNCF Scholarship

Purpose: To help African-American sophomores, juniors and seniors majoring in business with a concentration in marketing.

Eligibility: Applicants must have a minimum 3.0 GPA and attend United Negro College Fund (UNCF) member colleges and universities. Students must complete the Free Application for Federal Student Aid (FAFSA) and have unmet financial need that is verified by the college or university financial aid office. UNCF students are encouraged to complete the UNCF General Scholarship application to be matched with scholarships for which they meet the criteria.

How to Apply: Applications are available online.
Deadline: Varies.
Amount: Varies, based on need.
Number of Awards: Varies.

1080 • Doris and John Carpenter Scholarship

Purpose: To help African Americans with the most financial need.

Eligibility: Applicants must be freshmen at United Negro College Fund (UNCF) member colleges or universities and must have a minimum 2.5 GPA.

How to Apply: Applications are available online.
Deadline: Varies.
Amount: $2,000-$5,000.
Number of Awards: Varies.

1081 • Earl and Patricia Armstrong Scholarship

Purpose: To promote the health sciences among African-American students.

Eligibility: Applicants must major in pre-medicine, biology or health, have a minimum 2.5 GPA, complete the Free Application for Federal Student Aid (FAFSA) and have unmet financial need that is verified by the college or university financial aid office. UNCF students are encouraged to complete the UNCF General Scholarship application to be matched with scholarships for which they meet the criteria.

How to Apply: Applications are available online.
Deadline: Varies.
Amount: Up to $3,000.
Number of Awards: 1.

1082 • Mike and Stephanie Bozic Scholarship

Purpose: To assist African-American students with financial need.

Eligibility: Applicants must attend United Negro College Fund (UNCF) member colleges and universities, have a minimum 2.5 GPA, complete the Free Application for Federal Student Aid (FAFSA) and have unmet financial need that is verified by the college or university financial aid office. UNCF students are encouraged to complete the UNCF General Scholarship application to be matched with scholarships for which they meet the criteria.

How to Apply: Applications are available online.
Deadline: Varies.
Amount: Varies.
Number of Awards: Varies.

1083 • Raymond W. Cannon Memorial Scholarship

Purpose: To help African-American student leaders.

Eligibility: Applicants must be juniors majoring in pharmacy or pre-law at United Negro College Fund (UNCF) member colleges or universities or Historically Black Colleges or Universities (HBCU Schools) and who have shown leadership in high school and college.

How to Apply: Applications are available online.
Deadline: Varies.
Amount: $2,000-$5,000.
Number of Awards: Varies.

1084 • Robert Dole Scholarship for Disabled Students

Purpose: To help physically and/or mentally challenged African Americans at United Negro College Fund (UNCF) member colleges or universities.

Eligibility: Applicants must have a minimum 2.5 GPA, complete the Free Application for Federal Student Aid (FAFSA) and have unmet financial need that is verified by the college or university financial aid office. UNCF students are encouraged to complete the UNCF General Scholarship application to be matched with scholarships for which they meet the criteria.

How to Apply: Applications are available online.
Deadline: November 30.
Amount: $3,000.
Number of Awards: Varies.

1085 • United Negro College Fund Scholarships

Purpose: To enhance the quality of education by providing financial assistance to deserving students.

Eligibility: The UNCF general scholarship eligibility criteria are: Students must have a minimum 2.5 GPA and must have unmet financial need as verified by the Financial Aid Director. Students must also complete a Financial Aid Form (FAF) or a Family Financial Aid Statement (FFS) and request that the Student Aid Report (SAR) be sent to the financial aid office at their college or university.

How to Apply: Applications are available online.
Deadline: Varies.
Amount: Varies.
Number of Awards: Varies.

Related Scholarships:

Idaho State Board of Education
See #1314 · Minority and At-Risk Scholarship

Kansas Board of Regents
See #1360 · Kansas Ethnic Minority Scholarship

National Society of Professional Engineers
See #416 · Virginia D. Henry Memorial Scholarship

National Black Nurses Association
See #668 · Annual NBNA Scholarships

Medical Library Association
See #590 · MLA Scholarship for Minority Students

Women's Sports Foundation
See #174 · Linda Riddle/SGMA Scholarship

Delaware Higher Education Commission
See #1260 · Agenda for Delaware Women Trailblazer Scholarship

Educational Foundation for Women in Accounting
See #76 · Women in Transition Scholarship

Ethel Louise Armstrong Foundation
See #295 · Ethel Louise Armstrong Foundation Scholarship

Association for Women in Mathematics
See #603 · Alice T. Schafer Prize

Sons of Norway
See #477 · King Olav V Norwegian-American Heritage Fund

Clan MacBean Foundation
See #468 · Clan MacBean Foundation Grant Program

National Italian American Foundation
See #497 · National Italian American Foundation Scholarship

Association for Women in Mathematics
See #604 · AWM Biographies Contest

Minnesota Higher Education Services Office
See #1434 · Minnesota Indian Scholarship Program

American Bar Association
See #557 · Legal Opportunity Scholarship Fund

American Association for Respiratory Care
See #609 · Jimmy A. Young Memorial Education Recognition Award

Appraisal Institute
See #1086 · Minorities and Women Educational Scholarship

American Meteorological Society
See #1114 · AMS/Industry Minority Scholarships

American Physical Society
See #1122 · APS Minority Scholarship

Institute of Real Estate Management
See #1088 · George M. Brooker Collegiate Scholarship for Minorities

League of United Latin American Citizens
See #409 · GM Fund

Fisher Communications Inc.
See #531 · Fisher Broadcasting Scholarships for Minorities

National Society of Professional Engineers
See #412 · Auxiliary Scholarships

Medical Library Association
See #591 · MLA/NLM Spectrum Scholarship

National Association of Minority Engineering Program Administrators
See #410 · NAMEPA Scholarship Program

Oncology Nursing Society
See #685 · Bachelor's Scholarships

Henry Sachs Foundation
See #1255 · Henry Sachs Foundation Scholarship

Kosciuszko Foundation
See #473 · Tuition Scholarship Program

National Association of Women in Construction Founders' Scholarship Foundation
See #263 · Undergraduate Scholarship and Construction Crafts Scholarship

Special Libraries Association
See #592 · Affirmative Action Scholarship

Women In Defense

See #565 · *HORIZONS Foundation Scholarship*

Association for Women in Science

See #1127 · *Association for Women in Science Predoctoral Awards*

Educational Foundation for Women in Accounting

See #74 · *Laurel Fund*

Educational Foundation for Women in Accounting

See #75 · *Women in Need Scholarship*

Soroptimist International

See #928 · *Violet Richardson Award*

Association for Women in Science

See #181 · *Association for Women in Science College Scholarship*

Executive Women International (EWI)

See #204 · *Adult Students in Scholastic Transition (ASIST)*

American Dental Association Foundation

See #272 · *Minority Dental Student Scholarship*

Sons of Norway

See #476 · *General Heritage and Culture Grants*

Sons of Norway

See #478 · *Scholarships to Oslo International Summer School*

Radio and Television News Directors Association

See #550 · *Ken Kashiwahara Scholarship*

Ladies Auxiliary VFW

See #573 · *National Junior Girls Scholarships*

National Society Daughters of the American Revolution

See #677 · *Alice W. Rooke Scholarship And Irene And Daisy MacGregor Memorial Scholarship*

Girls Inc.

See #781 · *National Scholars and Awards Program*

Association for Women in Architecture

See #1220 · *AWA Scholarships*

Dow Jones Newspaper Fund

See #530 · *DJNF Summer Internships*

California Chicano News Media Association

See #1223 · *Frank del Olmo Memorial Scholarship*

Iota Sigma Pi (ISP)

See #222 · *Members-at-Large Reentry Award*

National Association of Blacks in Criminal Justice

See #727 · *William L. Hastie Award*

National Association of Blacks in Criminal Justice

See #725 · *Mary Church Terrell Award*

National Association of Blacks in Criminal Justice

See #726 · *Medger Evers Award*

National Medical Fellowships Inc. California Community Service Scholarship

See #1248 · *California Community Service Scholarship Program*

National Society of Hispanic MBAs

See #215 · *National Society of Hispanic MBAs Scholarship*

California Chicano News Media Association

See #1224 · *Joel Garcia Memorial Scholarship*

American Speech-Language-Hearing Foundation

See #642 · *Minority Student Scholarship*

Iota Sigma Pi (ISP) ND

See #223 · *Gladys Anderson Emerson Scholarship*

National Association of Blacks in Criminal Justice

See #724 · *Jonathan Jasper Wright Award*

Real Estate

Also See Scholarships Listed Under:
Business/Management

Appraisal Institute

550 W. Van Buren Street
Suite 1000
Chicago, IL 60607
Phone: 312-335-4100
Fax: 312-335-4400
Email: wwoodburn@appraisalinstitute.org
Website: http://www.appraisalinstitute.org

1086 • Minorities and Women Educational Scholarship

Purpose: To assist minority and women college students in pursuing degrees in real estate appraisal or related fields.

Eligibility: Applicants must be women or American Indians, Alaska Natives, Asians, African Americans, Hispanics or Latinos, Native Hawaiians or other Pacific Islanders. Applicants must be full- or part-time students enrolled in real estate courses and working toward degrees, have a minimum 2.5 GPA and demonstrate financial need.

How to Apply: Applications are available online.
Deadline: April 15.
Amount: $1,000.
Number of Awards: Varies.

Hopi Tribe Grants and Scholarship Program

P.O. Box 123
Kykotsmovi, AZ 86039
Phone: 800-762-9630
Fax: 928-734-9575
Email: info@hopi.nsn.us
Website: http://www.hopi.nsn.us

1087 • Tribal Priority Scholarship

Purpose: To encourage Hopi college students to obtain bachelor's and graduate degrees in subject areas of priority interest to the Hopi Tribe.

Eligibility: Applicants must be Hopi college juniors, seniors and graduate students who would like to obtain bachelor's or graduate degrees in specific subject areas. Contact the scholarship program for more information.

How to Apply: Applications are available by mail.
Deadline: Varies.
Amount: Varies.
Number of Awards: Varies.

Institute of Real Estate Management

IREM Foundation Administrator
430 N. Michigan Avenue
Chicago, IL 60611
Phone: 800-837-0706
Fax: 800-338-4736
Website: http://www.irem.org

1088 • George M. Brooker Collegiate Scholarship for Minorities

Purpose: To increase minority participation in the real estate industry.

Eligibility: Applicants must be minorities, be U.S. citizens, declare a major in real estate or a related field, have a minimum 3.0 GPA in the major and have completed two courses in real estate or plan to finish them. Applicants must submit a 500-word essay explaining their reason for pursuing a real estate career. Applicants must also submit three general letters of recommendation and a letter of recommendation from a local IREM chapter officer.

How to Apply: Applications are available online.
Deadline: March 31.
Amount: $1,000-$2,500.
Number of Awards: 3.

Religion and Churches

Also See Scholarships Listed Under:
Academics/General

Al-Ameen

14252 Culver Boulevard
Suite A714
Irvine, CA 92604
Email: alameenscholarship@yahoo.com
Website: http://www.alameen.edu/corporate/so_rel.htm

1089 • Al-Ameen Scholarship

Purpose: To insure that Muslim students do not need to discontinue their studies due to finances.
Eligibility: Applicants must be pursuing or plan to pursue higher education and submit applications including forms from their mosques. Students and their parents will be interviewed, and the awards are for tuition, books and uniforms.
How to Apply: Contact local mosques.
Deadline: July 1.
Amount: $3,000.
Number of Awards: 2.

American Atheists

P.O. Box 5733
Parsippany, NJ 07054
Phone: 908-276-7300
Fax: 908-276-7402
Website: http://www.atheists.org

1090 • Life Members' Scholarship

Purpose: To support Atheist students who are activists.
Eligibility: Applicants must be high school seniors or college students who are Atheists, have a minimum 2.5 GPA and be student activists. The award is based on the level of activism and requires a 500- to 1,000-word essay. In addition to the scholarship, the winner will receive a free trip to the American Atheists National Convention.
How to Apply: Applications are available online.
Deadline: January 31.
Amount: $2,000.
Number of Awards: 1.

American Baptist Churches USA

P.O. Box 851
Valley Forge, PA 19482
Phone: 800-222-3872
Fax: 610-768-2453
Email: karen.drummond@abc-usa.org
Website: http://www.nationalministries.org

1091 • Undergraduate Scholarships

Purpose: To support American Baptist students pursuing educational opportunities.
Eligibility: Applicants must be members of an American Baptist church for at least one year before applying for aid, be enrolled at an accredited educational institution in the U.S. or Puerto Rico, be U.S. citizens and retain a 2.75 GPA to remain eligible for the scholarships.
How to Apply: Applications are available by request.
Deadline: May 31.
Amount: $1,000-$2,000.
Number of Awards: Varies.

Catholic Aid Association

Scholarship Program
3499 Lexington Avenue N.
St. Paul, MN 55126
Phone: 800-568-6670
Email: caa@catholicaid.org
Website: http://www.catholicaid.com

1092 • Catholic Aid Association College Tuition Scholarship

Purpose: To award scholarships to members of the Catholic Aid Association.
Eligibility: Applicants must be members of the Catholic Aid Association for at least two years prior to the date of application, have completed high school and be entering their first or second year in any accredited college, university, state college or technical college other than a private, non-Catholic college/university.
How to Apply: Applications are available online.
Deadline: February 16.
Amount: $300-$500.
Number of Awards: Varies.

Catholic Workman Fraternal Benefit Society

Attn.: Scholarships
P.O. Box 47
New Prague, MN 56071
Phone: 800-346-6231
Email: info@catholicworkman.org
Website: http://www.catholicworkman.org

1093 • Catholic Workman Scholarship

Purpose: To assist insured members of Catholic Workman.
Eligibility: Applicants must be insured members of Catholic Workman for at least 12 months prior to application. Applicants may apply during their senior year in high school, or any year thereafter. Applicants must have a minimum GPA of 2.5.
How to Apply: Applications are available online.
Deadline: July 1.
Amount: $500-$1,000.
Number of Awards: 20.

Fadel Educational Foundation

P.O. Box 212135
Augusta, GA 30917-2135
Phone: 866-705-9495
Fax: 866-705-9495
Email: afadel@bww.com
Website: http://www.fadelfoundation.org

1094 • Fadel Educational Foundation Annual Award Program

Purpose: To support Muslim U.S. citizens and permanent residents.

Eligibility: Applicants must be non-incarcerated students pursuing higher education. Selection is based on need and merit. Applicants should provide application forms, two teacher recommendation forms, one masjid official recommendation letter and financial need reports.

How to Apply: Applications are available online.

Deadline: April 20.

Amount: $2,000.

Number of Awards: Varies.

Faith and Education Scholarship Fund

P.O. Box 25555
San Mateo, CA 94402
Phone: 650-341-8702
Email: chris@faithandeducation.org
Website: http://www.faithandeducation.org

1095 • Faith and Education Scholarship Fund

Purpose: To support students who are active members of churches of Christ.

Eligibility: Applicants must be active members of churches of Christ and be enrolled full-time at four-year liberal arts colleges or universities. Students must submit the application form, transcripts, copy of SAT or ACT scores from high school applicants and a recommendation letter from a leader of their congregation.

How to Apply: Applications are available online.

Deadline: April 28.

Amount: $5,000.

Number of Awards: Varies.

Fellowship of United Methodists in Music and Worship Arts

Robert A. Schilling
4702 Graceland Avenue
Indianapolis , IN 46208-3504
Phone: 800-952-8977
Fax: 615-749-6874
Email: info@fummwa.org
Website: http://www.fummwa.org

1096 • Fellowship of United Methodists in Music and Worship Arts Scholarship

Purpose: To support students who want to pursue church music and/or worship arts as a career.

Eligibility: Applicants must be full-time music students pursuing a career in sacred music who are either entering freshmen or already enrolled in an accredited college, university or school of theology or pursuing an academic education in worship; be members of the United Methodist Church or be employed in the United Methodist Church for at least a year before applying and show Christian character and participation in Christian activities. Students must also demonstrate musical or other artistic talent and leadership potential. Applicants must submit applications, transcripts, personal statements and three reference letters.

How to Apply: Applications are available online.

Deadline: March 1.

Amount: Varies.

Number of Awards: Varies.

Fund for Theological Education Inc.

825 Houston Mill Road, Suite 250
Atlanta, GA 30329
Phone: 404-727-1450
Fax: 404-727-1490
Email: fte@thefund.org
Website: http://www.thefund.org

1097 • Undergraduate Fellows Program

Purpose: To support students who are considering ministry as a possible career.

Eligibility: Applicants must be juniors or seniors in an accredited undergraduate program at a North American college or university who are considering ministry as a career, have a minimum 3.0 GPA and be citizens of the U.S. or Canada. Applicants are evaluated on the basis of ability and character.

Deadline: March 1.

Amount: $2,000.

Number of Awards: Up to 70.

General Commission on Archives and History, The United Methodist Church

P.O. Box 127
36 Madison Avenue
Madison, NJ 07940
Phone: 973-408-3189
Fax: 973-408-3909
Email: research@gcah.org
Website: http://www.gcah.org

1098 • Racial/Ethnic History Research Grant

Purpose: To promote excellence in research and writing in the history of Asians, Blacks, Hispanics and Native Americans in The United Methodist Church.

Eligibility: Applicants must submit an application in English which includes biographical information, a detailed description of the project, the expected date of completion, a budget and letters of recommendation.

How to Apply: Submit materials to the General Secretary at the address listed.

Deadline: December 31.

Amount: $750-$1,500.

Number of Awards: 1-2.

1099 • Women in United Methodist History Research Grant

Purpose: To provide seed money for research projects relating specifically to the history of women in the United Methodist Church.

Eligibility: Applicants must submit an application that includes a resume, a description of the project, a timetable for the project, a budget and letters of recommendation.

How to Apply: Submit materials to the General Secretary at the address listed.

Deadline: December 31.

Amount: $500-$1,000.

Number of Awards: 1-2.

1100 • Women in United Methodist History Writing Award

Purpose: To reward research and writing on the history of women in The United Methodist Church.

Eligibility: Applicants must submit completed, original manuscripts no longer than 20 double-spaced, typewritten pages with footnotes and bibliography about the history of women in the United Methodist Church or its antecedents.

How to Apply: Send manuscript to the General Secretary at the address listed.

Deadline: May 1.

Amount: $250.

Number of Awards: 1.

Kaplun Foundation

Essay Contest Committee
P.O. Box 234428
Great Neck, NY 11023
Website: http://www.kaplunfoundation.org/

1101 • Moris J. and Betty Kaplun Scholarship

Purpose: To award essays about Jewish-related topics.

Eligibility: Applicants must be in grades 7 through 12. Grades 7 through 9 are level one, and grades 10 through 12 are level two. Applicants must submit essays on Jewish-related topics listed on the website, and essays must be typed, double-spaced and a minimum of 250 words. Level one essays may not be more than 1,000 words. Level two essays may not be more than 1,500 words. A recent level one topic has been, "What person of importance to the Jewish people, past or present, would you like to meet and why?" A recent level two topic has been, "Anti-semitism plagues all Jews regardless of religious adherence. How do you see yourself reacting to it?"

How to Apply: Essays must be submitted by mail.

Deadline: March 15.

Amount: $1,800.

Number of Awards: 12.

Knights of Columbus

Department of Scholarships
P.O. Box 1670
New Haven, CT 06507
Phone: 203-752-4000
Email: info@kofc.org
Website: http://www.kofc.org

1102 • Vocations Scholarship Funds

Purpose: To support theology students on their path to the priesthood.

Eligibility: Applicants must be males studying with ecclesiastical approval at a major seminary for a diocese or religious institute in the United States, its territories and Canada. The Father Michael J. McGivney Vocations Scholarship Fund awards scholarships based on financial need, and applicants must provide proof of need. The Bishop Thomas V. Daily Scholarships Fund awards recipients on the basis of merit, and applicants must submit their most recent transcript and two letters of recommendation. Both funds give preference to Knights of Columbus members and their sons, but membership is not required.

How to Apply: Applications are available from seminary rectors and diocesan vocations directors starting in February.

Deadline: June 1.

Amount: $2,500.

Number of Awards: Varies.

Presbyterian Church (USA)

100 Witherspoon Street
Louisville, KY 40202
Phone: 888-728-7228 x5776
Email: fcook@ctr.pcusa.org
Website: http://www.pcusa.org

1103 • Continuing Education Grant/Loan Program

Purpose: To aid Presbyterian Church (U.S.A.) members pursuing post graduate educations.

Eligibility: Applicants must be PCUSA church members enrolled in a Ph.D. or equivalent postgraduate program in religious studies. Or, an applicant must be a Presbyterian Church minister or lay professional serving a congregation of at most 150 people for a minimum period of 3 years, who either intends to obtain certification or to work at a accredited institution or PC-sponsored national event.

How to Apply: Applications are available online.

Deadline: First come, first serve.

Amount: $100-$1,000.

Number of Awards: Varies.

1104 • Grant Programs for Medical Studies

Purpose: To aid Presbyterian Church (U.S.A.) members pursuing a post graduate education in a medical profession.

Eligibility: Applicants must be PCUSA church members who demonstrate financial need and are in good academic standing at an accredited institution at which they are enrolled full-time. A recommendation by a church pastor and an academic advisor from their institution is required.

How to Apply: Applications are available online.

Deadline: May 15.

Amount: $100-$1,000.

Number of Awards: Varies.

1105 • National Presbyterian College Scholarship

Purpose: To recognize young students preparing to enter as full-time incoming freshmen in one of the participating colleges related to the Presbyterian Church.

Eligibility: Applicants must be members of the Presbyterian Church, U.S. citizens or permanent residents and high school seniors planning to attend a participating college related to PCUSA. Applicants must also demonstrate financial need and take the SAT or ACT exam no later than December 15 of their senior year in high school. Applicants must have recommendations from both their church pastors and high school guidance counselors.

How to Apply: Applications are available online.

Deadline: January 31.

Amount: Varies.

Number of Awards: Varies.

Unitarian Universalist Association

25 Beacon Street
Boston, MA 02108
Phone: 617-742-2100
Email: info@uua.org
Website: http://www.uua.org

1106 • Stanfield and D'Orlando Art Scholarship

Purpose: To help graduate and undergraduate Unitarian Universalist artists.

Eligibility: Applicants must be preparing for a career in fine arts which includes painting, drawing, photography and sculpture. Applicants must submit applications, transcripts, recommendations, slide portfolios and a list of works.

How to Apply: Applications are available online.

Deadline: February 15.

Amount: Varies.

Number of Awards: Varies.

United Methodist Church

Office of Loans and Scholarships
P.O. Box 340007
Nashville, TN 37203
Phone: 615-340-7344
Fax: 615-340-7367
Email: scholarships@umcom.org
Website: http://www.umc.org

1107 • Foundation Scholars Program

Purpose: To support students attending a United Methodist-related school.

Eligibility: Applications and nominations will be accepted for candidates who have been active members of the UMC for at least one year and who will be enrolled in full-time study at a two- or four-year United Methodist-related school, college or university. A scholarship will be given to an applicant of each grade level at each school.

How to Apply: Applications may be obtained from your UM-related institution.

Deadline: September 1.

Amount: $1,000.

Number of Awards: 420.

1108 • Leonard M. Perryman Communications Scholarship for Ethnic Minority Students

Purpose: To assist undergraduate Christian students who intend on pursuing a career in religion journalism.

Eligibility: Applicants must be undergraduate students entering their junior or senior year of college, be Christian students who are pursuing a career in religion journalism and must major in religion journalism or communications. One scholarship will be given to the best Methodist applicant and one will be given to best overall. Applicants must submit letters of recommendation, a personal statement, photograph, and three samples of journalism work.

How to Apply: Applications are available online and by request.

Deadline: March 15.

Amount: $2,500.

Number of Awards: 2.

1109 • United Methodist Scholarship Programs

Purpose: To support students who are members of a United Methodist Church.

Eligibility: Applicants must be active, full members of a United Methodist Church for at least one year prior to applying, be admitted to a full-time degree program in an accredited college or university and have a minimum 2.5 GPA. Awards are available for older students, minority students and leadership.

How to Apply: Applications are available online.

Deadline: Varies.

Amount: Varies.

Number of Awards: Varies.

Related Scholarships:

California Masonic Foundation

See #1234 • California Masonic Foundation Scholarship

Unitarian Universalist Association

See #564 • Otto M. Stanfield Legal Scholarship

American Sephardi Federation

See #464 • Broome and Allen Boys Camp and Scholarship Fund

Sciences/Physical Sciences

Also See Scholarships Listed Under:
Engineering
Chemistry
Computer and Information Science
Mathematics

Academia Resource Management

535 E 4500 S, Suite D120
Salt Lake City, UT 84107-2988
Phone: 801-273-8911
Fax: 801-277-5632
Email: info@armanagement.org
Website: http://www.armanagement.org

1110 • ARM Undergraduate Student Fellowships

Purpose: To support scientific and technological study in non-academic settings under the guidance of mentors at sponsoring facilities.
Eligibility: Applicants must plan to be science or technology interns or fellows at national laboratories and sponsoring institutions and be undergraduates in any accredited institution within six months of the start of their award. The award is based on academic performance, career goals, recommendations and compatibility with the host facility. Applications, a recommendation letter, and transcripts are required. Applicants do not need to be enrolled in an ARM member institution to apply.
How to Apply: Applications are available online.
Deadline: February 15.
Amount: Varies.
Number of Awards: Varies.

American Council of Independent Laboratories

1629 K Street NW, Suite 400
Washington, DC 20006-1633
Phone: 202-887-5872
Fax: 202-887-0021
Email: jallen@acil.org
Website: http://www.acil.org

1111 • ACIL Scholarship

Purpose: To encourage students to enter the laboratory testing community.
Eligibility: Applicants must be college juniors or higher attending a four-year university or graduate school program and must major in physics, chemistry, engineering, geology, biology or environmental science. In addition to the applications, applicants should submit resumes, two recommendation letters, transcripts and any information about other scholarships received.
How to Apply: Applications are available online.
Deadline: April 4.
Amount: $1,000-$4,000.
Number of Awards: Varies.

American Meteorological Society

45 Beacon Street
Boston, MA 02108
Phone: 617-227-2426
Fax: 617-742-8718
Email: scholar@ametsoc.org
Website: http://www.ametsoc.org/AMS/

1112 • AMS Graduate Fellowship in the History of Science

Purpose: To support students writing dissertations on the history of atmospheric or related oceanic or hydrologic sciences.
Eligibility: Applicants must be graduate students who plan to write dissertations on the history of atmospheric or related oceanic or hydrologic sciences. Students must submit a cover letter with curriculum vitae, official transcripts, a typed description of the dissertation topic and three letters of recommendation.
How to Apply: Submit materials to address listed.
Deadline: February 10.
Amount: $15,000.
Number of Awards: Varies.

1113 • AMS Undergraduate Scholarships

Purpose: To encourage undergradute students to pursue careers in the atmospheric and related oceanic and hydrologic sciences.
Eligibility: Applicants must be full-time students majoring in the atmospheric or related oceanic or hydrologic science and entering their final undergraduate year, show intent to make the atmospheric or related sciences their career and have a minimum 3.25 GPA. For the Schroeder scholarship, applicants must demonstrate financial need. For the Murphy scholarship, applicants must demonstrate interest in weather forecasting through curricular or extracurricular activities and for the Crow scholarship, applicants must demonstrate interest in applied meteorology. The Glahn scholarship will be awarded to a student with a strong interest in statistical meteorology.
How to Apply: Applications are available online.
Deadline: February 10.
Amount: Varies.
Number of Awards: Varies.

1114 • AMS/Industry Minority Scholarships

Purpose: To support minority students who have been traditionally underrepresented in the sciences, especially Hispanic, Native American and Black students.
Eligibility: Applicants must be minority students who will be entering their freshman year of college in the following fall and must plan to pursue careers in the atmospheric or related oceanic and hydrologic sciences.
How to Apply: Applications are available online.
Deadline: February 10.
Amount: $3,000.
Number of Awards: Varies.

1115 • AMS/Industry/Government Graduate Fellowships

Purpose: To attract students to prepare for careers in the meteorological, oceanic and hydrologic fields.
Eligibility: Applicants must be entering their first year of graduate study the following year and plan to pursue advanced degrees in the atmospheric and related oceanic and hydrologic sciences. Awards are based on undergraduate performance.
How to Apply: Applications are available online or by mail.
Deadline: February 15.

Amount: $22,000.
Number of Awards: Varies.

1116 • Father James B. Macelwane Annual Awards in Meteorology

Purpose: To encourage interest in meteorology among college students.

Eligibility: Applicants must be enrolled as undergraduates and submit an original student paper on an aspect of atmospheric science. No more than two students from any one institution may enter papers in any one contest, and there is no application form needed.

How to Apply: Submit materials to address listed.
Deadline: July 7.
Amount: $300.
Number of Awards: 1.

1117 • Freshman Undergraduate Scholarship

Purpose: To encourage high school students to pursue careers in the atmospheric and related oceanic and hydrologic sciences.

Eligibility: Applicants must enter as full-time freshmen or sophomores the following fall and major in the atmospheric or related oceanic and hydrologic sciences.

How to Apply: Applications are available online.
Deadline: February 10.
Amount: $2,000-$3,000.
Number of Awards: Varies.

American Museum of Natural History

Central Park West at 79th Street
New York, NY 10024
Phone: 212-533-0222
Email: yna@amnh.org
Website: http://www.amnh.org

1118 • Young Naturalist Awards

Purpose: To reward students for their research-based essays to promote participation and communication in science.

Eligibility: Applicants must be students in grade 7 through 12 who are currently enrolled in a public, private, parochial or home school in the United States, Canada, the U.S. territories or in a U.S.-sponsored school abroad. The essays must be based on studies in school or an educational program and the theme that is the same every year: "Scientific Discovery Begins with Expeditions!" Students may choose a topic in biology, earth science or astronomy and take an expedition to an area where they can explore their topic. The expedition does not have to be complicated. Each essay must include a list of references. Essays are judged primarily on scientific merit.

How to Apply: Applications are available online, by mail, by phone or by email.
Deadline: May 1.
Amount: $2,500.
Number of Awards: 12.

American Nuclear Society

555 N. Kensington Avenue
La Grange Park, IL 60526
Phone: 708-352-6611
Fax: 708-352-0499
Email: hr@ans.org
Website: http://www.ans.org

1119 • ANS Graduate Scholarship

Purpose: To assist full-time graduate students who are pursuing advanced degrees in a nuclear-related field.

Eligibility: Applicants must be full-time students at an accredited graduate school in a program leading to an advanced degree in nuclear science, nuclear engineering or a nuclear-related field. There are also individual graduate scholarships. Applicants should submit applications, transcripts, recommendation letter and three reference forms.

How to Apply: Applications are available online.
Deadline: February 1.
Amount: Varies.
Number of Awards: Up to 29.

1120 • ANS Undergraduate Scholarship

Purpose: To assist undergraduate students who are pursuing careers in the field of nuclear science.

Eligibility: Applicants must be at least sophomores in an accredited university and must be enrolled in a program leading to a degree in nuclear science, nuclear engineering or a nuclear-related field.

How to Apply: Applications are available online.
Deadline: February 1.
Amount: Varies.
Number of Awards: Up to 4 for sophomores, up to 21 for juniors and seniors.

1121 • John and Muriel Landis Scholarship

Purpose: To assist disadvantaged students to seek careers in a nuclear-related field.

Eligibility: Applicants must be undergraduate or graduate students enrolled or planning to enroll in a U.S. college or university who are also planning a career in nuclear science, nuclear engineering or another nuclear-related field. Students must have greater than average financial need.

How to Apply: Applications are available online.
Deadline: February 1.
Amount: Varies.
Number of Awards: Up to 8.

American Physical Society

One Physics Ellipse
College Park, MD 20740
Phone: 301-209-3232
Website: http://www.aps.org

1122 • APS Minority Scholarship

Purpose: To assist minorities studying physics.

Eligibility: Applicants must be African-American, Hispanic American or Native American U.S. citizens or permanent residents who plan to or are majoring in physics. Applicants must be high school seniors, college freshmen or college sophomores.

How to Apply: Applications are available online.
Deadline: February 1.
Amount: $2,000-$3,000.
Number of Awards: 20-25.

American Physiological Society

Education Office
9650 Rockville Pike
Bethesda, MD 20814-3991
Phone: 301-634-7787
Fax: 301-634-7241

Email: education@the-aps.org
Website: http://www.the-aps.org

1123 • Undergraduate Student Summer Research Fellowships

Purpose: To support full-time summer study for undergraduate students in the laboratory of an established researcher.

Eligibility: Applicants must be enrolled in an undergraduate program, and faculty sponsor must be an active member of APS. Fellowships are awarded to students pursuing a career as a basic research scientist.

How to Apply: Applications are available online.

Deadline: February 3.

Amount: $3,000.

Number of Awards: Up to 12.

American Society for Photogrammetry and Remote Sensing

5410 Grosvenor Lane
Suite 210
Bethesda, MD 20814
Phone: 301-493-0290 x101
Fax: 301-493-0208
Email: scholarships@asprs.org
Website: http://www.asprs.org

1124 • Robert E. Altenhofen Memorial Scholarship

Purpose: To commend college students who display ability in the theoretical aspects of photogrammetry.

Eligibility: Applicants must be undergraduate or graduate students and submit several pieces with their applications including: a two-page statement regarding plans for continuing studies in theoretical photogrammetry, papers, research reports or other items written by the applicants and academic transcripts. Recipients are required to submit a report on the work they accomplish during the award period.

How to Apply: Applications are available online.

Deadline: December 1.

Amount: $2,000.

Number of Awards: 1.

1125 • Space Imaging Award for Application of High Resolution Digital Satellite Imagery

Purpose: To support remote sensing education and stimulate the development of applications of high-resolution digital satellite imagery for applied research by undergraduate or graduate students.

Eligibility: Applicants must be full-time undergraduate or graduate students at an accredited college or university with proper image processing facilities. Selection is based on the application, letters of recommendation and a brief two-page proposal. The structure for the proposal can be found on the website.

How to Apply: Applications are available online.

Deadline: December 1.

Amount: $2,000.

Number of Awards: 1.

1126 • William A. Fischer Memorial Scholarship

Purpose: To support graduate study in new uses of remote sensing data or techniques that relate to the natural, cultural or agricultural resources of the Earth.

Eligibility: Applicants must be prospective or current graduate students and submit letters of recommendation, a two-page statement detailing educational and career plans for continuing studies in remote sensing applications and transcripts. It is also recommended that applicants submit technical papers, research reports or other items that indicate their capabilities. Recipients must submit a report of their work during the award period.

How to Apply: Applications are available online.

Deadline: December 1.

Amount: $2,000.

Number of Awards: 1.

Association for Women in Science

1200 New York Avenue NW
Suite 650
Washington, DC 20005
Phone: 202-326-8940
Fax: 202-326-8960
Email: awis@awis.org
Website: http://www.awis.org

1127 • Association for Women in Science Predoctoral Awards

Purpose: To recognize female students enrolled in a behavioral, life, physical or social science or engineering program leading to a Ph.D. degree.

Eligibility: Three of the awards have limitations for students in certain fields and one is reserved for a student who interrupted her education for at least three years to raise a family. Awards are given based on academic achievement, the importance of the research question addressed, the quality of the research and the applicant's potential for future contributions to science or engineering.

How to Apply: Applications are available online.

Deadline: January 26.

Amount: $1,000.

Number of Awards: 5-10.

Astronaut Scholarship Foundation

6225 Vectorspace Boulevard
Titusville, FL 32780
Phone: 321-269-6101
Fax: 321-264-9176
Email: linnleblanc@astronautscholarship.org
Website: http://www.astronautscholarship.org

1128 • Astronaut Scholarship

Purpose: To ensure the United States' continued leadership in science by assisting promising physical science and engineering students.

Eligibility: Applicants must be junior or senior undergraduate or graduate students in physical science or engineering at Georgia Institute of Technology, Harvey Mudd College, Miami University, North Carolina A&T State University, North Carolina State University, North Dakota State University, Pennsylvania State University, Purdue University, Syracuse University, Texas A&M University, Tufts University, University of Central Florida, University of Colorado, University of Kentucky, University of Minnesota, University of Oklahoma, University of Washington or Washington University and must be nominated by faculty or staff. Applicants may not directly apply for the scholarship. Students must have excellent grades and performed research or lab work in their field.

How to Apply: Applicants must be nominated.

Deadline: Varies.

Amount: $10,000.

Number of Awards: One per school.

Astronomical League

7241 Jarboe
Kansas City, MO 64114
Phone: 816-444-4878
Email: carroll-Iorg@kc.rr.com
Website: http://www.astroleague.org

1129 • Jack Horkheimer Award

Purpose: To assist young Astronomical League members.

Eligibility: Applicants must be Astronomical League members under the age of 19 on the date of the application. The award is based on involvement in the organization.

How to Apply: Applications are available online.

Deadline: March 31.

Amount: $1,000.

Number of Awards: Varies.

1130 • National Young Astronomer Award

Purpose: To support young astronomers.

Eligibility: Applicants must be 14 to 19 years old, not yet enrolled in college at the award deadline and do not have to be members of an astronomy club or of the Astronomical League. International students of the same age are eligible if they are enrolled in a U.S. secondary school on the application deadline. The application consists of the application form, summary of astronomy related activities and optional exhibits.

How to Apply: Applications are available online.

Deadline: January 31.

Amount: Varies.

Number of Awards: 3.

Damon Runyon Cancer Research Foundation

675 Third Avenue, 25th Floor
New York, NY 10017
Phone: 212-455-0520
Fax: 212-455-0529
Email: awards@drcrf.org
Website: http://www.drcrf.org

1131 • Fellowship Award

Purpose: To support the training of postdoctoral scientists as they start their research careers.

Eligibility: Applicants must have completed one or more of the following degrees or its equivalent: M.D., Ph.D., M.D./Ph.D., D.D.S. or D.V.M. Applicants should submit an application cover sheet, sponsor's biographical sketch, CV, degree certificate, letter, research proposal, summary of research form, up to three reprints of work and four letters of reference. This is a three-year award with various deadlines and funding. The research must be conducted at a university, hospital or research institution. International candidates may apply to do their research only in the United States.

How to Apply: Applications are available online.

Deadline: March 15.

Amount: $174,000 over three years.

Number of Awards: Varies.

Department of Defense, American Society for Engineering Education

1818 N Street NW
Suite 600
Washington, DC 20036
Phone: 202-331-3516

Fax: 202-265-8504
Email: ndseg@asee.org
Website: http://www.asee.org

1132 • NDSEG Fellowship Program

Purpose: To award fellowships to those in science and engineering.

Eligibility: Applicants must pursue a doctoral degree in an area of Department of Defense interest: aeronautical and astronautical engineering, biosciences, chemical engineering, chemistry, civil engineering, cognitive, neural, and behavioral sciences, computer and computational sciences, electrical engineering, geosciences, materials science and engineering, mathematics, mechanical engineering, naval architecture and ocean engineering, oceanography and physics. Applicants must have completed no more than one academic year of graduate study as a part-time or full-time student or be in their final year of undergraduate studies. The award is based on academic achievement, personal statements, recommendations and Graduate Record Examination scores. Fellowships may be used only at U.S. institutions of higher education offering doctoral degrees.

How to Apply: Applications are available online.

Deadline: January 6.

Amount: $31,500.

Number of Awards: 200.

DuPont

The DuPont Challenge
Science Essay Awards Program, c/o General Learning Communications
900 Skokie Boulevard, Suite 200
Northbrook, IL 60062
Phone: 847-205-3000
Website: http://www.glcomm.com/dupont/

1133 • DuPont Challenge Science Essay Award

Purpose: To promote interest in scientific studies.

Eligibility: Applicants must be full-time students between grades 7 and 12 in a U.S. or Canadian school and write a 700- to 1,000-word essay about a scientific or technological development that interests them.

How to Apply: Applications are available online.

Deadline: February 12.

Amount: $100-$3,000.

Number of Awards: 10 plus honorable mentions.

Electrochemical Society

65 S. Main Street, Building D
Pennington, NJ 08534-2839
Phone: 609-737-1902
Fax: 609-737-2743
Email: awards@electrochem.org
Website: http://www.electrochem.org

1134 • Corrosion Division Morris Cohen Graduate Student Award

Purpose: To recognize graduate research in corrosion science and/or engineering.

Eligibility: Applicants must be graduate students who have completed all the requirements for their degrees within two years prior to the nomination deadline. Nomination may be made by the applicant's research supervisor or someone familiar with the applicant's research work. A summary of the applicant's master's or Ph.D. research work, reports, memberships and involvement with scientific societies, awards, an academic record and reprints of publications are required.

How to Apply: Application materials are listed online.
Deadline: December 15.
Amount: $1,000.
Number of Awards: 1.

Geological Society of America

Program Officer
Grants, Awards and Recognition
P.O. Box 9140
Boulder, CO 80301-9140
Phone: 303-357-1028
Email: awards@geosociety.org
Website: http://www.geosociety.org

1135 • Graduate Student Research Grants

Purpose: To support thesis and dissertation research for graduate students in geological science.

Eligibility: Applicants must currently be enrolled in a geological science graduate program at an institution in the United States, Canada, Mexico or Central America. Applicants must also be members of the Geological Society of America (GSA).

How to Apply: Applications are available online.
Deadline: February 1.
Amount: Varies.
Number of Awards: Varies.

1136 • Travel Grants

Purpose: To provide undergraduate and graduate students with grants to travel to GSA section meetings and to the GSA annual meeting.

Eligibility: Applicants must be members of GSA. Each regional section has its own application process.

How to Apply: Application information for each region is available online.
Deadline: Varies.
Amount: Varies.
Number of Awards: Varies.

1137 • Undergraduate Student Research Grants

Purpose: To provide research grants to undergraduate students studying geology who are members of GSA.

Eligibility: Applicants must be members of GSA and attend school in one of the following GSA sections: Northeastern, North-Central or Southeastern. Each section has a separate application process.

How to Apply: Application instructions for each region are available online.
Deadline: Varies.
Amount: Varies.
Number of Awards: Varies.

Intel Corporation and Science Service

1719 North Street NW
Washington, DC 20036
Phone: 202-785-2255
Fax: 202-785-1243
Email: sciedu@sciserv.org
Website: http://www.sciserv.org

1138 • Intel Science Talent Search

Purpose: To recognize excellence in science among the nation's youth and encourage the exploration of science.

Eligibility: Applicants must be high school seniors in the U.S., Puerto Rico, Guam, Virgin Islands, American Samoa, Wake or Midway Islands or the Marianas. U.S. citizens attending foreign schools are also eligible. Applicants must complete college entrance exams and complete individual research projects and provide a report on the research.

How to Apply: Applications are available by request.
Deadline: November.
Amount: $1,000-$100,000.
Number of Awards: 300.

1139 • International Science and Engineering Fair

Purpose: To reward outstanding high school science fair projects.

Eligibility: Students must participate in a regional science fair affiliated with Intel ISEF and be selected to advance to the Intel ISEF. The competition is open to students in the ninth to twelfth grade and has 18 categories: Animal Sciences, Behavioral and Social Sciences, Biochemistry, Cellular and Molecular Biology, Chemistry, Computer Science, Earth Science, Engineering: Electrical and Mechanical, Engineering: Materials and Bioengineering, Energy and Transportation, Environmental Management, Environmental Science, Mathematical Sciences, Medicine and Health, Microbiology, Physics and Astronomy, Plant Sciences and Team Projects.

How to Apply: Required forms are available online.
Deadline: Varies.
Amount: Up to $50,000.
Number of Awards: 600.

International Society for Optical Engineering

P.O. Box 10
Bellingham, WA 98227
Phone: 360-676-3290
Fax: 360-647-1445
Email: education@spie.org
Website: http://www.spie.org

1140 • SPIE Student Scholarships

Purpose: To promote students who have potential to contribute to the field of optics.

Eligibility: Applicants must be high school, undergraduate or graduate students enrolled full-time in programs in the field of optics, optical science and engineering. Students must be members of SPIE, although they may submit a membership application along with the scholarship application. Applicants must also submit two sealed letters of reference.

How to Apply: Applications are available online.
Deadline: January 30.
Amount: Varies.
Number of Awards: Varies.

1141 • Student Travel Contingency Grants

Purpose: To assist students who need support to travel to present at a SPIE meeting.

Eligibility: Applicants must be presenting an accepted paper at a SPIE-sponsored meeting and not have any other way of supporting their travel. Applicants must be full-time students who are not full-time employees in industry, government or academia. Applicants

must also submit a letter of recommendation and a written statement of support from the chair of the SPIE-sponsored meeting.
How to Apply: Applications are available online.
Deadline: 10 weeks prior to the start of meeting.
Amount: Varies.
Number of Awards: Varies.

Iron and Steel Society

Attn.: Lori Wharrey
ISS Foundation
186 Thorn Hill Road
Warrendale, PA 15086
Phone: 724-776-1535
Fax: 724-776-0430
Email: nicks@iss.org
Website: http://www.iss.org

1142 • ISS Scholarship Foundation
Purpose: To attract talented and dedicated students to careers within the iron and steel and steel-related industries.
Eligibility: Applicants must be full-time college juniors or seniors majoring in metallurgy, metallurgical engineering or materials science. Other related majors are considered with a letter from the academic adviser. Applicants must have a minimum 3.0 GPA in the major or a minimum 3.25 GPA if they are undeclared and be ISS student members or submit an application for membership with the scholarship application.
How to Apply: Applications are available online.
Deadline: April 30.
Amount: $2,000.
Number of Awards: 5.

Micron

c/o Scholarship Management Services
One Scholarship Way
P.O. Box 297
St. Peter, MN 56082
Phone: 800-537-4180
Website: http://www.micron.com

1143 • Science and Technology Scholars Program
Purpose: To reward academic excellence and leadership while encouraging careers in engineering, science and computer science.
Eligibility: Applicants must be high school seniors from Idaho, Utah, Texas, Colorado or Virginia planning to major in engineering, computer science, physics, chemistry or material sciences. They must have at least a 3.5 GPA and an SAT combined score of 1350 or an ACT composite score of 30. Applicants must also demonstrate leadership in school, work or extracurricular activities.
How to Apply: Applications are distributed to eligible students in November and are also available online.
Deadline: January 19.
Amount: $16,500-$55,000.
Number of Awards: Up to 13.

Microscopy Society of America

Undergraduate Research Scholarships
230 E. Ohio Street
Suite 400
Chicago, IL 60611

Phone: 800-538-3672
Fax: 312-622-8557
Email: businessoffice@microscopy.org
Website: http://www.microscopy.org

1144 • MSA Undergraduate Research Scholarship
Purpose: To help undergraduate students interested in pursuing microscopy as a career or for research.
Eligibility: Applicants must conduct research in microscopy at their school and complete their research before graduation. Applicants must also be full-time undergraduate students and achieve junior or senior standing by the time the research work is started.
How to Apply: Applications are available online.
Deadline: December 31.
Amount: $3,000.
Number of Awards: Varies.

National Association for Surface Finishing

1155 Fifteenth Street NW
Washington, DC 20005
Phone: 202-457-8401
Fax: 202-530-0659
Website: http://www.nasf.org

1145 • American Electroplaters and Surface Finishers Society Scholarship
Purpose: To award students whose education or research is related to surface finishing and plating technologies.
Eligibility: For the undergraduate scholarship program, applicants must be full-time undergraduates of at least junior standing majoring in chemistry, chemical engineering, environmental engineering, metallurgy, metallurgical engineering or materials science or engineering with the focus of the curriculum in surface science subjects. Applicants for the graduate scholarship program must have completed an undergraduate program leading to a master's or Ph.D. degree. Selection is based on motivation and interest in finishing technologies, scholarship potential and achievement.
How to Apply: Applications are available online.
Deadline: April 15.
Amount: $1,500.
Number of Awards: Varies.

National Radio Astronomy Observatory (NRAO)

NRAO Headquarters
520 Edgemont Road
Charlottesville, VA 22903
Phone: 434-296-0211
Fax: 434-296-0278
Email: info@nrao.edu
Website: http://www.nrao.edu

1146 • GBT Student Support Program
Purpose: To support student research at the Robert C. Byrd Green Bank Telescope (GBT).
Eligibility: GBT is the largest fully steerable single aperture antenna. Students begin the application process by completing a preliminary funding proposal form. If the proposal is accepted, they will be informed of further requirements.
How to Apply: Applications are available online.
Deadline: Varies.

Amount: Varies.
Number of Awards: Varies.

1147 • Graduate Summer Student Research Assistantship

Purpose: To allow graduate students to perform astronomical research at National Radio Astronomy Observatory (NRAO) sites.
Eligibility: Applicants must be first- or second-year graduate students interested in astronomical research. Recipients work on-site for 10 to 12 weeks, beginning in late May or early June.
How to Apply: Applications are available online.
Deadline: January 23.
Amount: $510 per week stipend.
Number of Awards: Varies.

1148 • Undergraduate Summer Student Research Assistantship

Purpose: To allow students to perform astronomical research at National Radio Astronomy Observatory (NRAO) sites.
Eligibility: Depending on the specific program, applicants must be either undergraduates or graduating college seniors. Recipients work on-site for 10 to 12 weeks, beginning in late May or early June.
How to Apply: Applications are available online.
Deadline: January 23.
Amount: $425 per week stipend.
Number of Awards: Varies.

Siemens Foundation

170 Wood Avenue South
Iselin, NJ 08330
Phone: 877-822-5233
Fax: 732-603-5890
Email: foundation.us@siemens.com
Website: http://www.siemens-foundation.org

1149 • Siemens Westinghouse Competition in Math, Science and Technology

Purpose: To provide high school students an opportunity to meet other students interested in math, science and technology and to provide monetary assistance with college expenses.
Eligibility: Students must submit research reports either individually or in teams of two or three members. Individual applicants must be high school seniors, but members of a team submission do not. Members of a team submission Projects may be scientific research, technological inventions or mathematical theories.
How to Apply: Applications are available online.
Deadline: October.
Amount: $1,000-$10,000.
Number of Awards: Varies.

Society of Physics Students

One Physics Ellipse
College Park, MD 20740
Phone: 301-209-3007
Fax: 301-209-0839
Email: sps@aip.org
Website: http://www.spsnational.org

1150 • Herbert Levy Memorial Scholarship

Purpose: To provide financial assistance for physics students in any year of undergraduate study.

Eligibility: Applicants must be physics majors, be members of SPS and demonstrate scholarly achievement and financial need.
How to Apply: Applications are available online or from SPS Chapter Advisors.
Deadline: February 15.
Amount: $2,000.
Number of Awards: 1.

1151 • Peggy Dixon Two-Year Scholarship

Purpose: To help students seeking a bachelor's degree in physics to transition from a two-year to a four-year program.
Eligibility: Applicants must be members of SPS. Students must have finished at least one semester or quarter of the introductory physics sequence and must be registered in the appropriate subsequent physics classes.
How to Apply: Applications are available online or from chapter advisors.
Deadline: February 15.
Amount: $2,000.
Number of Awards: 1.

1152 • SPS Leadership Scholarships

Purpose: To further the study of physics.
Eligibility: Applicants must be undergraduates at least in their junior year, physics majors and active members of SPS.
How to Apply: Applications are available online and from SPS Chapter Advisors.
Deadline: February 15.
Amount: $2,000-$5,000.
Number of Awards: 21.

Related Scholarships:

Armed Forces Communications and Electronics Association
See #253 • AFCEA General John A. Wickham Scholarships

Armed Forces Communications and Electronics Association
See #254 • AFCEA Ralph W. Shrader Scholarships

Maryland Higher Education Commission
See #1402 • Science and Technology Scholarship

American Institute of Aeronautics and Astronautics
See #93 • AIAA Foundation Undergraduate Scholarship Program

Massachusetts Office of Student Financial Assistance
See #1415 • CommonWealth Futures Grant Program

Minnesota Higher Education Services Office
See #1433 • Minnesota Academic Excellence Scholarship

American Chemical Society
See #935 • American Chemical Society Scholars Program

American Society of Naval Engineers

See #370 · ASNE Scholarship Program

Association for Women in Science

See #181 · Association for Women in Science College Scholarship

Barry M. Goldwater Scholarship and Excellence in Education Foundation

See #391 · Barry M. Goldwater Scholarship and Excellence in Education Program

National Inventors Hall of Fame

See #411 · Collegiate Inventors Competition

Society of Exploration Geophysicists

See #422 · SEG Scholarship

Triangle Education Foundation

See #830 · Rust Scholarship

Women In Defense

See #565 · HORIZONS Foundation Scholarship

EAA Aviation Center

See #101 · Payzer Scholarship

Armed Forces Communications and Electronics Association

See #707 · AFCEA Sgt Jeannette L. Winters, USMC Memorial Scholarship

Armed Forces Communications and Electronics Association

See #705 · AFCEA General Emmett Paige Scholarships

Armed Forces Communications and Electronics Association

See #706 · AFCEA ROTC Scholarships

International Society for Optical Engineering

See #408 · Michael Kidger Memorial Scholarship

Hispanic Heritage Awards Foundation

See #985 · Hispanic Heritage Youth Awards

Association of Engineering Geologists Foundation Marliave Fund

See #383 · Marliave Fund

ASM International Foundation

See #380 · George A. Roberts Scholarships

ASM International Foundation

See #377 · ASM Foundation Scholarship Awards

ASM International Foundation

See #381 · Nicholas J. Grant Scholarship

Society of Physics Students

See #341 · SPS Future Teacher Scholarship

American Physiological Society

See #945 · Explorations Summer Research Fellowships

Electrochemical Society

See #395 · Industrial Electrolysis and Electrochemical Engineering Engineering Division Student Achievement Awards

Fannie and John Hertz Foundation

See #190 · Hertz Foundation's Graduate Fellowship Award

National Consortium for Graduate Degrees for Minorities in Engineering and Science Inc. (GEM)

See #1026 · GEM Fellowship Program

Association of Engineering Geologists Foundation Tilford Fund

See #384 · Tilford Fund

ASM International Foundation

See #378 · ASM Foundation Technical and Community College Scholarship Awards

ASM International Foundation

See #379 · ASM Outstanding Scholars Awards

ASM International Foundation

See #382 · William Park Woodside Founder's Scholarship

Davidson Institute for Talent Development

See #20 · Davidson Fellows Award

Electrochemical Society

See #394 · Battery Division Student Research Award

Electrochemical Society

See #219 · Industrial Electrolysis and Electrochemical Engineering Division H.H. Dow Memorial Student Award

Electrochemical Society

See #220· SemiZone E-Learning Fellowships

Electrochemical Society

See #221· Student Poster Session Awards

Illuminating Engineering Society of North America

See #144· Robert E. Thunen Memorial Scholarships

Society of Mexican American Engineers and Scientists Inc. (MAES)

See #1052· MAES Scholarship Program

Social Science/History

Also See Scholarships Listed Under:
Education/Teaching
English/Writing
Foreign Language
Ethnic and Area Studies

American Center of Oriental Research (ACOR)

656 Beacon Street, 5th Floor
Boston, MA 02215
Phone: 617-353-6571
Fax: 617-353-6575
Email: acor@bu.edu
Website: http://www.bu.edu/acor

1153 • ACOR-CAORC Fellowships

Purpose: To assist master's and pre-doctoral students conducting research in Jordan.

Eligibility: Applicants must be graduate students researching topics involving scholarship in Near Eastern studies. Recipients are required to engage in scholarly and cultural activities while residing at the American Center of Oriental Research (ACOR) in Jordan. The fellowships last from two to six months. The award includes room and board at ACOR, transportation, a stipend and research funds.

How to Apply: Applications are available online.
Deadline: February 1.
Amount: $19,400.
Number of Awards: At least 5.

1154 • Harrell Family Fellowship

Purpose: To assist a graduate student with expenses on an archaeological project in Jordan.

Eligibility: Applicants must be graduate students in a program approved by a recognized academic review body.

How to Apply: Applications are available online.
Deadline: February 1.
Amount: $1,500.
Number of Awards: 1.

1155 • Jennifer C. Groot Fellowship

Purpose: To assist students with expenses on an archaeological project.

Eligibility: Applicants must be undergraduate or graduate students with little or no archaeological field experience. Recipients will travel to Jordan for the project.

How to Apply: Applications are available online but must be submitted by mail.
Deadline: February 1.
Amount: $1,500.
Number of Awards: At least 2.

1156 • Pierre and Patricia Bikai Fellowship

Purpose: To help graduate students in an archaeological project at the American Center of Oriental Research.

Eligibility: Applicants must be graduate students. The fellowship includes room and board at ACOR and $400 a month and may be combined with the Harrell and Groot fellowships. The fellowship does not support field work or travel. Recipients must live at the ACOR center in Jordan from June of one year to May of the next.

How to Apply: Applications are available online.
Deadline: February 1.
Amount: $400 plus room and board.
Number of Awards: Varies.

American Congress on Surveying and Mapping (ACSM)

6 Montgomery Village Avenue
Suite 403
Gaithersburg, MD 20879
Phone: 240-632-9716
Fax: 240-632-1321
Website: http://www.acsm.net

1157 • CaGIS Scholarships

Purpose: To support excellence in cartography or GIScience.

Eligibility: Applicants must be enrolled full-time in a four-year undergraduate or graduate degree program in cartography or geographic information science. Prior scholarship winners may apply. Applicants are judged on their records, statements, letters of recommendation and professional activities.

How to Apply: Applications are available online.
Deadline: January 22.
Amount: $1,000.
Number of Awards: Varies.

American Council of Learned Societies (ACLS)

633 Third Avenue
New York, NY 10017-6795
Phone: 212-697-1505
Fax: 212-949-8058
Email: sfisher@acls.org
Website: http://www.acls.org

1158 • Contemplative Practice Fellowship Program

Purpose: To support scholars interested in contemplative practices.

Eligibility: There are two awards, Contemplative Practice Fellowships and Contemplative Program Development Fellowships. The first is for $10,000, and the second is for $20,000. Applicants for the Contemplative Practice Fellowships must be scholars who are full-time faculty members at accredited U.S. academic institutions who want to integrate contemplative practices into their courses. Preferred applicants will have experience with contemplative practice. The fellowship is for a summer or semester. The Contemplative Program Development Fellowships is for scholars who are full-time faculty members and faculty-status administrators at accredited U.S. academic institutions who want to develop academic courses involving contemplative studies. The fellowship lasts for an academic year.

How to Apply: Applications are available online.
Deadline: November 10.
Amount: $20,000.
Number of Awards: Varies.

American Historical Association

400 A Street SE
Washington, DC 20003
Phone: 202-544-2422
Fax: 202-544-8307
Email: info@historians.org
Website: http://www.historians.org

1159 • J. Franklin Jameson Fellowship in American History

Purpose: To support one semester of scholarly research in the Library of Congress collections.
Eligibility: Applicants must hold a Ph.D. or equivalent, must have earned the degree within the past seven years and may not have published a book-length historical work. Projects should focus on American history.
How to Apply: Application instructions are available online.
Deadline: March 15.
Amount: $5,000.
Number of Awards: Varies.

1160 • Wesley-Logan Prize

Purpose: To award a prize to a scholarly/literary book focusing on the history of dispersion, relocation, settlement or adjustment of people from Africa; or on their return to that continent.
Eligibility: Books must have been published between May 1 of the previous year and April 30 of the entry year. Entries are mailed directly to committee members.
How to Apply: Application information is available on approximately March 30.
Deadline: May 15.
Amount: Varies.
Number of Awards: Varies.

American Institute for Economic Research

P.O. Box 1000
Attn.: Susan Gillette, Assistant to the President
Great Barrington, MA 01230
Phone: 413-528-1216
Fax: 413-528-0103
Email: fellowship@aier.org
Website: http://www.aier.org

1161 • Summer Fellowship Program

Purpose: To provide summer fellowships for college seniors entering a doctoral program in economics or economics-related studies.
Eligibility: Applicants must be college seniors who will enter a doctoral program in economics or an affiliated program.
How to Apply: Applications are available online.
Deadline: March 31.
Amount: Room and board, $250 per week.
Number of Awards: 12.

American Institute of Indian Studies

1130 E. 59th Street
Chicago, IL 60637
Phone: 773-702-8638
Email: aiis@uchicago.edu
Website: http://www.indiastudies.org

1162 • Junior Fellowships

Purpose: To support doctoral candidates at U.S. universities who wish to travel to India to conduct dissertation research on Indian aspects of their academic discipline.
Eligibility: Applicants must be doctoral candidates at a U.S. university. Junior fellows are affiliated with Indian universities and research mentors. Awards may last up to 11 months.
How to Apply: Applications are available by mail or email.
Deadline: July 1.
Amount: Varies.
Number of Awards: Varies.

American Numismatic Society

96 Fulton Street
New York, NY 10038
Phone: 212-571-4470
Fax: 212-571-4479
Email: info@numismatics.org
Website: http://www.amnumsoc.org

1163 • Donald Groves Fund

Purpose: To support publication in the field of early American numismatics, which involves materials created no later than 1800.
Eligibility: Funding is available for travel, research and publication costs.
How to Apply: Application instructions are available online. Applications should be mailed to the ANS, Attn.: Secretary of the Society.
Deadline: Varies.
Amount: Varies.
Number of Awards: Varies.

1164 • Frances M. Schwartz Fellowship

Purpose: To award fellowships in support of the study of numismatics and museum methodology at the American Numismatic Society.
Eligibility: Applicants must hold a B.A. or equivalent.
How to Apply: Applications are available online or by mail.
Deadline: Varies.
Amount: Up to $5,000.
Number of Awards: Varies.

American Research Institute in Turkey (ARIT)

3260 South Street
Philadelphia, PA 19104-6324
Phone: 215-898-3474
Fax: 215-898-0657
Email: leinwand@sas.upenn.edu
Website: http://ccat.sas.upenn.edu/ARIT

1165 • ARIT Fellowships for Research in Turkey

Purpose: To support scholars in their research in Turkey.
Eligibility: Applicants must be scholars or advanced graduate students involved in research on ancient, medieval or modern times in Turkey, in any field of the humanities and social sciences. Student applicants must have completed all requirements for the doctorate except the dissertation before beginning any ARIT-sponsored research. Non-U.S. applicants must be connected to an educational institution in the U.S. or Canada. Applicants should

submit applications, three letters of recommendation and graduate transcripts.

How to Apply: Applications are available online.
Deadline: November 1.
Amount: Varies.
Number of Awards: Varies.

American Sociological Association

1307 New York Avenue NW
Suite 700
Washington, DC 20005
Phone: 202-383-9005
Fax: 202-638-0882
Email: minority.affairs@asanet.org
Website: http://www.asanet.org

1166 • Minority Fellowship Program

Purpose: To provide pre-doctoral graduate education for sociology students.

Eligibility: Applicants must be enrolled in a Ph.D. program in sociology departments that have National Institute of Mental Health (NIMH) and National Institute of Drug Abuse (NIDA) relevant research programs and/or faculty who are currently engaged in research focusing on topics important to the NIMH and NIDA. Students may be earlier in their graduate career but must be accepted into a Ph.D. program in sociology. Recipients are selected on the basis of their commitment to research, the focus of their research experience, academic achievement, scholarship, writing ability, research potential, financial need and racial/ethnic minority background. Applicants must be members of one of the following racial/ethnic groups: African American, Latino, American Indian or Alaskan Native or Asian or Pacific Islander. An application, essay, three recommendation letters and transcripts are required.

How to Apply: Applications are available online.
Deadline: January 31.
Amount: $20,772.
Number of Awards: Varies.

1167 • Student Travel Award

Purpose: To help students with travel expenses to the ASA annual meeting.

Eligibility: Applicants must be pursuing an undergraduate or graduate sociology degree in an academic institution and current student members of ASA. Awards are based on participation in the annual meeting, purpose for attending, student need, availability of other forms of support, matching funds and the potential benefit to the student.

How to Apply: Applications are available online.
Deadline: May 1.
Amount: $200.
Number of Awards: 25.

Association of American Geographers (AAG) Hess Scholarship

1710 Sixteenth Street NW
Washington, DC 20009-3198
Phone: 202-234-1450
Fax: 202-234-2744
Email: grantsawards@aag.org
Website: http://www.aag.org

1168 • Darrel Hess Community College Geography Scholarship

Purpose: To support geography majors.

Eligibility: Applicants must be currently enrolled at a U.S. community college, junior college, city college or similar two-year educational institution, have completed at least two transfer courses in geography and plan to transfer to a four-year institution as a geography major. The award is based on academic excellence and promise. Applications, personal statements, two recommendation letters and transcripts are required.

How to Apply: Applications are available online.
Deadline: May 1.
Amount: $1,000.
Number of Awards: 2.

Association of American Geographers (AAG) Hoffman Award

Frostburg State University
101 Braddock Road
c/o George White
Frostburg, MD 21532-2303
Phone: 301-687-4000
Email: gwhite@frostburg.edu
Website: http://www.aag.org

1169 • George and Viola Hoffman Award

Purpose: To support graduate research in Eastern Europe.

Eligibility: Applicants must research toward a master's thesis or doctoral dissertation on a geographical subject in Eastern Europe which includes the countries of East Central and Southeast Europe from Poland south to Romania, Bulgaria and the successor states of the former Yugoslavia. The research topics may be historical or contemporary, systematic or regional, limited to a small area or comparative. Applicants must submit applications including a statement of the research topic, research methods, field of study, schedule and bibliography. Applicants should also submit a letter describing professional achievements and the goals and a letter of support from a sponsoring faculty member.

How to Apply: Application materials are described online.
Deadline: December 31.
Amount: $500.
Number of Awards: 1.

Bibliographical Society of America

P.O. Box 1537
Lenox Hill Station
New York, NY 10021
Phone: 212-452-2710
Email: bsa@bibsocamer.org
Website: http://www.bibsocamer.org

1170 • BSA Research Fellowship

Purpose: To provide financial assistance to those pursuing bibliographical studies.

Eligibility: Applicants must submit proposals for studying books as historical evidence or an examination of the history of book trades or publishing history.

How to Apply: Applications are available online.
Deadline: December 1.
Amount: $2,000.
Number of Awards: Varies.

Charles Babbage Institute

Center for the History of Information Processing
211 Andersen Library, University of Minnesota
222 - 21st Avenue South
Minneapolis, MN 55455
Phone: 612-624-5050
Email: yostx003@tc.umn.edu
Website: http://www.cbi.umn.edu

1171 • Adelle and Erwin Tomash Fellowship in the History of Information Processing

Purpose: To support a graduate student who is researching the history of computing.
Eligibility: Applicants must be graduate students who have completed all doctoral degree requirements except the research and writing of the dissertation. Students must submit a curriculum vitae and a five-page statement and justification of the research program.
How to Apply: Visit the website for more information.
Deadline: January 15.
Amount: $14,000 stipend.
Number of Awards: 1.

Crow Canyon Archeological Center

23390 Road K
Cortez, CO 81321-9908
Phone: 800-422-8975
Email: schoolprograms@crowcanyon.org
Website: http://www.crowcanyon.org

1172 • Florence C. and Robert H. Lister Fellowship

Purpose: To assist graduate students in the archeology of American Indian cultures of the Southwest.
Eligibility: Applicants must be enrolled in a North American Ph.D. program and have projects based on archaeological, ethnoarchaeological or paleoenvironmental research in the southwestern United States and northern Mexico.
How to Apply: Applications are available online.
Deadline: Varies.
Amount: $5,000.
Number of Awards: Varies.

Fund for American Studies

1706 New Hampshire Avenue NW
Washington, DC 20009
Phone: 800-741-6964
Email: admissions@tfas.org
Website: http://www.dcinternships.org

1173 • Fund for American Studies Internships

Purpose: To provide scholarships for students attending one of the Fund's internship programs.
Eligibility: There are programs in comparative political and economic systems, political journalism, business and government, philanthropy and international institutes. Each program includes classes, an internship and special events. Students take classes at Georgetown University and live in downtown Washington, DC. Summer and school-year programs are available.
How to Apply: Applications are available online.
Deadline: Varies.

Amount: Varies.
Number of Awards: Varies.

Gamma Theta Upsilon

Dr. Donald Zeigler
Old Dominion University
1181 University Drive
Virginia Beach, VA 23453
Website: http://www.gtuhonors.org

1174 • Gamma Theta Upsilon-Geographical Honor Society

Purpose: To support geography knowledge and awareness by awarding monetary assistance to college and graduate students.
Eligibility: Applicants must be initiated through a Gamma Theta Upsilon chapter.
How to Apply: Applications are available online.
Deadline: July.
Amount: $500.
Number of Awards: 5.

Hagley Museum and Library

Center for the History of Business, Technology and Society
P.O. Box 3630
Wilmington, DE 19807-0630
Phone: 302-655-2400
Fax: 302-658-3188
Website: http://www.hagley.org

1175 • Hagley-Winterthur Fellowships in Arts and Industries

Purpose: To support research fellowships for projects focusing on the relationship between economic life and the arts, including design architecture, crafts and the fine arts.
Eligibility: Fellowships last for one to six months and are available to students and independent professionals to perform serious scholarly research. Fellows may use collections of the Winterthur Museum, Gardens and Library and the Hagley Museum and Library.
How to Apply: Applications are available online. For more information, contact Dr. Philip Scranton at the museum at pscranton@hagley.org.
Deadline: December 1.
Amount: Up to $1,400 per month.
Number of Awards: Varies.

1176 • Henry Belin du Pont Dissertation Fellowship

Purpose: To provide four-month fellowships for doctoral students performing dissertation research.
Eligibility: Applicants must be doctoral students who have completed all course work and are performing dissertation research. Research topics should involve historical questions and should relate to the collections in the Hagley Library. Fellows will receive housing, office space a computer and Internet access. A presentation is required at the end of the residence period.
How to Apply: Applications are available online. For more information contact Dr. Roger Horowitz at rhorowitz@hagley.org.
Deadline: November 15.
Amount: $6,000.
Number of Awards: Varies.

Harry S. Truman Library Institute for National and International Affairs

Grants Administrator
500 W. U.S. Highway 24
Independence, MO 64050
Phone: 816-268-8248
Fax: 816-268-8299
Email: lisa.sullivan@nara.gov
Website: http://www.trumanlibrary.org

1177 • Harry S. Truman Research Grant

Purpose: To promote the Truman Library as a center for research.

Eligibility: Graduate students and post-doctoral scholars are most encouraged to apply, but others completing advanced research will be considered. Preference is given to research dealing with enduring public policy and foreign policy issues that have a high chance of being published or otherwise shared publicly. Applicants can receive up to two research grants in a five-year period. Grant winners must submit a report at the end of their studies.

How to Apply: Applications are available online.
Deadline: April 1 and October 1.
Amount: Up to $2,500.
Number of Awards: Varies.

1178 • Harry S. Truman Undergraduate Student Grant

Purpose: To promote the Truman Library as a center for research.

Eligibility: Applicants must be writing a senior thesis on an aspect of the life and career of Harry S. Truman or public and foreign policy issues that were prominent during the Truman years, describe in writing the proposed project and show how using the Truman Library for research will help their future development. Grant winners must submit a written report on their research.

How to Apply: There is no application form.
Deadline: September 30.
Amount: Up to $1,000.
Number of Awards: 1.

Herbert Hoover Presidential Library Association

P.O. Box 696
West Branch, IA 52358
Phone: 800-828-0475
Fax: 319-643-2391
Email: scholarship@hooverassociation.org
Website: http://www.hooverassociation.org

1179 • Herbert Hoover Presidential Library Association Travel Grant Program

Purpose: To provide financial aid to individuals to research at the Herbert Hoover Presidential Library in West Branch, Iowa.

Eligibility: Applicants must be current graduate students, post-doctoral scholars or independent researchers. Applicants must also ensure that the library's contents will meet their research needs before applying.

How to Apply: Applications are available online.
Deadline: March 1.
Amount: $500 - $1,500.
Number of Awards: Varies.

Holland and Knight Charitable Foundation

P.O. Box 2877
Tampa, FL 33601
Phone: 866-HK-CARES
Email: holocaust@hklaw.com
Website: http://www.holocaust.hklaw.com

1180 • Holocaust Remembrance Project Essay Contest

Purpose: To reward high school students who write essays about the Holocaust.

Eligibility: Applicants must be age 19 and under who are currently enrolled as high school students in grades 9 to 12 (including home-schooled students), high school seniors or students who are enrolled in a high school equivalency program and be residents of either the United States or Mexico or United States citizens living abroad. Applicants should submit essays about the Holocaust and entry forms. Every essay must include works cited, a reference page or a bibliography. First place winners will receive free trips to Washington, DC.

How to Apply: Essays may be submitted online or by mail.
Deadline: May 1.
Amount: $10,000.
Number of Awards: Varies.

Huntington Library, Art Collections and Botanical Gardens

1151 Oxford Road
San Marino, CA 91108
Phone: 626-405-2194
Fax: 626-449-5703
Email: cpowell@huntington.org
Website: http://www.huntington.org

1181 • Huntington Fellowships

Purpose: To provide fellowships to doctoral students and recipients in British and American history, literature, art history and the history of science and medicine.

Eligibility: Applicants must have a Ph.D. or equivalent or be doctoral candidates at the dissertation stage. Cover sheets, project descriptions, curriculum vitae and three letters of recommendation are required.

How to Apply: Application materials are described online.
Deadline: December 15.
Amount: $10,000.
Number of Awards: More than 100.

1182 • Huntington-British Academy Fellowships for Study in Great Britain

Purpose: To offer scholars exchange fellowships to research British and American history, literature, art history and the history of science and medicine.

Eligibility: Applicants must have a Ph.D. or equivalent. Applicants must submit cover sheets, project descriptions, curriculum vitae and three letters of recommendation.

How to Apply: There is no application form, and application materials are described online.
Deadline: December 15.
Amount: Varies.
Number of Awards: Varies.

1183 • W.M. Keck Foundation Fellowships for Young Scholars

Purpose: To provide fellowships to non-tenured faculty or doctoral candidates in British and American history, literature, art history and the history of science and medicine.

Eligibility: Applicants should be non-tenured faculty or doctoral candidates at the dissertation stage. Cover sheets, project descriptions, curriculum vitae and three letters of recommendation are required.

How to Apply: There is no application form, and application materials are listed online.

Deadline: December 15.

Amount: $11,500.

Number of Awards: Varies.

John F. Kennedy Library Foundation

Columbia Point
Boston, MA 02125
Phone: 617-514-1691
Email: profiles@nara.gov
Website: http://www.jfkcontest.org

1184 • John F. Kennedy Profile in Courage Essay Contest

Purpose: To encourage students to research and write about politics and John F. Kennedy.

Eligibility: Applicants must be in grades 9 through 12 in public or private schools or be home-schooled and write an essay about politics as it relates to John F. Kennedy's book "Profiles in Courage." Essays must have source citations. Applicants must register online before sending essays and have a teacher help with the essay. The winner and teacher will be invited to the Kennedy Library to accept the award, and the winner's teacher will receive a grant.

How to Apply: Essays may be sent online or by mail.

Deadline: January 7.

Amount: $500-$3,000.

Number of Awards: 7.

Lyndon B. Johnson Foundation

2313 Red River Street
Austin, TX 78705
Phone: 512-478-7829
Fax: 512-478-9104
Email: webmaster@lbjlib.utexas.edu
Website: http://www.lbjlib.utexas.edu

1185 • Lyndon B. Johnson Foundation Grants-in-Aid Research

Purpose: To assist with the travel and room-and-board expenses of those wishing to conduct research at the Lyndon B. Johnson Foundation Library.

Eligibility: Applicants must first contact the library to determine if their topic is appropriate for study at the facility. Applicants must also calculate the estimated amount of the grant before making a request.

How to Apply: Applications are available online.

Deadline: February 28.

Amount: $500-$2,000.

Number of Awards: Varies.

National Council for Geographic Education

Jacksonville State University
206-A Martin Hall
700 Pelham Road North
Jacksonville, AL 36265-1602
Phone: 256-782-5293
Fax: 256-782-5336
Email: ncge@ncge.org
Website: http://www.ncge.org

1186 • College/University Excellence of Scholarship Awards

Purpose: To recognize senior geography majors.

Eligibility: Every college or university geography department in North America may submit the name of its outstanding graduating senior geography majors. The students receive certificates.

How to Apply: Nomination materials are described online.

Deadline: April 1.

Amount: Varies.

Number of Awards: Varies.

1187 • Grades 7-12 Excellence of Scholarship Awards

Purpose: To recognize outstanding geography students.

Eligibility: Nominators must be NCGE members who teach grades 7-12 geography courses and who nominate students in their classes. Only one student in each section or class may be nominated.

How to Apply: Nominating materials are described online.

Deadline: March 25.

Amount: Varies.

Number of Awards: Varies.

National History Day

0119 Cecil Hall
University of Maryland
College Park, MD 20742
Phone: 301-314-9739
Fax: 301-314-9767
Website: http://www.nationalhistoryday.org

1188 • National History Day Contest

Purpose: To reward students for their scholarship, initiative and cooperation.

Eligibility: Applicants must be high school students who prepare throughout the school year history presentations based on an annual theme. Around February or March students compete in district History Day contests. District winners then prepare for the state contests, held usually in April or May. Those winners advance to the national contest held in June at the University of Maryland.

How to Apply: Applications are available online.

Deadline: February-March.

Amount: Varies.

Number of Awards: Varies.

National Security Agency (NSA)

9800 Savage Road, Suite 6779
Ft. George G. Meade, MD 20755-6779
Phone: 410-854-4725
Website: http://www.nsa.gov/careers/

1189 • Pat Roberts Intelligence Scholars Program for Intelligence Analysts

Purpose: To support students who plan to work in intelligence analysis.

Eligibility: Applicants must be college juniors who are pursuing the following specialties related to intelligence work: regional studies (Middle East, South, East or Central Asia); topical studies (terrorism, proliferation or related sciences, international banking and finance or telecommunications and information systems networks) and disciplines (intelligence analysis, philosophy or international relations). Familiarity with foreign languages, particularly Arabic, Chinese, Dari, Farsi, Hindi, Korean, Pashto, Urdu or a Central Asian language is preferred. Applicants studying social network analysis, library science or geographic information systems may also be considered. Recipients are expected to become full-time employees of NSA's Intelligence Analysis Development Program after graduation.

How to Apply: Applications are available online.
Deadline: October 30.
Amount: Up to $25,000.
Number of Awards: Varies.

National Society Daughters of the American Revolution

1776 D Street NW
Washington, DC 20006
Phone: 202-628-1776
Website: http://www.dar.org

1190 • American History Scholarship, Enid Hall Griswold Memorial Scholarship, J.E. Caldwell Centennial Scholarship

Purpose: To promote the study of history, political science, government and economics.

Eligibility: Applicants to the American History Scholarship must be high school students planning to major in American history. The award is up to $2,000 each year for up to four years. Applicants for the Enid Hall Griswold Memorial Scholarship must major in political science, history, government or economics. The award is $1,000. Applicants to the J.E. Caldwell Centennial Scholarship must be graduate students in historic preservation. The award is $2,000.

How to Apply: Applications are available by written request.
Deadline: February.
Amount: $1,000-2,000.
Number of Awards: 5.

National Society of the Sons of the American Revolution

1000 S. Fourth Street
Louisville, KY 40203
Phone: 502-589-1776
Email: contests@sar.org
Website: http://www.sar.org

1191 • Joseph S. Rumbaugh Historical Oration Contest

Purpose: To encourage students to learn more about the Revolutionary War and its impact on modern America.

Eligibility: Applicants must prepare a speech of five to six minutes on some aspect of the Revolutionary War. The contest is open to high school sophomores, juniors and seniors at public, private and parochial high schools, as well as home-schooled students. Eligibility for the national contest is determined by contests on the state and local level.

How to Apply: Applications are available from local chapters of Sons of the American Revolution.
Deadline: Varies.
Amount: $200-$3,000.
Number of Awards: Varies.

Organization of American Historians

112 N. Bryan Avenue
P.O. Box 5457
Bloomington, IN 47408
Phone: 812-855-9852
Fax: 812-855-0696
Email: awards@oah.org
Website: http://www.oah.org

1192 • ABC-CLIO America: History and Life Award

Purpose: The Organization of American Historians promotes the teaching and learning of history.

Eligibility: The History and Life Award grants money to an author of a published journal article that meets the organization's mission. Judges look for articles that suggest and explore new interpretations of historical events, places or people. The winning entry is presented at the OAH annual meeting. Both editors and authors may submit entries. This is a biennial award.

How to Apply: No application is required. Submit one copy of each entry (clearly labeled "ABC-CLIO America: History and Life Award Entry") directly to each of the judges. Their names and addresses are available online.
Deadline: December 1.
Amount: $750.
Number of Awards: 1.

1193 • Horace Samuel and Marion Galbraith Merrill Travel Grants in Twentieth-Century American Political History

Purpose: Named after a University of Maryland political historian and his wife, the Horace Samuel and Marion Galbraith Merrill Travel Grants seek to perpetuate the couple's desire to assist fledgling scholars and authors.

Eligibility: The award provides stipends, access to research collections and opportunities to interview current and former public figures in Washington D.C. Only applications from current OAH members are accepted.

How to Apply: A copy of a completed submission package (clearly labeled "Merrill Travel Grants") must be mailed directly to each selector. The required contents of the package and the names and addresses of the selectors are available online.
Deadline: December 1.
Amount: $500-$3,000.
Number of Awards: Varies.

Orgone Biophysical Research Laboratory

P.O. Box 1148
Ashland, OR 97520
Phone: 541-522-0118
Fax: 541-522-0118
Email: info@orgonelab.org
Website: http://www.orgonelab.org

1194 • Lou Hochberg Awards

Purpose: The Orgone Biophysical Research Lab offers a number of awards to students, scholars and journalists through a program set up by Louis Hochberg, a social worker who was dedicated to the sociological discoveries of Wilhelm Reich.

Eligibility: The Lou Hochberg Awards are given to winning theses and dissertations, university and college essays, high school essays and published articles that focus on Reich's sociological work. There are categories for students, scholars or journalists beginning at high school age through adulthood. A suggested list of topics and a bibliography is available online.

How to Apply: Each award has a specific set of instructions for submitting a package for consideration. Guidelines are listed online.

Deadline: Varies.
Amount: $500-$1,500.
Number of Awards: 5.

Pi Sigma Alpha

The Washington Center
2301 M Street NW, Fifth Floor
Washington, DC 20037-1427
Email: info@twc.edu
Website: http://www.apsanet.org/~psa/

1195 • Pi Sigma Alpha Washington Internship Scholarships

Purpose: To provide Pi Sigma Alpha members with scholarships to participate in summer or fall term internships in Washington, DC.

Eligibility: Applicants must belong to Pi Sigma Alpha and be nominated by their local chapter. The award is for a political science internship is based on academic achievement and service to the organization.

How to Apply: Applications are available online.
Deadline: April 15.
Amount: $2,000.
Number of Awards: 4.

Rural Poverty Research Center

Oregon State University
213 Ballard Hall
Corvallis, OR 97331-3601
Phone: 541-737-1442
Fax: 541-737-2563
Email: rprc@oregonstate.edu
Website: http://www.rprconline.org

1196 • Rural Poverty Research Center Undergraduate Fellowships

Purpose: To provide research opportunities for undergraduate students interested in rural poverty.

Eligibility: Applicants must have an interest in pursuing a career in rural poverty research or policy, be U.S. citizens or permanent residents, have a minimum 3.0 GPA in their major and be entering their final year of undergraduate study.

How to Apply: Contact RPRC for application information.
Deadline: Varies.
Amount: $500.
Number of Awards: Varies.

Related Scholarships:

U.S. Department of Health and Human Services National Institutes of Health

See #691 • NIH Undergraduate Scholarship Program

Institute for Humane Studies at George Mason University

See #36 • Humane Studies Fellowships

American Institute for Contemporary German Studies - (AICGS)

See #462 • DAAD/AICGS Research Fellowship Program

Minnesota Higher Education Services Office

See #1433 • Minnesota Academic Excellence Scholarship

American Federation of Teachers

See #1595 • Robert G. Porter Scholars Program

American Radio Relay League Foundation

See #229 • Donald Riebhoff Memorial Scholarship

American Society of Criminology

See #948 • American Society of Criminology Fellowships for Ethnic Minorities

American Society of Criminology Gene Carte Student Paper Competition

See #703 • Gene Carte Student Paper Competition

Association for Women in Science

See #1127 • Association for Women in Science Predoctoral Awards

General Commission on Archives and History, The United Methodist Church

See #1100 • Women in United Methodist History Writing Award

General Commission on Archives and History, The United Methodist Church

See #1099 • Women in United Methodist History Research Grant

General Commission on Archives and History, The United Methodist Church

See #1098 • Racial/Ethnic History Research Grant

Institute for Humane Studies at George Mason University

See #37 • Summer Graduate Research Fellowships

American Institute for Contemporary German Studies (AICGS)

See #461 • German Studies Research Grant

Institute for Humane Studies at George Mason University

See #535 · Young Communicators Fellowships

American Historical Association

See #92 · Fellowship in Aerospace History

Association of Government Accountants (AGA)

See #200 · AGA Scholarships

Davidson Institute for Talent Development

See #20 · Davidson Fellows Award

National Association of Negro Business and Professional Women's Clubs Inc.

See #1024 · Julianne Malveaux Scholarship

National Institutes of Health

See #674 · NIH Undergraduate Scholarship Program for Students from Disadvantaged Backgrounds

American School of Classical Studies at Athens

See #490 · Fellowships for Regular Program

National Council for Geographic Education

See #335 · Women in Geographic Education Scholarship

State of Residence - Alabama

State of Alabama

Commission on Higher Education
100 N. Union Street
P.O. Box 302000
Montgomery, AL 36130
Phone: 334-242-1998
Fax: 334-242-0268
Website: http://www.ache.state.al.us

1197 • Alabama Student Grant Program

Purpose: To assist Alabama residents planning to attend colleges in the state.

Eligibility: Applicants must be Alabama residents attending or planning to attend Birmingham-Southern College, Concordia College, Faulkner University, Huntingdon College, Judson College, Miles College, Oakwood College, Samford University, Selma University, Southeastern Bible College, Southern Vocational College, Spring Hill College, Stillman College or the University of Mobile.

How to Apply: Contact the college financial aid office.
Deadline: Varies.
Amount: Up to $1,200.
Number of Awards: Varies.

1198 • Two-Year College Academic Scholarship Program

Purpose: To assist students attending two-year colleges in Alabama.

Eligibility: Applicants must be accepted for enrollment at a public two-year postsecondary educational institution in Alabama. Selection is based on academic merit and is not based on financial need.

How to Apply: Contact the college financial aid office.
Deadline: Varies.
Amount: Award will not exceed the in-state tuition and books for a public two-year college.
Number of Awards: Varies.

Related Scholarships:

National Association for Campus Activities

See #1288 • NACA Southeast Region Student Leader Scholarship

State of Residence - Alaska

Alaska Commission on Postsecondary Education

3030 Vintage Boulevard
Juneau, AK 99801
Phone: 907-465-6741
Email: customer_service@acpe.state.ak.us
Website: http://alaskaadvantage.state.ak.us/

1199 • GEAR UP ALASKA Scholarship Program

Purpose: To provide financial aid to students in Alaska.

Eligibility: Applicants must be students under the age of 22 who have participated in GEAR UP Programs in 6th, 7th and 8th grade and who have met GEAR UP academic requirements. Students must be seniors at an Alaskan high school or have received a diploma or GED from an Alaskan high school. Applicants must complete the Free Application for Federal Student Aid (FAFSA) and then submit the Student Aid Report (SAR) and federal income tax forms with their application. The award is based on financial need.

How to Apply: Applications are available by contacting the scholarship coordinator.
Deadline: May 31.
Amount: $7,000 for full-time and $3,500 for part-time students.
Number of Awards: Varies.

Alaska Department of Education and Early Development

801 W. 10th Street, Suite 200
P.O. Box 110500
Juneau, AK 99811
Phone: 907-465-2800
Fax: 907-465-4156
Email: melora_gaber@eed.state.ak.us
Website: http://www.eed.state.ak.us

1200 • Robert C. Byrd Honors Scholarship Program - Alaska

Purpose: To support Alaskan high school students in their pursuit of higher education.

Eligibility: Applicants must be high school seniors with the promise of future excellence and achievement. They must be residents of Alaska and U.S. citizens accepted into a college, university or technical school as a full-time student. Applicants must not be in default on any federal student loans. They must include an essay on a social issue of importance to them and three letters of recommendation with their application.

How to Apply: Applications are available online.
Deadline: April 2.
Amount: $1,500.
Number of Awards: 18.

National Association for Campus Activities

13 Harbison Way
Columbia, SC 29212-3401
Phone: 803-732-6222
Fax: 803-749-1047

Email: info@naca.org
Website: http://www.naca.org

1201 • Lori Rhett Memorial Scholarship
Purpose: The scholarship recognizes the achievements of student leaders.
Eligibility: Applicants must hold a significant campus leadership position and demonstrate significant leadership skills and abilities. Students must also be making significant contributions through on- or off-campus volunteering and must attend school in Alaska, Idaho, Montana, Oregon or Washington.
How to Apply: Applications are available online.
Deadline: June 30.
Amount: Varies.
Number of Awards: 1.

Related Scholarships:

CIRI Foundation

See #974 • Foundation Scholarships

State of Residence – Arizona

Arizona Commission for Postsecondary Education

2020 N. Central Avenue, Suite 550
Phoenix, AZ 85004
Phone: 602-258-2435
Fax: 602-258-2483
Email: judi@azhighered.org
Website: http://www.azhighered.org

1202 • Arizona Private Postsecondary Education Student Financial Assistance Program (PFAP)
Purpose: To assist Arizona students earning baccalaureate degrees at private postsecondary schools.
Eligibility: Applicants must be residents of Arizona attending a licensed and accredited private postsecondary institution.
How to Apply: Applications are available through your school's financial aid office.
Deadline: Ongoing.
Amount: Varies.
Number of Awards: Varies.

1203 • Leveraging Educational Assistance Partnership (LEAP)
Purpose: State and federal agencies have partnered together to provide awards to Arizona college and graduate students attending Arizona schools.
Eligibility: Applicants must be Arizona residents attending participating Arizona postsecondary institutions full-time or half-time as undergraduate or graduate students. The award is based on financial need.
How to Apply: Apply through your financial aid office.
Deadline: Varies.
Amount: Varies.
Number of Awards: Varies.

Arizona Department of Education

1535 W. Jefferson Street
Phoenix, AZ 85007
Phone: 800-352-4558
Fax: 602-364-1532
Email: byrd@azed.gov
Website: http://www.ade.state.az.us/byrd/

1204 • Robert C. Byrd Honors Scholarship Program - Arizona
Purpose: To reward Arizona high school students who demonstrate academic excellence.
Eligibility: Applicants must be graduating high school seniors or students who have received a GED who have applied to or been accepted at a post-secondary institution as a full-time student. They must be Arizona residents and U.S. citizens or permanent residents.
How to Apply: Applicants must be nominated by their high schools.
Deadline: March 26.
Amount: $1,500.
Number of Awards: Varies.

Phoenix Suns Charities

P.O. Box 1369
Phoenix, AZ 85001
Website: http://www.suns.com

1205 • Sun Student College Scholarship Program

Purpose: As part of the series of grants offered by the Phoenix Suns to help children in Arizona, the Student College Scholarship Program assists Arizona high school seniors with their college expenses.

Eligibility: Eligible candidates must be seniors in an Arizona high school.

How to Apply: Contact the Phoenix Suns Charities via their website.

Deadline: Varies.

Amount: $1,000-$5,000.

Number of Awards: Varies.

Related Scholarships:

Bank of America

See #290• Bank of America ADA Abilities Scholarship Program

State of Residence - Arkansas

American Legion, Department of Arkansas

Department Oratorical Chairman, Roger Lacy
P.O. Box 3280
Little Rock, AR 72203
Phone: 501-375-1104
Fax: 501-375-4236
Email: alegion@swbell.net
Website: http://www.arlegion.org/Oratorical.html

1206 • Oratorical Contest

Purpose: To enhance high school students' experience with and understanding of the U.S. Constitution. The contest will help develop students' leadership skills and civic appreciation, as well as the ability to deliver thoughtful, insightful orations regarding U.S. citizenship and its inherent responsibilities.

Eligibility: Applicants must be high school students under the age of 20 who are U.S. citizens or legal residents and residents of the state. Students first give an oration within their state and winners compete at the national level. The oration must be related to the Constitution of the United States focusing on the duties and obligations citizens have to the government. It must be in English and be between eight and ten minutes. There is also an assigned topic which is posted on the website, and it should be between three and five minutes.

How to Apply: Applications are available online.

Deadline: December 15.

Amount: $3,500.

Number of Awards: Varies.

Arkansas Department of Education

4 Capitol Mall
Little Rock, AR 72201
Phone: 501-682-4475
Email: ade.communications@arkansas.gov
Website: http://www.arkansased.org

1207 • Robert C. Byrd Honors Scholarship Program - Arkansas

Purpose: To support high-achieving Arkansas high school graduates.

Eligibility: Applicants must be graduating seniors or recipients of the equivalent of a high school diploma. They must be residents of Arkansas admitted to a post-secondary school. Applicants must show current academic achievement with a promise of future achievement. Students with full scholarship awards or who will be attending military academies are not eligible for the scholarship.

How to Apply: Applications are available online.

Deadline: February 16.

Amount: $1,500.

Number of Awards: 62.

Arkansas Department of Higher Education

114 East Capitol
Little Rock, AR 72201-3818
Phone: 501-371-2050
Fax: 501-371-2001
Email: finaid@adhe.arknet.edu
Website: http://www.arkansashighered.com

1208 • Academic Challenge Scholarship

Purpose: To encourage Arkansas high school graduates to enroll in Arkansas colleges and universities.

Eligibility: Applicants must be graduating Arkansas high school seniors who meet academic minimum standards and income requirements.

How to Apply: Applications are available through your high school counselor.

Deadline: June 1.

Amount: Up to $3,500.

Number of Awards: Varies.

1209 • Arkansas Student Assistance Grant Program

Purpose: To help Arkansas students in need.

Eligibility: Applicants must complete the Free Application for Federal Student Aid (FAFSA) as a paper application, a renewal application or an electronic application. They must be eligible for a Pell Grant and meet the other general eligibility requirements for federal financial aid programs. They also must be attending a college within the state full-time. Awards are made on a first come, first served basis.

How to Apply: The FAFSA is available online at http://www.fafsa.ed.gov or by mail.

Deadline: April 1.

Amount: $600.

Number of Awards: Varies.

1210 • Governor's Scholars Program

Purpose: To assist outstanding Arkansas high school graduates to encourage them to attend postsecondary schools in Arkansas.

Eligibility: Applicants must be Arkansas graduating high school seniors who will attend an Arkansas college or university. Selection is based on academic achievement, test scores and leadership. A minimum ACT score of 27, SAT score of 1220 or 3.5 GPA in academic courses is required.

How to Apply: Applications are available through your high school counselor and online.

Deadline: February 1.

Amount: $4,000.

Number of Awards: At least 75.

Arkansas Single Parent Scholarship Fund

614 E. Emma, Suite 119
Springdale, AR 72764
Phone: 479-927-1402
Fax: 479-751-1110
Website: http://www.aspsf.org

1211 • Arkansas Single Parent Scholarship

Purpose: To help single parents attain a post-secondary education.

Eligibility: Applicants must be low-income Arkansas residents who are single parents with custody of a child who is a minor. Applicants must not have a four-year degree.

How to Apply: Applications are available from the ASPSF affiliate in your county.

Deadline: Varies.

Amount: Varies.

Number of Awards: Varies.

Related Scholarships:

Bank of America

See #290• Bank of America ADA Abilities Scholarship Program

National Association for Campus Activities

See #924• Markley Scholarship

State of Residence - California

American Legion Auxiliary, Department of California

401 Van Ness Avenue
Room 113
San Francisco, CA 94102
Phone: 415-861-5092
Fax: 415-861-8365
Email: calegionaux@calegionaux.org
Website: http://www.calegionaux.org

1212 • American Legion Auxiliary, Department of California $1,000 Scholarships

Purpose: To provide support to the children of U.S. Armed Forces members.

Eligibility: One of applicants' parents must have served in the U.S. Armed Forces during an eligible period. Applicants must be California resident high school seniors or graduates who have had to postpone school due to health or financial reasons and plan to attend a California college or university. Applicants must also demonstrate financial need.

How to Apply: Applications are available online.
Deadline: March 15.
Amount: $1,000.
Number of Awards: 5.

1213 • American Legion Auxiliary, Department of California $2,000 Scholarships

Purpose: To provide support to children of U.S. Armed Forces members.

Eligibility: One of applicants' parents must have served in the U.S. Armed Forces during an eligible period. Applicants must attend a California college or university, be California resident high school seniors or graduates who have not begun college because of illness or need and demonstrate need.

How to Apply: Applications are available online.
Deadline: March 15.
Amount: $2,000.
Number of Awards: 1.

1214 • American Legion Auxiliary, Department of California $500 Scholarships

Purpose: To provide support to the children of U.S. Armed Forces members.

Eligibility: One of applicants' parents must have served in the U.S. Armed Forces during an eligible period. Applicants must be California resident high school seniors or graduates who have had to postpone school due to health or financial reasons and plan to attend a California college or university. Applicants must also demonstrate financial need.

How to Apply: Applications are available online.
Deadline: March 15.
Amount: $500.
Number of Awards: 5.

1215 • Continuing/Re-entry Students Scholarship

Purpose: To provide support to children of U.S. Armed Forces members.

Eligibility: One of applicants' parents must have served in the U.S. Armed Forces during an eligible period. Applicants must be California residents planning to attend a California college or university and must be continuing or re-entry college students.

How to Apply: Applications are available online.
Deadline: March 15.
Amount: $1,000.
Number of Awards: 2.

1216 • Past Department Presidents' Junior Scholarship Award

Purpose: To reward American Legion Auxiliary Juniors.

Eligibility: Applicants must be California resident high school students planning to attend a California college or university, be American Legion Auxiliary members with three years as a Junior and be the children, grandchildren or great grandchildren of a veteran.

How to Apply: Applications are available online.
Deadline: April 15.
Amount: Varies.
Number of Awards: 1.

1217 • Past Presidents' Parley Nursing Scholarships

Purpose: To provide support to the U.S. Armed Forces members and their spouses and children.

Eligibility: Applicants be residents of California, enrolled or planning to enroll in a nursing program, and be the wife, husband, widow, widower or child of a veteran or be veterans themselves.

How to Apply: Applications are available online.
Deadline: April 5.
Amount: $500-$1,000.
Number of Awards: Varies.

American Legion, Department of California

401 Van Ness Avenue, Room 117
San Francisco, CA 94102
Phone: 415-431-2400
Fax: 415-255-1571
Email: calegion@pacific.net
Website: http://www.calegion.org

1218 • California Oratorical Contest

Purpose: To enhance high school students' experience with and understanding of the U.S. Constitution. The contest will help develop students' leadership skills and civic appreciation, as well as the ability to deliver thoughtful, insightful orations regarding U.S. citizenship and its inherent responsibilities.

Eligibility: Applicants must be high school students under the age of 20 who are U.S. citizens or legal residents and residents of the state. Students first give an oration within their state and winners compete at the national level. The oration must be related to the Constitution of the United States focusing on the duties and obligations citizens have to the government. It must be in English and be between eight and ten minutes. There is also an assigned topic which is posted on the website, and it should be between three and five minutes.

How to Apply: Applications are available by email.
Deadline: February 25.
Amount: Up to $2,700.
Number of Awards: Varies.

Asian Pacific Fund

225 Bush Street
Suite 590
San Francisco, CA 94104
Phone: 415-433-6859
Email: scholarship@asianpacificfund.org
Website: http://www.asianpacificfund.org

1219 • Lapiz Family Scholarship

Purpose: To support students from farm working backgrounds who attend the University of California.

Eligibility: Applicants must be full-time undergraduate students at University of California (preference given to students at UC Davis and UC Santa Cruz), be farm workers or the children of farm or migrant workers and have a minimum 3.0 GPA. The award is based on merit and financial need. Applicants should submit applications, transcripts, essays, resumes and Student Aid Reports.

How to Apply: Applications are available online.
Deadline: March 31.
Amount: $1,000.
Number of Awards: 2.

Association for Women in Architecture

22815 Frampton Avenue
Torrance, CA 90501-5304
Phone: 310-534-8466
Fax: 310-257-6885
Email: scholarship@awa-la.org
Website: http://www.awa-la.org

1220 • AWA Scholarships

Purpose: To support women studying architecture.

Eligibility: Applicants must be female residents of California or attend a California school and must be enrolled in one of the following majors: architecture, landscape architecture, urban and/or land planning, interior design, environmental design, architectural rendering and illustrating, civil, electrical, mechanical or structural engineering. Applicants must also have completed a minimum of 18 units in their major by the application due date. The award is based on grades, personal statement, financial need, recommendations and submitted materials. Applicants must be able to go to Los Angeles for interviews. Applications, two recommendation letters, transcripts, financial statements, personal statements and self-addressed stamped envelopes are required.

How to Apply: Applications are available online.
Deadline: April 27.
Amount: $2,500.
Number of Awards: Varies.

California Association of Private Postsecondary Schools

400 Capitol Mall
Suite 1560
Sacramento, CA 95814
Phone: 916-447-5500
Email: info@cappsonline.org
Website: http://www.cappsonline.org

1221 • CAPPS Scholarship Program

Purpose: To allow private postsecondary schools to offer tuition scholarships to students.

Eligibility: Applicants must be legal California residents who have fulfilled the admission requirements for the school that is pledging their CAPPS scholarship. Application is restricted to high school and adult students only. Recipients are chosen on the basis of application date and each individual school's judging standards.
How to Apply: Applications are available online.
Deadline: July 21.
Amount: Varies.
Number of Awards: Varies.

California Chicano News Media Association

USC Annenberg School of Journalism
One California Plaza
300 S. Grand Avenue, Suite 3950
Los Angeles, CA 90071-3175
Phone: 213-437-4408
Fax: 213-437-4423
Email: ccmainfo@ccnma.org
Website: http://www.ccnma.org

1222 • CCNMA Scholarships

Purpose: To support Latino students with career goals in journalism.

Eligibility: Applicants must be Latino and either California residents or be attending California schools. While the students' degree does not have to be in journalism, they must demonstrate plans to pursue a career in journalism. An interview and autobiographical essay are required. Awards are based also on financial need, academic achievement and a civic responsibility.

How to Apply: Applications are available online.
Deadline: April 3.
Amount: $500-$2,000.
Number of Awards: Varies.

1223 • Frank del Olmo Memorial Scholarship

Purpose: To assist California Latino college students who demonstrate a desire to pursue a career in journalism.

Eligibility: Applicants must be Latino, be either California residents or attending California schools and have an interest in pursuing a journalism career. An interview is required. Financial need, academic achievement and community involvement are also considered.

How to Apply: Applications are available online.
Deadline: April 3.
Amount: $500-$2,000.
Number of Awards: Varies.

1224 • Joel Garcia Memorial Scholarship

Purpose: To support Latino students studying journalism who are California residents or are attending California schools.

Eligibility: Applicants must be Latino and either attending California schools or be California residents attending out-of-state schools. Students must show an interest in journalism (broadcast, print, photo or online) and demonstrate financial need and academic achievement.

How to Apply: Applications are available online, by email, by mail or by phone.
Deadline: April.
Amount: $500-$2,000.
Number of Awards: Varies.

California Community Foundation

445 S. Figueroa Street, Suite 3400
Los Angeles, CA 90071-1638
Phone: 213-413-4130
Fax: 213-622-2979
Website: http://www.calfund.org

1225 • CalFund 150+ Scholarship Programs

Purpose: To assist California residents attending college or graduate school.

Eligibility: The fund has about $2 million which is disbursed through a variety of scholarships for California residents pursuing higher education through undergraduate or graduate work in or out of state. There are scholarships for students pursuing specific majors, with specific personal, academic or leadership qualities and that honor family members or colleagues.

How to Apply: Please contact your financial aid office for more information.

Deadline: Varies.

Amount: Varies.

Number of Awards: 150.

California Council of the Blind

578 B Street
Hayward, CA 94541
Phone: 510-537-7877
Fax: 510-537-7830
Email: ccotb@earthlink.net
Website: http://www.ccbnet.org

1226 • California Council of the Blind Scholarships

Purpose: To assist blind California residents for college, graduate or vocational studies.

Eligibility: Applicants must be legally blind residents of California attending an accredited college, university or vocational school full-time or with at least 12 units per term. The school does not have to be in California. Proof of blindness is required. A letter from the local chapter's president or member recommending the applicant is helpful. Award money can't be spent on food, clothing or shelter.

How to Apply: Applications are available online.

Deadline: June 15.

Amount: Varies.

Number of Awards: Varies.

California Health and Welfare Agency - Office of Statewide Health Planning and Development

Health Professions Education Foundation
818 K Street, Room 210
Sacramento, CA 95814
Phone: 916-324-6500
Fax: 916-324-6585
Email: hpef@oshpd.state.ca.us
Website: http://www.healthprofessions.ca.gov

1227 • Allied Healthcare Scholarship Program

Purpose: To increase the number of allied healthcare professional working in medically underserved areas of California.

Eligibility: Applicants must be enrolled in a California community college or university and be studying one of the following programs: medical imaging, occupational therapy, physical therapy, respiratory care, social work, pharmacy and diagnostic medical sonography, pharmacy technician, medical laboratory technologist, surgical technician or ultrasound technician. Those selected will complete a one-year service contract or work volunteer hours in a medically underserved area of California. Financial need, work experience, academic achievement and community involvement are considered. Preference is given to those who expect to graduate within two years of application.

How to Apply: Applications are available online.

Deadline: March, September.

Amount: Up to $4,000.

Number of Awards: Varies.

1228 • Associate Degree Nursing Scholarship Program

Purpose: To increase the number of registered nurses working in medically underserved areas of California.

Eligibility: Applicants must be California residents enrolled in an associate degree nursing program at a California school, agree to pursue a bachelor's degree in nursing within five years and be fluent in a language other than English. Financial need, work experience, community involvement and academic achievement are considered. Preference is given to those who will graduate within two years and to those who plan to remain in a medically underserved area past the service time required. Recipients must sign a two-year service contract to work in a medically underserved area as an RN.

How to Apply: Applications are available online.

Deadline: March, September.

Amount: $8,000.

Number of Awards: Varies.

1229 • Bachelor of Science Nursing Scholarship Program

Purpose: To increase the number of professional nurses practicing in medically underserved areas of California by assisting nursing students attending California schools.

Eligibility: Applicants must be attending a California undergraduate nursing program and be fluent in a language other than English. Financial need, work experience, academic achievement and community involvement are considered. A two-year service agreement to work in a medically underserved area of California is required. Preference is given to those who expect to graduate within two years and to those who plan to remain in a medically underserved area after the service agreement has expired.

How to Apply: Applications are available online.

Deadline: March, September.

Amount: $10,000.

Number of Awards: Varies.

1230 • Health Professions Education Scholarship Program

Purpose: To increase medical care to underserved areas of California by assisting residents who are studying to become dentists, dental hygienists, nurse practitioners, certified midwives and physician assistants.

Eligibility: Applicants must be California residents who have been accepted by or are enrolled in an accredited California program. Financial need, work experience and career goals are considered, and preference is given to applicants who plan to remain in a medically underserved area past the service time. Those selected must sign a two-year service agreement to work in a medically underserved area of California.

How to Apply: Applications are available online.
Deadline: March.
Amount: $10,000.
Number of Awards: Varies.

1231 • Pre-Nursing Scholarship Program

Purpose: To increase the number of registered nurses in medically underserved areas by providing assistance to pre-nursing students in Central Valley counties in California.

Eligibility: Applicants must be pre-nursing students who are fluent in a language other than English and enrolled in schools in the Central Valley counties of Fresno, Kern, Kings, Madera, Merced or Tulare. Financial need, academic achievement, work experience and community involvement are considered. Preference is given to applicants who plan to remain in a medically underserved area after the service term and Associate Degree Nursing candidates.

How to Apply: Applications are available online.
Deadline: March, September.
Amount: $4,000.
Number of Awards: Varies.

1232 • Youth for Adolescent Pregnancy Prevention-Leadership Recognition Program

Purpose: To assist California students who promote teen pregnancy prevention and healthy adolescent sexuality.

Eligibility: Applicants must be California residents between the ages of 16 and 24, have either a high school diploma or GED and plan to or are already enrolled in a health profession program. Recipients must sign a two-year service agreement to work in a medically underserved area within six months following graduation from the program.

How to Apply: Applications are available online.
Deadline: November.
Amount: $25,000.
Number of Awards: Varies.

California Interscholastic Federation (CIF)

CIF State Office
Attn.: CIF Scholar-Athlete of the Year
1320 Harbor Bay Parkway, Suite 140
Alameda, CA 94502
Phone: 510-521-4447
Fax: 510-521-4449
Email: info@cifstate.org
Website: http://www.cifstate.org

1233 • California Interscholastic Federation (CIF) Scholar-Athlete of the Year

Purpose: To recognize high school student-athletes with exemplary academic and athletic careers and personal standards.

Eligibility: Applicants must be high school seniors with a minimum 3.7 GPA, demonstrate outstanding athletic performance in a minimum of two years of varsity play in California and exhibit character, trustworthiness, respect, responsibility, fairness, caring and citizenship.

How to Apply: Applications are available by request.
Deadline: March.
Amount: Varies.
Number of Awards: 2.

California Masonic Foundation

1111 California Street
San Francisco, CA 94108
Phone: 415-776-7000
Email: gloffice@freemason.org
Website: http://www.freemason.org

1234 • California Masonic Foundation Scholarship

Purpose: To aid students in pursuit of a higher education.

Eligibility: Applicants must be U.S. citizens, be California residents for at least one year, be current high school seniors with a minimum 3.0 GPA, plan to attend an accredited two- or four-year college or university full-time and demonstrate financial need. There are a number of awards based on residence, career goals and general selection criteria.

How to Apply: Applications are available online.
Deadline: Varies.
Amount: $500-$12,000.
Number of Awards: Varies.

California Nurses Association

2000 Franklin Street
Oakland, CA 94612
Phone: 510-273-2200
Email: execoffice@calnurses.org
Website: http://www.calnurse.org

1235 • Shirley C. Titus Scholarship Fund

Purpose: To assist California nurses to make them better leaders in the nursing profession.

Eligibility: Applicants must submit an essay describing their educational goals and vision for healthcare, two letters of recommendation, curriculum vitae and a copy of current RN license. Applications are based on educational plans, professional vision and participation in CNA, nursing or health-related organizations.

How to Apply: Applications are available online.
Deadline: July 1.
Amount: Varies.
Number of Awards: Varies.

California School Library Association

1001 26th Street
Sacramento, CA 95816
Phone: 916-447-2684
Fax: 916-447-2695
Email: csla@pacbell.net
Website: http://www.schoollibrary.org

1236 • John Blanchard Memorial Scholarship

Purpose: To assist a school library paraprofessional in becoming a certified school library media teacher.

Eligibility: Applicants must be members of the California School Library Association who are currently working or have worked in the last three years in a classified library position. Candidates must be currently enrolled in a degree program for certification as a library media teacher and California residents planning to work in California after completing their programs. Three letters of recommendation are required.

How to Apply: Applications are available online.
Deadline: June 30.
Amount: $2,000.
Number of Awards: 1.

1237 • Leadership for Diversity Scholarship

Purpose: To encourage diversity in the library media teacher profession.

Eligibility: Applicants must be members of a traditionally underrepresented group attending or planning to attend an accredited library media teacher credential program and plan to work in California for three years after completing the program. Applicants must provide a 250-word statement about their qualifications, career goals, financial situation and commitment to supporting multicultural students and two letters of reference.

How to Apply: Applications are available online.
Deadline: June 30.
Amount: $1,500.
Number of Awards: 1.

California School Library Association Jewel Gardiner Memorial Scholarship

Chair
717 K Street
Suite 515
Sacramento, CA 95814
Email: ebell@pleasanton.k12.ca.us
Website: http://www.schoollibrary.org

1238 • Jewel Gardiner Memorial Scholarship

Purpose: To encourage students in library media teacher programs.

Eligibility: Applicants must be currently enrolled in a library media teacher program or have been enrolled at any time during the previous year. Preference is given to first-time award recipients, current California School Library Association members and candidates with teaching experience. Applicants may win the award twice.

How to Apply: Applications are available online.
Deadline: August 1 and November 1.
Amount: $1,000.
Number of Awards: 2 (1 for each semester).

California School Library Association Paraprofessional Scholarship

1001 26th Street
Sacramento, CA 95816
Phone: 916-447-2684
Fax: 916-447-2695
Email: csla@pacbell.net
Website: http://www.schoollibrary.org

1239 • Library Media Teacher Scholarship

Purpose: To encourage students who plan to become library media teachers.

Eligibility: Applicants must be currently enrolled in a school library media credential program or master's degree program. Candidates must be residents of the California School Library Association Southern Section region and must provide three letters of recommendation.

How to Apply: Applications are available online.
Deadline: March 11.
Amount: $1,500.
Number of Awards: 1.

1240 • Paraprofessional Scholarship

Purpose: To increase the number of trained and qualified library technicians in Southern California.

Eligibility: Applicants must be classified library media workers currently enrolled in a two-year paraprofessional program to become a certified library technician. Students must be Southern California residents planning to work in California as library media technicians after completing the program and be members of the California School Library Association. Three letters of recommendation are required.

How to Apply: Applications are available online.
Deadline: February 15.
Amount: $250.
Number of Awards: 1.

1241 • Paraprofessional-to-LMT Scholarship

Purpose: To support school library paraprofessionals who plan to become certified library media teachers.

Eligibility: Applicants must be working or have worked within the last three years in a classified library media position and be currently enrolled in a degree program for a Library Media Teacher credential. Candidates must also be Southern California residents planning to work as Library Media Teachers upon finishing the program and be members of the California School Library Association. Three letters of recommendation are required.

How to Apply: Applications are available online.
Deadline: March 11.
Amount: $500.
Number of Awards: 1.

California State PTA

930 Georgia Street
Los Angeles, CA 90015-1322
Phone: 213-620-1100
Fax: 213-620-1411
Website: http://www.capta.org

1242 • California State PTA Scholarship

Purpose: To support high school seniors who have contributed to the community.

Eligibility: Applicants must attend a public California high school, be high school seniors who have served their school and community and be members of the PTA.

How to Apply: Applications are available online.
Deadline: Varies.
Amount: Varies.
Number of Awards: Varies.

California Student Aid Commission

P.O. Box 419026
Rancho Cordova, CA 95741
Phone: 888-224-7268
Fax: 916-526-8002
Website: http://www.csac.ca.gov

1243 • Cal Grant Entitlement Award

Purpose: To support California resident students.

Eligibility: Applicants must complete the Free Application for Federal Student Aid (FAFSA) and file a verified grade point average with the California Student Aid Commission. Students must be California residents, be U.S. citizens or eligible noncitizens, meet U.S. Selective Service requirements, attend an eligible California postsecondary institution, be enrolled at least half-time, maintain satisfactory academic progress and not be in default on any student loan. Cal Grant A Entitlement Awards are for undergraduate institutions of not less than two academic years. Cal Grant B Entitlement Awards are for low-income students for living and transportation expenses, supplies and books at institutions of not less than one year. Cal Grant C Awards are for occupational or vocational programs. Cal Grant T Awards are for teacher credential candidates.

How to Apply: Applications are available by request.

Deadline: March 2.

Amount: Varies.

Number of Awards: Varies.

California Student Aid Commission (CSAC)

Attn.: Robert C. Byrd Honors Scholarship Program
P.O. Box 419029
Rancho Cordova, CA 95741-9029
Phone: 888-224-7268
Email: studentsupport@csac.ca.gov
Website: http://www.csac.ca.gov

1244 • Robert C. Byrd Honors Scholarship Program - California

Purpose: To aid outstanding California resident students.

Eligibility: Applicants must be legal residents of California who are U.S. citizens or eligible noncitizens. Applicants must enroll in and attend a U.S. postsecondary institution on a full-time basis as freshmen, have registered with the Selective Service System and submit a certification form attesting that they are not delinquent or in default on a federal scholarship or educational loan. The Commission reviews applicants by grade point average.

How to Apply: Students must apply through their high school program coordinator. Students not currently enrolled in a California high school may obtain an application directly from the California Student Aid Commission.

Deadline: April 27.

Amount: $1,500.

Number of Awards: Varies.

California Teachers Association (CTA)

CTA Human Rights Department
P.O. Box 921
Burlingame, CA 94011-0921
Phone: 650-697-1400
Fax: 650-552-5001
Website: http://www.cta.org

1245 • CTA César E. Chávez Memorial Education Awards Program

Purpose: To honor César Chávez by rewarding students and teachers who follow his vision and guiding principles.

Eligibility: A student or group of up to five students must submit an essay or visual piece under the supervision of a teacher or professor who is a member of the CTA. Students may be in kindergarten through high school or in community college. All works must focus on topics such as non-violence and their relationship to Chávez's legacy. Visit the website for a complete list of topics and specific essay and visual arts submission requirements.

How to Apply: Applications are available online.

Deadline: March 24.

Amount: Varies.

Number of Awards: Varies.

Chicana/Latina Foundation Scholarship Program

1419 Burlingame Avenue, Suite N
Burlingame, CA 94010
Phone: 650-373-1084
Fax: 650-373-1090
Email: info@chicanalatina.org
Website: http://www.chicanalatina.org

1246 • Chicana/Latina Foundation Scholarship

Purpose: To assist Latina students in completing their educations.

Eligibility: Applicants must be Chicana/Latina women who have lived in the Northern California counties for at least two years and are attending school at an accredited institution in the same region. Undergraduate applicants must be full-time students who have completed at least 15 semester units and earned a 2.5 GPA. Applicants must demonstrate leadership and community involvement and agree to volunteer at least five years in support of the Chicana/Latina Foundation if they receive the scholarship.

How to Apply: Applications are available online.

Deadline: March 20.

Amount: $1,500.

Number of Awards: Varies.

Consulting Engineers and Land Surveyors of California

1303 J Street
Suite 450
Sacramento, CA 95814
Phone: 916-441-7991
Fax: 916-441-6312
Website: http://www.celsoc.org

1247 • Engineering and Land Surveying Scholarships

Purpose: To help undergraduate and graduate students studying engineering or land surveying at California schools.

Eligibility: Applicants must be entering their third or fourth year (or fifth year of a five-year program) of undergraduate study for the upper division scholarships, or be entering or continuing graduate study for the graduate scholarships. Undergraduate students must be enrolled full-time and working toward a degree at an accredited engineering or land surveying program. Graduate students must be enrolled at least half time and working toward a degree at an accredited engineering or land surveying program. Students must submit application folders, including 500-word essays, transcripts, and recommendation forms.

How to Apply: Applications are available online.

Deadline: April 28.

Amount: $7,500.

Number of Awards: Varies.

National Medical Fellowships Inc. California Community Service Scholarship

The Chancery Building
564 Market Street
Suite 209
San Francisco, CA 94104
Phone: 415-397-2526
Fax: 415-397-2556
Email: info@nmfonline.org
Website: http://www.nmfonline.org

1248 • California Community Service Scholarship Program

Purpose: To allow minority students to participate in research or community-based clinical training to promote health issues of medically underserved communities in California.

Eligibility: Applicants must be African American, mainland Puerto Rican, Mexican American, Native Hawaiian, Alaska Native or American Indian second- or third-year students at California medical schools. The award is for the third or fourth year of medical school and is based on commitment to practice in California, interest in community-based primary care, academic performance, leadership and financial need. Recommendation letters, applications, statements, transcripts, financial aid documents and essays are required.

How to Apply: Applications are available online.

Deadline: January 15.

Amount: $7,500.

Number of Awards: Varies.

Related Scholarships:

Bank of America

See #290• Bank of America ADA Abilities Scholarship Program

American Society of Travel Agents (ASTA) Foundation Inc.

See #525• Southern California Chapter/Pleasant Hawaiian Holidays Scholarship

American Nursery and Landscape Association

See #113• Usrey Family Scholarship

California Teachers Association (CTA)

See #757• CTA Scholarship for Dependent Children

California School Library Association

See #588• Above and Beyond Scholarship

California Teachers Association (CTA)

See #759• L. Gordon Bittle Memorial Scholarship for Student CTA (SCTA)

California Teachers Association (CTA)

See #758• CTA Scholarship for Members

California Teachers Association (CTA)

See #760• Martin Luther King, Jr. Memorial Scholarship

State of Residence – Colorado

American Legion, Department of Colorado

7465 E. 1st Avenue, Suite D
Denver, CO 80230
Phone: 303-366-5201
Fax: 303-366-7618
Email: garylbarnett@comcast.net
Website: http://www.coloradolegion.org

1249 • Colorado Oratorical Contest

Purpose: To enhance high school students' experience with and understanding of the U.S. Constitution. The contest will help develop students' leadership skills and civic appreciation, as well as the ability to deliver thoughtful, insightful orations regarding U.S. citizenship and its inherent responsibilities.
Eligibility: Applicants must be high school students under the age of 20 who are U.S. citizens or legal residents and residents of the state. Students first give an oration within their state and winners compete at the national level. The oration must be related to the Constitution of the United States focusing on the duties and obligations citizens have to the government. It must be in English and be between eight and ten minutes. There is also an assigned topic which is posted on the website, and it should be between three and five minutes.
How to Apply: Applications are available online.
Deadline: March 10.
Amount: Up to $4,000.
Number of Awards: Varies.

Boettcher Foundation

600 Seventeenth Street
Suite 2210 South
Denver, CO 80202
Phone: 800-323-9640
Email: scholarships@boettcherfoundation.org
Website: http://www.boettcherfoundation.org

1250 • Boettcher Foundation Scholarship

Purpose: To recognize high school seniors who plan to make contributions to the people in the state of Colorado.
Eligibility: Applicants must be high school seniors and current, legal residents of the state of Colorado who will graduate in the top 5 percent of their class. Applicants must have a composite score of 27 on the ACT or 1200 on the SAT. Selection is based on academic merit, demonstration of leadership skills, community service and character.
How to Apply: Contact the Boettcher Foundation for more information.
Deadline: November 1.
Amount: Varies.
Number of Awards: Varies.

Colorado Commission on Higher Education

1380 Lawrence
12th Floor
Denver, CO 80204
Phone: 303-866-2723
Fax: 303-866-4266
Email: cche@state.co.us
Website: http://www.state.co.us/cche

1251 • Colorado Student Aid Program

Purpose: To assist Colorado student residents.
Eligibility: Applicants must be Colorado residents who plan to enroll or are enrolled in eligible programs at eligible Colorado postsecondary institutions. Applicants must make satisfactory academic progress and have not defaulted in educational loans or grants. Awards are need-based and merit-based and are made by institutions to students.
How to Apply: Contact your financial aid office.
Deadline: Varies.
Amount: Varies.
Number of Awards: Varies.

1252 • Colorado Undergraduate Merit Scholarships

Purpose: To help students attending Colorado state-supported institutions at the undergraduate level.
Eligibility: Applicants must be Colorado residents, demonstrate academic achievement and have not defaulted on any student loans. A transcript, test scores and application form are required. The award may be used for tuition, fees, room, board, books, supplies or other expenses related to attendance at participating Colorado institutions. A list of these institutions is available on the website.
How to Apply: Contact the financial aid office at participating institutions.
Deadline: Varies.
Amount: Varies.
Number of Awards: Varies.

1253 • Governor's Opportunity Scholarship

Purpose: To help Colorado college freshmen with financial need attend colleges in the state.
Eligibility: Applicants must be U.S. citizens or permanent residents, plan to attend college full-time and have an Expected Family Contribution or parental contribution of "0" on the Free Application for Federal Student Aid (FAFSA). Students should apply to their desired college and submit the FAFSA. Then, nominators and students must submit the Governor's Opportunity Scholarship nomination form to each institution to which the student is applying. A copy should also be sent to the Colorado Commission on Higher Education.
How to Apply: Nomination forms are available online.
Deadline: Varies.
Amount: Varies.
Number of Awards: 250.

Colorado Department of Education

Competitive Grants and Awards Unit
1560 Broadway, Suite 1450
Denver, CO 80202
Phone: 303-866-6243
Fax: 303-866-6647
Email: hitt_p@cde.state.co.us
Website: http://www.cde.state.co.us/cdeawards/byrd.htm

1254 • Robert C. Byrd Honors Scholarship Program - Colorado

Purpose: To promote academic excellence in Colorado high school seniors.

Eligibility: Applicants must be Colorado residents graduating from high school or receiving a GED. They must also be U.S. citizens or national or permanent residents of the U.S. Applicants must have an unweighted GPA of at least 3.8 or a weighted GPA of at least 4.0 and have received a score of 31 or above on the ACT or a score of 2040 or above on the SAT. Students receiving a GED must score in the top 5 percent of Colorado GED scores. Applicants must be accepted into an accredited post-secondary institution and provide proof of acceptance with the application.

How to Apply: Applications are available online.
Deadline: April 6.
Amount: $1,500.
Number of Awards: Varies.

Henry Sachs Foundation

90 S. Cascade Avenue
Suite 1410
Colorado Springs, CO 80903
Phone: 719-633-2353
Email: info@sachsfoundation.org
Website: http://www.sachsfoundation.org

1255 • Henry Sachs Foundation Scholarship

Purpose: To aid African American high school students in Colorado to obtain a college education.

Eligibility: Applicants must be African-American residents of Colorado for at least five years. Applicants must be either seniors in high school or have graduated in the last 3 years but are not currently attending college. Awards are based on high school grade point average and financial need. If selected, applicants must attend a personal interview in order to receive the grant money.

How to Apply: Applications are available online.
Deadline: March 1.
Amount: $4,000.
Number of Awards: 50.

Related Scholarships:

Alert Magazine

See #1567 • *Alert Scholarship*

State of Residence - Connecticut

Connecticut Department of Higher Education

61 Woodland Street
Hartford, CT 06105
Phone: 860-947-1855
Fax: 860-947-1311
Email: sfa@ctdhe.org
Website: http://www.ctdhe.org

1256 • Capitol Scholarship

Purpose: To assist Connecticut student residents.

Eligibility: Applicants must be Connecticut residents who are U.S. citizens or permanent resident aliens and high school seniors or graduates in the top 20 percent of their class or with a minimum SAT score of 1200. The award must be used at a Connecticut college or at colleges in states that have reciprocity agreements and is based on financial need.

How to Apply: Applications are available online.
Deadline: February 15.
Amount: Up to $2,000.
Number of Awards: Varies.

1257 • Connecticut Aid for Public College Students

Purpose: To assist Connecticut student residents.

Eligibility: Applicants must be Connecticut residents attending a public Connecticut college or university. The award is based on financial need.

How to Apply: Apply through your college financial aid office.
Deadline: Varies.
Amount: Up to amount of unmet financial need.
Number of Awards: Varies.

1258 • Connecticut Independent College Student Grant Program

Purpose: To assist Connecticut student residents.

Eligibility: Applicants must be Connecticut residents attending an independent Connecticut college or university. Awards are based on financial need.

How to Apply: Apply through your college financial aid office.
Deadline: Varies.
Amount: Up to $8,500.
Number of Awards: Varies.

1259 • Robert C. Byrd Honors Scholarship Program - Connecticut

Purpose: To assist Connecticut student residents.

Eligibility: Applicants must be Connecticut residents who are high school seniors ranking in the top 2 percent of their class or with SAT scores of at least 1400. Selection is based on SAT scores and class rank.

How to Apply: Applications are available online.
Deadline: April 1.
Amount: $1,500.
Number of Awards: Varies.

Related Scholarships:

Community Foundation of Western Massachusetts

See #1411 • Putnam Scholarship

New England Board of Higher Education

See #1421 • New England Regional Student Program

Big Y

See #1406 • Big Y Scholarships

State of Residence - Delaware

Delaware Higher Education Commission

Carvel State Office Building, 5th Floor
820 N. French Street
Wilmington, DE 19801
Phone: 800-292-7935
Fax: 302-577-6765
Email: dhec@doe.k12.de.us
Website: http://www.doe.state.de.us/high-ed/

1260 • Agenda for Delaware Women Trailblazer Scholarship

Purpose: To support female Delaware undergraduate students.

Eligibility: Applicants must be legal residents of Delaware who will enroll in a public or private nonprofit college in Delaware as an undergraduate with a minimum 2.5 GPA. Based 50 percent on financial need and 50 percent on community and school activities, vision, participation and leadership.

How to Apply: Applications are available online.

Deadline: April 12.

Amount: $2,500.

Number of Awards: 2.

1261 • Delaware Diamond State Scholarship

Purpose: To support Delaware student residents.

Eligibility: Applicants must be residents of Delaware, U.S. citizens or eligible non-citizens, high school seniors who rank in the upper quarter of their class and score a minimum of 1200 on the SAT or 27 on the ACT and enroll as full-time students in a degree program at a regionally accredited college.

How to Apply: Complete the Common Merit application from the Delaware Higher Education Commission, available online.

Deadline: March 31.

Amount: $1,250.

Number of Awards: 50.

1262 • Delaware Governor's Workforce Development Grant

Purpose: To assist students who are also working in Delaware.

Eligibility: Applicants must be residents of Delaware and U.S. citizens or eligible non-citizens who are 18 or older. Applicants must meet income requirements. Students must attend a participating school in Delaware on a part-time basis and be employed in Delaware full-time with a small employer, part-time, through temporary employment or through self-employment. Applicants must be employed by an eligible employer who contributes to the Blue Collar Training Fund Program. Academic progress is monitored.

How to Apply: Applications are available online.

Deadline: End of free drop/add period each semester.

Amount: Up to $2,000.

Number of Awards: Varies.

1263 • Delaware Scholarship Incentive Program

Purpose: To assist Delaware student residents.

Eligibility: Applicants must be legal residents of Delaware and U.S. citizens or eligible non-citizens who are enrolled full-time at a regionally-accredited undergraduate institution in Delaware or Pennsylvania. Other undergraduate and graduate students will be considered if their major is not available at a public college in Delaware. Students must demonstrate substantial financial need and have a minimum 2.5 GPA. Applicants must also submit the Free Application for Federal Student Aid (FAFSA).

How to Apply: Delaware residents are automatically considered for the scholarship when their FAFSA form is received.

Deadline: April 15.

Amount: $700-$2,220.

Number of Awards: Varies.

1264 • Legislative Essay Scholarship

Purpose: To reward Delaware high school seniors who submit winning essays.

Eligibility: Applicants must be seniors in public or private schools or in home school programs who plan to enroll full-time at nonprofit, regionally accredited colleges. Applicants should submit essays on a topic listed on the website.

How to Apply: Applications are available online.

Deadline: November 30.

Amount: $1,000.

Number of Awards: Up to 62.

1265 • Robert C. Byrd Honors Scholarship Program - Delaware

Purpose: To support Delaware resident students.

Eligibility: Applicants must be residents of Delaware, U.S. citizens or eligible noncitizens, high school seniors who rank in the upper quarter of their class or GED recipients who score at least 300 on the GED examination, score a minimum of 1200 on the SAT or 27 on the ACT and enroll at least half-time at a regionally-accredited institution of higher education. The program is dependent on U.S. Congressional funding.

How to Apply: Complete the Common Merit application from the Delaware Higher Education Commission, available online.

Deadline: March 31.

Amount: $1,500.

Number of Awards: 20.

Fresh Start Scholarship Foundation

P.O. Box 7784
Wilmington, DE 19803
Phone: 302-656-4411
Fax: 610-347-0438
Email: fsscholar@comcast.net
Website: http://www.wwb.org/freshstart.html

1266 • Fresh Start Scholarship

Purpose: To help women who are returning to school.

Eligibility: Applicants should be women at least 20 years old with financial need who have a high school diploma or G.E.D., have had at least a two year break in education either after finishing high school or during college studies and are enrolled in a Delaware college in a two- or four-year degree program at the undergraduate level. Applicants should have at least a C average if already in college.

How to Apply: Applications are available online or by mail and include a personal statement. A social service agency or college representative should recommend applicants.

Deadline: May 31.

Amount: Varies.

Number of Awards: Varies.

Related Scholarships:

National Association for Campus Activities

See #1482 • NACA East Coast Undergraduate Scholarship for Student Leaders

State of Residence – District of Columbia

DC Tuition Assistance Grant Office

441 4th Street NW
Suite 350 North
Washington, DC 20001
Phone: 202-727-2824
Website: http://www.tuitiongrant.dc.gov

1267 • District of Columbia Tuition Assistance Grant

Purpose: To make attending out-of-state, private and Historically Black schools more affordable for DC residents.

Eligibility: Applicants must be residents of the District of Columbia for at least 12 months before the start of their freshman year of college; high school graduates, GED recipients or enrolled in an eligible institution; enrolled at least half-time at an eligible institution; maintain satisfactory academic progress; not have defaulted on student loans; have registered with the Selective Service; be U.S. citizens or permanent residents have not already received a B.A. or B.S, and not incarcerated.

How to Apply: Applications are available online.

Deadline: June 30.

Amount: Up to $10,000 per year for students attending U.S. public colleges or universities.

Number of Awards: Varies.

Government of the District of Columbia

D.C. Tuition Assistance Grant Program
441 4th Street NW, Suite 350 North
Washington, DC 20001
Phone: 877-485-6751
Website: http://www.tuitiongrant.washingtondc.gov

1268 • D.C. Tuition Assistance Grant Program

Purpose: To provide financial assistance to students in the District of Columbia who wish to attend either a public university in a different state or a historically Black college or university.

Eligibility: Applicants must be residents who have lived in the District of Columbia for at least 12 months prior to the beginning of their freshman year of college. Applicants must also either plan to or be currently enrolled at least half-time in an undergraduate or certificate program.

How to Apply: Applications are available online.

Deadline: June 30.

Amount: Up to $10,000.

Number of Awards: Varies.

Related Scholarships:

Bank of America

See #290• Bank of America ADA Abilities Scholarship Program

National Association for Campus Activities

See #1482• NACA East Coast Undergraduate Scholarship for Student Leaders

Central Scholarship Bureau

See #1390• Shoe City-WB54/WB50 Scholarship

State of Residence - Florida

American Legion, Department of Florida

P.O. Box 547859
Orlando, FL 32854
Phone: 407-295-2631
Fax: 407-299-0901
Website: http://www.floridalegion.org

1269 • Florida Oratorical Contest

Purpose: To enhance high school students' experience with and understanding of the U.S. Constitution. The contest will help develop students' leadership skills and civic appreciation, as well as the ability to deliver thoughtful, insightful orations regarding U.S. citizenship and its inherent responsibilities.
Eligibility: Applicants must be high school students under the age of 20 who are U.S. citizens or legal residents and residents of the state. Students first give an oration within their state and winners compete at the national level. The oration must be related to the Constitution of the United States focusing on the duties and obligations citizens have to the government. It must be in English and be between eight and ten minutes. There is also an assigned topic which is posted on the website, and it should be between three and five minutes.
How to Apply: Applications are available by contacting the local American Legion Post.
Deadline: Varies.
Amount: Up to $4,000.
Number of Awards: Varies.

Florida Association of Postsecondary Schools and Colleges

150 S. Monroe Street, Suite 303
Tallahassee, FL 32301
Phone: 850-577-3139
Fax: 850-577-3133
Email: mail@fapsc.org
Website: http://www.fapsc.org

1270 • Florida Association of Postsecondary Schools and Colleges Scholarship Program

Purpose: To provide full and partial-tuition scholarships to Florida students.
Eligibility: Applicants must either be graduating from high school or receiving a GED in Florida.
How to Apply: Applications are available from guidance counselors and participating FAPSC schools.
Deadline: March 1.
Amount: Varies.
Number of Awards: Varies.

Florida Department of Education

Office of Student Financial Assistance
1940 N. Monroe Street
Suite 70
Tallahassee, FL 32303-4759
Phone: 888-827-2004
Fax: 850-245-9667
Email: osfa@fldoe.org
Website: http://www.floridastudentfinancialaid.org

1271 • Access to Better Learning and Education Grant Program

Purpose: To help undergraduate students from Florida who want to attend Florida private colleges or universities.
Eligibility: Applicants must be Florida residents for at least a year and first-time undergraduate students enrolled in degree programs (except theology or divinity degrees). Applicants must meet Florida's general state aid eligibility requirements. Participating institutions determine application procedures, deadlines and student eligibility.
How to Apply: Contact the financial aid office at eligible Florida colleges and universities.
Deadline: Varies.
Amount: Varies.
Number of Awards: Varies.

1272 • Critical Teacher Shortage Loan Forgiveness Program

Purpose: To help Florida public school teachers with loans.
Eligibility: Applicants should be teaching in the critical shortage area full-time at least 90 days of the school year under contract at a publicly funded Florida school, and they should have valid Florida teacher's certificates (temporary or professional) or Florida Department of Health licenses (temporary or permanent) in the same critical shortage area as teaching. Applicants must apply by the end of the first year of having both the critical shortage position and the critical shortage certificate or license. This program helps repay undergraduate and graduate educational loans that led to certification in a critical teacher shortage subject area, and the loans must have paid for courses before becoming a certified teacher. Applicants should submit applications and transcripts. A list of critical teacher shortage areas is listed online.
How to Apply: Applications are available online.
Deadline: July 15.
Amount: Varies.
Number of Awards: Varies.

1273 • Critical Teacher Shortage Tuition Reimbursement Program

Purpose: To help Florida full-time publicly-funded school employees get teacher's certification at a grade level and in a subject area designated as a critical teacher shortage subject area.
Eligibility: Applicants must have valid Florida Teacher's Certificates (temporary or professional) or Florida Department of Health Licenses (temporary or permanent) and be enrolled in undergraduate or graduate courses leading to certification.
How to Apply: Applications are available online.
Deadline: September 15.
Amount: Varies.
Number of Awards: Varies.

1274 • Ethics in Business Scholarship Program

Purpose: To help undergraduate college students who enroll at community colleges and eligible private Florida colleges or universities.
Eligibility: Applicants should contact financial aid offices at participating institutions for more information. Participating institutions determine deadlines, award amounts and eligibility.
How to Apply: Contact financial aid offices at participating institutions.
Deadline: Varies.
Amount: Varies.
Number of Awards: Varies.

1275 • Federal Academic Competitiveness Grant

Purpose: To help Florida students who have finished a rigorous secondary school program of study.

Eligibility: Applicants must be full-time Florida students eligible for Federal Pell Grants who have enrolled or been accepted by a two- or four-year degree-granting institution of higher education. The grants are available to students for the first and second years of college with up to $750 for the first year and up to $1,300 for the second year. Second year students must also have a minimum 3.0 GPA.

How to Apply: Contact the program for more information.
Deadline: Varies.
Amount: Up to $1,300.
Number of Awards: Varies.

1276 • First Generation Matching Grant Program

Purpose: To help Florida undergraduate students with financial need who are enrolled in state universities and whose parents have not earned bachelor's degrees.

Eligibility: Applicants must submit applications and the Free Application for Federal Student Aid (FAFSA). Each university determines its own deadline.

How to Apply: Applications are at the financial aid offices of state universities.
Deadline: Varies.
Amount: Varies.
Number of Awards: Varies.

1277 • Florida Bright Futures Scholarship Program

Purpose: Lottery-funded scholarships are awarded to Florida high school seniors as reward for academic achievements and to assist with postsecondary education.

Eligibility: Applicants must earn a Florida high school diploma or equivalent, have not been found guilty or pled no contest to a felony charge and meet the award's academic requirements. Applicants must also be Florida residents, U.S. citizens or eligible noncitizens and be accepted by and enrolled in an eligible Florida public or private college or vocational school at least quarter time. Application must be completed during the senior year of high school.

How to Apply: Apply by completing the Florida Financial Aid Application. The application is available online at www.floridastudentfinancialaid.org or from your high school guidance counselor.
Deadline: Varies.
Amount: Tuition and fees.
Number of Awards: Varies.

1278 • Florida Student Assistance Grant Program

Purpose: To help degree-seeking, Florida resident, undergraduate students who have financial need and who are enrolled in participating postsecondary institutions.

Eligibility: There are three student financial aid programs: The Florida Public Student Assistance Grant is for students who attend state universities and public community colleges. The Florida Private Student Assistance Grant is for students who attend eligible private, non-profit, four-year colleges and universities. The Florida Postsecondary Student Assistance Grant is for students who attend eligible degree-granting private colleges and universities that are ineligible under the Florida Private Student Assistance Grant. High school students in the top 20 percent of their classes receive priority funding.

How to Apply: Applicants must submit the Free Application for Federal Student Aid (FAFSA).
Deadline: Each school determines its own deadline.
Amount: $1,722.
Number of Awards: Varies.

1279 • Jose Marti Scholarship Challenge Grant

Purpose: To help Florida students in need who are of Hispanic origin.

Eligibility: Applicants must have been born in or have a natural parent who was born in either Mexico or Spain, or a Hispanic country of the Caribbean, Central or South America, regardless of race. Students must plan to attend Florida public or eligible private institutions as undergraduate or graduate students, but graduating high school seniors get preference.

How to Apply: Applicants must submit the initial student Florida Financial Aid Application by April 1 and the Free Application for Federal Student Aid (FAFSA) by May 15.
Deadline: April 1.
Amount: $2,000.
Number of Awards: Varies.

1280 • Mary McLeod Bethune Scholarship Program

Purpose: To help Florida-resident undergraduate students who attend or plan to attend Bethune-Coleman College, Edward Waters College, Florida A&M University or Florida Memorial University.

Eligibility: Applicants must show financial need as determined by the school and meet the application procedures and deadlines of the participating schools.

How to Apply: Applications may be obtained from the participating schools' financial aid offices.
Deadline: Varies.
Amount: $3,000.
Number of Awards: Varies.

1281 • Robert C. Byrd Honors Scholarship Program - Florida

Purpose: To support Florida high school graduates who show academic promise.

Eligibility: Applicants must meet Florida's residency requirements for receiving state financial aid as determined by the student's postsecondary school and must not be in default on federal or state student loan programs.

How to Apply: Applicants must be nominated by their high school principal, adult education director or principal or headmaster and complete the Florida Financial Aid Application.
Deadline: Varies.
Amount: Varies.
Number of Awards: Varies.

1282 • Rosewood Family Scholarship Program

Purpose: To help minority students especially direct descendants of Rosewood families.

Eligibility: Applicants must be full-time, undergraduate minority students (Black, Hispanic, Asian, Pacific Islander, American Indian or Alaskan native) who attend state universities, public community colleges or public postsecondary vocational-technical schools. Direct descendants of Rosewood families affected by the incidents of January, 1923 receive preference. The descendants must provide family information on the Florida Financial Aid Application.

How to Apply: Applicants must submit the Initial Student Florida Financial Aid Applications online by April 1. Florida residents must submit the Free Application for Federal Student

Aid (FAFSA) online by May 15. Non-residents must submit the FAFSA in time to receive the Student Aid Report (SAR) from the processor and send a copy of the SAR to the Office of Student Financial Assistance by May 15.
Deadline: April 1.
Amount: Varies.
Number of Awards: 25.

1283 • William L. Boyd, IV, Florida Resident Access Grant

Purpose: Provides monetary assistance to Florida undergraduate college students enrolled at eligible, private, non-profit Florida schools.
Eligibility: Applicants must attend an eligible private, nonprofit Florida college or university, be Florida residents and not be in default on any state or federal grant, loan or scholarship. Requirements vary by institution.
How to Apply: Contact your financial aid office.
Deadline: Varies.
Amount: Varies.
Number of Awards: Varies.

Florida Leader Magazine

College Student of the Year Inc.
P.O. Box 14081
Gainesville, FL 32604
Phone: 352-373-6907
Fax: 352-373-8120
Email: info@studentleader.com
Website: http://www.floridaleader.com/soty

1284 • Florida College Student of the Year Award

Purpose: To honor and reward students who are leaders and role models both on campus and in their communities.
Eligibility: Applicants must be enrolled at a Florida-based community college, college or university or accredited vocational, technical or business school, be attending school at least half-time and have at least 12 credit hours completed during the previous calendar year. Applicants must also have a minimum 3.25 GPA and demonstrate financial self-reliance by receiving scholarships or working. In addition to academic record and financial self-reliance, applicants will also be judged on the basis of campus and community service.
How to Apply: Applications are available online.
Deadline: February 1.
Amount: Varies.
Number of Awards: 20.

Florida's Office of Campus Volunteers

Florida Campus Compact
325 John Knox Road
Building F, Suite 210
Tallahassee, FL 32303
Phone: 850-488-7782
Fax: 850-922-2928
Email: info@floridacompact.org
Website: http://www.floridacompact.org

1285 • Excellence in Service Award

Purpose: To reward students who perform outstanding acts of service in their communities.
Eligibility: Applicants must be full-time undergraduate students at an accredited public or private institution of higher education within the state of Florida.
How to Apply: Applications are available online.
Deadline: April 30.
Amount: $1,000.
Number of Awards: 3.

McCurry Foundation Inc.

Scholarship Selection Committee
11645 Beach Boulevard, Suite 200
Jacksonville, FL 32246
Website: http://www.mccurryfoundation.org

1286 • McCurry Foundation Scholarship

Purpose: To provide assistance to college students who have demonstrated leadership, a responsible work ethic and academic excellence.
Eligibility: Applicants must be public high school seniors who have demonstrated leadership, a responsible work ethic, community involvement, service, and academic excellence, with a GPA of at least 3.0. Students must demonstrate financial need, with a maximum family income of $75,000. Preference is given to students from Clay, Duval, Nassau and St. Johns Counties in Florida and from Glynn County in Georgia.
How to Apply: Applications are available online.
Deadline: February 15.
Amount: Varies.
Number of Awards: Varies.

Miami Herald and El Herald Newspapers

One Herald Plaza
Miami, FL 33132
Phone: 305-376-2905
Email: silverknight@herald.com
Website: http://www.silverknightaward.com

1287 • Silver Knight Award

Purpose: To recognize students for their academic achievement and contributions to their school and community.
Eligibility: Applicants must be high school seniors in Miami-Dade and Broward counties in Florida and be nominated by their schools.
How to Apply: Contact your high school guidance counselor.
Deadline: Last Friday in January.
Amount: $500-$1,500.
Number of Awards: Varies.

National Association for Campus Activities

13 Harbison Way
Columbia, SC 29212-3401
Phone: 803-732-6222
Fax: 803-749-1047
Email: info@naca.org
Website: http://www.naca.org

1288 • NACA Southeast Region Student Leader Scholarship

Purpose: To provide financial assistance to Southeast student leaders.

Eligibility: Students must hold a significant campus leadership position, demonstrate significant leadership skills and abilities and make significant contributions through on- or off-campus volunteering. Students must attend school in Alabama, Florida, Georgia, Mississippi, North Carolina, South Carolina, Tennessee, Virginia or Puerto Rico.

How to Apply: Applications are available online.
Deadline: March 31.
Amount: Varies.
Number of Awards: Up to 4.

Southern Scholarship Foundation

322 Stadium Drive
Tallahassee, FL 32304
Phone: 850-222-3833
Fax: 850-222-6750
Email: info@southernscholarship.org
Website: http://www.southernscholarship.org/

1289 • Southern Scholarship Foundation Scholarship

Purpose: To provide rent-free housing scholarships to students attending Florida State, University of Florida, Florida A&M, Bethune-Cookman or Florida Gulf Coast University.

Eligibility: Applicants must have financial need, have a minimum 3.0 high school GPA or 2.85 college GPA, demonstrate high character and attend or plan to attend Florida State, the University of Florida, Florida Gulf Coast University, Florida A&M or Bethune-Cookman.

How to Apply: Applications are available online.
Deadline: March 1.
Amount: Varies.
Number of Awards: Varies.

Related Scholarships:

Bank of America

See #290• Bank of America ADA Abilities Scholarship Program

State of Residence - Georgia

American Legion, Department of Georgia

3035 Mt. Zion Road
Stockbridge, GA 30281
Phone: 678-289-8883
Fax: 678-289-8885
Email: amerlegga@bellsouth.net
Website: http://www.galegion.org

1290 • Georgia Oratorical Contest

Purpose: To enhance high school students' experience with and understanding of the U.S. Constitution. The contest will help develop students' leadership skills and civic appreciation, as well as the ability to deliver thoughtful, insightful orations regarding U.S. citizenship and its inherent responsibilities.

Eligibility: Applicants must be high school students under the age of 20 who are U.S. citizens or legal residents and residents of the state. Students first give an oration within their state and winners compete at the national level. The oration must be related to the Constitution of the United States focusing on the duties and obligations citizens have to the government. It must be in English and be between eight and ten minutes. There is also an assigned topic which is posted on the website, and it should be between three and five minutes.

How to Apply: Applications are available by contacting the local American Legion Post.
Deadline: March 3.
Amount: Up to $2,800.
Number of Awards: Varies.

Georgia Student Finance Commission

2082 E. Exchange Place
Tucker, GA 30084
Phone: 800-505-4732
Fax: 770-724-9089
Website: http://www.gsfc.org

1291 • Charles McDaniel Teacher Scholarship

Purpose: To support students in Georgia pursuing a degree in teaching.

Eligibility: Applicants must be full-time juniors or seniors at a public Georgia college or university. They must be admitted to their school's college or department of education and have a GPA of 3.25 or higher. Applicants must be legal residents of Georgia, have graduated from a Georgia high school, be U.S. citizens or permanent resident aliens, be in compliance with Selective Service requirements and not be in default on student financial aid. Eligible colleges and universities can nominate one student each year.

How to Apply: Applications are available online and from college education departments.
Deadline: July 15.
Amount: $1,000.
Number of Awards: 3.

1292 • Georgia Tuition Equalization Grant

Purpose: To support Georgia resident students.

Eligibility: Applicants must be full-time students at eligible private colleges or universities in Georgia or in out-of-state four-year public colleges within 50 miles of students' residences and be U.S. citizens.

How to Apply: Applications are available online.
Deadline: Varies.
Amount: Varies.
Number of Awards: Varies.

1293 • Governor's Scholarship Program

Purpose: To aid graduating Georgia high school seniors attend Georgia colleges or universities.
Eligibility: Applicants must be selected by the Georgia Department of Education or be a valedictorian, salutatorian or STAR student and enroll full-time as an undergraduate at a Georgia institution. A minimum 3.0 GPA is required for renewal.
How to Apply: Applications are available by telephone request.
Deadline: Varies.
Amount: Varies.
Number of Awards: Varies.

1294 • HOPE Scholarship Program

Purpose: To support students attending Georgia institutions.
Eligibility: Applicants must have graduated from high school and be attending or planning to attend college in Georgia.
How to Apply: Applications are available online.
Deadline: Varies.
Amount: Varies.
Number of Awards: Varies.

1295 • Leveraging Educational Assistance Partnership (LEAP) Grant

Purpose: To aid residents of Georgia with substantial financial need in attending postsecondary institutions in Georgia.
Eligibility: Applicants must demonstrate substantial financial need, be eligible to receive the Pell Grant and be enrolled at a Georgia college, university or technical college at least half-time. Applicants must also complete and submit the Free Application for Federal Student Aid (FAFSA) and for renewal must maintain satisfactory academic progress.
How to Apply: Applications are available by telephone request.
Deadline: Varies.
Amount: Varies.
Number of Awards: Varies.

1296 • Robert C. Byrd Honors Scholarship Program - Georgia

Purpose: To aid outstanding Georgia high school students.
Eligibility: Applicants must be U.S. citizens, have recently graduated from a Georgia secondary school and be enrolled at a postsecondary institution. Applicants must also demonstrate academic achievement.
How to Apply: Applications are available by telephone request.
Deadline: Varies.
Amount: Varies.
Number of Awards: 664.

Related Scholarships:

Bank of America

See #290 • Bank of America ADA Abilities Scholarship Program

National Association for Campus Activities

See #1288 • NACA Southeast Region Student Leader Scholarship

Family Circle Cup and L'Oreal

See #1529 • L'Oreal/Family Circle Cup

McCurry Foundation Inc.

See #1286 • McCurry Foundation Scholarship

State of Residence - Hawaii

Hawaii Community Foundation - Scholarships

1164 Bishop Street
Suite 800
Honolulu, HI 96813
Phone: 888-731-3863
Email: scholarships@hcf-hawaii.org
Website: http://www.hawaiicommunityfoundation.org

1297 • American Savings Bank Scholarship Program

Purpose: To assist Hawaii high school graduates with college expenses at state schools.

Eligibility: Applicants must be entering college freshmen and demonstrate scholastic aptitude, leadership, financial need and character. Four scholarships are awarded, one for the University of Hawaii College System, one for Chaminade University of Honolulu, one for Brigham Young University-Hawaii Campus and one for Hawaii Pacific University. Applicants must be full-time students and must have a minimum 3.0 GPA. The award is renewable and includes an offer of a paid internship.

How to Apply: Applications are available at any American Savings Branch.

Deadline: March 1.

Amount: $5,000.

Number of Awards: 4.

1298 • Hawaii Community Foundation Scholarships

Purpose: To help Hawaii residents who show financial need.

Eligibility: The Hawaii Community Foundation Scholarship Program has over 120 different scholarship funds covering areas such as vocational education, those in foster care, ethnicity, religion and major. Applicants must be Hawaii residents who plan to attend nonprofit two- or four-year colleges as either full-time undergraduate or graduate students. Applicants must also have academic achievement and good moral character. A personal statements, Student Aid Report, transcript, recommendation letter and essay may be required depending on the specific scholarship.

How to Apply: Applications are available online.

Deadline: March 1.

Amount: $1,800.

Number of Awards: Varies.

Hawaii Department of Education

Office of Curriculum, Instruction and Student Support
Student Support Section
641 18th Avenue V-201
Honolulu, HI 96816
Phone: 808-586-3230
Fax: 808-586-3234
Website: http://doe.k12.hi.us

1299 • Robert C. Byrd Honors Scholarship Program - Hawaii

Purpose: To promote academic excellence among Hawaii students.

Eligibility: Applicants must be graduating high school seniors or planning to earn a GED. They must have a GPA of 3.3 or higher and have scored above 1270 on the SAT and/or above 29 on the ACT. GED applicants must score at least 60 points. Applicants must be legal Hawaiian residents, but they attend high schools outside of Hawaii.

How to Apply: Applications are available online.

Deadline: March 15.

Amount: $1,500.

Number of Awards: Varies.

1300 • Sterling Scholar Award Program

Eligibility: Applicants must be graduating high school seniors and demonstrate leadership and citizenship in English, industrial arts, speech/drama, business education, foreign language, visual arts, mathematics, science, music, social science, Hawaiian studies or computer science and technology.

How to Apply: Applications are available from the department heads of each high school.

Deadline: December.

Amount: Varies.

Number of Awards: 65.

Hawaii Department of Education (DOE)

900 Fort Street Mall
Suite 1300
Honolulu, HI 96813
Phone: 808-566-5570
Email: hern@hawaii.edu
Website: http://doe.k12.hi.us

1301 • Community Scholarship Fund

Purpose: To assist college and graduate students majoring in arts, education, humanities or social science.

Eligibility: Applicants must demonstrate accomplishment, motivation, initiative, vision and intention to work in Hawaii and major in the arts, education, humanities or social science. Applicants must also submit a four-page application and financial form, a personal statement, transcript and recommendations.

How to Apply: Applications are available by written request.

Deadline: March 1.

Amount: Varies.

Number of Awards: Varies.

1302 • John M. Ross Foundation Scholarships

Purpose: To assist Hawaii resident students, with preference given to those with Big Island ancestry.

Eligibility: Applicants must be residents of Hawaii and entering freshman or undergraduate students. Preference is given to applicants with roots on the Big Island who plan to remain on or return to it.

How to Apply: Applications are available by written request.

Deadline: March 1.

Amount: Varies.

Number of Awards: Varies.

1303 • Rosemary and Nellie Ebrie Foundation

Purpose: To assist college and graduate students who have Hawaiian ancestry or were born or have been a long-time residents of the Island.

Eligibility: Applicants must be residents of the Island of Hawaii and be of Hawaiian or part-Hawaiian ancestry. Applicants must also submit a four-sheet application and financial form, personal statement, recommendations and transcript.

How to Apply: Applications are available by written request.

Deadline: March 1.

Amount: Varies.

Number of Awards: Varies.

Hawaii Hotel and Lodging Association

2250 Kalakaua Avenue
Suite 404-4
Honolulu, HI 96815
Website: http://www.hawaiihotels.org

1304 • Clem Judd, Jr., Memorial Scholarship

Purpose: To help Hawaiian residents majoring in hotel management.

Eligibility: Applicants must have a minimum 3.0 GPA, be able to prove Hawaiian ancestry and be enrolled full-time at a U.S. university or college.

How to Apply: Applications are available by written request beginning February 1.

Deadline: July 1.

Amount: $2,500.

Number of Awards: 1.

High School Athletic Association

P.O. Box 62029
Honolulu, HI 96839
Website: http://www.sportshigh.com

1305 • Nissan Hawaii High School Hall of Honor

Purpose: To support Hawaii high school seniors who are athletes.

Eligibility: Applicants must be graduating high school seniors and athletes in any organized sport in Hawaii. Selection is based primarily on sports achievements. Factors considered include contributions to the team, sportsmanship, character, participation in school activities and community involvement.

How to Apply: Applications are available by written request.

Deadline: Varies.

Amount: $2,000.

Number of Awards: 12.

Mamoru and Aiko Takitani Foundation

P.O. Box 10687
Honolulu, HI 96816
Email: info@takitanifoundation.org
Website: http://www.takitani.org

1306 • Mamoru and Aiko Takitani Foundation Scholarship

Purpose: To assist Hawaii resident students with business school, technical school, community college or four-year college expenses.

Eligibility: Applicants must be graduating high school seniors and Hawaii residents. Applicants must also demonstrate scholastic achievement, participation in activities and have been accepted into an accredited institution. Community service and financial need are also considered.

How to Apply: Contact your high school guidance counselor.

Deadline: March 1.

Amount: $1,000-$10,000.

Number of Awards: Varies.

Outrigger Duke Kahanamoku Foundation

Scholarship Committee
P.O. Box 2498
Honolulu, HI 96804
Phone: 808-545-4880
Fax: 808-532-0560
Email: info@dukefoundation.org
Website: http://www.dukefoundation.org

1307 • Duke Kahanamoku Outrigger Scholarship

Purpose: To support Hawaii students who are involved in water sports.

Eligibility: Applicants must be Hawaii residents and demonstrate financial need and athletic involvement. Preference is given to the water sports.

How to Apply: Applications are available online.

Deadline: March 15.

Amount: Varies.

Number of Awards: Varies.

Tsung Tsin Association

Chairperson, Scholarship Committee
47-701 Hui Alala Street
Kaneohe, HI 96744
Phone: 808-533-3998

1308 • Tsung Tsin Association Scholarship

Purpose: To help outstanding Hawaii students pay for college.

Eligibility: Applicants must be high school seniors, college undergraduates or graduate students and must be attending or planning to attend a post-secondary institution. Applicants must provide a transcript, SAT scores, recommendations and autobiographical sketch. Community service and career goals are taken into consideration.

How to Apply: Applications are available by written request.

Deadline: April 20.

Amount: $750.

Number of Awards: 1.

University of Hawaii

Student Services Center Room 413
2600 Campus Road
Honolulu, HI 96822
Phone: 808-956-4642
Email: seed@hawaii.edu
Website: http://www.hawaii.edu/diversity

1309 • Charles R. Hemenway Memorial Scholarship

Purpose: To assist residents of Hawaii with college education expenses.

Eligibility: Applicants must demonstrate financial need and be Hawaii residents. Applicants must also be enrolled at least half-time at any of the campuses of the University of Hawaii. Selection is based on character and "qualities of good citizenship."

How to Apply: Contact your financial aid office.

Deadline: Varies.

Amount: $2,000.

Number of Awards: Varies.

State of Residence - Idaho

Idaho State Board of Education

P.O. Box 83720
Boise, ID 83720
Phone: 208-334-2270
Fax: 208-334-2632
Email: dkelly@osbe.state.id.us
Website: http://www.boardofed.idaho.gov

1310 • Governor's Challenge Scholarship

Purpose: Monetary assistance is provided to Idaho resident high school seniors planning to attend state colleges.

Eligibility: Applicants must be Idaho high school seniors planning to attend Idaho colleges or universities full-time and have a minimum 2.8 GPA. Public service is a significant factor.

How to Apply: Applications are available online.

Deadline: December 15.

Amount: $3,000.

Number of Awards: 12.

1311 • Idaho Promise Category A Scholarship

Eligibility: Applicants must be Idaho residents, be graduating seniors of Idaho high schools and enroll full-time at an eligible Idaho college or university. Academic applicants must also be in the top 10 percent of their graduating class, have a minimum 3.5 GPA and a minimum ACT score of 28. Professional-technical applicants must have a minimum 2.8 GPA and take the COMPASS test.

How to Apply: Contact your high school guidance counselor.

Deadline: Varies.

Amount: $3,000.

Number of Awards: 25.

1312 • Idaho Promise Category B Scholarship

Purpose: Monetary assistance is provided to Idaho resident high school students with their freshman expenses at Idaho colleges or universities.

Eligibility: Applicants must have graduated from an Idaho high school, be entering freshmen at an eligible Idaho college or university, be residents of Idaho and have a minimum 3.0 GPA or minimum ACT score of 20. Applicants must also be younger than 22 years old and complete at least 12 credits per semester with a minimum 2.5 GPA to remain eligible for renewal.

How to Apply: Contact eligible college or university financial aid office.

Deadline: Varies.

Amount: $250.

Number of Awards: Varies.

1313 • Leveraging Educational Assistance State Partnership Program (LEAP)

Purpose: To aid students attending Idaho colleges or universities regardless of their states of residence.

Eligibility: Applicants must demonstrate financial need, attend eligible public or private colleges or universities in Idaho and take a minimum of six credits. Applicants may be residents of any state.

How to Apply: Contact your financial aid office.

Deadline: Varies.

Amount: $5,000.

Number of Awards: Varies.

1314 • Minority and At-Risk Scholarship

Purpose: To aid students who are "at-risk" of not being able to be college educated due to cultural, economic or physical circumstances.

Eligibility: Applicants must have graduated from an Idaho high school, and meet three of the following criteria: be a first-generation college student, be disabled, be a migrant farm worker or the dependent of one, demonstrate significant financial need or be a member of an ethnic minority underrepresented in Idaho higher education. Applicants must also attend an eligible Idaho college or university.

How to Apply: Applications are available by telephone request.
Deadline: Varies.
Amount: $3,000.
Number of Awards: Varies.

1315 • Robert C. Byrd Honors Scholarship Program - Idaho

Purpose: To recognize outstanding Idaho high school seniors.

Eligibility: Applicants must be U.S. citizens who are graduating seniors of Idaho high schools and who demonstrate outstanding academic achievement. Selection is based on merit.

How to Apply: Applications are available online.
Deadline: Varies.
Amount: $1,500.
Number of Awards: Varies.

Related Scholarships:

Bank of America

See #290 • Bank of America ADA Abilities Scholarship Program

Treacy Company

See #1452 • Treacy Company Scholarship

National Association for Campus Activities

See #1201 • Lori Rhett Memorial Scholarship

Alert Magazine

See #1567 • Alert Scholarship

State of Residence - Illinois

American Legion, Department of Illinois

P.O. Box 2910
Bloomington, IL 61702
Phone: 309-663-0361
Fax: 309-663-5783
Website: http://www.illegion.org/scholarship.html

1316 • American Essay Contest Scholarship

Purpose: To award outstanding 500-word essays written on assigned topics.

Eligibility: Applicants must be enrolled in an Illinois school in grades eight to twelve.

How to Apply: Application information is available by contacting the local American Legion Unit or Auxiliary.
Deadline: February 2.
Amount: Up to $75.
Number of Awards: Varies.

1317 • Illinois American Legion Scholarship Program

Purpose: To award scholarships to graduating students enrolled in Illinois high schools.

Eligibility: Applicants must be children or grandchildren of American Legion Illinois members and must be in their senior year of high school. Awards may be used to further education at an accredited college, university or technical school.

How to Apply: Application information is available by contacting the American Legion, Department of Illinois.
Deadline: March 15.
Amount: $1,000.
Number of Awards: 20.

1318 • Illinois Oratorical Contest

Purpose: To enhance high school students' experience with and understanding of the U.S. Constitution. The contest will help develop students' leadership skills and civic appreciation, as well as the ability to deliver thoughtful, insightful orations regarding U.S. citizenship and its inherent responsibilities.

Eligibility: Applicants must be high school students under the age of 20 who are U.S. citizens or legal residents and residents of the state. Students first give an oration within their state and winners compete at the national level. The oration must be related to the Constitution of the United States focusing on the duties and obligations citizens have to the government. It must be in English and be between eight and ten minutes. There is also an assigned topic which is posted on the website, and it should be between three and five minutes.

How to Apply: Application information is available by contacting the local American Legion Post or Illinois Department Headquarters.
Deadline: February.
Amount: Up to $1,600.
Number of Awards: Varies.

Chicago Scholars Foundation

333 W. Wacker Drive, 33rd Floor
Chicago, IL 60606
Phone: 312-917-6868
Fax: 312-917-7806
Email: chischolars@nuveen.com
Website: http://www.chicagoscholars.org

1319 • Chicago Scholars Award

Purpose: To recognize high school seniors in the Chicago area who have overcome considerable obstacles to succeed in high school and attend college.

Eligibility: One award is presented to one senior from each Chicago high school graduating class. Applicants must be nominated by their high school and be Chicago residents or attend a Chicago high school and have a minimum 3.5 GPA. Applicants' financial need is also a consideration.

How to Apply: Applicants must be nominated by their high schools.

Deadline: Varies.

Amount: $1,000.

Number of Awards: Varies.

Community Banker Association of Illinois

901 Community Drive
Springfield, IL 62703-5184
Phone: 800-736-2224
Email: bobbiw@cbai.com
Website: http://www.cbai.com

1320 • Community Banker Association of Illinois Annual Scholarship Program

Purpose: To assist Illinois high school seniors.

Eligibility: Applicants must write essays and be sponsored by a participating CBAI member bank. There is an essay topic related to community banking, and the short essays are judged on understanding of community banking philosophy, accurate information, clear and concise sentences, logical organization, proper grammar, correct punctuation and spelling and conclusion/summary.

How to Apply: A list of participating banks and more information is available by email.

Deadline: February 13.

Amount: $4,000.

Number of Awards: 13.

Edward Arthur Mellinger Educational Foundation Inc.

1025 E. Broadway
P.O. Box 770
Monmouth, IL 61462
Phone: 309-734-2419
Fax: 309-734-4435
Email: info@mellinger.org
Website: http://www.mellinger.org

1321 • Mellinger Scholarships

Purpose: The E. A. Mellinger Foundation supports education as a memorial to its namesake.

Eligibility: Applicants must live in Western Illinois or Eastern Iowa, submit the FAFSA form and demonstrate financial need and attend an accredited university. Awards are based on academic achievement. Part-time students are also eligible for scholarships, and loans are also available to graduate students.

How to Apply: Applications are available by mail or online. Application forms are only available from February 1 to May 1 each year.

Deadline: May 1.

Amount: $300-$1,200.

Number of Awards: Varies.

Governor's Office of the State of Illinois Michael Curry Summer Internship Program

107 William G. Stratton Building
Springfield, IL 62706
Phone: 217-782-5189
Website: http://www.illinois.gov/gov/intopportunities.cfm

1322 • Michael Curry Summer Internship Program

Purpose: To provide internships for college juniors, seniors or graduate students.

Eligibility: Applicants must be Illinois residents. Recipients work full-time in an agency under the jurisdiction of the Governor for 10 weeks during the summer.

How to Apply: Applications are available online or by mail.

Deadline: January 31.

Amount: Varies.

Number of Awards: Varies.

Illinois Department of Public Health

535 W. Jefferson Street
Springfield, IL 62761
Phone: 217-782-4977
Fax: 217-782-3987
Email: dph.mailus@illinois.gov
Website: http://www.idph.state.il.us

1323 • Allied Health Care Professional Scholarship Program

Purpose: To encourage more nurse practitioners, physician assistants and certified nurse midwives to set up practices in rural areas of Illinois.

Eligibility: Applicants must be accepted to or currently enrolled in an accredited Illinois school to become a nurse practitioner, physician assistant or certified nurse midwife. Students must demonstrate financial need, and they may be full-time or part-time students as long as part-time students are enrolled for at least a third of the hours required to be a full-time student. Scholarship recipients agree to set up their practice in designated shortage areas after graduation.

How to Apply: Applications are available online.

Deadline: June 30.

Amount: $7,500.

Number of Awards: Varies.

1324 • Golden Apple Scholars of Illinois (Illinois Scholars Program)

Purpose: To offer scholarships to promising students pursuing teaching degrees.

Eligibility: Applicants must be Illinois high school seniors or college sophomores at one of the 53 partner universities in Illinois who are interested in teaching. There are a limited number of spots for college sophomores, and all college students must be nominated by a university liaison. Students must commit to teaching in an Illinois school of need for five years after graduation.

How to Apply: Applications are available by calling 312-407-0433, extension 105.

Deadline: November 30.

Amount: Financial assistance for four years at one of 53 colleges in Illinois.

Number of Awards: Varies.

1325 • Illinois Incentive for Access (IIA) Program

Purpose: To aid Illinois students who have extreme financial need.

Eligibility: Applicants must be Illinois residents, be enrolled at least half-time as freshmen at a participating Illinois school and have an Expected Family Contribution (EFC) of zero.

How to Apply: Complete the Free Application for Federal Student Aid (FAFSA).

Deadline: As soon as possible after January 1.

Amount: $500.

Number of Awards: Varies.

1326 • Medical Student Scholarship Program

Purpose: To increase the number of medical professionals in rural areas of Illinois.

Eligibility: Applicants must be Illinois residents enrolled in an Illinois allopathic or osteopathic medical school. Students must be planning to practice in one or more of the following medical fields: family practice, general internal medicine, general pediatrics or obstetrics/gynecology. Applicants must show evidence of financial need. Scholarship recipients agree to set up practice in an area designated as having a shortage of primary care providers.

How to Apply: Applications are available online.

Deadline: May 15.

Amount: Tuition, fees and living expenses.

Number of Awards: Varies.

1327 • Merit Recognition Scholarship (MRS) Program

Purpose: To aid Illinois high school students.

Eligibility: Applicants must be graduating seniors or have graduated within a year of application from an Illinois high school, be ranked in the top 5 percent of their class OR received a ACT, SAT I or Prairie State Achievement Exam test score in the top 5 percent of all Illinois students who took the exam at the same time and attend a MAP-approved Illinois institution as an undergraduate at least half-time.

How to Apply: Qualifying students are automatically sent applications.

Deadline: Varies.

Amount: Varies.

Number of Awards: Varies.

1328 • Monetary Award Program (MAP)

Purpose: To provide grants to eligible Illinois undergraduate students.

Eligibility: Applicants must be residents of Illinois, enrolled at a MAP-approved Illinois institution and carry a minimum of three hours per term. Applicants must also demonstrate financial need and maintain satisfactory academic progress.

How to Apply: Complete the Free Application for Federal Student Aid (FAFSA).

Deadline: As soon as possible after January 1.

Amount: Varies.

Number of Awards: Varies.

1329 • Nursing Education Scholarship Program

Purpose: To increase the number of nurses in Illinois.

Eligibility: Applicants must be Illinois residents, having lived in the state for one year prior to applying and be U.S. citizens or permanent residents. Applicants must be accepted to or enrolled in an approved nursing program and demonstrate financial need. Scholarship recipients must agree to work as a nurse in Illinois after graduation.

How to Apply: Applications are available online.

Deadline: May 31.

Amount: Tuition and fees for nursing program.

Number of Awards: Varies.

1330 • Robert C. Byrd Honors Scholarship Program - Illinois

Purpose: To aid outstanding Illinois high school students.

Eligibility: Applicants must be U.S. citizens, be graduating Illinois high school seniors, demonstrate outstanding academic achievement and be enrolled or accepted for enrollment full-time as undergraduate students.

How to Apply: Applicants are nominated by their high schools.

Deadline: July 15.

Amount: $1,500.

Number of Awards: Varies.

Illinois Student Assistance Commission

1755 Lake Cook Road
Deerfield, IL 60015
Phone: 800-899-4722
Fax: 847-831-8549
Email: collegezone@isac.org
Website: http://www.collegezone.com

1331 • General Assembly Scholarship

Purpose: To assist Illinois students.

Eligibility: Applicants must be Illinois high school students planning to attend a state-supported university. They must contact their State Senator and State Representative to be considered for the award, and they must live within the legislative district of that Senator or Representative.

How to Apply: Applications are available from your State Senator and State Representative.

Deadline: Varies.

Amount: Full tuition for one to four years.

Number of Awards: 1-4 per district.

1332 • Illinois Future Teacher Corps (IFTC) Program

Purpose: To assist talented and financially needy students who are interested in pursuing a career in education.

Eligibility: Applicants must be Illinois residents who are U.S. citizens or eligible non-citizens. They must be enrolled as a junior or above in an approved teacher education program and maintain at least a 2.5 GPA. Applicants must submit a FAFSA form, comply with Selective Service requirements and not be in default on any student loans. Applicants are not eligible to receive the scholarship in the same year as receiving a Minority Teachers of Illinois (MTI) Scholarship or Illinois Special Education Teacher Tuition Waiver (SETTW). Scholarship recipients agree to teach in Illinois after graduating.

How to Apply: Applications are available online.

Deadline: March 1, but applications received after this date will be considered as funding allows.

Amount: $5,000-$15,000.

Number of Awards: Varies.

1333 • Nurse Educator Scholarship Program (NESP)

Purpose: To increase the number of nurse educators in Illinois.

Eligibility: Applicants must be Illinois residents and U.S. citizens or permanent residents who have earned a bachelor's degree and plan to pursue a graduate degree in nursing education at an approved college. Applicants must apply for federal financial aid, comply with all Selective Service requirements and not be in default on any student loans. Scholarship recipients agree to teach in the field of nursing education in Illinois after graduation.

How to Apply: Applications are available online.

Deadline: March 1, but applications received after that date will be considered if funding remains.

Amount: Tuition, fees and living stipend.

Number of Awards: Varies.

Township Officials of Illinois

408 S. 5th Street
Springfield, IL 62701
Phone: 217-744-2212
Fax: 217-744-7419
Email: bryantoi@toi.org
Website: http://www.toi.org

1334 • Township Officials of Illinois Scholarship

Purpose: To promote the ideas of quality local government and civic duty and to recruit young people into the TOI.

Eligibility: Applicants must be high school seniors attending an Illinois college or university in the fall.

How to Apply: Applications are available online in January.

Deadline: March 1.

Amount: Varies.

Number of Awards: Varies.

Related Scholarships:

Bank of America

See #290• Bank of America ADA Abilities Scholarship Program

State of Residence - Indiana

American Legion, Department of Indiana

777 N. Meridian Street
Indianapolis, IN 46204
Phone: 317-630-1300
Website: http://www.indlegion.org

1335 • Indiana Oratorical Contest

Purpose: To enhance high school students' experience with and understanding of the U.S. Constitution. The contest will help develop students' leadership skills and civic appreciation, as well as the ability to deliver thoughtful, insightful orations regarding U.S. citizenship and its inherent responsibilities.

Eligibility: Applicants must be high school students under the age of 20 who are U.S. citizens or legal residents and residents of the state. Students first give an oration within their state and winners compete at the national level. The oration must be related to the Constitution of the United States focusing on the duties and obligations citizens have to the government. It must be in English and be between eight and ten minutes. There is also an assigned topic which is posted on the website, and it should be between three and five minutes.

How to Apply: Application information is available from the local American Legion Post and online.

Deadline: December 8.

Amount: Up to $3,200.

Number of Awards: Varies.

Pacers Foundation

125 S. Pennsylvania Street
Indianapolis, IN 46204
Phone: 317-917-2864
Fax: 317-917-2599
Email: foundation@pacers.com
Website: http://www.nba.com/pacers/news/Foundation_Index.html

1336 • Pacers TeamUp Scholarship

Purpose: The Pacers TeamUp Scholarship rewards students for community service.

Eligibility: Applicants must be Indiana residents in their senior year of high school planning to attend an accredited four-year college or two-year community or junior college.

How to Apply: Application information is available by email at foundation@pacers.com, by phone at 317-917-2864 or online.

Deadline: March 1.

Amount: $2,000.

Number of Awards: 5.

State Student Assistance Commission of Indiana

150 W. Market Street
Suite 500
Indianapolis, IN 46204
Phone: 888-528-4719
Fax: 317-232-3260
Email: grants@ssaci.state.in.us
Website: http://www.in.gov/ssaci/

1337 • Frank O'Bannon Grant Program

Purpose: To aid Indiana students in attending eligible postsecondary schools.

Eligibility: Applicants must be high school graduates and attend or plan to attend eligible Indiana colleges or universities full-time.

How to Apply: Complete the Free Application for Federal Student Aid (FAFSA).

Deadline: March 10.

Amount: Varies.

Number of Awards: Varies.

1338 • Hoosier Scholar Award

Purpose: Monetary assistance is provided to Indiana resident high school seniors with freshman expenses at state schools.

Eligibility: Applicants must be graduating Indiana high school seniors, rank in the top 20 percent of their graduating class and plan to attend an Indiana institution of higher education full-time. Scholars are chosen by high school guidance counselors. Selection is based on educational merit.

How to Apply: Winners are selected by their high school.

Deadline: Varies.

Amount: $500.

Number of Awards: Varies.

1339 • Part-Time Grant Program

Purpose: To help part-time Indiana students pursue higher education.

Eligibility: Applicants must be undergraduates taking at least 6 but not more than 12 credit hours per term at eligible institutions. This is a need-based award.

How to Apply: Complete the Free Application for Federal Student Aid (FAFSA).

Deadline: Varies.

Amount: Varies.

Number of Awards: Varies.

1340 • Robert C. Byrd Honors Scholarship Program - Indiana

Purpose: Monetary assistance is provided to academically worthy Indiana resident high school seniors with their college expenses.

Eligibility: Applicants must be U.S. citizens who are graduating Indiana high school seniors and have a minimum SAT score of 1300 or a minimum ACT score of 29. Applicants must apply to and enroll in a higher education institution full-time.

How to Apply: Applications are available online.

Deadline: April 24.

Amount: $1,500.

Number of Awards: Varies.

State of Residence - Iowa

American Legion, Department of Iowa

720 Lyon Street
Des Moines, IA 50309
Phone: 800-365-8387
Fax: 515-282-7583
Email: programs@ialegion.org
Website: http://www.ialegion.org

1341 • Iowa Oratorical Contest

Purpose: To enhance high school students' experience with and understanding of the U.S. Constitution. The contest will help develop students' leadership skills and civic appreciation, as well as the ability to deliver thoughtful, insightful orations regarding U.S. citizenship and its inherent responsibilities.

Eligibility: Applicants must be high school students under the age of 20 who are U.S. citizens or legal residents and residents of the state. Students first give an oration within their state and winners compete at the national level. The oration must be related to the Constitution of the United States focusing on the duties and obligations citizens have to the government. It must be in English and be between eight and ten minutes. There is also an assigned topic which is posted on the website, and it should be between three and five minutes.

How to Apply: Applications are available online.

Deadline: February 18.

Amount: Up to $3,500.

Number of Awards: Varies.

Grand Lodge of Iowa, A.F. and A.M.

Scholarship Selection Committee
P.O. Box 279
Cedar Rapids, Iowa 52406-0279
Phone: 319-365-1438
Fax: 319-365-1439
Email: scholarships@gl-iowa.org
Website: http://www.gl-iowa.org

1342 • Masonic Scholarship Program

Purpose: To reward high school seniors from Iowa public high schools for academics and leadership skills.

Eligibility: Applicants must be pursuing a post-secondary education in any state at an institution which provides a two-year or four-year college program or vocational training. They do not need to have a Masonic connection. Selection is based on academic record, communication skills and financial need, but the most important is service to school and community with an emphasis on leadership roles. Finalists will be asked to appear before the committee for personal interviews.

How to Apply: Applications are available online or from guidance departments at Iowa public high schools.

Deadline: February 1.

Amount: $2,000.

Number of Awards: 60.

Herbert Hoover Presidential Library Association

P.O. Box 696
West Branch, IA 52358
Phone: 800-828-0475
Fax: 319-643-2391
Email: scholarship@hooverassociation.org
Website: http://www.hooverassociation.org

1343 • Herbert Hoover Uncommon Student Award

Purpose: To honor Herbert Hoover by rewarding students who live up to his ideal of the "uncommon man."

Eligibility: Applicants must be juniors in an Iowa high school or homeschool. Students must submit a project proposal and two letters of recommendation. Recipients must attend a weekend program during the summer and are expected to complete the proposed project. Grades, essays and test scores are not considered.

How to Apply: Applications are available online.
Deadline: March 31.
Amount: $750-$5,000.
Number of Awards: Approximately 15.

Iowa College Student Aid Commission

200 10th Street, 4th Floor
Des Moines, IA 50309
Phone: 515-242-3344
Fax: 515-242-3388
Email: info@iowacollegeaid.org
Website: http://www.iowacollegeaid.org

1344 • Iowa Grants

Purpose: To assist needy Iowa students.

Eligibility: Applicants must be enrolled in or planning to enroll at least part-time in an undergraduate program at eligible Iowa colleges, universities and community colleges and be U.S. citizens. Selection is based on need, with priority given to the neediest applicants.

How to Apply: Complete the Free Application for Federal Student Aid (FAFSA).
Deadline: As soon as possible after January 1.
Amount: $1,000.
Number of Awards: Varies.

1345 • Iowa Tuition Grants

Purpose: To help students attend Iowa's independent colleges and universities.

Eligibility: Applicants must be enrolled in or planning to enroll at least part-time in an eligible Iowa college or university and demonstrate financial need. Priority is given to the neediest applicants.

How to Apply: Complete the Free Application for Federal Student Aid (FAFSA).
Deadline: July 1.
Amount: $4,000.
Number of Awards: Varies.

1346 • Iowa Vocational-Technical Tuition Grants

Purpose: To aid those Iowa residents enrolled in vocational-technical programs at community colleges.

Eligibility: Applicants must be enrolled in or planning to enroll in a career education or option course of at least 12 weeks duration at an Iowa area community college and be U.S. citizens or permanent residents.

How to Apply: Complete the Free Application for Federal Student Aid (FAFSA).
Deadline: July 1.
Amount: $1,200.
Number of Awards: Varies.

1347 • Robert C. Byrd Honors Scholarship Program - Iowa

Purpose: To recognize top Iowa high school seniors.

Eligibility: Applicants must be ranked in the top 10 percent of their graduating Iowa high school class, have taken required academic courses, have a minimum ACT score of 28 or minimum SAT score of 1240 and have a minimum 3.5 GPA.

How to Apply: Applications are available from your high school guidance counselor and online.
Deadline: February 2.
Amount: $1,500.
Number of Awards: Varies.

1348 • State of Iowa Scholarships

Purpose: To recognize Iowa's top students.

Eligibility: Applicants must be Iowa residents ranked in the top 15 percent of their high school graduating class. Awards may only be used at eligible Iowa institutions. Selection is based on class rank and standardized test scores.

How to Apply: Applications are available online.
Deadline: November 3.
Amount: $400.
Number of Awards: Varies.

Vincent L. Hawkinson Foundation for Peace and Justice

324 Harvard Street S.E.
Minneapolis, MN 55414
Phone: 612-331-8125
Email: info@graceattheu.org
Website: http://www.graceattheu.org

1349 • Vincent L. Hawkinson Scholarship for Peace and Justice

Purpose: To provide financial assistance to undergraduate and graduate students who share the ideals of the Rev. Vincent L. Hawkinson, a leader of Grace University Lutheran Church for more than 30 years.

Eligibility: Applicants must advocate peace, reside in Iowa, Minnesota, North Dakota, South Dakota or Wisconsin and attend an interview in Minneapolis and fall awards ceremony.

How to Apply: Applications are available by sending a self-addressed, stamp envelope, by email or online.
Deadline: April 1.
Amount: $1,500.
Number of Awards: 1.

Related Scholarships:

Bank of America

See #290• Bank of America ADA Abilities Scholarship Program

Edward Arthur Mellinger Educational Foundation Inc.

See #1321• Mellinger Scholarships

State of Residence - Kansas

American Legion, Department of Kansas

1314 SW Topeka Boulevard
Topeka, KS 66612
Phone: 785-232-9315
Fax: 785-232-1399
Website: http://www.ksamlegion.org

1350 • Albert M. Lappin Scholarship

Purpose: To assist the education of needy and worthy children of American Legion and American Legion Auxiliary members.

Eligibility: Applicants must be high school seniors or college freshmen or sophomores who are average or better students. They must be the son or daughter of a veteran and enrolling or enrolled in a post-secondary school in Kansas. A parent must have been a member of the Kansas American Legion or American Legion Auxiliary for the previous three years. In addition, the children of deceased parents are eligible if the parent was a paid member at the time of death. Applicants must submit a 1040 income statement, documentation of parent's veteran status, three letters of recommendation, with only one from a teacher, an essay on the topic of "Why I Want to Go to College" and a high school transcript. Applicants must maintain a C average in college and verify enrollment at the start of each semester.

How to Apply: Applications are available online.
Deadline: February 15.
Amount: $1,000.
Number of Awards: 1.

1351 • Charles W. and Annette Hill Scholarship

Purpose: To provide financial assistance to needy and worthy children of members of the American Legion.

Eligibility: Applicants must be descendents of an American Legion member with a GPA of at least 3.0. Special consideration will be given to students studying science, engineering or business administration. Applicants must submit three letters of recommendation, with only one from a teacher, an essay on "Why I Want to Go to College," a high school transcript, documentation of parent's veteran status and a 1040 income statement. Applicants must maintain a 3.0 GPA in college and verify enrollment at the start of each semester.

How to Apply: Applications are available online.
Deadline: February 15.
Amount: $1,000.
Number of Awards: 1.

1352 • Hobble (LPN) Nursing Scholarship

Purpose: To assist future Kansas nurses.

Eligibility: Applicants must be Kansas residents attending an accredited Kansas school to receive a degree in Licensed Practical Nursing (LPN) and planning to practice their career in Kansas. Applicants must also demonstrate financial need and be 18 before taking the Kansas State Board examination.

How to Apply: Applications are available online and may be requested from Department Headquarters.
Deadline: February 15.
Amount: $300.
Number of Awards: 1.

1353 • Hugh A. Smith Scholarship Fund

Purpose: To provide assistance to needy and worthy children of American Legion and American Legion Auxiliary members.

Eligibility: Applicants must be average or better students who are high school seniors or college freshmen or sophomores enrolling or enrolled in a post-secondary school in Kansas. They must be the son or daughter of a veteran, and a parent must have been a member of the Kansas American Legion or American Legion Auxiliary for the past three years. The children of deceased parents are also eligible if the parent was a paid member at the time of death. Applicants must submit three letters of recommendation, including one from a teacher, an essay on "Why I Want to Go to College", high school transcript, a 1040 income statement and documentation of parent's veteran status.

How to Apply: Applications are available online.
Deadline: February 15.
Amount: $500.
Number of Awards: 1.

1354 • Kansas Oratorical Contest

Purpose: To enhance junior high and high school students' experience with and understanding of the U.S. Constitution. The contest will help develop students' leadership skills and civic appreciation, as well as the ability to deliver thoughtful, insightful orations regarding U.S. citizenship and its inherent responsibilities.

Eligibility: Applicants must be high school students under the age of 20 who are U.S. citizens or legal residents and residents of the state. Students first give an oration within their state and winners compete at the national level. The oration must be related to the Constitution of the United States focusing on the duties and obligations citizens have to the government. It must be in English and be between eight and ten minutes. There is also an assigned topic which is posted on the website, and it should be between three and five minutes.

How to Apply: Applications are available from schools and local American Legion Posts.
Deadline: January 15.
Amount: $150-$1,500.
Number of Awards: 4+local scholarships.

1355 • Music Committee Scholarship

Purpose: To support Kansas students who have distinguished themselves in the field of music.

Eligibility: Applicants must be Kansas residents who are currently high school seniors or college freshmen or sophomores. They must have a proven talent and background in music and be planning to major or minor in music at an approved Kansas post-secondary institution. Applicants must also be average or better students. Three letters of recommendation, with only one from a music teacher, a 1040 income statement, a high school transcript and a statement describing why they are applying for the scholarship are required. The scholarship will be awarded in two installments; recipients must maintain a C average to receive the second installment.

How to Apply: Applications are available online.
Deadline: February 15.
Amount: $1,000.
Number of Awards: 1.

1356 • Paul Flaherty Athletic Scholarship

Purpose: To support student athletes.

Eligibility: Applicants must be high school seniors or college freshmen or sophomores and have participated in high school athletics. Students must be average or better students and submit three letters of recommendation, one of which must be from a

coach, a high school transcript, a 1040 income statement and an essay on the topic, "Why I Want to Go to College."
How to Apply: Applications are available online.
Deadline: July 15.
Amount: $250.
Number of Awards: 1.

1357 • Rosedale Post 346 Scholarship

Purpose: To assist the children of members of the Kansas American Legion or American Legion Auxiliary.

Eligibility: Applicants must be high school seniors or college freshmen or sophomores who are enrolling or enrolled in an approved post-secondary school. They also must be average or better students who are the children of veterans. The children of deceased parents are also eligible if the parent was a paid member at the time of death. Applicants must submit three letters of recommendation, with at least one from a teacher, an essay on "Why I Want to Go to College," a 1040 income statement, documentation of parent's veteran status and a certified high school transcript.
How to Apply: Applications are available online.
Deadline: February 15.
Amount: $1,500.
Number of Awards: 2.

1358 • Ted and Nora Anderson Scholarships

Purpose: To support worthy and needy children of American Legion and American Legion Auxiliary members as they pursue their educations.

Eligibility: Applicants must be high school seniors or college freshmen or sophomores who are average or better students. They must be enrolling or enrolled in a post-secondary school in Kansas and the son or daughter of a veteran. At least one parent must have been a member of the Kansas American Legion or American Legion Auxiliary for the past three years. The children of deceased parents are also eligible as long as the parent was a paid member at the time of death. Applicants must submit three letters of recommendation, with only one from a teacher, a 1040 income statement, documentation of parent's veteran status, an essay on "Why I Want to Go to College" and a high school transcript.
How to Apply: Applications are available online.
Deadline: February 15.
Amount: $500.
Number of Awards: Up to 4.

Kansas Board of Regents

Curtis State Office Building
Suite 520
1000 SW Jackson Street
Topeka, KS 66612
Phone: 785-296-3421
Fax: 785-296-0983
Email: dlindeman@ksbor.org
Website: http://www.kansasregents.org

1359 • Kansas Comprehensive Grants

Purpose: To help needy Kansas students attend Kansas colleges and universities.
Eligibility: Applicants must be enrolled full-time at an eligible Kansas institution. Selection is based on financial need.
How to Apply: Complete the Free Application for Federal Student Aid (FAFSA).
Deadline: April 1.
Amount: $100-$3,000.
Number of Awards: Varies.

1360 • Kansas Ethnic Minority Scholarship

Purpose: To aid outstanding Kansas minority students with financial need.

Eligibility: Applicants must be African American, Native Indian or Alaskan Native, Asian or Pacific Islander or Hispanic. Priority is given to graduating high school seniors. Applicants must have one of the following: a minimum ACT score of 21 or SAT score of 816, a minimum 3.0 GPA, a top 33 percent ranking in their high school class, completion of Kansas Scholars Curriculum, selection by National Merit Corporation or selection by College Board as a Hispanic Scholar.
How to Apply: Applications are available online.
Deadline: April.
Amount: $1,850.
Number of Awards: Varies.

1361 • State Scholarship

Purpose: To aid needy Kansas students designated as state scholars.

Eligibility: Applicants must have taken the ACT, completed the Regents Scholars Curriculum and be graduating seniors. Applicants are ranked by an index combining ACT score and GPA. The top students are chosen.
How to Apply: Complete the Free Application for Federal Student Aid (FAFSA).
Deadline: May 1.
Amount: $1,000.
Number of Awards: Varies.

1362 • Vocational Scholarship

Purpose: To assist Kansas students to attend vocational colleges.
Eligibility: Applicants must be enrolled in approved vocational programs and take the vocational exam. Selection is based on exam scores.
How to Apply: Applications are available online.
Deadline: Varies.
Amount: $500.
Number of Awards: 250.

Kansas State Department of Education

120 SE 10th Avenue
Topeka, KS 66612
Phone: 785-296-3201
Fax: 785-296-7933
Email: contact@ksde.org
Website: http://www.ksde.org

1363 • Robert C. Byrd Honors Scholarship Program - Kansas

Purpose: To provide scholarship funds to high-achieving seniors in Kansas.

Eligibility: Applicants must be graduating high school seniors or have obtained the equivalent of a high school diploma. They must demonstrate academic achievement and show promise of continued academic achievement and be planning to attend a post-secondary school. Applicants must have an unweighted GPA of at least 3.85 and score of 22 or above on the ACT. Applicants must be U.S. citizens or legal residents.
How to Apply: Applications are available online. Two letters of reference and an essay are required.
Deadline: February 5.
Amount: $1,500.
Number of Awards: Varies.

Midwest Higher Education Commission

1300 S. Second Street
Suite 130
Minneapolis, MN 55454-1079
Phone: 612-626-8288
Fax: 612-626-8290
Email: mhec@mhec.org
Website: http://www.mhec.org

1364 • Midwest Student Exchange Program

Purpose: The program aims to make attending out-of-state schools more affordable for students in member states.

Eligibility: Applicants must currently live in Kansas, Michigan, Minnesota, Missouri, Nebraska or North Dakota and wish to attend a participating school in one of these states outside their own. Other eligibility requirements vary depending on the state and school.

How to Apply: Students must clearly mark that they are an MSEP student when applying to the school of their choice.

Deadline: Varies.

Amount: $500-$3,000.

Number of Awards: Varies.

Related Scholarships:

Bank of America

See #290 • Bank of America ADA Abilities Scholarship Program

State of Residence - Kentucky

Kentucky Higher Education Assistance Authority

P.O. Box 798
Frankfort, KY 40602
Phone: 800-928-8926
Email: blane@kheaa.com
Website: http://www.kheaa.com

1365 • College Access Program

Purpose: To aid Kentucky students with financial need.

Eligibility: Applicants must be Kentucky residents, be enrolled at least half-time in undergraduate academic programs and have an Expected Family Contribution (EFC) based on the FAFSA of lower than approximately $3,850.

How to Apply: Complete the Free Application for Federal Student Aid (FAFSA).

Deadline: Varies.

Amount: $1,400.

Number of Awards: Varies.

1366 • Educational Excellence Scholarship

Purpose: To reward outstanding Kentucky high school students.

Eligibility: Applicants must have a minimum 2.5 GPA, be graduating from eligible Kentucky high schools and meet high school graduation requirements. The scholarship amount is based on high school GPA and ACT composite score.

How to Apply: High schools send eligible students' GPAs to the Kentucky Department of Education.

Deadline: Varies.

Amount: Varies.

Number of Awards: Varies.

1367 • Kentucky Tuition Grant

Purpose: To provide grants to Kentucky residents to attend the Commonwealth's independent colleges.

Eligibility: Applicants must be full-time students enrolled at eligible private institutions. Students must not be enrolled in divinity, theology or religious education degree programs. This is a need-based program.

How to Apply: Complete the Free Application for Federal Student Aid (FAFSA).

Deadline: Varies.

Amount: $200-$2,600.

Number of Awards: Varies.

1368 • Robert C. Byrd Honors Scholarship Program - Kentucky

Purpose: To assist high-achieving high school seniors and GED recipients.

Eligibility: Applicants must be residents of Kentucky and U.S. citizens or nationals. Students must have a GPA of 3.5 or higher and a score of 23 or higher on the ACT or a score of 1060 or higher on the SAT. GED recipients must receive a score of 2700 or higher. Applicants must be nominated by a high school official or GED coordinator, can not be in default on a federal loan and males must be in compliance with Selective Service requirements.

How to Apply: Applications are available online.

Deadline: February 15 for high school and June 30 for GED.

Amount: $1,500.

Number of Awards: Varies.

Related Scholarships:

National Association for Campus Activities

See #1579 • Zagunis Student Leader Scholarship

State of Residence – Louisiana

Louisiana Department of Education

P.O. Box 94064
Baton Rouge, LA 70804
Phone: 877-453-2721
Fax: 225-342-0193
Website: http://www.doe.state.la.us

1369 • Robert C. Byrd Honors Scholarship Program - Louisiana

Purpose: To provide financial support to students who have demonstrated academic achievement.

Eligibility: Applicants must be high school students or GED recipients who are Louisiana residents and U.S. citizens. They must have a GPA of at least 3.5 and score above 23 on the ACT or above 970 on the SAT. GED recipients should have a score above 620. Applicants must be planning to attend an accredited post-secondary institution.

How to Apply: Applications are available from high school guidance counselors and GED coordinators.

Deadline: Varies.

Amount: $1,500.

Number of Awards: 124.

Louisiana Office of Student Financial Assistance

P.O. Box 91202
Baton Rouge, LA 70821
Phone: 800-259-5626
Email: custserv@osfa.state.la.us
Website: http://www.osfa.state.la.us

1370 • Honors Award

Purpose: To aid Louisiana student residents.

Eligibility: Applicants must be Louisiana residents and U.S. citizens, apply during their senior year in high school, use the award at a Louisiana college or university, have a minimum 3.5 GPA and have a minimum ACT score of 27 or equivalent SAT I score.

How to Apply: The application is the Free Application for Federal Student Aid (FAFSA). ACT or SAT I scores must also be reported.

Deadline: July 1.

Amount: Tuition plus $800.

Number of Awards: Varies.

1371 • Leveraging Educational Assistance Partnership (LEAP)

Purpose: To need-based grants to academically qualified Louisiana students.

Eligibility: Students must be U.S. citizens or eligible noncitizens and residents of Louisiana, earn a high school diploma with a minimum 2.0 GPA or GED score minimum and meet the selection criteria of their particular college. All applicants must have substantial financial need as demonstrated on the Free Application for Federal Student Aid (FAFSA) form.

How to Apply: Contact your school's financial aid office for specific information about their LEAP program.

Deadline: July 1.

Amount: $200-$2,000.

Number of Awards: Varies.

1372 • Opportunity Award

Purpose: To aid Louisiana student residents.

Eligibility: Applicants must be Louisiana residents, U.S. citizens, have a minimum 2.5 GPA, have a minimum ACT score of 20 or equivalent SAT I score and apply during their senior year in high school. Applicants must use the award at a Louisiana college or university.

How to Apply: The application is the Free Application for Federal Student Aid (FAFSA). ACT or SAT I scores must also be reported.

Deadline: July 1.

Amount: Varies.

Number of Awards: Varies.

1373 • Performance Award

Purpose: To aid Louisiana student residents.

Eligibility: Applicants must be Louisiana residents, U.S. citizens, apply during their senior year in high school, use the award at a Louisiana college or university, have a minimum 3.5 GPA and have a minimum ACT score of 23 or an equivalent SAT I score.

How to Apply: The application is the Free Application for Federal Student Aid (FAFSA). ACT or SAT I scores must also be reported.

Deadline: July 1.

Amount: Tuition plus $400.

Number of Awards: Varies.

1374 • Rockefeller Wildlife Scholarship

Purpose: To assist Louisiana students in wildlife, forestry or marine science.

Eligibility: Applicants must be Louisiana residents for at least one year, be enrolled as full-time undergraduate or graduate students in a Louisiana public college or university, earn a degree in wildlife, forestry or marine science and have a minimum 2.5 GPA. Applicants must also submit the Free Application for Federal Student Aid (FAFSA) and be U.S. citizens.

How to Apply: Applications are available online or by written request.

Deadline: July 1.

Amount: $1,000.

Number of Awards: Varies.

1375 • Technical Award

Purpose: To assist Louisiana resident students.

Eligibility: Applicants must be Louisiana residents, be U.S. citizens, apply during their senior year in high school, use the award at a Louisiana college, university or technical school that offers nonacademic skill training, have a minimum 2.5 GPA and have a minimum ACT score of 17 or an equivalent SAT I score.

How to Apply: The application is the Free Application for Federal Student Aid (FAFSA). ACT or SAT I scores must also be reported.

Deadline: July 1.

Amount: Tuition.

Number of Awards: Varies.

Related Scholarships:

National Association for Campus Activities

See #924• Markley Scholarship

State of Residence - Maine

American Legion, Department of Maine

21 College Avenue
Waterville, ME 04901
Phone: 207-873-3229
Email: legionme@me.acadia.net
Website: http://www.mainelegion.org

1376 • Children and Youth Scholarships

Purpose: To provide financial support to Maine students.

Eligibility: Applicants must be high school seniors or college students attending or planning to attend an accredited college or vocational school. Applicants must also demonstrate financial need and include two letters of recommendation and a personal statement.

How to Apply: Applications are available online.

Deadline: May 1.

Amount: $500.

Number of Awards: 7.

1377 • Daniel E. Lambert Memorial Scholarship

Purpose: To support the descendents of veterans who demonstrate financial need and who are residents of Maine.

Eligibility: Applicants must be enrolled in an accredited college or vocational technical school and be U.S. citizens. A parent or grandparent must be a veteran, verified by a copy of military discharge papers with the application. Applicants must have good character and believe in the American way of life.

How to Apply: Applications are available online.

Deadline: May 1.

Amount: $1,000.

Number of Awards: Up to 2.

1378 • James V. Day Scholarship

Purpose: To provide financial assistance to the children or grandchildren of American Legion, Department of Maine members.

Eligibility: Applicants must be U.S. citizens, residents of Maine and graduating high school seniors. They must be enrolled in an accredited college or vocational technical school and provide evidence of financial need. Applicants must demonstrate good character and a belief in the American way of life.

How to Apply: Applications are available online.

Deadline: May 1.

Amount: $500.

Number of Awards: 1.

1379 • Maine Oratorical Contest

Purpose: To enhance high school students' experience with and understanding of the U.S. Constitution. The contest will help develop students' leadership skills and civic appreciation, as well as the ability to deliver thoughtful, insightful orations regarding U.S. citizenship and its inherent responsibilities.

Eligibility: Applicants must be high school students under the age of 20 who are U.S. citizens or legal residents and residents of the state. Students first give an oration within their state and winners compete at the national level. The oration must be related to the Constitution of the United States focusing on the duties and obligations citizens have to the government. It must be in English and be between eight and ten minutes. There is also an assigned topic which is posted on the website, and it should be between three and five minutes.

How to Apply: Application information is available by contacting the local American Legion Post.
Deadline: Varies.
Amount: Varies.
Number of Awards: Varies.

Barking Foundation

P.O. Box 855
Bangor, ME 04401
Phone: 207-990-2910
Fax: 207-990-2975
Email: info@barkingfoundation.org
Website: http://www.barkingfoundation.org

1380 • Barking Foundation Grants and Scholarships

Purpose: To financially assist residents of Maine with their post-secondary education goals.
Eligibility: Applicants must be residents of Maine and have demonstrated financial need. There is no minimum GPA requirement for first-time applicants, but to reapply, recipients must have a minimum 3.0 GPA.
How to Apply: Printable applications are available online, but applications must be mailed.
Deadline: February 15.
Amount: $3,000.
Number of Awards: 50.

Maine Community Foundation

245 Main Street
Ellsworth, ME 04605
Phone: 207-667-9735
Fax: 207-667-0447
Email: jwarren@mainecf.org
Website: http://www.mainecf.org

1381 • Maine Community Foundation Scholarship Program

Purpose: To provide financial assistance to Maine students.
Eligibility: There are a number of scholarships in this program for Maine traditional and adult students to attend private high schools, undergraduate colleges or graduate schools. Many are limited to residents of a specific county or graduates of a certain high school.
How to Apply: Applications are available online.
Deadline: April.
Amount: Varies.
Number of Awards: Varies.

Maine Education Assistance Division

Finance Authority of Maine (FAME)
5 Community Drive
P.O. Box 949
Augusta, ME 04332
Phone: 800-228-3734
Fax: 207-623-0095
Email: education@famemaine.com
Website: http://www.famemaine.com

1382 • Maine State Grant Program

Purpose: To support Maine undergraduate students who have financial need.
Eligibility: Applicants must be U.S. citizens or eligible noncitizens, be Maine residents and submit the Free Application for Federal Student Aid (FAFSA) by May 1. If eligible, applicants will receive a notice of award in August.
How to Apply: Complete the FAFSA.
Deadline: May 1.
Amount: $500-$1,250.
Number of Awards: Varies.

1383 • Robert C. Byrd Honors Scholarship Program - Maine

Purpose: To provide support to high-achieving high school seniors.
Eligibility: Applicants must be graduating high school seniors. Home-schooled seniors are eligible if they submit GED scores and high school transcripts, if available. Applicants must be Maine residents who have demonstrated academic achievement and participation in community service activities. They must submit an essay and ACT or SAT scores.
How to Apply: Applications are available online.
Deadline: May 1.
Amount: $1,500.
Number of Awards: Varies.

Maine State Society Foundation of Washington, D.C.

3678 Bay Drive
Edgewater, MD 21037
Phone: 703-237-1031
Email: joanmbeach@aol.com
Website: http://www.mainestatesociety.org

1384 • Maine State Society Foundation Scholarship

Purpose: To provide financial assistance to Maine students.
Eligibility: Applicants must be full-time students who are at least sophomores and must attend an accredited, non-profit college or university located in Maine.
How to Apply: Applications are available by mail and online.
Deadline: April 1.
Amount: $1,000.
Number of Awards: Varies.

Mitchell Institute

22 Monument Square, Suite 200
Portland, ME 04101
Phone: 888-220-7209
Email: info@mitchellinstitute.org
Website: http://www.mitchellinstitute.org

1385 • Senator George J. Mitchell Scholarship Research Institute Scholarships

Purpose: To provide educational opportunities to students in Maine.
Eligibility: Applicants must be legal residents of Maine graduating from a public high school in Maine and attending a two- or four-year program at an accredited college. Scholarships are based on academic performance, community service and financial need.

One scholarship is given out at every Maine public high school, with one extra scholarship per county intended for first-generation college students. While the deadline for the application is April 1, supporting materials have a deadline of May 1.

How to Apply: Applications are available online.
Deadline: April 1.
Amount: $1,250-$1,500.
Number of Awards: Varies.

Related Scholarships:

New England Board of Higher Education

See #1421 · New England Regional Student Program

State of Residence - Maryland

Central Scholarship Bureau

1700 Reisterstown Road
Suite 220
Baltimore, MD 21208-2903
Phone: 410-415-5558
Fax: 410-415-5501
Email: info@centralsb.org
Website: http://www.centralsb.org

1386 • Chesapeake Urology Associates Scholarship

Purpose: To assist full-time Maryland undergraduate students pursuing a degree in pre-medicine, pre-nursing and ancillary health fields.

Eligibility: Applicants must be U.S. citizens or permanent residents, have a minimum 2.0 GPA and meet specified income requirements. The awards are based on commitment to the medical field, financial need and academic excellence. An application form, budget form, school bill, transcript, Student Aid Report, school financial aid award letter and essay are required.

How to Apply: Applications are available online.
Deadline: May 31.
Amount: $5,000.
Number of Awards: 3.

1387 • Ellen R. Clayton Scholarship for Nursing Students

Purpose: To assist full-time undergraduate or graduate students who are pursuing a degree in nursing.

Eligibility: Applicants must be Maryland residents, be U.S. citizens or permanent residents, meet specified income requirements and have a minimum 2.0 GPA. An application form, budget form, school bill, transcript, Student Aid Report, school financial aid award letter and essay are required.

How to Apply: Applications are available online.
Deadline: May 31.
Amount: $2,500.
Number of Awards: 2.

1388 • Lessans Family Scholarship

Purpose: To assist undergraduate Jewish students in Maryland.

Eligibility: Applicants must have already applied for a Central Scholarship Bureau interest-free loan for the current year, be enrolled at an accredited college, university or vocational school, have a certain income level and apply for financial aid and, if offered, accept a subsidized Stafford loan. An application form, budget form, copy of school bills, transcript, Student Aid Report, school financial aid award letter and essay are required. Selection is based on need and merit.

How to Apply: Applications are available online.
Deadline: May 31.
Amount: Varies.
Number of Awards: Varies.

1389 • Mary Rubin and Benjamin M. Rubin Scholarship Fund

Purpose: To help women from Maryland who plan to attend an accredited school.

Eligibility: Applicants must have been out of high school for at least a year and be permanent residents of Maryland. Selection is based on academic achievement, extracurricular activities and financial need. A transcript, recommendation, Student Aid Report (SAR), school financial aid letter, budget form and essay are required.

How to Apply: Applications are available online.
Deadline: March 1.
Amount: $2,500.
Number of Awards: Varies.

1390 • Shoe City-WB54/WB50 Scholarship

Purpose: To help high school seniors who live in Maryland or Washington, DC.

Eligibility: Applicants must be permanent residents of Maryland or Washington DC, plan to attend an accredited college or university full-time and demonstrate financial need. An application, budget form, school bill, transcript, school financial aid award letter and essay are required. Selection is based on financial need, teamwork/community service and academic excellence.

How to Apply: Applications are available online.
Deadline: May 31.
Amount: $1,500.
Number of Awards: 4.

CollegeBound Foundation

Scholarship, Research and Retention Services
300 Water Street
Suite 300
Baltimore, MD 21202
Phone: 410-783-2905
Fax: 410-727-5786
Email: info@collegeboundfoundation.org
Website: http://www.collegeboundfoundation.org

1391 • Last Dollar Grant

Purpose: To help Baltimore City public high school graduates who will attend Maryland colleges.

Eligibility: Applicants must be new graduates of Baltimore City public high schools, have family income of no more than $75,000 per year and contribute at least 15 percent of their college costs through self-help. Students must attend Bowie State University, Coppin State University, Frostburg State University, Morgan State University, St. Mary's College of Maryland, Towson University, University of Maryland College Park, University of Maryland Eastern Shore or Villa Julie College. Applicants must also attend the Transition to College Workshop and the Annual Scholars' Luncheon and other program events scheduled throughout the year. The Student Aid Report, college acceptance letters, financial aid award letter and transcript are required. The grant is given to students whose Expected Family Contribution and financial aid package are less than the cost to attend college. The award is renewable up to five years.

How to Apply: Applications are available online.
Deadline: March 19.
Amount: $3,000.
Number of Awards: Varies.

1392 • Leslie Moore - Baltimore and Howard County Scholarship

Purpose: To help Baltimore and Howard County public high school seniors who have performed community service.

Eligibility: Applicants must be accepted to community colleges, universities or technical schools. A transcript, essay, two recommendation letters and college acceptance letters are required,

and finalists should be available for interviews. One award is for a Baltimore county public high school senior, and the other award is for a Howard county public high school senior.

How to Apply: Applications are available online.
Deadline: March 19.
Amount: $2,500.
Number of Awards: 2.

Maryland Higher Education Commission

Office of Student Financial Assistance
839 Bestgate Road, Suite 400
Annapolis, MD 21401
Phone: 800 974-1024
Fax: 410-974-5994
Email: ssamail@mhec.state.md.us
Website: http://www.mhec.state.md.us/

1393 • Child Care Provider Scholarship

Purpose: To encourage and support students to enter the field of childhood development or early childhood education.

Eligibility: Applicants and their parents must be legal residents of the state of Maryland. Applicants must enroll at a two- or four-year Maryland college or university as a full-time or part-time degree-seeking undergraduate. Applicants must enter a child development program or an early childhood education program. Applicants must also sign a promissory note agreeing to provide child care services in Maryland at the rate of one year for each year of the award.

How to Apply: Complete and file a Child Care Provider Scholarship application.
Deadline: June 15.
Amount: $1,000-$2,000.
Number of Awards: Varies.

1394 • Delegate Scholarship

Purpose: To assist Maryland undergraduate and graduate students who can demonstrate financial need.

Eligibility: Applicants must be legal residents of the state of Maryland and complete the Free Application for Federal Student Aid (FAFSA). Some delegates have supplementary forms. Contact your delegate's office for complete details. Applicants must show financial need.

How to Apply: Complete and file the Free Application for Federal Student Aid (FAFSA). Contact delegate's office for specific application forms. The Office of Student Financial Assistance (OSFA) can provide a list of all State legislators.
Deadline: Varies.
Amount: $200-$2,000.
Number of Awards: Varies.

1395 • Distinguished Scholar Award

Purpose: To recognize high academic performing Maryland students.

Eligibility: Applicants must be high school juniors and U.S. citizens or eligible noncitizens. Finalists in the National Merit Scholarship and National Achievement Scholarship programs will automatically receive the award if they attend a Maryland institution. Applications must be submitted directly to your high school guidance counselor.

How to Apply: Applications may be obtained from the high school guidance counselor.
Deadline: February.
Amount: Varies.
Number of Awards: Varies.

#1396 • Educational Assistance (EA) Grant

Purpose: To help Maryland students with financial need afford college.

Eligibility: Applicants and their parents must both be legal residents of the state of Maryland, U.S. citizens or eligible noncitizens and complete the Free Application for Federal Student Aid (FAFSA).

How to Apply: Complete the FAFSA.

Deadline: March 1.

Amount: $400-$2,700.

Number of Awards: Varies.

#1397 • Graduate and Professional Scholarship Program

Purpose: To assist graduate and professional students who can demonstrate financial need.

Eligibility: Applicants must be U.S. citizens or eligible noncitizens, legal residents of the state of Maryland and complete the Free Application for Federal Student Aid (FAFSA). Applicants must contact the financial aid office of the institution attending and request to be considered for a Graduate and Professional Scholarship. Grants can only be used at the following schools: University of Maryland, Baltimore (UMB) Schools of Medicine, Dentistry, Law, Pharmacy, or Social Work; University of Baltimore School of Law; The Johns Hopkins University School of Medicine; The Virginia-Maryland Regional College of Veterinary Medicine or certain Maryland institutions offering a master's degree in nursing or social work.

How to Apply: Complete the FAFSA and contact the financial aid office.

Deadline: Varies.

Amount: $1,000-$5,000.

Number of Awards: Varies.

#1398 • Guaranteed Access (GA) Grant

Purpose: To help Maryland students with financial need afford college.

Eligibility: Applicants and their parents must both be legal residents of the state of Maryland. Applicants must be U.S. citizens or eligible noncitizens, complete the Free Application for Federal Student Aid (FAFSA) and the Guaranteed Access (GA) Grant application. Applicants and families must also meet the established income limits to qualify.

How to Apply: Complete the FAFSA.

Deadline: March 1.

Amount: $400-$10,200.

Number of Awards: Varies.

#1399 • Hope Community College Transfer Scholarship

Purpose: To help Maryland community college students who want to transfer into a four-year Maryland college or university.

Eligibility: Applicants must be U.S. citizens or eligible noncitizens and current Maryland community college students who will have completed at least 60 credits or who will have earned an associate's degree by the end of the semester in which they will transfer to a Maryland four-year institution.

How to Apply: Complete and file the Free Application for Federal Student Aid (FAFSA), and complete and file the HOPE Community College Transfer Scholarship application.

Deadline: January 1-March 1.

Amount: Varies.

Number of Awards: Varies.

#1400 • HOPE General Scholarship

Purpose: To help Maryland students who major in certain fields at Maryland colleges.

Eligibility: Applicants and their parents must be Maryland residents. All applicants must have an unweighted cumulative high school GPA of 3.0 or higher. Applicant's family income may not exceed $95,000 annually. Applicants must enroll at a two- or four-year Maryland college or university as a full-time, degree-seeking undergraduate student and major in an eligible program. Eligible programs include: agriculture and natural resources, area studies, business and management, communications, fine arts and applied arts, foreign languages, health professions, home economics, interdisciplinary, law, letters (English), psychology, public affairs, social sciences and theology. All applicants are ranked by cumulative grade point average.

How to Apply: Complete and file the Free Application for Federal Student Aid (FAFSA), and complete and file the HOPE Scholarship application.

Deadline: January 1-March 1.

Amount: $1,000-$3,000.

Number of Awards: Varies.

#1401 • Part-Time Grant

Purpose: To assist part-time, degree-seeking undergraduates or students who are simultaneously enrolled in a secondary school and an institution of higher education.

Eligibility: All applicants must be U.S. citizens or eligible noncitizens and legal residents of the state of Maryland. Part-time applicants must complete the Free Application for Federal Student Aid (FAFSA) and contact the financial aid office of the college attending and request to be considered for the Part-Time Grant. Dually enrolled students must contact the college financial aid office to determine the specific application process. This award is based on financial need.

How to Apply: Complete the FAFSA and contact the financial aid office.

Deadline: March 1.

Amount: $200-$1,000.

Number of Awards: Varies.

#1402 • Science and Technology Scholarship

Purpose: To assist Maryland students who are earning an undergraduate degree in the sciences.

Eligibility: Applicants and their parents must be Maryland residents. Applicants not currently enrolled in college must have a cumulative high school GPA of 3.0 or higher. All applicants enrolled in college must have a minimum 3.0 GPA. You must intend to enroll, or be enrolled, at a two- or four-year Maryland college or university as a full-time, degree-seeking undergraduate and major in one of the following degree programs: biological sciences, computer information science, engineering, mathematics or physical sciences.

How to Apply: Complete and file the HOPE Scholarship application.

Deadline: January 1-March 1.

Amount: $1,000-$3,000.

Number of Awards: Varies.

#1403 • Senatorial Scholarship

Purpose: To assist Maryland undergraduate and graduate students who can demonstrate financial need.

Eligibility: Applicants must be U.S. citizens or eligible noncitizens, legal residents of the state of Maryland and complete the Free Application for Federal Student Aid (FAFSA). Some senators have supplementary forms. Contact your area's senator's office for complete details. All applicants must enroll at a two- or four-year Maryland college or university as degree-seeking undergraduate or graduate student, or attend certain private career schools. Applicants must show financial need. High school applicants must also take the SAT I or the ACT.

How to Apply: Complete and file the Free Application for Federal Student Aid (FAFSA). Contact senator for specific application forms. The Office of Student Financial Assistance (OSFA) can provide a list of all State legislators.

Deadline: Varies.

Amount: $200-$2,000.

Number of Awards: Varies.

1404 • State Nursing Scholarship

Purpose: To assist Maryland undergraduates and graduate students who are earning a degree in nursing.

Eligibility: Applicants and their parents must be Maryland residents. Applicants must have a minimum cumulative GPA of 3.0 in high school or college. Applicants must enroll at a two- or four-year Maryland college or university as an undergraduate or graduate student in a program leading to a degree in nursing.

How to Apply: Applications are available by request.

Deadline: June 30.

Amount: Varies.

Number of Awards: Varies.

Maryland State Department of Education

William Cappe
200 W. Baltimore Street
Baltimore, MD 21201
Email: wcappe@msde.state.md.us
Website: http://www.msde.state.md.us

1405 • Robert C. Byrd Honors Scholarship Program - Maryland

Purpose: To recognize student achievement and scholastic excellence.

Eligibility: Applicants must be high school seniors who are Maryland residents and in the top 1 percent of their class. They must be admitted full-time to a post-secondary school, excluding military academies.

How to Apply: Applicants must be nominated by school officials.

Deadline: Varies.

Amount: $1,000-$1,500.

Number of Awards: 129.

Related Scholarships:

Bank of America

See #290• Bank of America ADA Abilities Scholarship Program

National Association for Campus Activities

See #1482• NACA East Coast Undergraduate Scholarship for Student Leaders

American Nursery and Landscape Association

See #110• Carville M. Akehurst Memorial Scholarship

State of Residence – Massachusetts

Big Y

Scholarship Committee
P.O. Box 7840
Springfield, MA 01102-7840
Phone: 413-504-4047
Website: http://www.bigy.com

1406 • Big Y Scholarships

Purpose: To reward students in the Big Y market area and those affiliated with Big Y.

Eligibility: Applicants must either be Big Y employees or their dependents or must reside or attend school in Western or Central Massachusetts, Norfolk County, Massachusetts or Connecticut. The scholarships are available to high school seniors, undergraduates, graduates, community college students and adult students. Applicants should submit transcripts, college entrance exams scores and two recommendation letters. Big Y employees must submit one recommendation from their supervisor. Selection is based on achievements, awards, community involvement, leadership positions and class rank. Eight scholarships are available specifically for dependents of law enforcement officers and firefighters.

How to Apply: Applications are available at any Big Y location from October through January each year. Applications are also available at guidance offices of schools within Big Y's market area.

Deadline: February 1.

Amount: Varies.

Number of Awards: 300.

Community Foundation of Western Massachusetts

1500 Main Street
P.O. Box 15769
Springfield, MA 01115
Phone: 413-732-2858
Fax: 413-733-8565
Email: scholar@communityfoundation.org
Website: http://www.communityfoundation.org

1407 • Diana and Leon Feffer Scholarship Fund

Purpose: To help residents of western Massachusetts to attend college or graduate school.

Eligibility: Applicants must attend a U.S. college or university part-time or full-time. Application forms, transcripts and Student Aid Reports are required. Selection is based on financial need and academic merit.

How to Apply: Applications are available online and by phone.

Deadline: March 31.

Amount: Varies.

Number of Awards: Varies.

1408 • James L. Shriver Scholarship

Purpose: To help students from western Massachusetts to pursue technical careers.

Eligibility: Applicants must attend a U.S. college or university part-time or full-time. Application forms, transcripts and Student Aid Reports are required. Selection is based on financial need and academic merit.

How to Apply: Applications are available online and by phone.
Deadline: March 31.
Amount: $500.
Number of Awards: 1.

1409 • James W. Colgan Loan

Purpose: To provide interest-free educational loans for students who have lived in Massachusetts for the past five years.
Eligibility: Applicants must be part-time or full-time undergraduate or graduate students. Students should provide application forms, transcripts and Student Aid Reports. Recipients will begin repaying the loan three months after graduation, and no interest is charged as long as the monthly payments are made on time.
How to Apply: Applications are available online and by phone.
Deadline: March 31.
Amount: Varies.
Number of Awards: Varies.

1410 • Kimber Richter Family Scholarship

Purpose: To help students of the Baha'i faith from western Massachusetts.
Eligibility: Applicants must attend a U.S. college or university part-time or full-time. Application forms, transcripts and Student Aid Reports are required. Selection is based on financial need and academic merit.
How to Apply: Applications are available online and by phone.
Deadline: March 31.
Amount: $500.
Number of Awards: 1.

1411 • Putnam Scholarship

Purpose: To help African-American and Latino students who live in western Massachusetts and Hartford County in Connecticut.
Eligibility: Applicants must attend a U.S. college or university part-time or full-time. Application forms, transcripts and Student Aid Reports are required. Selection is based on financial need and academic merit. A pastoral letter of reference from any denomination is highly recommended.
How to Apply: Applications are available online and by phone.
Deadline: March 31.
Amount: Varies.
Number of Awards: 7.

1412 • William A. and Vinnie E. Dexter Scholarship

Purpose: To help graduating high school seniors in western Massachusetts.
Eligibility: Applicants must plan to attend college part-time or full-time. Application forms, transcripts and Student Aid Reports are required.
How to Apply: Applications are available online and by phone.
Deadline: March 31.
Amount: Varies.
Number of Awards: Varies.

Massachusetts Department of Education

350 Main Street
Malden, MA 02148
Phone: 781-338-6304
Email: steixeira@doe.mass.edu
Website: http://www.doe.mass.edu

1413 • Robert C. Byrd Honors Scholarship Program - Massachusetts

Purpose: To reward academic achievement in high school seniors.
Eligibility: Applicants must be high school seniors or be earning the equivalent of a high school diploma. They must be Massachusetts residents, having lived in the state at least one year prior to beginning college. Applicants must apply to or be accepted at an accredited post-secondary institution. They must have a GPA of at least 3.5, and the scholarship committee will consider school activities, leadership, community service, employment, awards and honors.
How to Apply: Applications are sent to schools, and schools must nominate students.
Deadline: Varies.
Amount: $1,500.
Number of Awards: Varies.

Massachusetts Office of Student Financial Assistance

454 Broadway
Suite 200
Revere, MA 02151
Phone: 617-727-9420
Fax: 617-727-0667
Email: osfa@osfa.mass.edu
Website: http://www.osfa.mass.edu

1414 • Christian A. Herter Memorial Scholarship Program

Purpose: To provide educational opportunities to Massachusetts students who demonstrate academic promise and a desire to attend post-secondary institutions.
Eligibility: Applicants must be enrolled in a public or private secondary school in the Commonwealth of Massachusetts and be legal residents of the State. Applicants must have a cumulative grade point average of 2.5 and exhibit difficult personal circumstances, high financial need and strong academic promise to continue education beyond the secondary level.
How to Apply: Applications are available online.
Deadline: February-March.
Amount: Varies.
Number of Awards: Varies.

1415 • CommonWealth Futures Grant Program

Purpose: To encourage enrollment in high industry demand programs.
Eligibility: Applicants must be permanent legal residents of Massachusetts or an eligible out-of-state student. Applicants must agree to complete an eligible undergraduate or graduate degree program in one of the following areas: computer and information sciences engineering, engineering-related technologies, biological sciences/life sciences, mathematics, physical sciences or science technologies.
How to Apply: Contact the financial aid office at the institution attending or planning to attend for application forms and deadlines.
Deadline: Varies.
Amount: Varies.
Number of Awards: Varies.

1416 • DSS Adopted Children Tuition Waiver

Purpose: To lessen the financial burden on adopting parents in Massachusetts by extending tuition waivers at eligible schools.

Eligibility: Applicants must be under the age of twenty-four and adopted through the Department of Social Services by eligible Massachusetts residents. The tuition waiver encompasses 100 percent of tuition for state-supported courses at all of the Massachusetts public institutions of higher education, excluding graduate courses.

How to Apply: Contact the financial aid office at the institution attending or planning to attend for application forms and deadlines.

Deadline: Varies.

Amount: Tuition waiver.

Number of Awards: Varies.

1417 • Joint Admissions Tuition Advantage Program Waiver

Purpose: To encourage community college graduates to enter into a four year program by awarding a tuition waiver equal to 33 percent of the resident tuition rate at a State college or participating university.

Eligibility: Applicants must be enrolled in a State College or University and have completed an associate degree at a public community college within the prior calendar year as a participant in the Joint Admissions Program with a minimum GPA of 3.0.

How to Apply: Contact the financial aid office at the institution attending or planning to attend for application forms and deadlines.

Deadline: Varies.

Amount: Up to 33 percent of state tuition.

Number of Awards: Varies.

1418 • MASSGrant

Purpose: To provide need-based financial assistance to undergraduate students who reside in Massachusetts and who are enrolled in and pursuing a program of higher education.

Eligibility: Applicants must be permanent legal residents of Massachusetts and have an Expected Family Contribution (EFC) between $0 and $3,800. Applicants must be enrolled as full-time students in a certificate, associate or bachelor's degree program and not have received a prior bachelor's degree or its equivalent.

How to Apply: Complete and submit the Free Application for Federal Student Aid (FAFSA).

Deadline: May 1.

Amount: $300-$2,000.

Number of Awards: Varies.

1419 • Part Time-Grant program

Purpose: To provide need-based financial assistance to part-time students seeking an undergraduate degree or certificate.

Eligibility: Applicants must be permanent legal residents of Massachusetts for at least one year prior to the start of the academic year for which the grant is awarded. Applicants must be enrolled for at least six but fewer than twelve undergraduate credits per academic term in an eligible undergraduate degree program or eligible certificate program. Applicant must not have previously earned a baccalaureate or professional degree. Applicants must show financial aid need.

How to Apply: Complete and submit the Free Application for Federal Student Aid (FAFSA).

Deadline: May 1.

Amount: $200-full cost of tuition.

Number of Awards: Varies.

1420 • Tomorrow's Teachers Scholarship Program

Purpose: To provide scholarships to academically talented high school students who wish to pursue a teaching career.

Eligibility: Applicants must be permanent legal residents of Massachusetts and rank in the top 25 percent of their high school class. Applicants must agree to enroll and complete a four-year bachelor's degree program at an eligible college or university leading to teacher certification and agree to teach for four years in Massachusetts public schools.

How to Apply: Applications are available online.

Deadline: Varies.

Amount: Varies.

Number of Awards: Varies.

New England Board of Higher Education

45 Temple Place
Boston, MA 02111
Phone: 617-357-9620
Fax: 617-338-1577
Email: rsp@nebhe.org
Website: http://www.nebhe.org

1421 • New England Regional Student Program

Purpose: The program lowers tuition rates for New England students who must travel out of state for their desired major.

Eligibility: Students must be residents of Connecticut, Maine, Massachusetts, New Hampshire, Rhode Island or Vermont and attend a school in another of those states that offers an RSP program in their major. The major must not be available at an in-school state.

How to Apply: Students should note that they are interested in the RSP program on their regular college application.

Deadline: Varies.

Amount: Varies.

Number of Awards: Varies.

State of Residence - Michigan

American Legion, Department of Michigan

212 N. Verlinden Avenue
Lansing, MI 48915
Phone: 517-371-4720 x25
Fax: 517-371-2401
Email: programs@michiganlegion.org
Website: http://www.michiganlegion.org

1422 • Guy M. Wilson Scholarship

Purpose: To aid students who are the sons or daughters of veterans who plan to attend a Michigan college.

Eligibility: Applicants must be residents of Michigan who are planning to attend a Michigan college or university and who are the sons or daughters of veterans. Students must have a minimum GPA of 2.5 and must have demonstrated financial need. Applicants must provide proof of a parent's military service record and an indication of their abilities to fulfill their goals and intentions. They should send scholarship information to their county district committee person.

How to Apply: Applications are available online.
Deadline: January 5.
Amount: $500.
Number of Awards: Varies.

1423 • Michigan Oratorical Contest

Purpose: To enhance high school students' experience with and understanding of the U.S. Constitution. The contest will help develop students' leadership skills and civic appreciation, as well as the ability to deliver thoughtful, insightful orations regarding U.S. citizenship and its inherent responsibilities.

Eligibility: Applicants must be high school students under the age of 20 who are U.S. citizens or legal residents and residents of the state. Students first give an oration within their state and winners compete at the national level. The oration must be related to the Constitution of the United States focusing on the duties and obligations citizens have to the government. It must be in English and be between eight and ten minutes. There is also an assigned topic which is posted on the website, and it should be between three and five minutes.

How to Apply: Application information is available by contacting the appropriate American Legion Oratorical Zone Chairman.
Deadline: January 5.
Amount: Up to $1,000.
Number of Awards: Varies.

1424 • William D. and Jewell Brewer Scholarship

Purpose: To support Michigan students who are the sons, daughters or grandchildren of veterans.

Eligibility: Applicants must be sons, daughters or grandchildren of war-time veterans, residents of Michigan, have a minimum 2.5 GPA and plan to attend a college or university. Scholarships are based on financial need, academic standing and applicants' goals. Applicants must also provide proof of a parent's military service record. They should send scholarship information to the county district committee person.

How to Apply: Applications are available online.
Deadline: January 5.
Amount: $500.
Number of Awards: Varies.

Center for the Education of Women

330 E. Liberty
Ann Arbor, MI 48104-2289
Phone: 734-998-7080
Fax: 734-998-6203
Website: http://www.umich.edu/~cew

1425 • CEW Scholarships

Purpose: To support women who are returning to college after an interruption.

Eligibility: Applicants must be women who are returning to school after an interruption of at least 48 consecutive months or a total of 50 months excluding interruptions of less than 8 months. Candidates must be working toward a clear educational goal at any University of Michigan campus. Preference is given to women wishing to study in non-traditional fields such as mathematics, physical sciences and engineering.

How to Apply: Applications are available online.
Deadline: January 9.
Amount: $1,500-$8,000.
Number of Awards: Approximately 38.

Office of Scholarships and Grants, Bureau of Student Financial Assistance

P.O. Box 30462
Lansing, MI 48909
Phone: 888-4-GRANTS
Email: treasscholgrant@michigan.gov
Website: http://www.michigan.gov/mistudentaid

1426 • Adult Part-Time Grant

Purpose: To assist financially needy, independent undergraduates who have been out of high school for at least two years.

Eligibility: Applicants must be Michigan residents enrolled at a participating public or independent degree-granting Michigan college or university on a part-time basis. Applicants must be able to show financial need and not be in default on an educational loan. This award is distributed through each participating college.

How to Apply: For detailed information and application procedures contact the college or university financial aid office.
Deadline: Varies.
Amount: Varies.
Number of Awards: Varies.

1427 • Michigan Competitive Scholarship

Purpose: To assist students who plan to attend a Michigan public or private college.

Eligibility: Applicants must be Michigan residents since July 1 of the previous calendar year and have received a qualifying score on the ACT and a minimum 2.0 GPA. Applicants must also demonstrate financial need and be enrolled in an approved Michigan college or university. Applicants cannot be pursuing a degree in theology, divinity or religious education. This award is based on both financial need and academic merit.

How to Apply: File a Free Application for Federal Student Aid (FAFSA).
Deadline: February 21 or March 21.
Amount: Varies.
Number of Awards: Varies.

1428 • Michigan Educational Opportunity Grant

Purpose: To assist needy undergraduate students who enroll on at least a half-time basis at a Michigan public community college or university.

Eligibility: Applicants must be residents of Michigan and enrolled at least half-time in eligible undergraduate programs. Applicants must be able to demonstrate financial need and not be in default on an educational loan.

How to Apply: The college awards the funds. Qualifying students apply for this need-based aid by filing a Free Application for Federal Student Aid (FAFSA). The college's financial aid award letter is the means by which students are notified regarding eligibility.

Deadline: Varies.

Amount: Varies.

Number of Awards: Varies.

1429 • Michigan Tuition Grant

Purpose: To assist undergraduate and graduate students with financial need pay for tuition at Michigan colleges and universities.

Eligibility: Applicants must be Michigan residents and attend an approved Michigan college or university. Applicants must also demonstrate financial need and not be in default on an educational loan.

How to Apply: File a Free Application for Federal Student Aid (FAFSA). Priority will be given to students who apply before September 1.

Deadline: September 1.

Amount: Varies.

Number of Awards: Varies.

1430 • Postsecondary Access Student Scholarship (PASS)

Purpose: To assist Michigan students in meeting the cost of tuition and fees in pursuit of an associate's degree at a Michigan community college, college or university.

Eligibility: Applicants must be Michigan residents and enrolled in a program leading to an associate degree. Applicants must have scored at level 1 or level 2 on the Michigan Education Assessment Program (MEAP) tests in reading, writing, mathematics, and science. Applicants must also be eligible for a Federal Pell Grant. Applicants who meet all criteria except for the MEAP test level requirement are eligible for the PASS award for one year and may receive continued aid if satisfactory academic progress is maintained.

How to Apply: File a Free Application for Federal Student Aid (FAFSA).

Deadline: February 21 or March 21.

Amount: Varies.

Number of Awards: Varies.

1431 • Robert C. Byrd Honors Scholarship Program - Michigan

Purpose: To assist outstanding Michigan high school seniors.

Eligibility: Applicants must be U.S. citizens or eligible noncitizens, Michigan residents, high school seniors and demonstrate academic excellence.

How to Apply: Each Michigan high school principal may nominate one outstanding senior.

Deadline: Varies.

Amount: Varies.

Number of Awards: Varies.

Related Scholarships:

Midwest Higher Education Commission

See #1364• Midwest Student Exchange Program

National Association for Campus Activities

See #1579• Zagunis Student Leader Scholarship

State of Residence - Minnesota

American Legion, Department of Minnesota

Third Floor, Veterans Service Building
20 W. 12th Street, Room 300A
St. Paul, MN 55155
Phone: 651-291-1800
Fax: 651-291-1057
Email: department@mnlegion.org
Website: http://www.mnlegion.org

1432 • Minnesota Oratorical Contest

Purpose: To enhance high school students' experience with and understanding of the U.S. Constitution. The contest will help develop students' leadership skills and civic appreciation, as well as the ability to deliver thoughtful, insightful orations regarding U.S. citizenship and its inherent responsibilities.

Eligibility: Applicants must be high school students under the age of 20 who are U.S. citizens or legal residents and residents of the state. Students first give an oration within their state and winners compete at the national level. The oration must be related to the Constitution of the United States focusing on the duties and obligations citizens have to the government. It must be in English and be between eight and ten minutes. There is also an assigned topic which is posted on the website, and it should be between three and five minutes.

How to Apply: Application information is available by email.
Deadline: January 31.
Amount: Up to $1,200.
Number of Awards: 4.

Minnesota Higher Education Services Office

1450 Energy Park Drive
Suite 350
Saint Paul, MN 55108
Phone: 651-642-0567
Fax: 651-642-0675
Email: info@heso.state.mn.us
Website: http://www.mheso.state.mn.us

1433 • Minnesota Academic Excellence Scholarship

Purpose: To help students who have demonstrated outstanding ability, achievement and potential in selected areas of study.

Eligibility: Applicants must be Minnesota residents who have been admitted to a full-time program in an approved Minnesota college or university. Applicants must have demonstrated achievement in one of the following subjects: English or creative writing, fine arts, foreign language, math, science or social science.

How to Apply: For information about the status of this program, applicants should contact the schools they wish to attend.
Deadline: Varies.
Amount: Varies.
Number of Awards: Varies.

1434 • Minnesota Indian Scholarship Program

Purpose: To provide money to help Native American students pay for higher education.

Eligibility: Applicants must be at least one-fourth Native American, Minnesota residents and members of a federally recognized Indian tribe. Applicants must be a high school graduate or posses a GED and have been accepted by an approved college, university or vocational school in Minnesota.

How to Apply: This award is administered by the Minnesota Department of Children, Families, and Learning (CFL), and must be approved by the Minnesota Indian Scholarship Committee. To receive an application, contact your local tribal education office.
Deadline: Varies.
Amount: Varies.
Number of Awards: Varies.

1435 • Minnesota State Grant

Purpose: To help students from low and moderate income families pay for colleges or universities.

Eligibility: Applicants must be Minnesota residents who are high school graduates and will be 17 years of age or over by the end of the academic year. Applicants must be enrolled as undergraduates for at least three credits at one of more than 160 eligible schools in Minnesota.

How to Apply: Use the Free Application for Federal Student Aid (FAFSA) to apply for the Minnesota State Grant.
Deadline: Varies.
Amount: Varies.
Number of Awards: Varies.

1436 • Robert C. Byrd Honors Scholarship Program - Minnesota

Purpose: To assist outstanding Minnesota high school seniors.

Eligibility: Applicants must be U.S. citizens or eligible noncitizens, Minnesota residents, high school seniors and demonstrate academic excellence.

How to Apply: Minnesota Department of Children, Families, & Learning, sends out the nomination information in January. Applicants apply through their high school and should contact their principal or counselor for application forms.
Deadline: March.
Amount: Varies.
Number of Awards: 125.

Related Scholarships:

Vincent L. Hawkinson Foundation for Peace and Justice

See #1349• Vincent L. Hawkinson Scholarship for Peace and Justice

Midwest Higher Education Commission

See #1364• Midwest Student Exchange Program

State of Residence - Mississippi

Mississippi Department of Education

P.O. Box 771
Jackson, MS 39205
Phone: 601-359-3513
Email: webhelp@mde.k12.ms.us
Website: http://www.mde.k12.ms.us

1437 • Robert C. Byrd Honors Scholarship Program - Mississippi

Purpose: To recognize and promote academic excellence and achievement.

Eligibility: Applicants must be residents of Mississippi and U.S. citizens or permanent residents. They must be graduating high school seniors or have earned their GED during the application year and have applied or been accepted to a post-secondary school. Applications must include ACT or SAT scores, high school transcript or GED test results, extracurricular activities, leadership activities, honors and awards and a one-page essay.

How to Apply: Applications are available online.

Deadline: March 31.

Amount: $1,100-$1,500.

Number of Awards: 70-75.

Mississippi Office of Student Financial Aid

3825 Ridgewood Road
Jackson, MS 39211
Phone: 800-327-2980
Fax: 601-432-6527
Email: sfa@ihl.state.ms.us
Website: http://www.ihl.state.ms.us

1438 • Critical Needs Teacher Program

Purpose: To increase the supply of teachers for public schools in Mississippi.

Eligibility: Applicants must be enrolled as full-time students in programs leading to an 'A' level teaching license and must have a college GPA of 2.5 or higher. Applicants must be admitted to an eligible Mississippi institution at the time of application. Applicants must also agree to the service obligation, which calls for one year of service in a Mississippi public school district located in a critical teacher shortage area for each year the scholarship is received.

How to Apply: Contact the Mississippi Office of Student Financial Aid for an application.

Deadline: March 31.

Amount: Full tuition.

Number of Awards: Varies.

1439 • Higher Education Legislative Plan (HELP)

Purpose: To assist financially needy Mississippi students afford tuition.

Eligibility: Applicants must be U.S. citizens or eligible noncitizens, Mississippi residents and have a minimum college GPA of 2.5 and have graduated from high school within the past two years. Applicants must be attending an eligible Mississippi institution, must have a minimum ACT score of 20 and must document an average gross income of $36,000 or less over the prior two years, and must have the results of a processed Student Aid Report (SAR). Students who file the Free Application for Federal Student Aid (FAFSA) will receive a SAR report.

How to Apply: Contact the Mississippi Office of Student Financial Aid for an application.

Deadline: March 31.

Amount: Varies.

Number of Awards: Varies.

1440 • Mississippi Eminent Scholars Grant (MESG)

Purpose: To recognize academically high performing Mississippi students.

Eligibility: Applicants must be U.S. citizens or eligible noncitizens and current legal residents of Mississippi who are enrolled as full-time, 'first-time-in-college' undergraduates. Applicants must have a high school GPA of 3.5 and a minimum ACT of 29. National Merit/National Achievement semifinalists with a 3.5 grade-point average qualify without the test score.

How to Apply: Applicants must complete an MTAG/MESG application and either a FAFSA or a Statement of Certification (a waiver for completing the FAFSA).

Deadline: September.

Amount: Varies.

Number of Awards: Varies.

1441 • Mississippi Tuition Assistance Grant (MTAG)

Purpose: To assist financially needy Mississippi students afford tuition.

Eligibility: Applicants must be current legal residents of Mississippi who are enrolled as full-time undergraduates. Applicants must have a high school grade-point average of 2.5 and a minimum ACT of 15.

How to Apply: Applicants must complete an MTAG/MESG application and either a FAFSA or a Statement of Certification (a waiver for completing the FAFSA).

Deadline: September.

Amount: Varies.

Number of Awards: Varies.

1442 • William Winter Teacher Scholarship

Purpose: To increase the supply of teachers for public schools in Mississippi.

Eligibility: Applicants must be enrolled as full-time students in programs leading to a Class 'A' teaching license and must have a high school GPA of 3.0 or higher and an ACT score of 21 or higher. Sophomores, juniors, seniors and persons seeking a second baccalaureate degree leading to a Class "A" teaching license must have a cumulative college GPA of 2.5 or higher. Applicants must also agree to serve for one year in any Mississippi public school for each year they receive the scholarship. Awards are made on a first come, first served basis.

How to Apply: Contact the Mississippi Office of Student Financial Aid for an application.

Deadline: March.

Amount: $1,000-$3,000.

Number of Awards: Varies.

Related Scholarships:

National Association for Campus Activities

See #1288 • NACA Southeast Region Student Leader Scholarship

State of Residence - Missouri

American Legion, Department of Missouri

P.O. Box 179
Jefferson City, MO 65102
Phone: 800-846-9023
Fax: 573-893-2980
Email: bmayberry@missourilegion.org
Website: http://www.missourilegion.org/programs/oratorical.
htm

1443 • Missouri Oratorical Contest

Purpose: To enhance high school students' experience with and understanding of the U.S. Constitution. The contest will help develop students' leadership skills and civic appreciation, as well as the ability to deliver thoughtful, insightful orations regarding U.S. citizenship and its inherent responsibilities.

Eligibility: Applicants must be high school students under the age of 20 who are U.S. citizens or legal residents and residents of the state. Students first give an oration within their state and winners compete at the national level. The oration must be related to the Constitution of the United States focusing on the duties and obligations citizens have to the government. It must be in English and be between eight and ten minutes. There is also an assigned topic which is posted on the website, and it should be between three and five minutes.

How to Apply: Application information is available by email.
Deadline: November 30.
Amount: Up to $3,500.
Number of Awards: Varies.

Missouri Department of Elementary and Secondary Education

P.O. Box 480
Jefferson City, MO 65102
Phone: 573-751-1668
Fax: 573-751-8613
Email: webreplyqualtrr@dese.mo.gov
Website: http://www.dese.mo.gov

1444 • Robert C. Byrd Honors Scholarship Program - Missouri

Purpose: To recognize and promote academic excellence and achievement.

Eligibility: Applicants must be Missouri high school graduates or GED recipients. They must be U.S. citizens or permanent residents. Applicants must be in the top 10 percent of their class and score above the 90th percentile on the ACT.

How to Apply: Applications are available online.
Deadline: April 15.
Amount: $1,500.
Number of Awards: Varies.

Missouri Student Assistance Resource Services (MOSTARS)

Missouri Department of Higher Education
3515 Amazonas Drive
Jefferson City, MO 65109
Phone: 800-473-6757
Fax: 573-751-6635
Website: http://www.dhe.mo.gov

1445 • Charles Gallagher Student Financial Assistance Program

Purpose: To provide need-based grants for Missouri citizens to access Missouri postsecondary education.

Eligibility: Applicants must be U.S. citizens or eligible noncitizens, Missouri residents who are full-time undergraduates at an approved Missouri postsecondary schools and working toward their first baccalaureate degree. Applicants must demonstrate financial need.

How to Apply: Complete the Free Application for Federal Student Aid (FAFSA) by April 1 of the upcoming academic year.
Deadline: April 1.
Amount: Varies.
Number of Awards: Varies.

1446 • Higher Education Academic Scholarship Program (Bright Flight)

Purpose: This merit-based program encourages top-ranked high school seniors to attend approved Missouri postsecondary schools.

Eligibility: Applicants must be U.S. citizens or eligible noncitizens, Missouri residents and have an ACT or SAT score within the top 3 percent of all Missouri students taking those tests. Applicants must be high school seniors who enroll as first-time, full-time students at an approved Missouri postsecondary school.

How to Apply: For an application contact your high school counselor or MOSTARS.
Deadline: July 31.
Amount: Varies.
Number of Awards: Varies.

1447 • Marguerite Ross Barnett Memorial Scholarship

Purpose: This scholarship was established for students who are employed while attending school part-time.

Eligibility: Applicants must be U.S. citizens or eligible noncitizens, Missouri residents and enrolled at least half-time but less than full-time at a participating Missouri college or university. Applicants must also be employed for at least 20 hours per week and be able to demonstrate financial need.

How to Apply: Applications are available online.
Deadline: April 1.
Amount: Varies.
Number of Awards: Varies.

1448 • Missouri College Guarantee Program

Purpose: To assist Missouri students who have demonstrated financial need and high school or college academic achievement.

Eligibility: Applicants must be U.S. citizens or eligible noncitizens, Missouri residents and have a high school GPA of 2.5 and an ACT score of 20 or an SAT I score of 950. Applicants must have participated in high school extracurricular activities and be enrolled full-time at a participating Missouri college or university.

How to Apply: Complete the Free Application for Federal Student Aid (FAFSA) and have achieved the required ACT or SAT score and the other high school eligibility requirements by April 1.
Deadline: April 1.
Amount: Varies.
Number of Awards: Varies.

Related Scholarships:

Bank of America

See #290 • Bank of America ADA Abilities Scholarship Program

Midwest Higher Education Commission

See #1364 • Midwest Student Exchange Program

State of Residence - Montana

Montana Department of Education

The Montana Office of Public Instruction
P.O. Box 202501
Helena, MT 59620
Website: http://www.opi.state.mt.us

1449 • Robert C. Byrd Honors Scholarship Program - Montana

Purpose: To assist outstanding Montana high school seniors.
Eligibility: Applicants must be U.S. citizens or eligible noncitizens, Montana residents, high school seniors and have a GPA of at least 3.6 in a college preparatory curriculum, and a cumulative score of 1380 on the SAT or 30 on the ACT.
How to Apply: Applications are available at your high school counseling office or online.
Deadline: March.
Amount: Varies.
Number of Awards: Varies.

Student Assistance Foundation of Montana

2500 Broadway
Helena, MT 59601
Phone: 406-495-7800
Fax: 406-495-7880
Email: vsteiner@safmt.org
Website: http://www.safmt.org

1450 • MHEG- Montana Higher Education Grant

Purpose: To assist Montana students with financial need pay for college.
Eligibility: Applicants must be U.S. citizens or eligible noncitizens, Montana residents and have exceptional financial need. Grants are awarded through individual colleges and universities.
How to Apply: Complete the Free Application for Federal Student Aid (FAFSA). Contact your college's financial aid office for details.
Deadline: Varies.
Amount: Varies.
Number of Awards: Varies.

1451 • MTAP - Montana Tuition Assistance Program/Baker Grant

Purpose: To assist Montana students with financial need pay for college.
Eligibility: Applicants must be U.S. citizens or eligible noncitizens, residents of Montana who have earnings greater than $2,575 and an EFC of between $0 and $6,500.
How to Apply: Contact your college's financial aid office for details.
Deadline: Varies.
Amount: $100-$1,000.
Number of Awards: Varies.

Treacy Company

P.O. Box 1700
Helena, MT 59624
Phone: 406-443-3549

1452 • Treacy Company Scholarship
Purpose: To support students in Montana, Idaho, North Dakota and South Dakota.
Eligibility: Applicants must be freshmen or sophomores in college and reside in Montana, Idaho, North Dakota or South Dakota.
How to Apply: Applications are available by mail.
Deadline: Varies.
Amount: $400.
Number of Awards: Varies.

Related Scholarships:

National Association for Campus Activities

See #1201 • Lori Rhett Memorial Scholarship

Alert Magazine

See #1567 • Alert Scholarship

State of Residence - Nebraska

Lincoln Community Foundation

215 Centennial Mall South, Suite 100
Lincoln, NE 68508
Phone: 402-474-2345
Fax: 402-476-8532
Email: lcf@lcf.org
Website: http://www.lcf.org

1453 • Norman & Ruth Good Educational Endowment
Purpose: To assist Nebraska students.
Eligibility: Applicants must be attending a private college in Nebraska and must be in their junior or senior year. Applicants may not apply if the scholarship money is to be used for summer programs or schools that are not valid degree-granting institutions.
How to Apply: Applications are available online.
Deadline: April 15.
Amount: Varies.
Number of Awards: Varies.

Nebraska Coordinating Commission for Postsecondary Education

P.O. Box 95005
Lincoln, NE 68509
Phone: 402-471-2847
Fax: 402-471-2886
Website: http://www.ccpe.state.ne.us

1454 • Postsecondary Education Award Program (PEAP)
Purpose: To assist students (including out-of-state students) in attending a Nebraska college or university.
Eligibility: Applicants must be enrolled in a Nebraska college and qualify for a federal Pell grant. Applicants apply for the grant through their specific college or university.
How to Apply: Complete the Free Application for Federal Student Aid (FAFSA).
Deadline: Varies.
Amount: Varies.
Number of Awards: Varies.

1455 • Scholarship Assistance Program (SAP)
Purpose: To assist Nebraska students attend a Nebraska college or university.
Eligibility: Applicants must be residents of the state of Nebraska, qualify for a federal Pell grant and be enrolled in a Nebraska college. Applicants apply for the grant through their specific college or university.
How to Apply: Complete the Free Application for Federal Student Aid (FAFSA).
Deadline: Varies.
Amount: Varies.
Number of Awards: Varies.

1456 • State Scholarship Award Program (SSAP)

Purpose: To assist Nebraska students in attending a Nebraska college or university.

Eligibility: Applicants must be residents of the state of Nebraska, qualify for a federal Pell grant and be enrolled in a Nebraska college. Applicants apply for the grant through their specific college or university.

How to Apply: Complete the Free Application for Federal Student Aid (FAFSA).

Deadline: Varies.

Amount: Varies.

Number of Awards: Varies.

Nebraska Department of Education

301 Centennial Mall South
P.O. Box 94987
Lincoln, NE 68509
Phone: 402-471-2295
Email: mardi.north@nde.ne.gov
Website: http://www.nde.state.ne.us

1457 • Robert C. Byrd Honors Scholarship Program - Nebraska

Purpose: To honor academic excellence and potential.

Eligibility: Applicants must be Nebraska residents who are graduating from high school or receiving a GED with a minimum ACT score of 30. They must be U.S. citizens, nationals or permanent residents. Applicants must have applied or been accepted to a post-secondary school, planning to attend full-time. They must fulfill all Selective Service requirements and not be in default on any student loans.

How to Apply: Applications are available online.

Deadline: March 15.

Amount: Up to $1,500.

Number of Awards: 40.

Union Bank and Trust

18 W. 23rd Street
Attn.: Franny Madsen
Kearney, NE 68847
Phone: 308-237-7593
Website: http://www.ubt.com/personal/studentloans.htm

1458 • Money to Learn Scholarship

Purpose: To help Nebraska high school students.

Eligibility: Applicants must be Nebraska high schools seniors in the upper 1/3 of their graduating class or have a minimum ACT score of 20 and must plan to attend post-secondary institutions full-time in the state. Applicants should submit scholarship applications, proof of class rank and/or test scores and non-returnable photos for publicity purposes. Selection is based on meeting the minimum requirements and the quality of the essay.

How to Apply: Applications are available online.

Deadline: March 15.

Amount: $500.

Number of Awards: 24.

Related Scholarships:

Midwest Higher Education Commission

See #1364 • Midwest Student Exchange Program

State of Residence - Nevada

Nevada Department of Education

700 E. Fifth Street
Carson City, NV 89701
Phone: 775-687-9200
Fax: 775-687-9101
Website: http://www.nde.state.nv.us

1459 • Robert C. Byrd Honors Scholarship Program - Nevada

Purpose: To recognize and promote excellence and achievement among Nevada students.
Eligibility: Applicants must be legal residents of the State of Nevada, be Nevada High School Scholars Program recipients and be accepted into an institution of higher education.
How to Apply: Contact your high school guidance counselor.
Deadline: Varies.
Amount: $1,500.
Number of Awards: 60.

Nevada Women's Fund

770 Smithridge Drive
Suite 300
Reno, NV 89502
Phone: 775-786-2335
Fax: 775-786-8152
Email: info@nevadawomensfund.org
Website: http://www.nevadawomensfund.org

1460 • Nevada Women's Fund Scholarships

Purpose: To improve the lives of women and children in northern Nevada.
Eligibility: Northern Nevada residents and those attending northern Nevada schools receive preference.
How to Apply: Applications are available online or from several offices listed on the website.
Deadline: February 27.
Amount: $500 and up.
Number of Awards: Varies.

Related Scholarships:

Bank of America

See #290 • Bank of America ADA Abilities Scholarship Program

State of Residence - New Hampshire

New Hampshire Postsecondary Education Commission

3 Barrell Court, Suite 300
Concord, NH 03301
Phone: 603-271-6051
Fax: 603-271-2696
Website: http://www.state.nh.us/postsecondary/

1461 • New Hampshire Incentive Program

Purpose: To assist New Hampshire students attending eligible New England institutions.
Eligibility: Applicants must be New Hampshire residents, demonstrate financial need and be working towards their first bachelor's degree at an eligible New England institution.
How to Apply: Applicants must complete the Free Application for Federal Student Aid (FAFSA).
Deadline: May 1.
Amount: $125-$1,000.
Number of Awards: Varies.

1462 • Robert C. Byrd Honors Scholarship Program - New Hampshire

Purpose: To assist exceptional New Hampshire students in postsecondary study.
Eligibility: Applicants must be New Hampshire residents, U.S. citizens or eligible noncitizens and high school seniors who plan to be full-time college students.
How to Apply: Contact the New Hampshire Department of Education for more information and an application.
Deadline: First Friday in April.
Amount: $1,500.
Number of Awards: Varies.

1463 • Workforce Incentive Program

Purpose: To encourage New Hampshire students to enter career shortage areas in special education, foreign language, mathematics, chemistry, science, physics and nursing. The scholarship repays education loans.
Eligibility: Applicants must have completed at least one year of service in an approved shortage area for each year of repayment.
How to Apply: Applications are available online.
Deadline: October 31.
Amount: $1,500-$3,000.
Number of Awards: Varies.

Related Scholarships:

New England Board of Higher Education

See #1421 • New England Regional Student Program

State of Residence - New Jersey

American Legion, Department of New Jersey

135 W. Hanover Street
Trenton, NJ 08618
Phone: 609-695-5418
Fax: 609-394-1532
Email: adjudant@njamericanlegion.org
Website: http://www.njamericanlegion.org

1464 • Luterman Scholarship

Purpose: To award descendants of American Legion members with scholarships.

Eligibility: Applicants must be direct descendants of American Legion, Department of New Jersey members. Applicants must be high school seniors and use the award in the year it is received.

How to Apply: Applications are available by contacting the local Post or Department Headquarters.

Deadline: February 15.

Amount: Up to $4,000.

Number of Awards: Varies.

1465 • New Jersey Oratorical Contest

Purpose: To enhance high school students' experience with and understanding of the U.S. Constitution. The contest will help develop students' leadership skills and civic appreciation, as well as the ability to deliver thoughtful, insightful orations regarding U.S. citizenship and its inherent responsibilities.

Eligibility: Applicants must be high school students under the age of 20 who are U.S. citizens or legal residents and residents of the state. Students first give an oration within their state and winners compete at the national level. The oration must be related to the Constitution of the United States focusing on the duties and obligations citizens have to the government. It must be in English and be between eight and ten minutes. There is also an assigned topic which is posted on the website, and it should be between three and five minutes.

How to Apply: Application information is available by email: ray@njamericanlegion.org.

Deadline: March 18.

Amount: Up to $5,500.

Number of Awards: 5.

1466 • Safety Essay Contest

Purpose: To award students for exceptional essays regarding safety.

Eligibility: Applicants must be in the 6th, 7th or 8th grade and enrolled in a New Jersey school.

How to Apply: Application information is available from the local Department.

Deadline: March 23.

Amount: Varies.

Number of Awards: Varies.

1467 • Stutz Scholarship

Purpose: To award children of American Legion members with scholarships.

Eligibility: Applicants must be children of members of the American Legion, Department of New Jersey. Applicants must also be high school seniors and use the award in the year it is received.

How to Apply: Applications are available by contacting the local Post or Department Headquarters.

Deadline: February 15.

Amount: $4,000.

Number of Awards: 1.

Freehold Soil Conservation District

4000 Kozloski Road
P.O. Box 5033
Freehold, NJ 07728
Phone: 732-683-8500
Fax: 732-683-9140
Email: info@freeholdscd.org
Website: http://www.freeholdscd.org

1468 • Freehold Soil Conservation District Scholarship

Purpose: To support college juniors and seniors majoring in the conservation of natural resources.

Eligibility: Applicants must be residents of Middlesex or Monmouth County, New Jersey, entering the junior or senior year in the fall. Students must major in an area related to conservation of natural resources such as agriculture; forestry; conservation; environmental or soil science; environmental studies, education, or policy; resource management or geology.

Deadline: April 7.

Amount: $1,000.

Number of Awards: 3.

New Jersey Commission on Higher Education

20 W. State Street, 7th Floor
P.O. Box 542
Trenton, NJ 08625
Phone: 609-984-2709
Fax: 609-292-7225
Email: glang@che.state.nj.us
Website: http://www.state.nj.us/highereducation/

1469 • Educational Opportunity Fund

Purpose: To assist students from disadvantaged backgrounds to attend higher education institutions in New Jersey.

Eligibility: Applicants must be New Jersey residents who attend a school in the state and have poverty level incomes. Awards are available for undergraduate students and graduate students through the Graduate Grants, Martin Luther King Physician-Dentist Scholarship and C. Clyde Ferguson Law Scholarship.

How to Apply: Contact your financial aid office.

Deadline: Varies.

Amount: $2,100-$4,150.

Number of Awards: Varies.

New Jersey Higher Education Student Assistance Authority

P.O. Box 540
Trenton, NJ 08625
Phone: 800-792-8670
Website: http://www.hesaa.org

1470 • Edward J. Bloustein Distinguished Scholars

Purpose: To support the highest achieving New Jersey students.

Eligibility: Applicants must be high school seniors who are New Jersey residents, be ranked in the top 10 percent of their classes, have a minimum SAT score of 1260 and plan to attend an institution of higher education. Juniors who are ranked first, second or third in their class at the end of the year may also apply. Applicants who attend high schools in the state's urban and economically distressed areas, who rank in the top 10 percent of their class and who have a minimum 3.0 GPA may also be selected through funding from the Urban Scholars Program.

How to Apply: Applicants are nominated by their high schools and must complete and submit the Free Application for Federal Student Aid (FAFSA).
Deadline: October 1.
Amount: $1,000.
Number of Awards: Varies.

State of New Jersey Department of Education

P.O. Box 500
Trenton, NJ 08625
Phone: 609-292-4469
Website: http://www.state.nj.us/education

1471 • Robert C. Byrd Honors Scholarship Program - New Jersey
Purpose: To reward academic achievement in graduating seniors and GED recipients.
Eligibility: Applicants must be New Jersey residents who are U.S. citizens or permanent residents. Scholarships are awarded based on merit and are renewable for four years of undergraduate study.
How to Apply: Applications are available from the department of education and school officials.
Deadline: Varies.
Amount: Up to $1,500.
Number of Awards: Varies.

Related Scholarships:

National Association for Campus Activities
See #1482 • NACA East Coast Undergraduate Scholarship for Student Leaders

State of Residence - New Mexico

Albuquerque Community Foundation (ACF)

P.O. Box 36960
Albuquerque, NM 87176
Phone: 505-883-6240
Email: tflynn@albuquerquefoundation.org
Website: http://www.albuquerquefoundation.org

1472 • Excel Staffing Companies Scholarships for Excellence in Continuing Education
Purpose: To assist individuals who demonstrate a commitment to achieving a career goal.
Eligibility: Applicants must be at least 21 years old and be Albuquerque area residents. Applicants must also work a minimum of 30 hours a week, have a 3.0 minimum GPA and be in need of financial assistance to obtain a goal.
How to Apply: Applications are available online.
Deadline: July 1.
Amount: Up to $1,000.
Number of Awards: Varies.

1473 • Sussman-Miller Educational Assistance Award
Purpose: To assist New Mexico high school graduates and college undergraduates.
Eligibility: Students must be New Mexico residents for a minimum of one year, have been awarded a financial package that does not satisfy demonstrated need and be accepted by and have chosen to attend a U.S. post-secondary, accredited, nonprofit educational institution full-time. High school applicants need to graduate from an accredited public or private high school and have a 3.0 minimum GPA. Undergraduate applicants must have completed a minimum of one semester of undergraduate study with a 2.5 minimum GPA and cannot be applying for residency in another state.
How to Apply: Applications are available online.
Deadline: April 20 or June 2.
Amount: $500-$2,500.
Number of Awards: Varies.

New Mexico Commission on Higher Education

1068 Cerrillos Road
Santa Fe, NM 87505
Phone: 800-279-9777
Fax: 505-476-6511
Website: http://hed.state.nm.us

1474 • 3 Percent Scholarships
Purpose: To support New Mexico undergraduate and graduate students to attend postsecondary institutions in New Mexico.
Eligibility: Applicants must be undergraduate or graduate students who attend public postsecondary institutions in New Mexico. Each participating college or university has its own eligibility requirements.
How to Apply: Contact your financial aid office.
Deadline: Varies.
Amount: Up to full tuition and fees.
Number of Awards: Varies.

1475 • Legislative Endowment Scholarships

Purpose: To support New Mexico undergraduate students with financial need attend postsecondary institutions in New Mexico.

Eligibility: Applicants must be undergraduate students who are New Mexico residents and attending public postsecondary institutions at least half-time in the state. Preference is given to adult students and transfer students from two-year New Mexico public postsecondary institutions to four-year institutions.

How to Apply: Contact your financial aid office and complete the Free Application for Federal Student Aid (FAFSA).

Deadline: Varies.

Amount: $1,000-$2,500.

Number of Awards: Varies.

1476 • Lottery Success Scholarships

Purpose: To support graduating New Mexico high school seniors with financial need.

Eligibility: Applicants must be graduating high school seniors in New Mexico, enroll full-time at an eligible New Mexico public college or university and maintain a minimum 2.5 GPA during the first college semester.

How to Apply: Contact your financial aid office.

Deadline: Varies.

Amount: Up to full tuition.

Number of Awards: Varies.

1477 • New Mexico Scholars

Purpose: To support New Mexico undergraduate students with financial need attend postsecondary institutions in New Mexico.

Eligibility: Applicants must be undergraduate students attending selected New Mexico public institutions or designated private non-profit colleges, meet family income requirements, be under the age of 22 and have graduated in the top 5 percent of their high school class or have a minimum ACT score of 25.

How to Apply: Contact your financial aid office.

Deadline: Varies.

Amount: Up to full tuition.

Number of Awards: Varies.

1478 • Student Incentive Grants

Purpose: To support New Mexico undergraduate students with financial need to attend postsecondary institutions in New Mexico.

Eligibility: Applicants must be New Mexico resident undergraduate students and attend public and selected private nonprofit postsecondary institutions in New Mexico at least half-time.

How to Apply: Contact your financial aid office.

Deadline: Varies.

Amount: $200-$2,500.

Number of Awards: Varies.

New Mexico Public Education Department

300 Don Gaspar
Santa Fe, NM 87501
Phone: 505-827-5800
Website: http://www.ped.state.nm.us

1479 • Robert C. Byrd Honors Scholarship Program - New Mexico

Purpose: To recognize the educational accomplishments of outstanding students.

Eligibility: Applicants must be New Mexico residents who are graduating high school seniors or who have received a GED. They must have a GPA of at least 3.5 and score higher than 1220 on the SAT or higher than 27 on the ACT.

How to Apply: Applications are available from school officials and the public education department.

Deadline: Varies.

Amount: $1,500.

Number of Awards: 44.

Related Scholarships:

Bank of America

See #290• *Bank of America ADA Abilities Scholarship Program*

National Association for Campus Activities

See #924• *Markley Scholarship*

State of Residence - New York

American Legion, Department of New York

112 State Street, Suite 1300
Albany, NY 12207
Email: info@nylegion.org
Website: http://www.ny.legion.org

1480 • New York Oratorical Contest

Purpose: To enhance high school students' experience with and understanding of the U.S. Constitution. The contest will help develop students' leadership skills and civic appreciation, as well as the ability to deliver thoughtful, insightful orations regarding U.S. citizenship and its inherent responsibilities.

Eligibility: Applicants must be high school students under the age of 20 who are U.S. citizens or legal residents and residents of the state. Students first give an oration within their state and winners compete at the national level. The oration must be related to the Constitution of the United States focusing on the duties and obligations citizens have to the government. It must be in English and be between eight and ten minutes. There is also an assigned topic which is posted on the website, and it should be between three and five minutes.

How to Apply: Application information is available by contacting the local American Legion Post.

Deadline: March 10.

Amount: Varies.

Number of Awards: Varies.

Center for Women in Government and Civil Society

University at Albany, SUNY
135 Western Avenue
Draper Hall 302
Albany, NY 12222
Phone: 518-442-3900
Fax: 518-442-3877
Website: http://www.cwig.albany.edu

1481 • Fellowship on Women and Public Policy

Purpose: To encourage New York state graduate students to pursue jobs in public policy.

Eligibility: Students must be enrolled in a graduate program at an accredited college or university in New York and have completed at least 12 credits before applying but not be scheduled to graduate before the internship. Applicants must demonstrate an interest in improving the status of women and underrepresented populations.

How to Apply: Applications are available online.

Deadline: May 15, although applications will be considered throughout the fall.

Amount: $9,000 stipend and tuition assistance.

Number of Awards: Varies.

National Association for Campus Activities

13 Harbison Way
Columbia, SC 29212-3401
Phone: 803-732-6222
Fax: 803-749-1047
Email: info@naca.org
Website: http://www.naca.org

1482 • NACA East Coast Undergraduate Scholarship for Student Leaders

Purpose: To provide financial assistance to East Coast student leaders.

Eligibility: Students must hold a significant campus leadership position, demonstrate significant leadership skills and abilities and make significant contributions through on- or off-campus volunteering. Students must attend school in Delaware, New Jersey, Maryland, New York, Eastern Pennsylvania or Washington, DC.

How to Apply: Applications are available online.

Deadline: March 31.

Amount: Varies.

Number of Awards: 2.

New York Lottery LOT Scholarships

One Broadway Center
P.O. Box 7540
Schenectady, NY 12301-7540
Phone: 518-388-3415
Fax: 518-388-3423
Email: lotscholar@lottery.state.ny.us
Website: http://www.nylottery.org/lot

1483 • New York Lottery Leaders of Tomorrow Scholarship

Purpose: To help New York State high school seniors who plan to attend colleges in the state.

Eligibility: Applicants must have demonstrated leadership skills in their extracurricular activities and community service, have B averages and plan to be full-time students at New York State colleges, universities, community colleges or trade schools and maintain B averages there.

How to Apply: Applications are available from high school guidance counselors.

Deadline: March 9.

Amount: $4,000.

Number of Awards: Varies.

New York State Higher Education Services Corporation

NYS Education Department, Office of K-16 Initiatives and Access Programs
Scholarships and Grants Administration Unit
Room 1078 Education Building Addition
Albany, NY 12234
Phone: 518-486-1319
Website: http://www.hesc.com

1484 • Regents Health Care Opportunity Scholarships

Purpose: To assist medical and dental students who are New York residents.

Eligibility: Applicants must be U.S. citizens or eligible noncitizens, be New York State residents and study full-time in an eligible New York State medical or dental school. Priority is given to students who are economically disadvantaged and members of a minority group. Recipients must work one year for each year of payment received, with a minimum of two years, in a physician-shortage area of New York State.

How to Apply: Applications are available by written request.
Deadline: Varies.
Amount: $10,000.
Number of Awards: Varies.

New York State Higher Education Services Corporation (HESC)

One Commerce Plaza
99 Washington Avenue
Albany, NY 12255
Phone: 888-697-4372
Website: http://www.hesc.com

1485 • Aid for Part-Time Study

Purpose: To assist part-time undergraduate students at New York State institutions.

Eligibility: Applicants must meet income eligibility requirements, be enrolled for at least 3 but less than 12 semester hours per semester or at least 4 but less than 8 semester hours per quarter in an eligible undergraduate program, be New York State residents and be U.S. citizens or eligible noncitizens. Tuition charges must exceed $100 per year, and once payments begin, students must maintain a C average.

How to Apply: Contact the financial aid office to receive an APTS application.
Deadline: Varies.
Amount: Up to $2,000.
Number of Awards: Varies.

1486 • Robert C. Byrd Honors Scholarship Program - New York

Purpose: To assist outstanding New York State high school graduates.

Eligibility: Applicants must be high school seniors, New York residents, plan to attend an institution of higher education and have a minimum high school average of 95 or GED of 310 and minimum SAT score of 1250.

How to Apply: Contact your high school guidance counselor.
Deadline: Varies.
Amount: Up to $1,500.
Number of Awards: Varies.

1487 • Scholarships for Academic Excellence

Purpose: To assist outstanding New York State high school graduates.

Eligibility: Applicants must be New York residents who are high school seniors, plan to study at an eligible undergraduate program in New York State and are U.S. citizens or eligible noncitizens. Selection is based on grades in Regents exams.

How to Apply: Students are nominated by their high schools.
Deadline: Varies.
Amount: $500-$1,500.
Number of Awards: 8,000.

1488 • Tuition Assistance Program (TAP)

Purpose: To assist New York resident students in attending in-state postsecondary institutions.

Eligibility: Applicants must be U.S. citizens or eligible noncitizens, be legal residents of New York State, study full-time at an eligible New York State postsecondary institution as undergraduate or graduate students, meet income eligibility requirements and maintain a "C" average in college.

How to Apply: Complete the Free Application for Federal Student Aid (FAFSA), including a New York school on the application and then complete the Express TAP Application.
Deadline: May 1.
Amount: Up to $5,000.
Number of Awards: Varies.

New York State Higher Education Services Corporation Regents Professional Opportunity

NYS Education Department
Bureau of HEOP/VATEA/Scholarships
Education Building Addition Room 1071
Albany, NY 12234
Phone: 518-486-1319
Website: http://www.hesc.com

1489 • Regents Professional Opportunity Scholarships

Purpose: To assist students in professional programs who are New York residents.

Eligibility: Applicants must be U.S. citizens or eligible noncitizens, be New York State residents and study at an eligible professional program in New York State. Priority is given to students who are economically disadvantaged and members of a minority group. Recipients must work as a licensed professional for one year for each year of payment received in New York State.

How to Apply: Applications are available by written request.
Deadline: Varies.
Amount: $1,000-$5,000.
Number of Awards: Varies.

Random House Inc. Creative Writing Competition

c/o Scholarship America
One Scholarship Way
P.O. Box 297
St. Peter, MN 56082
Phone: 888-369-3434
Email: worldofexpression@randomhouse.com
Website: http://www.worldofexpression.org

1490 • Random House Inc. Creative Writing Competition

Purpose: To recognize students of New York City Public High Schools for creativity in literature.

Eligibility: Applicants must be seniors in a New York City Public High School who are 21 years old or younger and must not have family members employed by Bertelsmann or its subsidiaries. Students must submit a literary composition. Possible formats include poetry/spoken word, fiction/drama or personal essay/memoir. College essays, book reports, myths and legends will not be accepted. Foreign language submissions are not allowed, and all work must not have been previously published or awarded.

How to Apply: Applications are available online.
Deadline: February 9.
Amount: $500-$10,000.
Number of Awards: 34.

1491 • **World of Expressions Scholarship - Music**
Purpose: To recognize students of New York City Public High Schools for creativity in music.
Eligibility: Applicants must be seniors in a New York City Public High School who are 21 years old or younger and must not have family members employed by Bertelsmann or its subsidiaries.
How to Apply: Applications are available online.
Deadline: February 1.
Amount: $500-$10,000.
Number of Awards: Varies.

State of Residence - North Carolina

American Legion, Department of North Carolina

4 N. Blount Street
P.O. Box 26657
Raleigh, NC 27611
Phone: 919-832-7506
Fax: 919-832-6428
Email: nclegion@nc.rr.com
Website: http://nclegion.org/orate.htm

1492 • **North Carolina Oratorical Contest**
Purpose: To enhance high school students' experience with and understanding of the U.S. Constitution. The contest will help develop students' leadership skills and civic appreciation, as well as the ability to deliver thoughtful, insightful orations regarding U.S. citizenship and its inherent responsibilities.
Eligibility: Applicants must be high school students under the age of 20 who are U.S. citizens or legal residents and residents of the state. Students first give an oration within their state and winners compete at the national level. The oration must be related to the Constitution of the United States focusing on the duties and obligations citizens have to the government. It must be in English and be between eight and ten minutes. There is also an assigned topic which is posted on the website, and it should be between three and five minutes.
How to Apply: Application information is available by contacting the local post by email.
Deadline: Varies.
Amount: Varies.
Number of Awards: Varies.

College Foundation of North Carolina

P.O. Box 41966
Raleigh, NC 27629
Phone: 866-234-6400
Fax: 919-821-3139
Email: programinformation@cfnc.org
Website: http://www.cfnc.org

1493 • **Community College Grant and Loan Program**
Purpose: To assist North Carolina community college students.
Eligibility: Applicants must be North Carolina residents, demonstrate financial need and attend North Carolina community colleges for at least six credit hours per semester. Eligibility is based on the same criteria as for the Federal Pell Grants.
How to Apply: Complete the Free Application for Federal Student Aid (FAFSA).
Deadline: Varies.
Amount: Varies.
Number of Awards: Varies.

1494 • **Governor James B. Hunt College Scholarships and Governor James G. Martin College Scholarships**
Purpose: To assist outstanding North Carolina high school students.

Eligibility: Applicants must be high school seniors who reside in North Carolina and who plan to attend full-time a public or private four-year college or university in North Carolina.
How to Apply: Each postsecondary institution may nominate two students.
Deadline: March 15.
Amount: Varies.
Number of Awards: Varies.

1495 • Incentive Grant

Purpose: To assist outstanding North Carolina high school graduates.
Eligibility: Successful applicants must be North Carolina residents enrolled full-time at a state college or university. Study programs cannot be in preparation for a religious career. Students must demonstrate financial need and maintain adequate academic progress.
How to Apply: Contact your financial aid office.
Deadline: March 15.
Amount: $750.
Number of Awards: Varies.

Crumley and Associates

Attn.: Stephen M. Keaney, Community Relations and Business Development Manager
2400 Freeman Mill Road
Suite 300
Greensboro, NC 27406
Email: smkeaney@crumleyandassociates.com
Website: www.crumleyandassociates.com

1496 • Crumley and Associates - Crib to College Scholarship

Purpose: To help North Carolina high school seniors who have performed community service.
Eligibility: Applicants must plan to attend four-year colleges or universities. Transcripts, three recommendation letters, applications and essays are required. Winners also receive laptop computers. No phone calls, please.
How to Apply: Applications are available online.
Deadline: March 15.
Amount: $1,000.
Number of Awards: 5.

North Carolina Department of Public Instruction

Center for Recruitment and Retention
Division of Human Resource Management, Department of Public Instruction
301 N. Wilmington Street
Wilmington, NC 27601
Phone: 919-807-3300
Fax: 919-807-3362
Email: scholars@dpi.state.nc.us
Website: http://www.ncpublicschools.org

1497 • Robert C. Byrd Honors Scholarship Program - North Carolina

Purpose: To assist academically outstanding North Carolina high school students.
Eligibility: Applicants must be legal North Carolina residents, graduate from a North Carolina high school, have a minimum SAT score of 900 and a minimum 3.0 GPA and be accepted to an approved postsecondary institution in the U.S.
How to Apply: Students must be nominated by their schools. Contact your high school guidance counselor.
Deadline: February.
Amount: $1,500.
Number of Awards: 160.

North Carolina Federation of Republican Women

Joyce Glass, Chairman
4413 Driftwood Drive
Clemmons, NC 27012
Phone: 336-766-0067
Email: fglass@triad.rr.com
Website: http;//www.ncfederationofrepublicanwomen.org

1498 • Dottie Martin Teachers Scholarship

Purpose: To support education students.
Eligibility: Applicants must be current college students planning to enter the field of education. The scholarship committee is especially interested in students who want to go into the fields of child guidance and counseling to make a difference in the lives of North Carolina children. Applicants must include an essay addressing their reasons for applying, career goals, plans for teaching in North Carolina, a description of their financial situation, why they should receive the scholarship and information on their personal values.
How to Apply: Applications are available online.
Deadline: June 1.
Amount: $500.
Number of Awards: 1.

North Carolina PTA

3501 Glenwood Avenue
Raleigh, NC 27612
Email: office@ncpta.org
Website: http://www.ncpta.org

1499 • North Carolina PTA Scholarship

Purpose: To recognize outstanding high school students who are members of their PTA.
Eligibility: Applicants must be North Carolina graduating high school seniors who are members of their high school PTA or PTSA.
How to Apply: Applications are available online or through your PTA.
Deadline: January 15.
Amount: Varies.
Number of Awards: Varies.

Triangle Community Foundation

Scholarship Programs
P.O. Box 12834
Research Triangle Park, NC 27709
Phone: 919-474-8370
Fax: 919-941-9208
Email: info@trianglecf.org
Website: http://www.trianglecf.org

1500 • GlaxoSmithKlein Opportunity Scholarships

Purpose: To assist North Carolina students who have overcome significant adversity.

Eligibility: Applicants must have been residents of Chatham, Durham, Orange or Wake County for the past six months and must be legal residents of the U.S. Only those who have overcome significant adversity should apply. There are no age or income limitations, and the award may be used at technical or community colleges, four-year colleges or universities or vocational or trade programs.

How to Apply: Applications are available online.

Deadline: April 1.

Amount: Up to $5,000.

Number of Awards: Varies.

Related Scholarships:

BI-LO Corporation

See #1528• BI-LO Minority Scholarship Program

Bank of America

See #290• Bank of America ADA Abilities Scholarship Program

Family Circle Cup and L'Oreal

See #1529• L'Oreal/Family Circle Cup

National Association for Campus Activities

See #1288• NACA Southeast Region Student Leader Scholarship

State of Residence – North Dakota

North Dakota Department of Public Instruction

600 E. Boulevard Avenue, Dept. 201
Floors 9, 10, and 11
Bismarck, ND 58505
Phone: 701-328-2260
Fax: 701-328-2461
Website: http://www.dpi.state.nd.us

1501 • Robert C. Byrd Honors Scholarship Program - North Dakota

Purpose: To recognize outstanding academic achievement.

Eligibility: Applicants must be North Dakota residents who are graduating seniors or have earned a GED. Academic achievement, potential for future academic achievement, leadership, extracurricular involvement and community service will all be considered in awarding the scholarship.

How to Apply: Applications are available from school officials and the department of public instruction.

Deadline: Late April.

Amount: $1,500.

Number of Awards: At least 8.

North Dakota University System

10th Floor, State Capitol
600 E. Boulevard Avenue, Dept. 215
Bismarck, ND 58505
Phone: 701-328-2960
Fax: 701-328-2961
Email: ndus.office@ndus.nodak.edu
Website: http://www.ndus.edu

1502 • Scholars Program

Purpose: To assist outstanding North Dakota high school students.

Eligibility: Applicants must be North Dakota high school seniors, score in the top 20 percent of all students in North Dakota who take the ACT, be in the top 20 percent of their class and attend a North Dakota public or tribal college.

How to Apply: Applications are available by written request.

Deadline: Varies.

Amount: Full tuition.

Number of Awards: 40-45.

1503 • State Student Incentive Grant Program

Purpose: To assist North Dakota students with financial need.

Eligibility: Applicants must be U.S. citizens or permanent residents, North Dakota residents, high school graduates and attend an eligible college in North Dakota full-time.

How to Apply: Complete the Free Application for Federal Student Aid (FAFSA).

Deadline: April 15.

Amount: Varies.

Number of Awards: 3,800.

Related Scholarships:

Vincent L. Hawkinson Foundation for Peace and Justice

See #1349 • *Vincent L. Hawkinson Scholarship for Peace and Justice*

Midwest Higher Education Commission

See #1364 • *Midwest Student Exchange Program*

Treacy Company

See #1452 • *Treacy Company Scholarship*

Alert Magazine

See #1567 • *Alert Scholarship*

State of Residence - Ohio

Big 33 Scholarship Foundation

P.O. Box 213
511 Bridge Street
New Cumberland, PA 17070
Phone: 717-774-3303
Fax: 717-774-1749
Email: info@big33.org
Website: http://www.big33.org

1504 • Big 33 Scholarship Foundation Scholarships

Purpose: To provide need-based scholarships to high school seniors with well-rounded educational and extracurricular success.

Eligibility: Applicants must be high school seniors enrolled in a public or accredited private school in Ohio or Pennsylvania. Students must have at least a 2.0 grade point average from their sophomore and junior year and be planning to continue education beyond high school at a technical school or accredited higher education institution.

How to Apply: Applications are available online.

Deadline: March.

Amount: Varies.

Number of Awards: Varies.

Ohio Board of Regents

State Grants and Scholarships Department
P.O. Box 182452
Columbus, OH 43128
Phone: 888-833-1133
Fax: 614-752-5903
Website: http://regents.ohio.gov

1505 • Academic Scholarship Program

Purpose: To assist outstanding Ohio high school students.

Eligibility: Applicants must be Ohio high school seniors who plan to attend full-time an Ohio undergraduate institution and who meet academic requirements. Awarded to at least one student from each participating high school.

How to Apply: Contact your high school guidance counselor.

Deadline: February 23.

Amount: Varies.

Number of Awards: Varies.

1506 • Instructional Grant

Purpose: To assist Ohio undergraduate students with financial need.

Eligibility: Applicants must be Ohio residents, full-time undergraduate students and come from low or moderate income families.

How to Apply: Complete the Free Application for Federal Student Aid (FAFSA).

Deadline: October 1.

Amount: Up to approximately $5,500.

Number of Awards: Varies.

1507 • Part-Time Student Instructional Grant

Purpose: To assist part-time Ohio undergraduate students.
Eligibility: Applicants must be Ohio residents who attend an eligible Ohio public or private university part-time and who have financial need.
How to Apply: Contact your financial aid office.
Deadline: Varies.
Amount: Varies.
Number of Awards: Varies.

1508 • Student Choice Grant Program

Purpose: To assist Ohio students attending private nonprofit colleges and universities in Ohio.
Eligibility: Applicants must be Ohio residents who attend an eligible Ohio private university full-time.
How to Apply: Contact your financial aid office.
Deadline: Varies.
Amount: Varies.
Number of Awards: Varies.

Ohio Department of Education

25 S. Front Street
Columbus, OH 43128
Phone: 614-466-4590
Email: contact.center@ode.state.oh.us
Website: http://www.ode.state.oh.us

1509 • Robert C. Byrd Honors Scholarship Program - Ohio

Purpose: To assist outstanding Ohio high school students.
Eligibility: Applicants must be Ohio high school seniors who plan to attend an accredited U.S. undergraduate college or university. Awarded to at least one student in each of Ohio's congressional districts. Selection is based on academic achievement and participation in leadership activities.
How to Apply: Contact your high school guidance counselor.
Deadline: Second Friday in March.
Amount: Varies.
Number of Awards: Varies.

Related Scholarships:

National Association for Campus Activities

See #1579• Zagunis Student Leader Scholarship

State of Residence - Oklahoma

Oklahoma State Department of Education

Professional Services Division
Oliver Hodge Building
2500 North Lincoln Boulevard
Oklahoma City, OK 73105
Phone: 405-521-2808
Email: studentinfo@osrhe.edu
Website: http://www.okhighered.org

1510 • Robert C. Byrd Honors Scholarship Program - Oklahoma

Purpose: To assist outstanding Oklahoma high school students.
Eligibility: Applicants must be high school seniors who are outstanding academically, U.S. citizens or eligible noncitizens, legal residents of Oklahoma, plan to attend full-time an institution of higher education and meet academic requirements.
How to Apply: Contact your high school guidance counselor.
Deadline: Varies.
Amount: Varies.
Number of Awards: Varies.

Oklahoma State Regents for Higher Education

655 Research Parkway, Suite 200
Oklahoma City, OK 73104
Phone: 800-858-1840
Fax: 405-225-9230
Email: studentinfo@osrhe.edu
Website: http://www.okhighered.org

1511 • Academic Scholars Program

Purpose: To assist students in attending Oklahoma colleges and universities.
Eligibility: Applicants can qualify for the program by being Oklahoma or out-of-state students who are named National Merit Scholars, National Merit Finalists or U.S. Presidential Scholars, by being Oklahoma residents who score above the 99.5 percentile on the SAT or ACT or by being nominated by a public college or institution. Applicants must attend an Oklahoma college or university.
How to Apply: Applications are available from your high school guidance counselor, by telephone request and online.
Deadline: Varies.
Amount: Full tuition.
Number of Awards: Varies.

Oklahoma State Regents for Higher Education (OK)

Oklahoma Tuition Aid Grant Program (OTAG)
P.O. Box 108850
Oklahoma City, OK 73101
Phone: 877-662-6231
Email: otaginfo@otag.org
Website: http://www.okhighered.org

1512 • Oklahoma Tuition Aid Grant Program (OTAG)
Purpose: To assist Oklahoma students with financial need.
Eligibility: Applicants must be Oklahoma residents who attend eligible undergraduate or graduate institutions in Oklahoma and have financial need.
How to Apply: Complete the Free Application for Federal Student Aid (FAFSA).
Deadline: April 30-June 30.
Amount: $1,000-$1,300.
Number of Awards: Varies.

Related Scholarships:

Bank of America

See #290 • Bank of America ADA Abilities Scholarship Program

National Association for Campus Activities

See #924 • Markley Scholarship

State of Residence - Oregon

Oregon Student Assistance Commission

1500 Valley River Drive, Suite 100
Eugene, OR 97401
Phone: 541-687-7400
Email: awardinfo@mercury.osac.state.or.us
Website: http://www.osac.state.or.us

1513 • Benjamin Franklin/Edith Green Scholarship
Purpose: To assist Oregon high school students.
Eligibility: Applicants must be graduating Oregon high school seniors who plan to attend a four-year public Oregon college.
How to Apply: Applications are available online.
Deadline: March 1.
Amount: Varies.
Number of Awards: Varies.

1514 • Dorothy Campbell Memorial Scholarship
Purpose: To assist female Oregon high school students.
Eligibility: Applicants must be female graduates of an Oregon high school, have a minimum 2.75 GPA and attend a four-year Oregon college.
How to Apply: Applications are available online.
Deadline: March 1.
Amount: Varies.
Number of Awards: Varies.

1515 • Ford Opportunity Program Scholarship
Purpose: To assist Oregon residents who are single heads of households.
Eligibility: Applicants must be Oregon single heads of household with custody of dependent children, have a minimum 3.0 GPA or 2900 GED score and attend a four-year Oregon college or community college.
How to Apply: Applications are available online.
Deadline: March 1.
Amount: Varies.
Number of Awards: Varies.

1516 • Ford Scholars Scholarship
Purpose: To assist Oregon students.
Eligibility: Applicants must be graduating high school seniors, high school graduates who have not been full-time undergraduates or community college students who are entering their junior year at an Oregon four-year college. Applicants must also have a minimum 3.0 GPA or GED score of 2900.
How to Apply: Applications are available online.
Deadline: March 1.
Amount: Varies.
Number of Awards: Varies.

1517 • Jerome B. Steinbach Scholarship
Purpose: To assist Oregon undergraduate students.
Eligibility: Applicants must be Oregon residents entering their sophomore year or higher in college and have a minimum 3.5 college GPA.
How to Apply: Applications are available online.
Deadline: March 1.
Amount: Varies.
Number of Awards: Varies.

1518 • Oregon Scholarship Fund Community College Student Award

Purpose: To assist Oregon community college students.

Eligibility: Applicants must be Oregon residents enrolled or planning to enroll in a community college in Oregon.

How to Apply: Applications are available online.

Deadline: March 1.

Amount: Varies.

Number of Awards: Varies.

1519 • Robert C. Byrd Honors Scholarship Program - Oregon

Purpose: To assist Oregon high school students.

Eligibility: Applicants must be Oregon high school seniors, have a minimum 3.85 GPA or minimum GED score of 325 and have a minimum SAT score of 1300 or ACT score of 29.

How to Apply: Applications are available online.

Deadline: March 1.

Amount: Varies.

Number of Awards: Varies.

Related Scholarships:

Bank of America

See #290 • Bank of America ADA Abilities Scholarship Program

National Association for Campus Activities

See #1201 • Lori Rhett Memorial Scholarship

State of Residence - Pennsylvania

American Legion, Department of Pennsylvania

P.O. Box 2324
Harrisburg, PA 17105
Phone: 717-730-9100
Fax: 717-975-2836
Email: hq@pa-legion.com
Website: http://www.pa-legion.com

1520 • Pennsylvania Oratorical Contest

Purpose: To enhance high school students' experience with and understanding of the U.S. Constitution. The contest will help develop students' leadership skills and civic appreciation, as well as the ability to deliver thoughtful, insightful orations regarding U.S. citizenship and its inherent responsibilities.

Eligibility: Applicants must be high school students under the age of 20 who are U.S. citizens or legal residents and residents of the state. Students first give an oration within their state and winners compete at the national level. The oration must be related to the Constitution of the United States focusing on the duties and obligations citizens have to the government. It must be in English and be between eight and ten minutes. There is also an assigned topic which is posted on the website, and it should be between three and five minutes.

How to Apply: Applications are available from school coordinators and online.

Deadline: January 13.

Amount: $4,000-$7,500.

Number of Awards: 3.

Pennsylvania Higher Education Assistance Agency

P.O. Box 8114
Harrisburg, PA 17105
Phone: 800-692-7392
Website: http://www.pheaa.org

1521 • Robert C. Byrd Honors Scholarship Program - Pennsylvania

Purpose: To assist outstanding Pennsylvania high school students.

Eligibility: Applicants must be high school seniors, Pennsylvania residents, accepted for enrollment at an eligible institution of higher education and U.S. citizens or permanent residents. Applicants must also rank in the top 5 percent of their class, have a minimum 3.5 GPA and have a minimum SAT score of 1150, ACT score of 25 or GED score of 355.

How to Apply: Applications are available through your high school counselor or by written request.

Deadline: Varies.

Amount: Varies.

Number of Awards: Varies.

Pennsylvania Higher Education Assistance Agency (PHEAA)

1200 N. 7th Street
Harrisburg, PA 17102
Phone: 800-692-7392
Website: http://www.pheaa.org

1522 • State Grant Program

Purpose: To assist Pennsylvania undergraduate students with financial need.

Eligibility: Applicants must be Pennsylvania residents, enroll at least half-time at an eligible undergraduate institution and meet financial need criteria.

How to Apply: Complete the Free Application for Federal Student Aid (FAFSA).

Deadline: May 1.

Amount: Up to $1,650.

Number of Awards: Varies.

Related Scholarships:

Big 33 Scholarship Foundation

See #1504 • Big 33 Scholarship Foundation Scholarships

National Association for Campus Activities

See #1579 • Zagunis Student Leader Scholarship

National Association for Campus Activities

See #1482 • NACA East Coast Undergraduate Scholarship for Student Leaders

State of Residence - Rhode Island

Rhode Island Department of Elementary and Secondary Education

255 Westminster Street
Providence, RI 02903
Phone: 401-222-4600
Website: http://www.ridoe.net

1523 • Robert C. Byrd Honors Scholarship Program - Rhode Island

Purpose: To reward high scholastic achievement.

Eligibility: Applicants must be graduating high school seniors or GED recipients who are residents of Rhode Island and U.S. citizens. The scholarship is awarded based on academic achievements and the student's potential for continued achievement in post-secondary education.

How to Apply: Applications are available from the Department of Elementary and Secondary Education and from school officials.

Deadline: Varies.

Amount: $1,500.

Number of Awards: Varies.

Rhode Island Foundation

One Union Station
Providence, RI 02903
Phone: 401-274-4564
Fax: 401-331-8085
Email: libbym@rifoundation.org
Website: http://www.rifoundation.org

1524 • Lily and Catello Sorrentino Memorial Scholarship

Purpose: To assist adult students who are continuing their undergraduate studies at colleges or universities in Rhode Island.

Eligibility: Applicants must be residents of Rhode Island, be over 45 years of age and attend a non-parochial college or university in the state.

How to Apply: Applications are available online.

Deadline: May 14.

Amount: $350-$1,000.

Number of Awards: Varies.

1525 • Rhode Island Foundation Association of Former Legislators Scholarship

Purpose: To assist Rhode Island high school seniors with an excellent track record of community service.

Eligibility: Applicants must be Rhode Island high school seniors who have been accepted into college, have demonstrated need and have a substantial amount of community service.

How to Apply: Applications are available online.

Deadline: June 1.

Amount: $1,500.

Number of Awards: 5.

Rhode Island Higher Education Assistance Authority

560 Jefferson Boulevard
Warwick, RI 02886
Phone: 401-736-1100
Fax: 401-732-3541
Email: scholarships@riheaa.org
Website: http://www.riheaa.org

1526 • CollegeBoundfund Academic Promise Scholarship

Purpose: To assist outstanding Rhode Island high school students.
Eligibility: Applicants must be graduating Rhode Island high school seniors who plan to attend a postsecondary institution full-time and demonstrate academic achievement and financial need.
How to Apply: Complete the Free Application for Federal Student Aid (FAFSA).
Deadline: March 1.
Amount: Up to $10,000.
Number of Awards: Varies.

1527 • State Grant Program

Purpose: To assist Rhode Island students with financial need.
Eligibility: Applicants must be U.S. citizens or eligible noncitizens, Rhode Island residents, enrolled or accepted for enrollment in a degree or certificate program and attend the program at least half-time.
How to Apply: Complete the Free Application for Federal Student Aid (FAFSA).
Deadline: March 1.
Amount: $250-$750.
Number of Awards: Varies.

Related Scholarships:

New England Board of Higher Education

See #1421 • New England Regional Student Program

State of Residence - South Carolina

BI-LO Corporation

P.O. Box 1465
Taylors, SC 29687
Website: http://www.scholarshipprograms.org

1528 • BI-LO Minority Scholarship Program

Purpose: To support minority high school students who might be interested in a career at the BI-LO company.
Eligibility: Applicants must be minority high school seniors who plan to enroll as freshmen at Benedict College, Claflin University, Morris College, North Carolina A&T State University and South Carolina State University. Applicants must agree to participate in the BI-LO Cooperative Education Program for one semester in the summer following their sophomore year. Applicants must have a minimum 3.0 GPA, minimum SAT score of 900 and be interested in pursuing a career in the food retail industry, which may include accounting, business management, marketing, distribution management, communications, pharmacy, human resources, information systems, advertising and finance.
How to Apply: Applications are available online.
Deadline: February 15.
Amount: Varies.
Number of Awards: Varies.

Family Circle Cup and L'Oreal

161 Seven Farms Drives
Charleston, SC 29492
Phone: 843-856-7900
Fax: 843-856-7901
Email: bhutto@gjusa.com
Website: http://www.familycirclecup.com

1529 • L'Oreal/Family Circle Cup

Purpose: To recognize and reward the efforts of female high school students who make a difference in their communities through extracurricular activities, volunteer work and role modeling.
Eligibility: Applicants must be female high school students with a minimum 2.0 GPA who reside in the states of Georgia, North Carolina or South Carolina.
Deadline: February 6.
Amount: $2,500.
Number of Awards: 3.

Kittie M. Fairey Educational Fund Scholarship Program

4320-G Wade Hampton Boulevard
Taylors, SC 29687
Phone: 866-608-0001
Email: sandralee41@bellsouth.net
Website: http://www.scholarshipprograms.org

1530 • Kittie M. Fairey Educational Fund Scholarships

Purpose: To help South Carolina high school seniors who want to attend colleges or universities in the state.

Eligibility: Applicants must be high school seniors with a minimum combined SAT score of 900 who plan to be full-time students pursuing a bachelor's of arts or bachelor's of science degree. Selection is based on academic merit and financial need, and the applicants' parents' adjusted gross income must not exceed $40,000. A transcript, recommendation letter, essay and parents' tax documents are required. Employees of Wachovia Bank are not eligible.

How to Apply: Applications are available online.

Deadline: January 30.

Amount: Varies.

Number of Awards: Varies.

South Carolina Board for Technical and Comprehensive Education

1333 Main Street
Suite 200
Columbia, SC 29201
Phone: 803-737-2260
Fax: 803-737-2297
Email: mmdowell@che.sc.gov
Website: http://www.che400.state.sc.us

1531 • Lottery Tuition Assistance Program

Purpose: To assist South Carolina residents attending a two-year public or independent institution of higher learning.

Eligibility: Applicants must complete the Free Application for Federal Student Aid (FAFSA), be residents of South Carolina and be enrolled a minimum of six credit hours at a technical college.

How to Apply: Applications are available by telephone request.

Deadline: Varies.

Amount: Varies.

Number of Awards: Varies.

South Carolina Commission on Higher Education

1333 Main Street
Suite 200
Columbia, SC 29201
Phone: 803-737-2260
Fax: 803-737-2297
Email: shubbard@che.sc.gov
Website: http://www.che400.state.sc.us

1532 • Legislative for Future Excellence (LIFE) Scholarship Program

Purpose: Monetary assistance is provided to South Carolina resident students pursuing higher education.

Eligibility: Applicants must graduate from a high school in South Carolina or outside of South Carolina if parent is a legal resident of South Carolina, attend an eligible South Carolina public or private college full-time and be a resident of South Carolina. Entering freshmen must meet two of the following: have a minimum 3.0 GPA, a minimum SAT score of 1100 or ACT score of 24 or graduate in the top 30 percent of their class.

How to Apply: Your college will determine your eligibility based on your high school transcript. There is no application form.

Deadline: Varies.

Amount: $4,700.

Number of Awards: Varies.

1533 • Palmetto Fellows Scholarship Program

Purpose: Monetary assistance is awarded to academically talented South Carolina high school seniors in an effort to encourage them to go to South Carolina colleges.

Eligibility: Applicants must have a minimum SAT score of 1200 or ACT score of 27, have a minimum 3.5 GPA, rank in the top 5 percent of their class, be residents of South Carolina, be enrolled in a public or private high school, be U.S. citizens or permanent residents and plan to attend a college in South Carolina.

How to Apply: Applications are available through your high school guidance office.

Deadline: Varies.

Amount: $6,700.

Number of Awards: Varies.

1534 • South Carolina Hope Scholarship

Purpose: Monetary assistance is provided to those freshmen who do not qualify for LIFE or Palmetto Fellows Scholarships.

Eligibility: Applicants must attend an eligible South Carolina public or private college full-time, be South Carolina residents and have a minimum 3.0 GPA. The award is only applicable to the first year of college.

How to Apply: Your college will determine your eligibility based on your high school transcript. There is no application form.

Deadline: Varies.

Amount: Varies.

Number of Awards: Varies.

1535 • State Need-based Grants

Purpose: Monetary assistance for higher education is provided to South Carolina resident students.

Eligibility: Applicants must be obtaining their first baccalaureate or professional degree, complete the Free Application for Federal Student Aid (FAFSA) and be residents of South Carolina.

How to Apply: Complete the FAFSA and contact your college's financial aid office if you plan to attend a public college or the South Carolina Commission on Higher Education if you plan to attend a private college.

Deadline: Varies.

Amount: $2,500.

Number of Awards: Varies.

South Carolina Department of Education

Beth Cope, Education Associate
Suite 701
1429 Senate Street
Columbia, SC 29201
Phone: 803-734-8116
Fax: 803-734-8701
Email: info@ed.sc.gov
Website: http://www.ed.sc.gov

1536 • Robert C. Byrd Honors Scholarship Program - South Carolina

Purpose: To help outstanding high school seniors pursue higher education.

Eligibility: Applicants must be graduating seniors in a South Carolina high school. Public, private and home-schooled students are eligible. Applicants must have a score of at least 1300 on the SAT or a score of at least 29 on the ACT and a GPA of 3.5 or higher.

How to Apply: Schools and home-school associations select applicants.

Deadline: February 1.

Amount: $1,500.

Number of Awards: 96.

South Carolina Tuition Grants Commission

101 Business Park Boulevard
Suite 2100
Columbia, SC 29203
Phone: 803-896-1120
Fax: 803-896-1126
Email: info@sctuitiongrants.org
Website: http://www.sctuitiongrants.com

1537 • South Carolina Tuition Grants Program

Purpose: To assist students who wish to attend independent South Carolina colleges.

Eligibility: Students must be legal residents of South Carolina with financial need. High school seniors must graduate in the top 75 percent of their class or score a minimum of 900 on the SAT or 19 on the ACT. College applicants must complete and pass a minimum of 24 semester hours each year.

How to Apply: Fill out the FAFSA, which is available online.

Deadline: June 30.

Amount: Varies.

Number of Awards: Varies.

Related Scholarships:

Bank of America

See #290 • Bank of America ADA Abilities Scholarship Program

National Association for Campus Activities

See #1288 • NACA Southeast Region Student Leader Scholarship

State of Residence - South Dakota

South Dakota Department of Education and Cultural Affairs

700 Governors Drive
Pierre, SD 57501
Phone: 605-773-3426
Website: http://doe.sd.gov

1538 • Robert C. Byrd Honors Scholarship Program - South Dakota

Purpose: To assist outstanding South Dakota high school students.

Eligibility: Applicants must be South Dakota high school seniors who plan to attend full-time an eligible institution of higher education, meet course requirements, have a minimum 3.5 GPA and have a minimum ACT score of 24.

How to Apply: Applications are available online.

Deadline: May 1.

Amount: Varies.

Number of Awards: Varies.

Related Scholarships:

Treacy Company

See #1452 • Treacy Company Scholarship

Vincent L. Hawkinson Foundation for Peace and Justice

See #1349 • Vincent L. Hawkinson Scholarship for Peace and Justice

Alert Magazine

See #1567 • Alert Scholarship

State of Residence - Tennessee

Tennessee Student Assistance Corporation

404 James Robertson Parkway
Suite 1510, Parkway Towers
Nashville, TN 37243
Phone: 800-342-1663
Fax: 615-741-6101
Email: TSAC.aidinfo@state.tn.us
Website: http://www.state.tn.us/tsac/

1539 • Ned McWherter Scholars Program

Purpose: To assist Tennessee students with financial need.
Eligibility: Applicants must be Tennessee residents, high school seniors or recent graduates who plan to attend an eligible Tennessee undergraduate institution full-time, U.S. citizens and have a minimum 3.5 GPA and SAT or ACT scores in the top 5 percent nationally.
How to Apply: Applications are available from your high school guidance counselor and online.
Deadline: February 15.
Amount: Up to $6,000.
Number of Awards: Varies.

1540 • Robert C. Byrd Honors Scholarship Program - Tennessee

Purpose: To assist outstanding Tennessee high school students.
Eligibility: Applicants must be U.S. citizens or permanent residents, be Tennessee residents, be graduating high school seniors or GED recipients and have a minimum 3.5 GPA and minimum ACT score of 24.
How to Apply: Contact your high school guidance counselor.
Deadline: March 1.
Amount: Varies.
Number of Awards: Varies.

1541 • Student Assistance Award Program

Purpose: To assist Tennessee students with financial need.
Eligibility: Applicants must attend or be accepted at eligible undergraduate higher education institutions in Tennessee for at least half-time and demonstrate financial need.
How to Apply: Complete the Free Application for Federal Student Aid (FAFSA).
Deadline: May 1.
Amount: Varies.
Number of Awards: Varies.

Related Scholarships:

Bank of America

See #290 • Bank of America ADA Abilities Scholarship Program

National Association for Campus Activities

See #1288 • NACA Southeast Region Student Leader Scholarship

State of Residence - Texas

American Legion, Department of Texas

3401 Ed Bluestein Boulevard
Austin, TX 78721
Phone: 512-472-4138
Fax: 512-472-0603
Email: programs@txlegion.org
Website: http://www.txlegion.org

1542 • Texas Oratorical Contest

Purpose: To enhance high school students' experience with and understanding of the U.S. Constitution. The contest will help develop students' leadership skills and civic appreciation, as well as the ability to deliver thoughtful, insightful orations regarding U.S. citizenship and its inherent responsibilities.
Eligibility: Applicants must be high school students under the age of 20 who are U.S. citizens or legal residents and residents of the state. Students first give an oration within their state and winners compete at the national level. The oration must be related to the Constitution of the United States focusing on the duties and obligations citizens have to the government. It must be in English and be between eight and ten minutes. There is also an assigned topic which is posted on the website, and it should be between three and five minutes.
How to Apply: Application information is available online or by contacting the local post.
Deadline: November.
Amount: Varies.
Number of Awards: 4.

Career Colleges and Schools of Texas

P.O. Box 11539
Austin, TX 78711
Phone: 866-909-2278
Email: scholars@careerscholarships.org
Website: http://www.colleges-schools.org

1543 • Career Colleges and Schools of Texas Scholarship Program

Purpose: To help Texas high school seniors who want to attend trade or technical schools in the state.
Eligibility: Participating institutions, which are listed on the website, provide scholarships to students who choose to enroll at their schools. Since each school has its own guidelines, applicants should contact a particular school for more information.
How to Apply: Applicants should contact their high school counselors or participating schools.
Deadline: Varies.
Amount: $1,000.
Number of Awards: Varies.

Dallas Morning News

TACT/Community Services
P.O. Box 655237
Dallas, TX 75265
Phone: 214-977-7256
Website: http://tact.dallasnews.com/

1544 • Dallas Morning News Annual Teenage Citizenship Tribute

Purpose: To recognize Dallas-area students for exemplary performance in school and the community.

Eligibility: Applicants must be high school seniors from Collin, Dallas, Denton, Ellis, Hunt, Kaufman, Rockwell, Parker or Tarrant counties. Applicants are individually interviewed by judges and evaluated in terms of academics, extracurricular activities, leadership skills, volunteer activities, community involvement and commitment.

How to Apply: Applications are available online.

Deadline: February 13.

Amount: $500-$2,000.

Number of Awards: 20.

Texas Higher Education Coordinating Board

P.O. Box 12788
Austin, TX 78711
Phone: 512-427-6101
Fax: 512-427-6127
Website: http://www.collegefortexans.com

1545 • License Plate Insignia Scholarship

Purpose: To assist Texas students with financial need.

Eligibility: Applicants must be Texas residents who are enrolled at least half-time at eligible public or private nonprofit colleges or universities in Texas and must demonstrate financial need.

How to Apply: Complete the Free Application for Federal Student Aid (FAFSA).

Deadline: Varies.

Amount: Varies.

Number of Awards: Varies.

1546 • Robert C. Byrd Honors Scholarship Program - Texas

Purpose: To assist outstanding Texas high school students.

Eligibility: Applicants must be U.S. citizens or permanent residents who are Texas residents, graduating high school seniors or GED recipients and be nominated by their school.

How to Apply: Contact your high school guidance counselor.

Deadline: Varies.

Amount: Varies.

Number of Awards: Varies.

1547 • Texas Public Educational Grant

Purpose: To assist Texas students with financial need.

Eligibility: Applicants must attend public colleges or universities in Texas and demonstrate financial need. Individual institutions determine additional eligibility criteria.

How to Apply: Complete the Free Application for Federal Student Aid (FAFSA) and contact your financial aid office.

Deadline: Varies.

Amount: Varies.

Number of Awards: Varies.

1548 • Toward Excellence, Access and Success (TEXAS) Grant II Program (TGII)

Purpose: To assist Texas two-year college students with financial need.

Eligibility: Applicants must be Texas residents, enrolled at least half-time in a public Texas two-year community college, technical college or public state college and demonstrate financial need.

How to Apply: Complete the Free Application for Federal Student Aid (FAFSA).

Deadline: Varies.

Amount: $1,300 per semester.

Number of Awards: Varies.

1549 • Toward Excellence, Access and Success (TEXAS) Grant Program

Purpose: To assist Texas students with financial need who have received their associate's degree.

Eligibility: Applicants must be Texas residents, have earned their associate's degree and enroll in a Texas higher level undergraduate program at least 3/4 time and demonstrate financial need.

How to Apply: Complete the Free Application for Federal Student Aid (FAFSA).

Deadline: Varies.

Amount: $1,475 per semester.

Number of Awards: Varies.

1550 • Tuition Equalization Grant Program (TEG)

Purpose: To assist students with financial need in attending private nonprofit colleges or universities in Texas.

Eligibility: Applicants must be Texas residents or nonresident National Merit Finalists, enroll in a Texas institution at least half-time and demonstrate financial need.

How to Apply: Complete the Free Application for Federal Student Aid (FAFSA).

Deadline: Varies.

Amount: Varies.

Number of Awards: Varies.

Related Scholarships:

Bank of America

See #290• Bank of America ADA Abilities Scholarship Program

National Association for Campus Activities

See #924• Markley Scholarship

State of Residence – Utah

Utah Higher Education Assistance Authority

Board of Regents Building, The Gateway
60 South 400 West
Salt Lake City, UT 84101
Phone: 801-321-7200
Fax: 801-321-7299
Email: uheaa@utahsbr.edu
Website: http://www.uheaa.org

1551 • Leveraging Educational Assistance Partnership (LEAP) Grants
Purpose: To assist students in attending Utah colleges.
Eligibility: Applicants must demonstrate need according to the federal guidelines. Eligibility requirements differ by campus. It is recommended that students apply early because there are limited funds.
How to Apply: Complete the Free Application for Federal Student Aid (FAFSA).
Deadline: Varies.
Amount: Up to $2,500.
Number of Awards: Varies.

1552 • Utah Centennial Opportunity Program for Education (UCOPE) Grants
Purpose: To assist Utah students in attending Utah colleges.
Eligibility: Applicants must be residents of Utah attending schools in Utah. Eligibility requirements differ by campus. It is recommended that students apply early because there are limited funds.
How to Apply: Complete the Free Application for Federal Student Aid (FAFSA).
Deadline: Varies.
Amount: Varies.
Number of Awards: Varies.

Utah State Board of Regents

Board of Regents Building, The Gateway
60 South 400 West
Salt Lake City, UT 84101
Phone: 801-321-7107
Website: http://www.utahsbr.edu

1553 • New Century Scholarship
Purpose: To assist Utah high school students.
Eligibility: Applicants must be high school students who have completed the equivalent of an associate's degree at a Utah state institution of higher education by September 1 of their high school graduation year. The award provides assistance for the bachelor's degree at a state college.
How to Apply: Applications are available online.
Deadline: Varies.
Amount: Varies.
Number of Awards: Varies.

Utah State Office of Education

250 East 500 South
P.O. Box 144200
Salt Lake City, UT 84114
Website: http://www.usoe.k12.ut.us

1554 • Robert C. Byrd Honors Scholarship Program - Utah
Purpose: To recognize graduating seniors who have demonstrated academic excellence.
Eligibility: Applicants must be graduating high school seniors in Utah or have an equivalent certificate of graduation. They must be accepted at a post-secondary institution and be planning to attend full-time. Applicants must show evidence of outstanding academic achievement, including a GPA of at least 3.7 and an ACT score of 25 or higher. Applicants must be U.S. citizens or permanent residents.
How to Apply: Applications are available online.
Deadline: March 30.
Amount: $1,500.
Number of Awards: Varies.

State of Residence - Vermont

American Legion, Department of Vermont

P.O. Box 396
126 State Street
Montpelier, VT 05601
Phone: 802-223-7131
Fax: 802-223-0318
Email: alvthq@verizon.net
Website: http://www.legionvthq.com

1555 • Vermont Oratorical Contest

Purpose: To enhance high school students' experience with and understanding of the U.S. Constitution. The contest will help develop students' leadership skills and civic appreciation, as well as the ability to deliver thoughtful, insightful orations regarding U.S. citizenship and its inherent responsibilities.
Eligibility: Applicants must be high school students under the age of 20 who are U.S. citizens or legal residents and residents of the state. Students first give an oration within their state and winners compete at the national level. The oration must be related to the Constitution of the United States focusing on the duties and obligations citizens have to the government. It must be in English and be between eight and ten minutes. There is also an assigned topic which is posted on the website, and it should be between three and five minutes.
How to Apply: Applications are available from district representatives.
Deadline: Varies.
Amount: $100-$2,000.
Number of Awards: At least 2.

Vermont Student Assistance Corporation

10 E. Allen Street
P.O. Box 2000
Winooski, VT 05404
Phone: 888-253-4819
Fax: 802-654-3798
Email: info@vsac.org
Website: http://www.vsac.org

1556 • Incentive Grants

Purpose: To assist Vermont students.
Eligibility: Applicants must be Vermont residents who demonstrate financial need and plan to attend college full-time.
How to Apply: Applications are available online.
Deadline: Varies.
Amount: Up to $8,700.
Number of Awards: Varies.

1557 • Part-Time Grants

Purpose: To assist Vermont part-time students.
Eligibility: Applicants must be Vermont residents enrolled or planning to enroll in an undergraduate degree, diploma or certificate program and take fewer than 12 credits per semester.
How to Apply: Contact your financial aid office.
Deadline: Varies.
Amount: Varies.
Number of Awards: Varies.

1558 • Robert C. Byrd Honors Scholarship Program - Vermont

Purpose: To recognize students who achieve academic excellence.
Eligibility: Applicants must be graduating high school seniors who have demonstrated academic excellence and show promise for future academic achievements. They must attend an accredited post-secondary institution full-time. Applicants must be residents of Vermont and U.S. citizens or permanent residents.
How to Apply: Applications are available online.
Deadline: May 1.
Amount: $1,500.
Number of Awards: Up to 15.

Related Scholarships:

New England Board of Higher Education

See #1421 • New England Regional Student Program

State of Residence – Virginia

American Legion, Department of Virginia

1708 Commonwealth Avenue
Richmond, VA 23230
Phone: 804-353-6606
Fax: 804-358-1940
Website: http://www.valegion.org

1559 • Middle School Essay Contest

Purpose: To promote citizenship in young Virginia students.
Eligibility: Applicants must write an essay on an assigned topic. The essay should be written at the student's desk during school time and will be evaluated based on originality, sincerity and the student's ability to communicate meaning.
How to Apply: Applications are available online and from sponsoring Posts.
Deadline: Varies.
Amount: $100-$500.
Number of Awards: 3+local awards.

Lee-Jackson Foundation

P.O. Box 8121
Charlottesville, VA 22906
Phone: 434-977-1861
Website: http://www.lee-jackson.org

1560 • Lee Jackson Foundation Scholarship

Purpose: To honor the memories of Robert E. Lee and Thomas J. "Stonewall" Jackson and provide scholarships to Virginia students.
Eligibility: Applicants must be juniors, seniors or the equivalent in a Virginia public high school, private high school or homeschooling program and be residents of Virginia who plan to attend an accredited four-year college or university in the U.S. as full-time students. Financial need is not a basis for selection. Applicants must write an essay that demonstrates an appreciation for the character and virtues of Generals Robert E. Lee and Thomas "Stonewall" Jackson.
How to Apply: Applications are available online.
Deadline: December.
Amount: $1,000-$10,000.
Number of Awards: Varies.

State Council of Higher Education for Virginia

101 N. 14th Street
James Monroe Building
Richmond, VA 23219
Phone: 804-225-2600
Fax: 804-225-2604
Website: http://www.schev.edu

1561 • College Scholarship Assistance Program

Purpose: To assist Virginia students with extreme financial need.
Eligibility: Applicants must be U.S. citizens or eligible noncitizens, enrolled or planning to enroll at least half-time in a Virginia public or eligible private nonprofit two- or four-year college or university and be residents of Virginia.

How to Apply: Complete the Free Application for Federal Student Aid (FAFSA).
Deadline: Varies.
Amount: $400-$5,000.
Number of Awards: Varies.

1562 • Graduate and Undergraduate Assistance Program

Purpose: To assist students in attending Virginia schools.
Eligibility: Applicants must be admitted to an eligible Virginia college or university and demonstrate academic excellence. Applicants do not need to be Virginia residents.
How to Apply: Contact your financial aid office.
Deadline: Varies.
Amount: Varies.
Number of Awards: Varies.

1563 • Part-Time Assistance Program

Purpose: To assist part-time Virginia students with financial need.
Eligibility: Applicants must attend a school in Virginia's Community College System part-time (three to five hours), be Virginia residents and demonstrate financial need.
How to Apply: Contact your financial aid office.
Deadline: Varies.
Amount: Up to the cost of tuition and fees.
Number of Awards: Varies.

1564 • Virginia Commonwealth Award Program

Purpose: To assist Virginia students with financial need.
Eligibility: Undergraduate applicants must be admitted to a Virginia public two- or four-year college or university, be enrolled at least half-time, be residents of Virginia, be U.S. citizens or eligible noncitizens and demonstrate financial need. Graduate applicants must be enrolled full-time in an eligible Virginia graduate degree program.
How to Apply: Contact your financial aid office.
Deadline: Varies.
Amount: Varies.
Number of Awards: Varies.

1565 • Virginia Tuition Assistance Grant Program (VTAG)

Purpose: To assist Virginia students.
Eligibility: Applicants must be Virginia residents and enrolled full-time as undergraduate, graduate or professional students in an eligible private Virginia institution.
How to Apply: Applications are available online or contact your financial aid office.
Deadline: July 31.
Amount: $2,000-$2,600.
Number of Awards: Varies.

Virginia Department of Education

P.O. Box 2120
Richmond, VA 23218
Phone: 804-225-3349
Fax: 804-371-2456
Website: http://www.pen.k12.va.us

1566 • Robert C. Byrd Honors Scholarship Program - Virginia

Purpose: To assist Virginia high school students.
Eligibility: Applicants must be U.S. citizens or eligible noncitizens, Virginia residents, high school seniors and demonstrate academic excellence.
How to Apply: Contact your high school guidance counselor.
Deadline: Varies.
Amount: Varies.
Number of Awards: Varies.

Related Scholarships:

Bank of America

See #290• Bank of America ADA Abilities Scholarship Program

National Association for Campus Activities

See #1288• NACA Southeast Region Student Leader Scholarship

American Nursery and Landscape Association

See #110• Carville M. Akehurst Memorial Scholarship

State of Residence - Washington

Alert Magazine

P.O. Box 4833
Boise, ID 83711
Phone: 208-375-7911
Fax: 208-376-0770
Website: http://www.alertmagazine.org

1567 • Alert Scholarship

Purpose: To promote the prevention of drug and alcohol abuse.
Eligibility: Scholarships are awarded for the best editorials on the prevention of drug and alcohol abuse. Winning editorials will be published in Alert Magazine. Applicants must be high school students between the ages of 18 and 19 and residents of Colorado, Idaho, Montana, North Dakota, South Dakota, Washington or Wyoming.
How to Apply: No application necessary.
Deadline: Ongoing.
Amount: $500.
Number of Awards: Varies.

American Legion, Department of Washington

P.O. Box 3917
Lacey, WA 98509
Phone: 360-491-4373
Fax: 360-491-7442
Email: americanismchairman@americanism-alwa.org
Website: http://www.americanism-alwa.org

1568 • Washington Oratorical Contest

Purpose: To enhance junior high and high school students' experience with and understanding of the U.S. Constitution. The contest will help develop students' leadership skills and civic appreciation, as well as the ability to deliver thoughtful, insightful orations regarding U.S. citizenship and its inherent responsibilities.
Eligibility: Applicants must be high school students under the age of 20 who are U.S. citizens or legal residents and residents of the state. Students first give an oration within their state and winners compete at the national level. The oration must be related to the Constitution of the United States focusing on the duties and obligations citizens have to the government. It must be in English and be between eight and ten minutes. There is also an assigned topic which is posted on the website, and it should be between three and five minutes.
How to Apply: Application information is available online.
Deadline: January 15.
Amount: Varies.
Number of Awards: Varies.

College Success Foundation

1605 NW Sammamish Road
Suite 100
Issaquah, WA 98027
Phone: 425-416-2000
Fax: 425-416-2001
Email: info@collegesuccessfoundation.org
Website: http://www.collegesuccessfoundation.org

1569 • Washington State Achievers Program

Purpose: To provide financial assistance to students in high schools serving large low-income populations in Washington state, encouraging these high schools to raise efforts to improve academic achievement.

Eligibility: Applicants must be a junior or senior in high school at a foundation-designated Achievers high school in Washington state, have a family income that is in the lowest 35 percent of Washington state's family income level, and plan to enroll in a Washington public or independent college for at least two years of their college education.

How to Apply: Applications are available at the selected high schools and on the Washington Education Foundation's website at http://www.waedfoundation.org.

Deadline: Varies.

Amount: $5,000.

Number of Awards: Varies.

Edmund F. Maxwell Foundation

P.O. Box 22537
Seattle, WA 98122-0537
Email: admin@maxwell.org
Website: http://www.maxwell.org

1570 • Edmund F. Maxwell Foundation Scholarship

Purpose: The scholarship is intended to assist high-achieving students who follow the ideals of Edmund F. Maxwell: ability, aptitude and citizenship.

Eligibility: Applicants must be from Western Washington and plan to attend an accredited independent school that is primarily not tax-funded. Students must submit a FAFSA form and demonstrate financial need.

How to Apply: Applications are available online at http://www.maxwell.org/app.html.

Deadline: April 30.

Amount: $3,500.

Number of Awards: Varies.

Higher Education Coordinating Board

917 Lakeridge Way
P.O. Box 43430
Olympia, WA 98504
Phone: 360-753-7843
Fax: 360-753-6243
Email: info@hecb.wa.gov
Website: http://www.hecb.wa.gov

1571 • Washington State Scholars Grant Program

Purpose: To assist Washington high school students.

Eligibility: Applicants must be Washington high school seniors planning to enroll in an eligible Washington college or university. Based on academic achievements, leadership and community activities.

How to Apply: Students are nominated by their high schools.

Deadline: Varies.

Amount: Varies.

Number of Awards: Varies.

Office of Superintendent of Public Instruction

Old Capitol Building
P.O. Box 47200
Olympia, WA 98504
Phone: 360-725-6000
Website: http://www.k12.wa.us

1572 • Robert C. Byrd Honors Scholarship Program - Washington

Purpose: To assist outstanding Washington high school students.

Eligibility: Applicants must be U.S. citizens or eligible noncitizens, Washington residents, high school seniors and demonstrate academic excellence.

How to Apply: Contact your high school guidance counselor.

Deadline: Varies.

Amount: Varies.

Number of Awards: Varies.

Related Scholarships:

Bank of America

See #290 • *Bank of America ADA Abilities Scholarship Program*

National Association for Campus Activities

See #1201 • *Lori Rhett Memorial Scholarship*

State of Residence – West Virginia

Greater Kanawha Valley Foundation

1600 Huntington Square
900 Lee Street, East
Charleston, WV 25301
Phone: 304-346-3620
Fax: 304-346-3640
Email: tgkvf@tgkvf.org
Website: http://www.tgkvf.org

1573 • Greater Kanawha Valley Foundation Scholarship Program

Purpose: To provide financial assistance to prospective college students from the state of West Virginia.
Eligibility: Applicants must be residents of West Virginia, be full-time students (12 hours) and demonstrate good moral character. Many awards are available, and each individual award may have additional eligibility requirements.
How to Apply: Applications are available online at http://www.tgkvf.org/scholar.htm.
Deadline: February 17.
Amount: Varies.
Number of Awards: 70.

1574 • Norman S. and Betty M. Fitzhugh Fund

Purpose: To provide financial assistance to West Virginia residents wishing to earn a college education.
Eligibility: Applicants must be full-time students (12 hours and demonstrate good moral character and academic excellence.
How to Apply: Applications are available online at http://www.tgkvf.org/scholar.htm or by email at shoover@tgkvf.org.
Deadline: February 17.
Amount: $500.
Number of Awards: 1.

1575 • Paul and Grace Rhudy Fund

Purpose: To provide financial assistance to West Virginia residents who are interested in pursuing a college education.
Eligibility: Applicants must be residents of West Virginia, be full-time students (12 credit hours) and possess good moral character and proven academic achievement.
How to Apply: Applications are available online at http://www.tgkvf.org/scholar.htm or by email at shoover@tgkvf.org.
Deadline: February 17.
Amount: $500.
Number of Awards: 1.

1576 • R. Ray Singleton Fund

Purpose: To provide financial assistance to residents of Kanawha, Boone, Clay, Putnam, Lincoln and Fayette counties in West Virginia who are interested in pursuing a college education.
Eligibility: Applicants must be full-time students and possess good moral character as well as proven academic achievement.
How to Apply: Applications are available online at http://www.tgkvf.org/scholar.htm or via email at shoover@tgkvf.org.
Deadline: February 17.
Amount: $1,000.
Number of Awards: 5.

1577 • Ruth Ann Johnson Fund

Purpose: To provide financial assistance to West Virginia residents who are interested in pursuing a college education.
Eligibility: Applicants must be residents of West Virginia, be full-time students (12 credit hours) and possess good moral character and proven academic achievement.
How to Apply: Applications are available online or by emailing shoover@tgkvf.org.
Deadline: February 17.
Amount: $1,000.
Number of Awards: 39.

1578 • W.P. Black Scholarship Fund

Purpose: To aid West Virginia students.
Eligibility: Applicants must be residents of West Virginia who are full-time students, have a minimum 2.5 GPA, have a minimum ACT score of 20, be of good moral character and demonstrate significant financial need.
How to Apply: Applications are available online.
Deadline: February 17.
Amount: $1,000.
Number of Awards: 114.

National Association for Campus Activities

13 Harbison Way
Columbia, SC 29212-3401
Phone: 803-732-6222
Fax: 803-749-1047
Email: info@naca.org
Website: http://www.naca.org

1579 • Zagunis Student Leader Scholarship

Purpose: To provide financial assistance to student leaders.
Eligibility: Applicants must hold a significant campus leadership position, demonstrate significant leadership skills and abilities and make significant contributions through on- or off-campus volunteering. Students must attend school in Kentucky, Michigan, Ohio, West Virginia or Western Pennsylvania.
How to Apply: Applications are available online.
Deadline: November 1.
Amount: Varies.
Number of Awards: Varies.

PROMISE Scholarship Program

1018 Kanawha Boulevard, East
Suite 700
Charleston, WV 25301
Phone: 877-WV-PROMISE
Fax: 304-558-3264
Email: morgenstern@hepc.wvnet.edu
Website: http://www.promisescholarships.org

1580 • PROMISE Scholarships

Purpose: To assist outstanding West Virginia high school students.
Eligibility: Applicants must be West Virginia residents planning to attend an eligible West Virginia public or private college or university, graduate with a minimum 3.0 GPA and have a minimum ACT score of 21 or SAT score of 1000.

How to Apply: Applications are available online. Applicants must also complete the Free Application for Federal Student Aid (FAFSA).
Deadline: January 31 for PROMISE application and March 1 for FAFSA.
Amount: Varies.
Number of Awards: Varies.

West Virginia Higher Education Policy Commission

1018 Kanawha Boulevard, East
Fifth Floor
Charleston, WV 25301
Phone: 304-558-2101
Fax: 304-558-5719
Website: http://www.hepc.wvnet.edu

1581 • Higher Education Adult Part-Time Student (HEAPS) Grant Program
Purpose: To assist adult West Virginia students.
Eligibility: Applicants must be West Virginia residents, be U.S. citizens or permanent residents, be enrolled or accepted for enrollment in an undergraduate institution on a part-time basis and demonstrate financial need.
How to Apply: Complete the Free Application for Federal Student Aid (FAFSA).
Deadline: Varies.
Amount: Varies.
Number of Awards: Varies.

1582 • Higher Education Grant Program
Purpose: To assist West Virginia students with financial need.
Eligibility: Applicants must be West Virginia residents, be U.S. citizens, demonstrate financial need and enroll full-time at an eligible undergraduate college or university in West Virginia or Pennsylvania.
How to Apply: Complete the Free Application for Federal Student Aid (FAFSA) and the Common Application for State-Level Financial Aid Programs available online.
Deadline: March 1.
Amount: Up to $2,700.
Number of Awards: Varies.

1583 • Robert C. Byrd Honors Scholarship Program - West Virginia
Purpose: To assist outstanding West Virginia high school students.
Eligibility: Applicants must be U.S. citizens or eligible noncitizens, be West Virginia residents, be high school seniors and demonstrate academic excellence.
How to Apply: Contact your high school guidance counselor.
Deadline: March 1.
Amount: Varies.
Number of Awards: Varies.

Related Scholarships:

American Nursery and Landscape Association
See #110 · Carville M. Akehurst Memorial Scholarship

State of Residence - Wisconsin

American Legion, Department of Wisconsin

2930 American Legion Drive
P.O. Box 388
Portage, WI 53901
Phone: 608-745-1090
Fax: 608-745-0179
Email: info@wilegion.org
Website: http://www.wilegion.org

1584 • Americanism and Government Test Program
Purpose: To award outstanding performance on the Americanism and Government Test, a 50-question examination based on state and federal government and history.
Eligibility: Participants must be enrolled in a Wisconsin high school and in their sophomore, junior or senior year.
How to Apply: Application information is available by contacting your local principal, teacher or guidance counselor.
Deadline: Varies.
Amount: Up to $500.
Number of Awards: 32.

1585 • Schneider-Emanuel American Legion Scholarship
Purpose: To award scholarships to American Legion members and their children or grandchildren and members of the Sons of the American Legion or Auxiliary.
Eligibility: Applicants must have graduated from an accredited Wisconsin high school and plan to earn an undergraduate degree at a U.S. college or university. Applicants must also have participated in one or more American Legion-sponsored activities listed in the eligibility requirements.
How to Apply: Applications are available online.
Deadline: March 1.
Amount: $1,000.
Number of Awards: 3.

1586 • Wisconsin Oratorical Contest
Purpose: To enhance high school students' experience with and understanding of the U.S. Constitution. The contest will help develop students' leadership skills and civic appreciation, as well as the ability to deliver thoughtful, insightful orations regarding U.S. citizenship and its inherent responsibilities.
Eligibility: Applicants must be high school students under the age of 20 who are U.S. citizens or legal residents and residents of the state. Students first give an oration within their state and winners compete at the national level. The oration must be related to the Constitution of the United States focusing on the duties and obligations citizens have to the government. It must be in English and be between eight and ten minutes. There is also an assigned topic which is posted on the website, and it should be between three and five minutes.
How to Apply: Application information is available by contacting the local American Legion Post.
Deadline: February 3.
Amount: Varies.
Number of Awards: Varies.

State of Wisconsin Higher Educational Aids Board

P.O. Box 7885
Madison, WI 53707
Phone: 608-267-2206
Fax: 608-267-2808
Email: HEABmail@heab.state.wi.us
Website: http://heab.state.wi.us

1587 • Academic Excellence Scholarship

Purpose: To assist outstanding Wisconsin students.
Eligibility: Applicants must be Wisconsin high school seniors who plan to enroll full-time at an eligible Wisconsin college or university. The award is given to the student with the highest GPA in each public and private Wisconsin high school.
How to Apply: Contact your high school guidance counselor.
Deadline: Varies.
Amount: $2,250-Full tuition.
Number of Awards: Varies.

1588 • Higher Education Grant

Purpose: To assist Wisconsin students with financial need.
Eligibility: Applicants must be Wisconsin undergraduate students with financial need who attend Wisconsin colleges or universities at least half-time. Based on financial need.
How to Apply: Complete the Free Application for Federal Student Aid (FAFSA).
Deadline: Varies.
Amount: Up to $1,800.
Number of Awards: Varies.

1589 • Talent Incentive Program (TIP) Grant

Purpose: To assist Wisconsin students with financial need.
Eligibility: Applicants must be Wisconsin first-time college freshmen with financial need who plan to attend Wisconsin colleges or universities at least half-time.
How to Apply: Complete the Free Application for Federal Student Aid (FAFSA). Applicants must be nominated by their financial aid office or the Wisconsin Educational Opportunities Program.
Deadline: Varies.
Amount: Up to $1,800.
Number of Awards: Varies.

1590 • Tuition Grant

Purpose: To assist Wisconsin students with financial need who attend private Wisconsin colleges.
Eligibility: Applicants must be Wisconsin undergraduate students with financial need who attend private Wisconsin colleges or universities at least half-time.
How to Apply: Complete the Free Application for Federal Student Aid (FAFSA).
Deadline: Varies.
Amount: Varies.
Number of Awards: Varies.

Wisconsin Department of Public Instruction

125 S. Webster Street
P.O. Box 7841
Madison, WI 53707
Phone: 800-441-4563
Website: http://www.dpi.state.wi.us

1591 • Robert C. Byrd Honors Scholarship Program - Wisconsin

Purpose: To assist outstanding Wisconsin students.
Eligibility: Applicants must be U.S. citizens or eligible noncitizens, be Wisconsin residents, be high school seniors and demonstrate academic excellence.
How to Apply: Applicants are nominated by their high schools.
Deadline: Third week in February.
Amount: Varies.
Number of Awards: Varies.

Related Scholarships:

Vincent L. Hawkinson Foundation for Peace and Justice

See #1349 • Vincent L. Hawkinson Scholarship for Peace and Justice

State of Residence - Wyoming

Wyoming Department of Education

2300 Capitol Avenue
Hathaway Building, 2nd Floor
Cheyenne, WY 82002
Phone: 307-777-7675
Fax: 307-777-6234
Website: http://www.k12.wy.us

1592 • Robert C. Byrd Honors Scholarship Program - Wyoming

Purpose: To assist outstanding Wyoming students.

Eligibility: Applicants must be U.S. citizens or eligible noncitizens, be Wyoming residents, be high school seniors and demonstrate academic excellence.

How to Apply: Individual applications are NOT available from the Wyoming Department of Education. Contact your high school guidance counselor for an application.

Deadline: Varies.

Amount: Varies.

Number of Awards: Varies.

Related Scholarships:

Alert Magazine

See #1567 • Alert Scholarship

Unions

Also See Scholarships Listed Under:
Organizations/Clubs/Employers

Air Line Pilots Association

1625 Massachusetts Avenue NW
Washington, DC 20036
Phone: 703-689-2270
Website: http://www.alpa.org

1593 • ALPA Scholarship Program

Purpose: To support the children of medically retired, long-term disabled or deceased pilot members of the Air Line Pilots Association.
Eligibility: Applicants must be pursuing a baccalaureate degree. Selection is based on academic achievements and financial need. The award is renewable for four years with a minimum 3.0 GPA.
How to Apply: Applications are available by mail.
Deadline: April 1.
Amount: $3,000.
Number of Awards: 1.

American Federation of State, County and Municipal Employees (AFSCME) Family Scholarship Program

Attn.: Education Department
1625 L Street NW
Washington, DC 20036-5687
Phone: 202-429-1000
Fax: 202-429-1293
Email: education@afscme.org
Website: http://www.afscme.org

1594 • AFSCME Family Scholarship Program

Purpose: To offer financial assistance to the dependents of AFSCME members.
Eligibility: Applicants must be graduating high school seniors who are the daughters, sons or financially dependent grandchildren of AFSCME members who intend to enroll in a full-time, four-year degree program in any accredited college or university. Applicants should submit applications, essays, transcripts, test scores and recommendation letters. Selection is based on information provided on the application form, high school transcript, SAT/ACT scores and a required essay.
How to Apply: Applications are available online and by written request.
Deadline: December 31.
Amount: $2,000.
Number of Awards: 13.

American Federation of Teachers

555 New Jersey Avenue NW
Washington, DC 20001
Phone: 202-879-4400
Website: http://www.aft.org

1595 • Robert G. Porter Scholars Program

Purpose: To provide scholarships to AFT members' dependents.
Eligibility: Applicants must be graduating high school seniors. The award is merit-based and will consider academics, community service and performance on the required labor-related essay. Applicants' parents or guardians must be AFT members for at least one year.
How to Apply: Applications are available by written request.
Deadline: March 31.
Amount: $8,000.
Number of Awards: 4.

1596 • Robert G. Porter Scholars Program

Purpose: To provide grants to AFT members.
Eligibility: Applicants must be AFT members who have been in good standing for at least one year and intend to pursue courses in their field of work. Applicants must submit an essay on a labor-related topic.
How to Apply: Applications are available by written request.
Deadline: March 31.
Amount: $1,000.
Number of Awards: Varies.

American Federation of Television and Radio Artists

260 Madison Avenue
7th Floor
New York, NY 10016
Phone: 212-532-0800
Fax: 212-532-2242
Email: info@aftra.com
Website: http://www.aftra.com

1597 • AFTRA/Heller Memorial Foundation Scholarships

Purpose: To support AFTRA members and their children.
Eligibility: Applicants must be AFTRA members in good standing with five years of membership or the children of members. Scholarships are awarded based on academic achievement and financial need and can be used to study any academic field or for professional training in the performing arts at an accredited higher education institution.
How to Apply: Applications are available online or by sending a self-addressed, stamped envelope.
Deadline: May 1.
Amount: Up to $2,500.
Number of Awards: 12-15.

American Guild of Musical Artists

1430 Broadway, 14th Floor
New York, NY 10018
Phone: 212-265-3687
Fax: 212-262-9088
Email: agma@musicalartists.org
Website: http://www.musicalartists.org

1598 • Beatrice S. Jacobson Memorial Fund

Purpose: To provide scholarships to AGMA members.
Eligibility: Applicants must be AGMA members in good standing for at least two years who are full- or part-time, traditional or adult students working toward either undergraduate or graduate degrees.

The award is based on financial need and GPA. Applicants don't have to be music majors.

How to Apply: Applications are available by written request.

Deadline: April 1.

Amount: Varies.

Number of Awards: Varies.

Association of Flight Attendants

501 Third Street NW
Washington, DC 20001
Phone: 202-434-1300
Email: afatalk@afanet.org
Website: http://www.afanet.org

1599 • Association of Flight Attendants Annual Scholarship

Purpose: To provide financial assistance to the children of members of the AFA.

Eligibility: Applicants must be the dependents of AFA members in good standing. Applicants must also be in the top 15 percent of their class, have or expect to have excellent SAT/ACT scores, demonstrate financial need and provide a 300-word essay along with the completed application.

How to Apply: Applications are available online.

Deadline: April 10.

Amount: $5,000.

Number of Awards: 1.

Bakery, Confectionery, Tobacco Workers and Grain Millers International Union

10401 Connecticut Avenue
Kensington, MD 20895
Phone: 301-933-8600
Fax: 301-946-8452
Website: http://www.bctgm.org

1600 • BCTGM Scholarship Program

Purpose: To provide scholarships for the members and families of members of BTGCM.

Eligibility: Applicants must be members of the BCTGM in good standing or the children of such members. The scholarships are also open to office employees and children of those employed at the International Union office. Applicants must be high school students who will be attending an accredited college, technical college or vocational school for the first time, high school graduates who have never attended college or BCTGM members who have never applied to the program before who are currently enrolled or planning to begin or resume their studies in the fall. All applicants are required to take the SAT or an equivalent, such as the ACT.

How to Apply: Applications are available through your local BCTGM union office.

Deadline: March 31.

Amount: $1,000.

Number of Awards: 10.

Boilermakers, Iron Ship Builders, Blacksmiths, Forgers and Helpers, (IBB)

753 State Avenue
Suite 570
Kansas City, KS 66101

Phone: 913-371-2640
Website: http://www.boilermakers.org

1601 • Boilermakers, Iron Ship Builders, Blacksmiths, Forgers and Helpers, International Brotherhood of (IBB) Scholarship Awards

Purpose: To provide scholarships to the children of members of the International Brotherhood.

Eligibility: Applicants must be the children or dependents of members of the IBB and high school seniors who will be entering their first year of college as full-time students within one year of graduation from high school. U.S. applicants are required to take the SAT or ACT. Recipients are selected on the basis of academic achievement, career goals, extracurricular activities, outside school activities and essay.

How to Apply: Applications are available by written request.

Deadline: March 31.

Amount: $2,000-$5,000.

Number of Awards: Varies.

Brotherhood of Locomotive Engineers and Trainmen

3341 S. 112th Street
Omaha, NE 68144-4709
Phone: 402-330-6348
Email: bunziegia@cox.net
Website: http://www.ble.org

1602 • BLET Auxiliary Scholarships

Purpose: To provide scholarships to the children of members of the BLE.

Eligibility: Applicants must be the children of both a Grand International Auxiliary (GIA) and BLE member (living or deceased) and enrolled or accepted by an accredited university, college or institute of higher learning. If the applicant is a graduate student or returning to school as a sophomore, junior or senior, he or she must have a minimum 3.0 GPA. Selection is based on academic record, leadership, character and personal achievement. Applicants must have a parent participating in the IWC.

How to Apply: Applications are available online and by written request through your local GIA auxiliary or BLE division.

Deadline: April 1.

Amount: $1,000.

Number of Awards: Varies.

Chemical Workers Union Council, International, of the UFCW

Research and Education Department
1799 Akron Peninsula Road
Akron, OH 44313
Phone: 330-926-1444
Fax: 330-926-0816
Website: http://www.icwuc.org

1603 • Walter L. Mitchell Memorial Scholarship Awards

Purpose: To offer scholarships to the children or step-children of members of the UFCW.

Eligibility: Applicants must be children or step-children of members of at least a year who intend to enter college the fall following application. Recipients are selected on the basis of biographical information, ACT/SAT scores and high school records.

How to Apply: Applications are available online.
Deadline: March 2.
Amount: $1,500.
Number of Awards: 13.

Communications Workers of America

Attn.: George Kohl
501 Third Street NW
Washington, DC 20001
Phone: 202-434-1158
Fax: 202-434-1139
Email: kadams@cwa-union.org
Website: http://www.cwa-union.org

1604 • CWA Joe Beirne Foundation Scholarship

Purpose: To provide scholarships for CWA members and their families.

Eligibility: Applicants may be Communications Workers of America (CWA) members, their spouses, their children or their grandchildren. Applicants must be high school graduates or at least high school students who will graduate during the year in which they apply. Winners are selected by a lottery drawing. This is a two-year scholarship.

How to Apply: Contact a CWA Local or write (referencing CWA local number, member name and Social Security number) for an application. Applications are available online.
Deadline: March 31.
Amount: $3,000.
Number of Awards: 30.

Glass, Molders, Pottery, Plastics and Allied Workers International Union

608 E. Baltimore Pike
P.O. Box 607
Media, PA 19063
Phone: 610-565-5051
Fax: 610-565-0983
Email: gmpiu@ix.netcom.com
Website: http://www.gmpiu.org

1605 • Glass, Molders, Pottery, Plastics and Allied Workers Memorial Scholarship Fund

Purpose: To provide financial assistance to the children of members.

Eligibility: Applicants must be children, step-children or legally-adopted children of Glass, Molders, Pottery, Plastics and Allied Workers members.

How to Apply: Applications are available by written request or by contacting your local union office.
Deadline: November 1.
Amount: $4,000.
Number of Awards: Varies.

Graphic Communications International Union

1900 L Street NW
Washington, DC 20036
Phone: 202-462-1400
Fax: 202-721-0600
Website: http://www.gciu.org

1606 • Anthony J. DeAndrade Scholarship

Purpose: To provide scholarships for the dependents of members of the GCIU.

Eligibility: Applicants must be dependents of a member of GCIU, be graduating from high school during the year of the award or be a recent graduate who by Oct. 1 will not have completed more than one-half year of college.

How to Apply: Applications are available by contacting your local union office or by filling out an online request form.
Deadline: February.
Amount: $500.
Number of Awards: 10.

International Alliance of Theatrical Stage Employees, Artists and Allied Crafts of the U.S.

1430 Broadway
20th Floor
New York, NY 10018
Website: http://www.iatse-intl.org

1607 • Richard F. Walsh, Alfred W. DiTolla, Harold P. Spivak Foundation Award

Purpose: To provide scholarships for the children of IATSE members.

Eligibility: Applicants must be the sons or daughters of IATSE members in good standing, be high school seniors and apply for admission to an accredited college or university full-time leading towards a bachelor's degree.

How to Apply: Applications are available by written request (through an online form).
Deadline: December 31.
Amount: $1,750.
Number of Awards: 2.

International Association of Machinists and Aerospace Workers

9000 Machinists Place
Room 117
Upper Marlboro, MD 20772
Phone: 301-967-4500
Website: http://www.iamaw.org

1608 • International Association of Machinists and Aerospace Workers Scholarship for Members

Purpose: To offer scholarships to members of the International Association of Machinists and Aerospace Workers (IAM).

Eligibility: Applicants must have two years of continuous good standing membership and must be working for a company under contract with the IAM. Applicants may be entering college or vocational/technical school as a freshman or at a higher level with some college credits already completed. Grades, attitude, references, test scores, activities and participation in local lodge are considered in selecting scholarship recipients.

How to Apply: Applications are available by written request.
Deadline: Last Friday of February.
Amount: $2,000.
Number of Awards: Varies.

1609 • International Association of Machinists and Aerospace Workers Scholarship for Members' Children

Purpose: To offer scholarships to children of the members of the IAM.

Eligibility: Applicants' parent member must have two years of continuous good standing membership, and applicants must be in their senior year of high school. Selection is based on grades, attitude, references, test scores and activities outside of school.

How to Apply: Applications are available by written request.

Deadline: Last Friday of February.

Amount: $1,000-$2,000.

Number of Awards: Varies.

International Federation of Professional and Technical Engineers

8630 Fenton Street
Suite 400
Silver Spring, MD 20910
Phone: 301-565-9016
Fax: 301-565-0018
Website: http://www.ifpte.org

1610 • Professional and Technical Engineers, International Federation Scholarship

Purpose: To offer scholarships to the children and grandchildren of IFPTE members.

Eligibility: Applicants must be high school seniors who are the children or grandchildren of IFPTE members.

How to Apply: Applications are available by fax, phone or written request.

Deadline: March 15.

Amount: $1,500.

Number of Awards: 3.

International Organization of Masters, Mates and Pilots

700 Maritime Boulevard
Linthicum Heights, MD 21090
Phone: 410-850-8700
Website: http://www.bridgedeck.com

1611 • International Organization of Masters, Mates and Pilots Scholarship

Purpose: To provide financial assistance to the children of members of the MMP.

Eligibility: Applicants must be the children of an eligible offshore active or deceased member or eligible pensioner of the International Organization of Masters, Mates and Pilots. Recipients are chosen on the basis of high school records, extracurricular activities, SAT scores, character and leadership.

How to Apply: Applications are available by written request.

Deadline: November 30.

Amount: $5,000.

Number of Awards: 6.

International Union of Bricklayers and Allied Craftworkers (BAC)

Education Department
1776 Eye Street NW
Washington, DC 2006
Phone: 888-880-8222 x3111
Email: askbac@bacweb.org
Website: http://www.bacweb.org

1612 • Harry C. Bates Merit Scholarships

Purpose: To award scholarships to the children of BAC members.

Eligibility: U.S. applicants must be the children of a member, living or deceased, of BAC and among the semifinalists in the PSAT/NMSQT.

How to Apply: For U.S. students: There is no application. NMSQT semi-finalists should notify their local BAC office. The application for Canadian students is available online.

Deadline: Varies.

Amount: $800-$2,000.

Number of Awards: 3.

International Union of Painters and Allied Trades of the United States and Canada

1750 New York Avenue NW
Washington, DC 20006
Website: http://www.iupat.org

1613 • S. Frank Bud Raftery Scholarship

Purpose: To provide scholarships for the children of IUPAT members.

Eligibility: Applicants must be the children or legally-adopted dependents of an IUPAT member in good standing. Selection is based on a 1,000- to 2,000-word essay on a subject chosen by the IUPAT.

How to Apply: Applications are available by written request.

Deadline: Varies.

Amount: $2,000.

Number of Awards: 10.

Iron Workers, International Association of Bridge, Structural, Ornamental and Reinforcing

1750 New York Avenue NW
Suite 400
Washington, DC 20006
Phone: 203-383-4000
Fax: 202-638-4856
Website: http://www.ironworkers.org

1614 • John H. Lyons, Sr., Scholarship Program

Purpose: To offer scholarships to the children of members of the Iron Workers Union.

Eligibility: Applicants must be the children, stepchildren or adopted children of an active member of the Iron Workers who has had five or more years of continuous membership. Children of deceased members who were in members in good standing at the time of their death are also eligible. Applicants must also be in their senior year of high school and rank in the upper half of their graduating classes. Selection is based on academic record, SAT/ACT scores, extracurricular activities, references, leadership and citizenship.

How to Apply: Applications are available by written request.
Deadline: Varies.
Amount: Up to $2,500.
Number of Awards: 2.

IUE-CWA

1275 K Street NW
Suite 600
Washington, DC 20005
Phone: 202-513-6300
Fax: 202-513-6357
Website: http://www.iue-cwa.org

1615 • IUE-CWA International Paul Jennings Scholarship

Purpose: To provide scholarships for the children and grandchildren of local IUE-CWA union elected officials.

Eligibility: Applicants must be the children or grandchildren of IUE-CWA members who are now or have been local union elected officials. Applicants must also be accepted for admission or already enrolled as full-time students at an accredited college, university, nursing school or technical school offering college credit courses. All study must be completed at the undergraduate level. Applicants should demonstrate an interest in equality, improving the quality of life of others and community service. Applicants will also be evaluated on character, leadership and a desire to improve.

How to Apply: Applications are available online.
Deadline: March 31.
Amount: $3,000.
Number of Awards: 1.

National Alliance of Postal and Federal Employees (NAPFE)

1628 11th Street NW
Washington, DC 20001
Phone: 202-939-6325
Email: headquarters@napfe.org
Website: http://www.napfe.com

1616 • Ashby B. Carter Memorial Scholarship

Purpose: To aid the dependents of National Alliance members in furthering their education.

Eligibility: Applicants must be dependents of members of the National Alliance of Postal and Federal Employees who have been in good standing for at least three years. Applicants must take the Aptitude Test of the College Board Entrance Examination at their local high school before March 1 and be high school seniors.

How to Apply: Applications are available online.
Deadline: April 1.
Amount: $1,900-$5,000.
Number of Awards: 6.

National Association of Letter Carriers

100 Indiana Avenue NW
Washington, DC 20001
Phone: 202-393-4695
Email: nalcinf@nalc.org
Website: http://www.nalc.org

1617 • William C. Doherty Scholarship Fund

Purpose: To offer scholarships to the children of members of the Letter Carriers Union.

Eligibility: Applicants must be the children or legally adopted children of an active, retired or deceased letter carrier and high school seniors. Applicants' parents must be members in good standing at least one year prior to applying. Selection is based on SAT/ACT scores, high school transcript and questionnaire.

How to Apply: Preliminary applications are available online.
Deadline: December 31.
Amount: $4,000.
Number of Awards: 5.

Office and Professional Employees International Union

1660 L Street NW
Washington, DC 20036
Phone: 202-393-4464
Website: http://www.opeiu.org

1618 • Howard Coughlin Memorial Scholarship Fund

Purpose: To offer scholarships to OPEIU members and their children.

Eligibility: Applicants must either be a members of OPEIU in good standing, or the children, stepchildren or legally adopted children of an OPEIU member in good standing or associate members. Applicants must also be either high school seniors or high school graduates entering a college, university or a recognized technical or vocational post-secondary school as full-time students. Part-time scholarships are defined as a minimum of three credits and no more than two courses. Selection is based on transcripts, high school class rank, and SAT/ACT scores or evidence of an equivalent exam by a recognized technical or vocational post-secondary school.

How to Apply: Applications are available by written request.
Deadline: March 31.
Amount: $2,000-$5,000.
Number of Awards: 18 (12 full-time, 6 part-time).

1619 • John Kelly Labor Studies Scholarship Fund

Purpose: To offer scholarships to OPEIU members and associate members.

Eligibility: Applicants must be members of OPEIU in good standing or associate members, and applicants must be either undergraduate or graduate students in one of the following areas of study: labor studies, industrial relations, social sciences or a related field. The selections shall be based on recommendations of an academic scholarship committee.

How to Apply: Applications are available by phone or written request.
Deadline: Varies.
Amount: $2,000.
Number of Awards: 10.

Retail, Wholesale and Department Store Union District Council (RWDSU)

30 E. 29th Street
New York, NY 10016
Phone: 212-684-5300
Website: http://www.rwdsu.info

1620 • Alvin E. Heaps Memorial Scholarship

Purpose: To provide scholarships for RWDSU members and their children.

Eligibility: Applicants must be RWDSU members or their children. Recipients are determined through consideration of academic performance, involvement in extracurricular activities and completion of a 500-word essay.

How to Apply: Applications are available online or by written request.

Deadline: June 15.

Amount: Varies.

Number of Awards: Varies.

Screen Actors Guild Foundation

5757 Wilshire Boulevard
7th Floor
Los Angeles, CA 90036
Phone: 323-549-6708
Fax: 323-549-6710
Email: dlloyd@sag.org
Website: http://www.sagfoundation.org/index.shtml

1621 • John L. Dales Scholarship Fund

Purpose: To award scholarships to the families of the SAG.

Eligibility: Applicants must be members of the Screen Actors Guild or children of members. Members applying for a scholarship must have been members of the Guild for five years; however, the parent of an applicant must have been a member for ten years. Members must have a lifetime earnings of at least $30,000, earned in the guild's jurisdiction, while parents of an applicant must have lifetime earnings of at least $60,000, earned in the guild's jurisdiction. Applicants must be either students accepted by an accredited institution of higher learning or students already enrolled for at least 12 credit hours per quarter or semester at such an institution. Recipients will be chosen based upon SAT scores, high school/college academic record, a statement of family income and an essay of not less than 250 words.

How to Apply: Applications are available online.

Deadline: March 15.

Amount: Varies.

Number of Awards: Varies.

Seafarers International Union of North America

Ms. Kathleen Eno, Assistant Administrator
Seafarers Health and Benefits Plan-Scholarship Program
5201 Auth Way
Camp Springs, MD 20746
Phone: 301-899-0675
Fax: 301-899-7355
Website: http://www.seafarers.org

1622 • Charlie Logan Scholarship Program for Dependents

Purpose: To offer scholarships to the dependents of members of the SIU.

Eligibility: Applicants must be the dependent children or spouses of members of the Seafarers International Union. The union member must be eligible for the Seafarer's Plan and must have credit for 3 years with an employer who is obligated to make a contribution to the Seafarer's Plan on behalf of the employee. Recipients may attend any U.S. accredited institution. Selection is based upon review of secondary school records, SAT or ACT test scores, college transcripts, if any, character references, extracurricular activities and autobiography.

How to Apply: Applications are available by written request.

Deadline: April 15.

Amount: $5,000.

Number of Awards: 4.

Service Employees International Union

c/o Scholarship Program Administrators Inc.
P.O. Box 23737
Nashville, TN 37202
Phone: 615-320-3149
Email: info@spaprog.com
Website: http://www.seiu.org

1623 • SEIU-Jesse Jackson Scholarship Program

Purpose: To honor the Rev. Jesse Jackson by giving a scholarship to those SEIU members and their children who exemplify his values in the pursuit of social justice.

Eligibility: Applicants must be members or the children of members of the SEIU in good standing for at least one year and must be enrolled in an accredited two- or four-year college or university. The scholarship is for undergraduate work only.

How to Apply: Applications are available by written request.

Deadline: Varies.

Amount: $5,000.

Number of Awards: 1.

1624 • Service Employees International Union Scholarships

Purpose: To give financial assistance to members of the SEIU and their children.

Eligibility: Applicants must be members or the children of members of SEIU who have been in good standing for at least three years. Applicants must also be enrolled in an accredited college or university and should not have completed more than one year of college.

How to Apply: Applications are available by written request.

Deadline: Request application by March 3.

Amount: $750-$1,000.

Number of Awards: 50.

1625 • Union Women Summer School Scholarships

Purpose: To award scholarships to the female members of the SEIU.

Eligibility: Applicants must be female members of SEIU local unions, have demonstrated a committed level of activity in the local union and have the support of the local union president.

How to Apply: Applications are available by written request.

Deadline: Varies.

Amount: Full tuition plus room and board.

Number of Awards: Varies.

Sheet Metal Workers' International Association

1750 New York Avenue NW
6th Floor
Washington, DC 20006
Phone: 202-783-5880
Email: scholarship@smwia.org
Website: http://www.smwia.org

1626 • Sheet Metal Workers' International Scholarship Fund

Purpose: To provide scholarships for members of the SMWIA and their families.

Eligibility: Applicants must be SMWIA members, covered employees, or dependent spouses or children under the age of 25 of SMWIA members or covered employees. Applicants must also be full-time students or accepted to be full-time students at an accredited college or university. Only qualified applicants from local unions that participate in the one-cent check off are eligible for these four-year scholarships. Selection is based on information on SMWIA membership, including information on the local union's jurisdiction and family member's SMWIA membership, high school transcript, SAT/ACT scores or college transcript if already enrolled in college, an essay on the importance of SMWIA to the applicant's family and a letter of recommendation.

How to Apply: Applications are available by email and written request.

Deadline: March 1.

Amount: $4,000.

Number of Awards: 30.

Transport Workers Union of America

1700 Broadway, Second Floor
New York, NY 10019
Website: http://www.twu.org

1627 • Michael J. Quill Scholarship Fund

Purpose: To provide financial assistance to the dependents of TWU members.

Eligibility: Applicants must be high school seniors and may be the children of present, retired or deceased TWU members in good standing or meet other eligibility requirements. Recipients are selected by a public drawing.

How to Apply: Applications are available from local unions and the union publication.

Deadline: May 1.

Amount: $1,200.

Number of Awards: 10.

United Food and Commercial Workers Union

Scholarship Program - Education Office
1775 K Street NW
Washington, DC 20006
Email: scholarship@ufcw.org
Website: http://www.ufcw.org/scholarship/

1628 • UFCW Suffridge Scholarship

Purpose: To provide financial assistance for members of the UFCW and their children.

Eligibility: Applicants must be members of the UFCW with a membership of one continuous year or more or the unmarried children of a member. Applicants must also be graduating high school in the year of the competition and be less than 20 years old. Academic achievement, class rank, biographical questionnaire and test scores are considered.

How to Apply: Applications are available by written request.

Deadline: December 31.

Amount: $1,000.

Number of Awards: 7.

United Mine Workers of America/BCOA T.E.F.

8315 Lee Highway
5th Floor
Fairfax, VA 22031
Phone: 800-822-5833
Website: http://www.umwa.org

1629 • Lorin E. Kerr Scholarship Fund

Purpose: To offer scholarships to UMWA members and their families.

Eligibility: Applicants must be UMWA members, employees or dependents. Selection is based on academic potential and financial need.

How to Apply: Applications are available by phone or written request.

Deadline: Varies.

Amount: Varies.

Number of Awards: Varies.

1630 • UMWA/BCOA Training and Education Fund

Purpose: To offer scholarships to UMWA members and their families.

Eligibility: Applicants must be miners unemployed from the coal industry with at least five years in classified employment. The spouses or children (below age 25) of eligible unemployed or working miners are also eligible for benefits. Grants are awarded based on the recommendation of one or more panels chosen by UMWA and the Bituminous Coal Association.

How to Apply: Applications are available by phone or written request.

Deadline: Varies.

Amount: Varies.

Number of Awards: Varies.

United Transportation Union Insurance Association

UTUIA Scholarship Program
14600 Detroit Avenue
Cleveland, OH 44107
Website: http://www.utuia.org

1631 • United Transportation Union Scholarships

Purpose: To provide financial aid to the children and grandchildren of UTU/UTUIA members.

Eligibility: Applicants must be at least high school seniors or the equivalent and be age 25 or less. Applicants must also be UTU or UTUIA-insured members, the children or grandchildren of a UTU or UTUIA-insured member or the children of a deceased UTU or UTUIA-insured member. UTU or UTUIA-insured members must be U.S. residents. Applicants must be accepted for admittance or already enrolled for at least 12 credit hours per quarter or semester at a recognized institution of higher learning (university, college or junior college, nursing or technical school offering college credit). Scholarships are awarded on the basis of chance, not grades. A UTUIA scholar, however, is expected to maintain a satisfactory academic record to keep the scholarship for the full four years.

How to Apply: Applications are available from the UTU news or by written request.

Deadline: Last workday in March.
Amount: $500.
Number of Awards: 50.

Utility Workers Union of America

815 16th Street NW
Washington, DC 20006
Phone: 202-974-8200
Fax: 202-974-8200
Email: webmaster@uwua.net
Website: http://www.uwua.net

1632 • Utility Workers Union of America Scholarships

Purpose: To offer scholarships to the children of UWUA members.

Eligibility: Applicants must be the sons or daughters of active Utility Workers Union members. Recipients are selected from those who participate in the National Merit Scholarship Competition by taking the PSAT/NMSQT as high school juniors, complete high school and are enrolled in a regionally accredited college in the United States.

How to Apply: Applications are available by written request.
Deadline: Varies.
Amount: $500-$2,000.
Number of Awards: 2.

Related Scholarships:

National Institute for Labor Relations Research (NILRR)

See #538 • William B. Ruggles Right to Work Scholarship

Actors' Fund of America/Actor's Work Program

See #834 • Actors' Work Program

Career Transition for Dancers

See #850 • Caroline H. Newhouse Scholarship Fund

Vocational/Technical

Also See Scholarships Listed Under:
Construction Trades
Engineering
Computer and Information Science

Imagine America Foundation

1101 Connecticut Avenue NW
Suite 901
Washington, DC 20036
Phone: 202-336-6724
Fax: 202-408-8102
Email: kerryt@career.org
Website: http://www.imagine-america.org

1633 • Imagine America scholarship

Purpose: To help high school seniors pursue a postsecondary career education.
Eligibility: Applicants must have a minimum 2.5 high school GPA, demonstrate financial need and have demonstrated community service during the senior year.
How to Apply: Applications are available online.
Deadline: October 31.
Amount: $1,000.
Number of Awards: Varies.

International Executive Housekeepers Association (IEHA) Education Foundation

1001 Eastwind Drive, Suite 301
Westerville, OH 43081-3361
Phone: 800-200-6342
Fax: 614-895-1248
Email: excel@ieha.org
Website: http://www.ieha.org

1634 • IEHA Scholarship

Purpose: To support IEHA members who are pursuing undergraduate or associate's degrees or IEHA certification.
Eligibility: Applicants must submit a 2,000-word manuscript about an issue in the housekeeping industry. The winning manuscript will be selected by a panel of judges and published.
How to Apply: Applications are available online.
Deadline: January 10.
Amount: Up to $800.
Number of Awards: Varies.

James F. Lincoln Arc Welding Foundation

Secretary
P.O. Box 17188
Cleveland, OH 44117-9949
Website: http://www.jflf.org

1635 • Arc Welding Awards

Purpose: To award prizes for arc welding projects made by the applicant or a group of applicants.
Eligibility: Projects may fit into one of the following categories: home, recreational or artistic equipment; shop tool, machine or mechanical device; a structure; agricultural equipment or a repair. Applicants must submit a paper about the creation of the project and be enrolled in a shop class. Applicants must also be enrolled in high school, adult evening classes, two-year/community college, vocational school, apprentice program, trade school, in-plant training or technical school and may not be college students enrolled in a bachelor's or master's program.
How to Apply: Applications are available online.
Deadline: June 1.
Amount: Up to $2,000.
Number of Awards: 95.

Joe Francis Haircare Scholarship Foundation

P.O. Box 50625
Minneapolis, MN 55405
Phone: 651-769-1757
Fax: 651-459-8371
Website: http://www.joefrancis.com

1636 • Joe Francis Haircare Scholarship Program

Purpose: To provide barber and cosmetology students with financial aid.
Eligibility: Applicants must be sponsored by one of the following: a fully accredited, recognized barber or cosmetology school, a licensed salon owner or manager, a full-service distributor or a member of the International Chain Association, Beauty and Barber Supply Institute, Cosmetology Advancement Foundation or National Cosmetology Association. Applicants must be actively enrolled in cosmetology school or planning to enroll during or after the award month of August. Judging is based on financial need, motivation and character.
How to Apply: Applications are available online.
Deadline: June 1.
Amount: $1,000.
Number of Awards: Varies.

Specialty Equipment Market Association

1575 S. Valley Vista Drive
Diamond Bar, CA 91765
Phone: 909-396-0289
Fax: 909-860-0184
Email: education@sema.org
Website: http://www.sema.org

1637 • SEMA Memorial Scholarship

Purpose: To support the education of students pursuing careers in the automotive aftermarket.
Eligibility: Applicants must show financial need, have a minimum 2.0 GPA, pursue a career in the automotive aftermarket or related field and be U.S. citizens. For the scholarship that is a minimum of $1,500: Applicants must be currently enrolled in a four-year degree or graduate level program at a college and complete a minimum of 60 hours credit or be juniors or seniors at the time of scholarship application. For the $1,000 scholarship: Applicants can also be in a

two-year community college, or vocational-technical program and have completed a minimum of 30 hours or credit or be sophomores at the time of the scholarship application.

How to Apply: Applications are available online.
Deadline: May 1.
Amount: $1,000-$1,500.
Number of Awards: Varies.

Related Scholarships:

National Foster Parent Association
See #1027 • *National Foster Parent Association Vocational/Job Training Scholarship*

Catholic Aid Association
See #1092 • *Catholic Aid Association College Tuition Scholarship*

Kansas Board of Regents
See #1362 • *Vocational Scholarship*

Triangle Community Foundation
See #1500 • *GlaxoSmithKlein Opportunity Scholarships*

American Welding Society Foundation
See #198 • *James A. Turner, Jr. Memorial Scholarship*

Plumbing-Heating-Cooling Contractors–National Association
See #264 • *Delta Faucet Company Scholarships*

American Academy of Chefs
See #267 • *Chair's Scholarship*

Transportation Clubs International Scholarships
See #434 • *Hooper Memorial Scholarship*

Transportation Clubs International Scholarships
See #433 • *Denny Lydic Scholarship*

American Fire Sprinkler Association
See #6 • *American Fire Sprinkler Association Scholarship Program*

Jeannette Rankin Foundation
See #1005 • *Jeannette Rankin Foundation Award*

United Transportation Union Insurance Association
See #1631 • *United Transportation Union Scholarships*

South Carolina Board for Technical and Comprehensive Education
See #1531 • *Lottery Tuition Assistance Program*

Navy-Marine Corps Relief Society
See #734 • *VADM E. P. Travers Scholarship And Loan Program*

American Radio Relay League Foundation
See #228 • *Chicago FM Club Scholarships*

Aircraft Electronics Association
See #83 • *Bud Glover Memorial Scholarship*

Aircraft Electronics Association
See #85 • *Dutch and Ginger Arver Scholarship*

Aircraft Electronics Association
See #88 • *Lee Tarbox Memorial Scholarship*

Aircraft Electronics Association
See #90 • *Mid-Continent Instrument Scholarship*

USA Funds
See #577 • *USA Funds Access to Education Scholarships*

Gravure Education Foundation
See #865 • *Hallmark Graphic Arts Scholarship*

Seafarers International Union of North America
See #739 • *Charlie Logan Scholarship Program for Seamen*

Automotive Hall of Fame
See #386 • *Automotive Hall of Fame Scholarships*

Iowa College Student Aid Commission
See #1346 • *Iowa Vocational-Technical Tuition Grants*

Soroptimist International
See #1053 • *Women's Opportunity Awards Program*

California Student Aid Commission
See #1243 • *Cal Grant Entitlement Award*

Wachovia Education Finance
See #70 • *Gimme Five Scholarship Sweepstakes*

National Association of Women in Construction Founders' Scholarship Foundation
See #263 • *Undergraduate Scholarship and Construction Crafts Scholarship*

Plumbing-Heating-Cooling Contractors–National Association

See #265 • PHCC Educational Foundation Scholarship

EAR Foundation

See #294 • Minnie Pearl Scholarship

Transportation Clubs International Scholarships

See #432 • Charlotte Woods Memorial Scholarship

Fisher Communications Inc.

See #531 • Fisher Broadcasting Scholarships for Minorities

Japanese American Citizens League (JACL)

See #999 • Hagiwara Student Aid Award

International Association of Machinists and Aerospace Workers

See #1608 • International Association of Machinists and Aerospace Workers Scholarship for Members

Aircraft Electronics Association

See #84 • David Arver Memorial Scholarship

Aircraft Electronics Association

See #86 • Garmin Scholarship

Aircraft Electronics Association

See #87 • Johnny Davis Memorial Scholarship

Aircraft Electronics Association

See #89 • Lowell Gaylor Memorial Scholarship

EAA Aviation Center

See #98 • H.P. Milligan Aviation Scholarship

National Council of Farmer Cooperatives

See #132 • W. Malcolm Harding Scholarship, Philip F. French Scholarship and Owen Hallberg Scholarship

American Dental Association Foundation

See #271 • Dental Student Scholarship

Army Emergency Relief (AER)

See #708 • MG James Ursano Scholarship Fund

Montgomery GI Bill - Active Duty

See #723 • Montgomery GI Bill - Active Duty

Navy-Marine Corps Relief Society

See #733 • Admiral Mike Boorda Scholarship Program

Associated General Contractors of America

See #262 • AGC Undergraduate Scholarships

American Dental Association Foundation

See #270 • Allied Dental Health Scholarships

American Dental Association Foundation

See #272 • Minority Dental Student Scholarship

Gravure Education Foundation

See #863 • GEF Resource Center Scholarships

Gravure Education Foundation

See #862 • Corporate Leadership Scholarships

Golden Gate Restaurant Association

See #484 • Golden Gate Restaurant Association Scholarship

Gravure Education Foundation

See #866 • Werner B. Thiele Memorial Scholarship

Gravure Education Foundation

See #864 • Gravure Catalog and Insert Council Scholarship

Indexes to the Scholarships

To help you find awards that match your specific background and interests we have included several useful indexes. Browse these indexes to see how easy it is to find awards that fit you.

Career and Major Index

Engineering

HOPE General Scholarship • 1400

JTG Scholarship in Scientific and Technical Translation or Interpretation • 489

KOR Memorial Scholarship • 496

Minnesota Academic Excellence Scholarship • 1433

National Italian American Foundation Scholarship • 497

National Security Education Program David L. Boren Undergraduate Scholarships • 495

NJCL Scholarships • 498

Pat Roberts Intelligence Scholars Program for Intelligence Analysts • 1189

Pat Roberts Intelligence Scholars Program for Language Analysts • 500

Stokes Educational Scholarship Program • 50

Student Translation Award • 491

Translation Prize • 492

Workforce Incentive Program • 1463

Forestry/Fishing/Wildlife
Also see Conservation

ASF Olin Fellowships • 501

National Garden Clubs Scholarship • 138

Robert Felix Memorial Scholarship • 504

General Studies and Humanities

Academic Fellowships and Grants • 465

ACLS Digital Innovation Fellowships • 321

ACLS Fellowships • 322

American Architectural Foundation and Sir John Soane's Museum Foundation Traveling Fellowship • 142

BSA Research Fellowship • 1170

Charles A. Ryskamp Research Fellowships • 323

Community Scholarship Fund • 1301

Fellowships for Regular Program • 490

Frederick Burkhardt Residential Fellowships for Recently Tenured Scholars • 324

Grades 7-12 Excellence of Scholarship Awards • 1187

HOPE General Scholarship • 1400

Pat Roberts Intelligence Scholars Program for Language Analysts • 500

Geologists

American Geological Institute Minority Scholarship • 936

Association for Women in Science College Scholarship • 181

Association for Women in Science Predoctoral Awards • 1127

MESBEC Program • 968

Tilford Fund • 384

Government/Public Administration

ACJA/Lambda Alpha Epsilon Scholarship • 698

American History Scholarship, Enid Hall Griswold Memorial Scholarship, J.E. Caldwell Centennial Scholarship • 1190

APTF Transit Hall of Fame Scholarship Award • 910

Charles G. Koch Summer Fellow Program • 912

Fellowship on Women and Public Policy • 1481

Fund for American Studies Internships • 1173

Julianne Malveaux Scholarship • 1024

Pi Sigma Alpha Washington Internship Scholarships • 1195

Robert G. Porter Scholars Program • 1595

SSPI Scholarship Program • 251

Student Paper Competition • 699

Transatlantic Community Foundation Fellowship • 918

Tribal Business Management Program • 970

Truman Scholar • 931

Graphic Designers

Art Awards • 897

Computer Graphic Design Scholarships • 505

Computer Graphics Scholarship • 512

Corporate Leadership Scholarships • 862

FFTA Scholarship Competition • 506

GEF Resource Center Scholarships • 863

Gravure Catalog and Insert Council Scholarship • 864

Hallmark Graphic Arts Scholarship • 865

IFEC Scholarships Award • 486

Imation Computer Arts Scholarship Program • 508

Print and Graphics Scholarship • 507

Student Design Competition • 509

Visual and Performing Arts Achievement Awards • 794

Werner B. Thiele Memorial Scholarship • 866

Health Professions
Also see Medicine/Health Professions

Michael Dunaway Scholarship • 632

A.T. Anderson Memorial Scholarship • 937

AACN Educational Advancement Scholarship • 615

Academic Study Award • 617

ADAF Student Scholarship • 620

ADHA Institute Scholarship Program • 273

Alice W. Rooke Scholarship And Irene And Daisy MacGregor Memorial Scholarship • 677

Allied Dental Health Scholarships • 270

Allied Healthcare Scholarship Program • 1227

Alpha Mu Tau Fraternity Scholarships • 629

AMBUCS Scholars • 606

American Legion Auxiliary, Department of California $2,000 Scholarships • 1213

AmSECT Scholarship • 633

Annual NBNA Scholarships • 668

AORN Foundation Scholarship Program • 644

ARC-ST Scholarships • 646

ASCLS Student Award • 630

Associate Degree Nursing Scholarship Program • 1228

Association for Food and Drug Officials Scholarship Fund • 479

Association of Food and Drug Officials Scholarship Award • 643

AST National Honor Society Scholarship • 647

Bachelor of Science Nursing Scholarship Program • 1229

Bachelor's Scholarships • 685

Behavioral Sciences Student Fellowship • 660

Bill Kane Scholarship, Undergraduate • 608

BSN Scholarship • 645

Burlington Northern Santa Fe (BNSF) Foundation Scholarship • 939

California Community Service Scholarship Program • 1248

Campus Safety Health And Environmental Management Association Scholarship • 676

Caroline E. Holt Nursing Scholarship • 678

Chesapeake Urology Associates Scholarship • 1386

Clinical Research Pre-Doctoral Fellowship • 626

Collins Scholarship • 651

Continuing Education Award • 618

Dade-Behring/Coordinating Council on the Clinical Laboratory Workforce Scholarship • 631

David S. Bruce Awards for Excellence in Undergraduate Research • 177

Dental Student Scholarship • 271

Don King Student Fellowship • 192

Dorothy Budnek Memorial Scholarship • 628

Earl and Patricia Armstrong Scholarship • 1081

Eight and Forty Lung and Respiratory Nursing Scholarship Fund • 623

Ellen R. Clayton Scholarship for Nursing Students • 1387

ENA Foundation Undergraduate Scholarship • 657

Explorations Summer Research Fellowships • 945

FA Davis Student Award • 616

Fellowship Award • 1131

Forum for Concerns of Minorities Scholarship • 947

Foundation for Surgical Technology Advanced Education/Medical Mission Scholarship • 648

Foundation for Surgical Technology Student Scholarship • 649

Graduate Student Scholarship • 640

Grant Programs for Medical Studies • 1104

Grotto Scholarships • 656

HDSA Research Fellowships • 665

Health Professions Education Scholarship Program • 1230

Health Resources and Services Administration-Bureau of Health Professions Scholarships for Disadvantaged Students • 692

Health Sciences Student Fellowship • 661

Henry Hecaen and Manfred Meier Neuropsychology Scholarships • 627

HHMI-NIH Research Scholars (Cloister Program) • 664

HIMSS Foundation Scholarship • 257

Hobble (LPN) Nursing Scholarship • 1352

HOPE General Scholarship • 1400

International Science and Engineering Fair • 1139

International Student Scholarship • 641

James L. Shriver Scholarship • 1408

James P. Dearing Scholarship • 634

Jerry W. Richmond Memorial Scholarship • 635

Jimmy A. Young Memorial Education Recognition Award • 609

Juanita Robles-Lopez • 1022

Karen O'Neil Endowed Advanced Nursing Practice Scholarship • 658

History

See Social Sciences/History

Hospitality/Travel

Information Technology and Sciences

Insurance Industry

Also see Business and Management

Interior Designers

Journalism

Media/Radio/Television

Also see Communications

Military Careers

Musicians

Social Sciences and History

Common Interests Index

Amateur Radio
ARRL Scholarship Honoring Senator Barry Goldwater, K7UGA • 225
Charles Clarke Cordle Memorial Scholarship • 226
Charles N. Fisher Memorial Scholarship • 227
Chicago FM Club Scholarships • 228
Donald Riebhoff Memorial Scholarship • 229
Dr. James L. Lawson Memorial Scholarship • 230
Earl I. Anderson Scholarship • 231
Edmond A. Metzger Scholarship • 232
Francis Walton Memorial Scholarship • 233
General Fund Scholarships • 235
K2TEO Martin J. Green, Sr. Memorial Scholarship • 236
L. Phil Wicker Scholarship • 237
Mary Lou Brown Scholarship • 238
New England FEMARA Scholarships • 239
Paul and Helen L. Grauer Scholarship • 240
PHD ARA Scholarship • 241
Tom and Judith Comstock Scholarship • 242

Animals
American Quarter Horse Foundation Scholarship • 114
ASHA Youth Scholarships • 115
Federal Junior Duck Stamp Program and Scholarship Competition • 902
Harness Tracks of America Scholarship Fund • 127
Junior Scholarship Program • 109
Shaw-Worth Memorial Scholarship • 128

Art
Animoids 3D Animation Contest • 513
Art Awards • 897
Elizabeth Greenshields Foundation Grants • 856
Federal Junior Duck Stamp Program and Scholarship Competition • 902
Free Photo Contest • 510
Hagley-Winterthur Fellowships in Arts and Industries • 1175
Illustrators of the Future • 876
Imation Computer Arts Scholarship Program • 508
Minnesota Academic Excellence Scholarship • 1433

National Sculpture Society Scholarship • 891
Poster Contest for High School Students • 852
Stacey Scholarship Fund • 872
Stanfield and D'Orlando Art Scholarship • 1106
Visual and Performing Arts Achievement Awards • 794
Young American Creative Patriotic Art Awards Program • 877
Youth Free Expression Network Film Contest • 879

Band
Glenn Miller Scholarship Competition • 861
HAPCO Music Scholarship • 867
Morton Gould Young Composer Award • 844
Urban Outreach Grants • 842
Visual and Performing Arts Achievement Awards • 794
Women Band Directors International College Scholarships • 905
Young Artist Competition • 904
Young Jazz Composer Award • 845

Business
Allstudentloan.org College Scholarship Program for Business Students • 196
Best Buy Scholarship Program • 1072
Business Achievement Awards • 782
Cardinal Health Scholarship • 1075
Citigroup Fellows Program • 1078
Ford Motor Company Business and Leadership Scholarship • 786
Fund for American Studies Internships • 1173
Harry A. Applegate Scholarship • 203
HSF/General Motors Scholarship • 990
James A. Turner, Jr. Memorial Scholarship • 198
National Scholarship • 1025
Public Relations Scholarship • 594

Cars/Trucks
Automotive Hall of Fame Scholarships • 386

Choir
Constance Eberhardt Memorial Award, AIMS Graz Experience Scholarship and Banff Center School of Fine Arts Scholarship • 890
Glenn Miller Scholarship Competition • 861

Community Service
Barbara Wiedner and Dorothy Vandercook Memorial Peace Scholarship • 919
Bonner Scholarship • 915
BRICK Award • 570
Frank Newman Leadership Award • 566
Howard R. Swearer Student Humanitarian Award • 916
Imagine America scholarship • 1633
Kiwanis International Foundation Scholarships • 921
Phillips Foundation Ronald Reagan Future Leaders Program • 576
Prudential Spirit of Community Award • 927
Sam Walton Community Scholarship • 71
Samuel Huntington Public Service Award • 923
Target All-Around Scholarships for Students • 929
Third Wave Foundation Scholarship Program • 1057
Toyota Community Scholars • 930
Violet Richardson Award • 928
Washington State Scholars Grant Program • 1571

Computers
Apple Scholars Program • 8
Cardinal Health Scholarship • 1075
Engineering/Technology Achievement Awards • 785
International Science and Engineering Fair • 1139
Microsoft Tuition Scholarships • 259

Cooking/Baking
Chain des Rotisseurs Scholarship • 266
Chair's Scholarship • 267

Crafts
Art Awards • 897
Free Photo Contest • 510
Hagley-Winterthur Fellowships in Arts and Industries • 1175
Visual and Performing Arts Achievement Awards • 794

Dance
Caroline H. Newhouse Scholarship Fund • 850
Donna Reed Performing Arts Scholarships - National Scholarship • 854
Thelma A. Robinson Award in Ballet • 881
Visual and Performing Arts Achievement Awards • 794

Entrepreneurship
Apple Scholars Program • 8
BRICK Award • 570
Business Achievement Awards • 782
Ford Motor Company Business and Leadership Scholarship • 786
Harry A. Applegate Scholarship • 203
National Scholarship • 1025

Environment
BRICK Award • 570
Federal Junior Duck Stamp Program and Scholarship Competition • 902
International Science and Engineering Fair • 1139
Third Wave Foundation Scholarship Program • 1057

Fashion
Art Awards • 897
Visual and Performing Arts Achievement Awards • 794

Feminism
Third Wave Foundation Scholarship Program • 1057

Film/TV/Radio
Apple Scholars Program • 8
Art Awards • 897
Charles & Lucille King Family Foundation Scholarship • 243
College Television Awards • 833
Don and Gee Nicholl Fellowships in Screenwriting • 892
Film and Fiction Scholarships • 870
Free Photo Contest • 510
Grants for Research in Broadcasting • 245
Joel Garcia Memorial Scholarship • 1224
Julianne Malveaux Scholarship • 1024
Student Academy Awards • 893
Student Journalist Impact Award • 537
Visual and Performing Arts Achievement Awards • 794
Writing Awards • 457
Young Communicators Fellowships • 535
Youth Free Expression Network Film Contest • 879

Gardening
Spring Meadow Nursery Scholarship • 111
Timothy Bigelow and Palmer W. Bigelow, Jr. Scholarship • 112
Usrey Family Scholarship • 113

History
C-SPAN Scholarship Program • 1074
Donald Groves Fund • 1163

Index By Award Sponsor

Minority Scholarship Awards for Incoming College Freshmen • 944

National Student Design Competition • 351

American Institute of Indian Studies
Junior Fellowships • 1162

American Kennel Club
Junior Scholarship Program • 109

American Legion
American Legion Eagle Scout of the Year • 745

Eight and Forty Lung and Respiratory Nursing Scholarship Fund • 623

National Oratorical Contest • 7

American Legion Auxiliary
Girl Scout Achievement Award • 746

National President Scholarship • 700

National President's Scholarship • 701

American Legion Auxiliary, Department of California
American Legion Auxiliary, Department of California $1,000 Scholarships • 1212

American Legion Auxiliary, Department of California $2,000 Scholarships • 1213

American Legion Auxiliary, Department of California $500 Scholarships • 1214

Continuing/Re-entry Students Scholarship • 1215

Past Department Presidents' Junior Scholarship Award • 1216

Past Presidents' Parley Nursing Scholarships • 1217

American Legion Baseball
American Legion Baseball Scholarship • 149

American Legion, Department of Arkansas
Oratorical Contest • 1206

American Legion, Department of California
California Oratorical Contest • 1218

American Legion, Department of Colorado
Colorado Oratorical Contest • 1249

American Legion, Department of Florida
Florida Oratorical Contest • 1269

American Legion, Department of Georgia
Georgia Oratorical Contest • 1290

American Legion, Department of Illinois
American Essay Contest Scholarship • 1316

Illinois American Legion Scholarship Program • 1317

Illinois Oratorical Contest • 1318

American Legion, Department of Indiana
Indiana Oratorical Contest • 1335

American Legion, Department of Iowa
Iowa Oratorical Contest • 1341

American Legion, Department of Kansas
Albert M. Lappin Scholarship • 1350

Charles W. and Annette Hill Scholarship • 1351

Hobble (LPN) Nursing Scholarship • 1352

Hugh A. Smith Scholarship Fund • 1353

Kansas Oratorical Contest • 1354

Music Committee Scholarship • 1355

Paul Flaherty Athletic Scholarship • 1356

Rosedale Post 346 Scholarship • 1357

Ted and Nora Anderson Scholarships • 1358

American Legion, Department of Maine
Children and Youth Scholarships • 1376

Daniel E. Lambert Memorial Scholarship • 1377

James V. Day Scholarship • 1378

Maine Oratorical Contest • 1379

American Legion, Department of Michigan
Guy M. Wilson Scholarship • 1422

Michigan Oratorical Contest • 1423

William D. and Jewell Brewer Scholarship • 1424

American Legion, Department of Minnesota
Minnesota Oratorical Contest • 1432

American Legion, Department of Missouri
Missouri Oratorical Contest • 1443

American Legion, Department of New Jersey
Luterman Scholarship • 1464

New Jersey Oratorical Contest • 1465

Safety Essay Contest • 1466

Stutz Scholarship • 1467

American Legion, Department of New York
New York Oratorical Contest • 1480

American Legion, Department of North Carolina
North Carolina Oratorical Contest • 1492

American Legion, Department of Pennsylvania
Pennsylvania Oratorical Contest • 1520

American Legion, Department of Texas
Texas Oratorical Contest • 1542

American Legion, Department of Vermont
Vermont Oratorical Contest • 1555

American Legion, Department of Virginia
Middle School Essay Contest • 1559

American Legion, Department of Washington
Washington Oratorical Contest • 1568

American Legion, Department of Wisconsin
Americanism and Government Test Program • 1584

Schneider-Emanuel American Legion Scholarship • 1585

Wisconsin Oratorical Contest • 1586

American Mathematical Society
Frank and Brennie Morgan Prize for Outstanding Research in Mathematics by an Undergraduate Student • 601

American Medical Technologists
AMT Student Scholarship • 624

American Medical Women's Association
Wilhelm-Frankowski Scholarship • 625

American Meteorological Society
AMS Graduate Fellowship in the History of Science • 1112

AMS Undergraduate Scholarships • 1113

AMS/Industry Minority Scholarships • 1114

AMS/Industry/Government Graduate Fellowships • 1115

Father James B. Macelwane Annual Awards in Meteorology • 1116

Freshman Undergraduate Scholarship • 1117

American Military Retirees Association
Sergeant Major Douglas R. Drum Memorial Scholarship Fund • 702

American Montessori Society
Teacher Education Scholarship Fund • 325

American Museum of Natural History
Young Naturalist Awards • 1118

American Nuclear Society
ANS Graduate Scholarship • 1119

ANS Undergraduate Scholarship • 1120

John and Muriel Landis Scholarship • 1121

American Numismatic Society
Donald Groves Fund • 1163

Frances M. Schwartz Fellowship • 1164

American Nursery and Landscape Association
Carville M. Akehurst Memorial Scholarship • 110

Spring Meadow Nursery Scholarship • 111

Timothy Bigelow and Palmer W. Bigelow, Jr. Scholarship • 112

Usrey Family Scholarship • 113

American Nurses Association (ANA)
Clinical Research Pre-Doctoral Fellowship • 626

American Orchid Society
AOS Master's Scholarship Program • 175

American Orff-Schulwerk Association (AOSA)
Shields-Gillespie Scholarship • 326

American Speech-Language-Hearing Foundation
Graduate Student Scholarship • 640
International Student Scholarship • 641
Minority Student Scholarship • 642

American Statistical Association
Gertrude Cox Scholarship For Women In Statistics • 602

American String Teachers Association (ASTA) with National School Orchestra Association
Urban Outreach Grants • 842

American Theatre Organ Society
American Theatre Organ Society Scholarships • 843

American Translators Association
Student Translation Award • 491

American Water Ski Educational Foundation (AWSEF)
AWSEF Scholarship • 150

American Water Works Association
Abel Wolman Fellowship • 372
Academic Achievement Award • 373
Holly Cornell Scholarship • 374
Larson Aquatic Research Support (LARS) • 375
Thomas R. Camp Scholarship • 376

American Welding Society Foundation
James A. Turner, Jr. Memorial Scholarship • 198

American-Scandinavian Foundation
Academic Fellowships and Grants • 465
Translation Prize • 492

AMVETS Auxiliary
AMVETS National Ladies Auxiliary Scholarship • 747

Anchor Scholarship Foundation
Anchor Scholarship Foundation Scholarship • 704

AOPA Air Safety Foundation
Donald Burnside Memorial Scholarship • 94

McAllister Memorial Scholarship • 95

APICS-The Educational Society for Resource Management
Donald W. Fogarty International Student Paper Competition • 199

Appalachian Studies Association Carl A. Ross Student Paper Award
Carl A. Ross Student Paper Award • 466

Appaloosa Horse Club
Appaloosa Youth Association Art Contest • 117
Appaloosa Youth Association Essay Contest • 118
Appaloosa Youth Association Junior Journalist Contest • 119
Appaloosa Youth Association Speech Contest • 120
Larry Williams Photography and AYA Photo Contest • 121
Youth Program • 122

Apple Computer Inc.
Apple Scholars Program • 8

Appraisal Institute
Minorities and Women Educational Scholarship • 1086

ARA Scholarship Foundation Inc.
ARA Scholarship • 748

Arab American Institute Foundation
Al Muammar Scholarships for Journalism • 949

Arby's Foundation/Big Brothers Big Sisters Of America
Arby's-Big Brothers Big Sisters Scholarship Award • 749

Arizona Commission for Postsecondary Education
Arizona Private Postsecondary Education Student Financial Assistance Program (PFAP) • 1202
Leveraging Educational Assistance Partnership (LEAP) • 1203

Arizona Department of Education
Robert C. Byrd Honors Scholarship Program - Arizona • 1204

Arkansas Department of Education
Robert C. Byrd Honors Scholarship Program - Arkansas • 1207

Arkansas Department of Higher Education
Academic Challenge Scholarship • 1208
Arkansas Student Assistance Grant Program • 1209
Governor's Scholars Program • 1210

Arkansas Single Parent Scholarship Fund
Arkansas Single Parent Scholarship • 1211

Armed Forces Communications and Electronics Association
AFCEA General Emmett Paige Scholarships • 705
AFCEA General John A. Wickham Scholarships • 253
AFCEA Ralph W. Shrader Scholarships • 254
AFCEA ROTC Scholarships • 706
AFCEA Sgt Jeannette L. Winters, USMC Memorial Scholarship • 707
Computer Graphic Design Scholarships • 505

Armenian Educational Foundation Inc.
Richard R. Tufenkian Memorial Scholarship • 950

Armenian General Benevolent Union (AGBU)
AGBU Scholarship Program • 951

Armenian Relief Society Of North America Inc.
Armenian Relief Society Undergraduate Scholarship • 952

Armenian Students' Association of America
ASA Scholarships • 953

Armstrong Foundation
Armstrong Achievement Scholarships • 750

Army Emergency Relief (AER)
MG James Ursano Scholarship Fund • 708

ArtCarved Class Rings
ArtCarved Get Cash for College Scholarship • 9

ASCAP Foundation
Morton Gould Young Composer Award • 844
Young Jazz Composer Award • 845

Asian American Journalists Association
AAJA Newhouse National Scholarship And Internship Awards • 954
Mary Moy Quan Ing Memorial Scholarship • 955
National AAJA General Scholarship Awards • 956

Asian Pacific Fund
Lapiz Family Scholarship • 1219

ASM International Foundation
ASM Foundation Scholarship Awards • 377
ASM Foundation Technical and Community College Scholarship Awards • 378
ASM Outstanding Scholars Awards • 379
George A. Roberts Scholarships • 380
Nicholas J. Grant Scholarship • 381
William Park Woodside Founder's Scholarship • 382

Aspen Institute
William Randolph Hearst Endowed Scholarship for Minority Students • 957

Associated Builders and Contractors
Trimmer Foundation Student Scholarships • 260

Associated General Contractors of America
AGC Graduate Scholarships • 261
AGC Undergraduate Scholarships • 262

Associated Male Choruses of America
AMCA Music Scholarship • 846

Association for Education and Rehabilitation of the Blind and Visually Impaired
William and Dorothy Ferrell Scholarship • 288

Association for Food and Drug Officials
Association for Food and Drug Officials Scholarship Fund • 479

Broadcast Education Association
Broadcast Education Association Scholarship Program • 529

Brotherhood of Locomotive Engineers and Trainmen
BLET Auxiliary Scholarships • 1602

Brown Foundation Scholarship Program
Brown Foundation Scholarships • 962

Bureau of Indian Affairs
Higher Education Grant • 963

Business and Professional Association Foundation
Career Advancement Scholarship • 964

Calgon
Calgon, Take Me Away to College Scholarship Competition • 10

California Association of Private Postsecondary Schools
CAPPS Scholarship Program • 1221

California Chicano News Media Association
CCNMA Scholarships • 1222
Frank del Olmo Memorial Scholarship • 1223
Joel Garcia Memorial Scholarship • 1224

California Community Foundation
CalFund 150+ Scholarship Programs • 1225

California Council of the Blind
California Council of the Blind Scholarships • 1226

California Health and Welfare Agency – Office of Statewide Health Planning and Development
Allied Healthcare Scholarship Program • 1227
Associate Degree Nursing Scholarship Program • 1228
Bachelor of Science Nursing Scholarship Program • 1229
Health Professions Education Scholarship Program • 1230
Pre-Nursing Scholarship Program • 1231
Youth for Adolescent Pregnancy Prevention-Leadership Recognition Program • 1232

California Interscholastic Federation (CIF)
California Interscholastic Federation (CIF) Scholar-Athlete of the Year • 1233

California Library Association
Begun Scholarship • 585
CLA Reference Services Press Fellowship • 586
CLA Scholarship for Minority Students in Memory of Edna Yelland • 587

California Masonic Foundation
California Masonic Foundation Scholarship • 1234

California Nurses Association
Sandra R. Spaulding Memorial Scholarship • 652
Shirley C. Titus Scholarship Fund • 1235

California School Library Association
Above and Beyond Scholarship • 588
Jewel Gardiner Memorial Scholarship • 1238
John Blanchard Memorial Scholarship • 1236
Leadership for Diversity Scholarship • 1237
Library Media Teacher Scholarship • 1239
Paraprofessional Scholarship • 1240
Paraprofessional-to-LMT Scholarship • 1241

California State PTA
California State PTA Scholarship • 1242

California Student Aid Commission
Cal Grant Entitlement Award • 1243

California Student Aid Commission (CSAC)
Robert C. Byrd Honors Scholarship Program - California • 1244

California Teachers Association (CTA)
CTA César E. Chávez Memorial Education Awards Program • 1245
CTA Scholarship for Dependent Children • 757
CTA Scholarship for Members • 758

L. Gordon Bittle Memorial Scholarship for Student CTA (SCTA) • 759
Martin Luther King, Jr. Memorial Scholarship • 760

Campus Compact
Frank Newman Leadership Award • 566
Howard R. Swearer Student Humanitarian Award • 916

CAP Charitable Foundation
Ron Brown Scholar Program • 965

Career Colleges and Schools of Texas
Career Colleges and Schools of Texas Scholarship Program • 1543

Career Transition for Dancers
Caroline H. Newhouse Scholarship Fund • 850

Cargill
United Negro College Fund Cargill Scholarship-Internship Program • 966

Casualty Actuarial Society/ Society of Actuaries
Actuarial Scholarships for Minority Students • 967

Catching the Dream
MESBEC Program • 968
Native American Leadership Education Program • 969
Tribal Business Management Program • 970

Catholic Aid Association
Catholic Aid Association College Tuition Scholarship • 1092

Catholic Workman Fraternal Benefit Society
Catholic Workman Scholarship • 1093

CBC Spouses Program
CBC Spouses Program • 11

Center for Native American Studies
Memorial Scholarships for American Indian Students • 971

Center for the Education of Women
CEW Scholarships • 1425

Center for Women in Government and Civil Society
Fellowship on Women and Public Policy • 1481

Central Intelligence Agency
CIA Undergraduate Scholarship Program • 12

Central Scholarship Bureau
Chesapeake Urology Associates Scholarship • 1386
Ellen R. Clayton Scholarship for Nursing Students • 1387
Lessans Family Scholarship • 1388
Mary Rubin and Benjamin M. Rubin Scholarship Fund • 1389
Shoe City-WB54/WB50 Scholarship • 1390

Chair Scholars
Chair Scholars Scholarship • 291

Charles and Lucille King Family Foundation
Charles & Lucille King Family Foundation Scholarship • 243

Charles Babbage Institute
Adelle and Erwin Tomash Fellowship in the History of Information Processing • 1171

Chemical Workers Union Council, International, of the UFCW
Walter L. Mitchell Memorial Scholarship Awards • 1603

Cherokee Nation
Cherokee Nation PELL Scholarship • 972

Chicago Scholars Foundation
Chicago Scholars Award • 1319

Chicana/Latina Foundation Scholarship Program
Chicana/Latina Foundation Scholarship • 1246

Chickasaw Nation Education Foundation
Chickasaw Nation Education Foundation Program • 973

Chief of Naval Education and Training/NROTC
NROTC Scholarship Program • 710

Child Nutrition Foundation
CNF Professional Growth Scholarship • 480
GED Jump Start Scholarship • 481
Nancy Curry Scholarship • 482
Schwan's Food Service Scholarship • 483

Governor's Office of the State of Illinois Michael Curry Summer Internship Program
Michael Curry Summer Internship Program • 1322

Grand Lodge of Iowa, A.F. and A.M.
Masonic Scholarship Program • 1342

Grandmothers for Peace International
Barbara Wiedner and Dorothy Vandercook Memorial Peace Scholarship • 919

Grange Insurance Association
Grange Insurance Group Scholarship • 796

Graphic Arts Information Network
Print and Graphics Scholarship • 507

Graphic Communications International Union
Anthony J. DeAndrade Scholarship • 1606

Gravure Education Foundation
Corporate Leadership Scholarships • 862
GEF Resource Center Scholarships • 863
Gravure Catalog and Insert Council Scholarship • 864
Hallmark Graphic Arts Scholarship • 865
Werner B. Thiele Memorial Scholarship • 866

Greater Kanawha Valley Foundation
Greater Kanawha Valley Foundation Scholarship Program • 1573
Norman S. and Betty M. Fitzhugh Fund • 1574
Paul and Grace Rhudy Fund • 1575
R. Ray Singleton Fund • 1576
Ruth Ann Johnson Fund • 1577
W.P. Black Scholarship Fund • 1578

Guideposts Magazine
Young Writers Contest • 444

Guy and Gloria Muto Memorial Scholarship Foundation Inc.
Guy and Gloria Muto Memorial Scholarship • 797

Hagley Museum and Library
Hagley-Winterthur Fellowships in Arts and Industries • 1175
Henry Belin du Pont Dissertation Fellowship • 1176

HAPCO Music Foundation Inc.
HAPCO Music Scholarship • 867

Harness Horse Youth Foundation
Harness Racing Scholarship • 154

Harness Tracks of America
Harness Tracks of America Scholarship Fund • 127

Harry S. Truman Library Institute for National and International Affairs
Harry S. Truman Research Grant • 1177
Harry S. Truman Undergraduate Student Grant • 1178

Hawaii Community Foundation – Scholarships
American Savings Bank Scholarship Program • 1297
Hawaii Community Foundation Scholarships • 1298

Hawaii Department of Education
Robert C. Byrd Honors Scholarship Program - Hawaii • 1299
Sterling Scholar Award Program • 1300

Hawaii Department of Education (DOE)
Community Scholarship Fund • 1301
John M. Ross Foundation Scholarships • 1302
Rosemary and Nellie Ebrie Foundation • 1303

Hawaii Hotel and Lodging Association
Clem Judd, Jr., Memorial Scholarship • 1304

Headquarters
Army ROTC Four-Year Scholarship Program • 716
Army ROTC Green To Gold Scholarship Program • 717

Healthcare Information and Management Systems Society
HIMSS Foundation Scholarship • 257

Hebrew Immigrant Aid Society
HIAS Scholarship • 982

Hellenic Times Scholarship Fund
Hellenic Times Scholarship • 983

Hemophilia Resources of America
Hemophilia Resources of America • 298

Henkel Consumer Adhesives
Stuck at Prom Scholarship • 32

Henry Sachs Foundation
Henry Sachs Foundation Scholarship • 1255

Herb Society of America
HSA Research Grants • 191

Herbert Hoover Presidential Library Association
Herbert Hoover Presidential Library Association Travel Grant Program • 1179
Herbert Hoover Uncommon Student Award • 1343

Herff Jones
Principal's Leadership Award • 572

High School Athletic Association
Nissan Hawaii High School Hall of Honor • 1305

Higher Education Coordinating Board
Washington State Scholars Grant Program • 1571

Hispanic College Fund
Hispanic College Fund Scholarships • 984

Hispanic Heritage Awards Foundation
Hispanic Heritage Youth Awards • 985

Hispanic Outlook Magazine
Hispanic Outlook Scholarship • 986

Hispanic Scholarship Fund (HSF)
College Scholarship Program • 987
Community College Transfer Scholarship Program • 988
High School Scholarship Program • 989
HSF/General Motors Scholarship • 990

Hitachi Foundation
Yoshiyama Award • 920

Holland and Knight Charitable Foundation
Holocaust Remembrance Project Essay Contest • 1180

Honor Society of Phi Kappa Phi
Literacy Grants • 798
Phi Kappa Phi Fellowship • 799
Study Abroad Grants • 33

Hopi Tribe Grants and Scholarship Program
Hopi Scholarship • 991
Private High School Scholarship • 992
Standardized Test Fee Scholarship • 993
Tribal Priority Scholarship • 1087
Tuition and Book Scholarship • 994

Horace Mann Insurance Companies
Horace Mann Scholarship • 800

Horatio Alger Association
Horatio Alger Association Scholarship Program • 34

Horizons Foundation
GAPA's George Choy Memorial Scholarship • 995

Hospitality Sales and Marketing Association International (HSMAI)
HSMAI Foundation Scholarship • 527

Houston Symphony
Houston Symphony Ima Hogg National Young Artist Competition • 868

Howard Hughes Medical Institute
Research Training Fellowships for Medical Students (Medical Fellows Program) • 663

Howard Hughes Medical Institute Research Scholars
HHMI-NIH Research Scholars (Cloister Program) • 664

Humane Society of the United States
Shaw-Worth Memorial Scholarship • 128

Huntington Library, Art Collections and Botanical Gardens
Huntington Fellowships • 1181

National Archery Association

NAA College Scholarship • 157

National Association for Campus Activities

Lori Rhett Memorial Scholarship • 1201

Markley Scholarship • 924

Multicultural Scholarship Program • 1010

NACA East Coast Undergraduate Scholarship for Student Leaders • 1482

NACA Southeast Region Student Leader Scholarship • 1288

Scholarships for Student Leaders • 574

Tese Caldarelli Memorial Scholarship • 575

Zagunis Student Leader Scholarship • 1579

National Association for Gifted Children

A. Harry Passow Classroom Teacher Scholarship • 334

National Association for Surface Finishing

American Electroplaters and Surface Finishers Society Scholarship • 1145

National Association for the Advancement of Colored People

Agnes Jones Scholarship • 1011

Earl Graves Scholarship • 1012

Louis Stokes Scholarship • 1013

Roy Wilkins Scholarship • 1014

Sutton Scholarship • 1015

Willems Scholarship • 1016

National Association of Black Accountants

National Association of Black Accountants Scholarship Program • 1017

National Association of Black Journalists

National Association of Black Journalists Scholarship Program • 1018

National Association of Blacks in Criminal Justice

Jonathan Jasper Wright Award • 724

Mary Church Terrell Award • 725

Medger Evers Award • 726

William L. Hastie Award • 727

National Association of Broadcasters

Grants for Research in Broadcasting • 245

National Association of Hispanic Journalists

Maria Elena Salinas Scholarship Program • 1019

NAHJ Scholarships • 1020

Newhouse Scholarship Program • 1021

National Association of Hispanic Nurses

Juanita Robles-Lopez • 1022

NAHN Scholarship • 1023

National Association of Insurance Women (NAIW) Education Foundation

College Scholarships • 211

Professional Scholarships • 212

National Association of Intercollegiate Athletics (NAIA)

NAIA Scholarships • 158

National Association of Letter Carriers

William C. Doherty Scholarship Fund • 1617

National Association of Minority Engineering Program Administrators

NAMEPA Scholarship Program • 410

National Association of Negro Business and Professional Women's Clubs Inc.

Julianne Malveaux Scholarship • 1024

National Scholarship • 1025

National Association of Pediatric Nurse Practitioners (NAPNAP)

McNeil Rural Health Scholarship • 667

National Association of the Deaf

William C. Stokoe Scholarship • 302

National Association of Water Companies

National Association of Water Companies Scholarship • 213

National Association of Women in Construction Founders' Scholarship Foundation

Undergraduate Scholarship and Construction Crafts Scholarship • 263

National Athletic Trainers' Association

NATA Scholarship • 159

National Beta Club

National Beta Club Scholarship • 811

National Bicycle League (NBL)

Bob Warnicke Scholarship • 160

National Black Nurses Association

Annual NBNA Scholarships • 668

National Black Police Association

Alphonso Deal Scholarship Award • 728

National Center for Learning Disabilities

Anne Ford Scholarship Program • 303

National Coalition Against Censorship (NCAC)

Youth Free Expression Network Film Contest • 879

National Collegiate Athletic Association

Ethnic Minority and Women's Enhancement Scholarship • 161

NCAA Postgraduate Scholarship • 162

National Community Pharmacists Association

NCPA Foundation Presidential Scholarship • 669

National Conference of CPA Practitioners NCCPAP Scholarship

NCCPAP Scholarship • 79

National Consortium for Graduate Degrees for Minorities in Engineering and Science Inc. (GEM)

GEM Fellowship Program • 1026

National Council for Geographic Education

College/University Excellence of Scholarship Awards • 1186

Grades 7-12 Excellence of Scholarship Awards • 1187

Women in Geographic Education Scholarship • 335

National Council of Farmer Cooperatives

W. Malcolm Harding Scholarship, Philip F. French Scholarship and Owen Hallberg Scholarship • 132

National Council of Teachers of English

Achievement Award • 336

National Court Reporters Association

Council on Approved Student Education's Scholarship Fund • 562

National Dairy Shrine

Dairy Student Recognition Program • 133

Klussendorf Scholarship • 134

Marshall E. McCullough Scholarship • 135

Milk Marketing Scholarship • 136

National Defense Transportation Association-Scott St. Louis Chapter

National Defense Transportation Association, St. Louis Area Chapter Scholarship • 214

National Environmental Health Association and the American Academy of Sanitarians

NEHA/AAS Scholarship Awards • 670

National Exchange Club

Youth of the Year Award • 812

National Federation of Music Clubs (AR)

NFMC Wendell Irish Viola Award • 880

National Federation of Music Clubs (Coral Gables, FL)

Thelma A. Robinson Award in Ballet • 881

National Federation of Music Clubs (NC)

NFMC Hinda Honigman Award for the Blind • 304

National Federation of Music Clubs (NY)

Victor Herbert ASCAP Young Composers Awards and The NFMC Marion Richter American Music Composition Award • 882

National Federation of Music Clubs (FL)

NFMC Gretchen E. Van Roy Music Education Scholarship • 337

National Federation of Music Clubs (Miami, FL)

NFMC Claire Ulrich Whitehurst (Flanagan) Piano Award • 883

Public Relations Student Society of America
Betsy Plank/PRSSA Scholarship • 596
Gary Yoshimura Scholarship • 597
Lawrence G. Foster Award for Excellence in Public Relations • 598
Multicultural Affairs Scholarship Program • 1045
Professor Sidney Gross Memorial Award • 599

QuestBridge
College Match Program • 55
College Prep Scholarship for High School Juniors • 56

Quill and Scroll Society
Edward J. Nell Memorial Scholarships in Journalism • 546

Radio and Television News Directors Association
Abe Schechter Graduate Scholarship • 547
Carole Simpson Scholarship • 548
Ed Bradley Scholarship • 549
Ken Kashiwahara Scholarship • 550
Lou and Carole Prato Sports Reporting Scholarship • 551
Mike Reynolds Scholarship • 552
Undergraduate Scholarships • 553

Random House Inc. Creative Writing Competition
Random House Inc. Creative Writing Competition • 1490
World of Expressions Scholarship - Music • 1491

Recording for the Blind and Dyslexic
Marion Huber Learning Through Listening Awards • 315
Mary P. Oenslanger Scholastic Achievement Awards • 316

Reserve Officers Association of the U.S.
Henry J. Reilly Memorial Scholarship • 736

Retail, Wholesale and Department Store Union District Council (RWDSU)
Alvin E. Heaps Memorial Scholarship • 1620

Retired Officers Association (TROA)
TROA Scholarship • 737

Rhode Island Department of Elementary and Secondary Education
Robert C. Byrd Honors Scholarship Program - Rhode Island • 1523

Rhode Island Foundation
Lily and Catello Sorrentino Memorial Scholarship • 1524
Rhode Island Foundation Association of Former Legislators Scholarship • 1525

Rhode Island Higher Education Assistance Authority
CollegeBoundfund Academic Promise Scholarship • 1526
State Grant Program • 1527

Rhodes Scholarship Trust
Rhodes Scholar • 57

Rhythm and Hues Studios
Computer Graphics Scholarship • 512

Rolling Stone
Rolling Stone Annual College Journalism Competition • 554

Rotary International
Cultural Ambassadorial Scholarships • 58
Rotary International Ambassadorial Scholarship Program • 475

Rural Poverty Research Center
Rural Poverty Research Center Undergraduate Fellowships • 1196

Sallie Mae Fund
American Dream Scholarship • 1046
Community College Transfer Scholarships • 1047
First in My Family Scholarship • 1048
Writers of Passage Scholarship • 1049

Sallie Mae Fund Unmet Need Scholarship Program
Unmet Need Scholarship • 59

San Angelo Symphony
Sorantin Competition • 896

Scholarship Experts
Scholarship Experts Scholarship for High School Students • 60

Scholastic
Art Awards • 897
Writing Awards • 457

Screen Actors Guild Foundation
John L. Dales Scholarship Fund • 1621

Scripps Howard Foundation
Scripps Howard Top Ten Scholarship • 555

Seabee Memorial Scholarship Association
Seabee Memorial Scholarship • 738

Seafarers International Union of North America
Charlie Logan Scholarship Program for Dependents • 1622
Charlie Logan Scholarship Program for Seamen • 739

Sertoma International
Sertoma Communicative Disorders Scholarship • 688
Sertoma Hearing Impaired Scholarship • 317

Service Employees International Union
SEIU-Jesse Jackson Scholarship Program • 1623
Service Employees International Union Scholarships • 1624
Union Women Summer School Scholarships • 1625

Sheet Metal Workers' International Association
Sheet Metal Workers' International Scholarship Fund • 1626

Siemens Foundation
Siemens Westinghouse Competition in Math, Science and Technology • 1149

Sigma Alpha Epsilon (SAE)
Jones-Laurence Award for Scholastic Achievement • 821

Sigma Alpha Iota Philanthropies
Undergraduate Scholarships • 898

Sinfonia Foundation
Sinfonia Foundation Scholarship • 899

Slovenian Women's Union of America
Continuing Education Award • 1050
Slovenian Women's Union of America Scholarship Program • 1051

Society for Imaging Science and Technology
Raymond Davis Scholarship • 417

Society for Range Management (SRM)
Masonic-Range Science Scholarship • 140

Society for Technical Communication
Distinguished Service Award for Students • 249

Society of American Registered Architects
Student Design Competition • 148

Society of Automotive Engineers
Doctoral Scholars Forgivable Loan Program • 418
Long-Term Member Sponsored Scholarship • 419
SAE Engineering Scholarships • 420
Yanmar/SAE Scholarship • 421

Society of Broadcast Engineers
Youth Scholarship • 250

Society of Exploration Geophysicists
SEG Scholarship • 422

Society of Mexican American Engineers and Scientists Inc. (MAES)
MAES Scholarship Program • 1052

Society of Naval Architects and Marine Engineers
Society of Naval Architects and Marine Engineers Undergraduate Scholarships • 423

Society of Nuclear Medicine
Paul Cole Scholarship Award • 689

Society of Physics Students
Herbert Levy Memorial Scholarship • 1150
Peggy Dixon Two-Year Scholarship • 1151
SPS Future Teacher Scholarship • 341
SPS Leadership Scholarships • 1152

Society of Plastics Engineers
American Plastics Council (APC)/SPE Plastics Environmental Division Scholarship • 424

Scholarship Name Index

Index

About the Authors

Harvard graduates and husband and wife team Gen and Kelly Tanabe are the founders of SuperCollege and award-winning authors of nine books including: *1001 Ways to Pay for College, How to Write a Winning Scholarship Essay, Get into Any College, Accepted! 50 Successful College Admission Essays, 501 Ways for Adult Students to Pay for College* and *Accepted! 50 Successful Business School Admission Essays.*

Together, Gen and Kelly were accepted to every school to which they applied, including all the Ivy League colleges, and won over $100,000 in merit-based scholarships. They were able to graduate from Harvard debt-free.

Gen and Kelly give workshops across the country and write the nationally syndicated "Ask The SuperCollege.com Experts" column. They have made hundreds of appearances on television and radio and have served as expert sources for *USA Today,* the *New York Times, U.S. News & World Report, New York Daily News, San Jose Mercury News, Chronicle of Higher Education, CNN* and *Seventeen.*

Gen grew up in Waialua, Hawaii. A graduate of Waialua High School, he was the first student from his school to be accepted at Harvard, where he graduated *magna cum laude* with a degree in both History and East Asian Studies.

Kelly attended Whitney High School, a nationally ranked public high school in her hometown of Cerritos, California. She graduated *magna cum laude* from Harvard with a degree in Sociology.

The Tanabes approach financial aid from a practical, hands-on point of view. Drawing on the collective knowledge and experiences of students, they provide real strategies students can use to pay for their education.

Gen and Kelly live in Belmont, California with their son Zane and dog Sushi.